Preface

The New Perspectives Series' critical-thinking, problem-solving approach is the ideal way to prepare students to transcend point-and-click skills and take advantage of all that Adobe Photoshop CS6 has to offer.

In developing the New Perspectives Series, our goal was to create books that give students the software concepts and practical skills they need to succeed beyond the classroom. We've updated our proven case-based pedagogy with more practical content to make learning skills more meaningful to students.

With the New Perspectives Series, students understand *why* they are learning *what* they are learning, and are fully prepared to apply their skills to real-life situations.

"The format of the text lends itself to easy-to-follow explanations and step-by-step processes assisting students in reviews for concept assessments. The hands-on exercises reinforce the concepts covered, the ProSkills sections bring reality into the classroom and coursework, and the problems at the end of each chapter give variety and relevance to all elements presented."
—Joyce Porter
Weber State University

About This Book

This book provides thorough coverage of the new Adobe Photoshop CS6 software, and includes the following:

- Hands-on instruction of essential digital editing concepts, such as file formats, color modes, raster versus vector graphics, and the new CS6 features such as Content-Aware Move, layer filtering, and vector layers
- Coverage of important skills including drawing and using work paths; and filling text and objects with images, gradients, and patterns using selections and clipping masks
- Highlights of Adobe Photoshop innovations such as adjustment layers, layer comps and styles, painting and drawing tools, non-destructive editing techniques, filters, and masks

New for this edition!

- Coverage of the new Content-Aware Move feature
- New hands-on instruction of new layer filtering
- Introduction of the new Properties panel

System Requirements

This book assumes a typical installation of Adobe Photoshop CS6 and Microsoft Windows 7 Ultimate using an Aero theme. You will need a graphics card that supports OpenGL 2.0. The browser used for any steps that require a browser is Internet Explorer 9.

"The clear step-by-step instructions, real-world data files, and helpful figures make New Perspectives texts excellent for courses taught in the classroom, the hybrid/blended format, or entirely online."
—Sylvia Amito'elau
Coastline Community College

The New Perspectives Approach

Context
Each tutorial begins with a problem presented in a "real-world" case that is meaningful to students. The case sets the scene to help students understand what they will do in the tutorial.

Hands-on Approach
Each tutorial is divided into manageable sessions that combine reading and hands-on, step-by-step work. Colorful screenshots help guide students through the steps. **Trouble?** tips anticipate common mistakes or problems to help students stay on track and continue with the tutorial.

VISUAL OVERVIEW

Visual Overviews
New for this edition! Each session begins with a Visual Overview, a new two-page spread that includes colorful, enlarged screenshots with numerous callouts and key term definitions, giving students a comprehensive preview of the topics covered in the session, as well as a handy study guide.

PROSKILLS

ProSkills Boxes and Exercises
New for this edition! ProSkills boxes provide guidance for how to use the software in real-world, professional situations, and related ProSkills exercises integrate the technology skills students learn with one or more of the following soft skills: decision making, problem solving, teamwork, verbal communication, and written communication.

KEY STEP

Key Steps
New for this edition! Important steps are highlighted in yellow with attached margin notes to help students pay close attention to completing the steps correctly and avoid time-consuming rework.

INSIGHT

InSight Boxes
InSight boxes offer expert advice and best practices to help students achieve a deeper understanding of the concepts behind the software features and skills.

TIP

Margin Tips
Margin Tips provide helpful hints and shortcuts for more efficient use of the software. The Tips appear in the margin at key points throughout each tutorial, giving students extra information when and where they need it.

REVIEW
APPLY

Assessment
Retention is a key component to learning. At the end of each session, a series of Quick Check questions helps students test their understanding of the material before moving on. Engaging end-of-tutorial Review Assignments and Case Problems have always been a hallmark feature of the New Perspectives Series. Colorful bars and brief descriptions accompany the exercises, making it easy to understand both the goal and level of challenge a particular assignment holds.

REFERENCE
TASK REFERENCE
GLOSSARY/INDEX

Reference
Within each tutorial, Reference boxes appear before a set of steps to provide a succinct summary and preview of how to perform a task. In addition, a complete Task Reference at the back of the book provides quick access to information on how to carry out common tasks. Finally, each book includes a combination Glossary/Index to promote easy reference of material.

www.cengage.com/ct/newperspectives

Our Complete System of Instruction

BRIEF

INTRODUCTORY

COMPREHENSIVE

Coverage To Meet Your Needs

Whether you're looking for just a small amount of coverage or enough to fill a semester-long class, we can provide you with a textbook that meets your needs.

- Brief books typically cover the essential skills in just 2 to 4 tutorials.
- Introductory books build and expand on those skills and contain an average of 5 to 8 tutorials.
- Comprehensive books are great for a full-semester class, and contain 9 to 12+ tutorials.

So if the book you're holding does not provide the right amount of coverage for you, there's probably another offering available. Go to our Web site or contact your Course Technology sales representative to find out what else we offer.

COURSECASTS

CourseCasts – Learning on the Go. Always available…always relevant.

Want to keep up with the latest technology trends relevant to you? Visit our site to find a library of podcasts, CourseCasts, featuring a "CourseCast of the Week," and download them to your mp3 player at http://coursecasts.course.com.

Our fast-paced world is driven by technology. You know because you're an active participant—always on the go, always keeping up with technological trends, and always learning new ways to embrace technology to power your life.

Ken Baldauf, host of CourseCasts, is a faculty member of the Florida State University Computer Science Department where he is responsible for teaching technology classes to thousands of FSU students each year. Ken is an expert in the latest technology trends; he gathers and sorts through the most pertinent news and information for CourseCasts so your students can spend their time enjoying technology, rather than trying to figure it out. Open or close your lecture with a discussion based on the latest CourseCast.

Visit us at http://coursecasts.course.com to learn on the go!

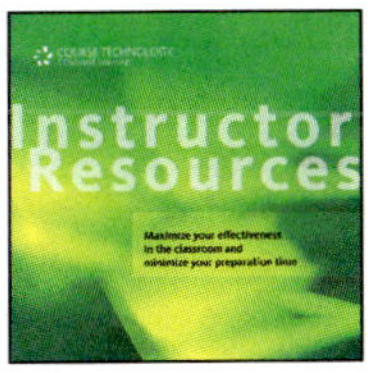

Instructor Resources

We offer more than just a book. We have all the tools you need to enhance your lectures, check students' work, and generate exams in a new, easier-to-use and completely revised package. This book's Instructor's Manual, ExamView testbank, PowerPoint presentations, data files, solution files, figure files, and a sample syllabus are all available on a single CD-ROM or for downloading at login.cengage.com.

Acknowledgments

I'd like to thank the following reviewers, who provided invaluable feedback to help make the book the best it can be. Their experience teaching Photoshop in the classroom was very helpful: DeAnnia Clements, Joyce Porter, and Samantha Brodie. I'd also like to thank everyone on the New Perspectives Team, including Kathy Finnegan, who encouraged me to write the book in the first place, and Leigh Hefferon, who managed all the moving parts with patience and expertise. Special thanks go to Mary Pat Shaffer, my editor, whose insights and eye for detail are always invaluable. Thanks also to Khaled, who didn't mind being "Photoshopped," Anya and Cyn, who provided some of the photos, and Maya, who gave me an excuse to go to Italy and take pictures.
– Jane Hosie-Bounar

TABLE OF CONTENTS

TUTORIAL 1

Getting Started with Adobe Photoshop CS6

Introducing Graphics and Photoshop CS6

OBJECTIVES

Session 1.1

- Understand the role of Photoshop in professional production
- Define raster versus vector graphics
- Start and exit Photoshop, and explore the workspace
- Examine Photoshop Help
- Open, rename, and close files
- Navigate and arrange file windows

Session 1.2

- Set Photoshop Preferences
- Work with the Photoshop interface, tools, and tool presets
- Work with panels and use the panel menu
- Choose a preset workspace
- Display and use rulers, guides, and the grid
- Add content to the canvas

Case | *Mirabeau Media*

Mirabeau Media is a consulting firm in Burlington, Vermont, that was founded in 2010 by Sarah Alward, a 2008 college graduate with a double major in journalism and graphic design. Sarah spent two years working for a local news organization, but decided her interest really lay in using her skills to help clients promote their products and companies through brochures, print ads, and Web-based media.

Sarah's firm uses Adobe Photoshop along with the other applications in the Adobe Creative Suite to create logos, flyers, brochures, catalogs, and online advertising for various clients in the Burlington area. You have recently been hired by Sarah to help in all areas of the company's activities, from design to production. Sarah knows you don't have experience using Photoshop, but based on your interview, she has decided that you are a quick learner with a lot to offer.

STARTING DATA FILES

Photoshop1 →

Tutorial
ExpertInsurance.psd
ExpertText.psd
FireInsurance.psd
LightningInsurance.psd
RainbowInsurance.psd
RainbowInsurance2.jpg
SingingInsurance.psd
Travel.psd
UnexpectedBolt.psd

Review
FireUnlit.psd
LightningInsurance.psd
UnexpectedBolt.psd

Case1
Harbour.psd

Case2
SeafoodDish.psd

Case3
Airplane.psd

Case4
ExploreMore.psd

SESSION 1.1 VISUAL OVERVIEW

The **Document window** is where Photoshop displays the images you open or create.

The Help menu lets you access **Adobe Community Help**, an online forum for information about Adobe Creative Suite features.

The **options bar** displays the settings for the currently selected tool.

A tool includes a hidden tool group if it displays a small triangle on the lower-right corner.

The **Tools panel** includes tools for zooming, panning, selecting, and working with colors and bitmap and vector objects.

The **status bar** displays information about the current file, such as magnification, size, and resolution.

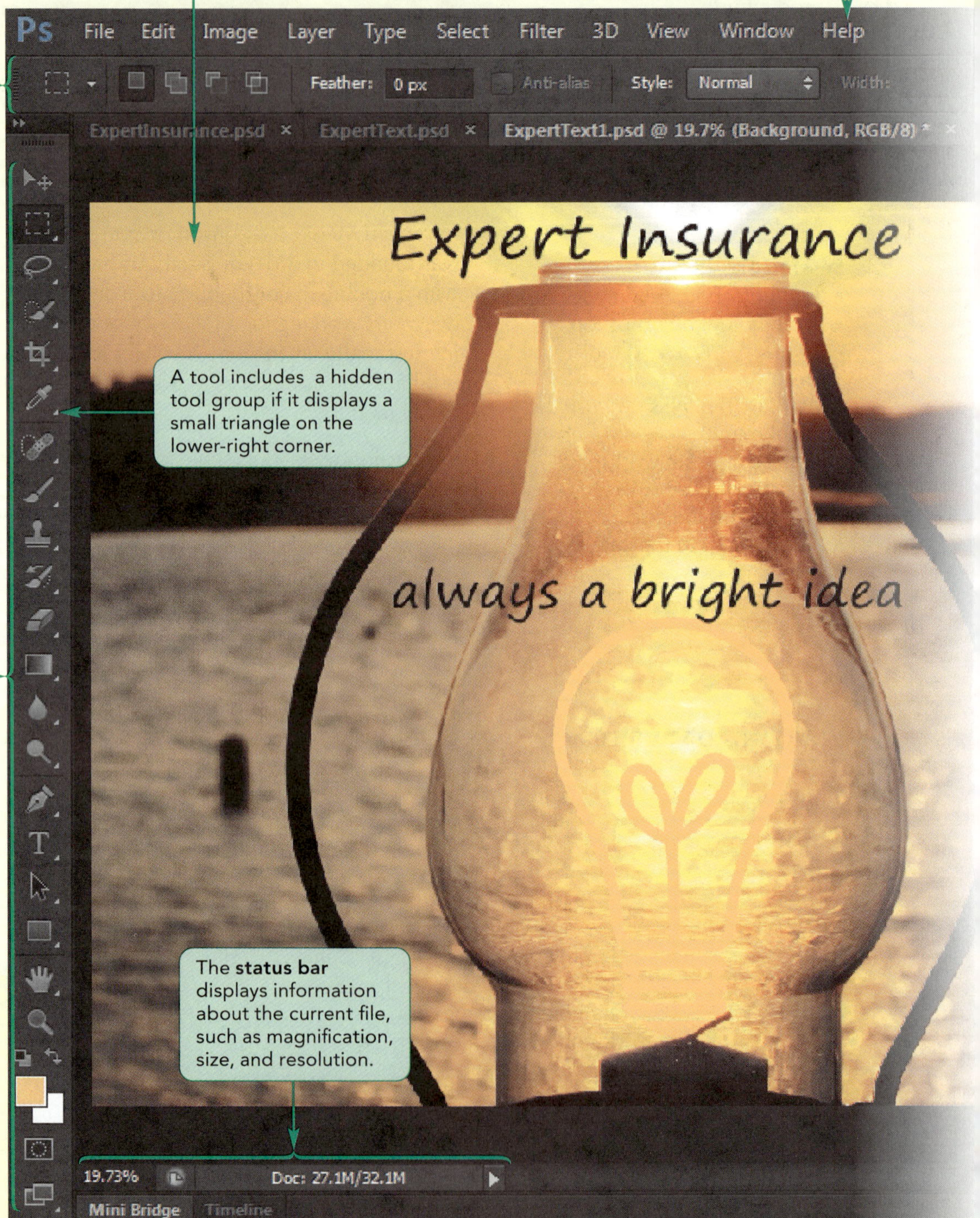

Jane Hosie-Bounar

You can click a **panel tab** to display and access the tools in a panel.

PHOTOSHOP PROGRAM WINDOW

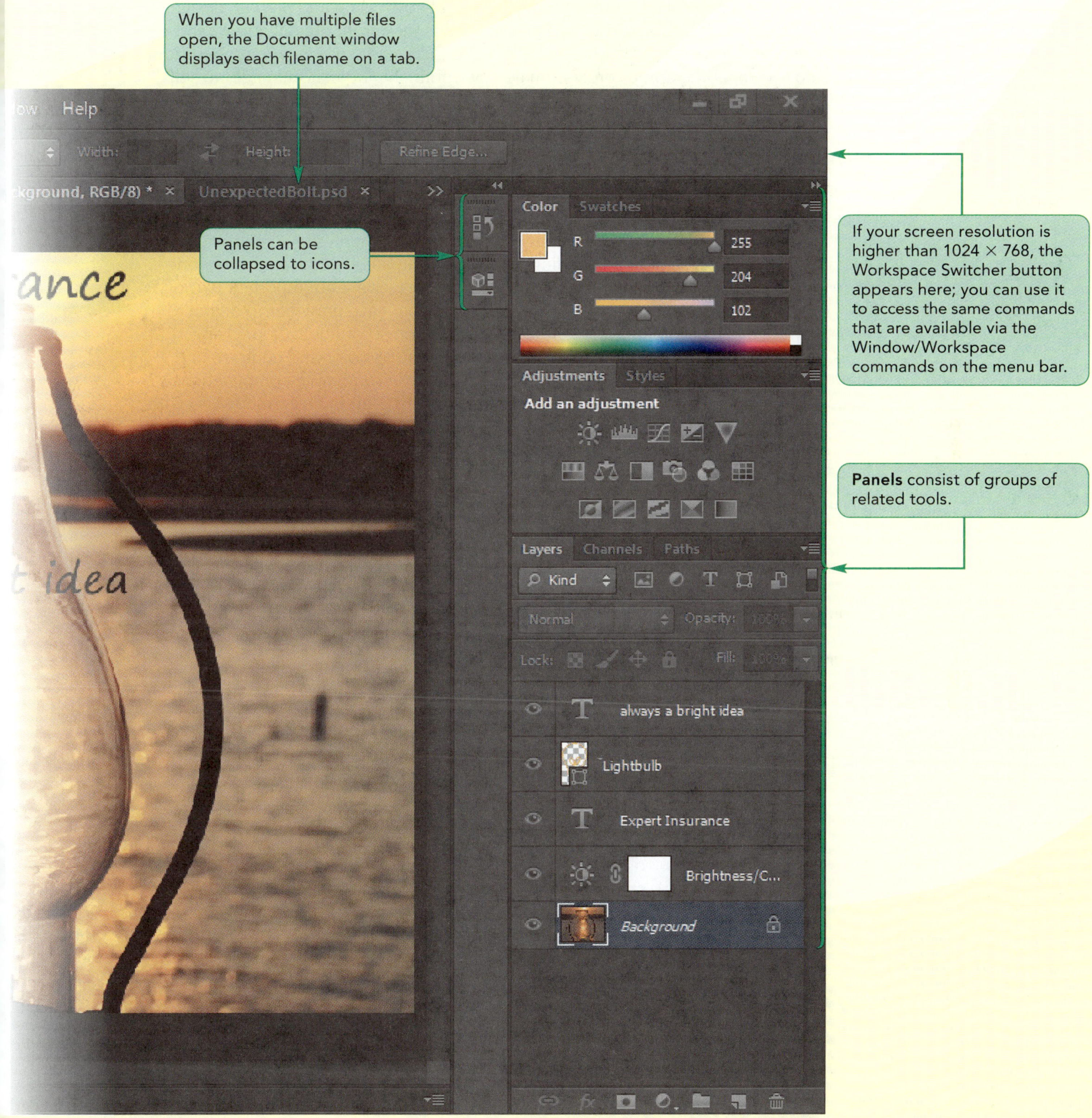

Introducing Graphics and Photoshop CS6

Over 20 years ago, Photoshop 1.0 was released exclusively for the Macintosh operating system. It has since become a standard for both Mac and PC image editing, and it is widely used by graphics professionals at advertising and graphic design agencies, news organizations, educational institutions, nonprofit organizations, and countless other businesses. Over the years, the product's name has even morphed from a noun to a verb, and graphics professionals now routinely *Photoshop* images to sell products, market ideas, and educate consumers.

How Graphics Are Used to Enhance Communications

Think for a moment about how images are used every day in print and Web media. You might use an image to add interest to a printed page by illustrating a story or by showing a product. You might also use an image to teach the mechanics of something—for example, an image of someone kneading bread dough in a cookbook or of someone changing an oil filter in a how-to book on car repair. Images are an important part of how we communicate—and they always have been, from cave drawings to digital photography. This fact explains a great deal about the appeal of Photoshop. Using Photoshop, you can remove the flaws in an image, refine its color and contrast, and modify it in a variety of other ways. You can also compose something completely new by combining digital photographs, text, and other artwork—all in Photoshop. And with the popularity of mobile devices and apps, you can instantly share your composition with relatives, friends, or colleagues—a feat that was unimaginable only a decade ago.

The Role of Photoshop in Professional Production

Since its inception, Photoshop has grown from a relatively straightforward digital image-editing program to a multifaceted, powerful tool used in many industries, from professional photography to Web design to advertising. A **digital image** is a photograph or drawing in electronic form—in other words, a digital image can be displayed on a computer monitor or on the LCD screen of a camera or mobile device. An **image-editing program** is software that lets you manipulate a digital image and then save it with the changes you have made. Many enhancements and adjustments can be achieved with the click of a mouse. Figure 1-1 shows two versions of a photograph enhanced merely by adding an adjustment and applying a filter. Furthermore, Photoshop lets you save images in different file formats—using different color settings and different resolutions depending on whether your output will be print or digital media.

Figure 1-1 **Image enhanced in Photoshop**

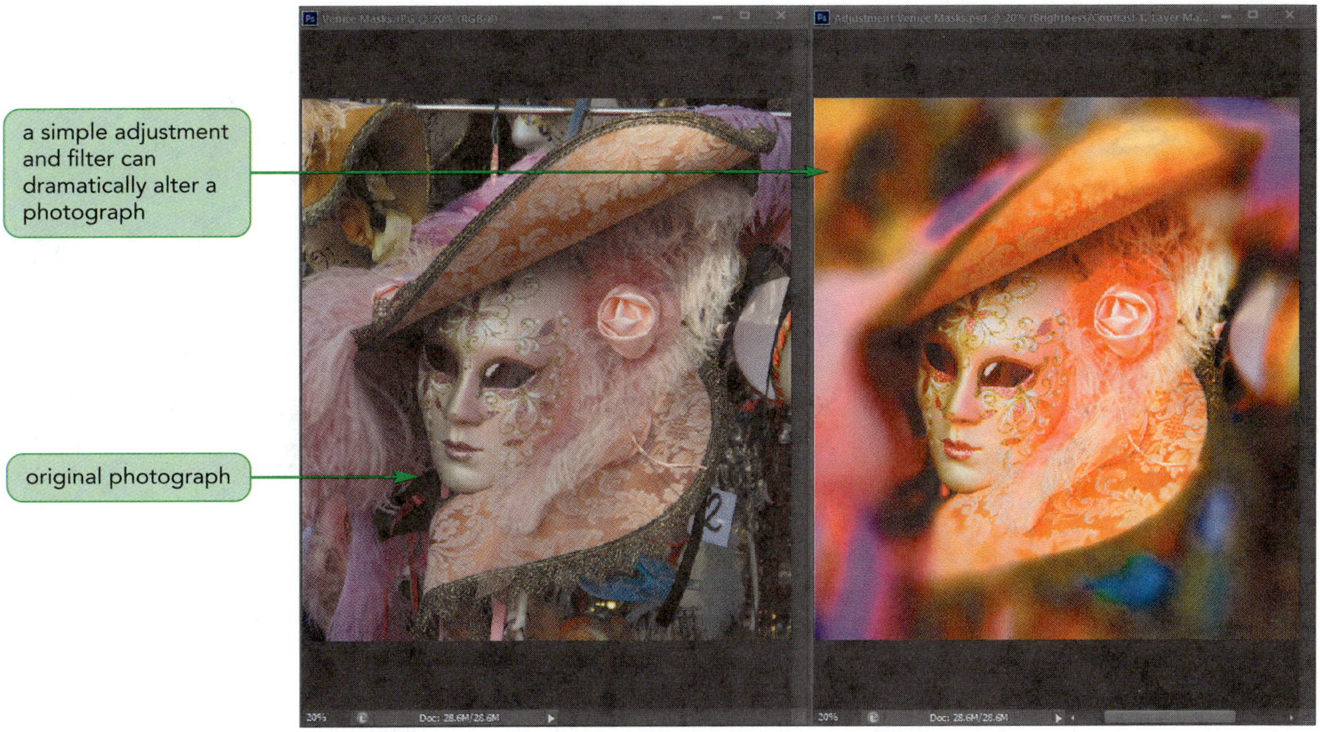

Jane Hosie-Bounar

Mirabeau Media's newest client is a small, local insurance company interested in running an ad campaign that will help it expand its business nationally. Sarah has asked you to learn the basics of digital photography and Photoshop so you can help her mock up a series of proposed ads for the business.

Bitmap vs. Vector Graphics

Digital images consist of two types of graphics—bitmap and vector. A **bitmap** graphic (also called a **raster** graphic) consists of closely spaced rows of pixels, the smallest element in a digital image. Each **pixel** (short for *picture element*) is a square that defines a color. Multiple pixels laid out in a rectangular grid give the illusion of continuity and smoothness in an image. They are the building blocks of any image. The human eye cannot distinguish between pixels unless the image is enlarged so much or the quality is so poor that the individual pixels and the spaces between them are visible. See Figure 1-2.

Resolution is the level of detail in an image, and it is measured in pixels per inch (ppi). The higher the resolution (the more pixels per inch), the sharper the image appears. The default resolution for a Web image is 72 ppi, which is also the default resolution for a new file created in Photoshop. If you plan to use an image for anything other than a Web page, you should create your new Photoshop file with a higher resolution. For example, the resolution required for a professional-quality printed photograph is usually around 300 ppi.

Figure 1-2 **Comparing pixels in an enlarged bitmap image**

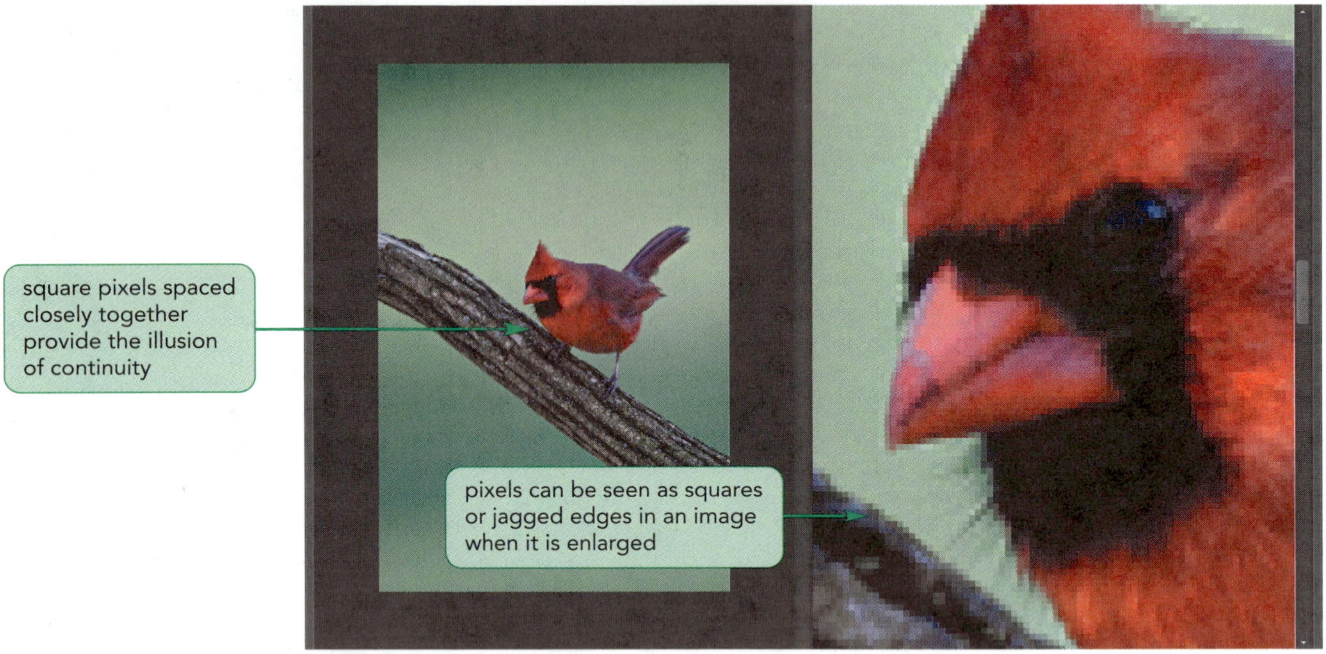

© 2012 Joe Milmoe/DCNature.com

The **file size** of a digital image is dependent both on its resolution and on its physical dimensions. For example, a 300-ppi photo that is 4 by 6 inches has a smaller file size than a 300-ppi photo that is 8 by 12 inches. Photoshop calculates file size by multiplying the number of pixels running across an image by the number of pixels running down an image. Because there are usually millions of pixels in an image, we often use the term **megapixel** (mega means millions) when we talk about file size.

A **vector** graphic is a collection of points, lines, curves, and shapes stored as a set of mathematical instructions. You can create vector graphics in a drawing program such as Adobe Illustrator, but you can also create them in Photoshop, which includes a number of vector tools in its Tools panel. The mathematical instructions in a vector graphic define the lines and curves that make up the graphic. They also define the object's colors and its position on the screen. Text is one example of a vector graphic. You can compose images in Photoshop that include both vector and bitmap graphics. Because of the way vector graphics are stored on a computer, you can resize them proportionally and maintain their quality. See Figure 1-3.

Figure 1-3 **Enlarged bitmap loses quality but vector stays crisp**

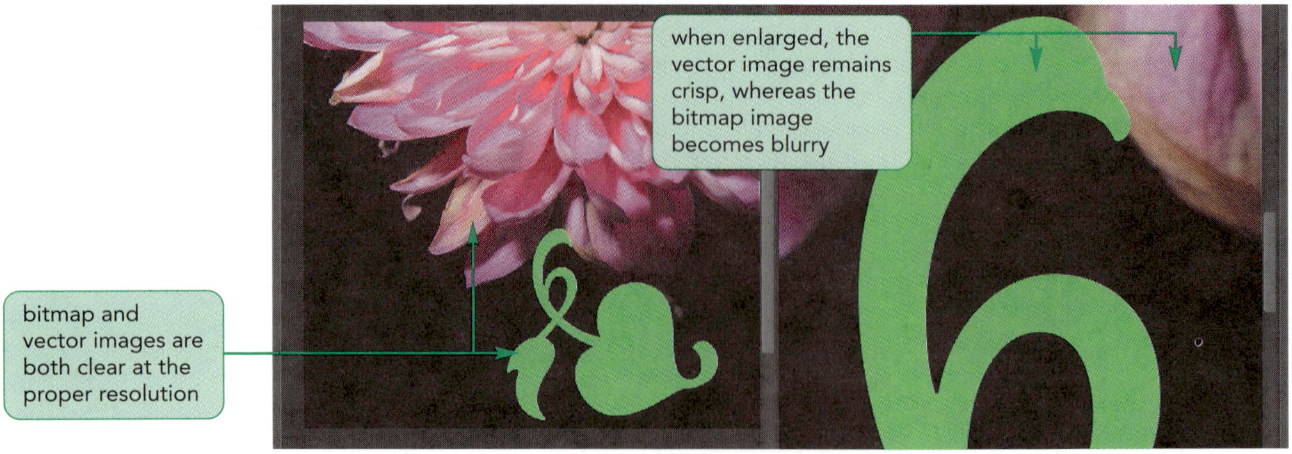

Jane Hosie-Bounar

PROSKILLS

Decision Making: Knowing When Enough Is Enough

Photoshop is a fun program to work with, and by using its features correctly and in moderation you can create interesting and exciting compositions. However, because Photoshop's image-editing possibilities are limitless, it is easy to get carried away. As a Photoshop user in the business world, it will be your responsibility to decide when an image is finished. For example, if you are providing artwork for a repair manual, your photographs should be clear representations of the device and its workings. Fancying up a repair manual with special effects photography would be counterproductive and a waste of your time. On the other hand, sometimes altering a photograph or combining it with another actually makes it stronger. For example, a photograph might be in need of minor color or brightness adjustments to improve its appearance. An image for an advertisement might need to be altered drastically so that the product you are showcasing stands out. As you decide how to manipulate an image in Photoshop, you should keep three things in mind: the message, the client, and the intended audience. Careful decision making will produce positive results.

Now that you have a better sense of what kinds of graphics you can work with in Photoshop, Sarah suggests that you start Photoshop and explore the workspace.

Starting Photoshop and Touring the Photoshop Workspace

When you start Photoshop CS6 for the first time, it opens with the default workspace displayed. In subsequent sessions, restarting Photoshop will display the workspace and settings that were in effect when you exited your last session. The **workspace** includes every element of the Photoshop program window, including the Document window, panels, and other elements that you'll explore in this tutorial.

TIP

You can restore Photoshop's defaults by pressing and holding the Ctrl+Alt+Shift keys while starting the application.

TIP

Depending on your screen resolution, some elements may have a different appearance in your Photoshop window.

To start Photoshop and view the Photoshop program window:

1. Click the **Start** button on the taskbar, click **All Programs**, and then click **Adobe Photoshop CS6** while pressing and holding the **Ctrl+Alt+Shift** keys. When you are prompted to delete the Adobe Photoshop settings, click **Yes**.

   Trouble? If you see an Adobe Creative Suite name, such as Adobe Design Premium CS6, listed before Adobe Photoshop CS6 on the All Programs menu, click the suite name and then click Adobe Photoshop CS6.

   Trouble? If you can't find Adobe Photoshop CS6 on the All Programs menu, navigate to the Adobe folder in the Program Files folder on your hard drive, double-click the Adobe Photoshop CS6 folder, and then double-click Photoshop.exe.

   Trouble? If a User Account Control dialog box appears asking if you want to allow Photoshop to make changes to your computer, click No. Then, restart Photoshop, making sure to press and hold the Ctrl+Alt+Shift keys immediately *after* clicking Adobe Photoshop CS6 so you are prompted to delete the Photoshop settings file.

   Trouble? If the Adobe Product Activation dialog box opens, click the appropriate option button, click Continue, enter the information requested, and then click the Register button. If you do not know your serial number or need additional assistance, ask your instructor or technical support person for help.

Trouble? If you see a message about a problem with the display driver on your computer, click the OK button.

The Photoshop program window opens and displays the default workspace, which is called Essentials. The largest area of the workspace, the Document window, is empty.

TIP

If you're working at a resolution greater than 1024 × 768, you can also click the Workspace Switcher button on the right side of the options bar to access the Workspace commands.

2. On the menu bar, click **Window**, point to **Workspace**, and then click **Reset Essentials** to reset the default workspace layout. On the far left side of the options bar, right-click the **Rectangular Marquee Tool** button, and then click **Reset All Tools**. When you are asked if you want to reset all tools to the default settings, click the **OK** button.

3. If necessary, click the **Maximize** button on the title bar to maximize the Photoshop program window. See Figure 1-4.

Figure 1-4 Photoshop program window

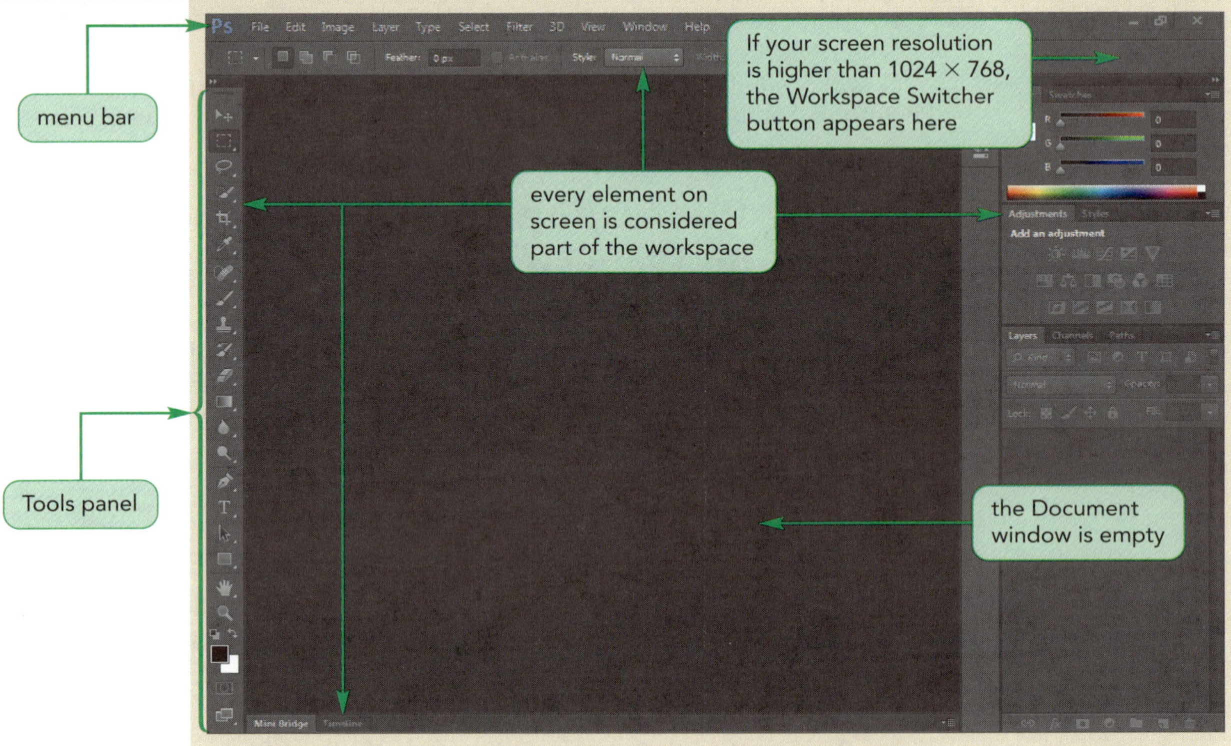

Opening a File

You open a file in Photoshop using the File command on the menu bar. Sarah has given you two Photoshop files that you can open to begin exploring Photoshop.

To open the files and tour the Photoshop workspace:

1. On the menu bar, click **File**, and then click **Open**. The Open dialog box opens.

2. Navigate to the Photoshop1\Tutorial folder included with your Data Files, click **LightningInsurance.psd** in the files list, and then click the **Open** button. The LightningInsurance document opens in the Document window.

   Trouble? If you don't have the starting Data Files, you need to get them before you can proceed. Your instructor will either give you the Data Files or ask you to obtain them from a specified location (such as a network drive). In either case, make a backup copy of the Data Files before you start so that you will have the original files available in case you need to start over. If you have any questions about the Data Files, see your instructor or technical support person for assistance.

   So that you can see how Photoshop handles multiple open files at a time, you'll also open a second file.

3. On the menu bar, click **File**, and then click **Open**. The Open dialog box opens.

   Because the last file you opened was in the Photoshop1\Tutorial folder, the Open dialog box opens to the Photoshop1\Tutorial folder.

4. Double-click **ExpertInsurance.psd**. The ExpertInsurance file opens on a new tab in the Document window, but you can still see the LightningInsurance file's tab behind the current tab. See Figure 1-5.

Figure 1-5 **Most recently opened file is visible**

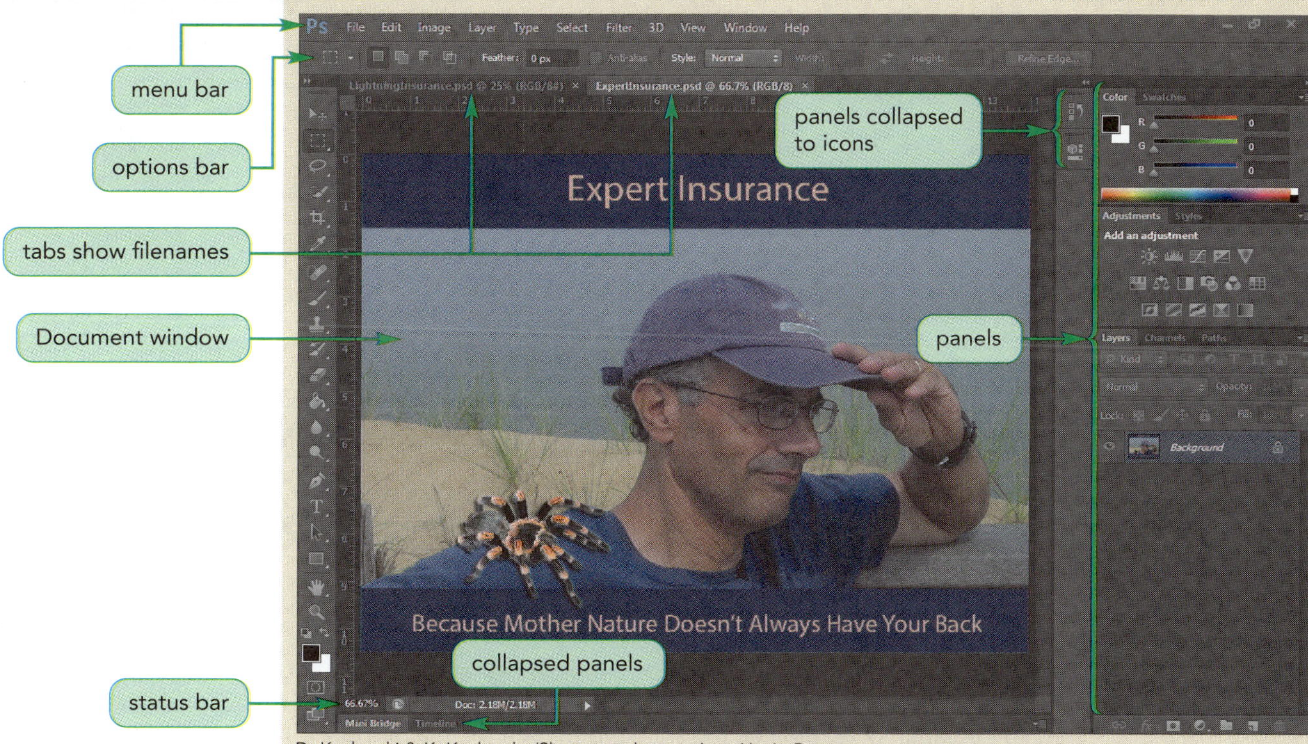

D. Kucharski & K. Kucharska/Shutterstock.com; Jane Hosie-Bounar

You opened two files so that you could see how the Photoshop tools and panels are laid out around the Document window, which contains the images you'll be working with. Now you'll tour the Photoshop workspace so you understand the function of its different elements.

Touring the Photoshop Workspace

The main components of the Photoshop workspace are the menu bar, the Tools panel, the options bar, the Document window, and any panels displayed in the currently selected workspace. In the Essentials workspace, the default panels are Color, Swatches, Adjustments, Styles, Layers, Channels, and Paths. The History and Properties panels also appear, but they are collapsed. (The Properties panel is new to Photoshop CS6 and is covered in detail in Tutorial 2.) At the bottom of the Photoshop workspace, the Mini Bridge and Timeline panels appear, also collapsed. You'll explore all of these panels in later sessions as you work toward becoming a Photoshop expert.

Menu Bar

The menu bar displays a list of 11 commands that open drop-down menus, similar to the menus you find in other applications. To select a menu command, you can either click the command, or press the Alt key and then press the key for the letter you see underlined on the menu bar. Figure 1-6 describes the commands found on the menu bar.

Figure 1-6 **Menu bar**

Menu Name	Use To
File	Browse files in Bridge and Mini Bridge; open, close, and save files; import and export files; print and perform other file-related commands; and exit Photoshop
Edit	Undo and redo changes; cut, copy, and paste objects; transform and format objects; assign and convert color profiles; and adjust user preferences
Image	Change the color mode; apply image adjustments; adjust image and canvas size; rotate, crop, and trim an image; and use other analysis tools
Layer	Add, duplicate, arrange, group, and ungroup layers; merge layers; align and distribute layers; and create layer-based slices for the Web; among other things
Type	Work with characters, paragraphs, fonts, and languages on text layers
Select	Save, edit, refine, and transform selections
Filter	Apply a filter to a layer or a selection; and browse online for additional filters
3D	Work with 3D layers and effects
View	Work with proofing tools; adjust the zoom level of a displayed image; change the screen modes; and display and hide rulers and guides
Window	Arrange windows; switch workspaces; and display and hide different panels
Help	Access local and online help; get software updates; and participate in online Photoshop community discussions

Tools Panel

TIP

To display the Tools panel in two columns, click the double arrows directly above the panel. To go back to a one-column display, click the double arrows again.

The Tools panel contains tools for creating vector images such as geometric shapes, selecting portions of a document, adding text, adding brushstrokes, and modifying pixels in bitmap images. Related tools are grouped in the panel. For example, tools for selecting pixels and colors appear in the top section. You can display the Tools panel as a single column (the default) or in two columns. When you point to a tool in the Tools panel, Photoshop displays a **tooltip**, which includes the name of the tool plus any shortcut key for selecting the tool. For example, the shortcut key for selecting the Zoom tool is Z.

The Tools panel also includes hidden tools. In fact, any tool with a small triangle displayed in the lower-right corner has other tools hidden beneath it, as shown in the Session 1.1 Visual Overview. To display a list of hidden tools, point to the top-level tool in the Toolbar, click and hold the mouse button, and then click the tool you want to make active.

Options Bar

The options bar includes the controls, or options, for the current tool. For example, if you select the Horizontal Type tool in the Tools panel, Photoshop displays options for text orientation, font, style, and size, among others. If you are working at a resolution higher than 1024 × 768, the options bar also displays the Workspace Switcher, which you use to create a new workspace, delete a workspace, reset a workspace, or switch to a different workspace.

Document Window

The Document window displays the current file. When you have multiple files open, the Document window displays each filename on a tab along the top of the window by default. Clicking a tab displays the document named on the tab. You can also use the Arrange command on the Window menu to display open files tiled in a grid or side by side vertically or horizontally. As soon as you open a file in the Document window, the status bar appears near the lower-left corner of the window. By default, the status bar displays the current zoom percentage as well as the document size (in kilobytes or megapixels). You can change what is displayed on the status bar by clicking the arrow to the right of the document size, and then clicking the information you want to display (for example, the document dimensions or the name of the currently selected tool).

Panels

Panels consist of groups of related tools. For example, the Swatches panel displays samples of colors available in the current color mode and stores the most frequently used colors. You can change the set of swatches displayed in the panel or add your own swatches to an existing set. The Adjustments panel lets you modify your images by adjusting different settings, such as brightness and contrast, or by changing a photograph from color to black and white. You'll explore panels and how to arrange them in Session 1.2.

Sarah suggests you make use of Photoshop's Help system to help you master the features of Photoshop. You decide to spend time exploring Help now so that you can use it efficiently in the future.

Getting Help in Photoshop

Photoshop includes an online Help system that lets you access information posted by Adobe as well as information posted by members of **Adobe Community Help**, a forum where you can find resources such as tips, videos, and other information from professional photographers and designers willing to share their insights. Some of the topics are written by Adobe and Adobe partners, but others are not. To access Help, you can use the Photoshop Online Help command on the Help menu, or you can press the F1 key.

When you first open Adobe Help using the Photoshop Online Help command, Photoshop displays a list of topics in the browser window. You can explore Adobe-authored Help by clicking the links. You can also search for specific information by typing a term in the Search Help box on the left. When you click a link, the relevant information is displayed.

You'll explore Help to find more about workspaces in Photoshop.

TIP

You can also press the F1 key to access Photoshop Help.

To get help in Photoshop:

1. On the menu bar, click **Help**, and then click **Photoshop Online Help**. The Photoshop Help/Help and tutorials window opens in your browser. See Figure 1-7.

Figure 1-7 **Adobe Community Help**

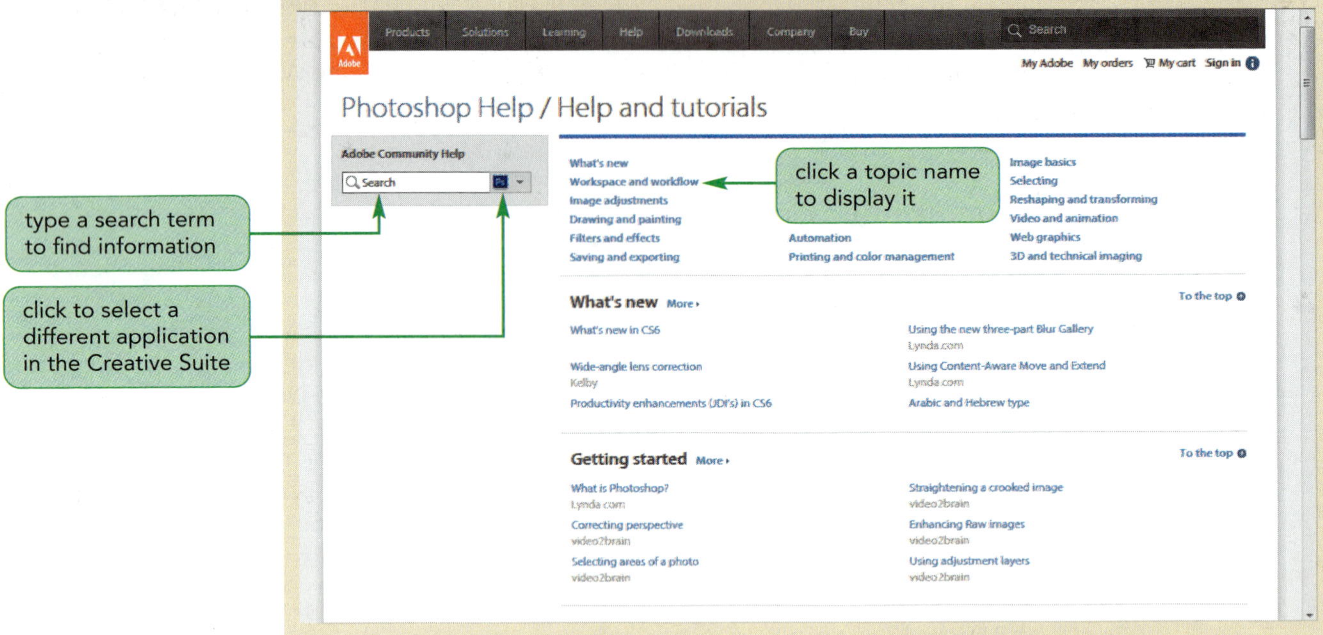

2. In the list of topics on the right, click **Workspace and workflow**, and then click **Workspace basics**.
3. Click **Manage windows and panels**. Photoshop displays detailed information about managing windows and panels. See Figure 1-8.

Figure 1-8 **Help topic**

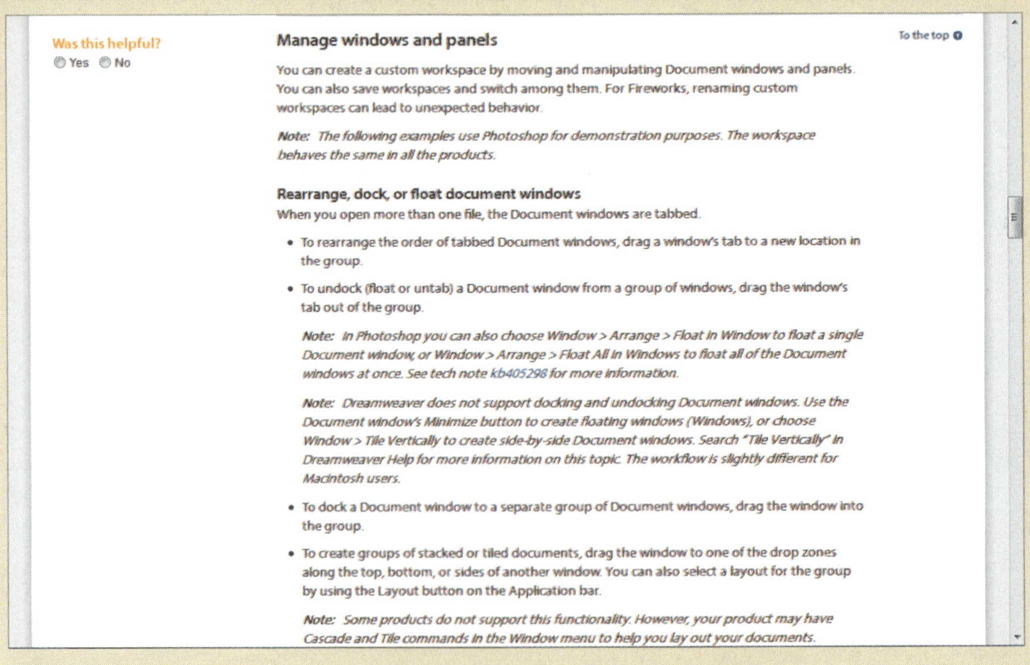

4. Scroll through and read the **Rearrange, dock, or float document windows** topic. Photoshop shows detailed information about working with Document windows. Notice that some of the information presented is about other products in the Adobe Creative Suite. Once you know how to manage the elements in Photoshop, you will recognize many of the same elements in other Adobe products, such as Dreamweaver.

5. Click the Close button [X] on the Adobe Community Help window title bar to close your browser. The Help system closes, and the Photoshop program window is now displayed.

INSIGHT

Searching for Information and Using External Help

You can use the Help system to search the Web for information on using Adobe Photoshop. To do so, at the top of the Help browser window, type a term in the Search box and then press the Enter key. Keep in mind that when you do this, the information you find is not necessarily approved by Adobe (even though it appears in the Search results) and, therefore, might not be as accurate as the information within the Help system itself. For the most reliable help, click the Only Adobe content option button above the list of search results.

Now that you have a sense of how to find information about any tool you need to use in Photoshop, you'll practice working with multiple files.

Working with Multiple Files

Photoshop not only allows you to edit and transform existing images, but it also lets you combine elements to create a completely new photo composition. When you do this kind of complex work, you will most likely need to have multiple files open at one time. You open, save, and close Photoshop files in the same way you perform file-handling tasks in many other applications, so some of the commands might be familiar to you.

REFERENCE

Opening Multiple Files at Once

- On the menu bar, click File, and then click Open (or press the Ctrl+O keys).
- To open contiguous files (files listed next to each other), click the first filename, press and hold the Shift key, click the last filename, and then release the Shift key.
- To open noncontiguous files, click the first filename, press and hold the Ctrl key, and then click any other file(s) in the list.
- Click Open (or press the Enter key).

Sarah has given you a number of photographs and photo compositions that she wants you to review so that you can better understand the power of Photoshop.

To open multiple files:

1. On the menu bar, click **File**, and then click **Open**. The Open dialog box opens. You can select multiple files and apply the Open command to all of them at once.

Be sure to press the Ctrl key and not the Shift key. If you press the Shift key, all the files in between will be selected as well.

2. Navigate to the Photoshop1\Tutorial folder included with your Data Files, if necessary. Click **FireInsurance.psd**, press and hold the **Ctrl** key, scroll down the files list, if necessary, and then click **UnexpectedBolt.psd**.

3. Click the **Open** button. Photoshop opens both files at once, each on its own tab in the Document window. See Figure 1-9.

Figure 1-9 Multiple open files

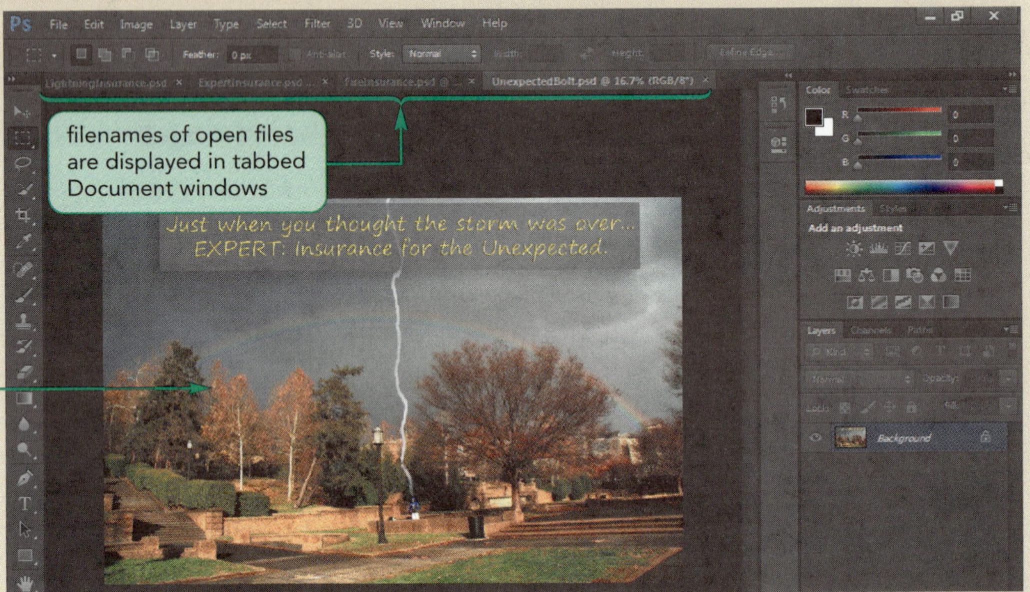

© 2012 Chadwick Cipiti/DCNature.com

The last file you selected, UnexpectedBolt, is visible. The other file you selected, FireInsurance, is behind it, as are the two files you opened previously, ExpertInsurance and LightningInsurance.

Sarah explains that because you will often modify files in Photoshop, it is best to preserve the original file so that you can reuse it or backtrack if you make and then save unwanted changes. Therefore, she asks you to save the UnexpectedBolt file with a new name.

Saving a File with a New Name

When you save files in Photoshop, you have many different options. You can save a file with the same name and file format (for example, JPEG), which overwrites the original file. You can save a file with a new name in the same file format. You can also save a file with a new name in a new format. No matter which option you choose, it is best to save your work often in Photoshop so you don't lose your changes should something unexpected occur.

TIP

You can also press the Shift+Ctrl+S keys to open the Save As dialog box.

To save a file with a new name:

1. Make sure the **UnexpectedBolt** tab is selected in the workspace, and then on the menu bar, click **File**, and then click **Save As**. The Save As dialog box opens. You can save the file in a different format, or as a copy of the original file. You'll explore a number of these save options in later tutorials, but for now, you'll save the file in the same format, with a new name.

Trouble? If the Photoshop Format Options dialog box opens, click the OK button to accept the default options to maximize compatibility.

2. Select the text in the File name box, and then type **NewUnexpected** to overwrite the existing filename. You don't need to type the .psd file extension because Photoshop automatically adds the selected file type's extension to the filename.
3. Click the **Save** button. Photoshop saves the file with a new name. To confirm that the original file is still intact, you can open the Open dialog box.
4. Press the **Ctrl+O** keys, navigate to the Photoshop1\Tutorial folder and then scroll to the bottom of the files list, if necessary. Notice that the new file, NewUnexpected, and the original file, UnexpectedBolt, both appear in the files list in the Tutorial folder. Any changes that you make to the newly saved file will not affect the original.
5. Click the **Cancel** button to close the Open dialog box.

Now that you've practiced opening and saving files, Sarah explains that you need to learn how to best arrange the Document windows and navigate through open files so you can work efficiently in Photoshop.

Navigating and Arranging File Windows

Photoshop provides many different ways to navigate through and arrange the files you are working with. You can navigate by clicking the Document window tabs, or you can use predefined key combinations. You can also use a menu to select a file and switch to it.

Navigating Open File Windows and Changing Tab Order

You can move from one open file to another by clicking the Document window tabs. Photoshop also provides two key combinations for navigating open files. Pressing the Ctrl+Tab keys cycles through the open files in the order in which they were opened. Pressing the Ctrl+Shift+Tab keys cycles through the open files in reverse.

To navigate the open file windows:

1. Click the **LightningInsurance** Document window tab. Photoshop displays the LightningInsurance photograph.
2. Click the **ExpertInsurance** tab.
3. Press the **Ctrl+Tab** keys. Photoshop displays the FireInsurance document.
4. Press and hold the **Ctrl+Shift** keys, and then press the **Tab** key two times. Photoshop cycles through the files in reverse order.
5. On the menu bar, click **File**, click **Open Recent**, and then click **UnexpectedBolt.psd**. Because you have more files open in the Document window than Photoshop has room to display tabs, a new window element appears on the right side of the tab area—a double arrow pointing to the right.
6. Click the **double arrow** >>. Photoshop displays a list of all open files. The active file has a check mark next to the filename. See Figure 1-10.

Trouble? Your view might vary depending on the size and resolution of your monitor. Such differences shouldn't cause problems as you complete these steps. However, if you don't see the double arrow », read but don't perform Step 6.

Figure 1-10 Open file list displayed

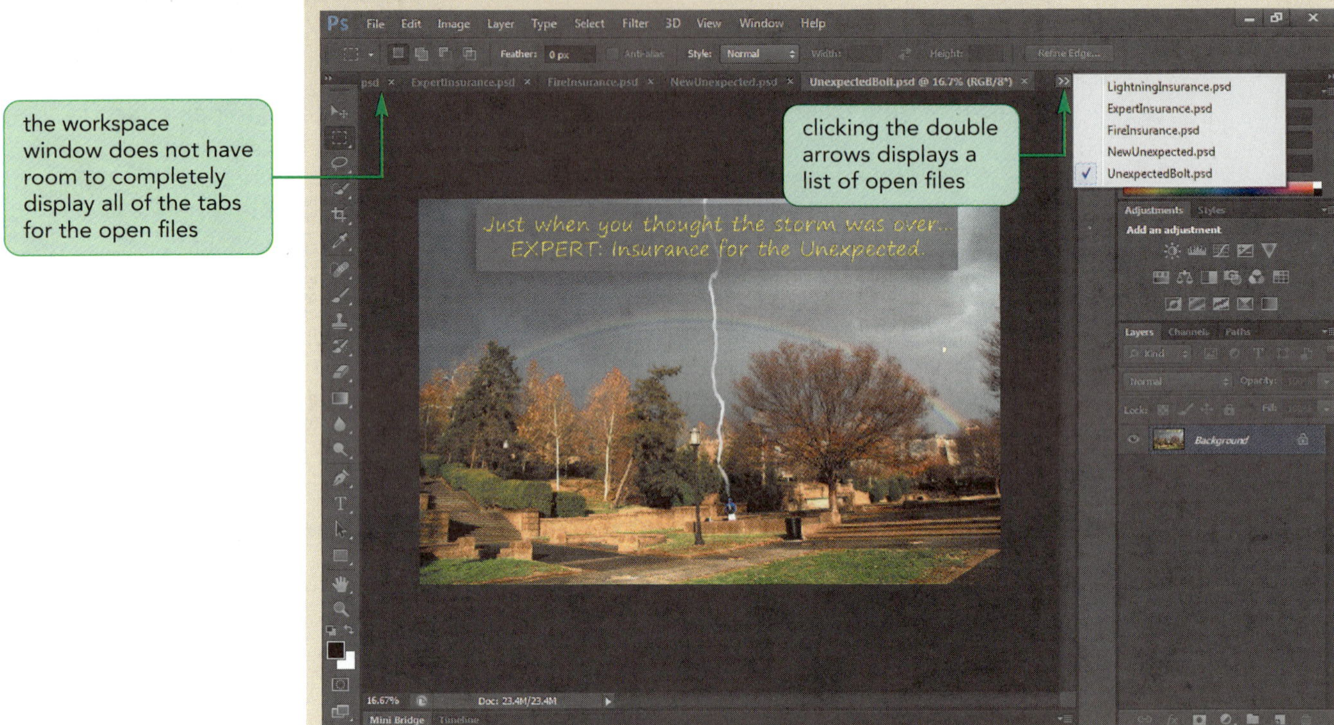

You can display an image by clicking its name on the list.

7. In the list of open files, click **LightningInsurance**, which is the file whose tab you cannot see. Photoshop displays the LightningInsurance image.

You might want to change the order of tabs in the Document window so you can navigate more easily between related files. You can change the tab order by clicking and dragging the tabs with the mouse.

To change the tab order:

1. Point to the **LightningInsurance** tab, click and hold the mouse button, and then drag to the right along the tab bar until the LightningInsurance tab appears to the right of the FireInsurance tab. See Figure 1-11.

Figure 1-11 Moving a tab

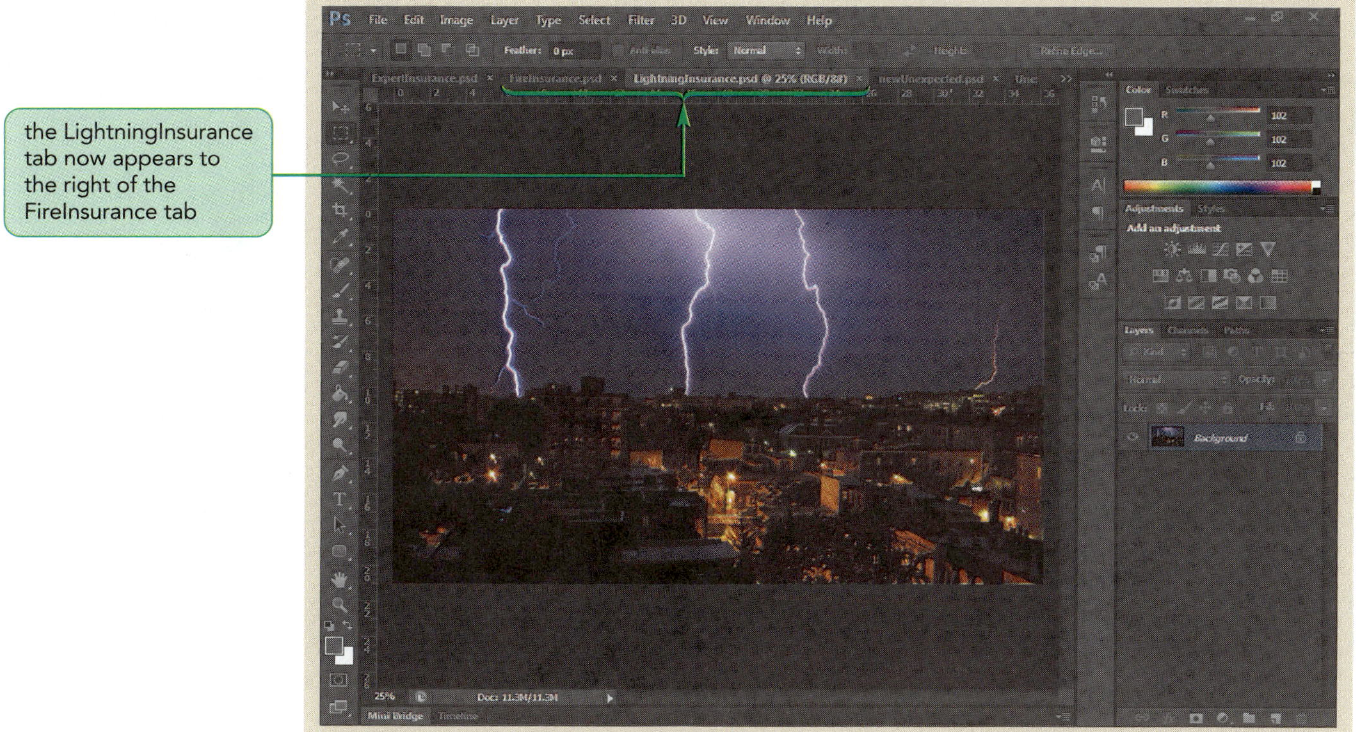

© 2012 Brian Gratwicke/DCNature.com

2. Release the mouse button.

   Dragging a tab changes its position, but it does not change the order in which you cycle through the files using the shortcut keys. They will always cycle from first opened to last opened when you press the Ctrl+Tab key combination.

Arranging File Windows

You can arrange file windows so that multiple files appear in the Document window at one time. You can display images in floating Document windows and drag them around the workspace, or you can arrange the files using the commands on the Arrange Documents menu.

Next, you'll explore how to work with floating Document windows, and then you'll arrange the windows in one of the arrangement choices provided by Photoshop.

To float the Document window:

1. Point to the **ExpertInsurance** tab, click and hold the mouse button, drag the tab down to the middle of the workspace, and release the mouse button. The Document window "detaches" from the other tabs and appears in its own free-floating Document window. See Figure 1-12.

Figure 1-12 **Free-floating Document window**

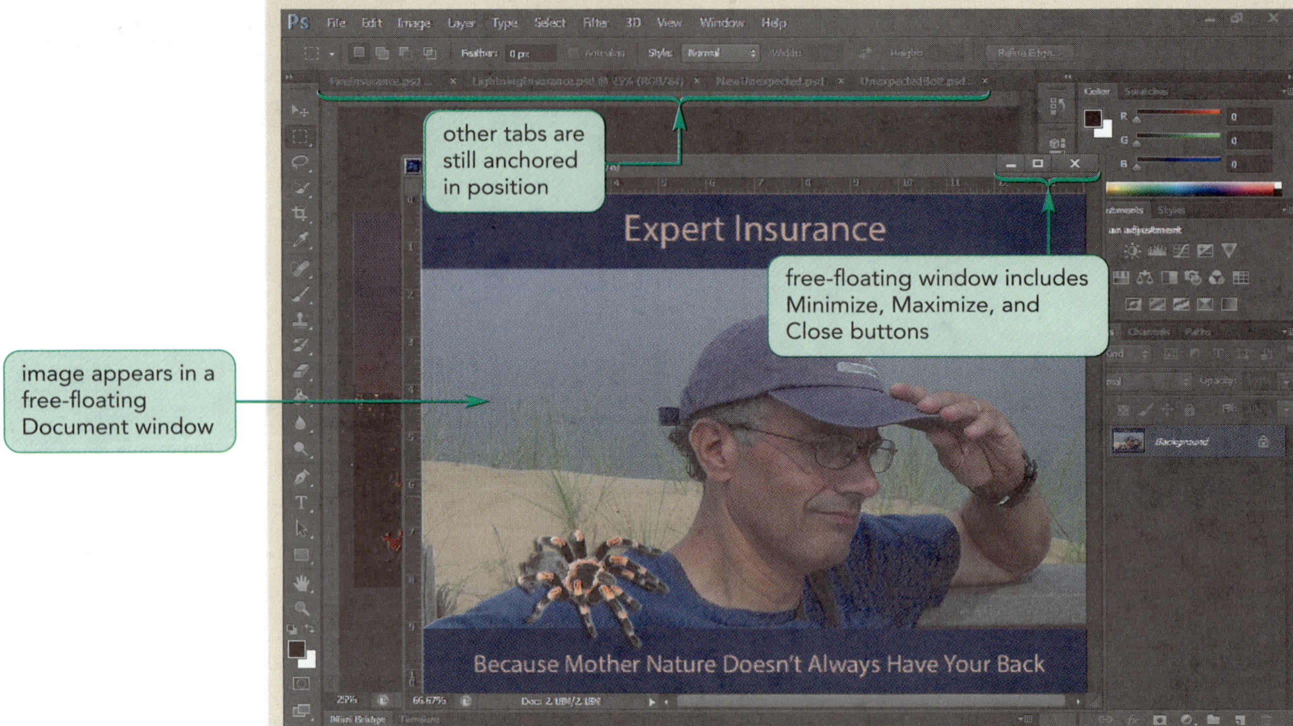

© 2012 Brian Gratwicke/DCNature.com; D. Kucharski & K. Kucharska/Shutterstock.com; Jane Hosie-Bounar

2. Click the **Minimize** button in the floating Document window title bar. The ExpertInsurance window seems to disappear from the Photoshop program window.
3. Point to the **Photoshop** program icon on the Windows 7 taskbar, and you will see that the ExpertInsurance document is still there, but minimized. Click the thumbnail. The ExpertInsurance Document window is restored to its floating size.
4. Click the **Maximize** button for the ExpertInsurance file. The file is maximized in its own window and covers the Photoshop program window.
5. Click the **Restore** button . The file again floats in its own Document window.
6. Point to the title bar of the floating Document window, click and hold the mouse button, and then drag the Document window up to the tabs until the window is surrounded by a blue outline. Release the mouse button. The ExpertInsurance Document window is now one of the tabbed windows.

Photoshop also provides a variety of predefined arrangements for viewing your open documents. You can find the different choices on the Arrange Documents menu.

To arrange the documents using the Arrange Documents menu:

1. On the menu bar, click **Window**, and then point to **Arrange**. Photoshop displays a menu of options with icons, each representing a window arrangement, as well as a series of commands for displaying your files in the Document window. The available options change based on the number of open files. For example, notice that the 6-up command is grayed out because you have fewer than six windows open. The default arrangement is Consolidate All to Tabs, which is the arrangement you have been working in.
2. Click **Tile**. Photoshop arranges the Document window so that all open files are visible. Notice that Photoshop does not change the zoom levels for any of the images. It merely fits each file in a smaller window so that less of each image is visible.
3. On the menu bar, click **Window**, point to **Arrange**, and then click **2-up Vertical** [icon]. Photoshop arranges the topmost file and the next file in the tab order into two windows in the Document window. You can view the other open files by clicking the double arrow to display the files list. See Figure 1-13.

Figure 1-13 2-up Vertical arrangement

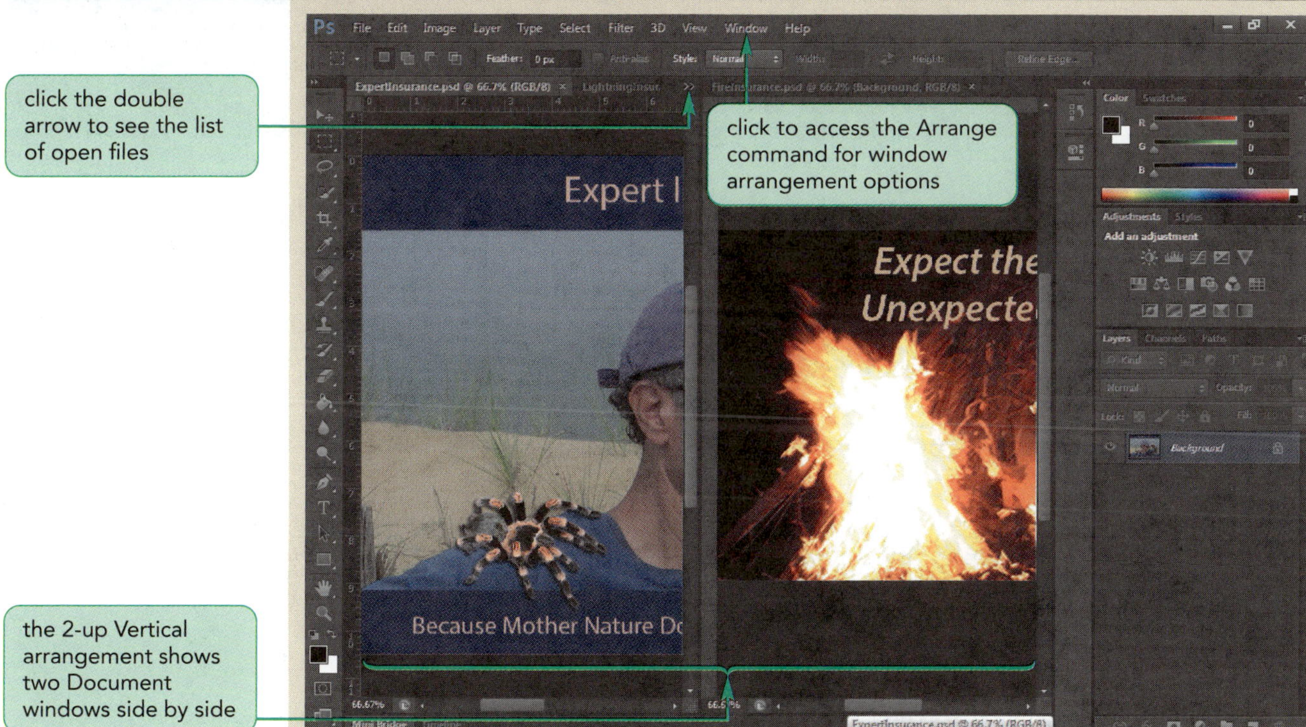

D. Kucharski & K. Kucharska/Shutterstock.com; Jane Hosie-Bounar; A. H. Bounar

4. On the menu bar, click **Window**, point to **Arrange**, and then click **Float All in Windows**. Photoshop stacks all of the files in free-floating Document windows. To navigate these windows, you click their title bars.
5. Click the **LightningInsurance** title bar. The LightningInsurance Document window moves to the front. See Figure 1-14.

Figure 1-14 Stacked floating windows

click a window title bar to display the file; your file arrangement might be different

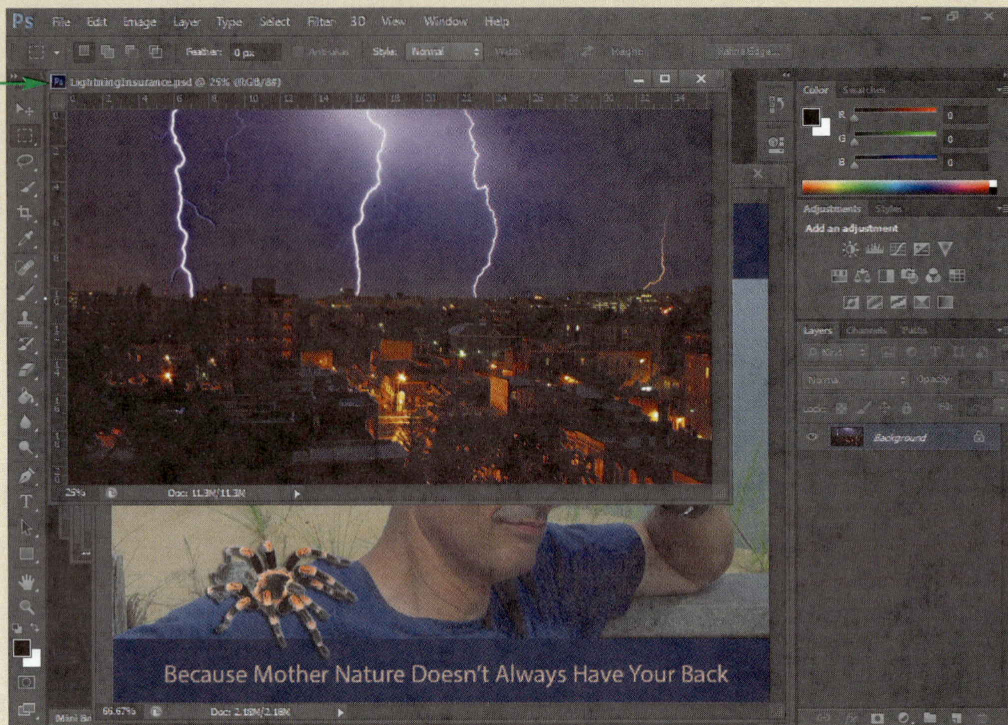

Although you can no longer see the title bars of the other files, and there is no double-headed arrow displayed, you can still access these files using the Window menu.

6. On the menu bar, click **Window**, and then click **ExpertInsurance** in the list of files at the bottom of the menu. The ExpertInsurance window is now on top.
7. On the menu bar, click **Window**, point to **Arrange**, and then click **Consolidate All to Tabs** to return to tabbed windows.

Now that you have spent time exploring the Photoshop workspace and have learned some of the basics of working with files and file windows, Sarah suggests you close all the files you have opened.

Closing Files

After you finish working on a file, you should close it. This saves system resources on your computer.

To close all the open files:

1. On the menu bar, click **File**, and then click **Close**. The top file closes.

   Trouble? If you are prompted to save the file, you might have inadvertently changed the file while you were exploring the workspace. Click No to close the file without saving it.

2. Click the **Close** button on the current Document window tab. The file closes.
3. On the menu bar, click **File**, and then click **Close All** to close the rest of the open files. The Photoshop window is now empty. You can open additional files, or you can exit Photoshop.

Exiting Photoshop

If you are no longer working in Photoshop, you should exit the application. This saves system resources as you work in other programs. You can also exit Photoshop without first closing the files. When you do, Photoshop asks you if you want to save any modified files before they are closed.

To exit Photoshop:

1. On the menu bar, click **File**, and then click **Exit**. Photoshop closes.

In this session, you learned how to start Photoshop, and you explored the program window. You also learned how to open and close files, how to find the information you need in Help, how to arrange windows, and how to exit Photoshop.

Now that you know the basics of working with files and Document windows, Sarah asks you to spend time learning about some additional features of Photoshop. In the next session, you will explore preference settings, panels, grids, and guides.

REVIEW

Session 1.1 Quick Check

1. Photoshop is a(n) ________________ program.
2. Explain how a bitmap graphic is different from a vector graphic.
3. The smallest unit in a bitmap graphic is called a(n) ________________.
4. What is the name of the default workspace in Photoshop?
5. The ________________ panel on the left side of the program window provides options for creating and modifying vector graphics and modifying the pixels in bitmap graphics in your Photoshop file.
6. True or False. You can only have one Photoshop file open at a time.
7. The ________________ command on the Window menu lets you tile open documents within the Document window.

SESSION 1.2 VISUAL OVERVIEW

The ruler displays the measurement of your document in pixels, inches, centimeters, or other units.

Dragging a title bar in a stack will move all of the panels in the stack together.

A **stack**, a collection of floating panel groups joined top to bottom, can improve workflow.

Use the Shape tools to draw vector objects.

Use vector tools to add a drawing to your image.

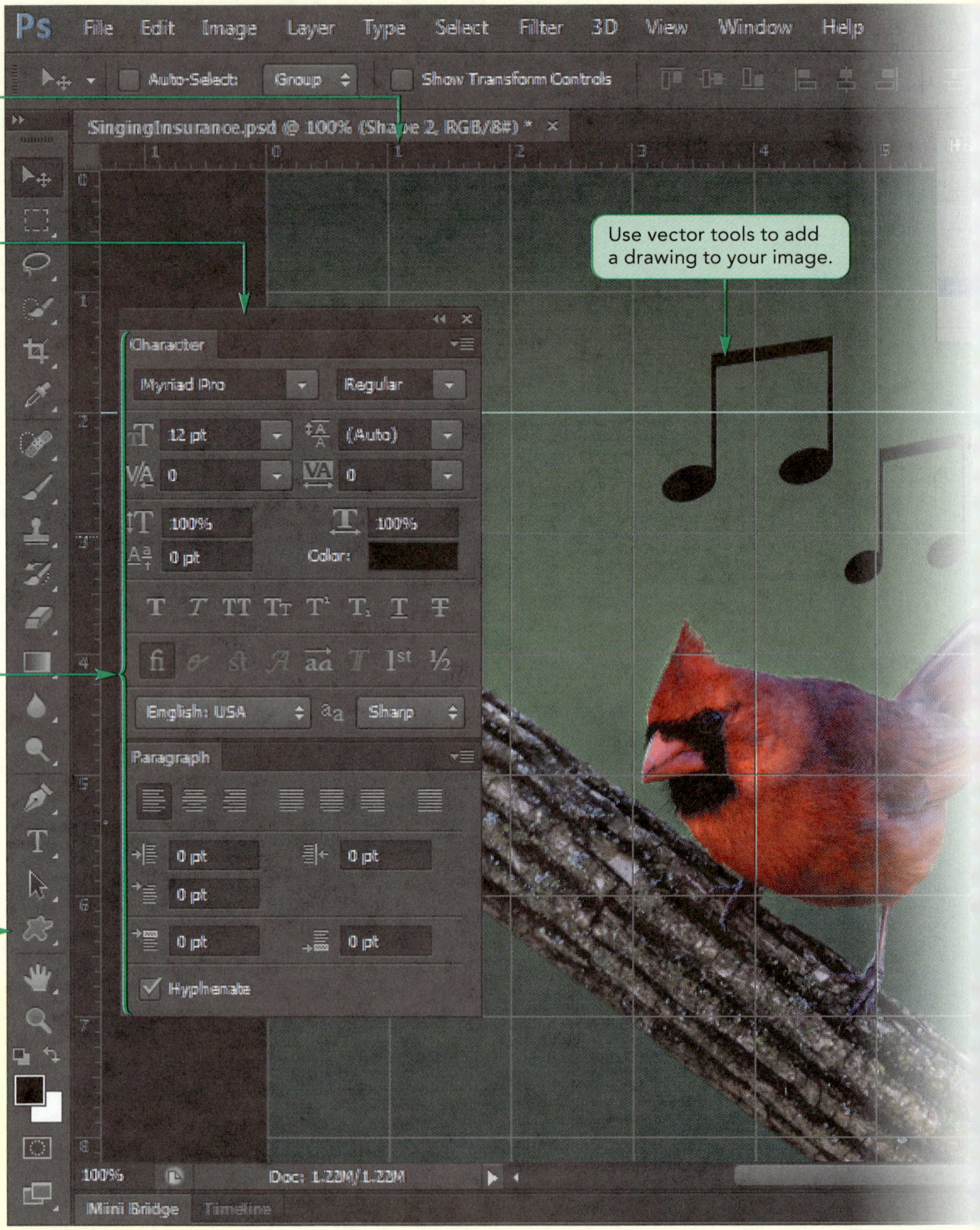

© 2012 Joe Milmoe/DCNature.com

GRIDS, GUIDES, AND PANELS

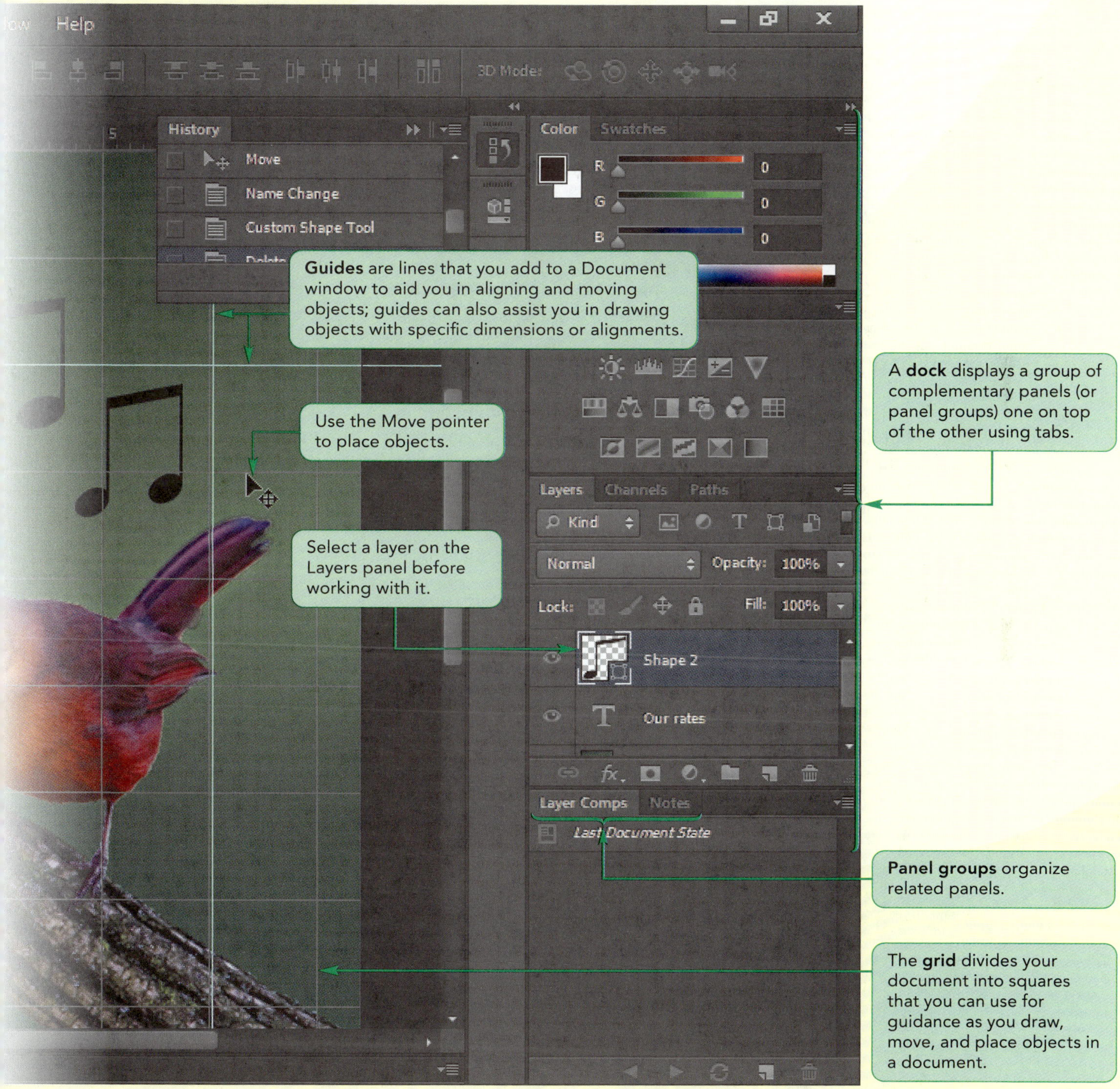

Viewing and Changing Photoshop Preferences

Once you have some experience working with Photoshop, you will find that you develop certain preferences for how the program window is set up. Photoshop lets you customize those preferences and save them for different tasks.

Now that you understand how to arrange and manipulate the display of files in the Document window, Sarah suggests you learn about Photoshop Preferences.

REFERENCE

Setting Photoshop Preferences

- On the menu bar, click Edit, point to Preferences, click General, and then click the Next button until you reach the panel you want to work with.
- Set preferences in the panel, and click the OK button to close the panel and save the preferences, or click the Next button or the Prev button to display the next or previous Preferences panel.

or

- On the menu bar, click Edit, point to Preferences, and then click the name of the panel you want to work with.
- Set preferences in the panel, and click the OK button to close the panel and save the preferences, or click the Next button or the Prev button to display the next or previous Preferences panel.

Photoshop includes plenty of options for customizing its tools, performance, file handling, and interface. Many of those options are covered in later tutorials, but it's important to know that they exist and where to access them so you can use them as your expertise in Photoshop grows.

Sarah suggests that you begin to explore the preferences in Photoshop by changing one of the Preferences settings.

To set Photoshop Preferences:

1. Start Photoshop while pressing the **Ctrl+Alt+Shift** keys. When you are prompted to delete the Adobe Photoshop Settings File, click **Yes**. On the menu bar, click **Window**, point to **Workspace**, and then click **Reset Essentials** to reset the default workspace layout. On the options bar, right-click the **Rectangular Marquee Tool** button, and then click Reset All Tools. When you are asked if you want to reset all tools to the default settings, click the **OK** button.
2. Navigate to the Photoshop1\Tutorial folder, and open the file **SingingInsurance.psd**.
3. On the menu bar, click **Edit**, point to **Preferences**, and then click **General**. All of the preferences are available in different panels of the Preferences dialog box. See Figure 1-15.

Figure 1-15 Preferences dialog box

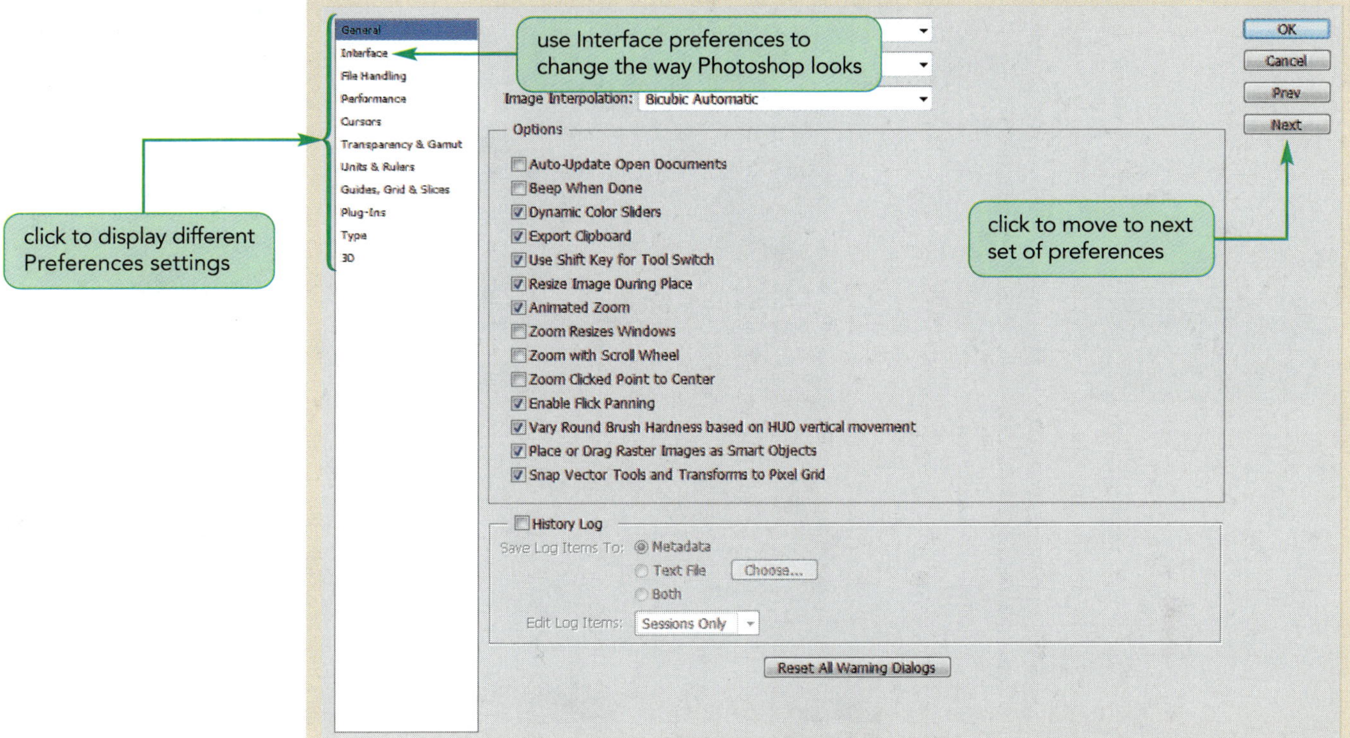

You change panels by clicking panel names in the left pane of the dialog box, or by clicking the Next button or the Prev button in the right pane.

4. In the left pane of the dialog box, click **Interface**. The Interface settings let you change the way Photoshop looks. You will change the color of the standard screen, which is the area that appears around a file.

5. In the Appearance section, click the **Standard Screen Mode Color arrow**, click **Light Gray**, and then click the **OK** button. The area around the document in the Document window is now light gray. See Figure 1-16.

Figure 1-16 Changing an Interface setting

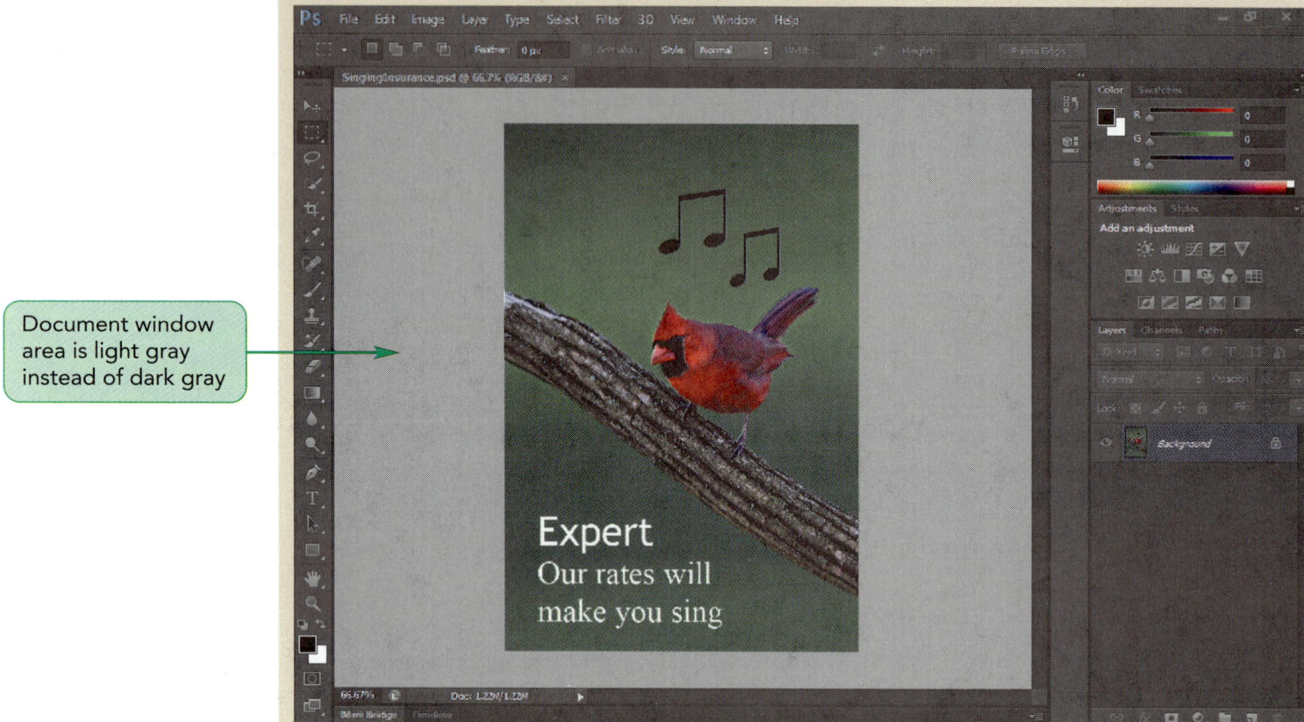

© 2012 Joe Milmoe/DCNature.com

6. On the menu bar, click **Edit**, point to **Preferences**, and then click **Interface**.
7. In the Appearance section, click the **Standard Screen Mode Color arrow**, click **Default**, and then click the **OK** button. The area around the file in the Document window is now dark gray, the default setting.

INSIGHT

Understanding File Handling Preferences

Photoshop CS6 has new file-handling preference settings that let users define how, where, and how often files and file backups are saved. The Save in Background option in the File Handling section of the Preferences dialog box ensures that even in the case of a crash or power failure, you won't lose your work. The Save in Background freature also allows you to continue working while Photoshop is saving a large file. In addition, you have the option to auto-save your work as frequently as every 5 minutes—another safeguard against losing the image-editing effects you may have spent hours trying to achieve.

Restoring Default Photoshop Preferences

If you make changes to Photoshop Preferences but later decide you want to restore the defaults, you do not have to go back to the individual Preferences panels and undo each change individually. Instead, you can simply exit Photoshop and restart it while pressing and holding the Ctrl+Alt+Shift keys. When you are prompted to delete the Adobe Photoshop Settings File, click Yes. When Photoshop opens, the default preferences will be restored.

Working with Panels

You have seen how you can arrange Document windows in different ways. You can also customize the workspace by rearranging the panels in the workspace or by opening panels that don't appear by default in a particular workspace. Furthermore, you can increase your work area by hiding and collapsing panels or by floating panels and then dragging them out of the way. See Figure 1-17.

Figure 1-17 Panel groups and docks

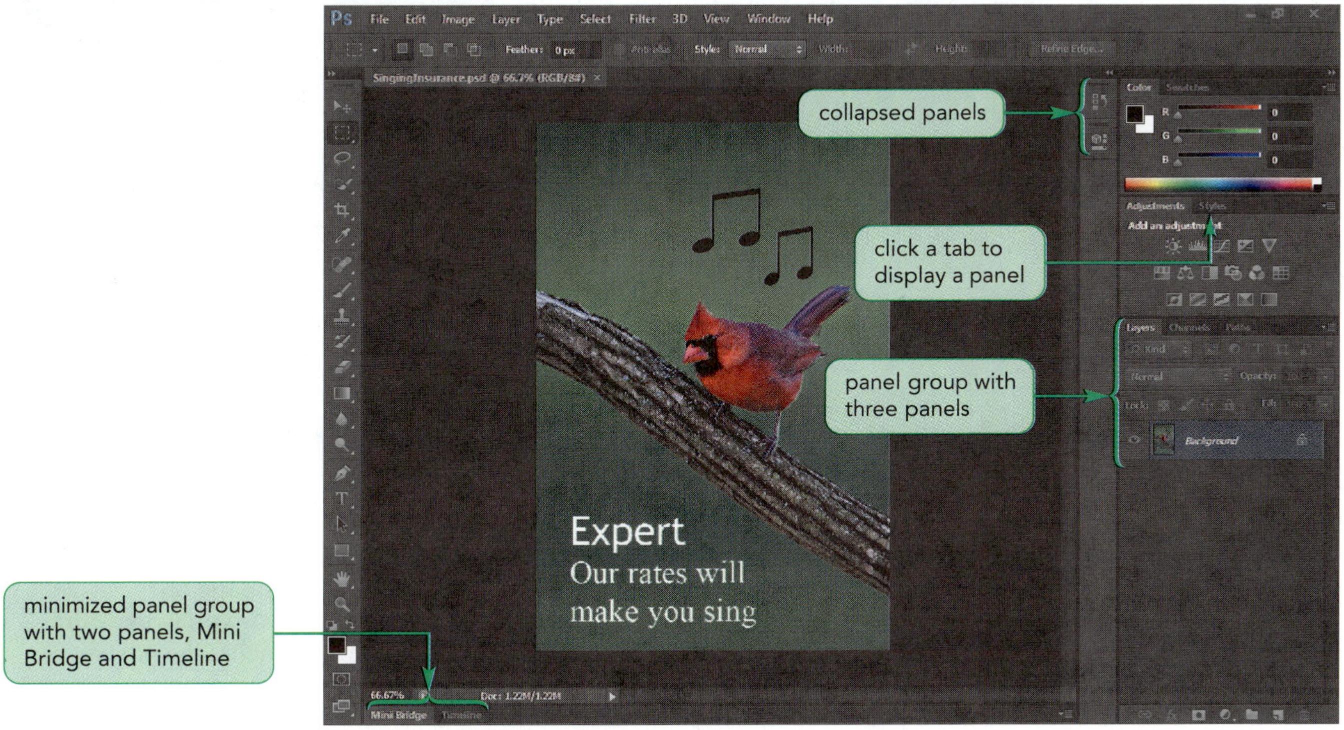

Each panel in Photoshop is a collection of related tools and settings, and panel groups organize related panels. Beyond that, groups of panels are often collected in docks. For example, in the Essentials workspace, the Layers, Channels, and Paths panels are displayed in a group by default because those panels are often used together. In turn, they are docked with two other panel groups: Adjustments and Styles, and Color and Swatches. Two collapsed panels, History and Properties, are also docked on the left side of the Color and Swatches panel group in the Essentials workspace. An additional panel group, Mini Bridge and Timeline, appears at the bottom of the window, collapsed. The default Essentials workspace also includes the Tools panel to the left of the Document window. You move from one docked panel to another by clicking the tabs.

Panels can also be displayed in stacks, which are collections of floating panel groups. The panels in a stack share a title bar, and you can drag the title bar to move the stack anywhere in the Photoshop window. See Figure 1-18.

Figure 1-18 **Panel stack**

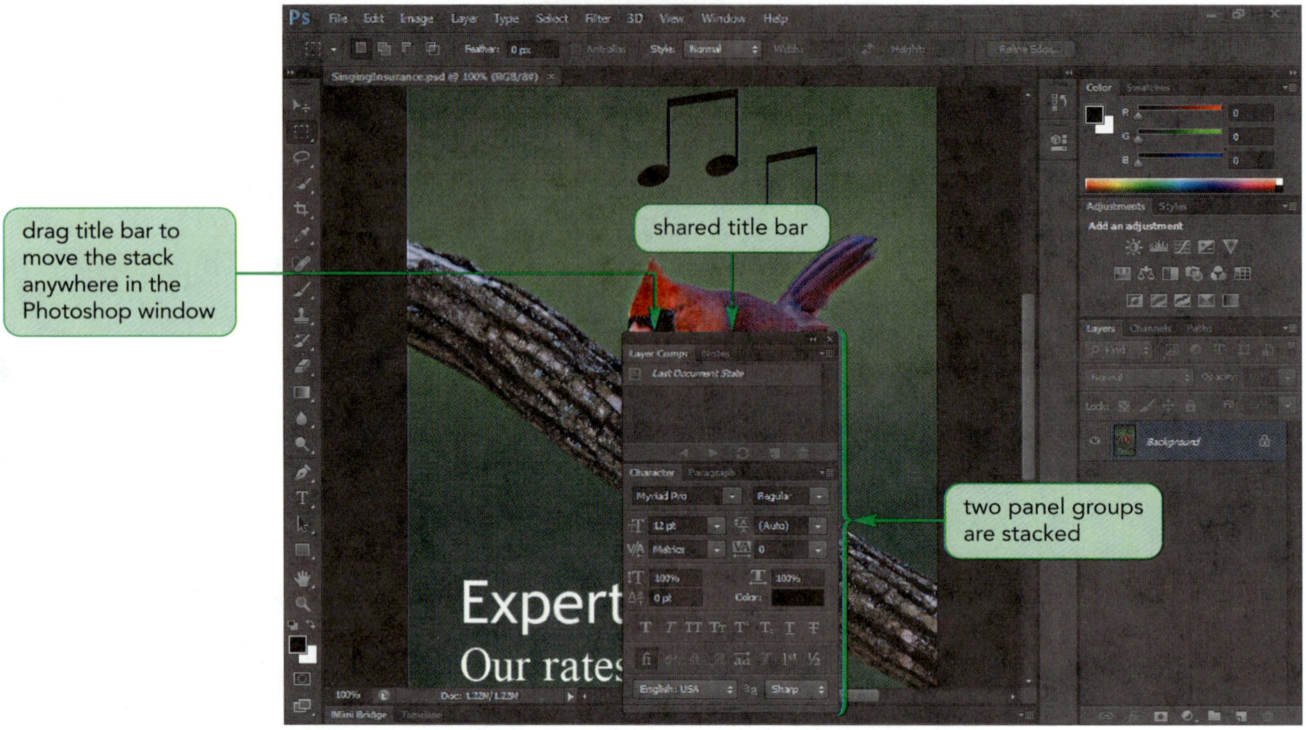

As you become more familiar with Photoshop, you will develop a preference for how you want your panels displayed, depending on what you are working on.

The way you work with the tabs in open panels is similar to the way you work with Document window tabs: You click a panel tab to move from one panel to the next in a group.

Now that you have a general idea of how a Photoshop workspace is set up, Sarah wants you to practice rearranging the Photoshop interface and working with some of the tools.

To choose a tab in an open panel:

1. Open **UnexpectedBolt.psd**, located in the Photoshop1\Tutorial folder. The file opens on top of the SingingInsurance file in the Essentials workspace. The workspace includes four panel groups, two collapsed panels, and the Tools panel. The top panel group includes the Color and Swatches panels.
2. In the top panel group, click the **Swatches** tab. The Swatches panel displays a set, or palette, of frequently used colors.
3. In the middle panel group, click the **Styles** tab. The Styles panel displays options for formatting layers in the current file.
4. On the menu bar, click **Window**, point to **Workspace**, and then click **Reset Essentials**. The Essentials workspace returns to its default settings, with the Color panel on top in the top panel group, and the Adjustments panel on top in the middle panel group.

Displaying and Closing a Panel

You do not always have to work with the default panels provided in a workspace. You can open and close panels at will. To access any of the panels not displayed in the current workspace, click Window on the menu bar to display a list of available panels, including panels for working with color, text, and brushes.

Sarah wants you to explore some of the panels that are not open by default in the Essentials workspace so you can learn how to open and close panels as you need them when working on projects in the future.

To display and close panels:

1. On the menu bar, click **Window**. The Window menu includes commands for arranging the windows and changing the workspace. It also includes a list of panels ranging from 3D to Tool Presets. The options bar and the Tools panel are listed separately at the end of the list of panels. Finally, the Window menu displays a list of open files. See Figure 1-19.

Figure 1-19 Window menu

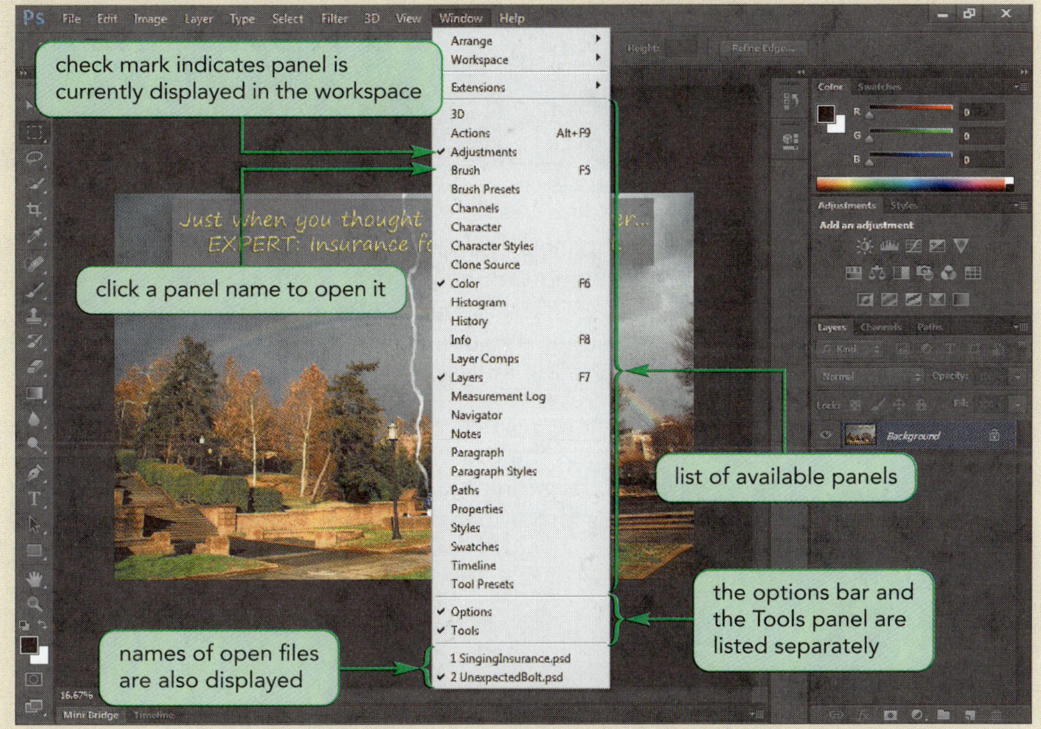

Any panel name preceded by a check mark is currently open in the workspace. To open a panel that isn't visible in the workspace, click its name.

2. Click **Brush**. The Brush panel opens in the workspace. See Figure 1-20.

TIP

You can also open the Brush panel by pressing the F5 shortcut key.

Figure 1-20 Brush panel

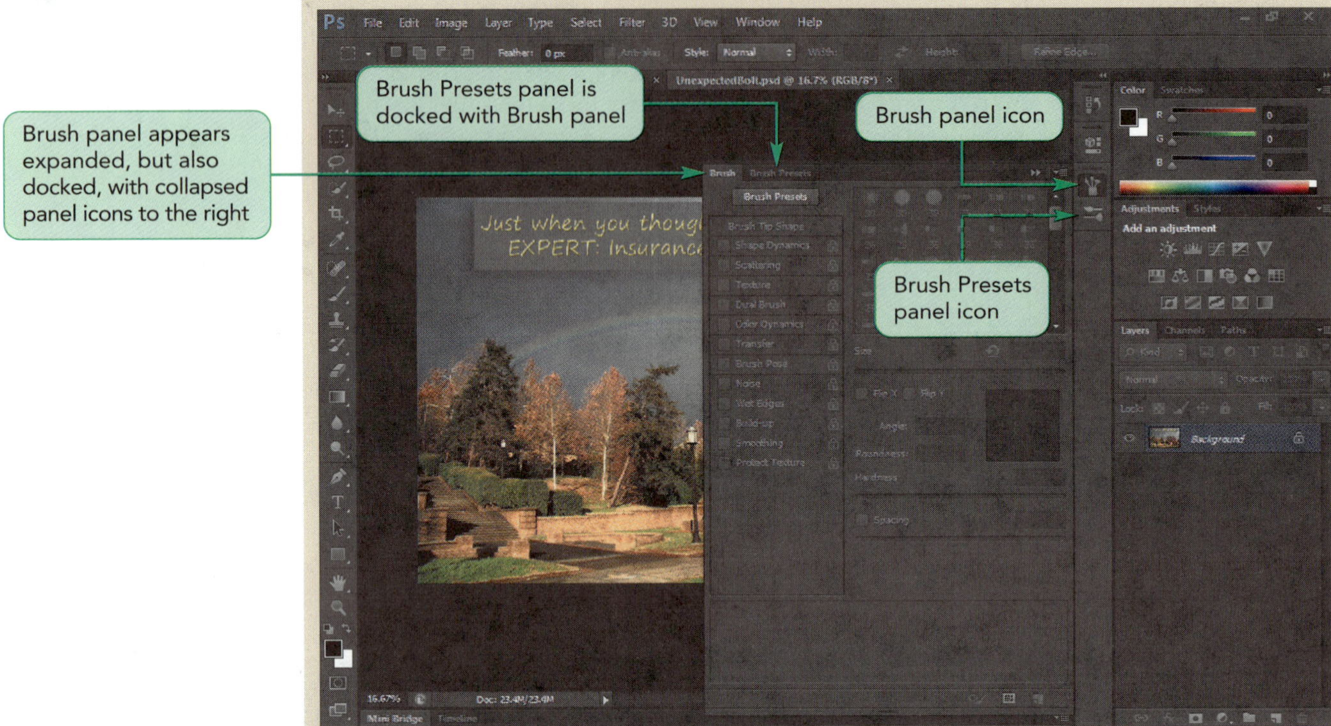

Most panels open in logical groups when you select one of the panels from the Window menu. In this case, the Brush Presets panel opens with the Brush panel. Notice that Photoshop has docked the panel to the left of the Adjustments panel, and that a Brush panel icon appears to the right of the Brush panel. Below that icon is the Brush Presets icon.

3. On the menu bar, click **Window**, and then click **Character**. Photoshop collapses the Brush panel, and the Character panel opens in a dock, with the Paragraph panel behind it. Panel icons for the Character and Paragraph panels also appear to the left of the default panels. See Figure 1-21.

Figure 1-21 **Character panel**

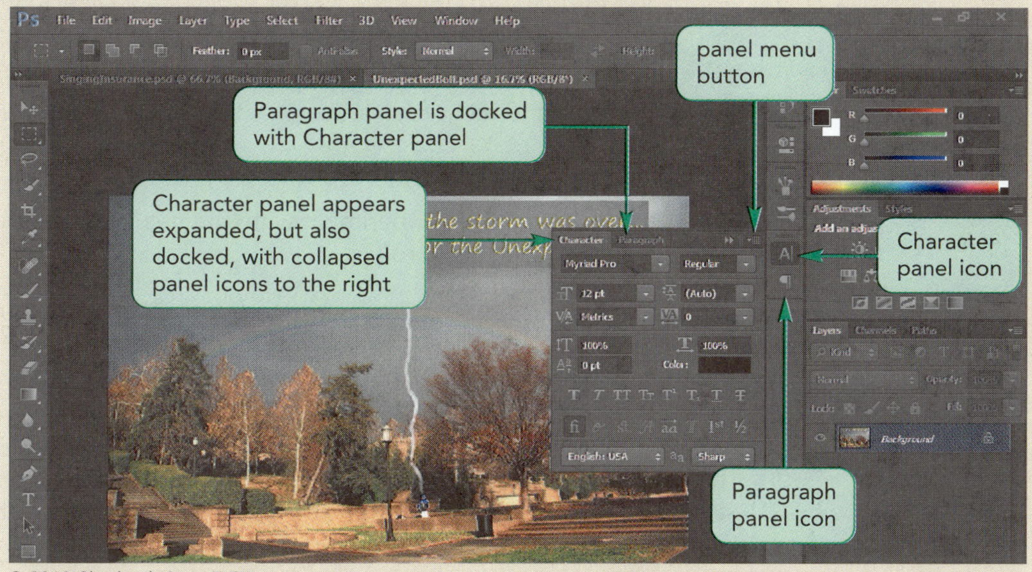

4. In the Character panel, click the **panel menu** button, and then click **Close** to close the panel. The Character panel closes, but the Paragraph panel, which was docked with it, remains open.

5. In the Color panel, click the **panel menu** button, and then click **Close Tab Group**. The Color panel group closes. See Figure 1-22.

Figure 1-22 **Closing a panel group**

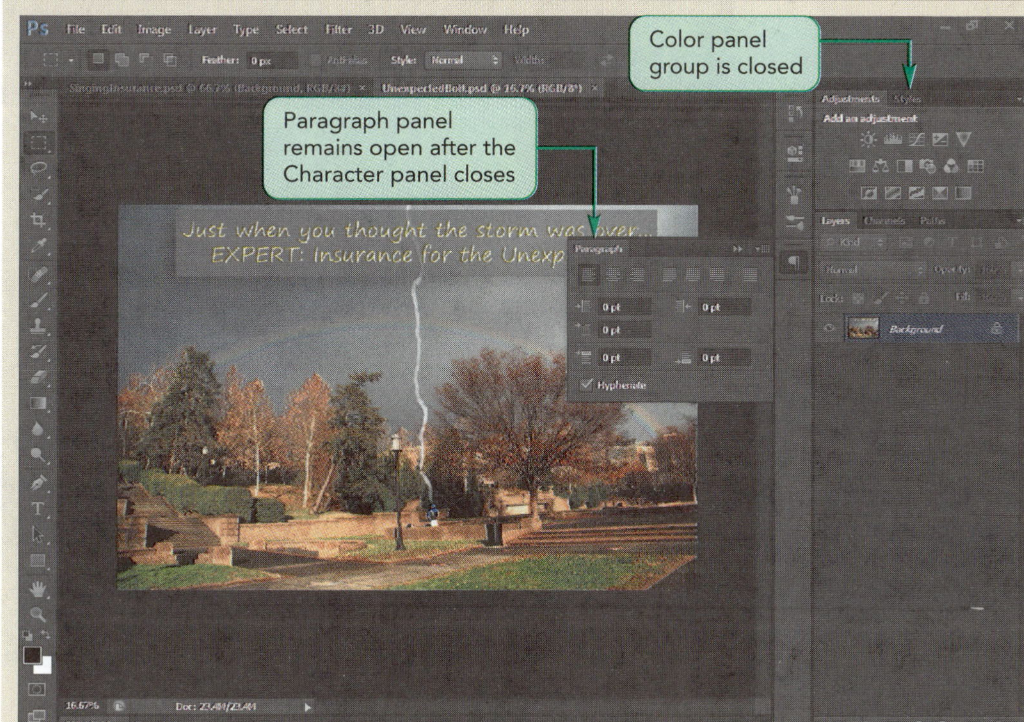

You can also use the Window menu to close a panel.

6. On the menu bar, click **Window**, and then click **Tools** to deselect the panel and remove the check mark. The Tools panel closes, and the Document window fills the space on the left side of the window.
7. Click Window on the menu bar, point to **Workspace**, and then click **Reset Essentials** to reset the workspace. All of the default panels reopen, and the Paragraph panel closes.

Sarah suggests that you experiment with minimizing, hiding, and redisplaying panels before you tackle a project.

Minimizing, Hiding, and Redisplaying Panels

As you work in Photoshop, you'll often find that you want more of the workspace area to display your file, and you'll also come to realize that you don't need all of the panels that might be displayed in the current workspace all of the time. To save real estate on your screen, you can minimize open panels or even hide them temporarily. This flexibility streamlines your work in Photoshop, and lets you work the way that suits you best.

To minimize, hide, and redisplay panels:

1. On the right side of the title bar for the docked panels, click the **Collapse to Icons** button. The panels collapse, and the Document window expands to fill the space. See Figure 1-23.

Figure 1-23 Collapsed panel groups

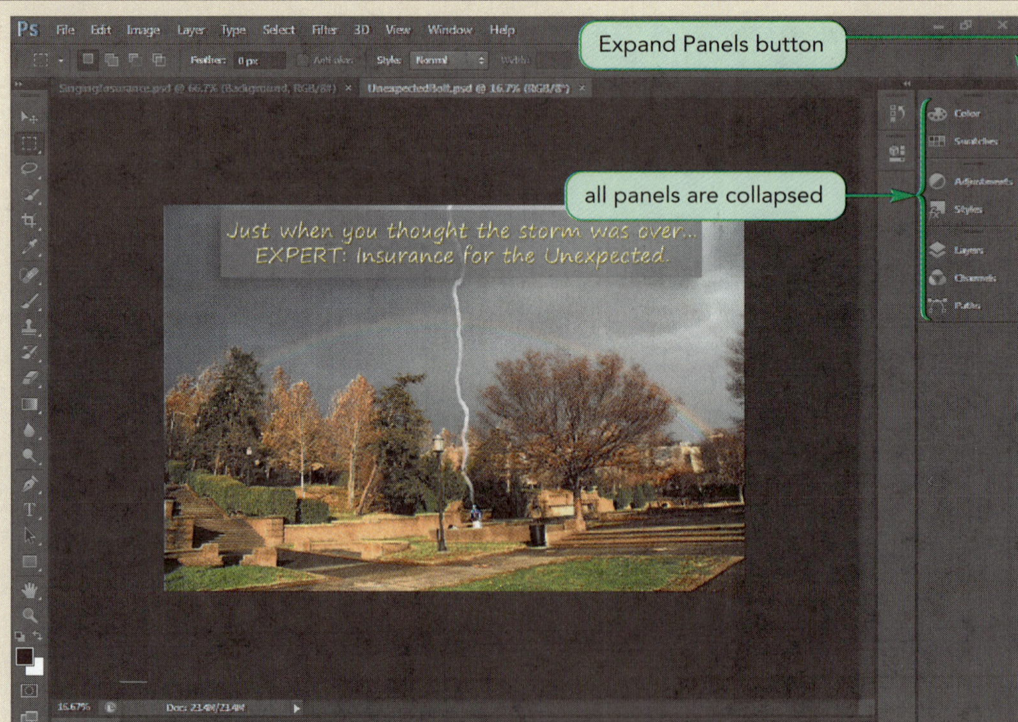

© 2012 Chadwick Cipiti/DCNature.com

2. On the right side of the title bar for the collapsed panels, click the **Expand Panels** button to restore the panels to their original display.

Trouble? If you click the wrong Expand Panels button, the History and Properties panels will expand. To correct this, click the Collapse to Icons button for those panels, and then click the Expand Panels button on the right side of the screen.

For even more screen real estate, you can temporarily hide all panels.

3. Press the **Tab** key. All of the panels in the workspace are now hidden. Only the menu bar and the status bar are visible. See Figure 1-24.

Figure 1-24 **Hiding all panels**

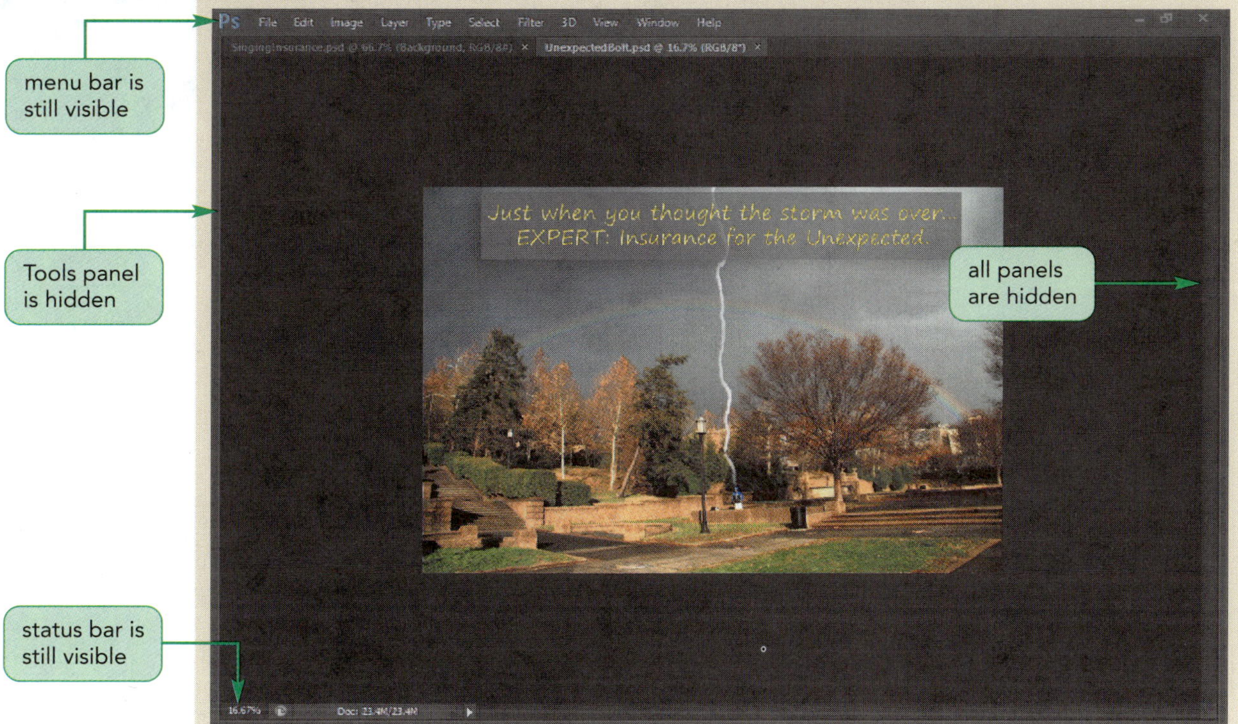

© 2012 Chadwick Cipiti/DCNature.com

4. Press the **Tab** key. All of the hidden panels are now visible.

Sarah has explained that you will sometimes want to group panels in ways that are different than the groupings in any of Photoshop's predefined workspaces. Because of this, she would like you to experiment with moving and stacking panels.

Moving and Stacking Panels

Because everyone has different work habits and preferences, Photoshop provides even more ways to manipulate panels. For example, you can move panels in the workspace, and you can create custom groups of panels by stacking them.

To move the panels:

1. On the menu bar, click **Window**, and then click **Brush** to open the Brush panel group.
2. Point to the **panel bar** to the right of the Brush Presets tab.

3. Click and hold the mouse button, and drag the panel group to the left and then up, into the Document window. A "ghost" version of the panel appears, and a blue border indicates the original location of the panel. See Figure 1-25.

Figure 1-25 **Moving a panel group**

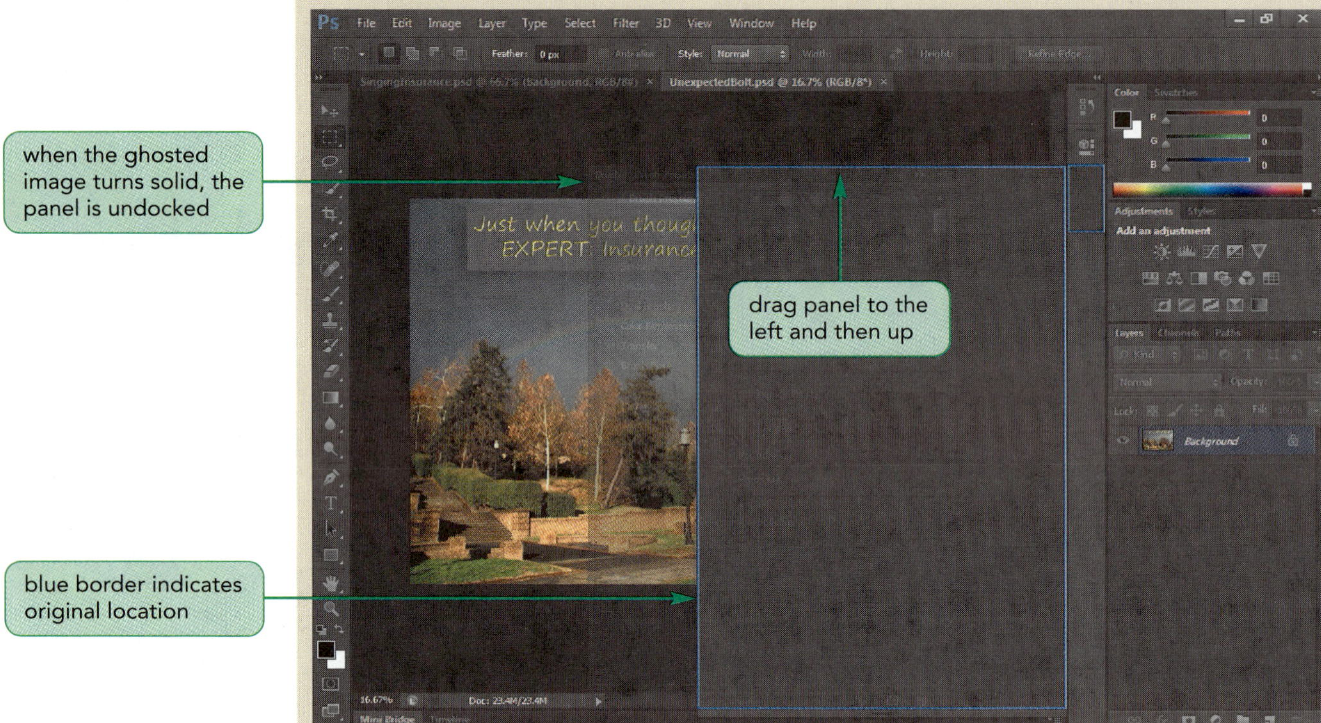

© 2012 Chadwick Cipiti/DCNature.com

When the ghosted version and the blue border disappear and a "solid" version of the panel appears, you have dragged the panel far enough from the dock to undock it so that it floats in the Document window. At that point, you can release the mouse button.

4. Release the mouse button. The panel is now floating in the middle of the Document window. Notice that the floating panel now has its own title bar that includes a Collapse to Icons button ▸▸ and a Close button ✕.

Stacking Panels

By stacking panel groups, you can move multiple panels and panel groups as a single unit. Next, you'll experiment with stacking panels so you can move groups of panels together around the Photoshop program window as you work.

To stack panels:

1. In the Layers, Channels, and Paths panel group, point to the right of the word Paths, click the **panel bar**, and drag the **Layers, Channels, and Paths** panel group to the left and under the Brush panel group until you see a blue line between the two panel docks. See Figure 1-26.

Figure 1-26 Stacking panels

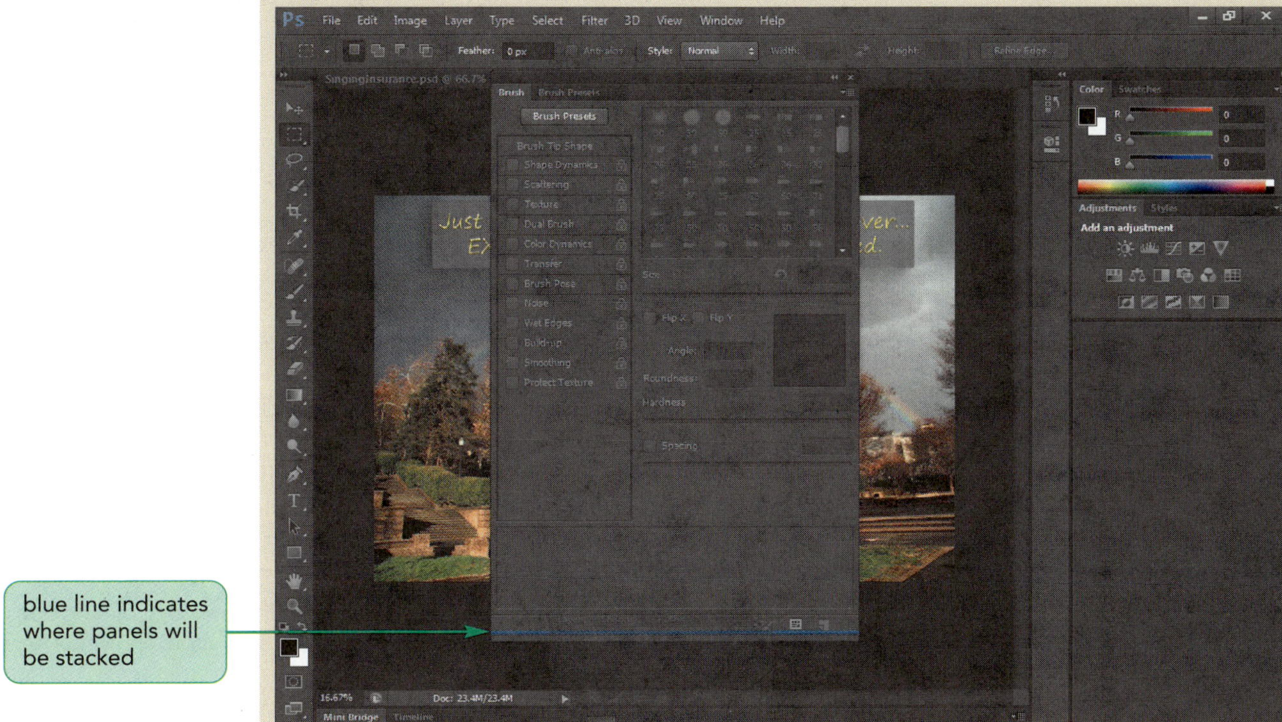

© 2012 Chadwick Cipiti/DCNature.com

2. Release the mouse button. The panels are now stacked.
3. Point to the stacked panels title bar, click the mouse button, and drag the stack up and to the right. The entire stack moves as you drag.

Preset Workspaces

As you have seen, the Photoshop workspace is customizable so you can change the way it appears based on your preferences. As you become more comfortable in Photoshop, you might find that you prefer one layout to another, depending on the task at hand. So far, you have been working in and modifying the default Essentials workspace. However, Photoshop also comes with a number of other predefined workspaces that you will explore throughout this book. For example, the Painting workspace opens six panels on the right side of the screen: Swatches, Navigator, Brush Presets, Layers, Channels, and Paths. It also displays collapsed History, Brush, Clone Source, and Tool Presets panels. These panels give you many different options for painting in Photoshop, including brush shape, color, and texture. The Typography workspace displays the Character and Paragraph panels, which give you multiple text formatting options when you add text to a file, as well as the Paragraph Styles and Character Styles panels, which let you create and save styles that you can apply to other text in your files. It also displays Layers, Channels, Paths, History, Info, Swatches, and Styles panels, all useful for working with text. Unless otherwise noted, the figures in this book show the workspace in the default Essentials layout.

Photoshop comes with seven preset workspaces. You can switch workspaces at any point in an editing session, and then switch back, depending on your current task. To switch workspaces, you click Window on the menu bar, click Workspace, and then click a workspace on the menu. See Figure 1-27 for a description of all the available preset workspace layouts.

Figure 1-27 Workspace layouts

Workspace Layout	Description
Essentials	Displays the most frequently used panels for accomplishing basic tasks in Photoshop, such as manipulating layers and channels, working with paths, applying image adjustments, and setting colors
New in CS6	Displays the new CS6 panels, as well as panels with new features, and highlights new commands on the menu
3D	Displays panels for working with imported 3D objects and converting 2D layers to 3D objects; 3D features are only available in Photoshop Extended
Motion	Displays panels that let you create motion effects and animate 3D objects
Painting	Displays panels with tools and settings for working with painting features, such as brushes, brush presets, and colors
Photography	Displays advanced panels for making fine adjustments to photographs, including modifying color balance, hue, and saturation; applying filters; and mixing color channels
Typography	Displays panels for working with type, including the Character and Paragraph panels, which allow you to make quick formatting changes to text, and the Character Styles and Paragraph Styles panels, which let you save text formatting and quickly apply it to new text

Sarah explains that depending on what your focus will be in an editing session, you might find you need to work in a different workspace. She suggests that you explore some of the other available workspaces.

TIP

If you're working at a resolution greater than 1024 × 768, you can also click the Workspace Switcher button and then click Typography.

To choose a preset workspace:

1. On the menu bar, click **Window**, point to **Workspace**, and then click **Typography**. Panels specific to working extensively with text appear. See Figure 1-28.

Figure 1-28 Typography workspace

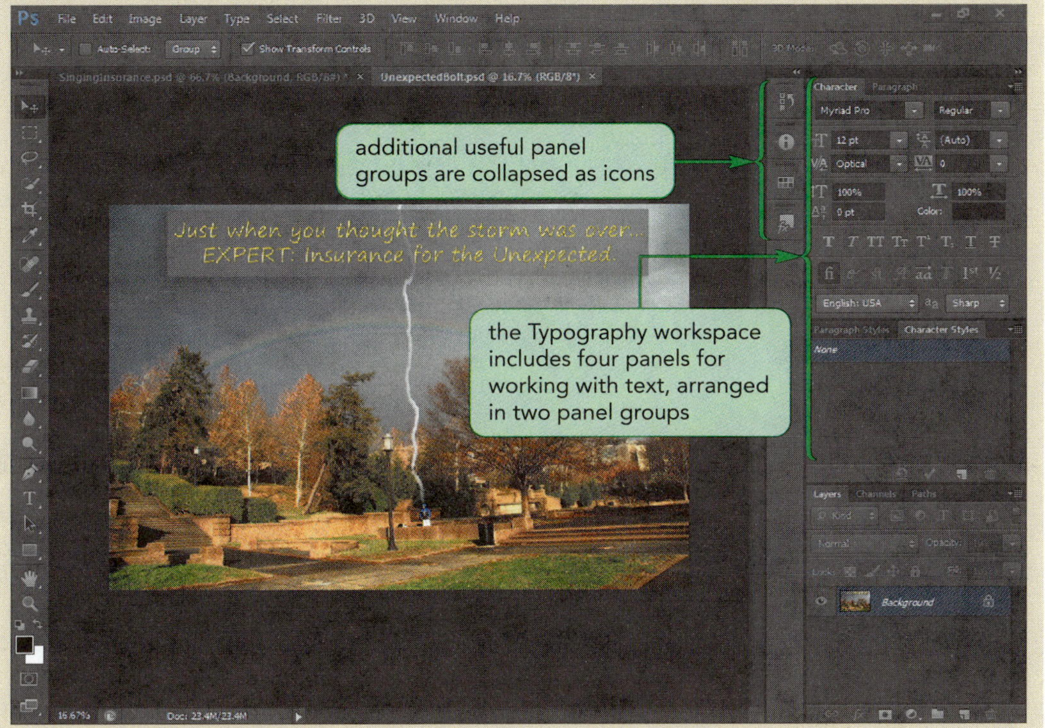

Trouble? If you can't see the Window menu, drag the panel stack down. If your window doesn't look like the figure, then click Window, point to Workspace, and then click Reset Typography.

2. On the menu bar, click **Window**, point to **Workspace**, and then click **Painting**. The workspace changes again to include tools and settings that are most helpful for working with the various brush and pencil tools in the Tools panel. Notice that in addition to the Brush Presets panel, which is docked by itself, the Brush panel appears collapsed to the left of the Swatches panel.
3. Click the **Brush Tool** button in the Tools panel. The Brush Presets panel display changes to show active settings appropriate for the Brush Tool.

You have explored a number of the workspaces Photoshop provides by default, but now you'll explore the other workspace options you might need in your work for Mirabeau Media.

INSIGHT

Saving, Redisplaying, and Deleting a Custom Workspace

In Photoshop, you can save **custom workspaces** to display the panels and tools you need for specific tasks, such as working on a photograph for a brochure or designing a poster. To create a custom workspace, make the changes you want—for example, by opening additional panels, closing panels you don't want, and rearranging the docks or stacks to your liking. When you have designed the workspace you want, click Window on the menu bar, point to Workspace, and then click New Workspace, or click the Workspace Switcher and then click New Workspace. Type a name for the new workspace, and then click the Save button. The next time you display the Workspace menu, your new workspace will be displayed in the workspace list. By using custom workspaces, you can improve your work flow and become more efficient.

Using the Rulers, Guides, and Grid

Photoshop provides a number of tools for keeping track of the measurements of your document, as well as guiding you as you make selections or add and position objects. For example, you might use the rulers to help you position an element in your composition. In addition, if you are adding an object such as text or a vector drawing to an image, you can first draw guides so you can place the object exactly at their intersection. **Smart Guides** are lines that appear automatically on the Document window as you move an object on one layer to align it with an object on another layer. For example, if you are aligning a small rectangle with a large rectangle, a Smart Guide runs through the center of the large rectangle as you drag the small rectangle, or appears when the bottom of the small rectangle is exactly aligned with the bottom of the large rectangle. You can also display another tool, called the grid, to help you quickly align multiple objects added to an image.

Sarah has suggested you experiment with rulers, guides, and the grid as you continue to experiment with other tools in Photoshop.

Showing the Rulers

You can display rulers so that you can measure objects in the Document window. The rulers show inches by default, but you can change the unit of measurement on the rulers by right-clicking a ruler and then clicking another unit of measurement, for example Pixels or Centimeters.

Sarah has provided you with a photograph of a pelican that she intends to use in one of her print ads for a travel agency. You'll use that image to experiment with the rulers and guides.

To show the rulers:

1. Close all open files, display the Essentials workspace, and then reset it.
2. Open **Travel.psd**, located in the Photoshop1\Tutorial folder included with your Data Files.
3. On the menu bar, click **View**, and then click **Fit on Screen**. The image fills the available area on the screen.
4. On the menu bar, click **View**, and then click **Rulers**. Two rulers appear around the Document window, one along the top, and one along the left side. See Figure 1-29.

TIP

You can also press the Ctrl+R keys to display and hide the rulers.

Figure 1-29 Displaying rulers

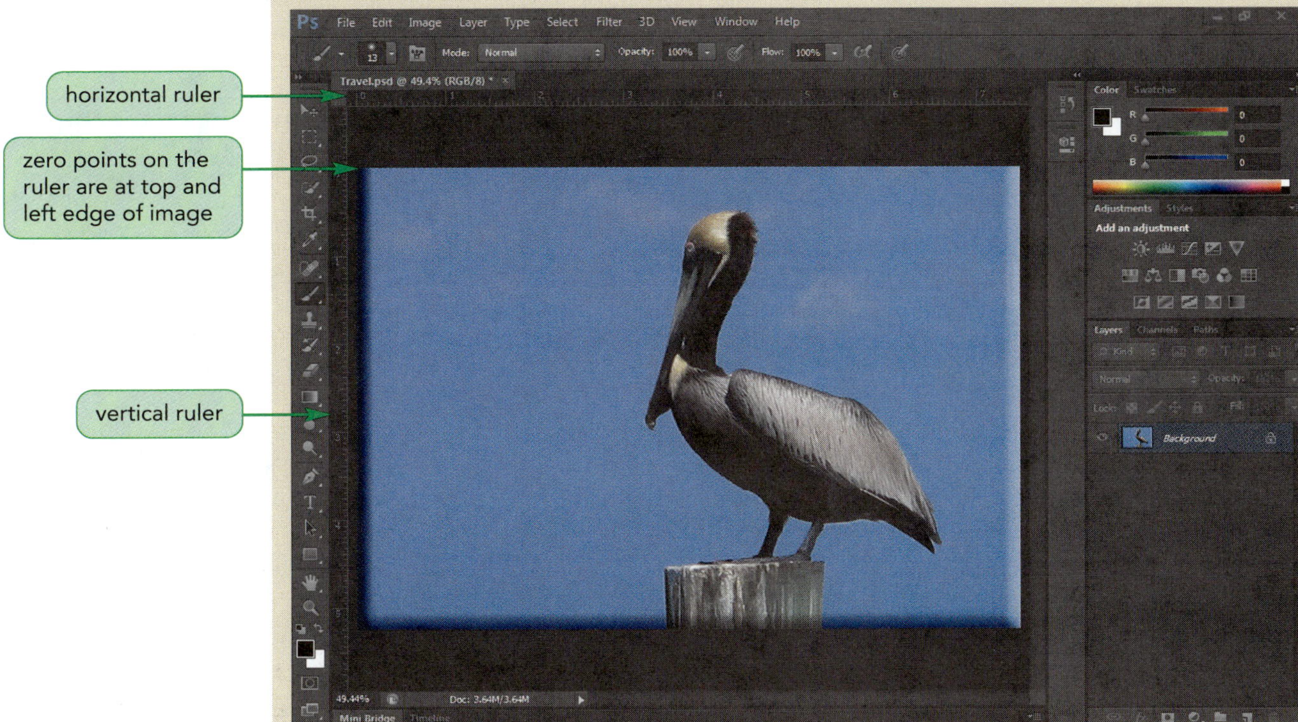

Jane Hosie-Bounar

By default, the rulers' zero points are at the upper-left corner of the document.

Adding Guides

Guides are another tool for measuring or aligning objects in an image. You can customize the location of guides and place them exactly where you want them. There are two ways to place guides in your document. You can use the View command on the menu bar, or you can drag guides from the rulers.

You'll experiment with guides as you continue to improve your Photoshop skills.

To add guides:

1. On the menu bar, click **View**, click **New Guide**, click the **Horizontal** option button, if necessary, type **.5** in the Position box, and then click the **OK** button. A horizontal guide appears at the half-inch mark on the vertical ruler and runs from one side of the Document window to the other.

   You can also add a guide by dragging from the ruler. To add a vertical guide, you drag from the vertical ruler. To add a horizontal guide, you drag from the horizontal ruler.

2. Point to the **horizontal ruler**, click and hold the mouse button, and then drag down toward the bottom of the pelican's beak, to about the **3-inch mark** on the vertical ruler.

3. Release the mouse button. Photoshop adds a horizontal guide to the Document window. See Figure 1-30.

Figure 1-30 Adding guides

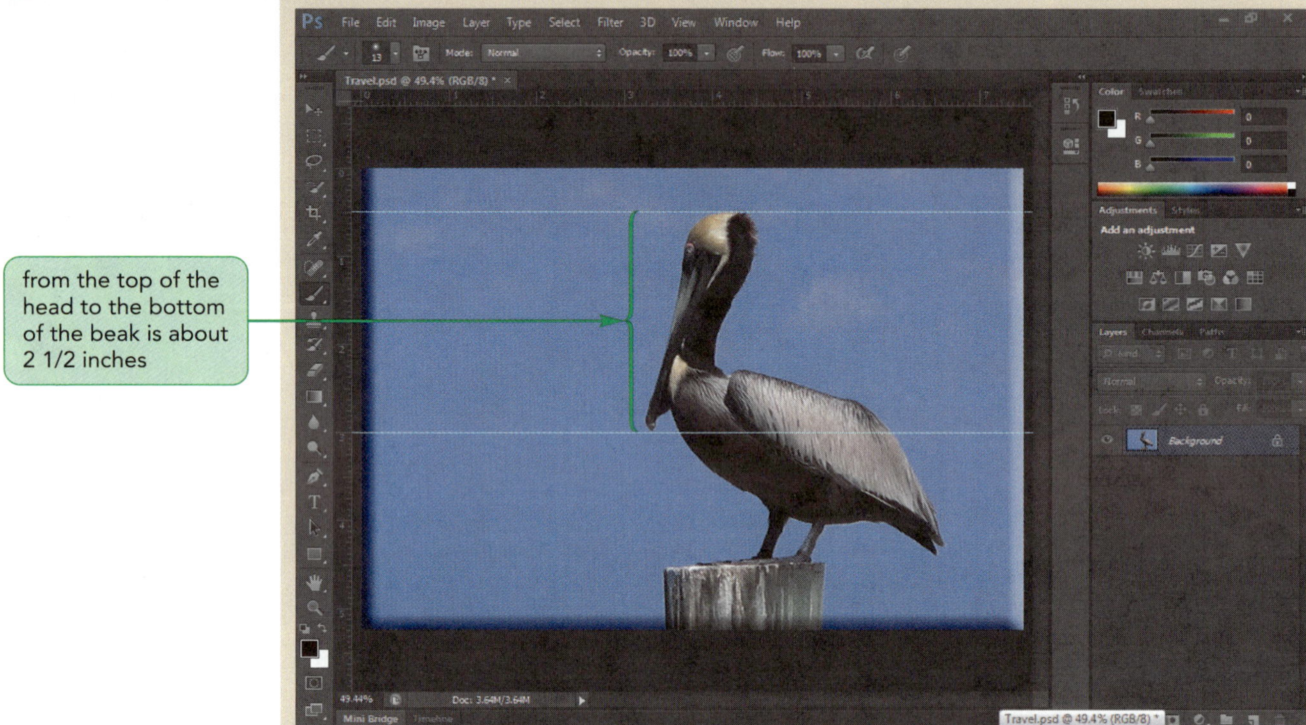

Jane Hosie-Bounar

Using the guides and the ruler, you can see that from the top of the pelican's head to the tip of its beak is about 2 ½ inches.

4. On the menu bar, click **View**, and then click **Actual Pixels**.

5. Drag the vertical scroll bar up until you can see the top guide and the top of the pelican's head, and drag the horizontal scroll bar to the right so that the beak nearly touches the vertical ruler. See Figure 1-31.

Figure 1-31 **Actual pixels display size**

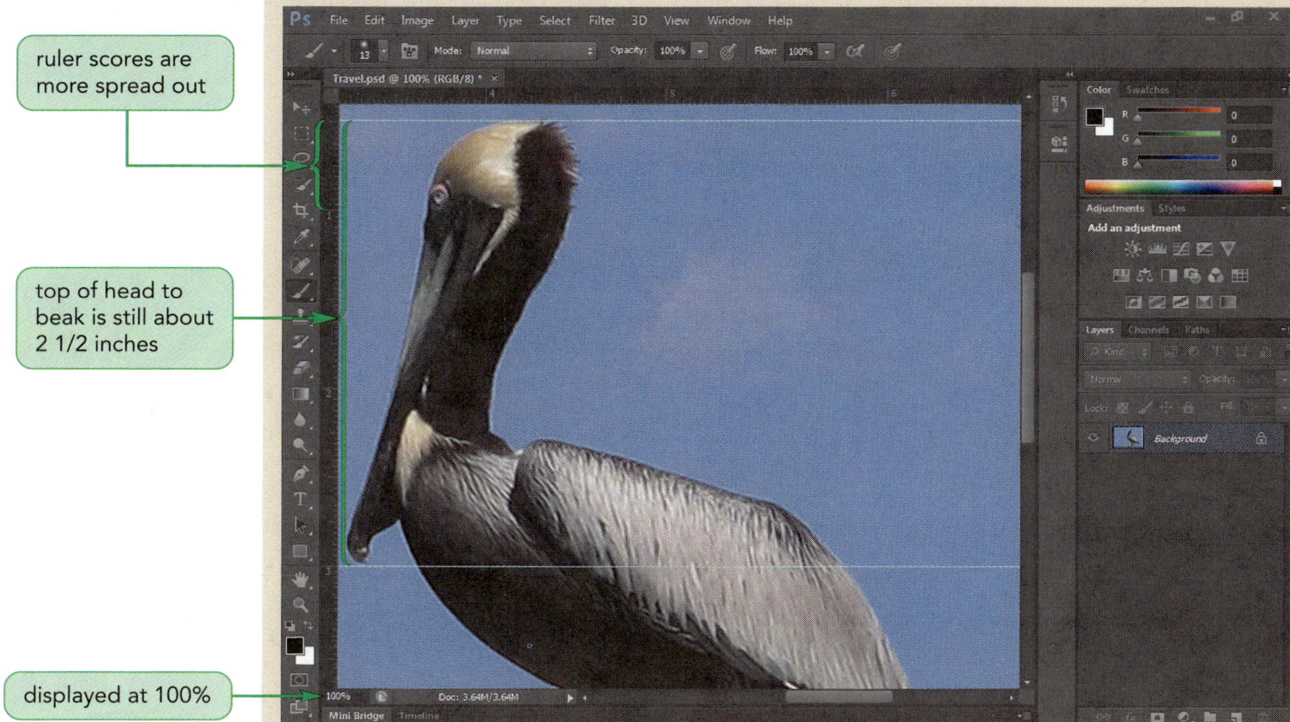

Jane Hosie-Bounar

The picture is enlarged to 100% of its size. Notice that the ruler markings are more spread out, and that the measurement from the top of the head to the bottom of the beak is still about 2 ½ inches.

6. Move the mouse pointer around the Document window. Notice that dotted lines slide along both rulers to indicate the position of the mouse pointer as you move it. This feature is helpful in determining the exact point at which you begin making a selection or drawing a vector object.

7. On the menu bar, click **View**, point to **Show**, and then click **Guides** to remove the check mark and turn off the display of the guides. Turning off the display of the Guides hides them, but does not delete them from the file. You can repeat this command to redisplay the guides at any time.

   You can delete a guide by pointing to the guide until the mouse pointer changes to ↕ or ↔ and then dragging the guide either up over the ruler, or to the left or right until it is off the image. You can also click View, and then click Clear Guides.

8. Save the file as **TravelGuides.psd**, and then close it. When you close a file, the rulers and any guides disappear from the workspace. Since the rulers were displayed when the TravelGuides file was saved, the next time you open that file, they will be redisplayed.

You can change the **origin** of the rulers (where the number 0 appears) by pointing to the intersection of the rulers until a crosshair pointer appears, and then dragging diagonally down and to the right. The crosshairs indicate the new intersection of the rulers, and 0 appears at the spot where you release the mouse button. To reset the ruler, double-click the intersection of the rulers.

You can also work with the grid to help you align objects in a document, which you'll do next.

Showing and Hiding the Grid

The grid helps you align multiple objects or arrange them exactly where you want them in your document. It can also help you make an exact selection. You show and hide the grid using commands on the View menu.

To show and hide the grid:

1. Open **ExpertText.psd**, located in the Photoshop1\Tutorial folder, and then save it as **ExpertText1.psd**.
2. Click **View** on the menu, click **Fit on Screen**, and make sure the rulers are displayed.

   Trouble? If Photoshop displays a message about missing fonts, click the OK button and let Photoshop make a substitution.
3. On the menu bar, click **View**, point to **Show**, and then click **Grid**. Photoshop displays a pattern of equally spaced horizontal and vertical lines. These lines can be especially useful if you want to align two or more objects exactly. Notice that the major gridlines appear as solid dark gray lines, and the minor gridlines appear as dashed white lines.

   You'll modify the Preferences to display only the major gridlines to make them easier to work with.
4. On the menu bar, click **Edit**, point to **Preferences**, and then click **Guides, Grid & Slices**. In the Grid section of the Preferences dialog box, select the text in the Subdivisions box, type **1**, and then click the **OK** button. The gridlines are now spaced one inch apart. See Figure 1-32.

Figure 1-32 Turning off the minor gridlines

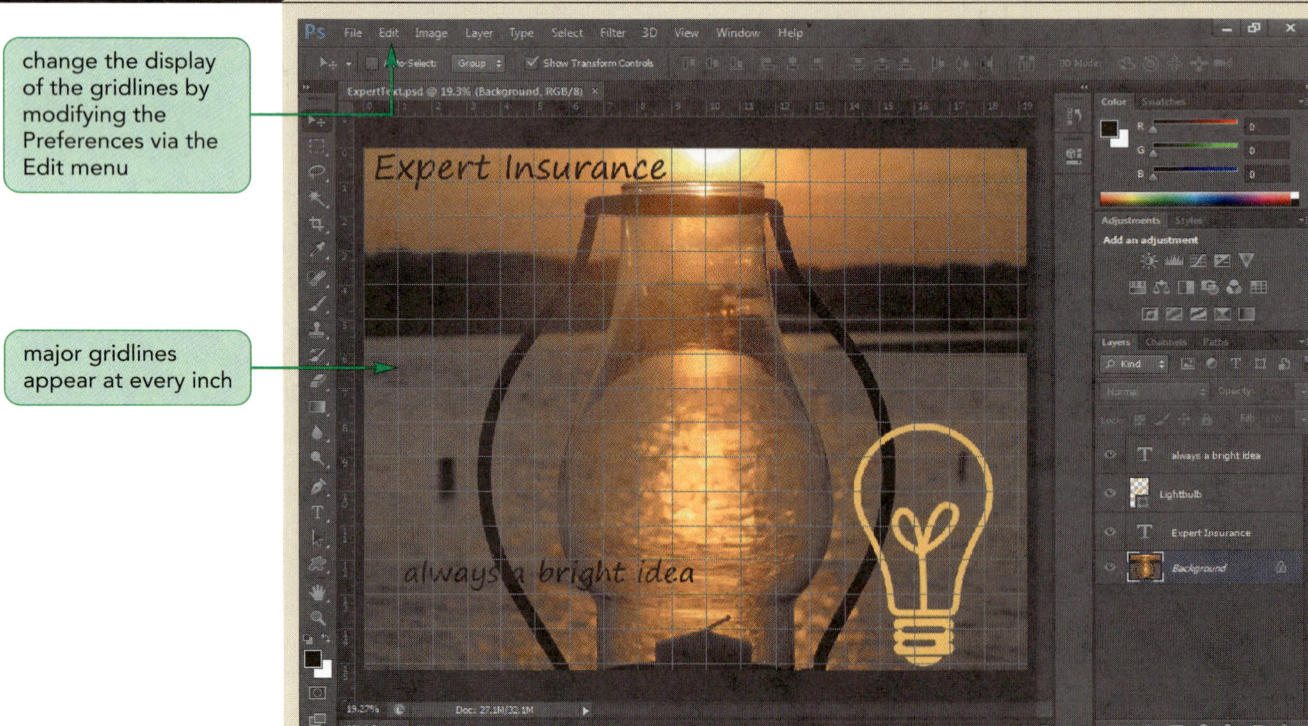

Jane Hosie-Bounar

Photoshop uses the Layers panel to store different elements in a composition on layers that can be edited and manipulated separately. You'll select a layer in the Layers panel to move it, using the grid to guide the placement of the layer.

5. In the Layers panel, click the **Layers** tab, if necessary, to expand the Layers panel, and then click the **Expert Insurance** layer to select it. You must always select a layer before you can work with it in Photoshop.
6. In the Tools panel, click the **Move Tool** button, if necessary, and then move the mouse pointer over the document. The move pointer appears.
7. Point to the **Expert Insurance** text, click and hold the mouse button, and then drag the text to the right so that the *E* is aligned with the fifth vertical gridline, resting on the first horizontal gridline. Notice that Photoshop provides additional guidance in the form of arrows and numbers that appear in a black box as you drag, indicating how many inches you have dragged an object from its original location, and in what direction.
8. In the Layers panel, click the **Lightbulb** layer, point to the **lightbulb** on the canvas, and drag it to the left and up slightly so that the bottom of the bulb is centered on the horizontal and vertical gridlines that intersect at the bottom of the candle wick.
9. In the Layers panel, click the **always a bright idea** layer to select it. The Move tool is still active.
10. Point to the **always a bright idea** text on the canvas, click and hold the mouse button, and then drag the text to the left and up so that the first *a* in *always* is aligned with the same vertical gridline as the *E* in *Expert*, resting on the horizontal gridline at the top of the lightbulb. See Figure 1-33.

TIP

You can also press the V key to select the Move tool.

Figure 1-33 **Aligning objects on the grid**

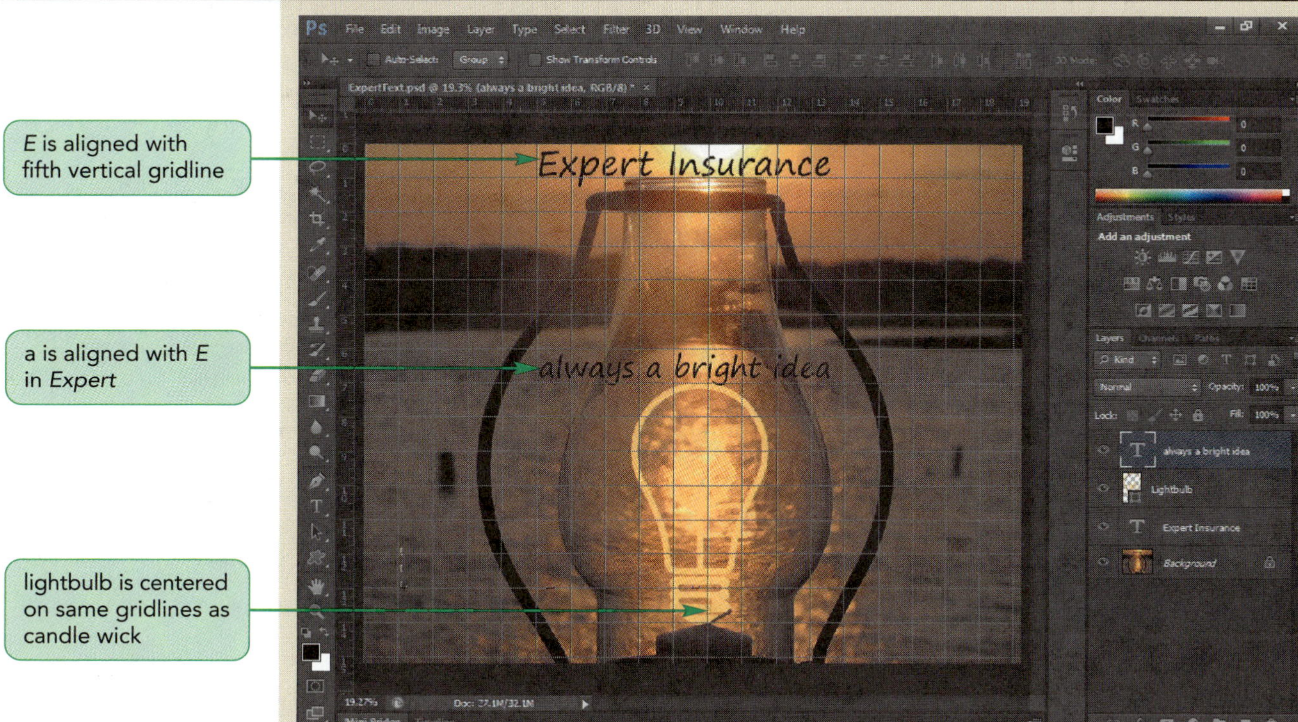

Jane Hosie-Bounar

11. Press the **Ctrl+'** keys to turn off the grid, and then save and close the file.

INSIGHT

Snapping to the Grid and Guides

Photoshop includes a **Snap To** feature that lets you easily align objects with gridlines or guides. Snap To "magnetizes" the lines so that when you drag a selection or shape, or move an object, the object aligns to the closest gridlines or guides. You can turn the Snap To feature on and off by clicking View on the menu bar, clicking Snap To, and then clicking the choice you want to turn on or off.

Using Tools in the Tools Panel

You might have noticed while you were working with panels earlier in this tutorial that there is one panel, the Tools panel, that appears on the left side of the window, whereas all of the other panels appear on the right by default. As you become more familiar with Photoshop, you'll use the Tools panel constantly; having it appear in a consistent place no matter what workspace you're currently working in makes it convenient to find the tools you use over and over again. Because Photoshop provides so many tools in its Tools panel, some of the tools are grouped to improve your work flow. The triangle on the lower-right corner of a tool in the Tools panel indicates that there are additional tools, called a **tool group**, hidden beneath the tool you see in the panel. You display the hidden tools either by right-clicking the top tool (the tool that is displayed in the panel) or by pointing to the tool and clicking and holding the mouse button until a menu of additional tools appears.

Sarah notes that much of your work will involve fine-tuning images and that this kind of work might require you to zoom in and pan an image. She explains that you can find the tools for this kind of work in the Tools panel.

Selecting and Using Tools

You select a tool in the Tools panel by clicking it with the mouse. Some tools also have shortcut keys assigned. For example, earlier in this tutorial, you saw that pressing the V key activates the Move tool. When you select a tool, the mouse pointer changes to reflect the selection.

To select and use a tool:

1. Open **RainbowInsurance.psd**, located in the Photoshop1\Tutorial folder included with your Data Files, and turn off the ruler display if necessary. Notice on the status bar that the photograph is displayed in the Document window at a low zoom percentage, depending on your monitor.

2. Click the **Zoom Tool** button in the Tools panel, and then move the mouse pointer over the photograph. The mouse pointer changes to the Zoom In pointer, a magnifying glass with a plus sign in the center.

TIP

You can also press the Z key to select the Zoom tool.

3. Click the center of the photograph. The photograph is enlarged in the window and centered at the place you clicked.
4. On the status bar in the lower-left corner of the Document window, click in the **zoom percentage** box, double-click the current zoom percentage to select it, type **300**, and then press the **Enter** key. The image zooms in again. Because the zoom percentage is so high, the image looks blurry, or pixelated.
5. Click the **Hand Tool** button in the Tools panel. The Hand tool lets you drag a file within the Document window to display different areas.
6. Point to the center of the **lightning bolt**, and then drag the image all the way to the right until the lightning is no longer visible.
7. Click the **Zoom Tool** button, press and hold the **Alt** key, and point to the center of the Document window. The Zoom In pointer changes to the Zoom Out pointer when you press the Alt key.
8. Click the **center** of the document. The image zooms out.
9. Press the **Ctrl+1** keys. The image zooms to 100%.
10. Press the **Ctrl+0** keys. The image now fits on the screen.

TIP

Pressing the Spacebar while using any other tool changes the pointer temporarily to the Hand tool pointer.

INSIGHT

Changing the Zoom Level

When you work to modify individual pixels in an image—for example, to change their color—the zoom feature will be an important tool for your work. The maximum zoom percentage for an image is 3200%. You will rarely need to zoom in this much, but if you are doing extremely precise work—for example, pixel-by-pixel corrections on an image—the ability to zoom in this much is an advantage. You might also find that you need to zoom way out (decrease the zoom percentage) on a very large image in order to see the overall effect of changes you have made. The minimum zoom percentage is .36%, which you'll probably never use. However, it is often helpful to have this much flexibility in zooming in and zooming out on an image.

Using the Options Bar to Change Tool Settings

Many tools in the Tools panel let you modify the default options using the options bar, which appears beneath the menu bar in the Photoshop window. The options bar changes depending on which tool is selected in the Tools panel. Using the options bar, you can define custom settings for the tool.

Now that you're comfortable with the Photoshop environment, Sarah asks you to try modifying some elements on the canvas. She would like you to start by erasing the faint lightning bolt in the RainbowInsurance file.

To use the options bar:

1. In the Layers panel, click **Layer 1** to select it, and then click the **Eraser Tool** button in the Tools panel. The options bar displays the default settings for the Eraser tool or the settings in effect the last time the tool was used.

2. On the left side of the options bar, right-click the **Eraser Tool** button, and then click **Reset Tool**. This command ensures that the default settings are in effect.

3. On the options bar, click the **Brush Preset picker** button (to the right of the number 13) to open the Brush Preset picker. See Figure 1-34.

   Trouble? If the Brush Preset picker button isn't visible, confirm that the mode is set to Brush and not Pencil or Block. To change the mode, click the Mode button on the options bar, and then click Brush.

Figure 1-34 Eraser tool settings and Brush Preset picker

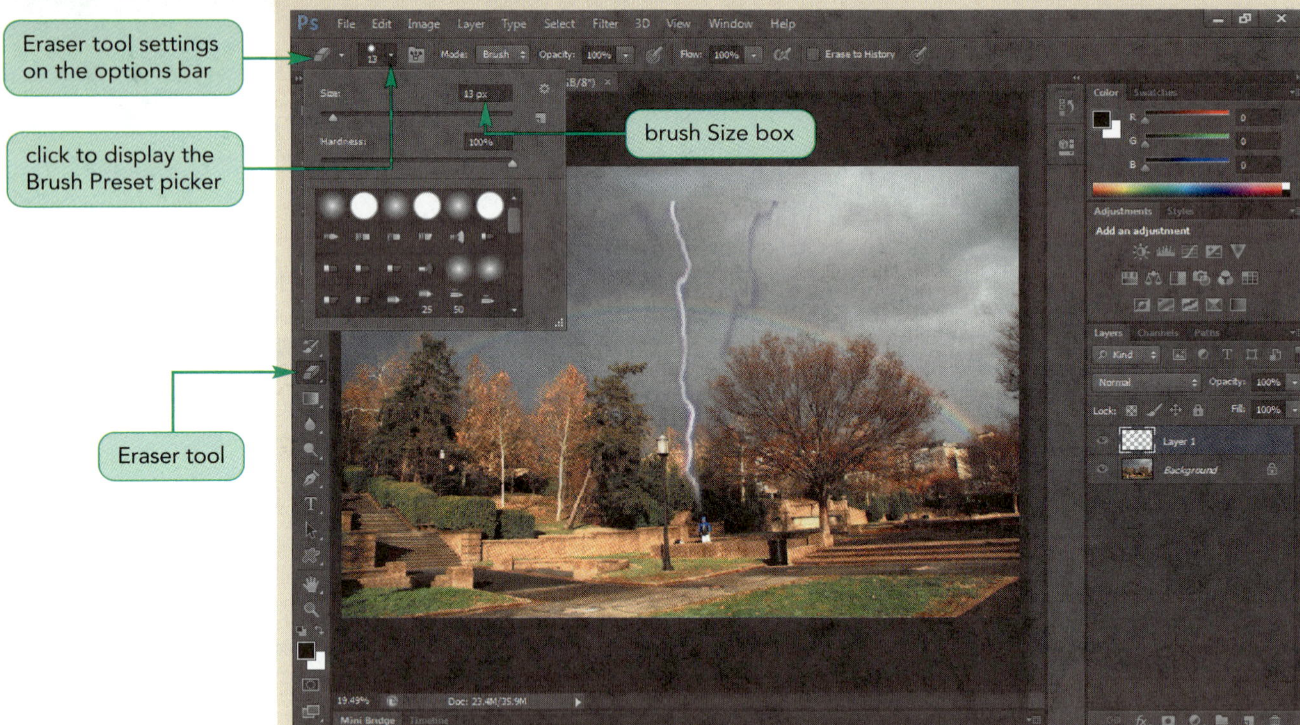

You can change the diameter of the brush by dragging the Size slider, by typing in the Size box, or by selecting one of the **brush presets**, which are commonly used Photoshop brush sizes. Presets are discussed later in this tutorial.

4. Select the text in the Size box, and then type **100**.

5. Click the **Brush Preset picker** button again to close the Brush Preset picker. You are now ready to use the Eraser Tool.

6. Position the **Eraser Tool** pointer over the bottom of the faint lightning bolt, and then click. The lightning disappears where you clicked.

7. Drag the **Eraser Tool** pointer over the lightning image until it has disappeared entirely. If you miss any parts of the lightning bolt, you can drag over the area again. The faint lightning bolt has been removed from the image. See Figure 1-35.

Figure 1-35 Using the Eraser tool

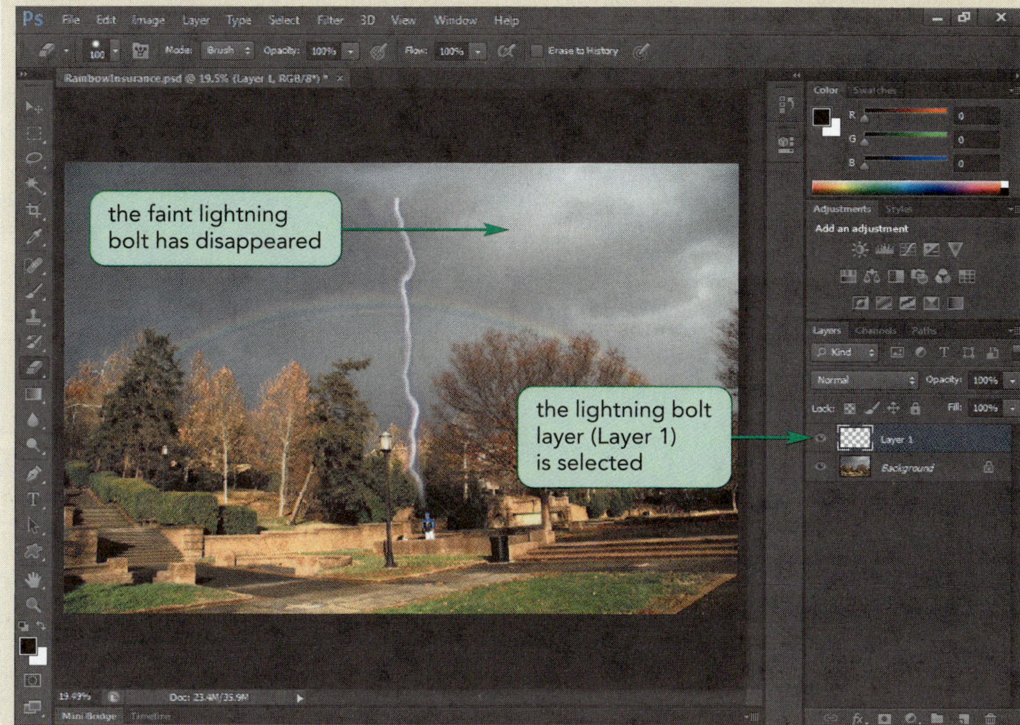

8. Save the file as **OneBolt.psd** in the Photoshop1\Tutorial folder, and then close it.

Adding Content to the Canvas and Using Tool Presets

You can use the drawing tools in the Tools panel to add content to the canvas. **Tool presets** are custom settings for tools that you can save to use again and again. For instance, you might want specific text—for example, a company name—to always appear in the same font and font color, no matter what document you are working in. You can set these options on the options bar for the Horizontal Type tool and then save the settings as a preset. When you need the settings again, you can open the preset after you select the tool. Photoshop also comes with its own presets. For example, when you used the Eraser tool earlier, you saw that it had brush size presets associated with it.

Sarah wants you to learn how to work with custom shapes and add them to the canvas. She gives you the image of the rainbow you used earlier and asks you to add a vector lightning bolt to the image for the insurance company campaign she's working on. To draw a lightning bolt, you can use the Custom Shape Tool, which is hidden under the Rectangle tool in the Tools panel.

To add content to the canvas:

1. Open **RainbowInsurance2.jpg**, located in the Photoshop1\Tutorial folder included with your Data Files.

2. In the Tools panel, point to the **Rectangle Tool** button, and then click and hold the mouse button. Photoshop displays a list of hidden tools.
3. Click the **Custom Shape Tool** button.
4. On the left side of the options bar, right-click the **Custom Shape Tool** button and then click **Reset Tool**. The options bar displays the default settings for the Custom Shape Tool.
5. On the right side of the options bar, click the **Custom Shape picker** button to open the Custom Shape picker. See Figure 1-36.

Figure 1-36 Custom Shape picker

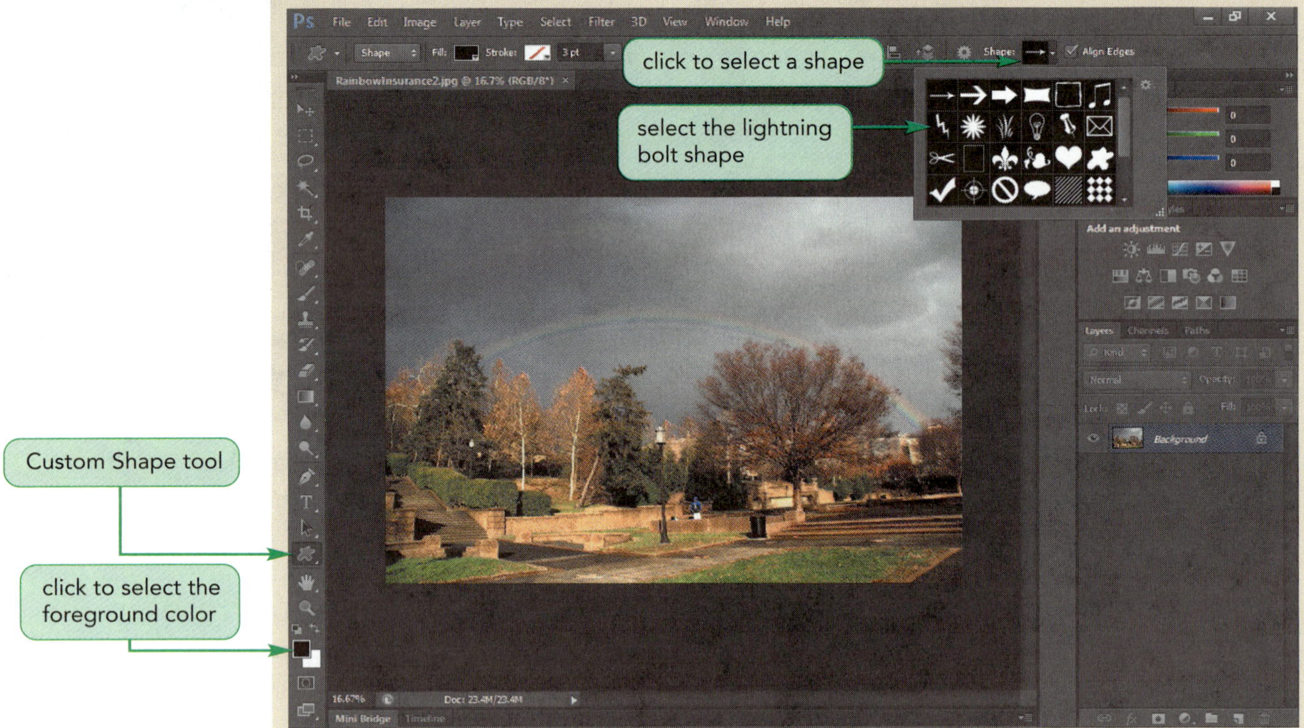

6. Double-click the **lightning bolt** in the first column, second row of the picker, to select that shape. You can now set the color for the shape.
7. On the options bar, click the **Fill** button to open a palette of fill colors.
8. Click a **yellow** box. See Figure 1-37.

Figure 1-37 Fill color palette

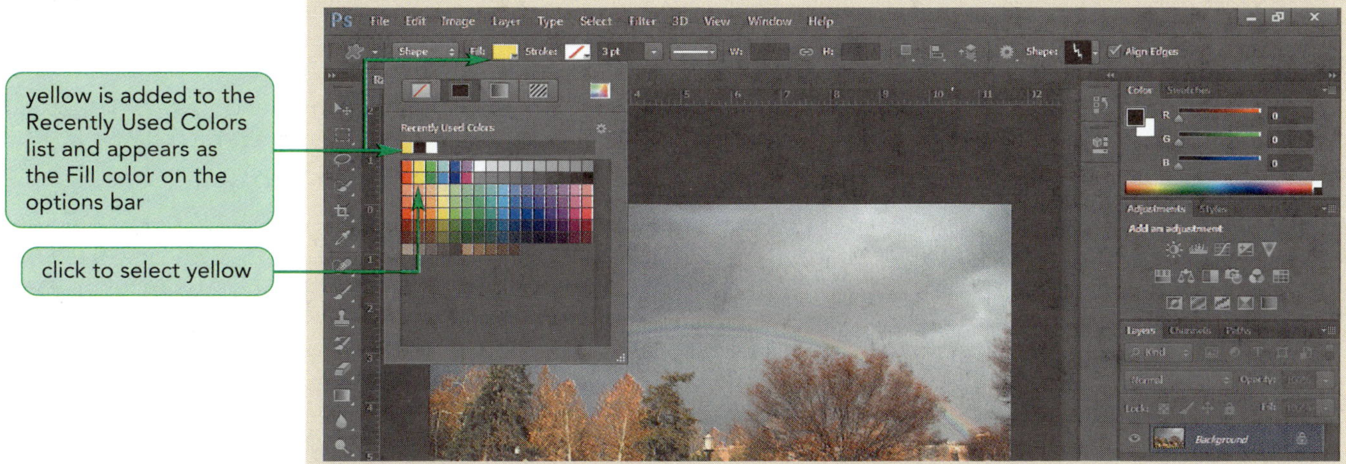

© 2012 Chadwick Cipiti/DCNature.com

9. On the options bar, click the **Fill** button to close the palette. The lightning bolt brush is now set to paint in yellow.

10. Drag from slightly to the left of the top center of the photograph down to the top of the person in the image, and then release the mouse button. You added a custom shape to the file. See Figure 1-38.

Figure 1-38 Brush panel

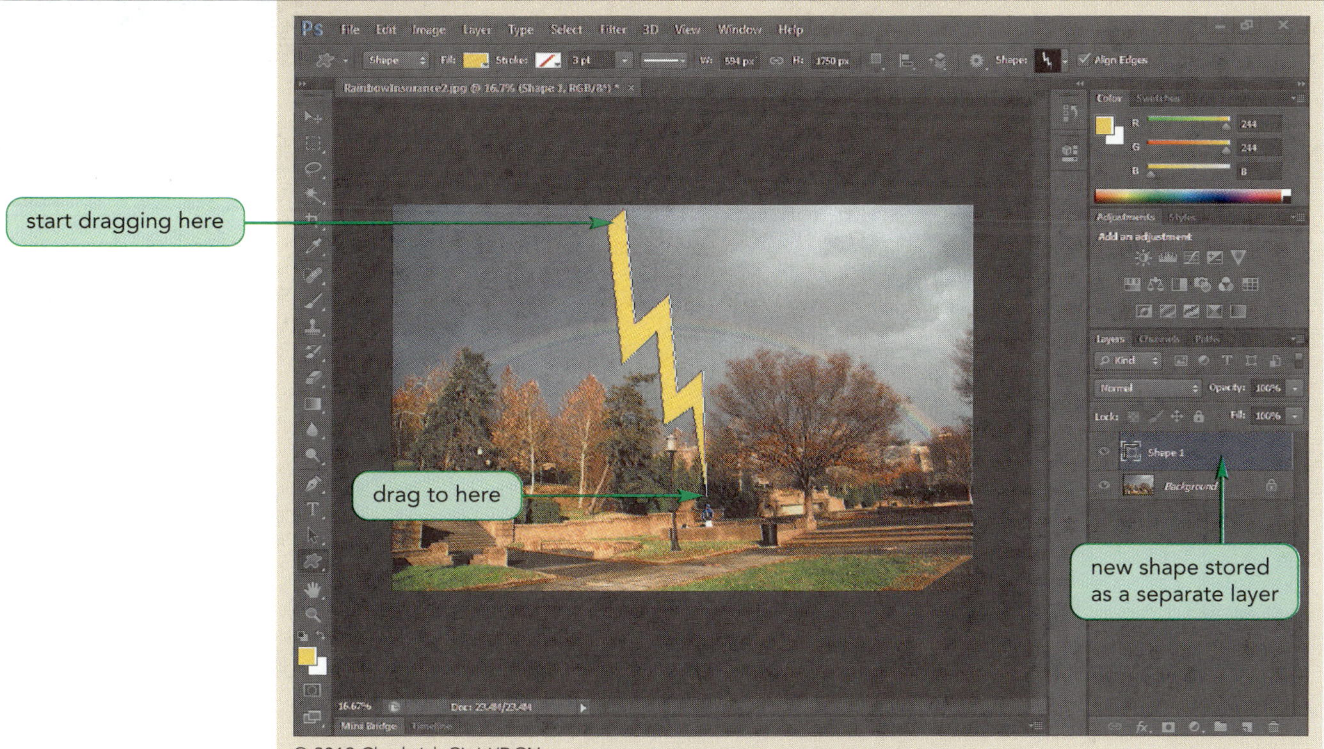

© 2012 Chadwick Cipiti/DCNature.com

The new shape is stored as a new layer on top of the Background layer.

When you set the options for the lightning bolt, you were making changes to the options bar for the lightning shape that you can now save as a tool preset.

To save a tool preset:

1. On the options bar, click the **Tool Preset picker** button, and then click the **Create new tool preset** button to the right of the preset list. The New Tool Preset dialog box opens. See Figure 1-39.

Figure 1-39 New Tool Preset dialog box

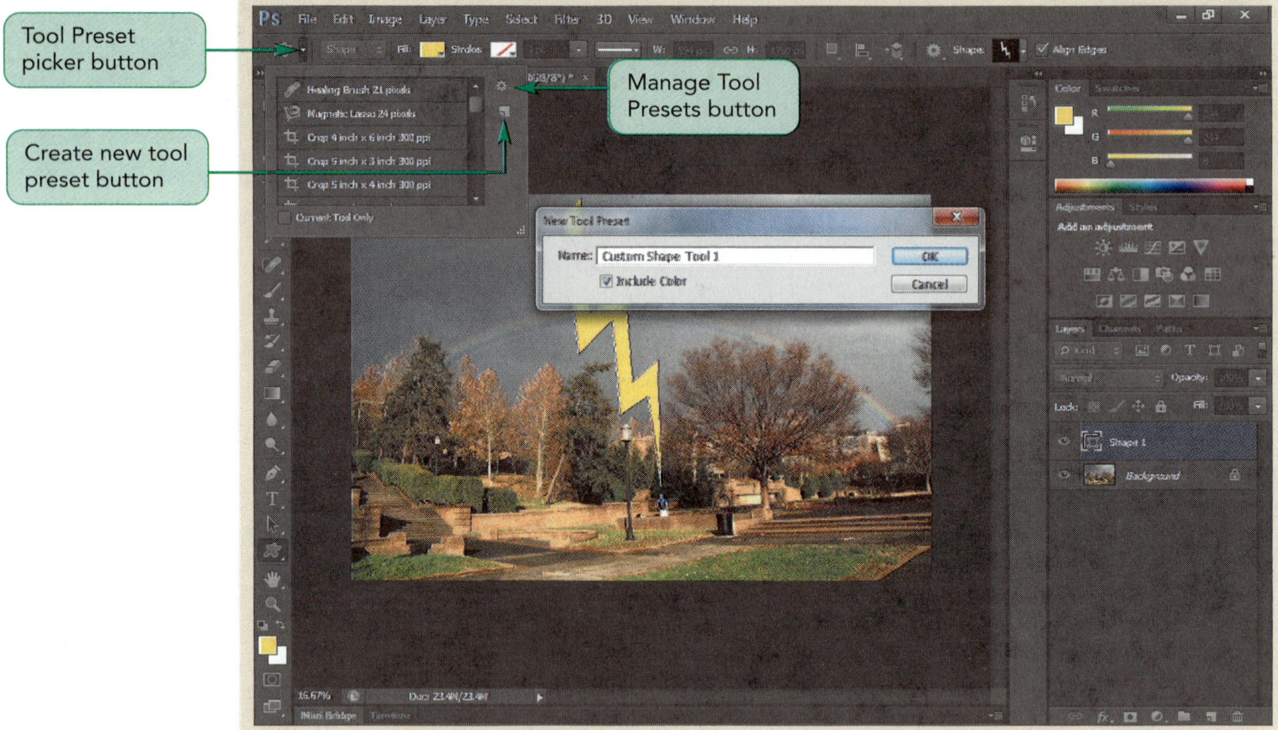

2. Type **Bolt preset** in the Name box, click the **Include Color** check box to select it, if necessary, and then click the **OK** button. The preset is added to the Tool Preset picker list. See Figure 1-40.

Figure 1-40 Tool preset added to Tool Preset picker list

new tool preset

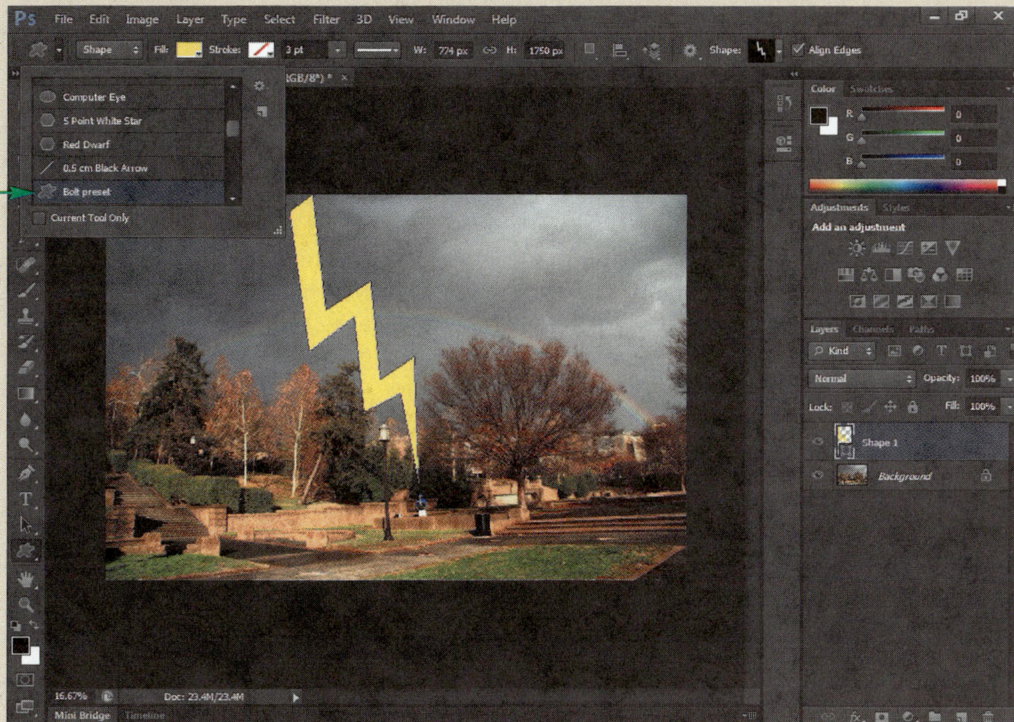

The next time you choose the Custom Shape Tool, the options will be set to a yellow lightning bolt.

3. Click the **Tool Preset picker** button again to close the list.

You might use a custom tool preset frequently while working on a particular project, but then find that you no longer need it once the project is finished. In that case, you can easily delete the custom tool preset from the Tool Preset picker list.

To delete a tool preset:

1. On the options bar, click the **Tool Preset picker** button.
2. Click the **Bolt preset** on the list, click the **Manage Tool Presets** button to the right of the preset list, and then click **Delete Tool Preset**.
3. Save the file as **Rainbow.psd** in the Photoshop1\Tutorial folder, and then close it.
4. Exit Photoshop.

In this session, you learned how to set Photoshop Preferences and then to restore the default preferences. You also worked with different elements of the Photoshop interface, including panels, workspaces, and tools. You learned how to display and use rulers, guides, and the grid; how to customize and save a workspace; and how to define and use tool presets. You also added content to the canvas.

PROSKILLS

Decision Making: Understanding Permissions

If you don't have a photograph that's appropriate for the job you need to accomplish, the Web provides a limitless supply—or does it? Just because an image is easy to download from the Web, does that mean it is free to use in any way you want? Think about it. If you're writing a paper for a class, you may easily find online sources, but can you copy paragraphs wholesale and not give credit to the original author?

As you acquire images, keep in mind that copyright law also applies to photographs (as well as video, music, and sound files). You should always operate under the assumption that every image on the Web is protected by copyright. Therefore, before you use someone else's work, you may need to obtain permission for its use, give credit or **attribution**, and, in some cases, pay a fee. You might be required to pay a **royalty** each time you use an image. Images that are **royalty-free** may still require payment, but usually it's a one-time fee. Some photographers assign a flexible copyright license that allows others to use their work. This might seem like an easy agreement to follow, but even a color correction would be considered an alteration, and would constitute copyright infringement if the photographer did not grant you the right to modify the photograph. Some government images and older works that are no longer protected by copyright law are in the **public domain**, and can be used however you want.

As you search for images to use in your work, you need to keep all of these issues in mind and make sure to read any licensing agreements or conditions posted by the owner of the photograph before you download an image. Two of the best resources for finding images you might be able to use are morgueFile and Creative Commons. Finally, if you plan to use one of your own photographs in any work, and would like to ensure that people understand that you hold the copyright, you can simply add the word *Copyright* or the copyright symbol ©, followed by the year. You can place this information directly on a photograph using the Text tools, or you can add it as a caption above or beneath the photograph.

By taking the time to understand copyright law and any pertinent licensing agreements, you can make the right decisions about the images you use in your projects.

REVIEW

Session 1.2 Quick Check

1. The Preferences command is found on the ____________ menu.
2. A ____________ displays a group of panels one on top of the other using tabs.
3. A ______________ is a collection of panels or panel groups joined top to bottom and sharing a title bar.
4. You can modify a predefined workspace in Photoshop and save it as a ______________ workspace.
5. What is a grid, and why would you use it in a Photoshop document?
6. ______________ are lines that you can add to the Document window to aid you in aligning and moving objects.
7. True or False. Any image that you can download from the Web is free to use in any manner.

Practice the skills you learned in the tutorial using the same case scenario.

PRACTICE

Review Assignments

Data Files needed for the Review Assignments: FireUnlit.psd, LightningInsurance.psd, UnexpectedBolt.psd

Sarah has given you some files that she plans to include in the Expert Insurance campaign so you can use them to familiarize yourself with the Photoshop interface, toolbars, and commands. She would also like you to create an image—using a photograph of a campfire—that she can use to present to her client as an idea for a new ad. Complete the following steps:

1. Start Photoshop while pressing the Ctrl+Alt+Shift keys. When you are prompted to delete the Adobe Photoshop Settings File, click Yes. Reset Photoshop to the Essentials workspace, and then reset all tools.
2. Open the **FireUnlit.psd**, **LightningInsurance.psd**, and **UnexpectedBolt.psd** files located in the Photoshop1\Review folder provided with your Data Files.
3. Save UnexpectedBolt as **RevUnexpected.psd** and FireUnlit as **FireLit.psd** in the Photoshop1\Review folder.
4. Switch to a 2-up Horizontal view of the files, and then switch back to the Consolidate All to Tabs view to view a single file in the Document window.
5. Open the original files, **UnexpectedBolt.psd** and **FireUnlit.psd**, so that you have five files open in the Document window.
6. Switch to the FireLit file.
7. Rearrange the tabs so the UnexpectedBolt file and the RevUnexpected file are next to each other and the FireUnlit file and the FireLit file are next to each other. Press the Alt+Print Screen keys to capture an image of the current Photoshop window; then open WordPad, which is available on the Accessories menu of the All Programs menu in Windows 7; and press the Ctrl+V keys to paste the image into a new file. Save the WordPad file as **PSTabs.rtf** in the Photoshop1\Review folder provided with your Data Files.
8. Display FireUnlit in a free-floating Document window.
9. Stack the Color panel group on top of the Layers panel group on the left side of the Document window. Press the Alt+Print Screen keys to capture an image of the current Photoshop window, switch to WordPad, and then press the Ctrl+V keys to paste the image into the PSTabs file you created in Step 7.
10. Consolidate all of the documents in the Document window to tabs with the FireLit file on top, and then switch to the Photography workspace.
11. Change the Guides, Grid & Slices preferences so that the Grid color is Medium Blue, and then display the grid.
12. Switch to the Essentials workspace, and reset the workspace.
13. Display the rulers; then, in the FireLit file, add a horizontal guide at 4 ½ inches on the vertical ruler and add a vertical guide at 6 inches on the horizontal ruler. Use the Custom Shape tool to add a shape that looks like fire on top of the wood. (*Hint*: Use the Grass 2 custom shape, which is in the second row, third column of the Custom Shape picker, and assign it an orange color to look like fire.)
14. With the Shape 1 layer selected, select the Move tool, and on the options bar, click to select the Show Transform Controls check box. Use the Move tool to center the drawing at the intersection of the horizontal and vertical guides. Press the Alt+Print Screen keys to capture an image of the current Photoshop window, switch to WordPad, and press the Ctrl+V keys to paste the image into the PSTabs file you created in Step 7.
15. Save your work in the **PSTabs.rtf** file, and then close WordPad.
16. Save your work in the **FireLit.psd** file, and then exit Photoshop.
17. Submit the results of the preceding steps to your instructor either in printed or electronic form, as requested.

Use your skills to create a magazine ad for an investment firm.

APPLY

Case Problem 1

Data File needed for this Case Problem: Harbour.psd

Safe Harbour Securities Maria Velasco, the marketing manager at Safe Harbour Securities, wants to place an ad for the company in a travel magazine. She asks you to create a mock-up for a magazine ad that would appeal to readers of a travel magazine. Complete the following steps:

1. Start Photoshop while pressing the Ctrl+Alt+Shift keys. When you are prompted to delete the Adobe Photoshop Settings File, click Yes. Reset Photoshop to the Essentials workspace, and then reset all tools.
2. Open **Harbour.psd**, located in the Photoshop1\Case1 folder provided with your Data Files, and then save the file as **SafeHarbour.psd** in the same folder.
3. Fit the image on the screen, and show the rulers.
4. Add guides at 6 inches on the horizontal ruler and at 2 inches and 4 inches on the vertical ruler.
5. Select the Background layer and then use the Custom Shape tool to draw an orange banner (Banner 3) that is 2 inches high and 6 inches wide, within the boundaries of the three guides on the left side of the screen.
6. Select the text layer, and use the Move tool to position the "Safe Harbour Securities…" text on top of the banner.
7. Add guides at 5 inches on the vertical ruler and 3 inches on the horizontal ruler.
8. Select the Background layer, and then use the Custom Shape tool to add a red heart below the banner, centered at the intersection of the two guides you just added.
9. Turn off the display of the guides to see what your ad will look like in final form.
10. Turn on the grid, and then turn the guides back on.
11. Save your work, and then exit Photoshop.
12. Submit the results of the preceding steps to your instructor, either in printed or electronic form, as requested.

Use Help to learn about and use tools to modify a photograph for a restaurant.

CHALLENGE

Case Problem 2

Data File needed for this Case Problem: SeafoodDish.psd

Yaya's Restaurant Yaya Venizia, the owner of Yaya's Restaurant, wants to modify a photograph of a lobster dish and change the image background for an upcoming ad. She wants you to help her make the necessary changes. Yaya thinks the Smudge tool will do what she wants, but she asks you to research the tool in Help before using it. Complete the following steps:

1. Start Photoshop while pressing the Ctrl+Alt+Shift keys. When you are prompted to delete the Adobe Photoshop Settings File, click Yes. Reset Photoshop to the Essentials workspace, and then reset all tools.
2. Open **SeafoodDish.psd**, located in the Photoshop1\Case2 folder provided with your Data Files. Fit the image on screen, and then save the file as **Yayas.psd** in the same folder.
3. EXPLORE Search Adobe Community Help for information on the Smudge Tool. Read the information provided by Adobe. (*Hint*: The topic should be called "Smudge image areas.")
4. EXPLORE Select the Seafood layer, and select the Smudge Tool. (*Hint*: The Smudge tool is hidden beneath the Blur tool in the Tools panel.) Set the brush size to 50 pixels and make sure Sample All Layers and Finger Painting check boxes on the options bar

are not selected. Using Figure 1-41 as a guide, smudge the edges of the image so that the photograph blends with the red border along all four sides of the photo image. Smudge every part of the seafood image except the lobster body and its claws so that the food looks as if it's surrounded by paint. (*Hint*: If you make a mistake, press the Ctrl+Z keys to undo your last action or click Edit on the menu bar and then click Step Backward.)

Figure 1-41 **YaYa's Restaurant image**

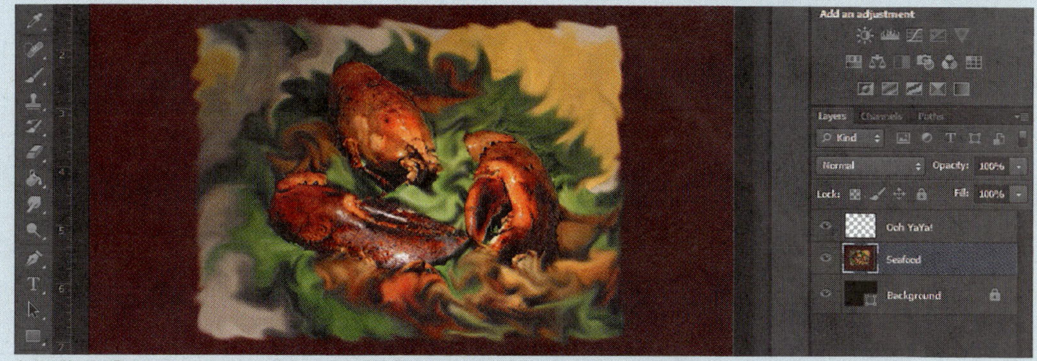

Jane Hosie-Bounar

5. Display the rulers and add guides at 5 ½ inches on the horizontal ruler and 8 inches on the vertical ruler.
6. Select the Ooh YaYa! layer, and then select the Move tool.

EXPLORE

7. Select the Show Transform Controls check box on the options bar, if necessary, and make the text ½ inch taller by dragging the center top control up. Press the Enter key to accept the size change.
8. Drag the text down so that the center bottom control is on the intersection of the two guides.

EXPLORE

9. Select the Paint Bucket tool in the Tools panel. (*Hint*: The Paint Bucket tool is hidden beneath the Gradient tool in the Tools panel.) Select the Seafood layer in the Layers panel, and then click the red border band surrounding the seafood with the Paint Bucket tool pointer to change the red border to black.
10. Save your work, and then exit Photoshop.
11. Submit the results of the preceding steps to your instructor, either in printed or electronic form, as requested.

Using Figure 1-42 as a guide, enhance a photograph for a placement agency.

CREATE

Case Problem 3

Data File needed for this Case Problem: Airplane.psd

Career Centers Fiona Friedman runs a career placement agency and wants to create a new brochure to promote her company. She asks you to modify a photograph that includes the company's trademark phrase so she can use the new image as the cover for the brochure. Figure 1-42 shows the final result.

Figure 1-42 Career Centers image

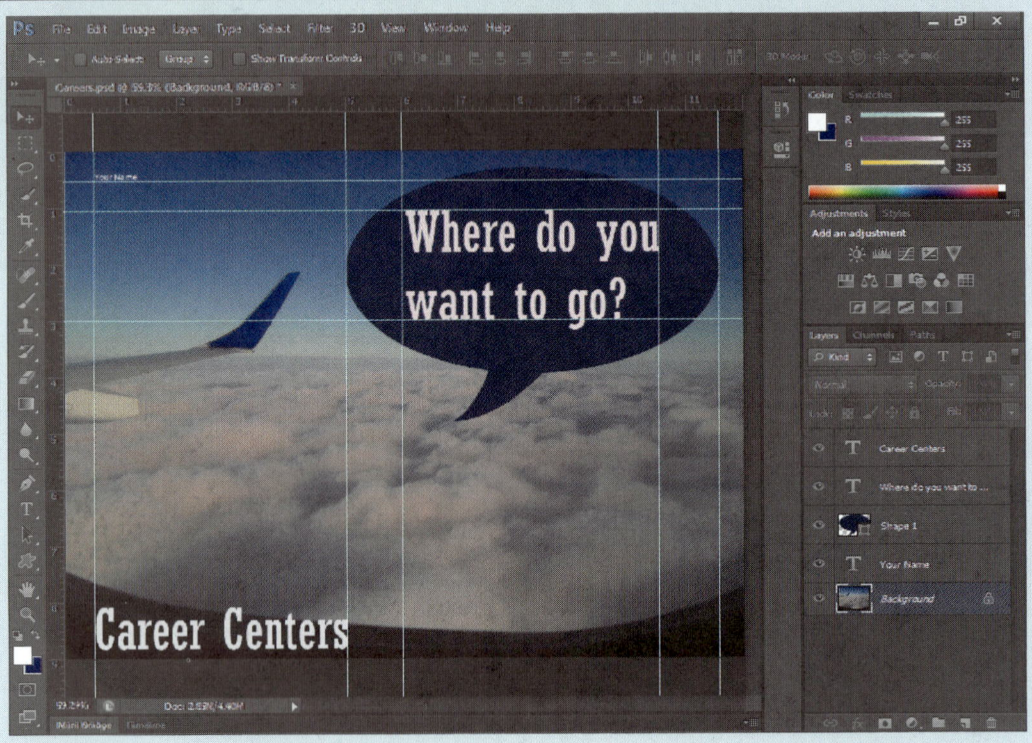

A. H. Bounar

Complete the following steps:

1. Start Photoshop while pressing the Ctrl+Alt+Shift keys. When you are prompted to delete the Adobe Photoshop Settings File, click Yes. Reset Photoshop to the Essentials workspace, and then reset all tools.
2. Open **Airplane.psd**, located in the Photoshop1\Case3 folder provided with your Data Files, and then save the file as **Careers.psd** in the same folder.
3. Zoom the image to fit on the screen.
4. Show the rulers, and add guides to the Document window, as shown in Figure 1-42.
5. Select the Background layer, and then add the blue shape shown in the figure.
6. Save the shape settings as a preset named **Bubble**.
7. Drag the "Where do you want to go?" text so that it is centered in the blue shape. Use the guides to position the text as shown in the figure.
8. Reset all of the tools.
9. Drag the "Career Centers" text to position it as shown in the figure, and then select the Background layer.

10. Select the Horizontal Type tool in the Tools panel, reset the tool, and make sure the foreground color is white. Click in the upper-left corner of the image, and then type your name. Drag your name so that it starts at the guide that is at the half-inch mark on the horizontal ruler and rests on the guide that is at the half-inch mark on the vertical ruler.
11. Delete the Bubble tool preset.
12. Save your work, and then exit Photoshop.
13. Submit the results of the preceding steps to your instructor, either in printed or electronic form, as requested.

Using Figure 1-43 as a guide, enhance a photograph for a travel agency.

CREATE

Case Problem 4

Data File needed for this Case Problem: ExploreMore.psd

Explore More Travel Hamid Brahim has hired you to help him with a new advertising campaign for his travel agency. He asks you to add text and drawings to a photograph that he has already "posterized," or adjusted to look like a painting rather than a photograph. Figure 1-43 shows the final result.

Figure 1-43 **Explore More Travel image**

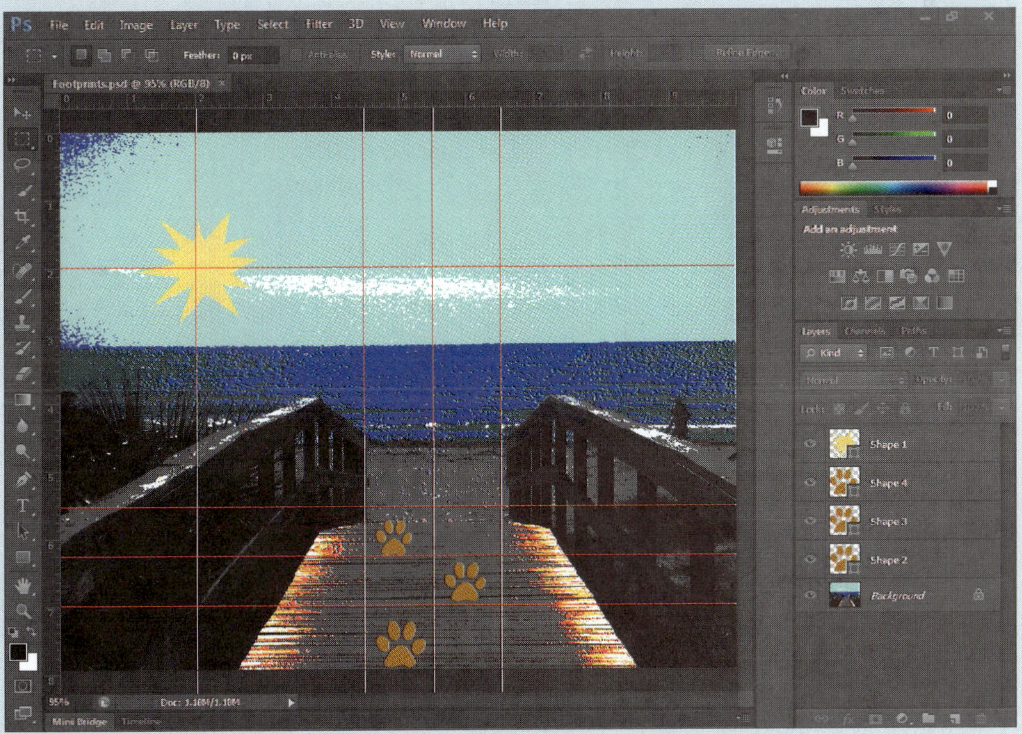

A. H. Bounar

Complete the following steps:

1. Start Photoshop while pressing the Ctrl+Alt+Shift keys. When you are prompted to delete the Adobe Photoshop Settings File, click Yes. Reset Photoshop to the Essentials workspace, and then reset all tools.
2. Open **ExploreMore.psd**, located in the Photoshop1\Case4 folder provided with your Data Files, and save the file as **Footprints.psd** in the same folder.
3. Zoom the image so it fills the Document window, and show the rulers, if necessary.

4. Change the Preferences so that the color of guides is Light Red, and then add guides to the Document window, as shown in Figure 1-43.
5. Draw a yellow starburst at the position indicated by the guides in the figure.
6. Draw three footprints at the positions indicated in the figure. Choose a color that you think works well with the image.
7. Zoom the image to 300%, and then pan until the starburst is at the center of the screen.
8. Press the Alt+Print Screen keys to capture an image of the current Photoshop window, then open WordPad and press Ctrl+V to paste the image into a new file. Save the file as **Starburst.rtf** in the Photoshop1\Case4 folder provided with your Data Files. Close WordPad.
9. Change the zoom to 95%.
10. Save your work, and close the file.
11. Submit the results of the preceding steps to your instructor either in printed or electronic form, as requested.

ENDING DATA FILES

Photoshop1 →

Tutorial
ExpertText1.psd
NewUnexpected.psd
OneBolt.psd
Rainbow.psd
TravelGuides.psd

Review
FireLit.psd
PSTabs.rtf
RevUnexpected.psd

Case1
SafeHarbour.psd

Case2
Yayas.psd

Case3
Careers.psd

Case4
Footprints.psd
Starburst.rtf

TUTORIAL 2

Working with Image Files

Working with File Sizes, Color Modes, and Image Adjustments

OBJECTIVES

Session 2.1

- Learn about file formats and their uses
- Change file type, file size, and resolution
- Examine Bridge and Mini Bridge
- Understand and change color modes
- Create new files using document presets and custom settings
- Place an image in a new file

Session 2.2

- Modify an image using adjustment layers
- Change canvas size
- Zoom and pan an image
- Rotate and flip an image

Case | *GreenHouse Construction*

GreenHouse Construction, an environmental construction firm in Fort Myers, Florida, was founded in 1992 by C. J. Kohl. The company designs "green" homes and buildings, so its building plans usually include features such as photovoltaic (solar) panels, automatic dimming fluorescent lights, double-paned windows, rooftop gardens, and plenty of natural lighting.

In the past, C. J. has created his own promotional materials. However, he thinks he needs help updating the materials to broaden his client base. He wants you to work with him on campaigns for both Web and print advertising. As you do, you'll explore various file sizes and color modes and determine which resolutions are best for which media. You'll also place images in files, make adjustments to images, and modify canvas and image size.

STARTING DATA FILES

Photoshop2 →

Tutorial
GreenDream.psd
GreenHouseConstruction.tif
GreenHouseText.psd
GreenHouseText2.psd
HeatCosts.psd
HeatCosts2.psd
Hi_Res.jpg
LeaderboardText.psd
Sun.psd
WireCutter.jpg
Wrench.jpg

Review
GreenHouseText.psd
Hammer.psd

Case1
ConcertHall.jpg

Case2
Eye.tif
EyeMask.psd

Case3
Mash.jpg
RockNRoll.psd

Case4
Cupcake.jpg
FinnText.psd
FinnText2.psd

SESSION 2.1 VISUAL OVERVIEW

A JPEG is one type of **file format**, which determines how the information (or data) in your file is organized when it is stored on a storage device such as a camera's memory card, a hard drive, or a flash drive.

When you save a JPEG file, you can specify the Quality setting, which determines the file size. The lower the Quality setting, the more Photoshop will **compress** the image, which reduces the file size.

You can select an option for how the file will load in a Web browser.

Photoshop previews the file size based on the JPEG settings you specify.

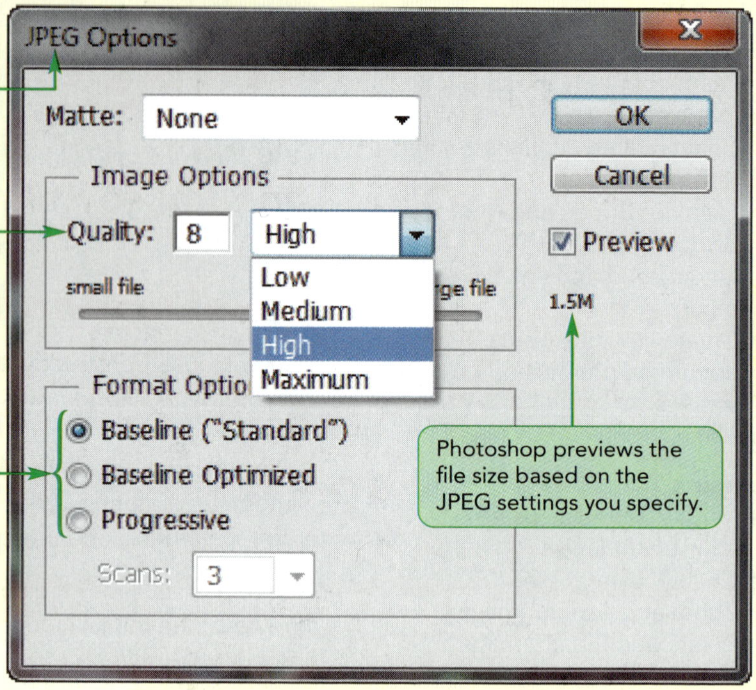

The Image Size dialog box provides options for changing the image size, resolution, and interpolation method, among other things.

When you change the resolution of an image, Photoshop **resamples** the image, which changes the number of pixels in the image.

The **interpolation method** determines how Photoshop will add or subtract pixels when you resample an image.

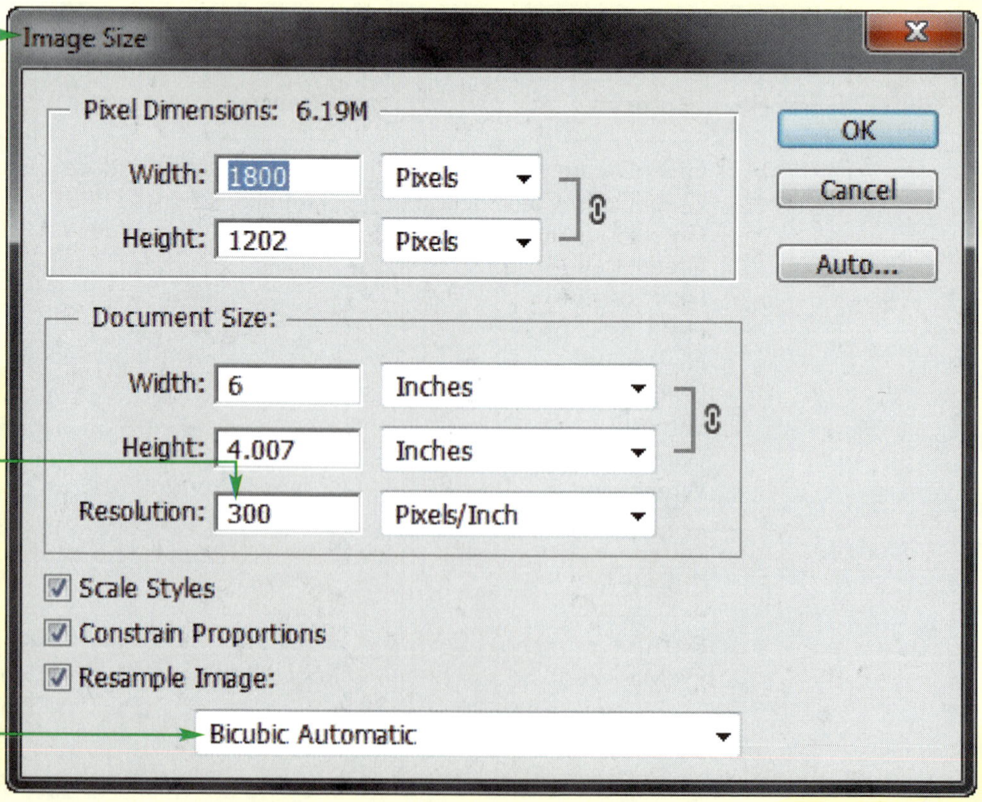

FORMAT AND SIZE OPTIONS

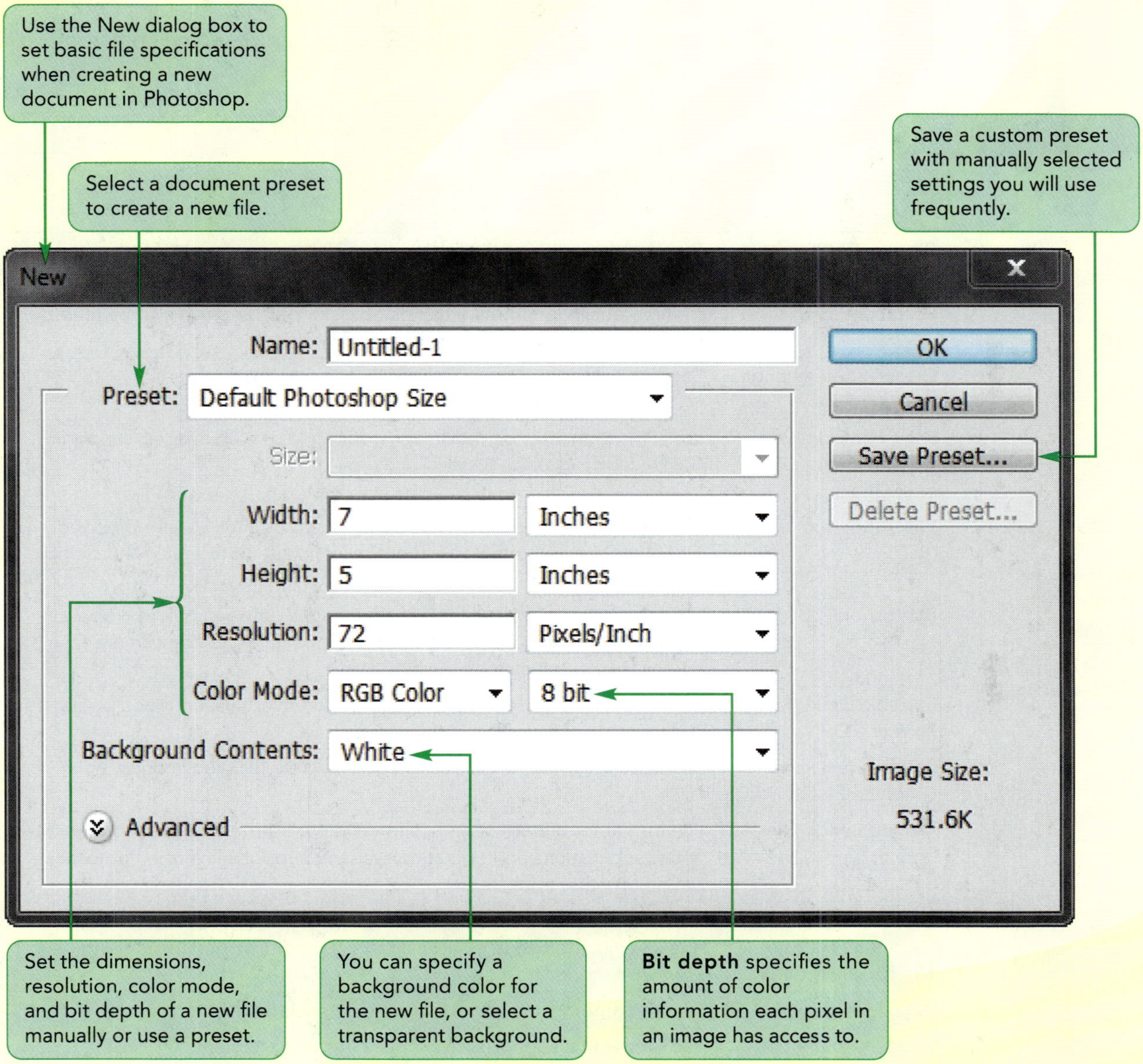

Understanding File Formats and Their Uses

You can open and save images in Photoshop in well over a dozen file formats. In an image-editing program like Photoshop, the file format, or file type, determines how much space an image takes up in memory, how it handles color, and how it is printed as output.

Although files with different formats might look the same in the Photoshop Document window, certain characteristics of each format can affect upload time on the Web, the print quality of a finished piece, and even the Photoshop features you can use to manipulate the file. The number of file formats might seem overwhelming at first, but as you continue to work with Photoshop, you'll find that choosing the right file format will eventually become second nature. Figure 2-1 summarizes some commonly used file formats.

Figure 2-1 **File formats**

Format	Details
Bitmap (BMP)	Bitmap image file format for Windows; does not support CMYK color
Encapsulated PostScript (EPS)	File format that supports both vector and bitmap graphics; can be used for high-quality printouts on a PostScript printer; and can also be read by most graphics, illustration, and layout programs
Graphics Interchange Format (GIF)	Lossless format for bitmap images; suitable for Web images
Joint Photographic Experts Group (JPEG or JPG)	Lossy file format for bitmap images; suitable for Web images; supports CMYK, RGB, and Grayscale
Photoshop format (PSD)	File format that supports all Photoshop features and is easily imported by other Creative Suite applications; can include both vector and bitmap graphics
Photoshop Raw (RAW)	File format that allows you to transfer images between different applications and operating systems; includes metadata, including camera type and exposure, but cannot contain layers
Portable Document Format (PDF)	File format that can display images in different applications and operating systems
Portable Network Graphics (PNG)	Lossless file format for bitmap images; suitable for Web images
Tagged Image File Format (TIFF, TIF)	File format for bitmap images; allows you to transfer images between different applications and operating systems; supports layers in Photoshop, but not in other applications
Digital Imaging and Communications in Medicine (DICOM)	Medical scan file format; each frame or slice of a scan is converted to a layer in Photoshop, which can then be edited or adjusted using Photoshop tools
Digital Negative (DNG)	File format that contains raw image data, including metadata
Large Document Format (PSB)	File format that supports large documents—up to 300,000 pixels
Desktop Color Separations (DCS)	File format that saves the color separations in a file; related to the EPS format, it saves vector and bitmap graphics and is used for high-quality printouts
OpenEXR	High-quality file format used in movie production
Cineon	File format developed by Kodak that lets you import a file from film to digital and then output it back to film
Targa (TGA)	An RGB format developed for use with TrueVision technology

Each file format has its own advantages and disadvantages. Some file formats support only vector graphics, whereas others support only bitmap graphics. **PSD**, the default Photoshop format, stands for Photoshop document. The PSD format, which can hold both vector and bitmap data, stores multiple image components and enhancements on separate elements called **layers** so you can make changes to one part of a composition while leaving the other parts intact. **GIF** (Graphics Interchange Format), **PNG** (Portable Network Graphics), and **JPEG** (Joint Photographic Experts Group, sometimes written as JPG) formats are **flat formats** consisting of single layers of bitmap data. These file types work best for the Web because they tend to have smaller file sizes, so they upload more quickly. Other file types, such as **TIFF** (Tagged Image File Format) and **EPS** (Encapsulated PostScript), contain a great deal of data and are used to output high-quality print pieces.

Some file formats are **proprietary**, meaning they can only be edited in the program in which they were created. For example, the PSD file type is a proprietary file type; the .psd extension indicates a file is **native** to—or created in—Photoshop. PSD files can be easily manipulated in other Adobe applications such as Adobe Illustrator, Adobe Flash, and Adobe Fireworks, but many drawing, Web design, and image-editing programs do not support the PSD file format. If you need to use a PSD file in a program that doesn't support the PSD format, you must save it in a compatible format so you can open and manipulate it in the other application. When you convert a file to another format, you might lose some features—for example, Photoshop layers—that are supported in the original file. However, you also gain some benefits, such as the ability to use a file in many different applications. You can save an image in different formats for use in different media, such as in a four-color printed piece, on a Web page, or in a newspaper advertisement.

Changing File Type, File Size, and Resolution

In Photoshop, you have the flexibility to change the properties of a file not only by changing its file type, but also by changing its file size and its resolution. You can do this in a number of different ways, including by compressing a file and by resampling a file. As you learn the nuances of the different file types in Photoshop, you'll be able to achieve the results you want for each project by using the appropriate file type, size, and resolution.

Optimizing an Image

When you edit or enhance images in Photoshop, each layer of editing you add can increase the size of a file by many megabytes. Larger file sizes are a necessity if you want to print high-quality images; to achieve the most accurate colors and the sharpest printout, you need the layers of detail and color data stored with an image. However, on the Web, large image file sizes can result in painfully slow download times for the end user, as well as file storage challenges. Because of this, images on Web sites are often compressed to allow for quicker download times. Finding the right balance between image quality and file size is called **optimization**.

The three image file formats most commonly used on the Web—GIF, JPEG, and PNG—all use compression to optimize images and reduce the size of image files. The JPEG format uses **lossy compression** to reduce file size by throwing out, or "losing," some of the original data in an image. For example, it reduces the number of colors in an image and uses a process called **dithering** to replace the discarded colors with colors from the new, smaller color palette. A file format that uses lossy compression is called a **lossy file format**. The GIF file format is a **lossless file format**; it uses **lossless** compression, which means it doesn't discard data when it compresses the file. Instead, it stores data more efficiently—for example, by mapping all colors to a color table instead of storing each pixel's color information with the pixel itself.

It's wise to make edits to an image file while working in a high-resolution, non-lossy format. Doing so gives you more editing options. Then, when you have finished editing the image, you can optimize it by saving it in a file format, such as JPEG, that is better suited to Web use. When you save a file as a JPEG, the JPEG Options dialog box opens, as shown in Figure 2-2.

Figure 2-2 **JPEG Options dialog box**

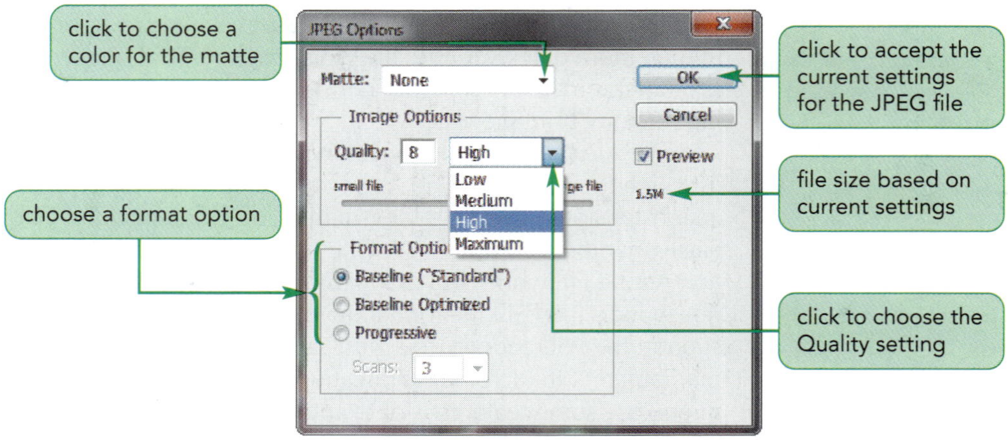

In the JPEG Options dialog box, you can select the **matte**, which is the color that will appear in the background of an image as it downloads while a user is trying to view it on the Web. You can also specify the quality of the image. The lower the quality, the smaller the file size and the faster the download time; however, you should always confirm that you haven't compromised the image quality on your Web site for the sake of a smaller file size. The JPEG Options dialog box offers three format options, including Baseline ("Standard"), which saves the file in a format most browsers can read. Baseline Optimized optimizes the color and results in a smaller than standard file size; however, not all browsers support optimized images. The Progressive format option results in an image that will initially be displayed with little detail, and then increase in detail as the file loads. In other words, it will appear as the ghost of an image, and then be filled in as the file loads. With the Progressive format option, you can specify three, four, or five **scans**, or stages, that the viewer will see before the image has finished loading. If you select the Preview check box, Photoshop calculates the approximate size of the file based on the selections you have made and displays it beneath the check box.

TIP

Always keep a copy of the original, unedited image file so it is available for other projects.

C. J. has an image that he'd like to use on the company's Web site. He asks you to save the file in a format that is suitable for Web use. You'll save the file as a JPEG and then use the JPEG Options dialog box to see the effect that compression has on file size.

To save the file in a lossy file format:

1. Start Photoshop while pressing the **Ctrl+Alt+Shift** keys. When you are prompted to delete the Adobe Photoshop Settings File, click **Yes**. On the menu bar, click **Window**, point to **Workspace**, and then click **Reset Essentials** to reset the default Essentials workspace layout. On the options bar, right-click the **Rectangular Marquee Tool** icon 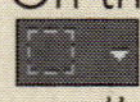, and then click **Reset All Tools**. When you are asked if you want to reset all tools to the default settings, click the **OK** button.
2. On the menu bar, click **File**, click **Open** to display the Open dialog box, and then navigate to the Photoshop2\Tutorial folder included with your Data Files.

3. In the Open dialog box, click the **View Menu** button, and then click **Details** to select it, if necessary.
4. Click **GreenHouseConstruction.tif**. Scroll to the right, if necessary, to see the Size column. Notice that this file is large, over 19 megabytes (MB).

   Trouble? If the Size column does not appear in the Open dialog box, right-click any column header and then click Size on the context menu to add the Size column to the dialog box.
5. Click the **Open** button. The GreenHouseConstruction.tif file opens in the Photoshop Document window.

   The TIFF file has several layers, including a shape layer and a text layer with special effects. Preserving these layers in a TIFF file lets you modify them at a later point. You'll learn more about layers in Tutorial 3.

   Trouble? If you get a message about missing fonts, click the OK button, and let Photoshop make the substitution.
6. On the menu bar, click **File**, and then click **Save As**. The Save As dialog box opens with the Layers check box selected, indicating that the file includes layers.
7. Click the **Format** arrow, and then click **JPEG (*.JPG;*.JPEG;*.JPE)** in the list of available image file formats. The filename changes to GreenHouseContruction.jpg. See Figure 2-3.

Figure 2-3 Save As dialog box

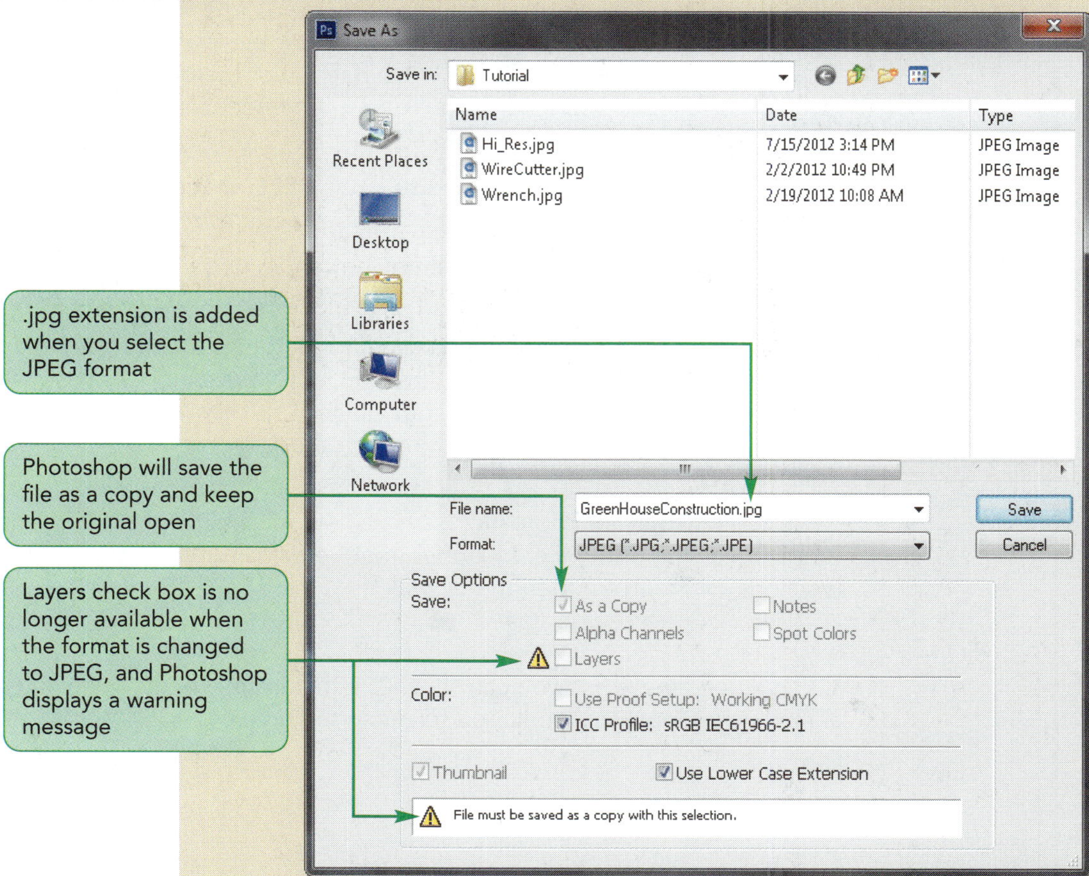

When you select JPEG as the file format, the Layers check box is cleared and is no longer available; at the bottom of the dialog box, next to an exclamation point, Photoshop displays a message indicating the file must be saved as a copy. When Photoshop saves the file, it will save it with the same name plus a .jpg extension in the current folder, but it will keep the original TIFF file open. To see the saved file, you'll need to open it in Photoshop.

8. Navigate to the Photoshop2\Tutorial folder, if necessary, and click the **Save** button. The JPEG Options dialog box opens, as shown in Figure 2-4.

Figure 2-4 **Changing JPEG options when saving**

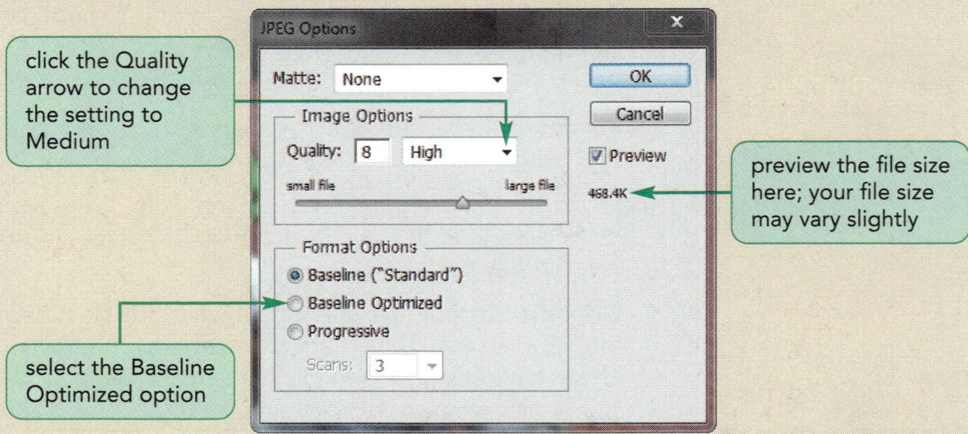

If you save the file with the default JPEG settings, the file size is reduced to around 468.4 kilobytes (KB), as shown under the Preview check box in the JPEG Options dialog box. This is a fraction of the original TIFF file size (which was over 19 MB). Next, you'll see what effect changing the Quality and Format Options has on file size.

Trouble? If you can't see the file size in the JPEG Options dialog box, click the Preview check box to select it and show the file size.

9. Click the **Quality** arrow, click **Medium**, and then, under Format Options, click **Baseline Optimized**. Photoshop previews the file size at around 295 KB.

The new file size is only about 60 percent as large as the file size that results from using the default settings in the JPEG Options dialog box. It is also less than 2 percent of the size of the original file. This difference should give you a very clear idea of how important optimization can be when you prepare images for the Web.

10. Click the **OK** button. Photoshop saves a copy of the file in JPEG format. The original version of the file, in TIFF format, remains open. To view the JPEG version, you need to open the new file.

Next, you'll open the file so you can show C. J. that in spite of the huge difference in file size, the images look very similar on screen.

To compare the two GreenHouseConstruction files:

1. On the menu bar, click **File**, and then click **Open**. The Open dialog box opens.

   Notice that the size of the GreenHouseConstruction.jpg file is even smaller than it was in the preview, and is listed at around 284 KB. This is because when Photoshop saves the file to disk, it compresses it even more. When you open it, it will expand slightly in memory for better display, and return to about 295 KB. (Your file sizes may vary slightly.)

2. Double-click the **GreenHouseConstruction.jpg** file to open it. Notice in the Layers panel that this file consists of a single layer labeled *Background*.
3. On the menu bar, click **Window**, point to **Arrange**, and then click **2-up Vertical** .
4. Press the **Tab** key to hide all panels so the images appear larger.
5. On the status bar of the GreenHouseConstruction.jpg window, type **35** in the zoom percentage box, and then press the **Enter** key to zoom GreenHouseConstruction.jpg to 35%.
6. On the status bar of the GreenHouseConstruction.tif window, type **35** in the zoom percentage box, and then press the **Enter** key to zoom GreenHouseConstruction.tif to 35%. See Figure 2-5.

Figure 2-5 JPEG and TIFF files displayed side by side

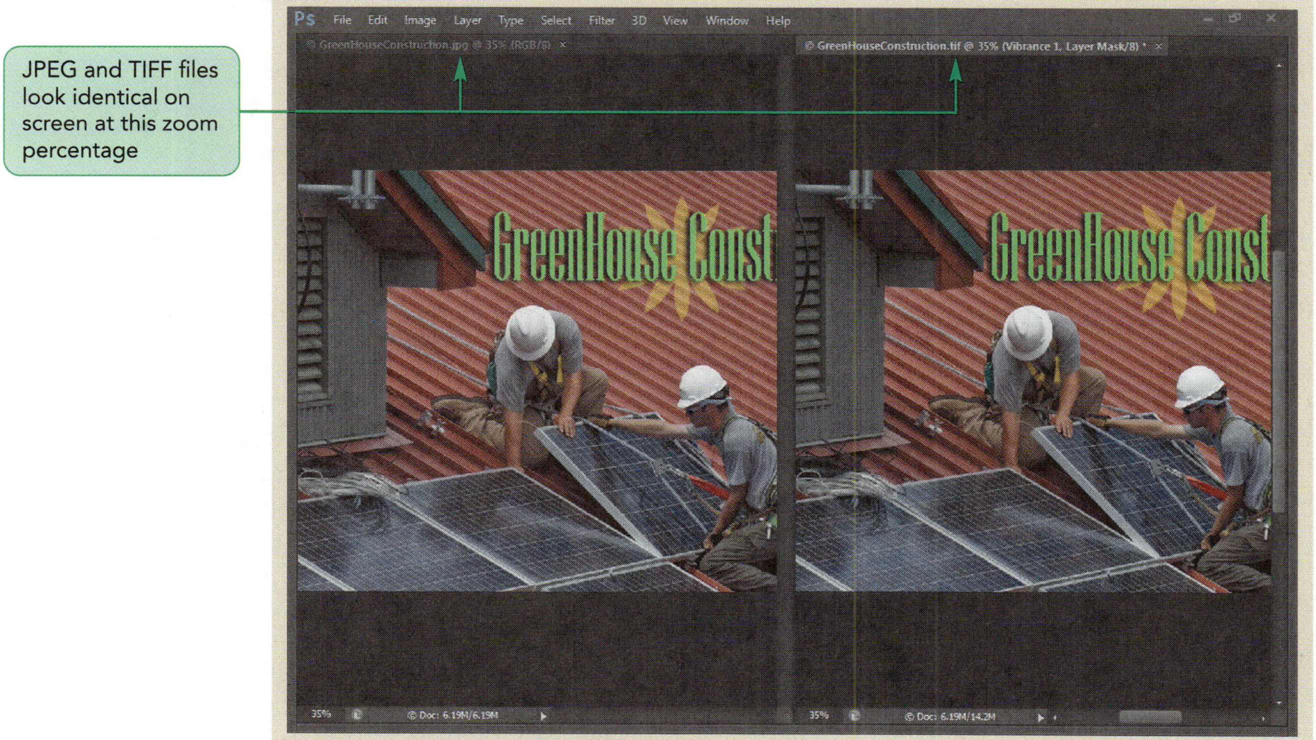

© 2009 Alex Snyder/Wayne National Forest

Even though the JPEG file is a small fraction of the size of the TIFF file, the two files look identical on screen at a 35% zoom setting.

7. Press the **Ctrl+1** keys to zoom the TIFF file to 100%, click the **GreenHouseConstruction.jpg** tab, and then press the **Ctrl+1** keys to zoom the JPEG file to 100%. Although the JPEG file has been compressed and is slightly less crisp than the TIFF file at such a high zoom percentage, it is still suitable for viewing on a computer monitor.

   Given that images on Web pages take up only a fraction of the display area available on a monitor, you can be sure that this file will work well on C. J.'s Web site.

8. Close GreenHouseConstruction.tif. Leave the GreenHouseConstruction.jpg file open, and press the **Tab** key to redisplay the panels.

Changing Image Resolution

Because different projects require files with different resolutions, Photoshop gives you the option of changing the resolution of a file. To change resolution, you open the Image Size dialog box and type in a new value. See Figure 2-6.

Figure 2-6 Image Size dialog box

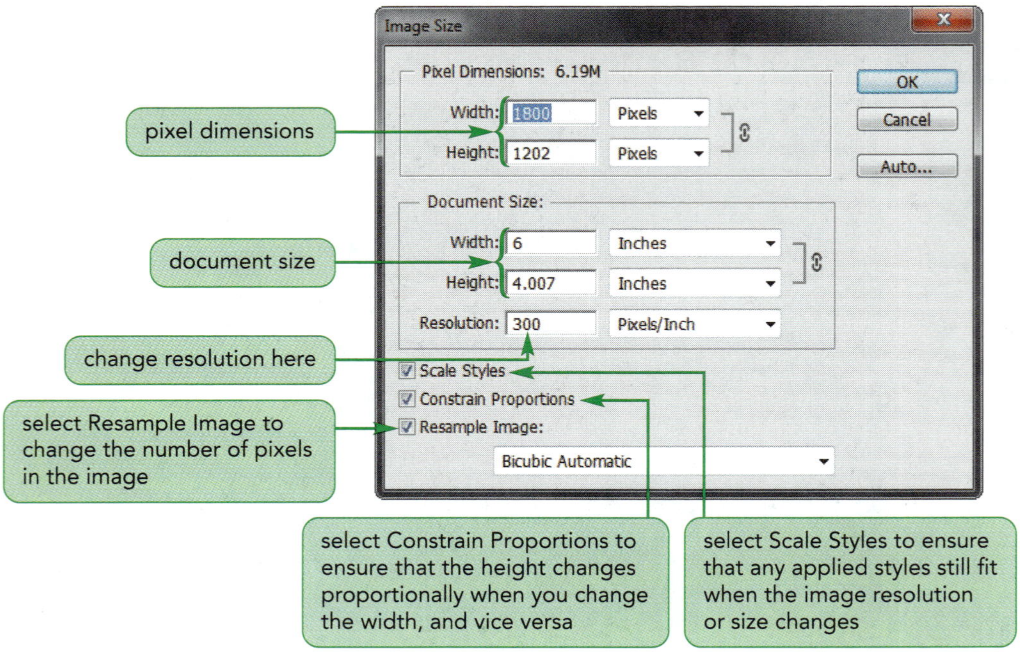

TIP

You can upsample a low-resolution image to increase the dimensions of a photo, but you'll achieve better results if you simply start with a high-resolution image.

Remember that resolution is measured in pixels per inch, so when you change an image's resolution, you are changing the number of pixels per inch. Photoshop uses a process called resampling to achieve the new resolution. You can resample an image in two different directions, depending on whether you want to decrease or increase the resolution. If you **upsample** an image, Photoshop adds pixels to the image so that there are more pixels per inch. It does this using a mathematical algorithm that uses interpolation to calculate what each added pixel should look like based on the surrounding pixels. The different interpolation methods are outlined in Figure 2-7.

Figure 2-7 Interpolation methods

Method	Details
Nearest Neighbor	Makes exact copies of pixels when upsampling; can result in jagged edges
Bilinear	Averages the color values of surrounding pixels to create new pixels
Bicubic	Uses complex calculations to determine values for new pixels; higher quality than Nearest Neighbor or Bilinear
Bicubic Smoother	Uses more complex calculations to calculate values for new pixels; higher quality than Nearest Neighbor, Bilinear, or Bicubic
Bicubic Sharper	Sharpens an image using a calculation similar to Bicubic Smoother; can result in edges that are too sharp
Bicubic Automatic	The default interpolation method; automatically chooses the best resampling method for you based on the resizing options you choose

Upsampling can't improve the quality of a blurry image because the interpolation algorithm can only use the information already contained in the file. If the existing pixels display an imperfect image, the upsampled image will be imperfect as well.

If you **downsample** an image by decreasing the resolution, Photoshop throws out pixels to keep the document the same physical dimensions—for example, 6 × 4 inches. What do you think might happen to the size of a file if you decrease the number of pixels per inch by downsampling? Rather than thinking in terms of pixels, think of a high-resolution photograph as a bucket of pebbles—with dozens of evenly spaced pebbles completely covering the bottom of the bucket. Now consider what happens to the weight of the bucket when you take some pebbles out so that the remaining pebbles are still evenly spaced, but no longer touching—the bucket will be lighter. When you downsample, you are decreasing the resolution (you have fewer pixels per inch), which results in a "lighter" file.

INSIGHT

PPI vs. DPI

Note that *ppi*, or pixels per inch, is different from the *dpi* (dots per inch) setting used to describe printer resolution. On a printer, one pixel can be created by multiple dots, depending on the resolution of your printer. In other words, there is not a one-to-one correspondence between ppi and dpi. A resolution of 300 ppi is excellent for a high-quality print piece, but 300 dpi could result in a grainy-looking printout if an image includes many different color gradations. An image with a resolution of 300 pixels per inch printed on a high-resolution printer might very well have 1200, or even 2880, dots per inch. It is a good idea to make sure everyone involved in a project is using these terms correctly so the final output quality meets the project's requirements.

You can also decrease the resolution of an image without resampling to increase the physical dimensions of your image. For example, you can change the resolution of a 4 × 6-inch photograph from 300 ppi to 150 ppi. If you deselect Resample Image in the Image Size dialog box, Photoshop will achieve the new resolution by spreading out the pixels over a larger area. Cutting the resolution in half will result in an image that is twice the dimensions of the original—or, using this example, 8 × 12 inches. This decrease in resolution will *not* result in a smaller file size because the image will still have the same number of pixels. If we return to the bucket analogy, you'll be carrying around a bucket with the same number of pebbles in it, but the bucket itself will be twice the size of the original, and the pebbles will be more spread out. Depending on your needs, this method might produce an acceptable image. However, if you plan to use the image in a printed piece, remember that spreading out pixels can result in poorer image quality.

REFERENCE

Changing Image Resolution Using Resampling

- On the menu bar, click Image, and then click Image Size.
- Confirm that the Resample Image check box is selected in the Image Size dialog box.
- Type a new value in the Resolution box.
- Click the OK button to change the resolution.
- Save the file with a new filename.

You'll experiment with different resolution settings so you are familiar with the different options available for the various advertising media C. J. plans to use.

To change the resolution of the GreenHouseConstruction.jpg image using resampling:

1. Make sure that the GreenHouseConstruction.jpg file is open in Photoshop at 100% magnification.
2. On the menu bar, click **Image**, and then click **Image Size**. The Image Size dialog box opens. It displays the pixel dimensions of the image (1800 pixels wide × 1202 pixels high). It also displays the document size, which is the size at which the image is currently set to print. At present, the document size is about 6 × 4 inches.
3. Click the **Resample Image** check box to select it, if necessary. Highlight **300** in the Resolution box to select it, and then type **150**. Leave the default interpolation method, Bicubic Automatic, unchanged. See Figure 2-8.

Figure 2-8 **Changing the resolution**

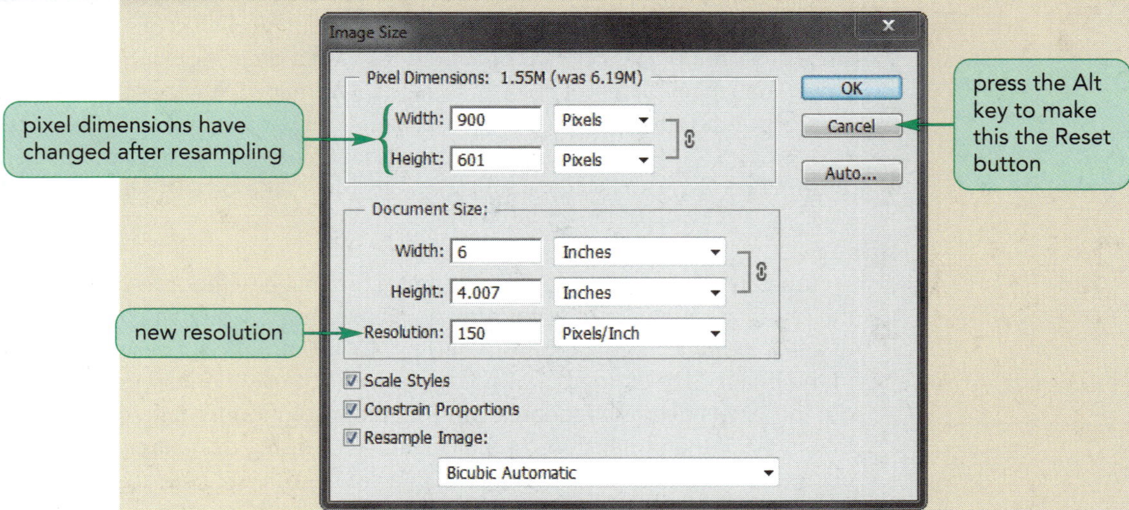

Trouble? If you make a mistake while working in the Image Size dialog box, press and hold the Alt key and then click the Reset button in the dialog box to return to the original settings.

When the Resample Image option is selected, Photoshop throws out pixels to reach the lower resolution (fewer pixels per inch). The pixel dimensions are now 900 × 601, or exactly half the pixel dimensions of the 300 ppi image.

4. Click the **OK** button, and then press the **Ctrl+0** keys to fit the image on the screen.

   Trouble? If the Open dialog box appears, you pressed the letter O instead of the number zero. Click the Cancel button to close the dialog box and press the Ctrl+0 keys.

Be sure to save the file with the new name so you still have a copy of the original high-resolution file, which you'll need for later steps.

5. Save the file as **GreenHouseConstruction150ppi.jpg** in the Photoshop2\Tutorial folder, and then click the **OK** button to accept the settings in the JPEG Options dialog box.

   A resolution of 150 ppi will be appropriate for a newspaper ad or for a 4 × 6-inch photograph printed on your home printer. You can also resave the file at a lower resolution appropriate for Web graphics.

6. On the menu bar, click **Image**, and then click **Image Size**.
7. Highlight **150** in the Resolution box to select it, and then type **72**. The pixel dimensions are now 432 × 289, or a little less than half the pixel dimensions of the 150-ppi image. This resolution will be sufficient for displaying the construction image on the Web.
8. Click the **OK** button to close the Image Size dialog box, and then save the file as **GreenHouseConstruction 72ppi.jpg** in the Photoshop2\Tutorial folder using the current JPEG settings.
9. Close GreenHouseConstruction 72ppi.jpg.

PROSKILLS

Decision Making: What Is the Best Resolution for Your Needs?

You already know that the resolution you need for an image is determined by how you plan to use the image, but which resolutions are best for which needs? If you are going to display the image on the Web, a relatively low resolution of 72 ppi is the standard. If your image will appear in black and white in a newspaper, 150 ppi is acceptable. If you are going to print an image on your color printer and want it to look good enough to frame, the resolution should be 240 ppi or above. Finally, if your image will appear in a magazine or professional journal, 300 ppi is your safest bet. At a lower resolution, you risk having your image look grainy. A resolution higher than 300 ppi adds many megabytes to the file size, but not much in terms of quality.

These guidelines can help you make decisions about which images you'll use for a project, but you also need to decide in advance whether you'll manipulate resolution in Photoshop, or whether you'll start with a file that already fits the bill. Many factors will go into making this decision, including time constraints (you are on a deadline), client needs (you are required to use the images provided), and budget (the client cannot afford to send a photographer into the field to shoot a new image or cannot afford to purchase a different image). Familiarizing yourself with all of your options ahead of time will ensure that you make the best decision to meet the needs of any given project.

Managing Multiple Image Files with Adobe Bridge and Mini Bridge

After you have worked with Photoshop for a while, you are bound to have dozens or even hundreds of different image files on your computer, but how do you organize them? Photoshop ships with a file management application called Adobe Bridge that simplifies storing, finding, sorting, and filtering your images. You work with Bridge outside of Photoshop, and you can use it in much the same way you use Windows Explorer to navigate folders on your computer. See Figure 2-9.

Figure 2-9 Adobe Bridge

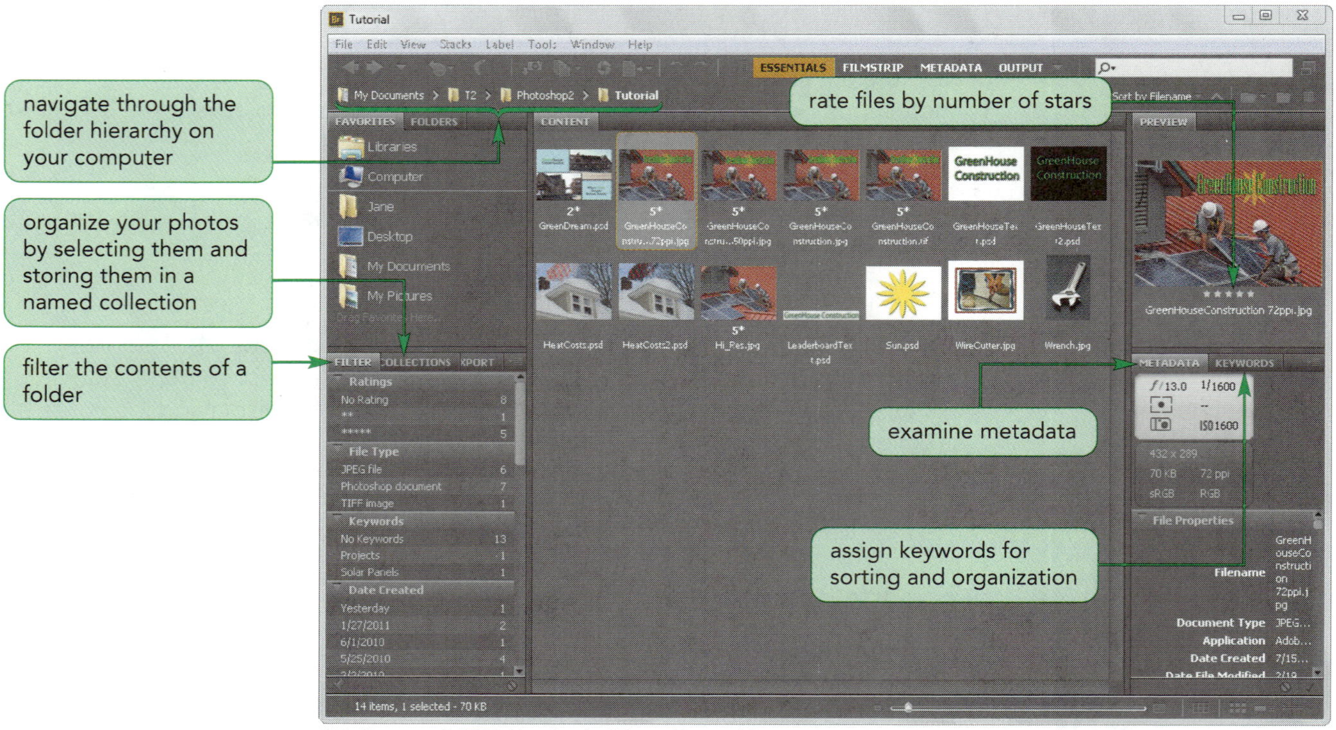

C.H. Gorman; © 2009 Alex Snyder/Wayne National Forest; Jane Hosie-Bounar; © 2009 Alex Snyder/Wayne National Forest; Garsya/Shutterstock.com

Bridge also has powerful tools that let you use metadata and keywords to categorize your images. In general terms, **metadata** is data about data—for example, information describing how data is formatted or how it was collected. In Bridge, metadata information could include details about the camera that a photographer used to shoot a photograph, the lighting conditions in which a photograph was taken, the date a file was created, the date a file was modified, file dimensions, resolution, color mode, bit depth, and copyright information, among other things. You can use the tools in Bridge to categorize your images with **keywords**, or words that describe your photographs in some way. For example, you might assign the keyword *People* to all photographs of people. You can also rate your photographs using a system of stars. A five-star image is better than a two-star image. You can then use this information to filter a folder containing photographs. A **filter** hides all files except those specified by the filter. So, you could filter by keyword so that only photos assigned the keyword *People* are listed, or you could filter by rating to display only the five-star photographs. You can also sort your images by rating, by filename, by file type, or by a number of other sort options. Another feature in Bridge lets you select files from many different folders and then add them to a custom object called a collection. A **collection** allows you to access photos stored in multiple locations with the click of a mouse. Bridge is fully integrated with Photoshop, so it is easy to switch between the two applications.

Photoshop also includes a stripped-down version of Bridge called Mini Bridge that opens directly in Photoshop. Adobe Mini Bridge is the "pocket-sized" version of Adobe Bridge. It has some, but not all, of the features of Bridge. For example, you can't assign a rating to a file in Mini Bridge, but you can view ratings, navigate folders, filter images, and search for and preview images without leaving the Photoshop workspace. You can also preview a file in Full Screen mode before you open it in Photoshop or see a slide show of all of the files in a folder before opening them. Review Mode displays the currently selected image in a new window, with the other images in the folder stacked behind it. You can navigate through those images using navigation buttons. You can also use Review mode to add photos to a named collection, or to zoom in on different areas of an image.

When it first opens, Mini Bridge displays the folder path of the current Windows user in the navigation area on the left. You can display a list of recently used folders by clicking the Computer button in the navigation area and then clicking Recent Folders. You can also click Recent Files to display a list of recently used files. When you do, the navigation area displays the names of any Creative Suite applications you have installed. When you click an application name such as Photoshop, the preview area displays a list of the digital image files you have recently worked with in Photoshop.

TIP

You can also click the Browse in Mini Bridge command on the File menu to expand Mini Bridge.

To use Mini Bridge:

1. Click the **Mini Bridge** tab at the bottom of the Photoshop window. The Mini Bridge panel expands under the Document window and displays a message indicating that Bridge must be open in order to use Mini Bridge.
2. In the Mini Bridge panel, click the **Launch Bridge** button. Photoshop displays the message "Waiting for Bridge CS6." Then Mini Bridge displays the navigation area on the left and the preview area on the right. By default, the navigation area displays a Computer button and a list of the drives on your computer. You can click the Computer button to display Favorites and recently visited folders.
3. In the navigation area on the left, click the **Computer** button, and then click **Favorites**. Mini Bridge displays a list of favorites in the navigation area including Computer, Desktop, My Documents, and My Pictures. If you have specified any Favorites in Windows, it displays those folders as well.

   Trouble? If the button in the navigation area is labeled something other than Computer, clicking it will still display the current user's main Windows folder, Favorites, Recent Folders, Recent Files, and Collections.
4. In the Favorites list, click **My Pictures**. Mini Bridge displays the contents of the My Pictures library.
5. In the navigation area click the **Favorites** button, click **Recent Files**, and then click **Photoshop**. See Figure 2-10.

Figure 2-10 Adobe Mini Bridge

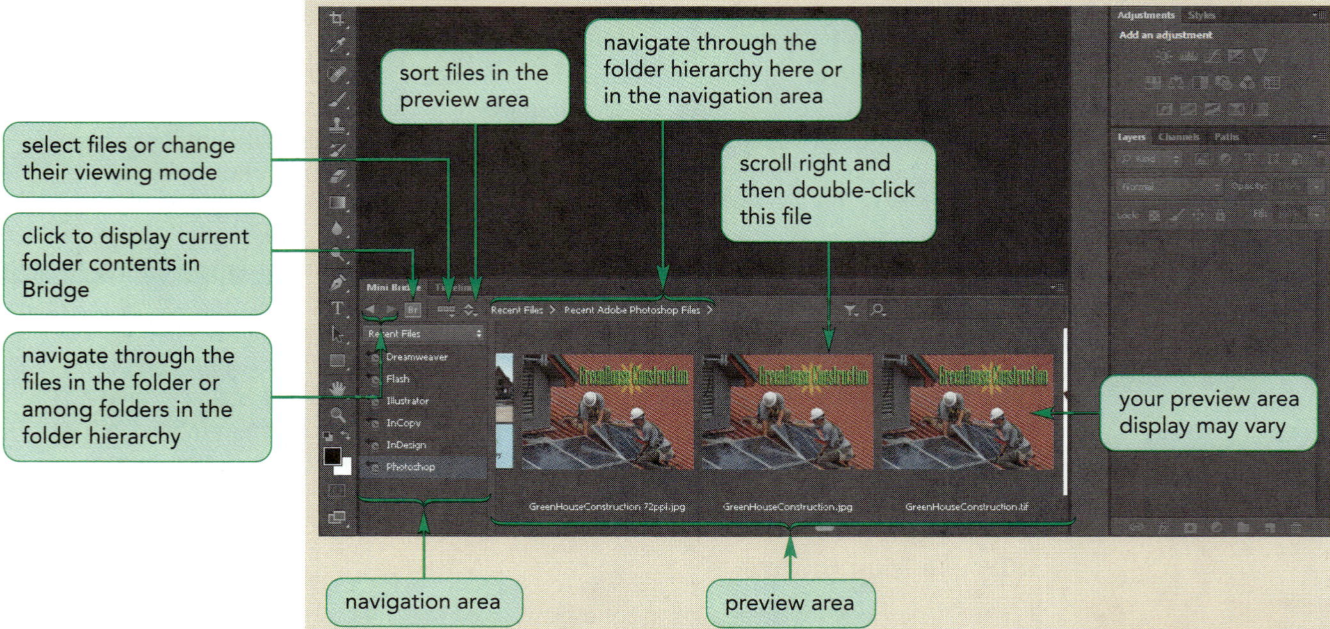

C.H. Gorman; © 2009 Alex Snyder/Wayne National Forest

TIP

You can also open a file by dragging it from Mini Bridge into the Document window.

6. In the preview area, scroll right if necessary, and then double-click **GreenHouseConstruction.jpg**. The GreenHouseConstruction.jpg file opens in the Document window.
7. Double-click the **Mini Bridge** tab. The Mini Bridge panel collapses.
8. On the menu bar, click **File**, and then click **Browse in Bridge**. In Bridge, click **File** on the menu bar, and then click **Exit**. Bridge closes.

Now that you have a good understanding of file formats, resolution, and file size, and know how to find and sort files in Mini Bridge, C. J. asks you to spend some time learning about the different color modes available in Photoshop so you'll be able to meet the needs of his advertising campaign on the Web, in four-color printed pieces, and in black-and-white newspapers.

INSIGHT

Adding User Information and Metadata in the File Info Dialog Box

Photoshop offers many options for viewing and adding metadata to a file. You have already seen that you can categorize and add metadata to files using Bridge. You can also open the File Info dialog box from the File menu to view camera and image data and add metadata such as keywords, ratings, and descriptions. You can view camera data such as camera model, image resolution, image size, and exposure, and if your camera has GPS capabilities, you can view GPS information for an image. If you are working with a medical image, you can use the DICOM tab to enter information such as a patient's name, ID number, and date of birth. Whether you choose to use the File Info dialog box or Bridge, it is always a good idea to enter as much information about a file as possible in case you need to reference it later.

Understanding Color Modes and Intensities

Color mode is an important setting that you must take into consideration when preparing an image in Photoshop. The color modes in Photoshop are based on a variety of industry-standard color models. A **color model** is a set of mathematical values that numerically represent color. Each color model consists of a few **primary**, or starting, colors (for example, red, green, and blue) that you can combine in different intensities to create hundreds of thousands, or even millions, of other colors. Common color models are RGB, CMYK, and grayscale. To understand how many color choices you can end up with using different combinations of only a few colors, consider the RGB model. The RGB color model uses only three colors—red, green, and blue—but each of these colors can be assigned a value from 0 (for no color) to 255 (for maximum color intensity). In Photoshop, **intensity** simply refers to the value you have assigned to one of the primary colors. That means you have 256 choices—or intensities—for red (remember that 0 is a choice), 256 choices for green, and 256 choices for blue. That's 256 × 256 × 256 color possibilities, or about 16.7 million choices. See Figure 2-11.

Figure 2-11 **Differing color intensities**

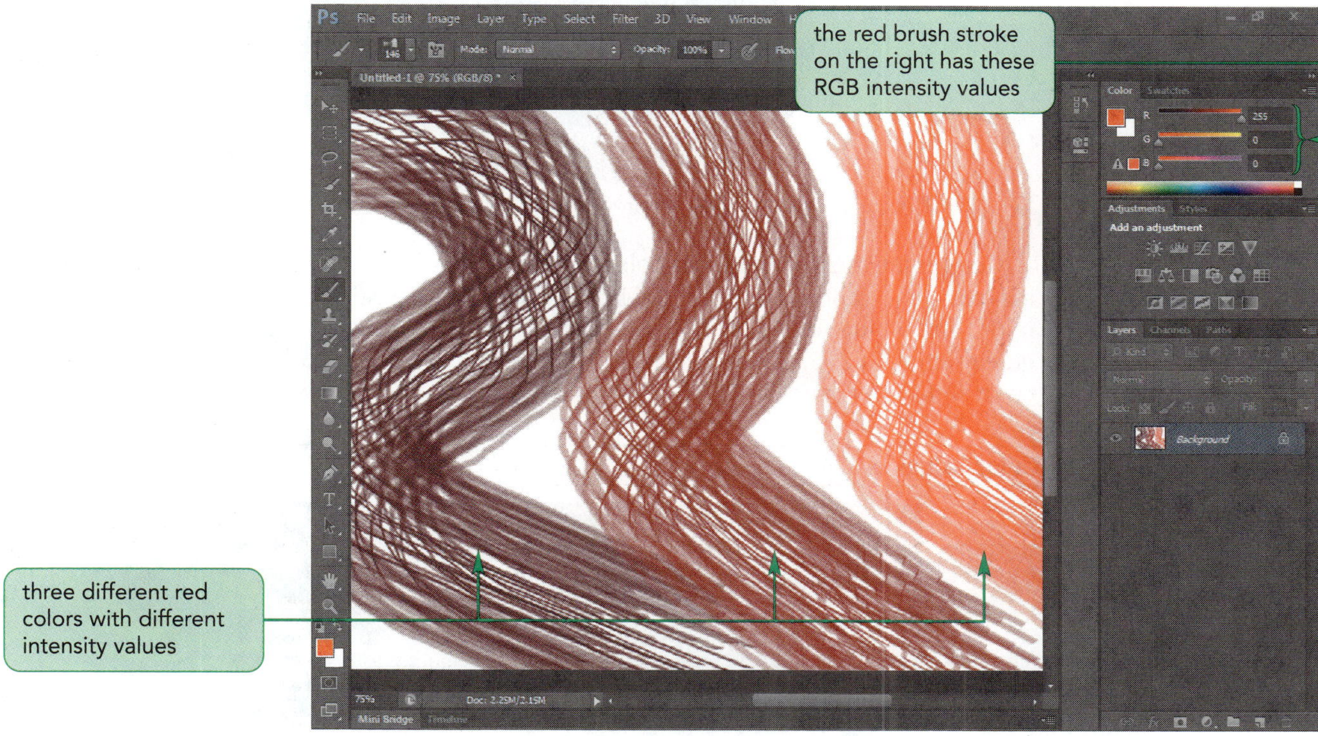

You can think of intensity in terms of paint. If you dip your brush in red paint and then paint on a canvas, you'll get one version of red paint. However, if you first put a bit of blue paint on your brush, and then dip the brush in the red paint, you'll get a different red with a different intensity. Finally, if you first dip your brush in a bit of green and then dip it in the red paint, you get still another version of the color red. Now imagine that you mix that first deep color of red thoroughly with a deep blue, but no green. You'll get a color that is neither red, nor blue, nor green, but a combination of red and blue. Or perhaps you combine it with green, but not blue. You'll get a different color.

Photoshop lets you specify the intensity of colors using numbers. Each color mode uses a different numbering system, but the results are similar: You start with a few color settings, but you wind up with a seemingly unlimited palette of colors to choose from. Different media require different color modes, and although the orange color you see on screen and the orange color you see on a printed page might look identical, they are created in completely different ways, by combining different colors in different color modes.

Understanding the RGB Color Mode

By default, new files in Photoshop use the RGB color mode, which is based on the RGB color model. The **RGB** (red, green, blue) color mode is an additive color mode. As you might expect, an **additive color mode** adds colors together to create a different color. See Figure 2-12.

Figure 2-12 RGB color mode

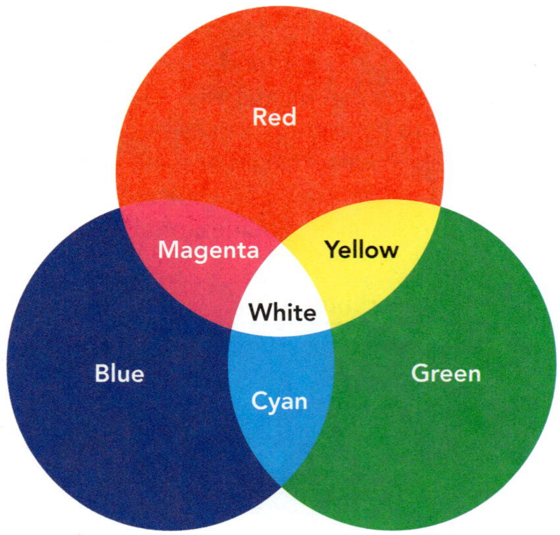

Combining the three primary colors in varying intensities results in the colors cyan, magenta, and yellow. For example, in Photoshop, a red setting of 142, a green setting of 61, and a blue setting of 151 results in an intense magenta. A red setting of 255, a green setting of 255, and a blue setting of 0 results in a yellow color, as shown in the color sliders in Figure 2-13.

Figure 2-13 Color values

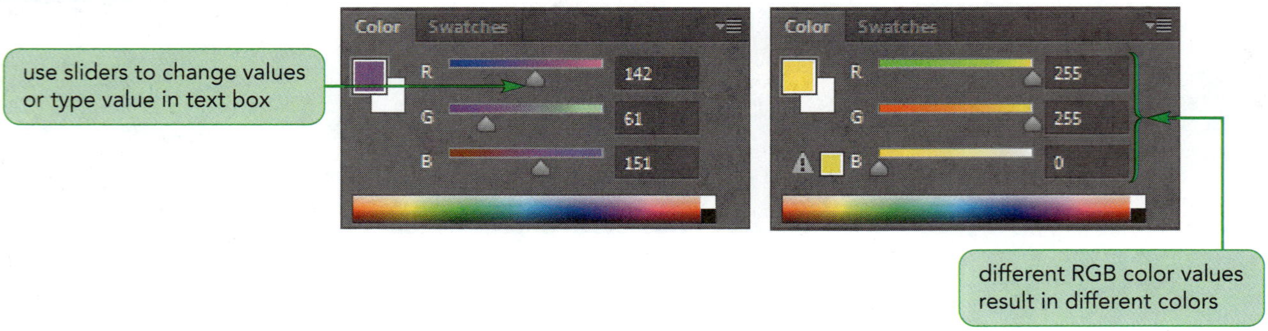

You have seen that red, green, and blue additive colors can create cyan, magenta, and yellow, but where do the colors white and black come from? If you have ever taken a physics course, you know that white light contains all of the colors in the color spectrum, and black is the absence of color. In fact, the RGB color mode follows the laws of physics; combining all three colors at their maximum intensities (255, 255, 255) results in white. Specifying a setting of 0 for all three colors (0, 0, 0) results in the color black.

Understanding the CMYK Color Mode

CMYK (cyan, magenta, yellow, key) is a color mode specifically meant for printed output. CMYK is a **subtractive color mode** because each color subtracts the light from the white page on which it's printed. Because printed output involves putting ink on white paper, the CMYK mode might make more sense to you than RGB. You don't need to have studied physics to understand CMYK. In fact, you learned all you need to know about this mode in kindergarten, where you discovered that mixing two paint colors together results in a third color, but mixing all paint colors together results in black. See Figure 2-14.

Figure 2-14 **CMYK color mode**

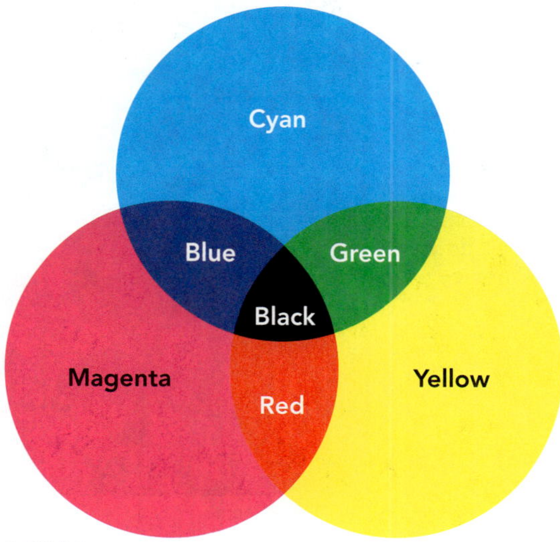

In the CMYK color mode, you specify color combinations in terms of percentages rather than intensity values, but CMYK still involves combining the primary colors of the mode, which in this case are cyan, magenta, yellow, and black.

You might wonder why the mode is called CMYK (for key) instead of CMYB (for black). In the CMYK color mode, *key* does refer to black, which is the color used on the key plate in the four-color printing process. The **key plate** is the plate in the printing process used to print the details in an image. To understand how printed output might look without the color black (and to understand why black is "key"), see Figure 2-15.

Figure 2-15 Image with and without black, a "key" color

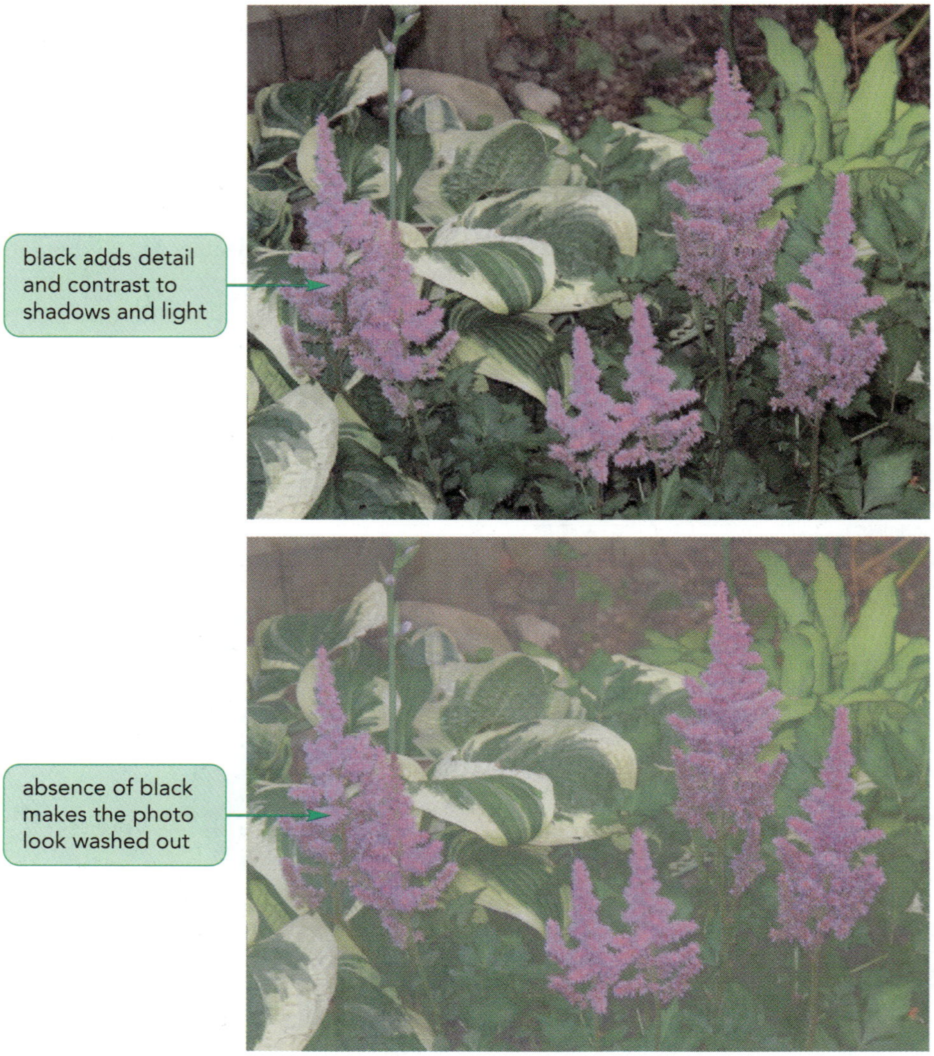

Jane Hosie-Bounar

> **TIP**
>
> Some inkjet printers print in RGB color mode rather than CMYK. Although the quality of these printers is not sufficient for a professional project, it is usually acceptable for home use.

The photograph on the top of the figure includes the key color (black). The photograph on the bottom shows the image as it would look without any black. You can see that the key color is essential to a crisp, clean image.

Because CMYK involves one more color than RGB, the file size of a CMYK image can be about 50 percent larger than its RGB counterpart, depending on optimization settings. Therefore, if you are only using a file for the Web, it's wise to use RGB.

Understanding Indexed Colors

The 8-bit Indexed color model uses a palette of 256 colors, which might seem limited given the millions of colors available in other models. However, for many uses, such as for Web animations and Web pages, 256 colors are more than enough. The advantage of using an Indexed color model rather than RGB is smaller file size. When you convert a file to the Indexed color model, Photoshop analyzes the colors in the image and then creates a **color lookup table (CLUT)** of 256 colors. The CLUT can consist of any of the colors in the image you are converting. For example, if you are converting from RGB, Photoshop creates the CLUT using just 256 of the 16.7 million color choices. See Figure 2-16.

Figure 2-16 **Color lookup table (CLUT)**

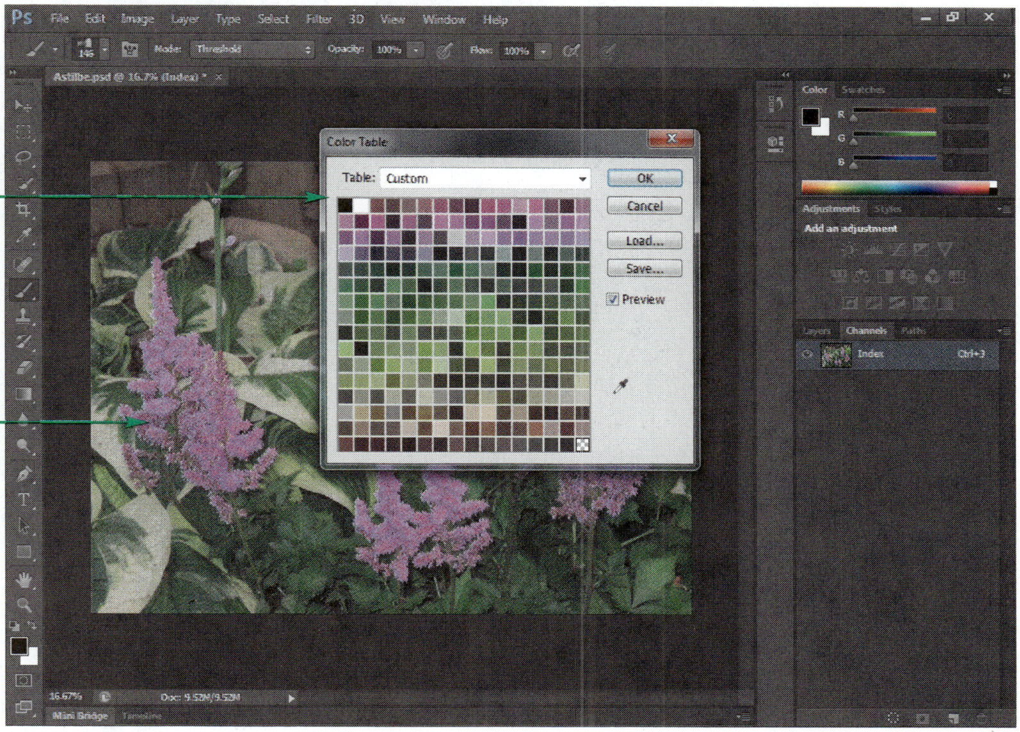

Jane Hosie-Bounar

If a color in the image matches a color stored in the table, Photoshop maps the pixel to that cell in the table. If a color has no matches in the table, Photoshop chooses the closest color from the table, or maps it to two or more indexed colors to simulate the color needed in the image. Switching an image to the Indexed color model in Photoshop is another way to optimize an image. Furthermore, the Indexed color model is supported by many different applications and, therefore, "travels" well from application to application. Your challenge is to ensure that the reduction of color choices doesn't result in a reduction in image quality.

Understanding the Grayscale Color Mode

When you convert an image from one of the other Photoshop color modes to Grayscale mode, Photoshop translates every intensity or shade of every color to a different shade, or **tone**, of gray. White is 0 percent, and black is 100 percent gray. See Figure 2-17.

Figure 2-17 Grayscale color percentages

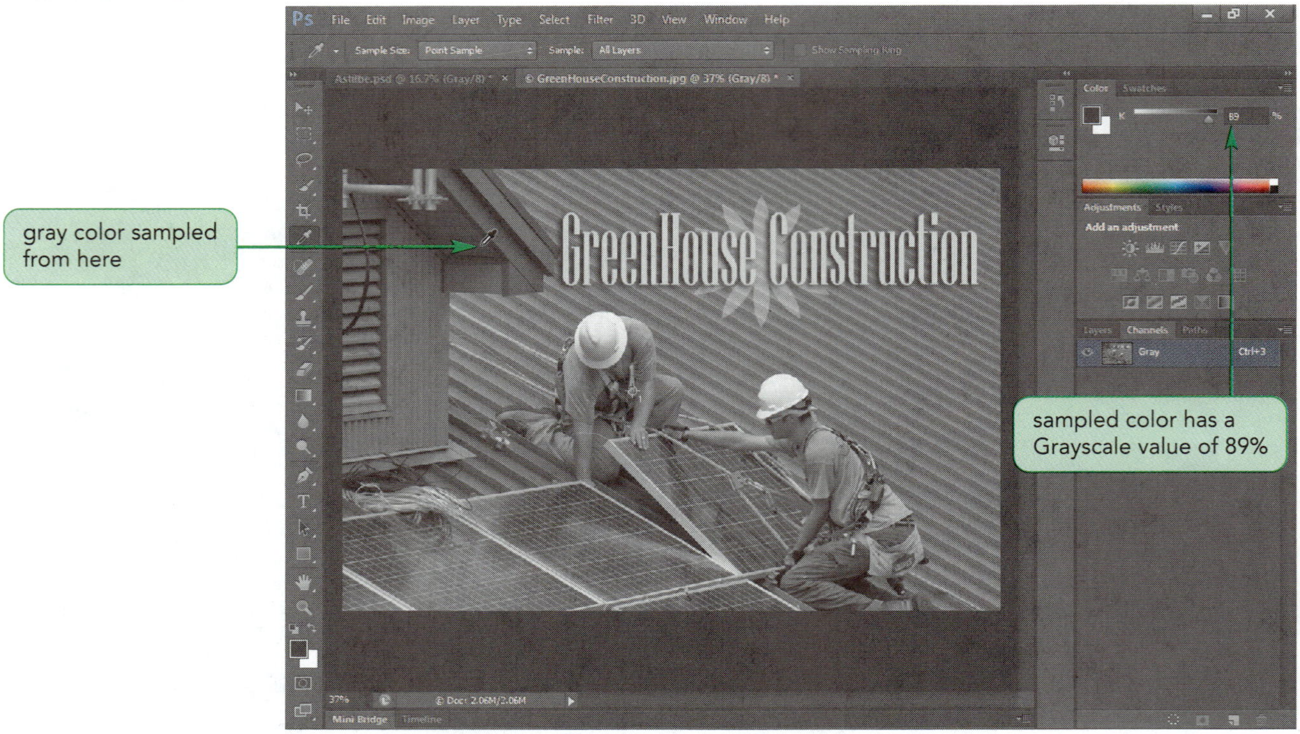

© 2009 Alex Snyder/Wayne National Forest

You can modify the tones of gray in an image converted to Grayscale mode—in other words, make them lighter or darker—but you cannot get the original color back once you save the file and close it. Converting the color mode to Grayscale in Photoshop is an example of **destructive editing**—all of the original color information is discarded when you save and close the file. Therefore, when you convert a file to Grayscale mode, you should immediately save it with a new name so you do not overwrite your original color file with the grayscale file.

Understanding How Bit Depth Combined with Color Mode Affects File Size

Each pixel in an image represents a single color. When the eye views hundreds or thousands of pixels together, the colors blend together and appear to transition smoothly from one part of the image to the next. Images with higher bit depths result in more realistically colored images because they have more available colors for shading and variations. Figure 2-18 explains the relationship between bit depth and color mode for some of the most commonly used Photoshop color modes.

Figure 2-18 **Bit depth and color mode**

Color Mode	Bit Depth	Number of Colors
Black and White	1	Each pixel in a black-and-white image has two possible values, black (0) or white (1), resulting in 2^1 possible colors—in other words, two.
Grayscale	8	The bit depth of a grayscale image in Photoshop is 8, which allows you to access 2^8, or 256 shades of gray.
RGB	8	An RGB image with a bit depth of 8 has a possible 16.7 million colors, 2^8 (or 256) choices of red, times 2^8 (or 256) choices of green, times 2^8 (or 256) choices of blue.
CMYK	8	A CMYK image with a bit depth of 8 has 256 times the number of colors available in an RGB image. In other words, it has over 4.2 billion possible colors (256 × 256 × 256 × 256).

Photoshop also supports 32-bit and 16-bit images, but not all of its features are available at these bit depths. Typically, you would use a 32-bit image, also called a **high dynamic range** or **HDR image**, in a computer graphics scene that requires a high level of detail and great contrast between dark and light areas; you might also use 32-bit images in 3D imagery. HDR image files are very large, and if you're using Photoshop for print pieces and Web ads, you are safe sticking with 8-bit imagery.

Changing Color Modes

You can change color mode in Photoshop based on your needs. For example, if you have a CMYK image that you would also like to use on the Web, you can switch from CMYK mode to RGB mode. To do so, you use the Mode command on the Image menu. If you switch from CMYK or RGB to the Indexed color mode, Photoshop will confirm that you want to flatten your image because Indexed color doesn't support layers; when you flatten an image, Photoshop merges all the layers into one. If you switch from any color mode to Grayscale, Photoshop will display a warning asking you to confirm that you want to discard the color information in the file.

C. J. wants you to save his GreenHouseConstruction.jpg image so that it is suitable for a newspaper ad. To do so, you'll convert it to Grayscale mode and decrease the resolution.

To change the color mode and decrease the resolution of the GreenHouseConstruction.jpg image:

1. Press the **Ctrl+0** keys to fit the photo on screen, and then save GreenHouseConstruction.jpg as **BWGreenHouse.jpg** in the Photoshop2\Tutorial folder, selecting **High** quality and **Baseline ("Standard")** in the JPEG Options dialog box.
2. On the menu bar, click **Image**, point to **Mode**, and then click **Grayscale**. Photoshop displays a dialog box prompting you to confirm that you want to discard color information. See Figure 2-19.

Figure 2-19 Discarding color information

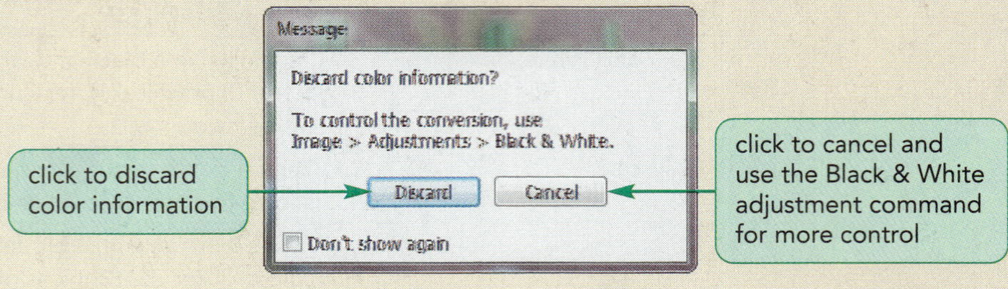

The dialog box also informs you that if you want more control over how each color is converted to grayscale, you can use the Black & White adjustment command instead. In this case, a simple conversion is fine for your needs.

3. In the dialog box, click **Discard**. See Figure 2-20.

Figure 2-20 Discarding color information

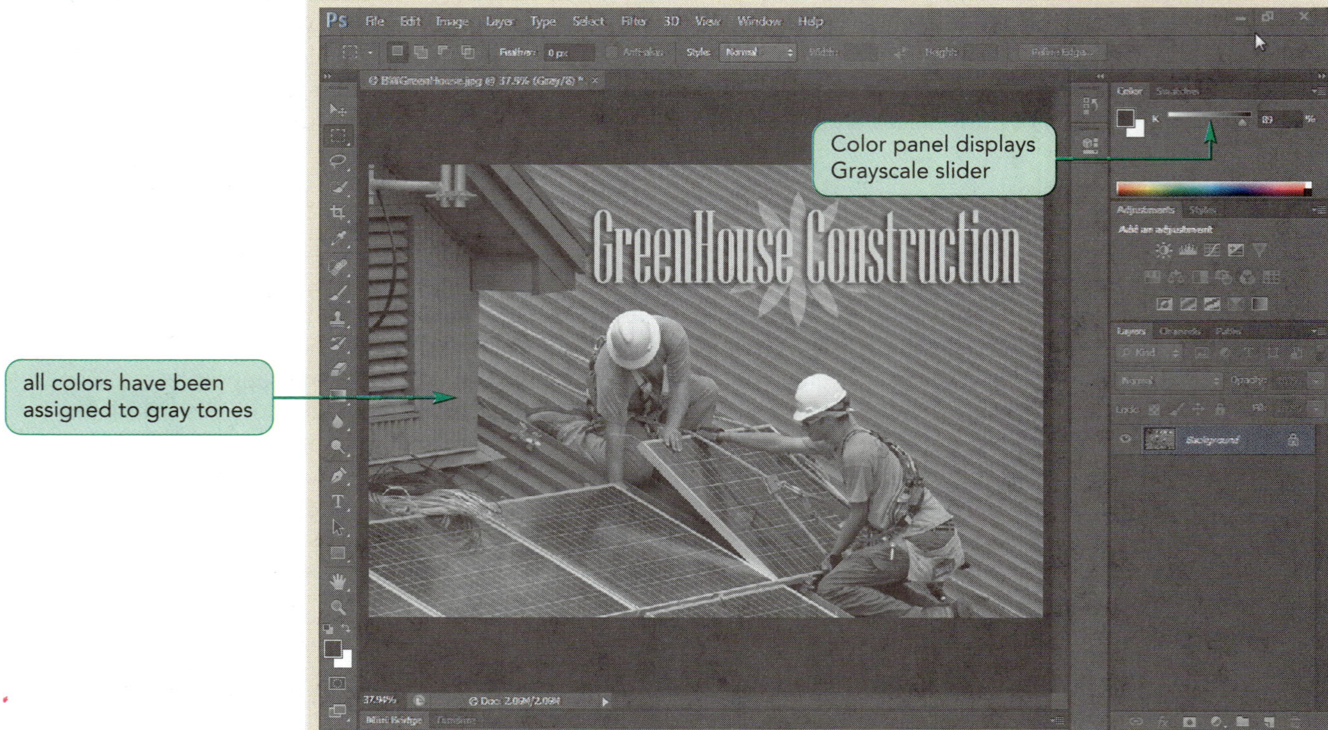

© 2009 Alex Snyder/Wayne National Forest

The photograph is now in grayscale. However, it is still 300 ppi, which is a larger file size than you need for a newspaper ad.

4. On the menu bar, click **Image**, click **Image Size**, and then change the resolution to **150** pixels per inch. Leave the other image size settings intact, and click the **OK** button to accept the changes.
5. Press the **Ctrl+1** keys to display the image at 100% zoom. The image now has the proper color mode and resolution for a newspaper ad.
6. Save BWGreenHouse.jpg, and then close it.

C. J. wants you to experiment with creating a few new files of your own so you are more familiar with the options available in Photoshop, and so you can feel confident making choices based on project needs.

Creating a New File

So far, you have only opened existing files in Photoshop. However, it's easy to open a new blank file in Photoshop and create your own composition. Before you create a new file in Photoshop, you should decide on the document's size, resolution, and background color based on the needs of your project. You can always modify a file's specifications later, but it will save you time and effort to set them up properly in advance. See Figure 2-21.

Figure 2-21 **Default settings for a new file**

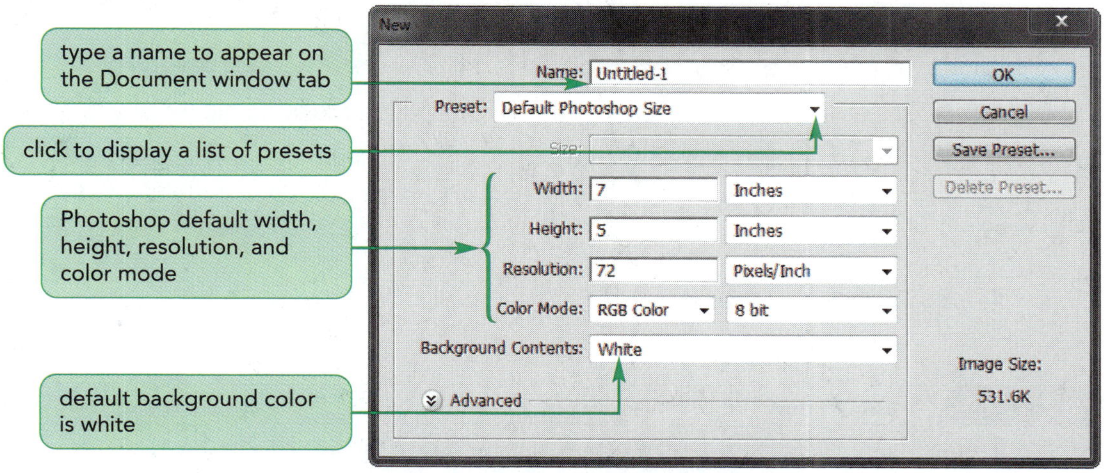

By default, Photoshop will create a new 7 × 5-inch file—using the RGB color mode, a bit depth of 8, and a white background. Once you have created the new file, you can add to it using the tools in the Tools panel, or you can copy an image from another file and paste it into the Document window. You can also place an image in the file.

Placing an Image in a New File

When you create a new file, you can think of yourself as an artist starting with a blank canvas. The **canvas** in Photoshop is the blank area in the middle of the Photoshop Document window, on which you can "paint" with bitmap images, vector graphics, and text. You can use vector drawing tools to paint on the canvas, but you can also copy and paste bitmap images or vector objects, or place them on the canvas. When you **place** an image in Photoshop, you import a copy of the image file that is still linked to the original. If you open and then edit the original file—for example, if you adjust a dark image by increasing its brightness—that change is reflected in the placed image in your new document file as well. You can open the original image file using the File command, or you can double-click the thumbnail of the placed image in the Layers panel.

A placed object is an example of a Photoshop feature called a **Smart Object**, which gives you the flexibility to transform the *placed* object in some way—for example, you can **transform** a placed image by rotating it or distorting it by making it wider or taller—without affecting the *original* object. To place an image file in a Photoshop document, you use the Place command on the File menu.

REFERENCE

Creating a New File Using a Preset

- On the menu bar, click File, and then click New. The New dialog box opens.
- In the Name box, type a name for the new file.
- Click the Preset arrow, and select the desired preset.
- Click the OK button to create the new file.

C. J. has asked you to create three new files, each based on a different design need. First, you'll create a variation of the company's logo for a Web-based campaign, using two separate files. You will not be making any changes to the placed images.

To create a new file and place an image:

1. On the menu bar, click **File**, and then click **New**. The New dialog box opens.
2. In the Name box, type **Logo1**. This is the name that will appear on the Document window tab. It will also appear as the default filename in the Save As dialog box, although you can choose to change the filename prior to saving it.
3. Click the **Preset** arrow. Photoshop displays a list of available presets. See Figure 2-22.

Figure 2-22 Available new file presets

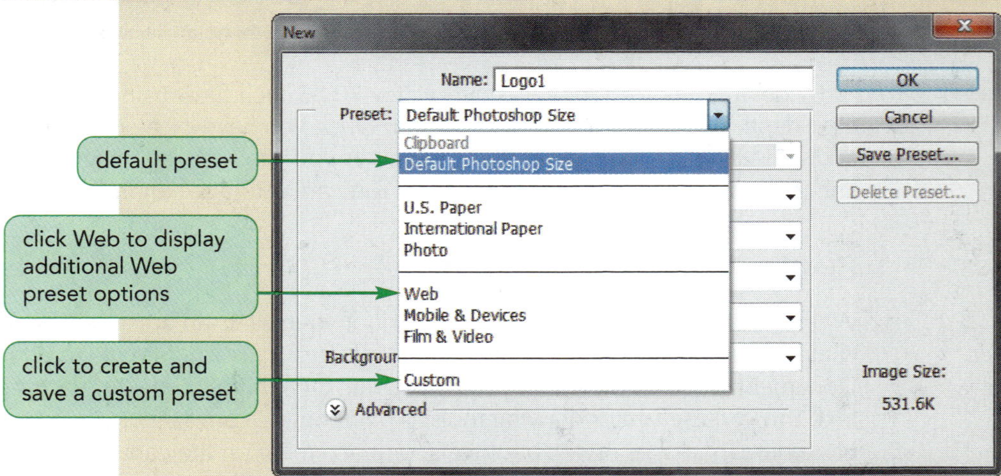

4. Click **Default Photoshop Size**, if necessary. The Default Photoshop Size preset creates a document that is 7 × 5 inches, with a resolution of 72 ppi.
5. Click the **OK** button. Photoshop creates the new file and displays the blank canvas at 100% zoom in the Document window.
6. On the menu bar, click **File**, and then click **Place**. The Place dialog box opens.
7. Navigate to the Photoshop2\Tutorial folder, click **Sun.psd**, click the **Place** button, and then press the **Enter** key. The sun image is placed at the center of the new file. Next, you'll place text on top of this image.

8. On the menu bar, click **File**, and then click **Place**. Navigate to the Photoshop2\Tutorial folder, click **GreenHouseText.psd**, click the **Place** button, and then press the **Enter** key. See Figure 2-23.

Figure 2-23 **Default new Photoshop file with placed images**

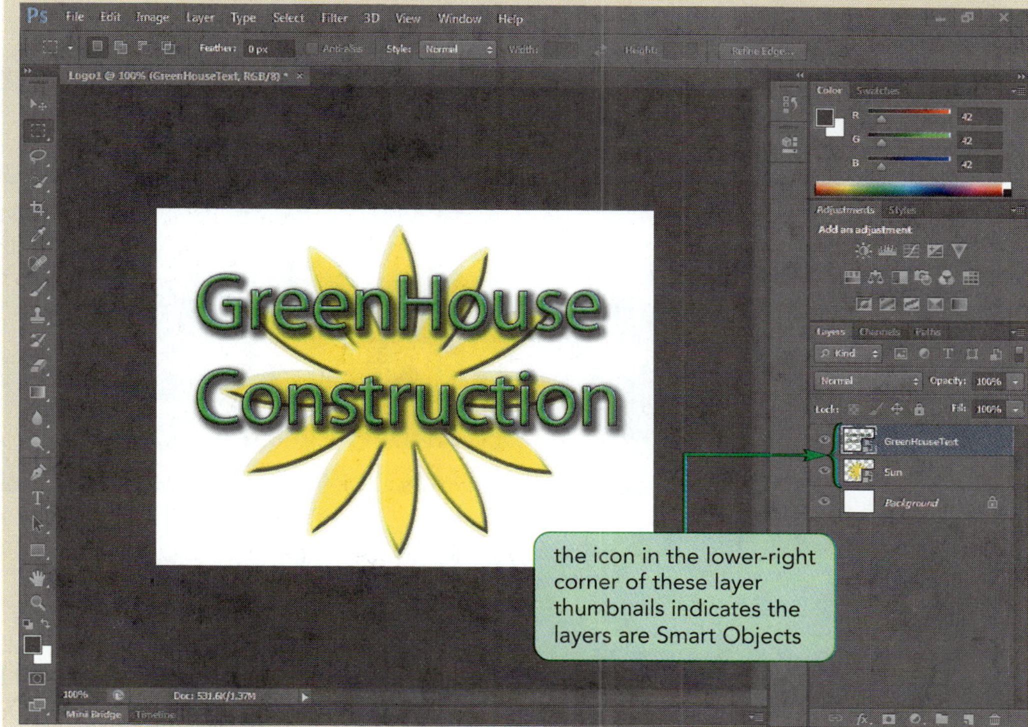

You created a new file using the default Photoshop settings and placed two images in it. You'll save this file and present it to C. J. as a possible new logo for the company's Web site.

9. Save the file as **Logo1.psd** in the Photoshop2\Tutorial folder, and then close the file.

You can also create a new file using a Web preset, which will create a file with dimensions suitable for displaying in a Web browser. Photoshop includes Web presets for low-resolution monitors (640 pixels by 480 pixels), high-resolution monitors (1600 pixels by 1200 pixels), and many resolutions in between. It also includes file sizes appropriate for navigation bars and **leaderboards**, which are advertising banners that often appear at the top of a Web page.

C. J. wants you to create a leaderboard for the company name. You'll create a new file with the proper dimensions and then place the text on the canvas.

To create the file using the Leaderboard Web preset:

1. On the menu bar, click **File**, and then click **New**. The New dialog box opens.
2. In the Name box, type **Leaderboard**.
3. Click the **Preset** arrow, and then click **Web**.
4. Click the **Size** arrow, click **Leaderboard, 728 x 90**, and then click the **OK** button to create the new file.

5. On the menu bar, click **File**, and then click **Place**.
6. Navigate to the Photoshop2\Tutorial folder, click **LeaderboardText.psd**, click **Place**, and then press the **Enter** key. The text is now placed in the new file. See Figure 2-24.

Figure 2-24 **Leaderboard file with placed image**

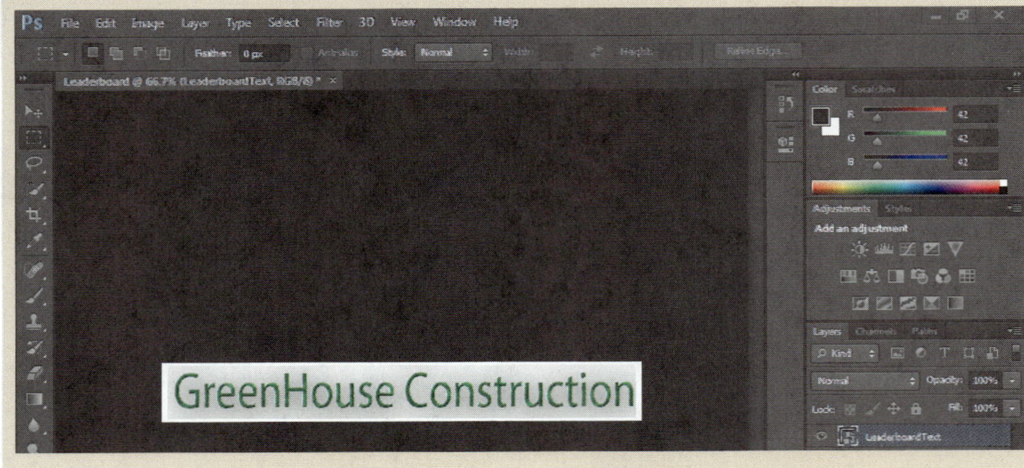

7. Save the file as **Leaderboard.psd** in the Photoshop2\Tutorial folder, and close the file.

C. J. will be able to use this file as an advertising banner on a Web site.

PROSKILLS

Decision Making: Using a Standard or a Nonstandard Size for a Photoshop Document

Photoshop gives you the flexibility to create documents using any dimensions. It provides presets for the Web or for printing photographs, but you might want to create a brochure with three panels, and no preset exists for that. You can easily create a new file using any dimensions you want, but it is wise to first check with your commercial printer to see if they have a standard size for a three-panel brochure. If they do, you need to decide whether following your original vision is worth the extra expense you're sure to incur if you use a nonstandard size for your piece. By exploring the options available in Photoshop and conferring with your printer before you start a project, you can ensure that you will make a decision about the size of your final document that results in a visually appealing marketing piece, while staying within your project budget.

C. J. frequently creates images that he then makes into posters for use at trade shows, so he asks you to create a document preset that you can use for trade show posters. You'll create and save a custom document preset for this project.

Creating a Custom Document Preset

You might find that the new document presets that come with Photoshop aren't exactly what you need for a particular project. You can specify custom options in the New dialog box and then save them as presets. Once you save a preset, it is listed along with all of the other presets in the New dialog box. If at any time you decide you will no longer use a particular custom preset, you can delete it.

REFERENCE

Saving a Custom Document Preset

- On the menu bar, click File, and then click New. The New dialog box opens.
- In the Name box, type a name for the new file.
- In the Width box, type a width for the canvas, and then specify the unit of measurement (such as pixels or inches).
- In the Height box, type a value for the height of the canvas.
- In the Resolution box, enter the resolution.
- Click the Save Preset button. The New Document Preset dialog box opens.
- Name the preset, and then select the necessary options in the New Document Preset dialog box.
- Click the OK button to save the custom preset.

To save a custom document preset for trade show posters:

1. On the menu bar, click **File**, and then click **New**. The New dialog box opens.
2. In the Name box, type **PosterPresetExample**.
3. Click the **Width** arrow, click **Inches**, if necessary, and then type **24** in the Width box. Notice that the setting for Height also changes to Inches.
4. In the Height box, type **36**.
5. In the Resolution box, type **300**.
6. Click the **Save Preset** button. The New Document Preset dialog box opens. See Figure 2-25.

Figure 2-25 Saving a new file preset

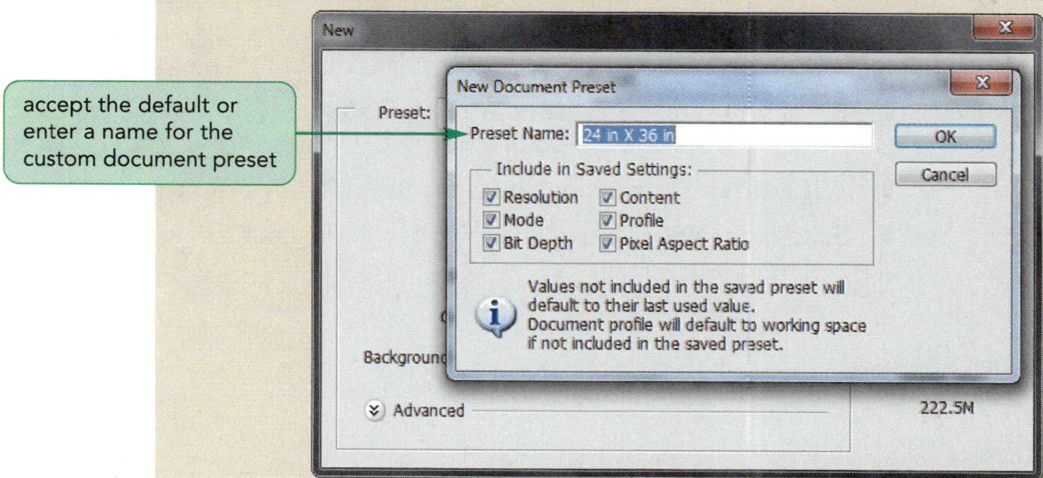

You can leave the default preset name, which is the dimensions of the new document, or you can type a new name.

7. In the Preset Name box, type **PosterPreset**, accept the default settings (all check boxes checked) so that every setting is saved with the preset, and then click the **OK** button.

8. In the New dialog box, click the **Preset** arrow.

   The new preset name appears in the Preset list. It will be available for all your future Photoshop sessions unless you delete it.

9. Click **PosterPreset**, and then click the **OK** button. Photoshop opens the blank canvas with the custom dimensions and resolution you entered.

10. On the menu bar, click **File**, and then click **Place**.

11. Navigate to the Photoshop2\Tutorial folder, click **Logo1.psd**, click **Place**, and then press the **Enter** key to place the logo. Use the Move tool to center the logo at the top of the poster.

12. Save the file as **PosterPresetExample.psd** in the Photoshop2\Tutorial folder, and then close the file.

You have shown your preset to C. J., and he wants to change it substantially. Because you will not be using this preset again, you can delete it to prevent a cluttered preset list.

REFERENCE

Deleting a Custom Document Preset

- On the menu bar, click File, and then click New.
- Click the Preset arrow, and then click the custom preset you want to delete.
- Click the Delete Preset button, and then click Yes in the dialog box to confirm that you want to delete the preset.
- Click the OK button.

To delete the custom preset:

1. On the menu bar, click **File**, and then click **New**.
2. In the New dialog box, click the **Preset** arrow, and then, if necessary, click **PosterPreset**, which is the preset you want to delete.
3. Click the **Delete Preset** button. A dialog box opens asking you to confirm that you want to delete the preset.
4. Click **Yes**. Photoshop deletes the PosterPreset custom preset.
5. Click the **OK** button, close the open file without saving it, and then exit Photoshop.

REVIEW

Session 2.1 Quick Check

1. Name one advantage of using the PSD file format.
2. The higher the resolution, the ____________ the file size.
3. Finding the right balance between image quality and file size is called ____________.
4. True or False. A JPEG version of an image is larger than a PSD version of the same image.
5. The default resolution for a new Photoshop file is ____________ ppi.
6. True or False. Resampling does not alter the number of pixels in the image.
7. ____________ specifies the amount of color information for each pixel in an image.

SESSION 2.2 VISUAL OVERVIEW

Open the Image menu to access the Image Rotation command; you can rotate your image or flip it horizontally or vertically on the canvas.

Rotate your image using presets of 90 degrees clockwise and counterclockwise.

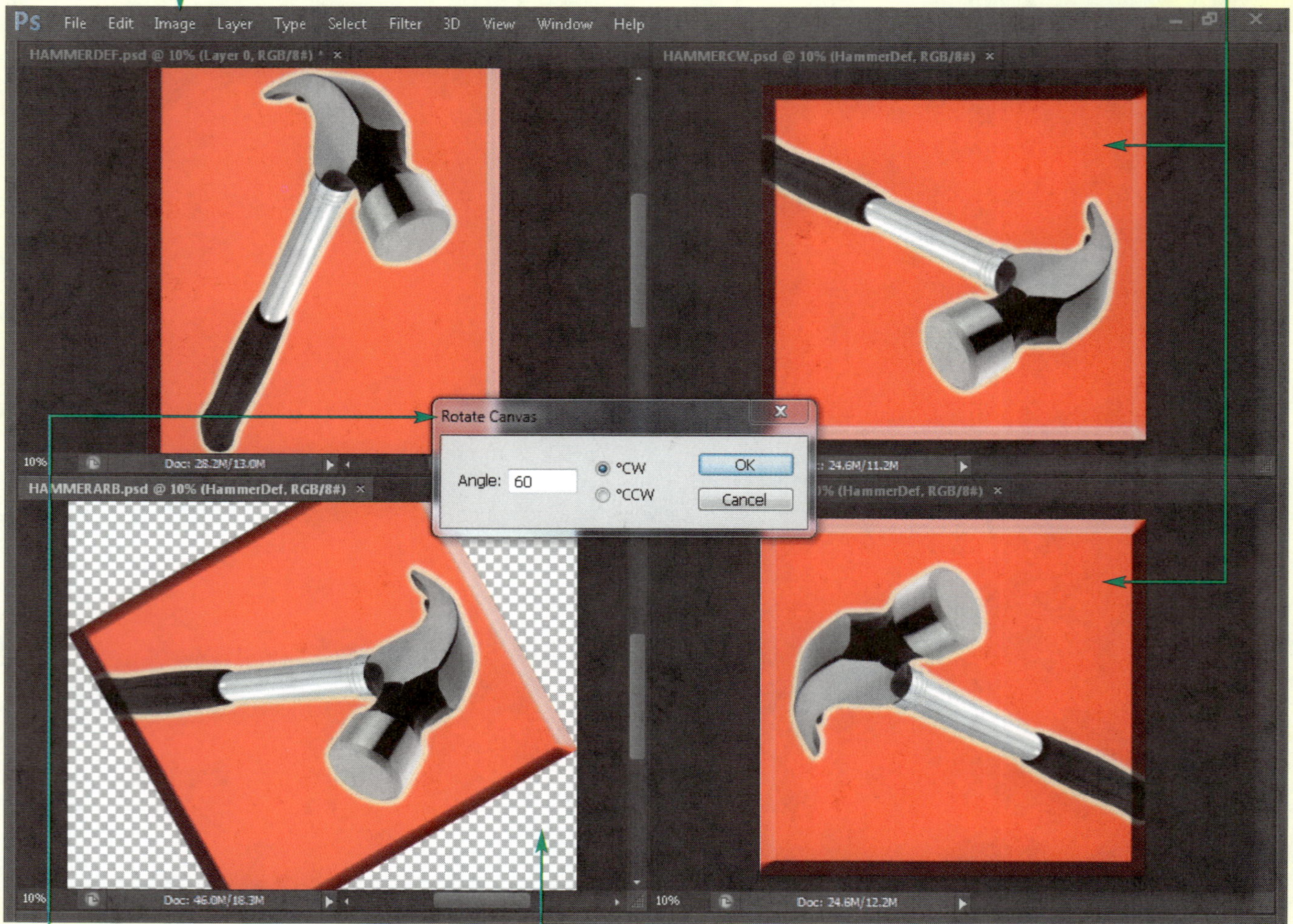

Use the Rotate Canvas dialog box to specify an angle of rotation, and whether to rotate clockwise or counterclockwise.

If you rotate your image by an **arbitrary angle**, which is an angle that you specify, Photoshop increases the dimensions of the canvas to compensate for the change.

Fotonic/Shutterstock.com

ADJUST, VIEW, AND ROTATE IMAGES

Many image adjustments include multiple presets for you to choose from.

The **Properties panel** is a new feature in Photoshop CS6 that lists the **properties**, or settings, of the adjustment layer selected in the Layers panel.

The Brightness/Contrast adjustment lets you change the lighting and modify the contrast between dark and light in your image.

The **adjustments** feature in Photoshop lets you easily manipulate an image and preview an adjustment as you make it.

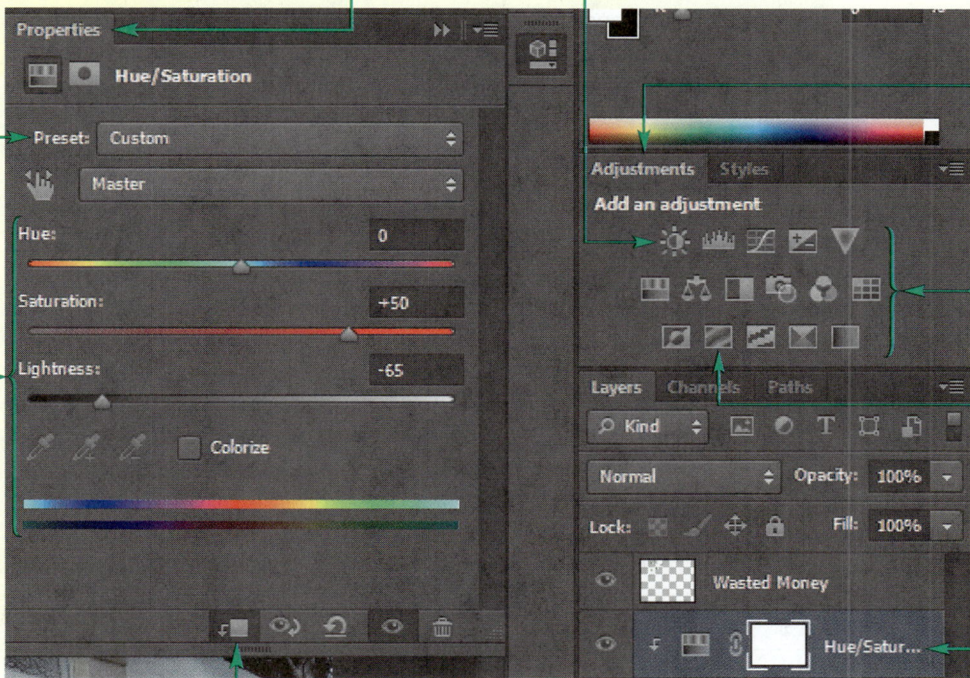

Clicking any of these adjustments adds an adjustment layer to your file.

The Posterize adjustment turns an image into a stylized painting that resembles a poster.

An **adjustment layer** changes your image in a nondestructive way.

You can modify preset properties for even more adjustment options.

You can click the Clip to layer icon to **clip** an adjustment to the layer directly beneath the adjustment layer so that other layers are unaffected by the adjustment.

In the Navigator, you can **pan** your image, which means to move the image within the Document window so that a different part of the image is visible.

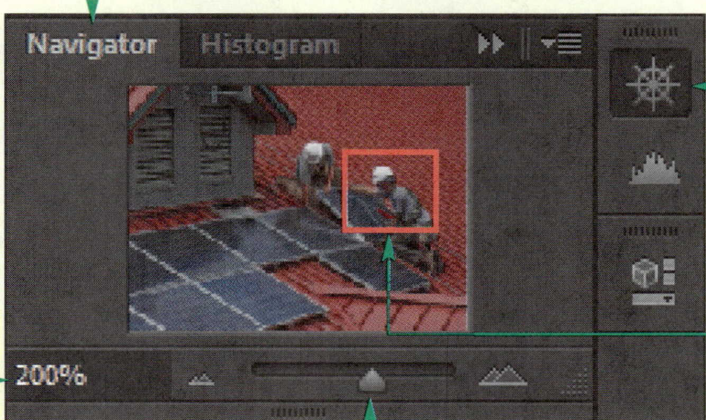

The Navigator can be collapsed to an icon.

The **view box** outlines the area of the image that is displayed in the Document window.

Type the zoom percentage in this zoom box or in the zoom box on the status bar.

Drag the Zoom slider to change the zoom setting.

Making Image Adjustments

As you work with digital images, you'll often find that an image is *almost* what you're looking for, but not quite. For example, perhaps the colors are a bit off or the image is overexposed. Maybe you'd prefer more shadows, or more light, or even a red door on a house instead of a blue door. Using Photoshop's adjustments feature, you can easily modify an image by making changes to the color and tone, among other things. If you make an image adjustment using the Adjustment command on the Image menu, the adjustment is made directly on the selected layer. This kind of adjustment is called a **destructive image adjustment** because it actually changes the pixels in the image. Once you save a file with this kind of adjustment, you have permanently changed the file. Unless you save the adjusted file with a different name, there is no way to return to the original. If this makes you nervous, it should. However, Photoshop has a feature called nondestructive image editing that should put you at ease. **Nondestructive image adjustments** are stored as layers on top of the original image. They are applied to the image, but rather than altering the pixels in the image, they are overlaid on the image as separate layers. As a result, you can easily turn them on or off or even delete them without harming the image itself. This session gives you a brief introduction to the Adjustments panel. As with many of the features in Photoshop, the Adjustments panel offers countless possibilities for editing your images, including adjusting the brightness and contrast of an image using the Brightness/Contrast adjustment.

The Adjustments panel includes icons for 16 different adjustments. Each adjustment has its own set of options, which appear on its Properties panel when you first select the adjustment or if you later select the adjustment layer to modify it. Some adjustments have additional presets, which also appear in the Properties panel. For example, if you select the Levels adjustment (the second icon in the first row), Photoshop adds an adjustment layer called Levels 1 and displays the Properties panel for that new layer. See Figure 2-26.

Figure 2-26 Adjustment panel icons and Properties panel for an adjustment layer

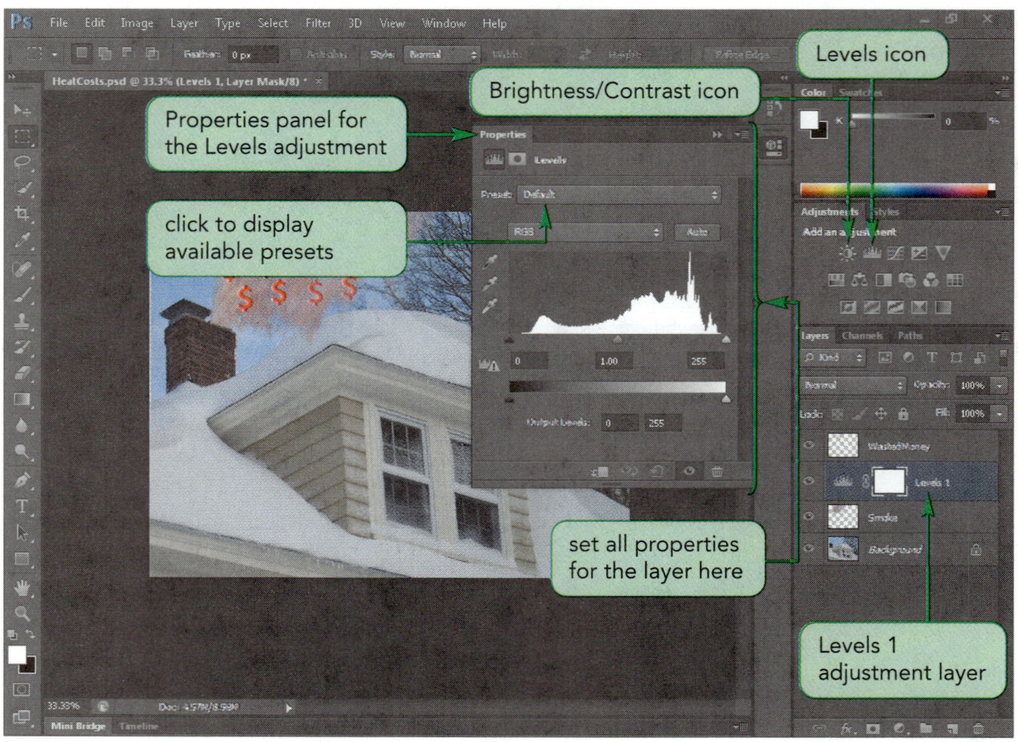

Jane Hosie-Bounar

The Properties panel displays the default settings for the Levels adjustment, but it also includes multiple presets that you can display by clicking the Preset arrow, and then clicking the name of the preset you want to apply.

C. J. is working on a campaign to persuade consumers to switch from gas and oil heat to solar and geothermal heat. He has started to compose an image meant to convince people that continuing with their current heating plans will cost them money and have a negative effect on the environment. He would like you to adjust the image so it has more impact. You'll experiment with brightness, contrast, and levels settings to see if those changes make the image stronger. You'll also experiment with a black-and-white preset to see how dramatic the change would be.

To add the Brightness/Contrast adjustment layer:

1. Start Photoshop while pressing the **Ctrl+Alt+Shift** keys, and click **Yes** to delete the Settings File when prompted. Reset Photoshop to the default Essentials workspace layout, and then reset all tools.
2. Navigate to the Photoshop2\Tutorial folder, and open **HeatCosts.psd**.
3. In the Layers panel, click the Background layer, if necessary, and then click the **Brightness/Contrast** icon. Photoshop adds an adjustment layer above the Background layer, and the Properties panel for the Brightness/Contrast adjustment opens. See Figure 2-27.

TIP

You can also work with adjustment layers using the New Adjustment Layer command on the Layer menu.

Figure 2-27 Brightness/Contrast settings

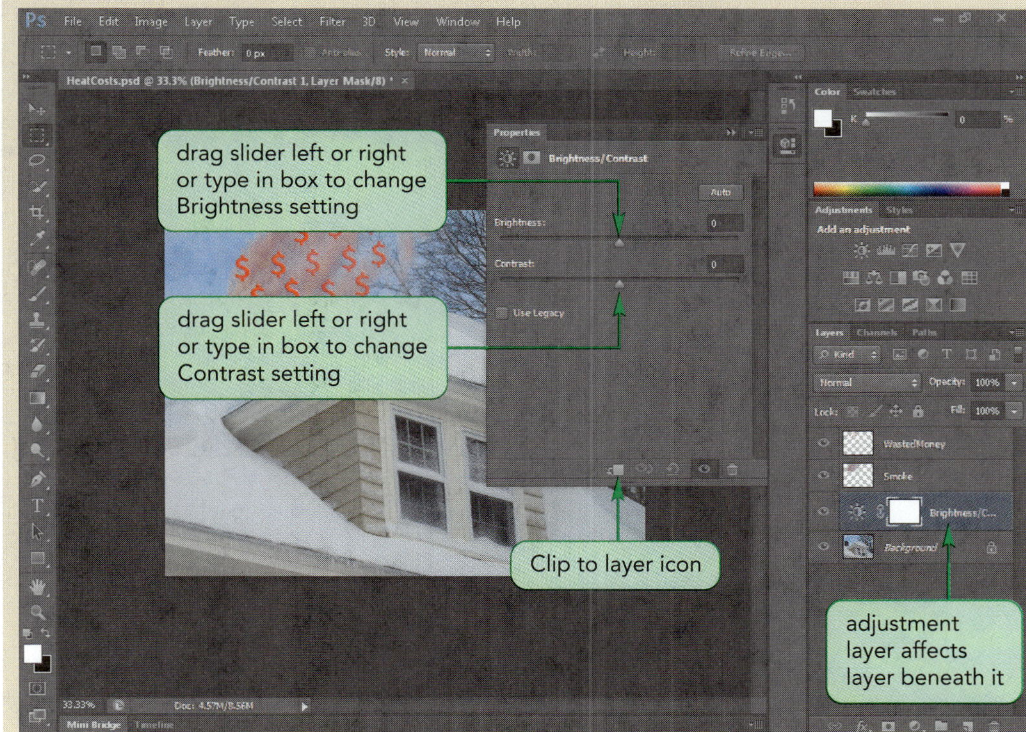

Jane Hosie-Bounar

An adjustment layer affects any layers beneath it in the Layers panel by default. If you have multiple layers beneath an adjustment layer but only want to affect the layer directly beneath the adjustment, you can clip it to that layer by clicking the Clip to layer icon at the bottom of the Properties panel.

Next, you'll use the slider to adjust the Brightness of the image, and you'll type a new Contrast value to see the effect of these changes.

4. In the Properties panel for the Brightness/Contrast adjustment, drag the **Brightness** slider to the left until the value reads **-45**.
5. In the Contrast box, type **85**.

   Notice that the color of the smoke hasn't changed because the Smoke layer is above the adjustment layer.
6. Click the **Smoke** layer to select it. Notice that the Properties panel is now blank because only adjustment layers have properties.
7. In the Adjustments panel, click the **Hue/Saturation** icon, and then in the Properties panel, click the **Clip to layer** icon to direct Photoshop to clip the adjustment to the selected layer.

   The Clip to layer icon changes to .
8. In the Properties panel, click the **Preset** button, click **Strong Saturation**, and then drag the **Lightness** slider to the left until the box reads -65. See Figure 2-28.

Be sure to select the Clip to layer icon. If you don't, the adjustment will also be applied to the Background layer, which you don't want to change.

Figure 2-28 Hue/Saturation adjustment layer clipped to Smoke layer

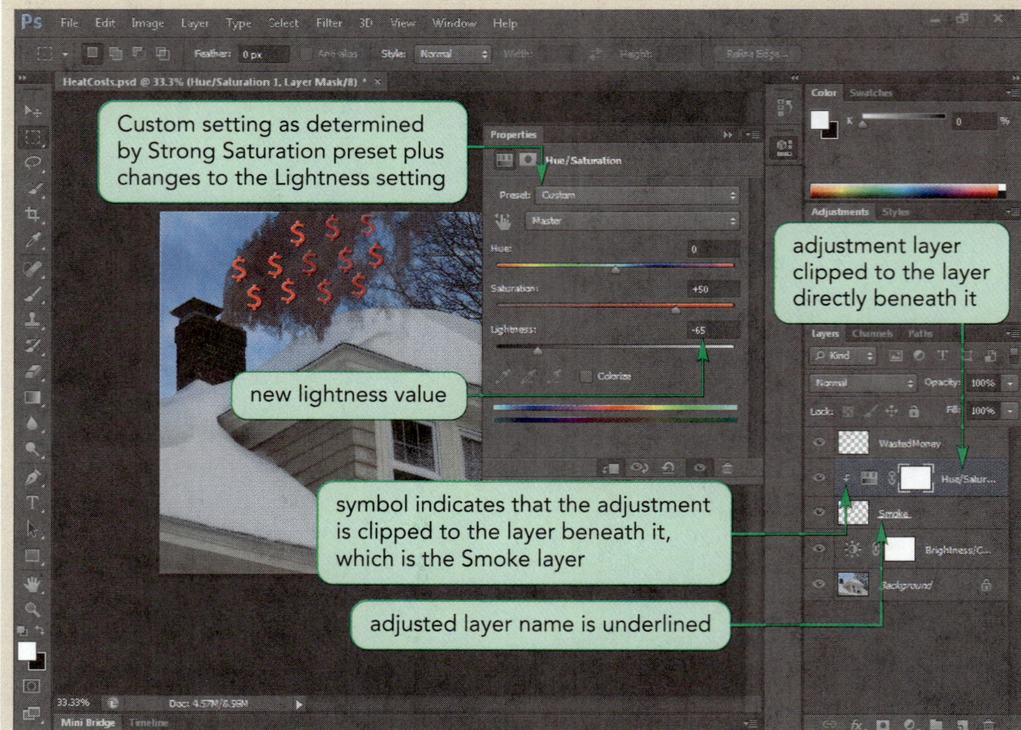

Jane Hosie-Bounar

The Smoke layer is now much darker, but because the adjustment was clipped only to that layer, the rest of the image is unchanged.

9. Save the file as **AdjustHeatCosts.psd** in the Photoshop2\Tutorial folder.

After seeing the changes you made to this image, C. J. has decided that the original brightness and contrast of the Background layer looks fine, so you'll delete the Brightness/Contrast layer.

To delete the adjustment:

1. In the Layers panel, click the **Hue/Saturation** layer, drag it to the lower-right corner of the Layers panel until it is over the Delete layer icon, and then release the mouse button. See Figure 2-29.

Figure 2-29 **Dragging the adjustment layer to delete it**

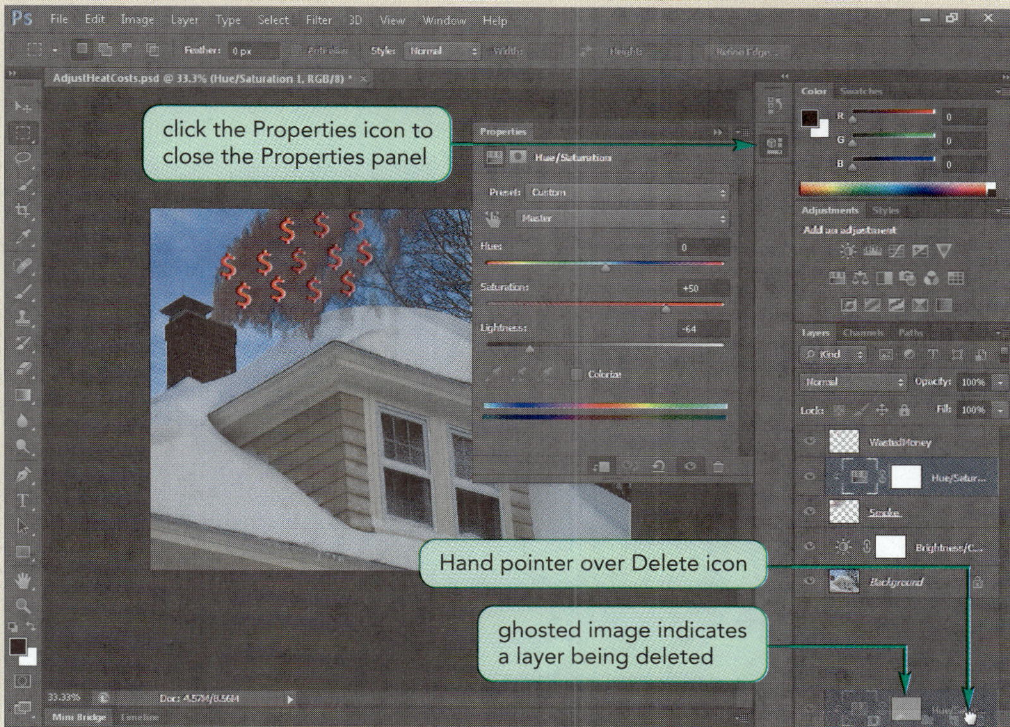

Jane Hosie-Bounar

The Hue/Saturation layer is deleted and the smoke returns to its original color. However, this is not the layer you really want to delete, so you'll undo the deletion and select the Brightness/Contrast layer to delete it.

2. Press the **Ctrl+Z** keys to undo the deletion. The smoke is now the darker, adjusted color.
3. In the Layers panel, click the **Brightness/Contrast** layer, and then press the **Delete** key to delete that layer. The Background layer reverts to its original brightness and contrast levels.
4. Click the **Properties panel** icon to close the Properties panel, and then save the file and close it.

You can also use adjustment layer presets as is, without any modifications, to get an entirely new effect with the click of a button. Next, you'll use a black-and-white preset to see if it will convey the message of your image more powerfully.

TIP

It is a good practice to clip adjustment layers when you apply them so they only affect the layers you want them to affect.

To use the Black & White adjustment layer preset:

1. Navigate to the Photoshop2\Tutorial folder, and open **HeatCosts2.psd** and then in the Layers panel, click the **Background** layer to select it, if necessary.
2. In the Adjustments panel, click the **Black & White** icon, and in the Properties panel, click the **Preset** button to see a list of Black & White presets.
3. Click **High Contrast Red Filter** to apply the preset, click the **Clip to layer** icon, and then close the Properties panel. See Figure 2-30.

Figure 2-30 Black & White adjustment applied to the Background layer

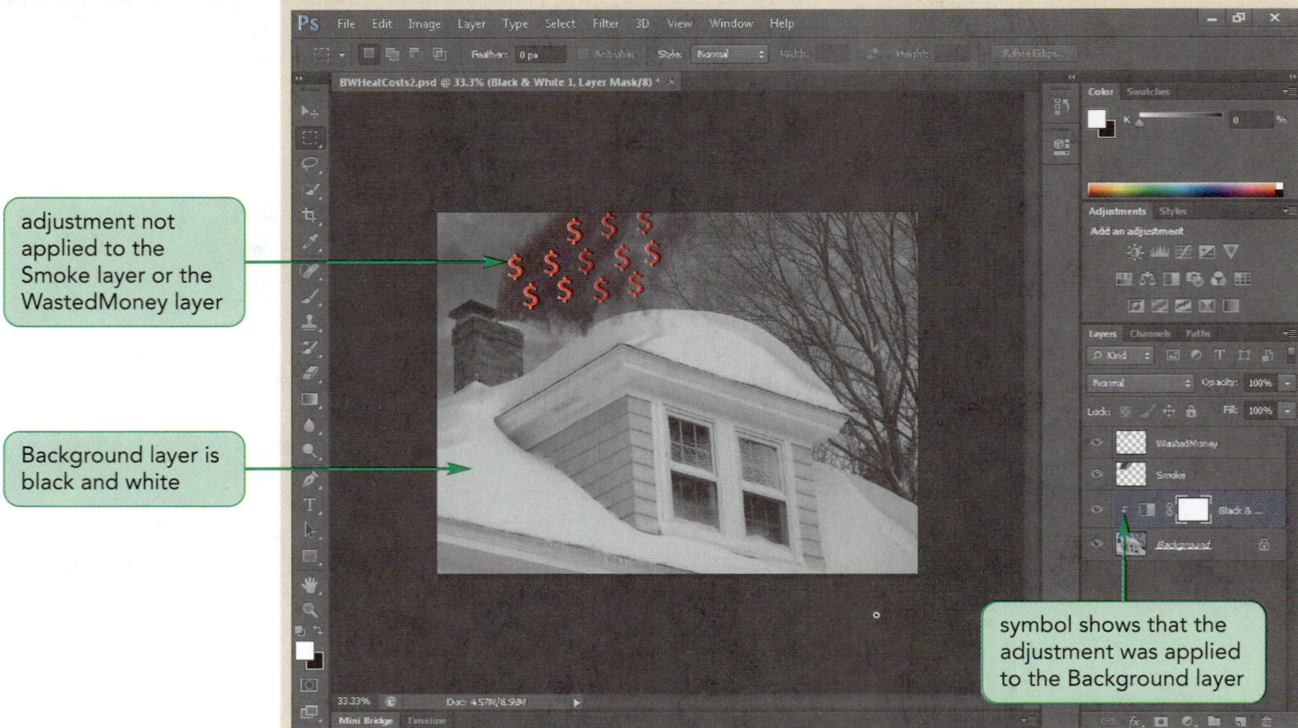

Jane Hosie-Bounar

Most of the image changes to black and white. Notice that the Smoke layer and the WastedMoney layers are unaffected by this adjustment because they are above the Black & White adjustment layer in the Layers panel.

4. Save the file as **BWHeatCosts2.psd** in the Photoshop2\Tutorial folder, and then close the file.

PROSKILLS

Problem Solving: Acquiring an Image from a Scanner

You might have a project that requires you to acquire photographs taken before the days of digital imaging. In fact, what if the ideal photograph for your project was taken in 1959? How can you get that image into Photoshop and use it in your work? The fact is that you don't have to start with a digital file to end up with a digital file. You can use a scanner to scan a printed photograph directly into Photoshop, or you can scan the image to a storage device on your computer and then open the file in Photoshop. (Keep in mind that you shouldn't scan a copyrighted photo without obtaining permission.) If the scanner uses its own software to scan the image to your hard drive, make sure to specify the file format you want. If you have a scanner that includes a Photoshop plug-in such as TWAIN, make sure to install the plug-in software. You can then import the file directly into Photoshop. If your scanner has a preview option, it's a good idea to preview the image before you scan it because previewing lets you adjust scanner settings such as dimensions, color mode, and resolution, and saves you time and effort.

A scanner works by illuminating, or shining light at, a photograph you place face down on the glass surface of the scanner. When you start the scan, the scan head moves across the photo one or more times and uses reflected light and two or more mirrors to direct image information to a lens that then converts the information into digital format. In simple terms, a scanner takes a digital photograph of your printed photograph and then transfers the digital data it to your computer.

Once you scan an image, you haven't necessarily finished with the file. You might find that the image needs adjusting to make it work in your project. With Photoshop's image-adjustment features, your problem is solved: Not only have you performed magic by digitizing an image that was made before the digital age, you have actually repurposed the image to suit your needs using Photoshop's image-editing features. In fact, being required to use an old photograph for a project isn't much of a problem at all. Scanning the photograph to digitize it, and then manipulating it with Photoshop, can bring any photograph, no matter how old, into the twenty-first century.

Working with the Canvas

You saw earlier in this tutorial that when you create a new file, you often start with a blank canvas. As you create your composition, you might find that you need more or less room on the canvas to finalize your work. To enlarge the canvas, you can use the Canvas Size command on the Image menu to open the Canvas Size dialog box.

In the Canvas Size dialog box, you specify the new dimensions for your canvas. If you select the Relative check box, you can specify the width and height measurements you want to add to the canvas, rather than the final dimensions of the canvas. You can also select an anchor position for your image. The **anchor** determines whether the existing content on the canvas will remain in the center of the extended canvas, or whether it will be aligned with an edge or a corner of the canvas.

You have created a mock-up for a postcard campaign based on a sketch that C. J. provided, and you need to increase the canvas size so you can add a border around the composition.

REFERENCE

Extending the Canvas

- With an image file open, on the menu bar, click Image, and then click Canvas Size. The Canvas Size dialog box opens.
- With the Relative check box deselected, specify the final Width and Height measurements for the canvas.
- Click an Anchor setting to determine where the existing image will appear on the larger canvas.
- Click the Canvas extension color arrow, click an option and then click the OK button.

or

- With the Relative check box selected, specify the additional Width and Height measurements you want to add to the canvas size.
- Click an Anchor setting to determine where the existing image will appear on the larger canvas.
- Click the Canvas extension color arrow, click an option, and then click the OK button.

To extend the canvas:

1. Navigate to the Photoshop2\Tutorial folder, and open **GreenDream.psd**. The file opens in the Document window. The image consists of the composition (photographs, text, and rectangles) and a white Background, which is not visible because it is covered by the other elements in the document. The image size and the canvas size are identical.
2. On the menu bar, click **Image**, and then click **Canvas Size**. The Canvas Size dialog box opens showing the Current Size, which is a little less than 9 inches × 6 inches. See Figure 2-31.

Figure 2-31 **Canvas Size dialog box**

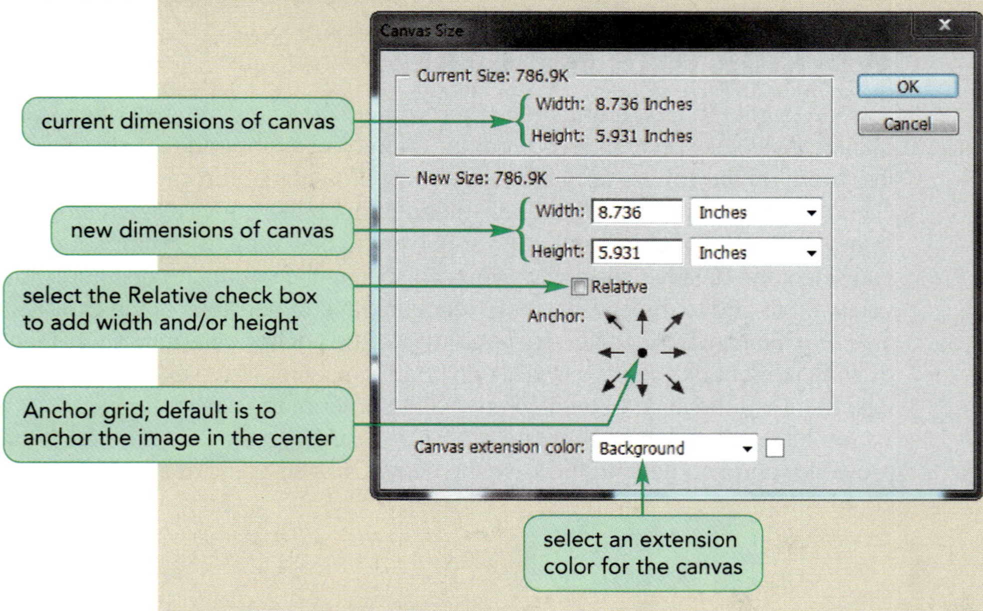

You need to add a half-inch border around the postcard image. To do so, you must increase the canvas size one inch in height and one inch in width.

3. Click the **Relative** check box to select it. When the Relative check box is selected, you can specify the width and height you want to add to the canvas, rather than the final width and height. Notice that under New Size, the Width and Height settings are now both 0 because you haven't yet specified what dimensions you want to add.
4. Verify that Inches is selected, and in the Width box, type **1**, and then in the Height box, type **1**. This will make the canvas ½ inch larger on all four sides of the current composition.

   If you wanted to anchor the image at the top, bottom, or side of the larger canvas, you could click one of the anchor buttons. Because you want to create a border of equal width around all four sides of the image, leave the anchor setting in the center. You also want the extension to be black, so you'll change the Canvas extension color setting.
5. Click the **Canvas extension color** arrow, click **Black**, and then click the **OK** button.

   The canvas increases in size with the image anchored in the middle of the canvas. The canvas extension color is black. See Figure 2-32.

Figure 2-32 Extending the canvas

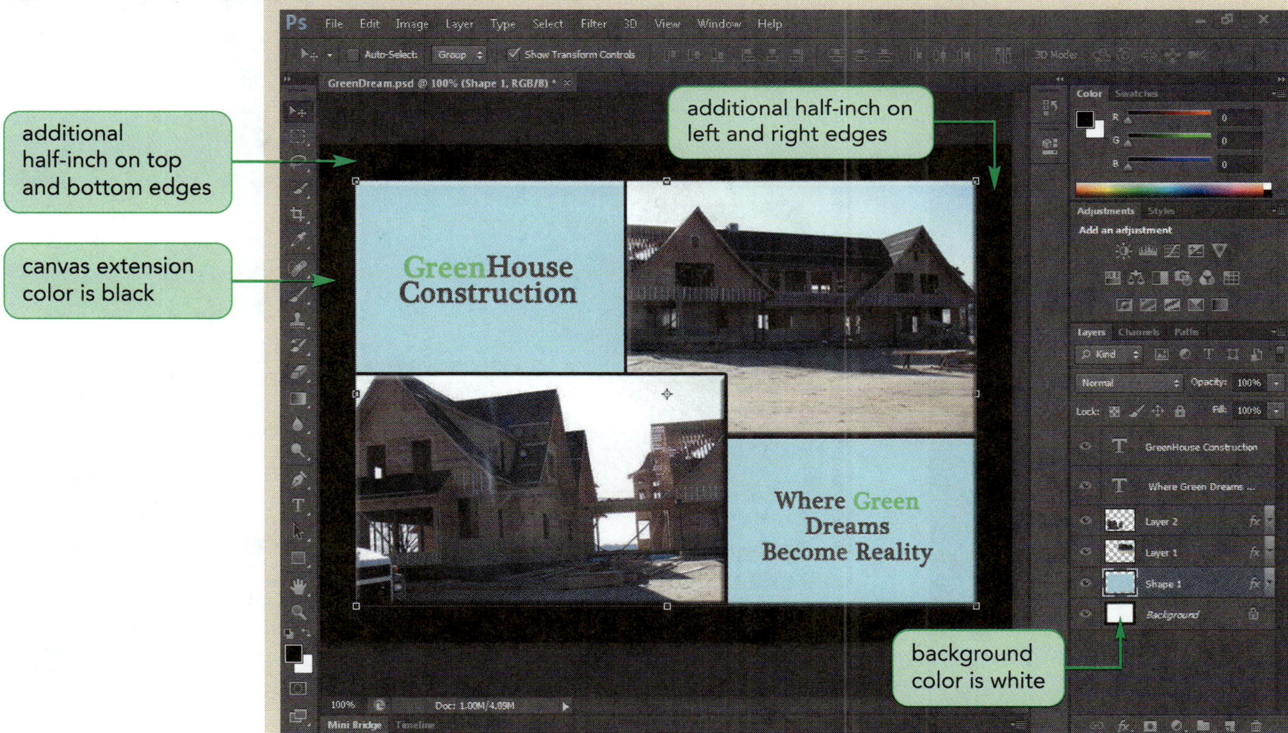

C.H. Gorman

6. Save the file as **CanvasSize.psd** in the Photoshop2\Tutorial folder, and close the file.

You can also trim a canvas to make an image smaller. Choosing Trim from the Image menu opens the Trim dialog box, where you can specify the color on which you want to base the trim, as well as indicate whether you want Photoshop to trim the top, bottom, left, or right of the image, or some combination of these choices.

C. J. has given you a second file for a solar panel advertising campaign that he would like you to trim so there's no white space around the image.

REFERENCE

Trimming the Canvas

- On the menu bar, click Image, and then click Trim. The Trim dialog box opens.
- Click the option button for the pixel color on which to base the trim—Transparent Pixels, Top Left Pixel Color, or Bottom Right Pixel Color.
- Specify which areas to trim by selecting or deselecting check boxes in the Trim Away section.
- Click the OK button to trim the image.

To trim the canvas:

1. Navigate to the Photoshop2\Tutorial folder, and open **WireCutter.jpg**. Notice that the image has extra white space on all sides.
2. On the menu bar, click **Image**, and then click **Trim**. The Trim dialog box opens. See Figure 2-33.

Figure 2-33 Trimming the canvas

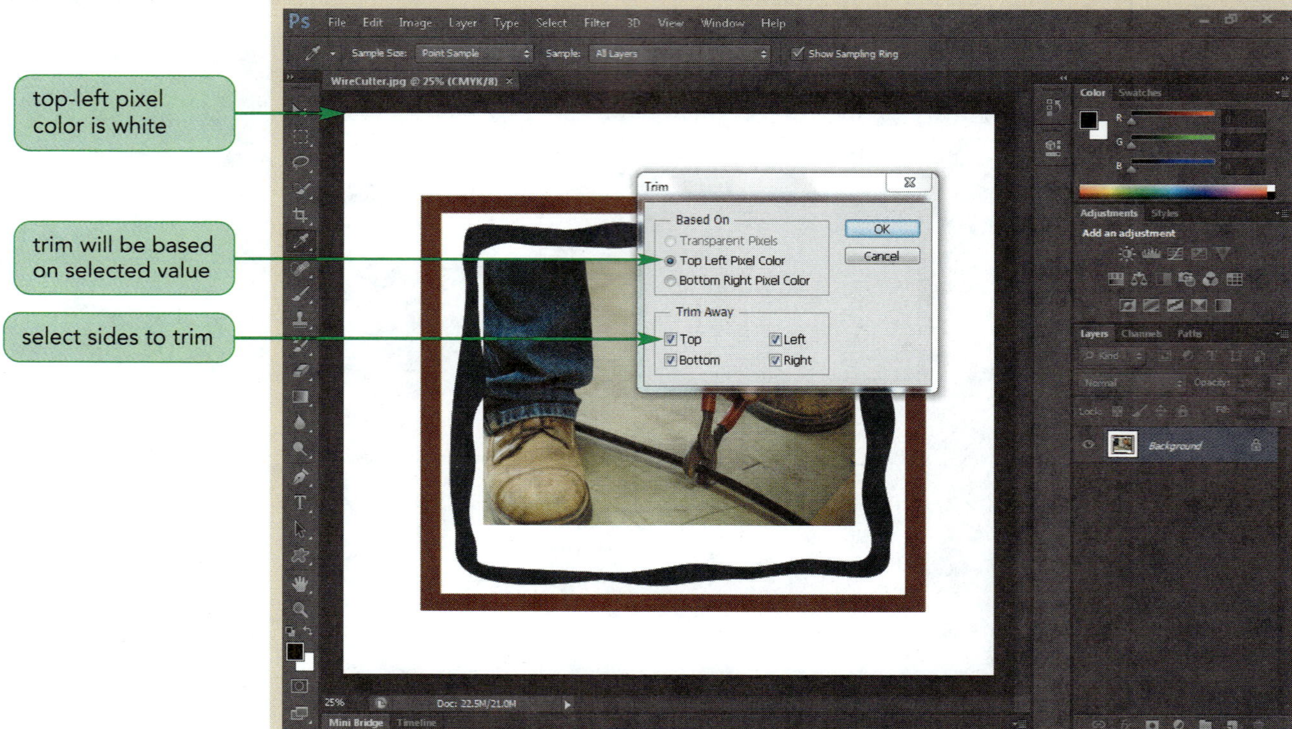

You can trim an image based on pixel colors. Photoshop will start trimming at the edges of the image based on either transparent pixels (if any), or the top-left or bottom-right pixel color. In this case, the top-left and bottom-right pixel colors are both white.

3. Click the **Top Left Pixel Color** option button to select it, if necessary. You can trim the top, left, bottom, or right part of the canvas, or any combination of those choices. For this image, you want to trim all sides of the image, so leave all four check boxes selected.
4. Click the **OK** button. Photoshop trims the canvas. See Figure 2-34.

Figure 2-34 Trimming the canvas

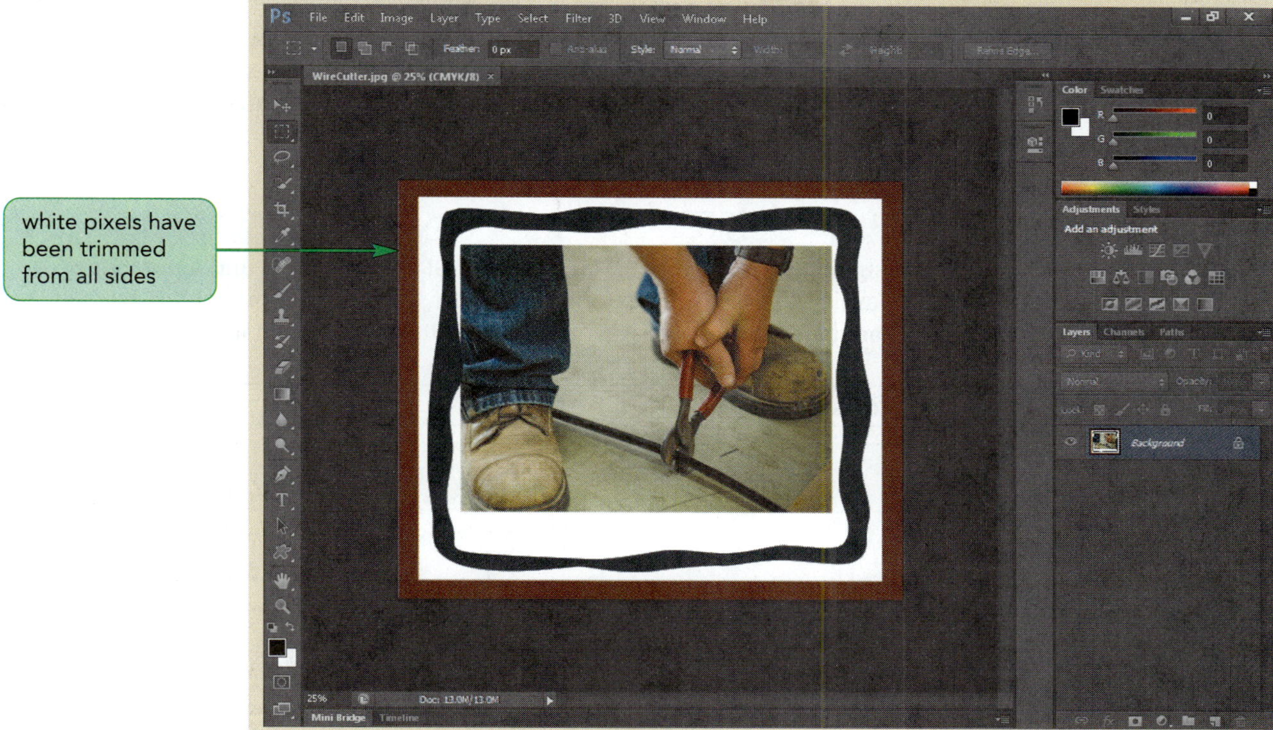

© 2009 Alex Snyder/Wayne National Forest

5. Save the file as **Trim.jpg** in the Photoshop2\Tutorial folder using the current JPEG settings, and then close the file.

INSIGHT

Trimming vs. Cropping

When you trim an image, you are cutting out image data by removing pixels in the image based on the criterion you specify in the Trim dialog box. For example, you can specify that Photoshop will trim away transparent pixels or that it will trim away pixels the color of the corner pixels in the image. When you **crop** an image, you can choose to delete the cropped pixels or save them. You can also control additional features. For example, you can specify the dimensions of the crop, rotate the cropping marquee, or straighten the image. In addition, you can control whether or not you want to transform the perspective of an image. When you **transform perspective**, you remove the distortion produced by taking a photograph at an angle. For example, you have probably seen a photograph of a tall building shot directly in front of the building, looking up. The photograph makes the building appear wider at the bottom than at the top. The Crop tool lets you correct this distortion and square the corners of the building so that it appears that the photograph was shot straight on, rather than at an angle. There will be times when you want this kind of detailed control over the image you're working with, and you'll choose to crop rather than trim.

Zooming and Panning an Image

As you spend more time working in Photoshop, you'll find that you use its zoom feature frequently. You can zoom in on an image to select, copy, or modify individual pixels. Zooming gives you the flexibility to fine-tune an image in ways not possible if you were always looking at a photograph displayed at its actual screen or print size. Panning lets you keep the image at a high magnification while quickly moving to the next area of the image you want to modify.

Zooming an Image

There are many ways to zoom an image in or out in Photoshop, and a number of these are available on the Zoom tool options bar. When the Zoom tool is selected, the options bar changes to reflect available zoom settings, as shown in Figure 2-35.

Figure 2-35 Zoom options

Option	Details
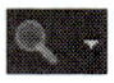	Indicates currently selected tool; click the arrow to open the Tool Preset picker.
	Select to zoom in.
	Select to zoom out.
Resize Windows to Fit	Resizes the window automatically when you zoom in or out.
Zoom All Windows	When you have multiple documents open, zooming one image zooms all the other images the same amount.
Scrubby Zoom	Only available with an Open GL video card; drag to the left to zoom out, or drag to the right to zoom in.
Actual Pixels	Shows the image at 100% magnification.
Fit Screen	Fits the image in the Document window.
Fill Screen	Fills the document window top to bottom; if the image is taller than it is wide, there will be space on either side of the image; if the image is wider than it is tall, the sides of the image will not show in this view.
Print Size	Displays the file in the size at which it will print.

TIP

You can also press the Ctrl++ keys to zoom in on the image and the Ctrl+- keys to zoom out.

To use the Zoom In pointer (a magnifying glass with a plus sign), position the pointer over the area on which you want to zoom in, and then click. How much the image is zoomed depends on your monitor size and the starting zoom percentage. For example, for an image displayed at a 25% zoom on a 19-inch monitor, clicking the Zoom In pointer once increases the zoom percentage to 33.33%. (The zoom percentage is also called the magnification level.) Clicking it a second time increases the zoom to 50%. Additional clicks result in 66.67% and then 100% zoom settings.

If you have a video card that supports OpenGL and if you have selected Animated Zoom in the General Preferences, you can zoom continuously rather than zooming in increments. When you zoom continuously, you achieve the same effect you see when you use your digital camera's zoom feature to zoom in on a scene to get a close-up photograph. To zoom continuously in Photoshop when the Zoom tool is active, point to the area of the image you want to zoom in on, and then press and hold the mouse button until you zoom to the level you want. If you press and hold the Alt key while zooming, you can achieve a similar animated zoom effect while zooming out continuously.

Photoshop provides another useful way to examine an image close up. Dragging a zoom selection marquee simplifies the zooming process and is often more practical than clicking the image repeatedly with the Zoom In pointer. To zoom in on a specific rectangular area of an image, activate the Zoom tool and then position the Zoom In pointer over the area on which you want to focus and drag a box, called a **selection marquee**, around the area. Photoshop zooms the image so the area inside the marquee is centered in and fills the Document window. If your computer is equipped with a video card that supports OpenGL, dragging the pointer will zoom continuously rather than draw a marquee.

When the Zoom tool is selected, you can also zoom an image using Zoom preset buttons on the options bar, including Actual Pixels, Fit Screen, Fill Screen, and Print Size. Zoom In, Zoom Out, Fit on Screen, Actual Pixels, and Print Size are also available on the View menu.

To zoom the image using presets:

1. Navigate to the Photoshop2\Tutorial folder, and open **Hi_Res.jpg**, display the rulers, and change the zoom setting to 50%, if necessary.
2. In the Tools panel, click the **Zoom Tool** button to display the zoom options on the options bar.
3. On the options bar, click the **Actual Pixels** button to display the image at a 100% zoom setting.

   If you have a large monitor, the inches on the rulers might appear wider than the inches on a real ruler. Because this image has a resolution of 240 pixels per inch and is five inches wide, what you see on screen is 1200 pixels across the width of the Document window. (5 inches times 240 pixels per inch equals 1200 pixels.) If you have a smaller monitor, or if you haven't maximized the Photoshop window, the inches on the ruler might appear smaller than real inches.
4. Click the **Print Size** button on the options bar. The image is now displayed at a lower zoom setting. Again, the actual setting depends on the size of your monitor. Notice that the ruler measurements are closer together. When the zoom is set to Print Size, an inch on the ruler is a true inch.
5. Click the **Fit Screen** button on the options bar. Photoshop enlarges the image so it is as large as possible but still fits on screen.
6. Click the **Fill Screen** button on the options bar. The image fills the Document window area.

Because zooming often hides parts of an image with which you might want to work, sometimes you need to pan an image to see an area that was previously hidden.

Panning an Image

TIP

You can temporarily turn off the panning feature by pressing the Ctrl key to change the pointer to the Zoom In pointer, or by pressing the Alt key to change it to the Zoom Out Pointer.

When you are doing detail work on an image and have zoomed in to a high magnification level, there will often be large parts of the image that you can't see. To move from one part of the image to another, you could zoom out, find the area of the photo you want to work with, and then zoom in again. However, it is much simpler to pan the image so that you can see a different area of the image.

Panning an image is like looking at a photograph on your desk using a magnifying glass. You can only see a part of the image at the high magnification the magnifying glass provides. To see another area, you can either slide the photo across the desk, or move the magnifying glass to a different part of the photo. Either way, you are panning the image.

The Hand tool in the Tools panel is one of the most convenient ways to pan an image. To use the Hand tool, click it in the Tools panel; the pointer takes the shape of a hand. You can click the mouse button and drag in the direction you want to pan the photo. As you drag, a different part of the image comes into view. If you drag to the right, the left part of the image comes into view. If you drag to the left, the right part of the image comes into view. Dragging up displays the bottom of the image, while dragging down displays the top.

C. J. is working on a new stationery letterhead, and thinks it would be interesting to use the grid of solar panels as part of the company logo. You'll use the Hand tool to pan the image when it is zoomed in and then you'll select the solar panels and copy them to use in a new file.

To use the Hand tool to pan the Hi_Res.jpg image:

1. Press the **Ctrl++** keys to zoom to 200%.
2. Click the **Hand Tool** button in the Tools panel.

   Trouble? If you can't see the Hand Tool button, click the Rotate View Tool button, hold down the mouse button until you see the tools list, and then click the Hand Tool button.
3. Move the mouse pointer over the Document window. When it is over the Document window, the pointer changes to a hand.
4. Click the mouse button and drag to the right until the coil of wires is completely visible.
5. Point to the coil of wires, click the mouse button, and drag up until the wires are no longer visible.
6. Click the **Rectangular Marquee Tool** button and drag a selection marquee over part of the solar panel, as shown in Figure 2-36.

Figure 2-36 Making a selection

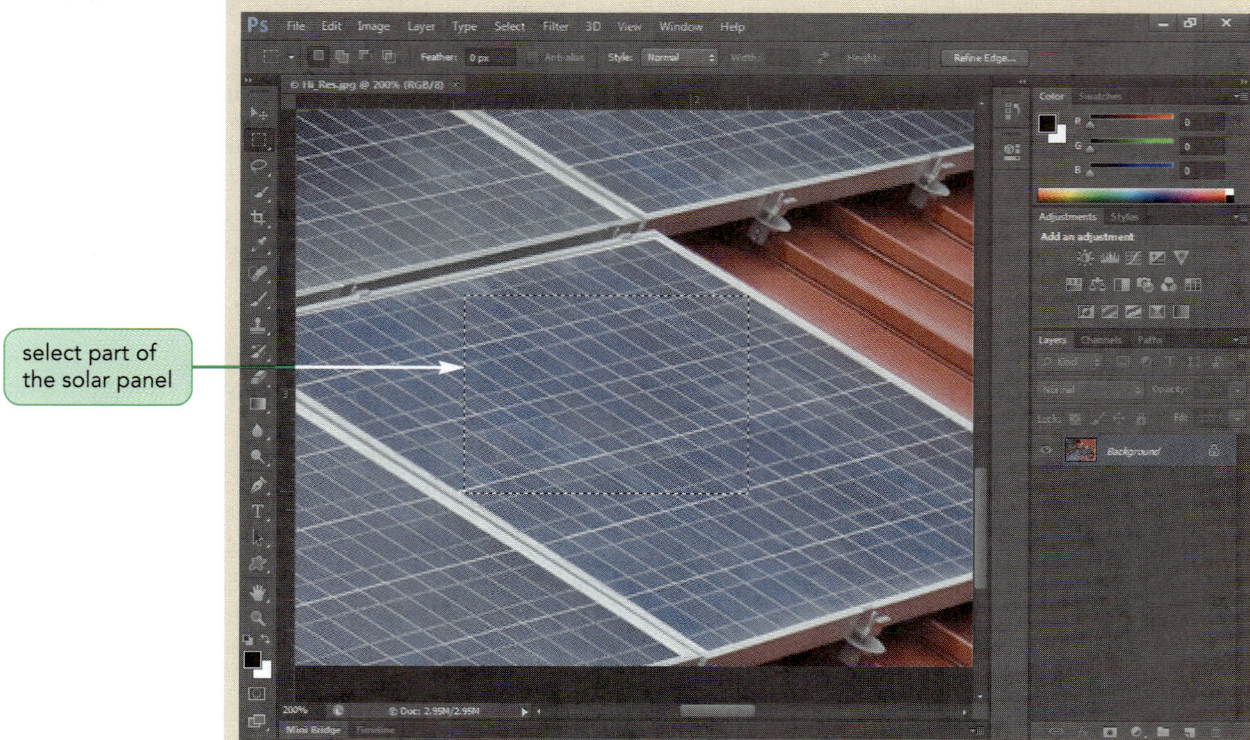

7. Press the **Ctrl+C** keys to copy the selection to the Clipboard.
8. On the menu bar, click **File**, and then click **Open**.
9. Navigate to the Photoshop2\Tutorial folder, and open **GreenHouseText2.psd**. In the Layers panel, click the **Background Layer**, and then press the **Ctrl+V** keys to paste the copied solar panel into the file.
10. Use the Move tool to move the copied panel so it is centered below the text.
11. Save the file as **SolarText.psd** in the Photoshop2\Tutorial folder, and then close the file.

The Navigator is another excellent tool for zooming and panning an image. It is especially useful because it displays a thumbnail of the entire image so you can easily choose your next "destination," or the place on the image to where you want to pan. You access the Navigator from the Window menu.

You'll work with the Navigator to become more comfortable focusing on different areas of a complex image. This skill will come in handy when you do detailed pixel-editing work for C. J. in the future.

To use the Navigator to pan and zoom the image:

1. Hi_Res.jpg should still be open at 200% in the Document window. On the menu bar, click **Select**, and then click **Deselect** to deselect the solar panel selection.
2. On the menu bar, click **Window**, and then click **Navigator**. The Navigator opens to the left of the Adjustments panel group. It is grouped with the Histogram panel. Notice the thumbnail of the open photograph and the red box, called the proxy preview area or view box, which outlines the portion of the image currently displayed in the Document window. The size of the view box changes based on the magnification. The lower the magnification, the larger the box because a larger part of the image is being displayed in the Document window.
3. Drag the **view box** in the Navigator up and to the right so that it encloses the man on the right. See Figure 2-37.

Figure 2-37 Using the Navigator

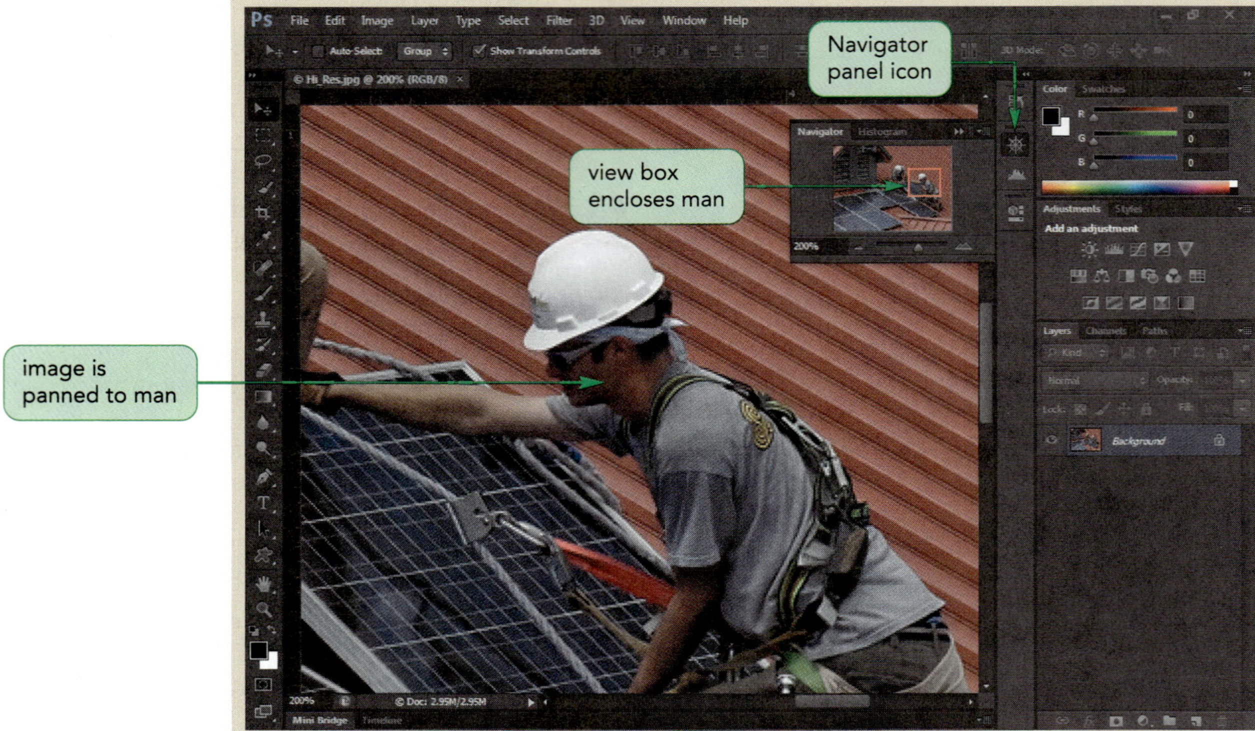

Dragging the view box pans the image.

4. Press the **Ctrl++** keys to change the zoom percentage to 300%. Notice that the view box has gotten smaller in the Navigator because a smaller portion of the image appears in the Document window.
5. Click the **Zoom Tool** button, if necessary, and then on the options bar, click the **Fit Screen** button. The view box in the Navigator is as large as the document in the Document window because the entire image is visible.
6. Click the **Actual Pixels** button on the options bar. The view box appears smaller on the thumbnail because by zooming in, you are viewing a smaller part of the image.

   You can also use the settings in the Navigator to zoom your image.
7. In the box in the lower-left corner of the Navigator, type **500**, and then press the **Enter** key. The image in the Document window zooms to a 500% magnification level. The view box on the thumbnail decreases substantially in size.
8. Drag the **Zoom** slider at the bottom of the Navigator all the way to the left, and then all the way to the right. The maximum zoom setting allowed by Photoshop is 3200%. Notice that the view box has nearly disappeared because you are focused on such a small part of the image.
9. Close the file without saving it, click **Window** on the menu bar, point to **Workspace**, and then click **Reset Essentials**.

Rotating and Flipping an Image

TIP

If you want to rotate the view while you are working, but don't want to permanently rotate the photo and alter the pixels, you can use the Rotate View tool if you have an OpenGL video card.

There might be times when you have the perfect image for a project—with one small problem: The door of the house needs to be on the right, not the left, or the photographer took the photograph with the camera held sideways in order to fit a tall person in the photo. As a result, the orientation is wrong. Or maybe you have photographs of two different people that you want to put in a composition so that they are facing each other. Unfortunately, each person is facing to the left. What can you do to fix this problem so the two people are facing each other? You can rotate or flip one of the images. It's important to note that rotating and flipping an image is a destructive form of editing: That is, it permanently alters the pixels in the photograph.

Photoshop provides a number of options for rotating and flipping images. You can access the rotation commands on the Image menu by clicking Image Rotation and then making a selection. Figure 2-38 shows the six options available for image rotation.

Figure 2-38 **Image rotation options**

Option	Details
180°	Flips the image so it is upside down and facing in the opposite direction
90°CW 90°CCW	Rotates the image 90 degrees clockwise or 90 degrees counterclockwise, respectively
Arbitrary	Lets you specify an angle of rotation for your image and whether you want to rotate the image clockwise or counterclockwise; when you rotate an image at an angle other than 90° or 180°, Photoshop increases the size of the canvas to accommodate the image
Flip Canvas Horizontal	Flips the image around an imaginary vertical line drawn through the center of the image
Flip Canvas Vertical	Flips the image around an imaginary horizontal line drawn through the center of the image

C. J. wants you to experiment with rotating and flipping an image of a wrench so that you are prepared to manipulate other images as needed on future projects.

To rotate and flip the image of the wrench:

1. On the options bar, reset all tools. Navigate to the Photoshop2\Tutorial folder, and open **Wrench.jpg**, display the rulers, if necessary, and fit the image on the screen. A photograph of a wrench that is about 8 1/2 inches wide and 13 inches high appears in the Document window.
2. On the menu bar, click **Image**, and then click **Image Rotation**. Photoshop displays the commands for rotating an image.
3. Click **90°CW**. See Figure 2-39. The photograph is now 13 inches wide by about 8 1/2 inches high.

Figure 2-39 Rotated image

image is now 13″ wide and about 8 1/2″ high

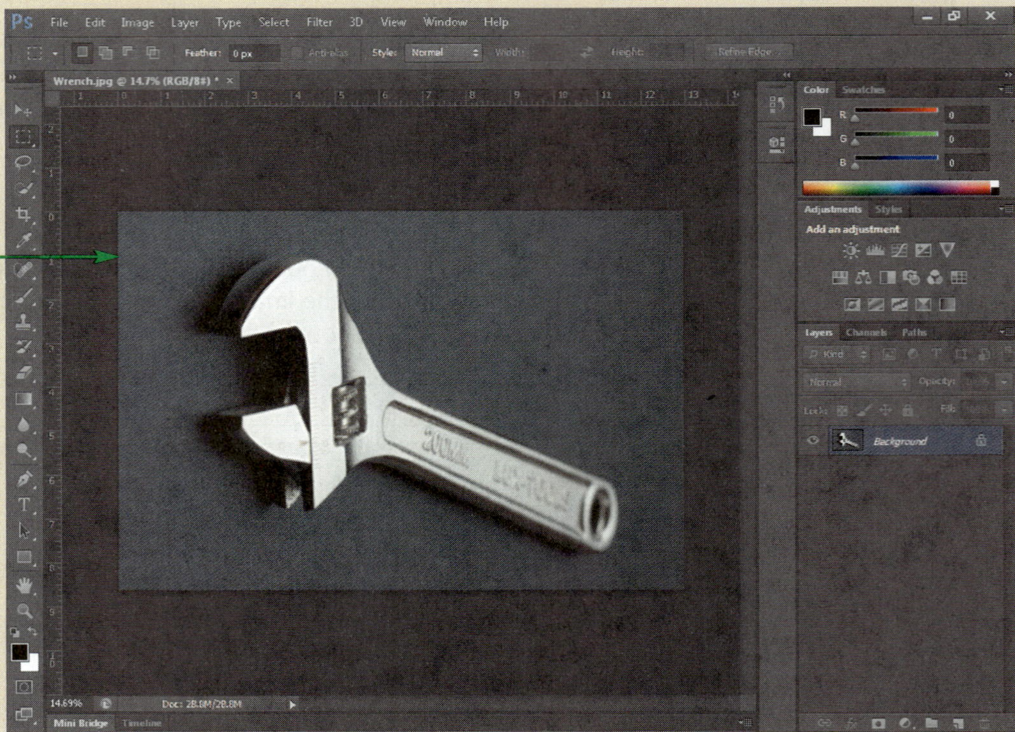

Garsya/Shutterstock.com

4. On the menu bar, click **Edit**, and then click **Undo Rotate Canvas**.
5. On the menu bar, click **Image**, click **Image Rotation**, and then click **Arbitrary**. The Rotate Canvas dialog box opens. You can specify the angle and direction (clockwise or counterclockwise) of the rotation.
6. In the Angle box, type **60**, click the **°CCW** option button to rotate the image 60 degrees counterclockwise, and then click the **OK** button. The image rotates 60 degrees counterclockwise, and Photoshop expands the dimensions of the canvas to accommodate the rotation.
7. In the Tools panel, click the **Zoom Tool** button, if necessary, and then click the **Fit Screen** button on the options bar. See Figure 2-40.

Figure 2-40 **Extended canvas accommodates rotation**

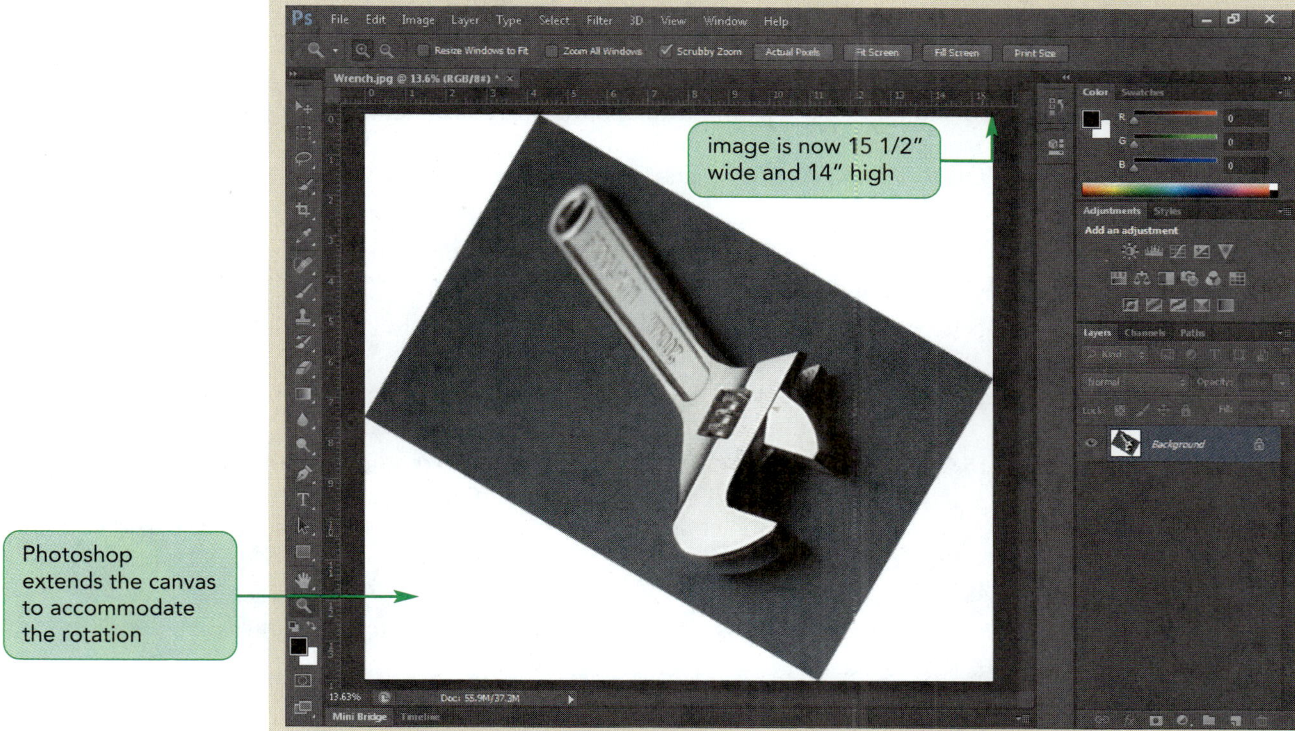

Garsya/Shutterstock.com

The canvas is now 15 1/2 inches wide and 14 inches high, and Photoshop has added to the canvas to accommodate the new angle of the image.

8. Save the file as **WrenchRotate.jpg** in the Photoshop2\Tutorial using the current JPEG settings, close the file, and then exit Photoshop.

In this session, you learned how to use the Adjustments panel to quickly make adjustments to an image. You also learned how to pan and zoom an image and how to rotate an image.

REVIEW

Session 2.2 Quick Check

1. What is the difference between destructive image edits and nondestructive image edits?
2. Nondestructive image edits are stored in the ______________ panel.
3. Brightness/Contrast settings for an image can be found in the ______________ panel.
4. When you drag an image within the Document window to see an area that was previously hidden, you are ______________ the image.
5. True or False. The keyboard shortcut Ctrl+- increases the zoom magnification of an image.
6. The ______________ provides a convenient way to zoom and pan an image.
7. The Image Rotation command can be found on the ______________ menu.

Practice the skills you learned in the tutorial using the same case scenario.

PRACTICE

Review Assignments

Data Files needed for the Review Assignments: Hammer.psd, GreenHouseText.psd

C. J. wants you to continue exploring Photoshop on your own so that you become more comfortable working with and making adjustments to images. He suggests you work with an image of a hammer that he is thinking of including on a postcard he plans to send to his customers. Complete the following steps:

1. Start Photoshop while pressing the Ctrl+Alt+Shift keys, and click Yes to delete the Settings File when prompted. Reset Photoshop to the default Essentials workspace layout, and then reset all tools.
2. Open **Hammer.psd**, located in the Photoshop2\Review folder provided with your Data Files.
3. Add a Hue/Saturation adjustment layer to the Hammer layer, and select the Cyanotype preset. Clip the adjustment to the layer.
4. Add a Brightness/Contrast adjustment layer so it adjusts all the layers in the image. (*Hint*: The Brightness/Contrast layer should appear at the top of the Layers panel, and it should not be clipped to any other layers.) Set the Brightness to 100 and the Contrast to 30. Save the file as **HammerAdjust.psd** in the Photoshop2\Review folder.
5. Delete the Brightness/Contrast layer, and collapse the Properties panel.
6. Rotate the image 90° clockwise.
7. Increase the canvas size half an inch on every side, and set the Canvas extension color to gray.
8. Save the file as **HammerExtend.psd** in the Photoshop2\Review folder.
9. Save the file again as **HammerExtend.jpg** in the Photoshop2\Review folder using Medium quality and 3 Progressive scans.
10. Open **HammerExtend.jpg** and view both files in 2-up Vertical view. Zoom both files to 100% view, and then fit them on screen. Close **HammerExtend.jpg**.
11. Delete the Hue/Saturation layer in the **HammerExtend.psd** file, and then change **HammerExtend.psd** to Grayscale mode and flatten it. Save the file as **GrayHammer.psd**.
12. Zoom the image to 110%, and use the Navigator to center the face of the hammer (the part that hits the nail) in the Document window.
13. Reduce the zoom to 45%, and then pan to display the entire head of the hammer in the Document window. Close the Navigator tab group.
14. Use the Rectangular Marquee tool to select the portion of the image that appears in the window, and then copy the selection to the Clipboard.
15. Create a new file using the Clipboard preset and a black background and paste the portion of the image you copied into the file. (*Hint*: Press the X key before you open the New dialog box to change the background color to black.) Save the new file as **HammerHead.psd** and close it.
16. Zoom to 20% in the GrayHammer.psd file. Place **GreenHouseText.psd**, located in the Photoshop2\Review folder, at the top of **GrayHammer.psd** so that it fits in the top black canvas area without overlapping the hammer.
17. Save **GrayHammer.psd**, and exit Photoshop.
18. Submit the results of the preceding steps to your instructor either in printed or electronic form, as requested.

Use your skills to modify a photograph for a presentation.

APPLY

Case Problem 1

Data File needed for this Case Problem: ConcertHall.jpg

Sound Plan Engineering Sound Plan Engineering is an organization of acoustic, audio, and noise control consultants in Santa Fe, New Mexico. The firm specializes in acoustic and audiovisual system design. The firm was founded by Manuel Ramirez in 2002 and has grown from 10 employees to 150 in less than a decade. You have been tasked with preparing variations on an image of the firm's most recent work to present at a meeting with board members. Complete the following steps:

1. Start Photoshop while pressing the Ctrl+Alt+Shift keys, and click Yes to delete the Settings File when prompted. Reset Photoshop to the default Essentials workspace layout, and then reset all tools.
2. Open **ConcertHall.jpg**, located in the Photoshop2\Case1 folder provided with your Data Files, and fit the image on the screen.
3. Trim the image based on the top-left pixel color. Do not trim away the bottom part of the image, as this is where text for the final piece will go.
4. Select the Zoom tool, and drag a zoom selection marquee around the piano and the chairs surrounding it. (*Hint*: If your computer is equipped with a video card that supports OpenGL, dragging the pointer will zoom continuously rather than draw a marquee. Zoom so that you can see the area described in Step 4.)
5. Open the Navigator. Press the Alt+Print Screen keys to capture an image of the current Photoshop window, then open WordPad, which is available on the Accessories menu of the All Programs menu in Windows 7, and press the Ctrl+V keys to paste the image into a new file. Save the WordPad file as **Marquee.rtf** in the Photoshop2\Case1 folder.
6. Use the Navigator to pan to the seats in the audience on the lower-right side of the image. Press the Alt+Print Screen keys to capture an image of the current Photoshop window, switch to WordPad, create a new file, and press the Ctrl+V keys to paste the image into the new file. Save the WordPad file as **Navigator.rtf** in the Photoshop2\Case1 folder.
7. Collapse the Navigator. Fit the image on screen, and then apply the Black & White adjustment using the Neutral Density preset.
8. Zoom out to fit the image on screen and then save the file as **BWConcertHall.jpg** using Maximum quality and the Baseline ("Standard") format option.
9. Delete the black-and-white adjustment layer.
10. Add a Brightness/Contrast adjustment, and change the Brightness setting to -15 and the Contrast setting to 10.
11. Save the file as a JPEG image named **ConcertHallAdjust.jpg** in the Photoshop2\Case1 folder, using the same JPEG options you used in Step 8. Remember that saving a file as a JPEG merges all of the layers into a single layer, so when you open this file later, you'll see that it only has one layer.
12. Close ConcertHall.jpg without saving it, and exit Photoshop.
13. Submit the results of the preceding steps to your instructor either in printed or electronic form, as requested.

Use your skills to create an image for an online costume company.

APPLY

Case Problem 2

Data Files needed for this Case Problem: EyeMask.psd, Eye.tif

FrightSite Darron Murtha owns FrightSite, an online costume company specializing in exotic masks, based in Columbus, Ohio. Darron recently hired you to work in FrightSite's Marketing Department. Currently, you are working on a composition that will combine an image of a mask with an image of an eye, and you want to use Photoshop to achieve the creepy effect you're looking for. Complete the following steps:

1. Start Photoshop while pressing the Ctrl+Alt+Shift keys, and click Yes to delete the Settings File when prompted. Reset Photoshop to the default Essentials workspace layout, and then reset all tools.
2. Open **EyeMask.psd**, located in the Photoshop2\Case2 folder provided with your Data Files.
3. EXPLORE Place **Eye.tif**, located in the Photoshop2\Case2 folder, on top of the Background layer, and resize and move the image so that it fits in the eye socket on the left. (*Hint*: Click the Show Transform Controls check box on the options bar when using the Move tool, and press the Shift key when resizing to constrain proportions if desired.)
4. EXPLORE Deselect Show Transform Controls, if necessary, and add adjustments to create a creepy effect for the eye. (*Hint*: To adjust only the eye, make sure you clip the adjustment to the Eye layer. For a creepy effect, try adjusting the hue and saturation.) If you are unhappy with an adjustment, you can delete it from the Layers panel.
5. Adjust the text layer by changing its Brightness to 120.
6. Place another copy of **Eye.tif** in the file and resize it and move it so that it fits between the two lines of text. (*Hint*: The Eye layer should appear at the top of the Layers panel.) Adjust the eye by changing its hue to 95 and its saturation to 90.
7. Merge each layer and its adjustment. (*Hint*: Select the first Eye layer and its adjustment, by clicking the Eye layer and then pressing and holding the Ctrl key and then clicking the adjustment layer. Then, right-click and then click Merge Layers on the context menu. Do the same for the two other layers and their adjustment layer.)
8. Switch the image to RGB mode and flatten the image.
9. Change the image size to 5 inches wide, and constrain the proportions to ensure that the height and width change proportionally. Change the resolution to 72 ppi, select Scale Styles, and resample the image using the Bicubic (best for smooth gradients) interpolation method.
10. Zoom the image to 100%, and then change the canvas size to 4 inches wide, anchoring the image at the center. (*Hint*: Allow clipping when prompted, and make sure to deselect the Relative check box if necessary.)
11. Save the file as **Fright.jpg** in the Photoshop2\Case2 folder, using Medium quality, and a Baseline ("Standard") for optimization.
12. Close the file, and exit Photoshop.
13. Submit the results of the preceding steps to your instructor either in printed or electronic form, as requested.

Use your skills to create different versions of a profile photo.

APPLY

Case Problem 3

Data Files needed for this Case Problem: Mash.jpg, RockNRoll.psd

MashMatch Music MashMatch Music is an online site for sharing original music and creating mashups with other musicians. You have joined the site as a solo musician, and want to post a profile photo showcasing your instrument. You plan to use the same composition for a newspaper ad and for a poster that you'll hang up around town. Complete the following steps:

1. Start Photoshop while pressing the Ctrl+Alt+Shift keys, and click Yes to delete the Settings File when prompted. Reset Photoshop to the default Essentials workspace layout, and then reset all tools.
2. Open **Mash.jpg**, located in the Photoshop2\Case3 folder provided with your Data Files.
3. Change the size of the image to 15 × 10 inches.
4. Change the Saturation setting of the image to –20 to tone down the bright red of the guitar.
5. Extend the canvas to add two inches to the bottom only, and make the extension color black.
6. Place the file **RockNRoll.psd**, located in the Photoshop2\Case3 folder in the file, and position the text so it is centered in the black area at the bottom of the image.
7. Apply a Posterize adjustment to the Background layer using the default settings.
8. Save the file as **Poster.jpg** in the Photoshop2\Case3 folder, using Medium quality and Baseline ("Standard") format.
9. Delete the Posterize adjustment layer.
10. Change image size to 5 × 4 inches at 72 ppi. When you resize, scale styles, constrain proportions, and resample the image using the default settings. Zoom the image to 100%.
11. Save the resized image as **WebProfile.jpg** at Medium quality with an optimized baseline.
12. Change the color mode to Grayscale, rasterize and flatten the image, and discard color information.
13. Save the file as **GrayRock.jpg** with the current JPEG settings in the Photoshop2\Case3 folder, close the file, and exit Photoshop.
14. Submit the results of the preceding steps to your instructor either in printed or electronic form, as requested.

Use the skills you learned, plus some new skills, to modify a photograph and add text.

CHALLENGE

Case Problem 4

Data Files needed for this Case Problem: Cupcake.jpg, FinnText.psd, FinnText2.psd

Finnegan's Cakes You are the sole proprietor of Finnegan's Cakes, a neighborhood bakery in Northport, New York. You are just learning Photoshop, and want to use your new skills to modify an image for the cover of the menu. You'll create a color menu for in-house customers and a black-and-white menu for takeout. Complete the following steps:

1. Start Photoshop while pressing the Ctrl+Alt+Shift keys, and click Yes to delete the Settings File when prompted. Reset Photoshop to the default Essentials workspace layout, and then reset all tools.
2. Open **Cupcake.jpg**, located in the Photoshop2\Case4 folder provided with your Data Files.
3. Zoom in on one of the blue confetti circles on the cupcake.

EXPLORE

4. Change the background color in Photoshop to the blue from the confetti. (*Hint*: Click the blue confetti on the cake using the Eyedropper pointer. Then switch the foreground and background colors by pressing the X key so the confetti blue becomes the background color; the foreground color and background color squares in the Color panel will switch.)

5. Fit the image on screen. Extend the canvas by increasing the canvas by 4 inches in height, with no change in width. Leave the image anchored in the center, and use the Background color for the canvas extension. Fit the image on screen again, if necessary, so you can see the blue border at the top and bottom.
6. Place **FinnText.psd**, located in the Photoshop2\Case4 folder, in the blue rectangle at the top of the canvas.
7. EXPLORE Use the Eyedropper tool, located in the Tools panel, to click the pink frosting on the cupcake to sample its color and assign it as the foreground color. The foreground color square in the Color panel should change to pink.
8. Use the Rectangle tool (*not* the Rectangular Marquee tool) to draw a pink rectangle over the blue rectangle at the bottom of the image so that it is as wide as the image, and about one inch tall. Center it vertically in the blue area.
9. Place **FinnText2.psd** located in the Photoshop2\Case4 folder, at the bottom of the canvas, centered on the pink rectangle.
10. EXPLORE Display the Styles panel, and apply the Basic Drop Shadow style to the text you just placed at the bottom of the canvas. (*Hint*: Basic Drop Shadow is in the third row in the Styles panel, and is the last button on the right. You may need to scroll to see the button.)
11. Convert the image to CMYK mode, and rasterize and flatten it.
12. Save the file as **Menu.tif** in the Photoshop2\Case4 folder, using the default TIFF settings.
13. Change the color mode to Grayscale.
14. Adjust the Brightness to –10 and the Contrast to 75.
15. Save the file as **GrayCake.jpg** in the Photoshop2\Case4 folder, with the current JPEG settings. Close Menu.tif without saving, and exit Photoshop.
16. Submit the results of the preceding steps to your instructor either in printed or electronic form, as requested.

ENDING DATA FILES

Photoshop2 →

Tutorial
AdjustHeatCosts.psd
BWGreenHouse.jpg
BWHeatCosts2.psd
CanvasSize.psd
GreenHouseConstruction72ppi.jpg
GreenHouseConstruction150ppi.jpg
GreenHouseConstruction.jpg
Leaderboard.psd
Logo1.psd
PosterPresetExample.psd
SolarText.psd
Trim.jpg
WrenchRotate.jpg

Review
GrayHammer.psd
HammerAdjust.psd
HammerExtend.jpg
HammerExtend.psd
HammerHead.psd

Case1
BWConcertHall.jpg
ConcertHallAdjust.jpg
Marquee.rtf
Navigator.rtf

Case2
Fright.jpg

Case3
GrayRock.jpg
Poster.jpg
WebProfile.jpg

Case4
GrayCake.jpg
Menu.tif

TUTORIAL 3

Layering Content to Compose Images

Working with Layers in Compositions

OBJECTIVES

Session 3.1
- Select, add, duplicate, and delete layers
- Change layer properties and visibility
- Move, align, and distribute layers
- Hide and redisplay layers
- Place, resize, and reposition an image on a layer

Session 3.2
- Lock layer content
- Work with layer comps
- Apply blending modes and adjust opacity
- Create layer groups
- Merge layers and flatten an image

Case | *Cooking the Books Publishing*

Cooking the Books Publishing is a small publishing house based in Madison, Wisconsin. The company was founded by Elena Genoa in 2008, and currently has 25 titles on its list. Upcoming titles include *The Fruit Fantastic: Recipes for the Adventurous Palate*, and *The New Old-Fashioned: 19th Century Recipes with a 21st Century Twist*. You are an assistant to Art Director Kaye Eastman. Because it's a small company, you and Kaye are tasked with creating all of the artwork for the publishing house, including illustrations and covers. Kaye has asked you to work on some cover and illustration ideas for the new titles. You'll use layers in Photoshop to develop a series of possible compositions to present to her at your next meeting.

STARTING DATA FILES

Photoshop3 →

Tutorial
- AlignStars.psd
- Citrus.jpg
- CitrusRecipes.psd
- DistributeStars.psd
- FruitDraft.psd
- FruitFantastic.psd
- FruitFantastic2.psd
- Grapes.psd
- HeavenSent.psd

Review
- BakeRectangle.psd
- BakeRectangle2.psd
- Breads.jpg
- Cover.jpg
- Perfection.psd

Case1
- NewHome.jpg
- NortonCo.psd
- Ruins.jpg

Case2
- AlwardArt.psd

Case3
- Clouds.jpg
- Clouds1.jpg
- Plane1.psd
- Plane2.psd

Case4
- Keys1.jpg
- Keys2.jpg

SESSION 3.1 VISUAL OVERVIEW

The Align icons on the options bar let you choose how to **align**, or line up, selected objects along their centers or edges.

Select the Show Transform Controls check box to see **transform controls**, the squares at each corner and along the sides of a selection that let you change the shape and size of an object.

Display **layer edges** to see where a layer begins and ends on the canvas.

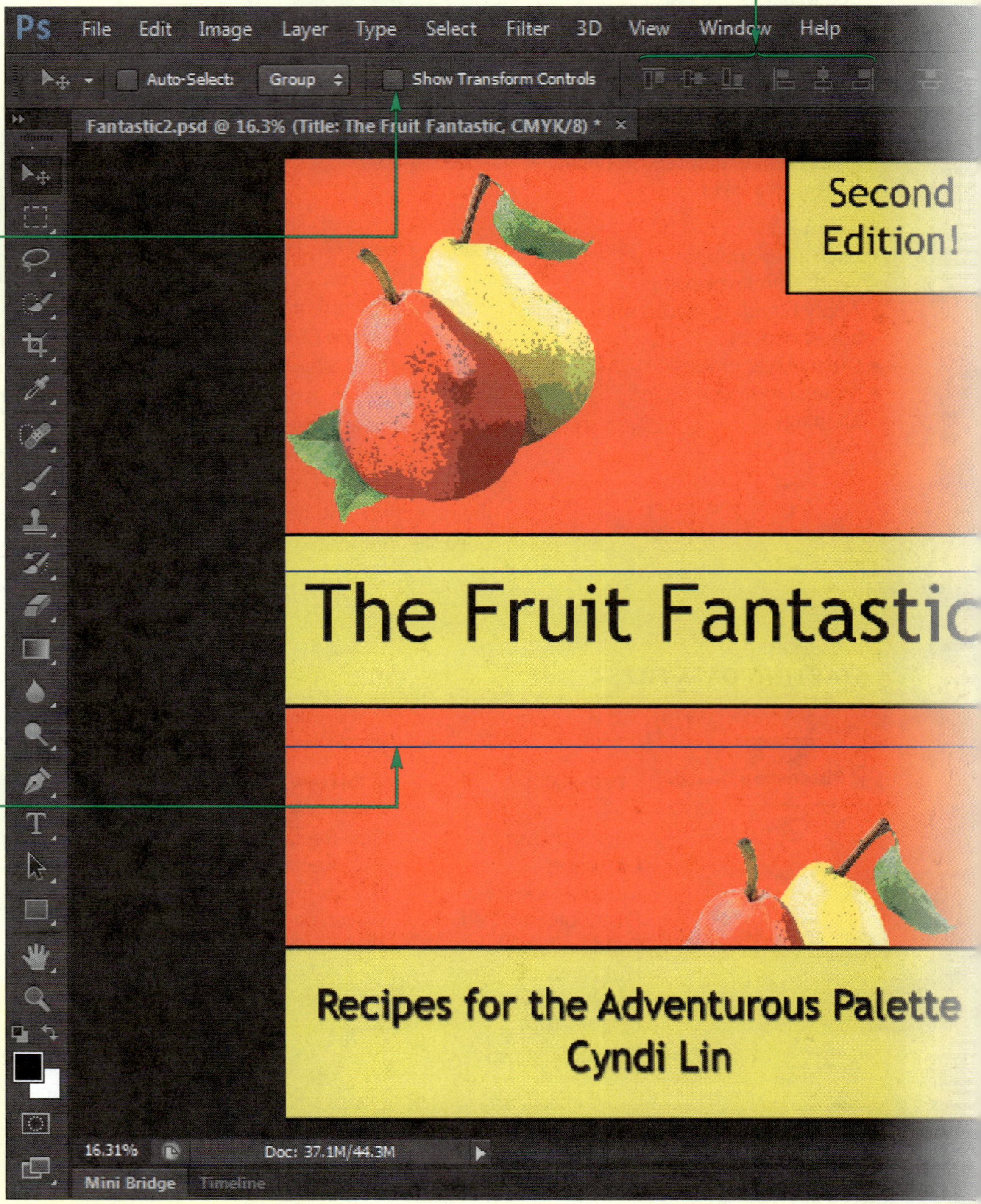

Anna Kucherova/Shutterstock.com

WORKING WITH MULTIPLE LAYERS

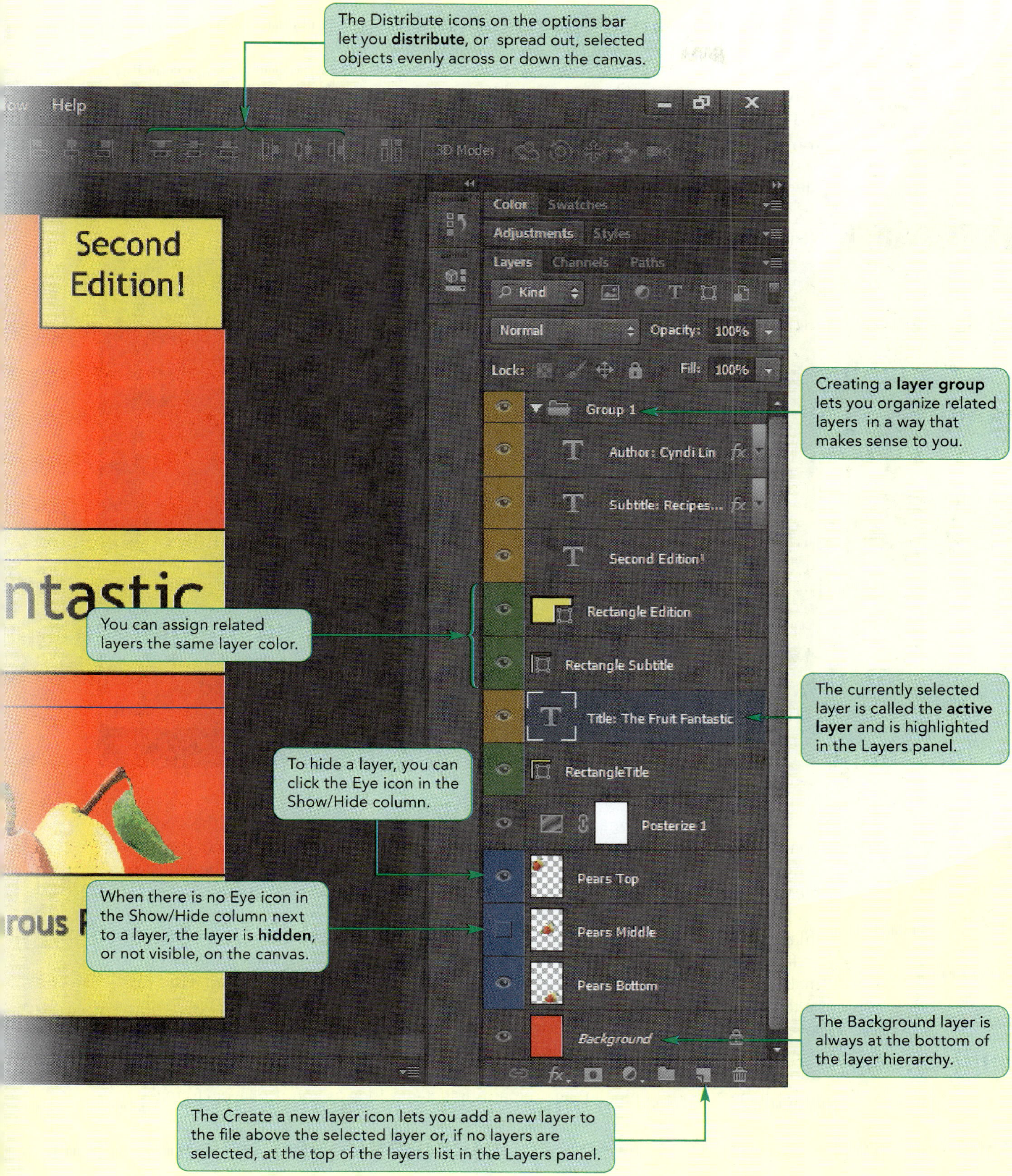

Understanding Layers

TIP

To hide a layer, click the Eye icon in the Show/Hide column to the left of the layer's thumbnail in the Layers panel. To redisplay a hidden layer, click the empty square to the left of the thumbnail.

You have already witnessed the power of layers in Photoshop. In Tutorial 2, when you placed an image in a file, it appeared on its own layer. When you added an image adjustment, you were actually adding it as a layer on top of the layer to which it was clipped. An adjustment layer changes the way an image looks, but it is a nondestructive edit; it does not alter the pixels in the image. Adding an adjustment layer is like placing a sheet of clear plastic over the original image with the changes etched on it. Through this virtual layer of plastic, it appears as if the image has changed in some fundamental way. However, if you want to restore that image to its original appearance, all you have to do is delete or hide the layer containing the adjustment—as if you were removing the sheet of plastic containing your changes. See Figure 3-1.

Figure 3-1 **Nondestructive editing with an adjustment layer**

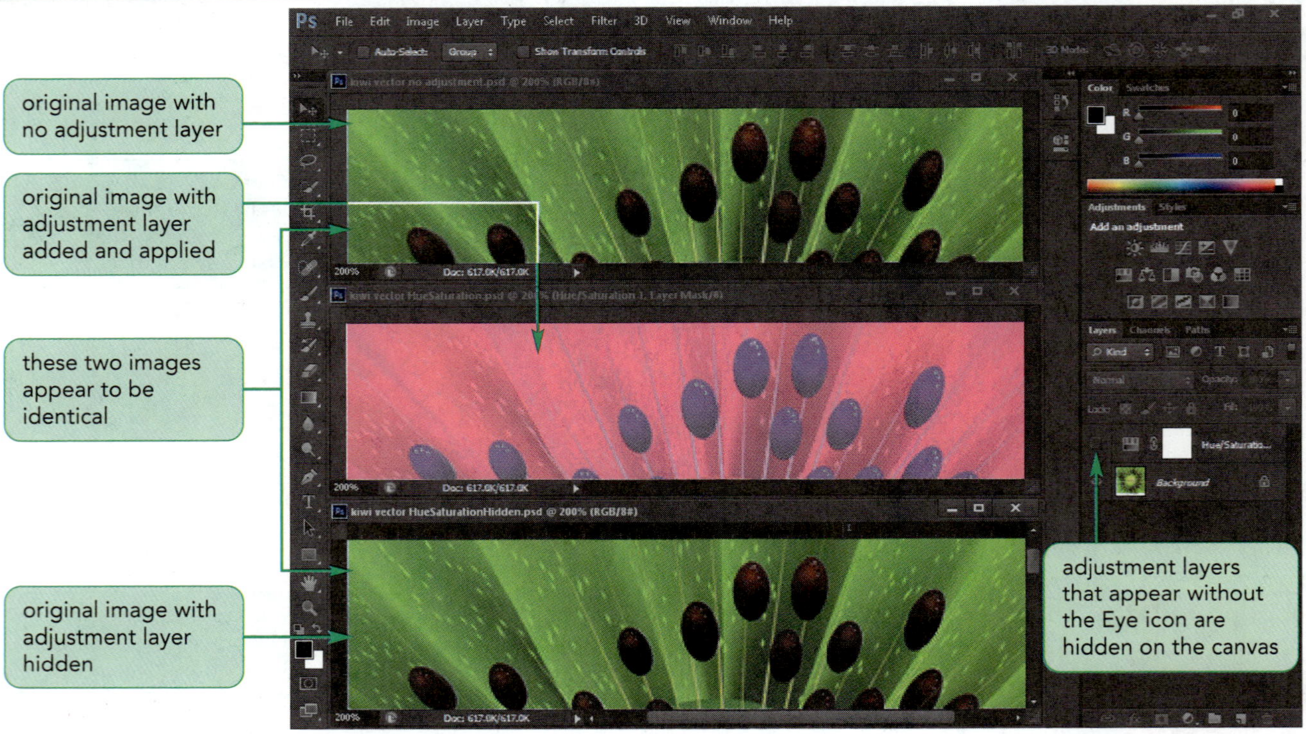

averych/Shutterstock.com

Figure 3-1 shows an image opened for the first time in Photoshop, then the same image with a Hue/Saturation adjustment layer applied, and a third version of the same image with the Hue/Saturation layer "turned off," or hidden. When the adjustment layer is visible, as shown in the middle image, it looks as if the underlying image itself has changed. However, when you hide the adjustment layer, you can see that the image pixels remain the same—with or without the adjustment layer.

If you do not make use of the layers functionality in Photoshop, any changes you make to an image are permanent after you save the file. If you haven't saved a backup of the original file, there is no way to go back to the original version of the file. With layers, however, you can experiment endlessly with a file by adding layer upon layer of changes, hiding layers, redisplaying layers, saving the file, working on it the next day and the next, and then deleting any layers you decide you don't want. Even with multiple changes, your original image remains intact—as long as you use layers to make those changes nondestructively.

Understanding Layer Positioning

As a rule, if no layer is selected in the Layers panel, any new layer that you add to a document appears at the top of the layers list in the Layers panel. If you first select a layer and then add a layer, the new layer appears directly above the selected layer. This is important to know because the order of layers in the Layers panel affects the way the image looks. Layers on top of other layers in the Layers panel appear on top of those layers in the composition itself. See Figure 3-2.

Figure 3-2 The importance of layer order

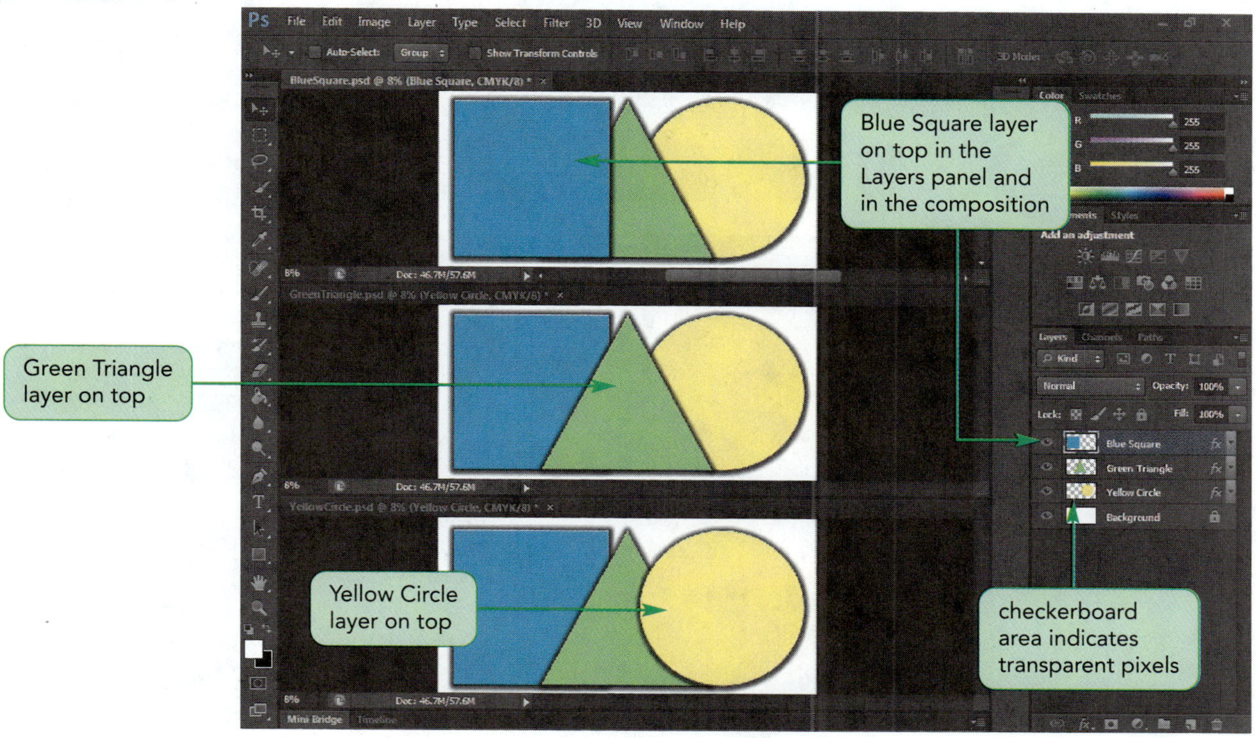

In the first file in Figure 3-2, the Blue Square layer is at the top of the list of layers in the Layers panel, followed by the Green Triangle layer and then the Yellow Circle layer. In the next file, the Green Triangle layer has been moved to the top of the list of layers, and appears on the top of the stacked objects in the document. In the third file, the Yellow Circle layer has been moved to the top of the Layers panel and appears on top in the document.

Notice that the thumbnail for each of these shapes in the Layers panel shows a checkerboard pattern around the shape. The checkerboard design in Photoshop indicates that the pixels in the checkerboard area are **transparent**, so you can see through them. Imagine that each of the shapes in Figure 3-2 has been painted on a rectangle of clear glass. Any area beneath the glass, except where the shape appears, is visible through the glass.

The position of adjustment layers in the Layers panel affects how the adjustments are applied to a file. An adjustment at the top of the Layers panel will affect all the layers beneath it, including the Background layer, unless it is clipped to a particular layer. As noted in Tutorial 2, when an adjustment is clipped to a layer in the Layers panel, it affects only that layer. See Figure 3-3.

Figure 3-3 Adjustment clipped to one layer and clipped to all layers beneath it

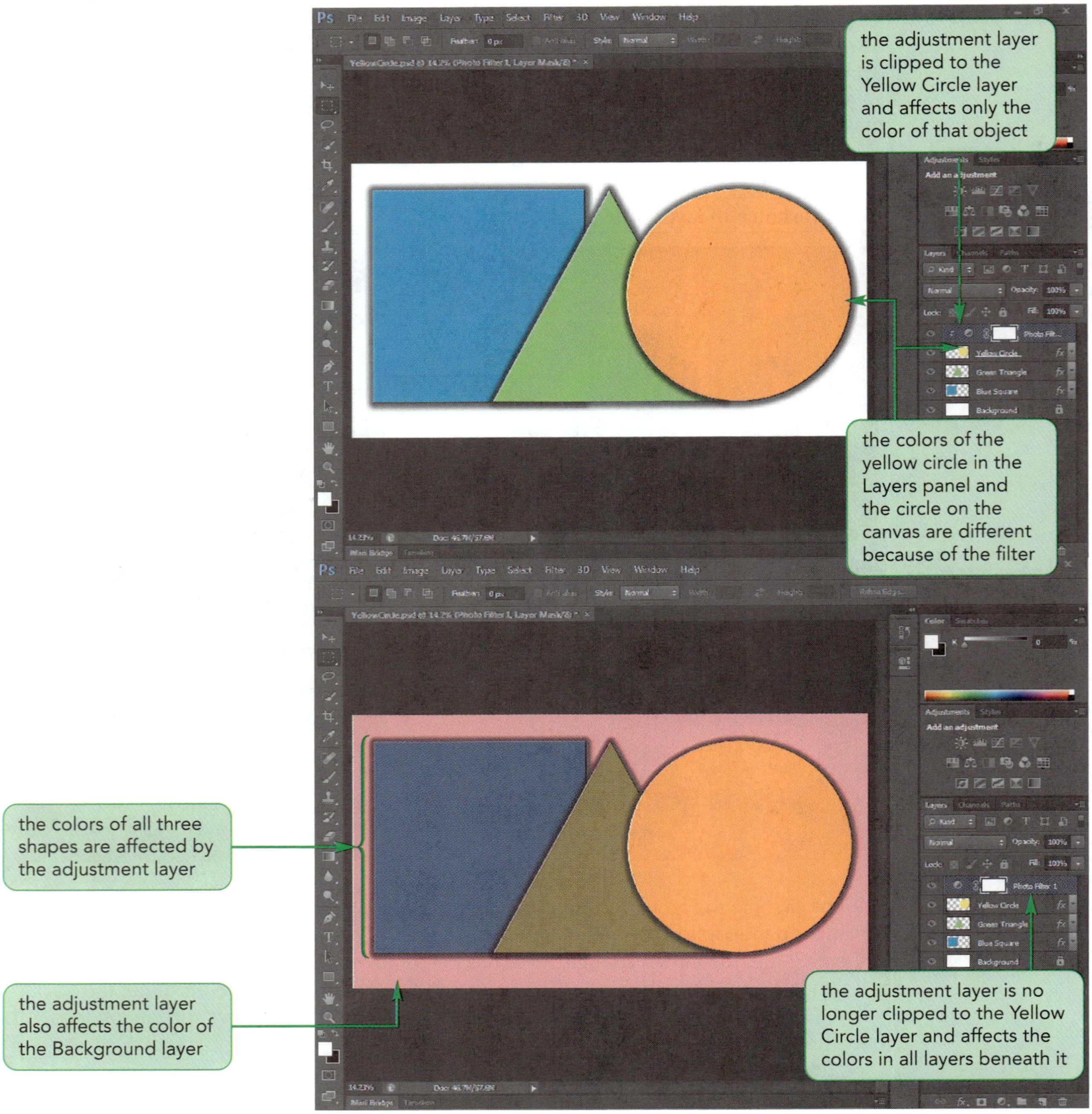

The Deep Red Photo Filter adjustment used in Figure 3-3 has the same effect on the colors in an image that putting a colored filter over your camera lens would have: It changes the colors of the objects in the image. In the top image, the Photo Filter adjustment layer is clipped to the layer beneath it (the yellow circle). As a result, the circle in the image appears orange rather than yellow. However, the color of the circle in the Layers panel thumbnail is still yellow. In the bottom image, the same Photo Filter adjustment layer has been unclipped from the Yellow Circle layer, so it affects *all* layers beneath it; each of the shapes and the background appear to have changed color.

You'll find that most of the work you do in a complex document involves layers. You will frequently add, duplicate, select, name, and move layers. You'll group layers in the Layers panel so their organization is logical, and you'll hide and redisplay them to compare their impact or effect. In this session, you'll learn many of the basic layer tasks you'll perform in Photoshop.

Selecting and Deselecting Layers

To work with any layer in a Photoshop file, you first need to select it so it becomes active. More than one layer can be active at a time, and a layer must be active if you want to work with it. It's a common mistake to start working on an image with a particular goal in mind only to realize that you are not actually working with the correct layer. See Figure 3-4.

Figure 3-4 **Trying to copy pixels in an unselected layer**

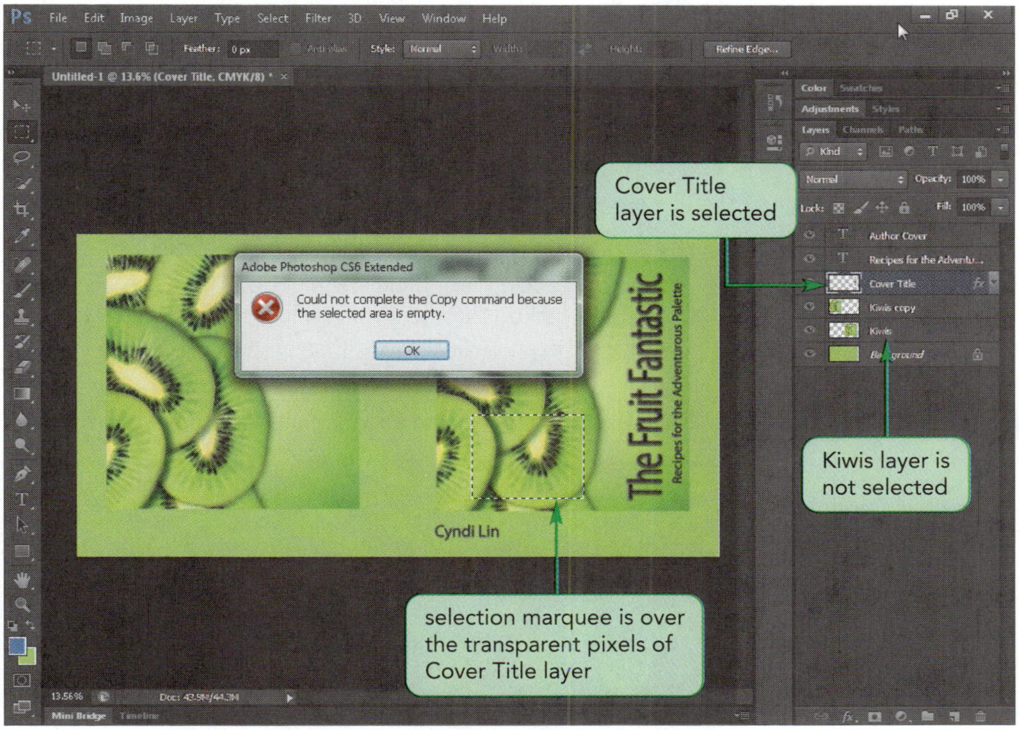

Subbotina Anna/Shutterstock.com

In Figure 3-4, the selection marquee appears around a portion of the image of the kiwi fruit. It is logical to think that you could use the Copy command on the Edit menu to copy the selection to the Clipboard. However, although the selection marquee is over the kiwi image, the Cover Title layer is the selected layer. If you hid all the layers except the Cover Title layer, you would see that the selected area consists of transparent pixels. In other words, there is nothing to copy. If you try to copy a selection that is empty, Photoshop displays the error message shown in the figure.

Selecting and Deselecting Single Layers

Often, you will need to select a single layer so you can make changes that affect that layer only. When you select certain layers in an image, a **bounding box** shows the borders of the layer; the transform controls are the squares on the sides and at each corner of the bounding box. Bounding boxes do not appear on **locked layers**, which are layers (such as the Background layer, which is locked by default) that you cannot move or resize. If you want to move or make changes to the locked Background layer, you can convert it to a regular layer by right-clicking the Background layer and selecting the Layer from Background option on the context menu.

Kaye has created a couple of mock-ups for the new *Fruit Fantastic* cookbook, and she wants you to experiment with the layers in her composition to see if you can improve on her ideas. You'll start by selecting and deselecting layers in order to make changes on a single layer at a time.

To select a single layer:

1. Start Photoshop while pressing the **Ctrl+Alt+Shift** keys, and click **Yes** to delete the Settings File when prompted. Reset Photoshop to the default Essentials workspace layout, and then reset all tools.
2. In the Tools panel, click the **Move Tool** button, and then click the Show Transform Controls check box to select it.
3. Click **File** on the menu bar, click **Open**, navigate to the Photoshop3\Tutorial folder included with your Data Files, open **FruitFantastic.psd**, and press the **Ctrl+0** keys to fit the image on the screen.
4. Minimize the **Color** panel group and the **Adjustments** panel group by double-clicking the panel tabs, and then expand the **Layers** panel, if necessary.

   The Layers panel lists all of the layers in the file, including text layers, image layers, an adjustment layer, and the Background layer. You'll select The Fruit Fantastic layer so you can change its font.

5. In the Layers panel, click the **Title: The Fruit Fantastic** layer to select it. The text layer is selected in the panel and in the document, as indicated by the bounding box and the transform controls. See Figure 3-5.

Figure 3-5 **Text layer selected in the Layers panel and on the canvas**

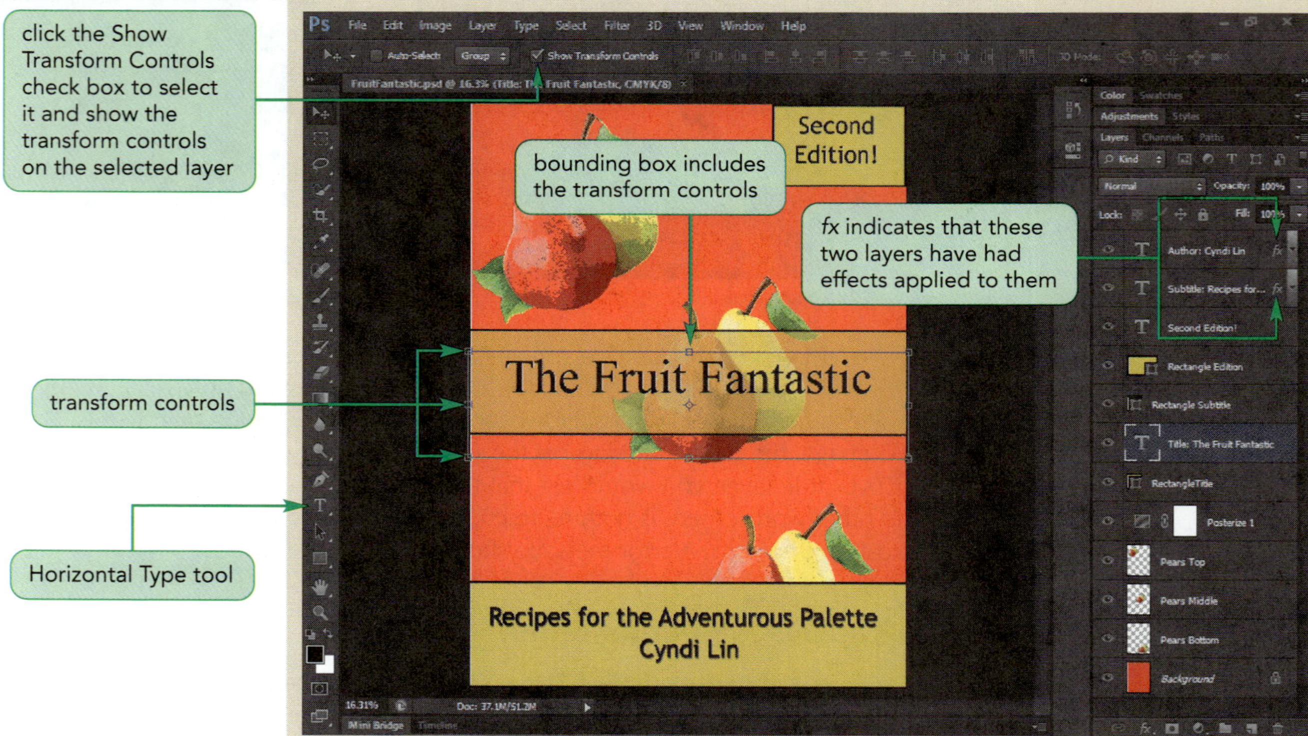

Anna Kucherova/Shutterstock.com

If you select the Horizontal Type tool to make changes to one or more text layers, the options for the Horizontal Type tool appear on the options bar, indicating that Photoshop is in text-edit mode. In **text-edit mode**, you can modify text on a layer by changing the font style and color, among other things. You'll make a change to the font on one of the text layers next.

To make changes to a single layer and deselect a layer:

1. In the Tools panel, click the **Horizontal Type Tool** button, and then on the options bar, click the **Set the font family** arrow.
2. In the font list, scroll down, if necessary, and then click **Trebuchet MS**. The title font changes to Trebuchet MS.

   Trouble? If Trebuchet MS does not appear on the font list, click a different font.
3. In the Tools panel, click the **Move Tool** button, and then in the Layers panel, click the **Pears Top** layer. The text layer is deselected, and the layer with the image of the pears in the upper-left corner of the composition is selected in the Layers panel and in the document, where a bounding box appears around the layer.
4. In the Layers panel, click the **Background** layer. The Background layer is selected in the Layers panel, but no bounding box appears in the document. This is because the Background layer is a locked layer and can't be moved or resized (as indicated by the lock icon that appears in the Layers panel).
5. In the Layers panel, click the **Posterize 1** layer. The Posterize 1 layer is selected in the Layers panel, but there is no selection in the document. This is because the Posterize 1 layer is an adjustment layer. It affects the layers beneath it, but doesn't appear as an object in the composition. However, it can be moved in the Layers panel so that it affects different layers in the composition.
6. On the menu bar, click **Select**, and then click **Deselect Layers**. Now there are no layers selected in the Layers panel.

TIP

You can also press and hold the Ctrl key and then click a layer to deselect it.

To work more efficiently, you can change many layers in a file at one time. To do so, you'll select multiple layers at once.

Selecting and Deselecting Multiple Layers

You will often find that you want to apply the same effect to multiple layers in a document. You could select the first layer, apply the effect, select the next layer, apply the effect, and so on. However, it's faster to select multiple layers at the same time and apply an effect to all of them at once. You can apply an effect to many layers at the same time by selecting all of the layers you want to work with to make them all active. For example, you might want to add a style to some of the text layers in your composition using the same settings. The subtitle and author name shown in Figure 3-5 were selected together and then had the Basic Drop Shadow style applied to them at the same time.

REFERENCE

Selecting Multiple Layers

- To select contiguous layers, in the Layers panel, click the first layer, press and hold the Shift key, and then click the last layer.
- To select noncontiguous layers, in the Layers panel, click the first layer, press and hold the Ctrl key, and then click each additional layer.

or

- To select all of the layers in the Layer panel, on the menu bar, click Select, and then click All Layers.

You can also select similar layers using a filter. **Similar layers** are layers with common characteristics. For example, all adjustment layers in the Layers panel would be considered similar layers, as would all image layers and all text layers. In the Layers panel, you can use a filter to display only those layers that are similar in some way, and then to select and make changes to all of those layers at the same time. You can filter by layer kind (for example, adjustment layer, type [or text] layer, or vector layer), layer name (for example, layers with the word *Title* in their name), or layer effect (for example, a layer with a shadow or bevel effect). Other filter options include mode, attribute, and color, all of which you'll learn about later in this tutorial.

Kaye asks you to see what the composition will look like if all of the rectangles behind the text are a different color. Notice that currently in the Layers panel, the rectangle layers are not next to each other. You'll use a filter to make it easy to select all the rectangles in the file at the same time to make the change.

To filter and display similar layers:

1. At the top of the Layers panel, click the **Filter for shape layers** icon. Photoshop hides all of the layers in the Layers panel except the three shape layers in the composition, the rectangles that are used as backgrounds for the text.
2. In the Layers panel, click the **Rectangle Edition** layer, press and hold the **Shift** key, and then click the **RectangleTitle** layer. All three rectangle layers are selected, so you can modify all three layers at the same time.
3. In the Tools panel, click the **Rectangle Tool** button, and then on the options bar, click the yellow **Fill** button. In the panel, click a bright green color for the rectangles, and then click the **Fill** button, which is now green, again to close the panel of swatches.

   The color of all three rectangles changes at the same time. See Figure 3-6.

Figure 3-6 Filtering and modifying similar layers

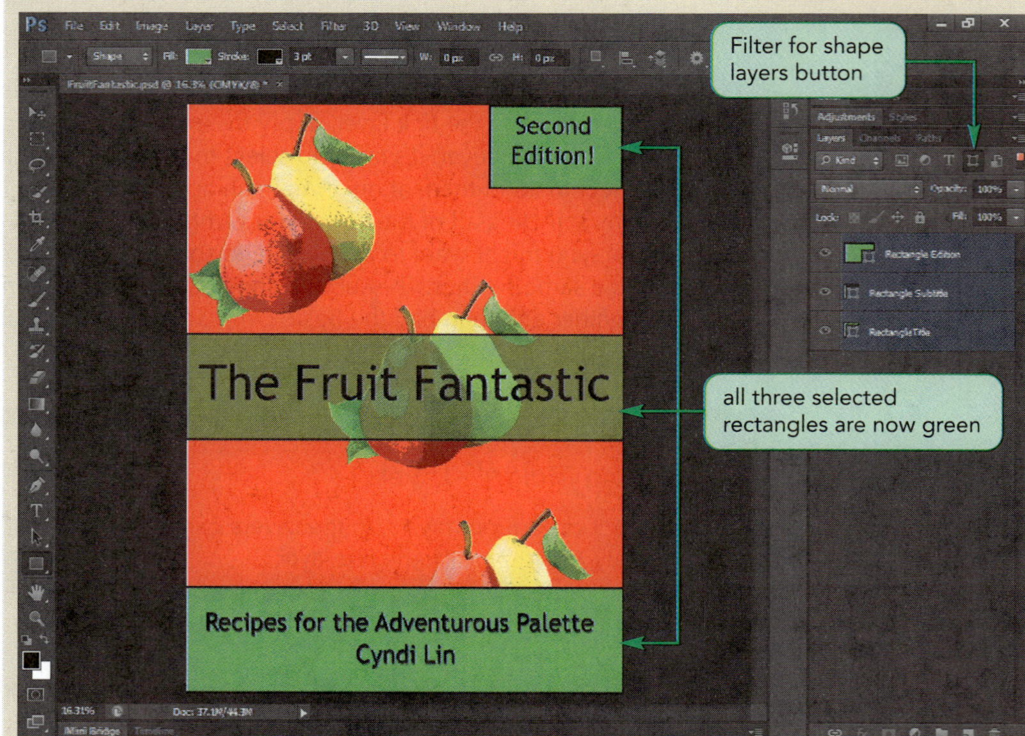

Anna Kucherova/Shutterstock.com

4. In the Layers panel, click the **Filter for shape layers** icon to deselect it and turn off layer filtering. All of the layers are redisplayed in the Layers panel.

   Next, you'll filter and select layers by name.

5. At the top of the Layers panel, click the **Kind** button, and then click **Name**. The layer Kind icons at the top of the Layer panel are replaced by a text box.
6. In the Name box, type **Pears**. Photoshop displays only the layers with the word *Pears* in their name.
7. In the Layers panel, click the **Turn layer filtering on/off** button to turn off filtering and redisplay all of the layers.
8. Save the file as **Fantastic2.psd** in the Photoshop3\Tutorial folder, and leave it open in the Photoshop workspace.

PROSKILLS

Teamwork: Knowing When to Call in Help

No matter how good your digital image-editing skills are, there will be times when you need to reach out to another person on your team to help you do your best work. Not only are teams useful for providing feedback on the work you do, but every good team has people who specialize in different areas. Being a Photoshop expert doesn't necessarily mean you have the artistic skills to create vector drawings at a professional level. Furthermore, although Photoshop's drawing tools might be sufficient for adding simple vector shapes to an image file, it is certainly not the best drawing tool for creating a professional composition—Illustrator is. When you need to create a challenging graphic for your composition, it is a good idea to call in a graphic designer or a visual artist if you need help. For example, if you need a vector drawing for a comp you are working on for a client, you could fumble around with the drawing tools in Photoshop and create a pretty good drawing—but why not shoot for excellent instead? Calling on an expert from your team for support will not only result in the best final product, but will also show that you have the decision-making and problem-solving skills necessary to get a job done right, the team player mentality to advance your organization's interests, and the potential to lead that team in the future.

Adding and Duplicating Layers

You can add a layer to a file in many ways. You can add an empty layer and then fill it with content. You can duplicate a selected layer so an exact copy of the layer appears in the Layers panel and in the composition. You can add a layer by drawing a vector object or by using the Type tools in the Tools panel. You can cut or copy a selection on one layer—or even in another file—and paste it into your composition to add it as a new layer. You can use the options in the Adjustments panel to add an adjustment layer. You can also add an **effects layer** by applying a style to a layer. In addition, you can add a fill layer to fill the background of a composition with a color, pattern, or gradient.

Adding an Empty Layer

To add a layer before adding any content or making an adjustment, use the Create a new layer icon at the bottom of the Layers panel. You can then place a photograph, enter text, or draw a vector object in the new layer, and it will appear on the canvas on top of the Background layer.

Kaye has asked you to develop some additional options for the *Fruit Fantastic* book cover by starting with a plain background and adding some new layers.

To add an empty layer and add a shape to the new layer:

1. Open **FruitDraft.psd**, located in the Photoshop3\Tutorial folder, and size it to fit the screen.
2. At the bottom of the Layers panel, click the **Create a new layer** icon. Photoshop creates a new layer, named Layer 1, above the Background layer.

   Next, you'll add a shape to the empty layer.

3. In the Tools panel, click the **Rectangle Tool** button, if necessary. The options bar changes to display settings for the Rectangle tool.
4. On the options bar, click the black **Fill** button. A swatches panel opens.
5. In the Swatches panel, click a pastel blue color, and then click the Fill button again to close the panel.
6. On the canvas, use the outer guides to draw a rectangle similar in size to the one shown in Figure 3-7.

Figure 3-7 **Drawing a rectangle in an empty layer**

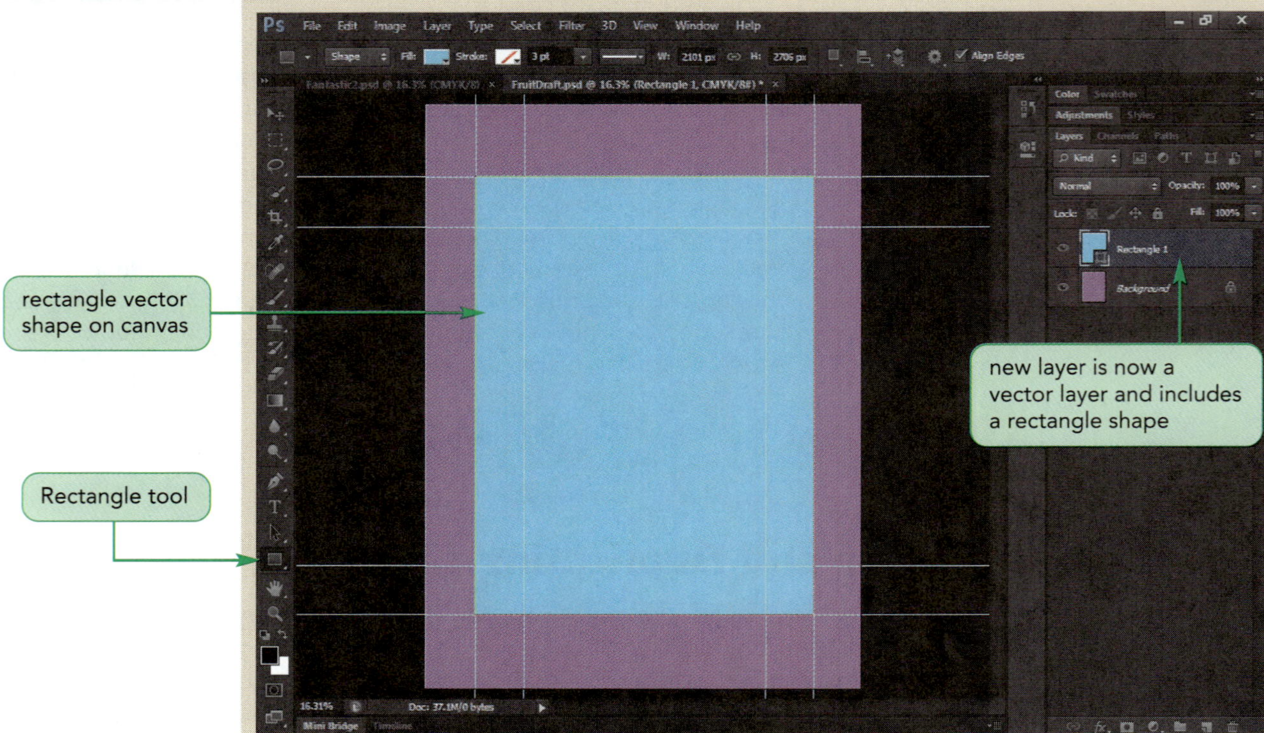

Adding a Vector Layer and an Effects Layer

When you use any of the vector drawing tools in the Tools panel when there are no layers selected, Photoshop places each vector object you draw on its own vector layer. When you modify the layer by adding an effect or applying a style, Photoshop adds an effects layer indented underneath the layer you are modifying and adds an ***fx*** designation next to the layer name. A **style** is a preset grouping of effects that are applied together. For example, a style might include a bevel and emboss effect as well as some sort of pattern or texture.

To add more interest to your cover design, you'll add another layer by drawing another shape in the file and then you'll apply one of the style presets to the new layer.

To add a vector layer and an effects layer:

1. Using the Rectangle tool and the inner guides, draw another rectangle inside the blue rectangle. Photoshop adds the rectangle to the document and places it on its own layer (Rectangle 2) in the Layers panel. You'll make the new rectangle stand out by applying a style to it.
2. Click the **Styles** tab behind the Adjustments tab to display the Styles panel.
3. In the Styles panel, click the **Tie-Dyed Silk (Texture)** icon to add the Tie-Dyed Silk style to the new layer. See Figure 3-8.

   Trouble? If you don't see the Tie-Dyed Silk (Texture) icon in the Styles panel, click the panel menu button, click Reset Styles, and then click the OK button to replace the current styles with the default styles. If prompted to save changes to the current styles before replacing them, click the No button. Repeat Step 3.

Figure 3-8 Tie-Dyed Silk effect applied to new layer

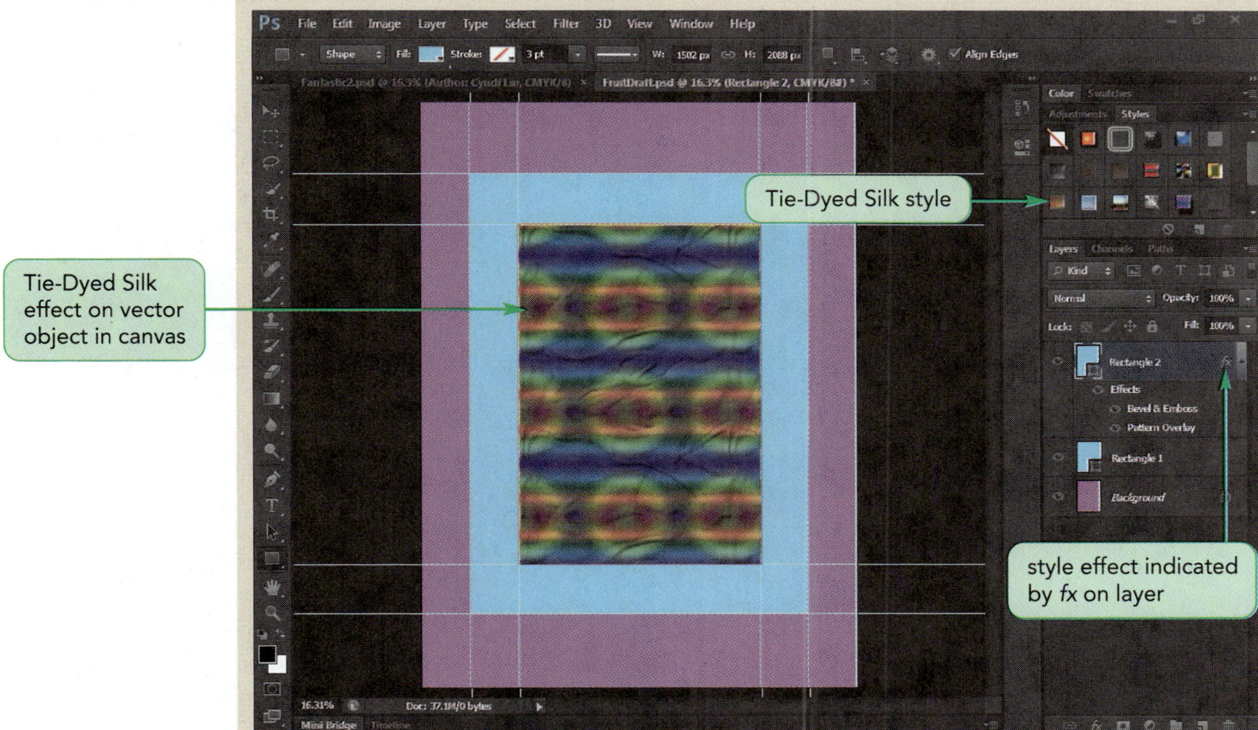

The Tie-Dyed Silk style includes two effects—a Bevel & Emboss effect, which gives the rectangle a three-dimensional look, as if it is wrinkled, and a Pattern Overlay effect, which fills the rectangle with an image of tie-dyed silk.

4. Save the file as **FruitDraft2.psd** in the Photoshop3\Tutorial folder, and keep the file open.

Creating a New Layer by Cutting or Copying and Pasting a Selection

You might find that you want to reuse part or all of an image, either in the current composition or in another composition. To do so, you can use one of the selection marquee tools to select the part of an image that you want to reuse, and then copy or cut the selection to the Windows Clipboard, which stores the selection in memory so you can paste it into the current file or another file. When you paste a selection, Photoshop puts the object on a new layer in the Layers panel. You can then use the Move tool to position the object where you want it to appear on the canvas.

To continue creating your mock-up for the cookbook cover, you'll copy some grapes from a PSD file to the FruitDraft2 file and paste them on a new layer.

To create a layer by copying and pasting:

1. Open **Grapes.psd** from the Photoshop3/Tutorial folder, and then size it to fit the screen.
2. In the Tools panel, click the **Rectangular Marquee Tool** button, and then drag a marquee around some of the grapes in the bunch of grapes. See Figure 3-9.

Figure 3-9 Copying a rectangular marquee selection

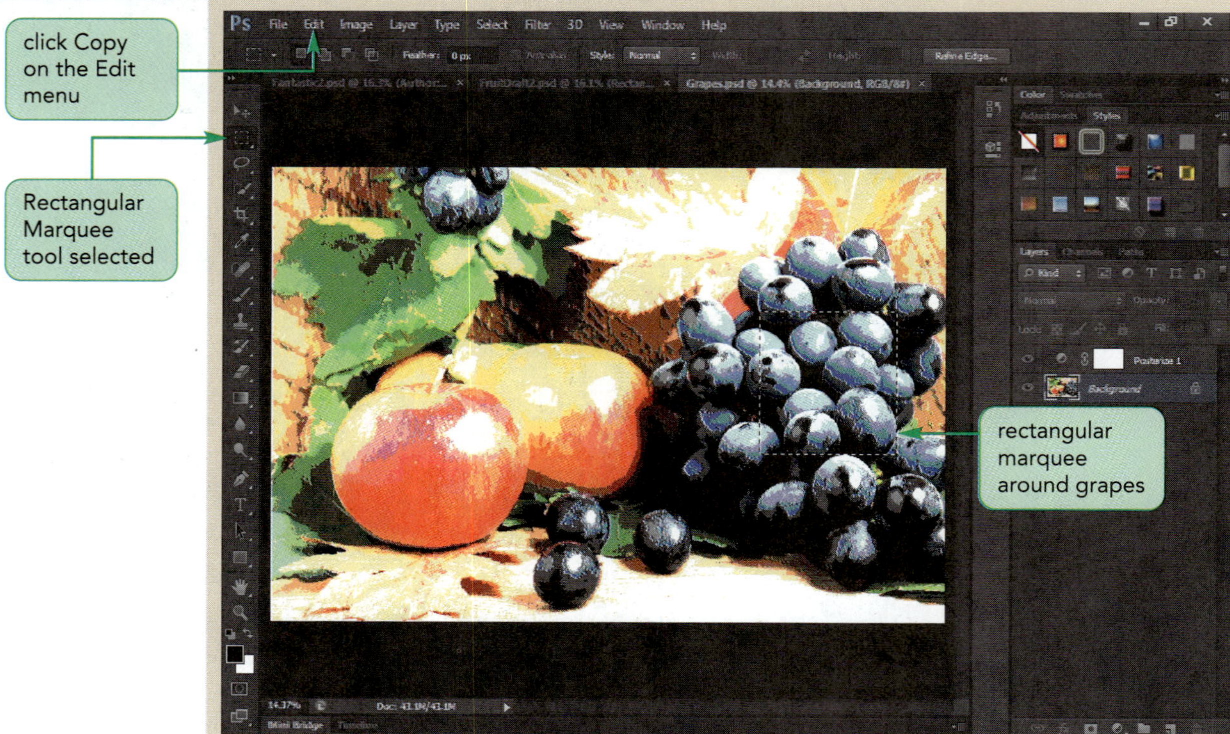

Chianuri/Shutterstock.com

3. On the menu bar, click **Edit**, and then click **Copy**.
4. Switch back to the **FruitDraft2.psd** file.
5. On the menu bar, click **Edit**, and then click **Paste**. Photoshop pastes the selection in the file and on a new layer. Note that you selected and copied only the grapes, not the Posterize effect that was applied to them in the original file. See Figure 3-10.

TIP

You can also press the Ctrl+C keys to copy. You can press the Ctrl+V keys to paste.

Figure 3-10 **Pasting a selection on the canvas**

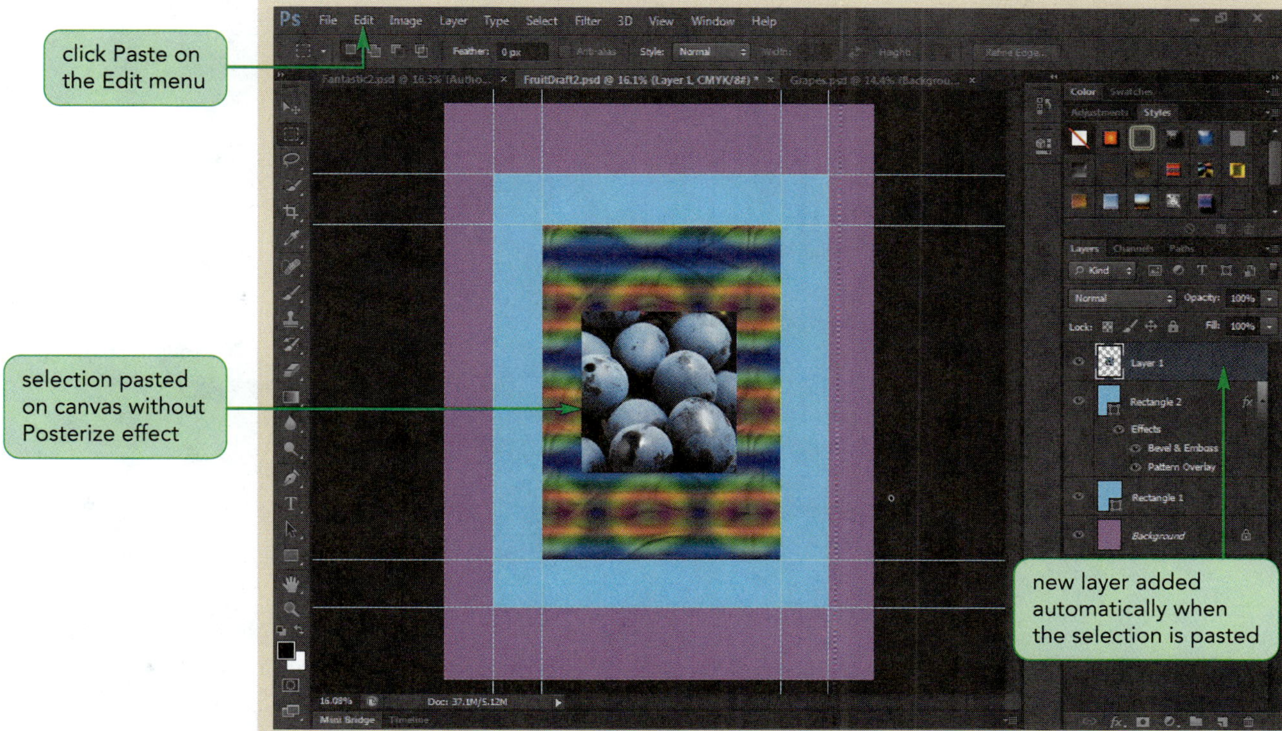

Chianuri/Shutterstock.com

Duplicating a Layer

When you duplicate a layer, you make an exact copy of its contents and any formatting or effects applied to it. For example, if you duplicate a shape layer that has a style applied to it, the new layer will include not only the vector shape but also the style. You can enter a name for the duplicate layer in the Duplicate Layer dialog box. You can also specify whether the duplicate should be added to the current file or another file, called a destination. A **destination file** can be any currently open file or a new file. You select the destination for a duplicate in the Duplicate Layer dialog box.

To duplicate a layer:

1. In the Layers panel, click the **Rectangle 2** layer to select it.
2. On the menu bar, click **Layer**, and then click **Duplicate Layer**. The Duplicate Layer dialog box opens. See Figure 3-11.

Figure 3-11 Duplicating a layer

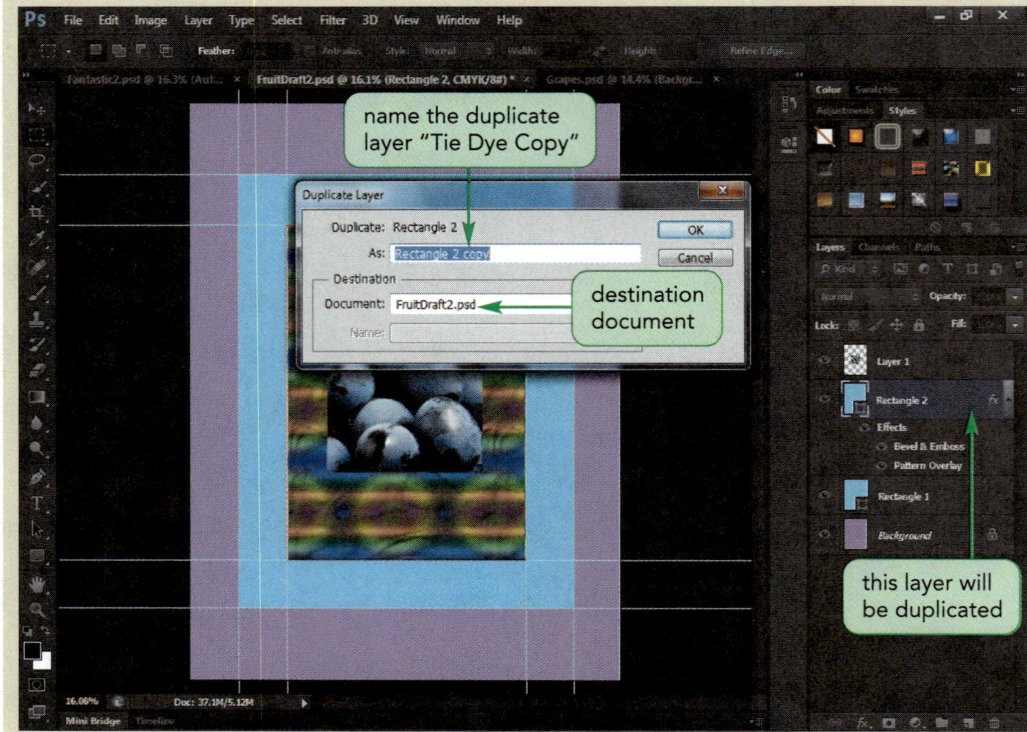

Chianuri/Shutterstock.com

3. In the As box, type **Tie Dye Copy**, confirm that the destination document is FruitDraft2.psd, and then click the **OK** button.

   Photoshop creates an exact copy of the Rectangle 2 layer, including the tie-dyed effect you added, and adds it to the Layers panel, with the name Tie Dye Copy. Because the duplicate is directly on top of the original layer on the canvas, you can't yet see it.

4. In the Tools panel, click the **Move Tool** button, point to the tie-dyed rectangle on the canvas, and then drag it up and to the top-left corner of the canvas.

5. In the Layers panel, right-click the **Tie Dye Copy** layer, and then click **Duplicate Layer** on the context menu.

6. Name the new layer **Tie Dye Copy 2**, and click the **OK** button. In the Document window, drag the new layer down and to the bottom-right corner of the canvas. See Figure 3-12.

Figure 3-12 Document with two duplicate layers

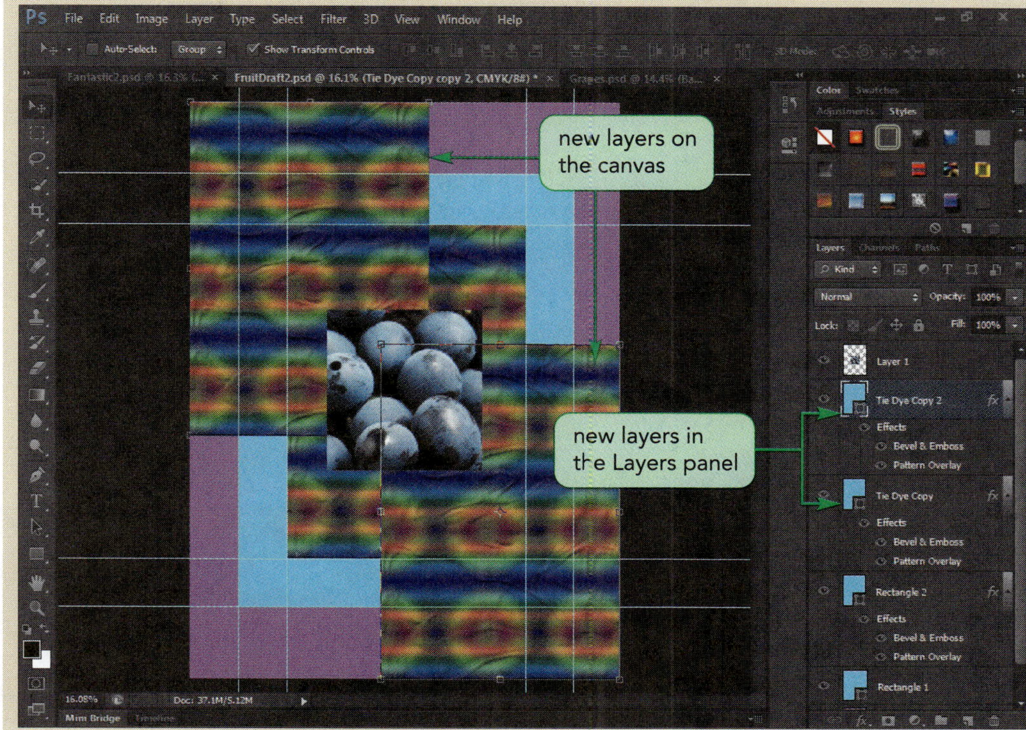

Chianuri/Shutterstock.com

Changing Layer Properties

When you are working in a file with many layers, it is helpful to give each layer a descriptive name that helps you remember its purpose or context. By default, Photoshop names generic layers by number: *Layer 1*, *Layer 2*, *Layer 3*, and so on. When you create a text layer, Photoshop names it using the actual text you have typed, and places a text icon (the letter *T*) in the thumbnail. When you draw a shape, Photoshop names the shape layer *Shape* 1, *Shape* 2, *Shape* 3, and so on. For example, when you draw a Rectangle, the first rectangle layer is given the name *Rectangle 1*. You can change the default name to make it more descriptive.

You can also change the color of a layer. Note that when you change the color of a layer, you are not changing the way the layer content looks on the canvas; rather, you are changing the color of the background of the Eye icon in the Show/Hide column in the Layers panel. If you assign the same color to related layers, you provide yourself with an easy visual overview of the organization of your document. For example, in the Session 3.1 Visual Overview, all text layers have a yellow color assigned to them, as does the group that contains the text layers; all digital images have been assigned a blue color; and all shape layers have been assigned a green color.

Kaye suggests that you organize your file by changing layer properties. You'll change the names and colors of the layers in your draft file so you can keep track of them more easily.

To change the name of a layer:

1. Press the **V** key to activate the Move tool, if necessary.
2. In the Layers panel, click **Layer 1** to select it, if necessary, and then point to the layer name, *Layer 1*, and double-click. The layer name appears highlighted in a box.
3. Type **Grapes** and then press the **Enter** key. Photoshop renames the layer.
4. In the Layers panel, click the **Rectangle 1** layer to select it. On the menu bar, click **Layer**, and then click **Rename Layer**.
5. Type **Blue Rectangle**, and then press the **Enter** key.
6. Change the name of the Rectangle 2 layer to **Tie Dye**, and then deselect all layers. Collapse the Adjustment and Styles panel group if necessary to see all of the layers in the Layers panel. See Figure 3-13.

Figure 3-13 **Renaming layers**

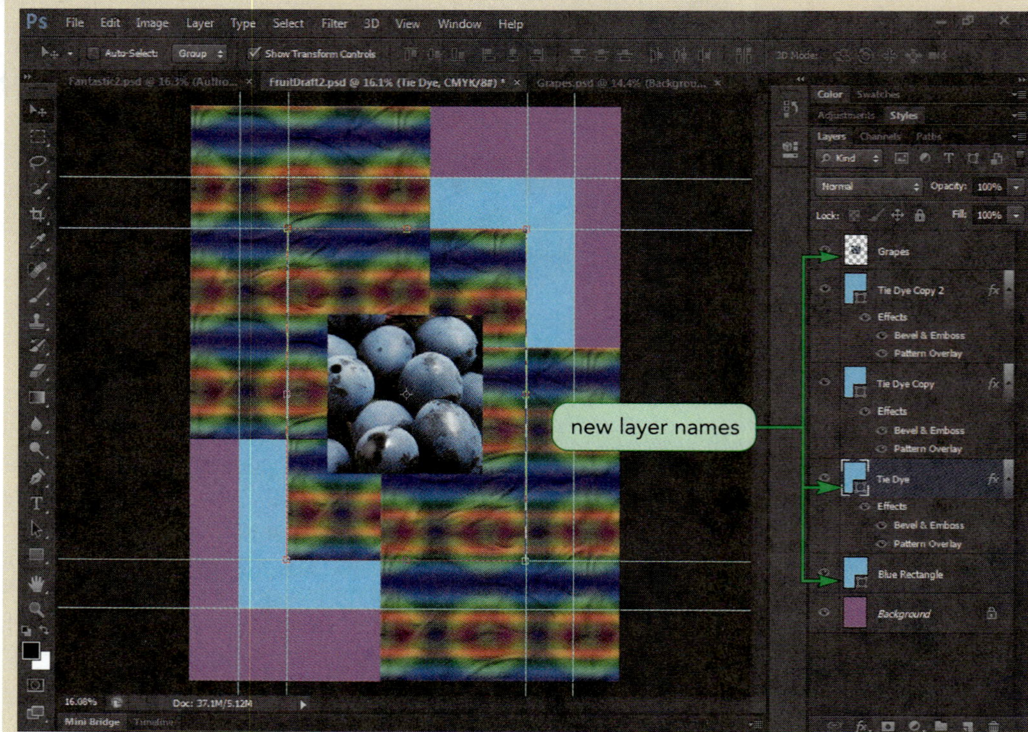

Chianuri/Shutterstock.com

The layers in the Layers panel now have names that help you identify them quickly. Next, you'll assign layer colors to the FruitDraft2.psd file to keep it organized.

To change the color of a layer:

1. In the Layers panel, right-click the **Grapes** layer, and then click **Violet**. Photoshop changes the color of the box in the Show/Hide column in the Layers panel to violet.
2. Change the color of all three Tie Dye layers to **Orange**. Photoshop assigns the orange color to the Tie Dye layers and their associated effects layers.
3. Change the color of the Blue Rectangle layer to **Blue**. See Figure 3-14.

Figure 3-14 **Changing layer colors**

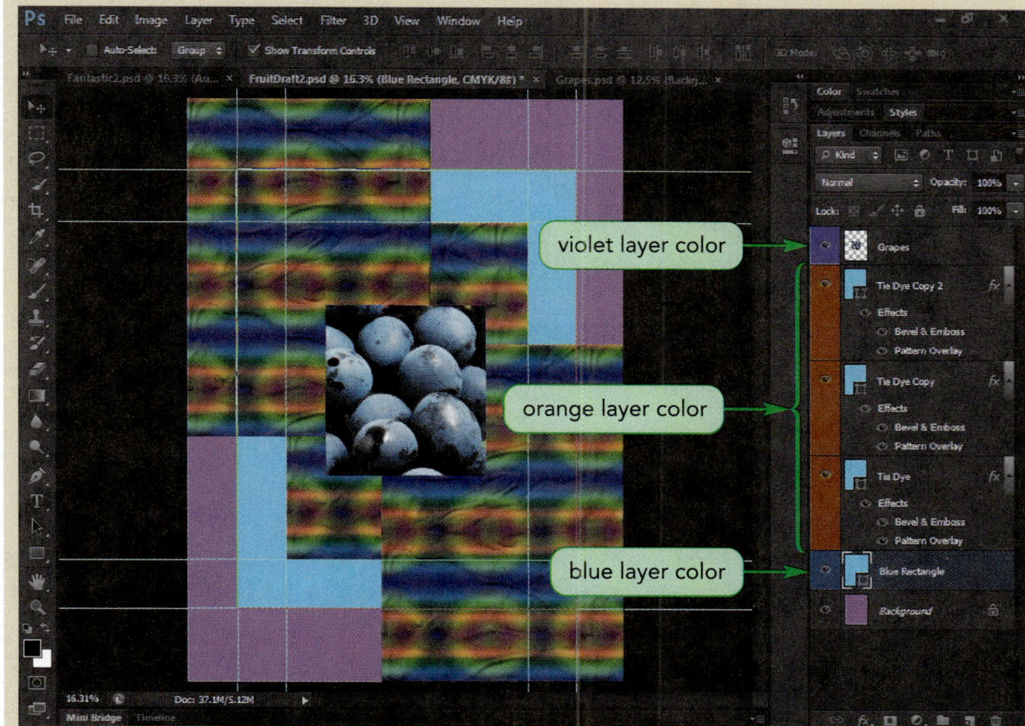

Chianuri/Shutterstock.com

4. Save FruitDraft2.psd in the Photoshop3\Tutorial folder, and then close the file. Close the Grapes.psd file without saving it.

INSIGHT

Keeping the Layers Panel Manageable

If you add many layers to your composition, and apply many adjustments to those layers, the Layers panel might become unwieldy. You can organize your layers by grouping them and color-coding them, but it can be tempting to go overboard when you do. For example, if you have one each of many different kinds of layers (shapes, text, adjustment), you should ask yourself whether it's worth the time and effort to change the color properties or even the names of each layer. Each composition will dictate its own best practice, and as you continue to familiarize yourself with Photoshop, you'll develop the insight you need to be able to determine which tools you should make use of in each situation.

Displaying Layer Edges

It is often helpful to be able to see where a layer begins and ends on the canvas. For some layers, you can see a bounding box when the layer is selected and you turn on the display of transform controls with the Move tool selected. When you select more than one layer, the bounding box expands to encompass the area enclosing all of the layers. When you turn on the display of layer edges, however, each layer selected in the Layers panel is enclosed in its own box in the Document window. To see the boundaries of all of the layers, select them all.

To display layer edges in the Fantastic2.psd file:

1. On the menu bar, click **Select**, and then click **Deselect Layers** to deselect all of the layers of the Fantastic2.psd file, if necessary.

   To make it easier to see the layer edges, you can turn off the Show Transform Controls setting.

2. Press **V** to activate the Move tool, if necessary, and then, on the options bar, click the **Show Transform Controls** check box to deselect it.
3. On the menu bar, click **View**, point to **Show**, and then click **Layer Edges**.
4. Fit the document on the screen if necessary, and then, in the Layers panel, click the **Pears Top** layer to select it.

   Layer edges appear as a blue box around the layer. You might have expected the edges to appear only around the picture of the pears, but the transparent pixels in the layer are also counted within the image boundaries.

5. In the Layers panel, click the **Title: The Fruit Fantastic** layer. Edges appear around the text layer.
6. On the menu bar, click **Select**, and then click **All Layers** to select all of the layers in the document except the Background layer. Photoshop displays the edges of all of the selected layers. See Figure 3-15.

Figure 3-15 Showing layer edges

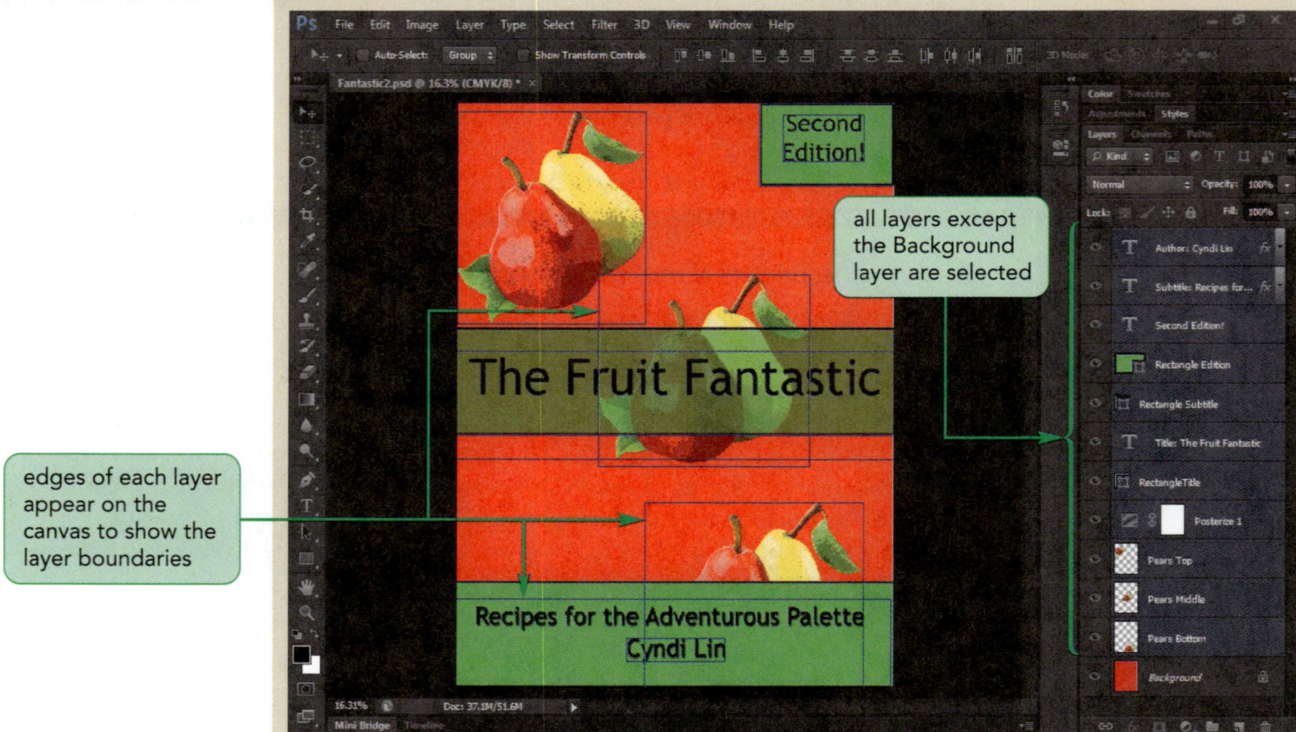

Anna Kucherova/Shutterstock.com

7. On the menu bar, click **View**, point to **Show**, and then click **Layer Edges** to turn off the display of layer edges.

Moving a Layer in the Layers Panel to Change Its Visibility

A layer's position in the Layers panel affects its appearance in the document. If it is near the bottom of the panel, it might be partially or completely hidden on the canvas by the layers above it. If a layer is at the top of the panel, it might obscure the layers underneath it.

REFERENCE

Moving a Layer in the Layers Panel to Change Its Visibility

- In the Layers panel, select a layer.
- Drag the layer down or up in the Layers panel to change its visibility on the canvas.

or

- On the menu bar, click Layer, click Arrange, and then click Bring to Front, Bring Forward, Send Backward, or Send to Back to change the position of the selected layer in the Layers panel. You can also click Reverse to reverse the order of two or more selected layers.

Kaye suggests that you experiment with the position of the layers in the Layers panel in the Fantastic2.psd file to see how changing their visibility affects the overall look of the composition.

TIP

You can also press the Ctrl+[keys to move the layer down or press the Ctrl+] keys to move the layer up in the Layers panel.

To move a layer in the Layers panel to change its visibility:

1. In the Layers panel, click the **Pears Middle** layer, and then drag it up. As you drag, a ghosted image of the Pears Middle layer indicates its new position in the Layers panel.
2. When the **Pears Middle** layer is above the Title: The Fruit Fantastic layer, release the mouse button.

   The Pears Middle layer appears above the Pears Top layer, the RectangleTitle layer, and the Title: The Fruit Fantastic layer in the Layers panel. Because of the change in layer order, the pears now obscure part of the book's title in the document. And because the Pears Middle layer is now also above the Posterize 1 adjustment layer in the Layers panel, it no longer has the Posterize adjustment applied to it. See Figure 3-16.

Figure 3-16 Moving a layer in the Layers panel

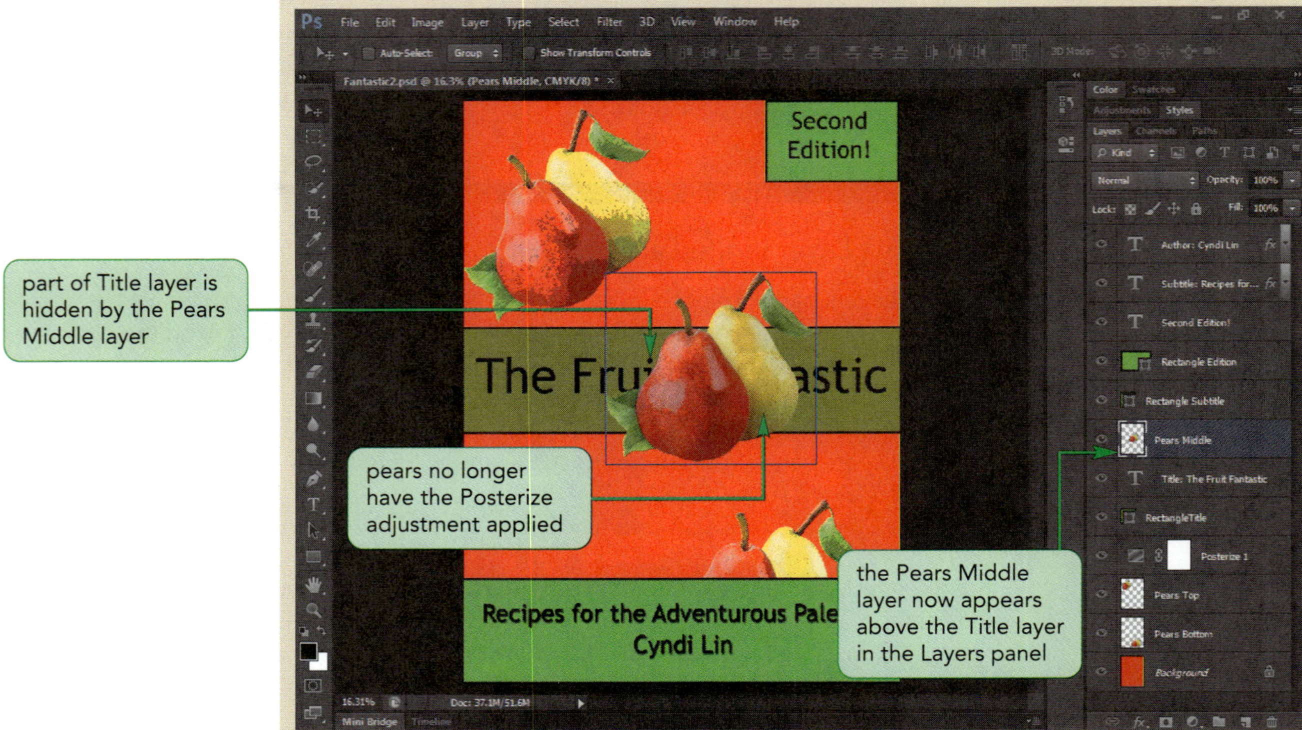

Anna Kucherova/Shutterstock.com

3. On the menu bar, click **Edit**, and then click **Undo Layer Order**. The Pears Middle layer is once again beneath the title, the rectangle, and the Posterize adjustment.
4. Click the **Background** layer and drag it to the top of the Layers panel. As you drag, the mouse pointer changes to the unavailable pointer ⃠, which indicates the action you are trying to perform is not allowed. Because the Background layer is locked, you can't move it—unless you change it to a regular layer.
5. Release the mouse button. The Background layer remains at the bottom of the panel.
6. Drag the **Posterize 1** layer under the Pears Top layer. See Figure 3-17.

Figure 3-17 Dragging an adjustment layer

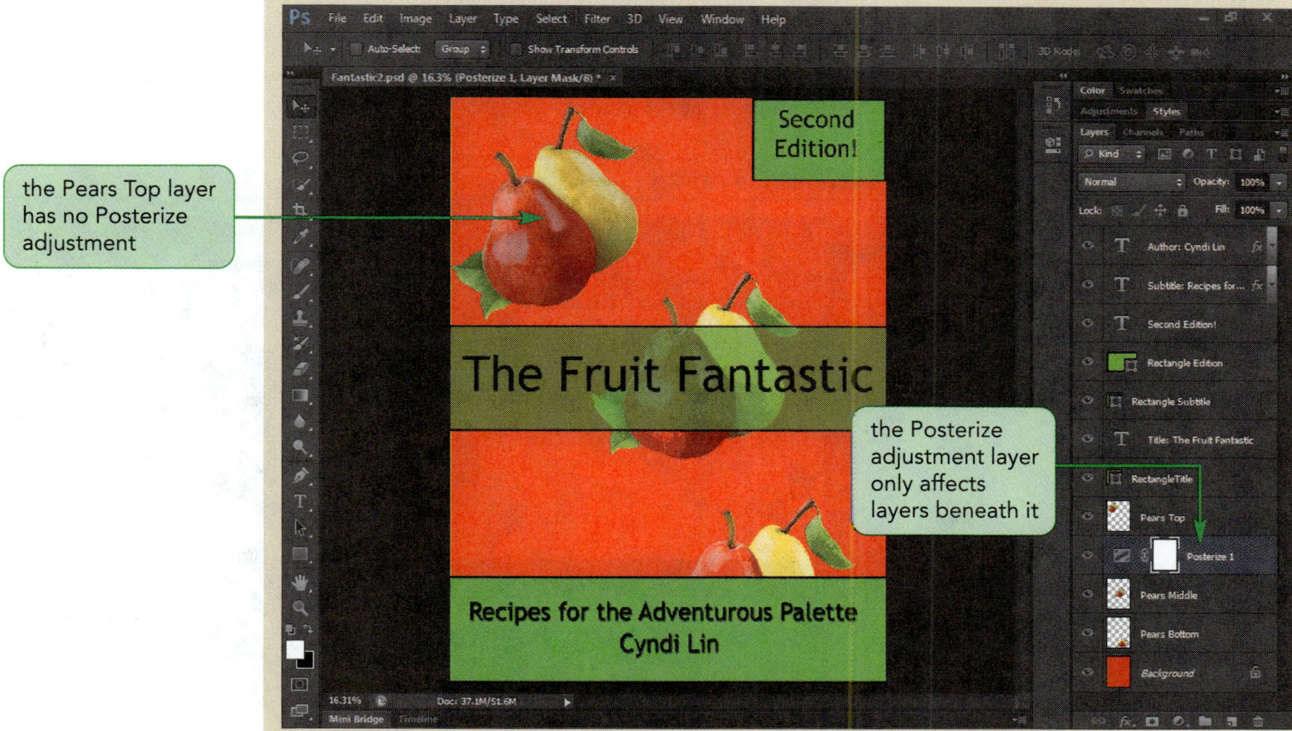

Anna Kucherova/Shutterstock.com

Dragging an adjustment layer changes which layers are affected by the adjustment. The Posterize adjustment is no longer applied to the Pears Top layer because it appears beneath it in the Layers panel. Only the Pears Middle, Pears Bottom, and Background layers are posterized.

7. On the menu bar, click **Edit**, and then click **Undo Layer Order** to move the Posterize 1 layer back to its original position.

Moving a Layer to Change Its Position on the Canvas

You can drag a layer to change its position on the canvas by selecting the layer in the Layers panel and using the Move tool to drag the image, drawing, or text to where you want it to appear on the canvas. If a portion of the layer ends up outside of the canvas area when you reposition it, that part will not show in the final composition and will be cropped when you finalize the image. You'll learn how to finalize an image later in this tutorial.

Kaye asks you to move some of the images on the canvas to see if you can improve the composition.

To move a layer to change its position on the canvas:

1. In the Layers panel, click the **Subtitle** text layer, point to the subtitle (Recipes for the Adventurous Palette) on the canvas, press the mouse button, and drag the text up so it is directly under the title.

2. In the Layers panel, click the **Author: Cyndi Lin** text layer, point to the name on the canvas, and then drag it until it is under the subtitle.
3. In the Layers panel, click the **RectangleTitle** layer, and then on the canvas, drag the green rectangle around the title down so the subtitle and author name also fit in it. See Figure 3-18.

Figure 3-18 Moving layers on the canvas

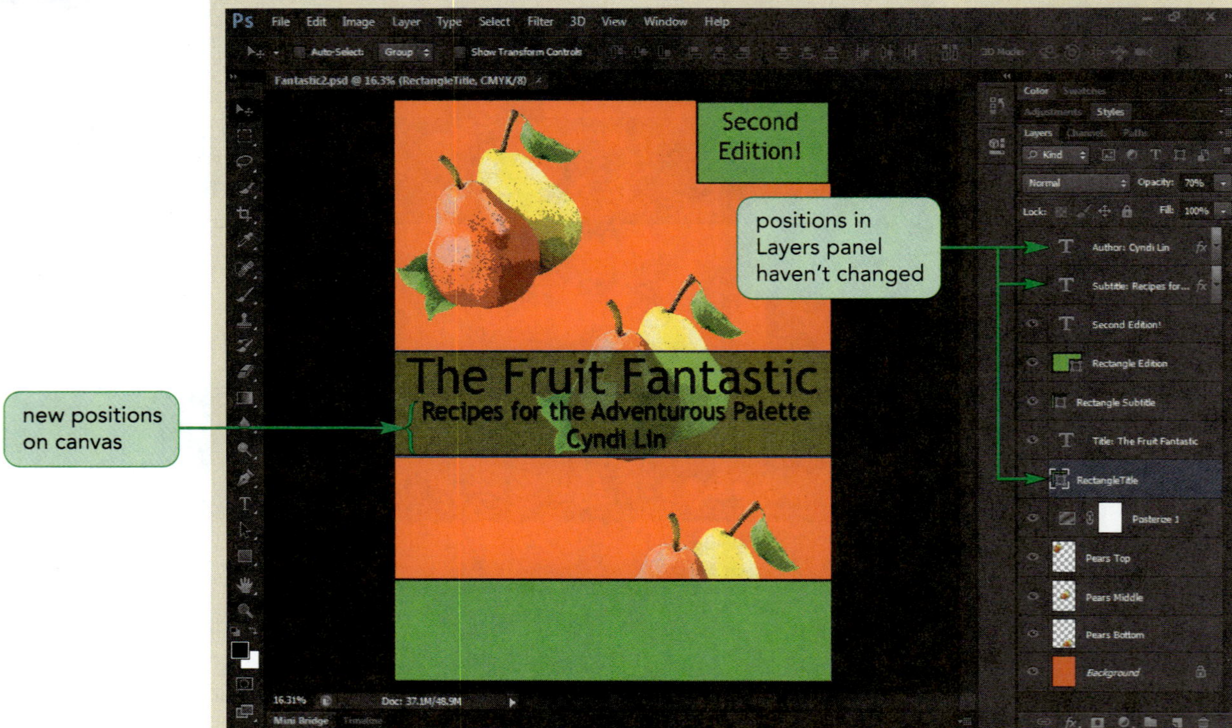

Anna Kucherova/Shutterstock.com

4. Save the file as **Fantastic3.psd** in the Photoshop3\Tutorial folder, and close the file.

Aligning and Distributing Layers

In Tutorial 1, you used the grid and guides to help you align and place images and text in a document. Photoshop offers a number of additional tools to help you align and place objects. To align or distribute selected layers, you can use commands on the Layers menu or icons on the Move tool options bar, shown in Figure 3-19.

Figure 3-19 Alignment and distribution icons and commands

Icon	Command
	Layer, Align, Top Edges
	Layer, Align, Vertical Centers
	Layer, Align, Bottom Edges
	Layer, Align, Left Edges
	Layer, Align, Horizontal Centers
	Layer, Align, Right Edges
	Layer, Distribute, Top Edges
	Layer, Distribute, Vertical Centers
	Layer, Distribute, Bottom Edges
	Layer, Distribute, Left Edges
	Layer, Distribute, Horizontal Centers
	Layer, Distribute, Right Edges

When you align layers, you can line them up along their top, bottom, left, or right edges, or you can align them based on their center points. When you distribute layers, you place them an equal distance apart along either an invisible horizontal or vertical axis.

REFERENCE

Aligning Layers in a Composition

- In the Layers panel, click the layers you want to align.
- On the menu bar, click Layer, point to Align, and then click an alignment option.

or

- With the Move tool selected, click one of the alignment icons on the options bar.

Kaye has given you a file of yellow star fruits on a green background. She'd like to create a logo to put next to any star fruit recipes in the book, but isn't sure how she wants to arrange the images. You'll experiment with aligning them to find the best arrangement.

To align the layers:

1. Open **AlignStars.psd**, located in the Photoshop3\Tutorial folder. Make sure the Move tool 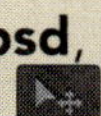 is selected in the Tools panel, and then click the Show Transform Controls check box on the options bar to select it. Turn on Layer Edges.
2. In the Layers panel, select the **Small Star Fruit**, **Medium Star Fruit**, and **Large Star Fruit** layers.

3. On the menu bar, click **Layer**, point to **Align**, and then click **Top Edges**. The top three star fruits are now aligned along the top edges of their layers.
4. In the Layers panel, select the **Small Star Fruit 2**, **Medium Star Fruit 2**, and **Large Star Fruit 2** layers.
5. On the options bar, click the **Align vertical centers** icon. The bottom three star fruits are now aligned along the vertical centers of their layers. See Figure 3-20.

Figure 3-20 Using the alignment options

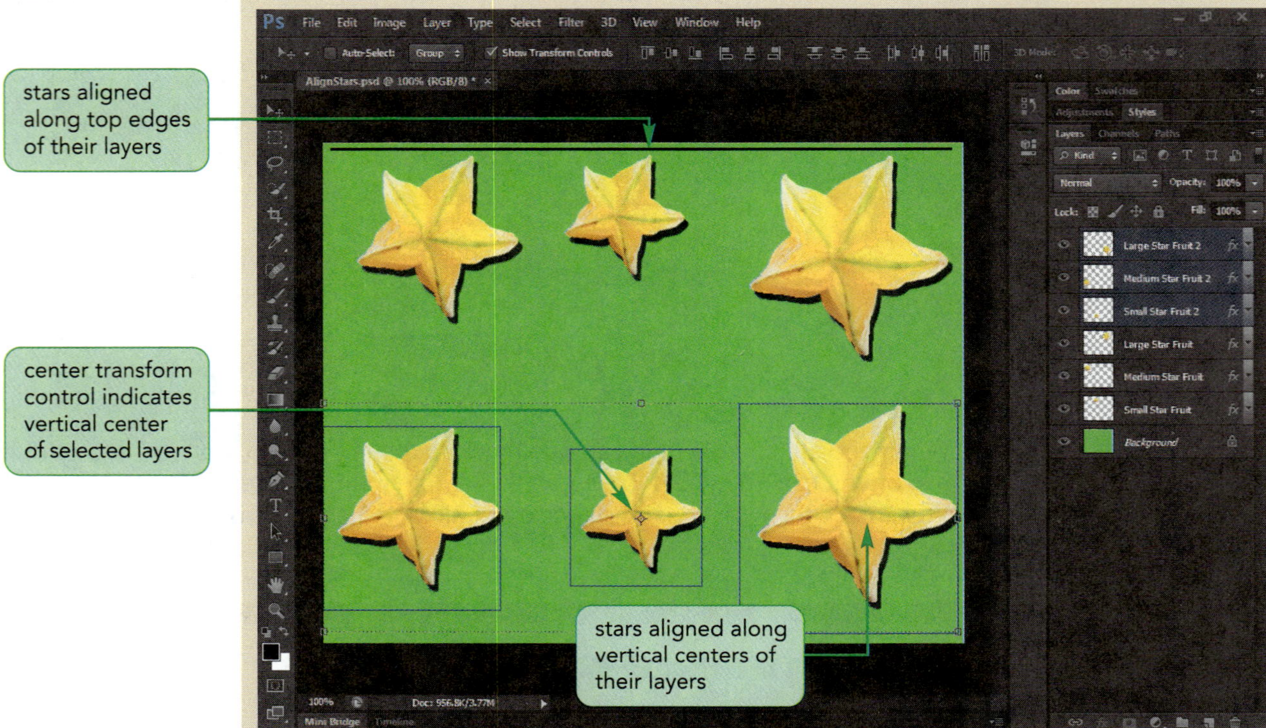

Viktar Malyshchyts/Shutterstock.com

6. Save the file as **StarsAligned.psd** in the Photoshop3\Tutorial folder, and then close the file.

Using the layer alignment options provided in Photoshop ensures that compositions you create are balanced and have the intended visual effect.

REFERENCE

Distributing Layers in a Composition

- In the Layers panel, click the layers you want to distribute. You must select at least three layers to distribute them.
- On the menu bar, click Layer, point to Distribute, and then click a distribute option.

or

- With the Move tool selected, click one of the distribute icons on the options bar.

Kaye has also given you a different star fruit file to see if you can come up with an idea for a logo to highlight or distinguish different elements in the book. This file includes three of the same size star fruits. You'll distribute them to see if the result is acceptable.

To distribute the star fruit layers:

1. Open **DistributeStars.psd**, located in the Photoshop3\Tutorial folder.
2. In the Layers panel, click the **Star Fruit 1** layer, press and hold the **Shift** key, and then click the **Star Fruit 3** layer to select all three Star Fruit layers.
3. On the menu bar, click **Layer**, point to **Distribute**, and then click **Vertical Centers**. Photoshop distributes the star fruits so they are evenly spaced.
4. Save the file as **StarsDistributed.psd** in the Photoshop3\Tutorial folder, and then close the file.

You'll show this image to Kaye for possible use on the chapter opener page for the star fruit recipes in the book or in the table of contents alongside the start fruit chapter title and contents.

Kaye has created another possible cover for *The Fruit Fantastic* book; this file contains even more layers and images in the composition. She wants you to decide whether the composition works with all of the different layers, or if some of the image layers should be deleted.

Hiding and Redisplaying Layers

In the Layers panel, the Eye icon in the Show/Hide column indicates that a layer is currently visible in the document. If you click the Eye icon, the icon disappears, and the layer is hidden on the canvas. If you click in the column again, the Eye icon reappears and the layer is redisplayed in the Document window.

To hide and redisplay a layer:

1. Open **FruitFantastic2.psd**, located in the Phostoshop3\Tutorial folder, and fit it on the screen. This file includes multiple images of fruit, three text layers, two shape layers, and a Posterize adjustment layer.
2. In the Layers panel, scroll down to the bottom of the list of layers, and then click the **Eye** icon in the Show/Hide column to the left of the Pears Middle layer. The Eye icon disappears, and the layer no longer appears on the canvas.
3. Click the empty **Eye** icon box in the Show/Hide column to the left of the Pears Middle layer. The Eye icon reappears and the middle photo of the pears reappears on the canvas.
4. In the Layers panel, click the **Eye** icon to the left of the Posterize 1 layer. The Eye icon disappears, and the posterize adjustment no longer affects the layers beneath it.
5. Click the empty **Eye** icon box . The Eye icon reappears and the Posterize adjustment is once again applied to the layers beneath it.

You can hide all of the layers but one by pressing and holding the Alt key and then clicking the Eye icon for the layer you want to stay visible. Photoshop hides all layers but the one you click. If you press and hold the Alt key and click the icon again, Photoshop redisplays the hidden layers. This is very convenient if you want to focus only on a single layer—to make detailed pixel corrections, for example, or to make a careful selection.

Next, you'll hide all of the layers except the Pears Middle layer.

To hide all but one layer and then redisplay all layers:

1. Click the **Pears Middle** layer, if necessary, press and hold the **Alt** key, and then click the **Eye** icon for the Pears Middle layer. All of the layers are hidden except the Pears Middle layer. See Figure 3-21.

Figure 3-21 **Hiding all but one layer**

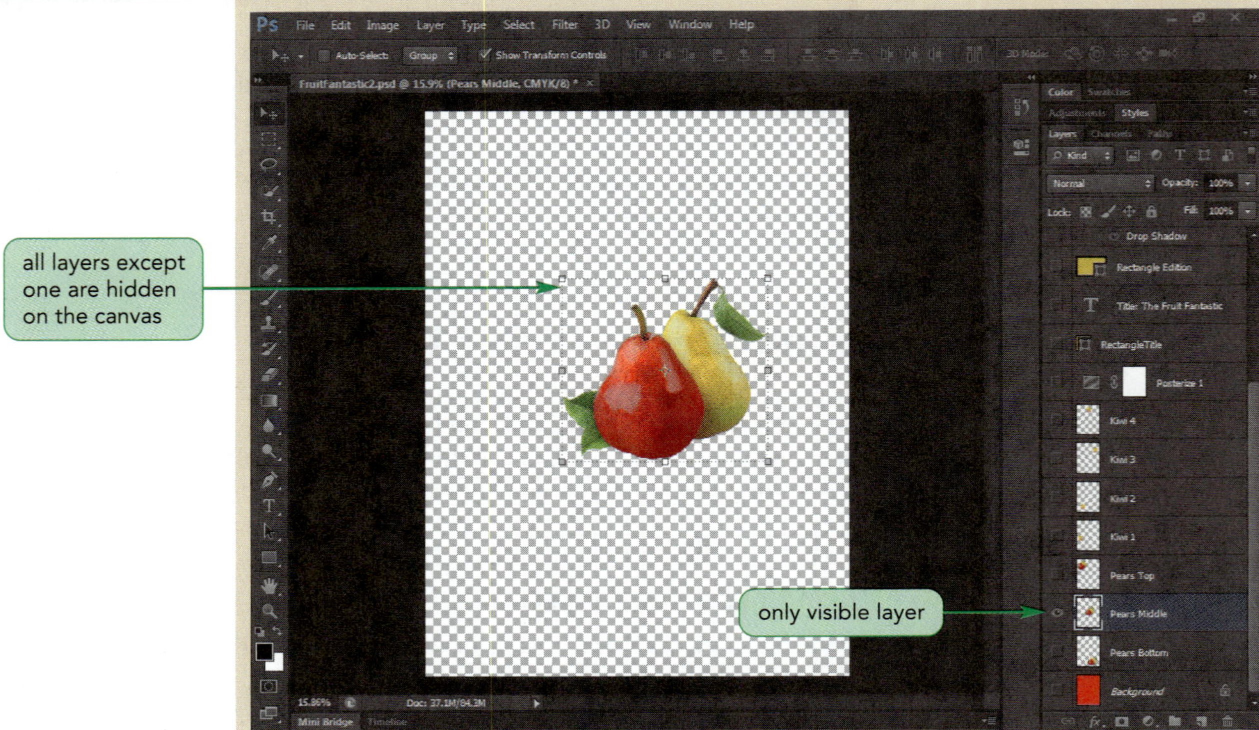

Anna Kucherova/Shutterstock.com

2. Alt-click the **Eye** icon to the left of the Pears Middle layer. The rest of the layers are redisplayed in the panel and on the canvas.

You can also drag down the Show/Hide column in the Layers panel. As you drag, the Eye icon for each layer disappears and the layer is hidden. To redisplay all of the layers, you can drag back over the column and the Eye icons reappear.

To hide and redisplay layers by dragging:

1. In the Layers panel, scroll up to the top of the list of layers, point to the **Eye** icon for the Author: Cyndi Lin layer, press and hold the mouse button, drag down the Show/Hide column to the Background layer, and then release the mouse button. All of the layers are hidden.

2. Point to the Show/Hide column to the left of the Background layer, press and hold the mouse button, drag up the column to the Author: Cyndi Lin layer, and then release the mouse button. All of the layers are redisplayed.

Now that Kaye has seen what the composition looks like with some of the layers hidden, she wants you to hide and then delete some layers so that they will no longer be saved with the file.

Deleting a Layer

One of the benefits of working with layers is that you can experiment with many different images, vector objects, and adjustments in the same composition, and then hide them, move them, and redisplay them to judge their effect. However, eventually you'll want your image to include only the layers that you want in the final composition. If you have added an adjustment, an image, or a vector object that you decide you no longer want to include, you can delete it from the Layers panel, which deletes it from the document.

To delete a layer:

1. In the Layers panel, scroll down, click the **Posterize 1** layer, and then press the **Delete** key. Photoshop deletes the adjustment layer without prompting you for confirmation.
2. Click the **Pears Middle** layer, and then click the **Delete layer** icon at the bottom of the Layers panel. Photoshop prompts you to confirm the deletion.
3. Click the **Yes** button to confirm the deletion. Photoshop deletes the Pears Middle layer. Save the file as **FruitFantastic3.psd** in the Photoshop3\Tutorial folder, and then close it.

Placing, Resizing, and Positioning an Image on a Layer

As you saw in Tutorial 2, you can place an image in a file to add it to your composition. When you place an image, Photoshop places the image on a new layer, positioned in the center of the canvas. The placed image is bounded by a box, and has diagonal lines running from corner to corner through a center point. You can use the options bar to change the placement and size of the image, as well as the angle at which it is rotated on the canvas. When you are satisfied with the placement of an image, you can click the Commit button on the options bar. See Figure 3-22.

Figure 3-22 **Placing an image**

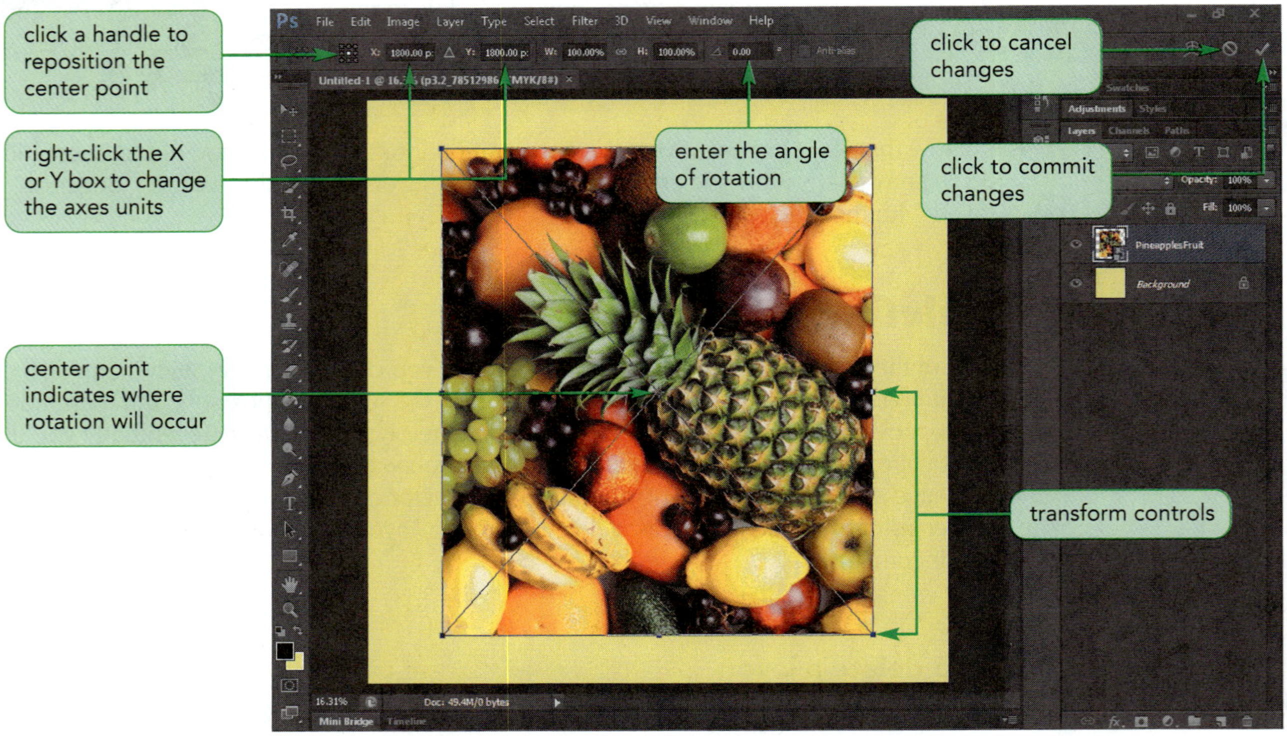

Shutter Lover/Shutterstock.com

In Photoshop, the **center point** is the point at which a placed image will rotate if you change its angle on the canvas. By default, the center point is located in the exact center of the image, but you can change its location by clicking a handle on the Center Point icon on the options bar, or by dragging the center point to a new location.

When you place an image, make sure it is the same resolution as the file into which you're placing it, or you'll see unexpected results. For example, a low-resolution file placed in a high-resolution file will be very small on the canvas, and a high-resolution file placed in a low-resolution file will be very large.

Kaye wants you to set up a chapter opener page for the section on citrus recipes. You'll place an image of oranges and kiwis on the canvas, and then you'll size and rotate it.

To place the image:

1. Open **CitrusRecipes.psd**, located in the Photoshop3\Tutorial folder.
2. On the menu bar, click **File**, and then click **Place**.
3. In the Place dialog box, select **Citrus.jpg**, located in the Photoshop3\Tutorial folder, and then click **Place**. Photoshop places the image in the center of the canvas.

   Right now, the image fills the entire canvas. See Figure 3-23.

Do not press the Enter key after you place the file. Doing so will place the image in the file without giving you any options to transform it or modify its placement.

Figure 3-23 Options bar for placing an image

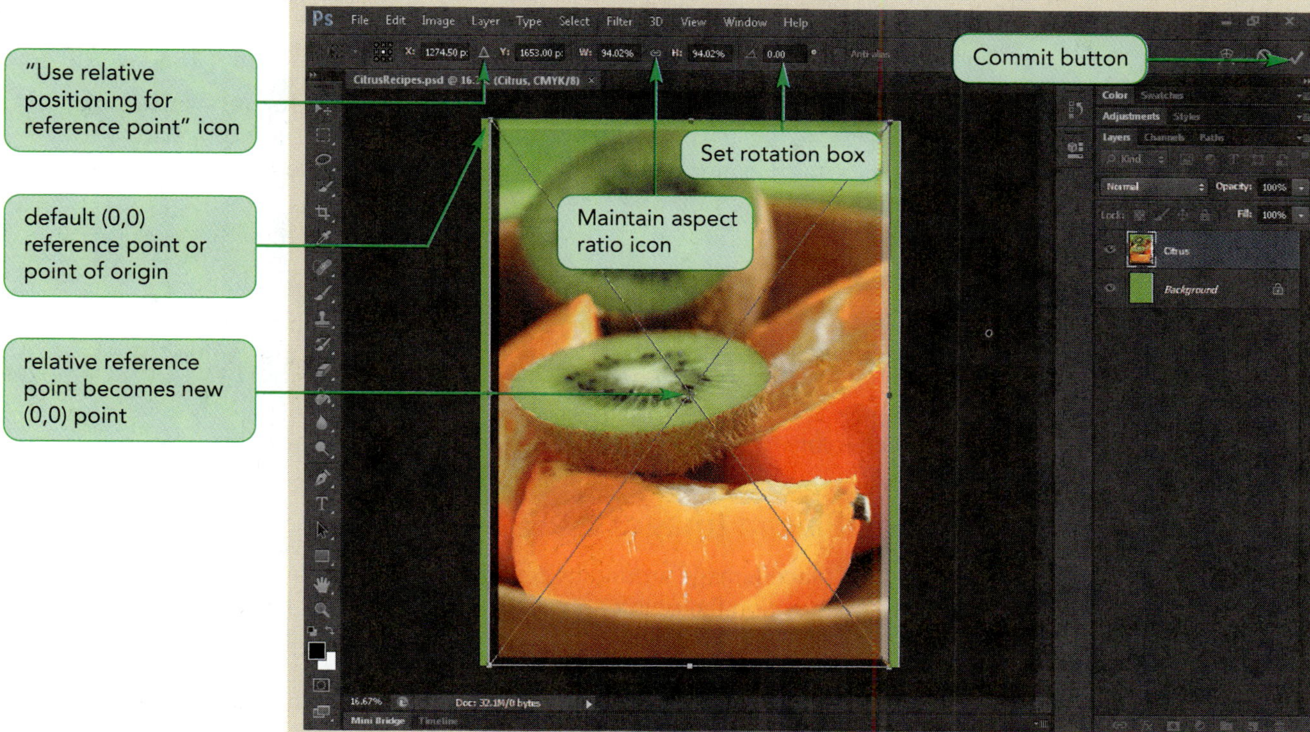

grintan/Shutterstock.com

You can resize a placed image using the width and height options on the options bar. To ensure that the image does not become distorted when you resize it, you need to maintain the aspect ratio. The **aspect ratio** is the relationship between the width and the height of an image. If the height of an image is two times greater than the width, it will still be two times greater than the width if you maintain the aspect ratio when resizing the image.

TIP

You can also press the Shift key while dragging a transform control to maintain the aspect ratio when resizing an image.

To resize the placed image:

1. On the options bar, click the **Maintain aspect ratio** icon to select it.
2. In the W box on the options bar, highlight the current value, type **50**, and then press the **Enter** key. You changed the width of the image to 50% of its original width, and because you chose to maintain the aspect ratio, the height of the image is also set to 50%.

To reposition a placed image, you can point inside the image with the mouse and drag the image to where you want it on the canvas. However, to place the image exactly, you can use the reference point on the canvas and the X, Y settings on the options bar.

The **reference point** is located at the (0,0) point on invisible x- and y-axes and is the point from which Photoshop will measure any change in position. If you have worked with graphs, you know that the (0,0) point is also called the origin. By default, Photoshop places the reference point in the upper-left corner of the document, as indicated in Figure 3-23. (This is also where it places the 0 mark on the rulers.) However, if you select the Use relative positioning for reference point icon on the options bar, the center point of the placed file becomes the new reference point.

To allow room for text to be added to the bottom of the chapter opener, Kaye suggests you move the image up one inch.

To reposition the placed image:

1. On the options bar, click the **Use relative positioning for reference point** icon to select it. The X and Y boxes on the options bar both change to zero values, indicating that the center point of the placed file is the new origin or reference point.
2. Right-click the **Y** box and then click **Inches** on the context menu to select it, if necessary.
3. In the Y box on the options bar, highlight the current value, type **-1**, and then press the **Enter** key. The image moves up one inch on the canvas.

Next, you'll rotate the placed image to see if that improves the effect.

Rotating a Placed Image

You can rotate a placed image around its center point in two ways. To rotate an image using the mouse, position the pointer outside of the image until it changes to a curved arrow, and then drag in the direction you want to rotate the image. This is called a **free transform** rotation. You can constrain a free transform rotation to 15-degree increments by pressing and holding the Shift key as you drag. You can also type a value for the rotation in the Rotation box on the options bar.

To rotate a placed image:

1. Place the mouse pointer outside of the image on the upper-right corner of the canvas until it turns into the rotate pointer.
2. Press and hold the **Shift** key and drag counterclockwise until the Set rotation box on the options bar reads -30.00.

   You can also rotate the image by an exact amount by entering the degrees rotation in the Set rotation box on the options bar.
3. In the Set rotation box on the options bar, select the value and then type **45**. The image rotates 45 degrees clockwise from its original position.
4. On the options bar, click the **Commit** button.
5. Save the file as **CitrusRecipes2.psd** in the Photoshop3\Tutorial folder, and then close the file and exit Photoshop.

The cover you've started has a completely different look than the covers you worked on previously, but it's an interesting one. Kaye would like you to present this possible cover image along with the other covers you've been working on at the next staff meeting so she can decide how to proceed with the book design.

You've spent a lot of time working with layers and should now have a good understanding of their benefits. You have also learned how nondestructive editing works in a Photoshop file. In the next session, you'll continue to work with and finalize the layers in the files that Kaye has given you, and you'll create some files of your own.

REVIEW

Session 3.1 Quick Check

1. What is nondestructive editing?
2. True or False. Adjustments in the Adjustments panel directly affect the image pixels.
3. A checkerboard display on the canvas or in a thumbnail in Photoshop is an indication of ______________ pixels.
4. True or False. When an adjustment is clipped to the layer beneath it, it affects all of the layers in the composition.
5. In Photoshop, the selected layer is also called the ______________ layer.
6. True or False. The Background layer is locked by default.
7. To move a layer on the canvas, you must first ______________ it in the Layers panel.
8. What does it mean to distribute layers?

SESSION 3.2 VISUAL OVERVIEW

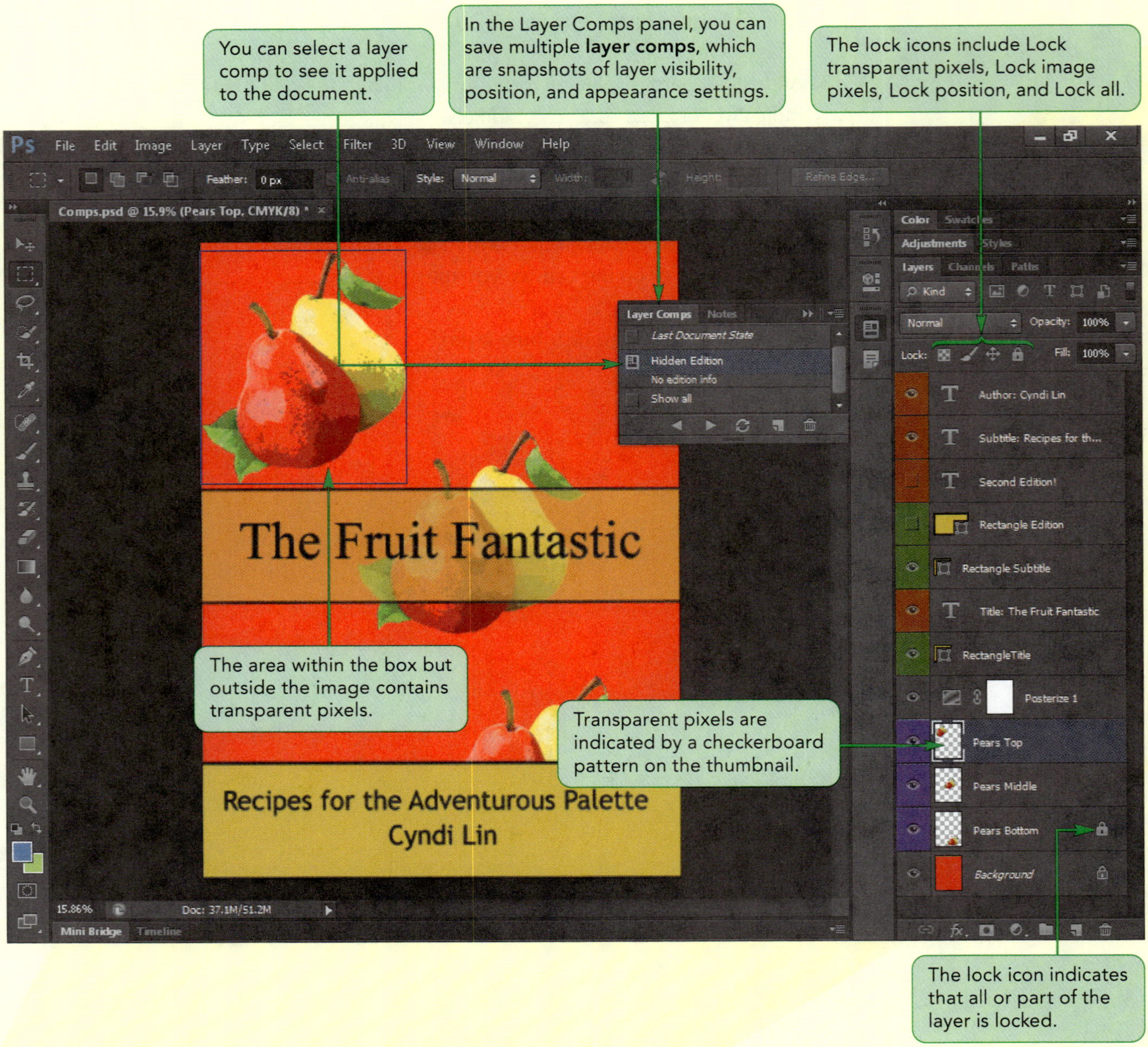

Anna Kucherova/Shutterstock.com

BLENDING AND FINALIZING LAYERS

The star fruit image is blended with the night sky image beneath it.

Blending modes are listed in the Layers panel; **blending modes** determine how the colors in a layer **blend**, or interact, with the colors in the layers beneath that layer.

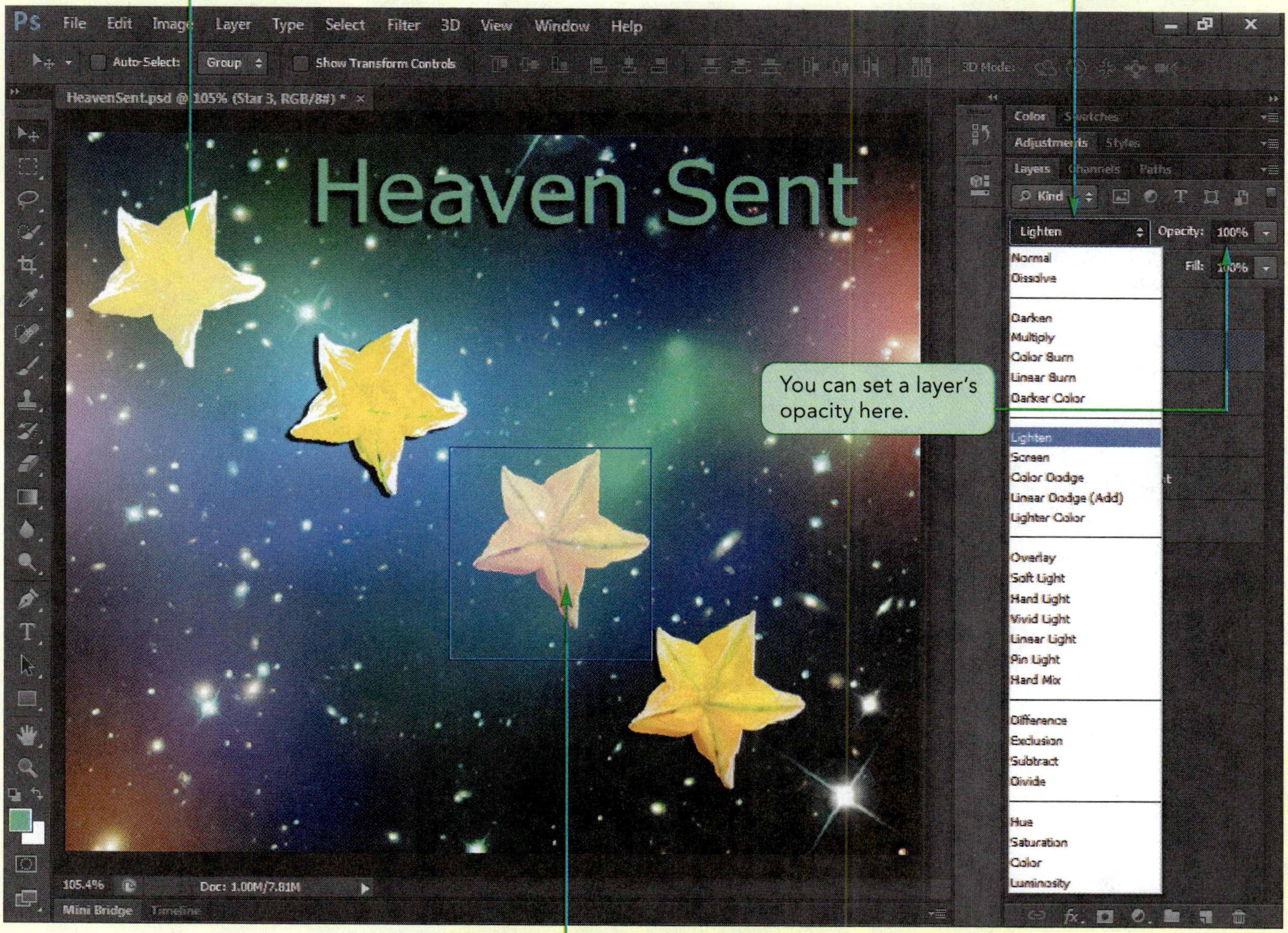

You can set a layer's opacity here.

Each star fruit layer has a different blending mode applied; each mode is determined by a different mathematical **algorithm**, or formula.

Viktar Malyshchyts/Shutterstock.com; NASA

Locking and Unlocking Layer Content

After you have finished working with a layer, it is a good idea to lock it so you don't make any unintended changes to that layer. When locking a layer, you can choose among four options:

- You can lock the transparent pixels so nothing can be added in those areas.
- You can lock the image pixels so the image itself cannot be altered.
- You can lock a layer in position so it cannot be moved or resized.
- You can lock the entire layer: transparent pixels, image pixels, and image position.

To lock a layer, you select it, and then click one of the lock icons at the top of the Layers panel. See Figure 3-24.

Figure 3-24 Locking layer content

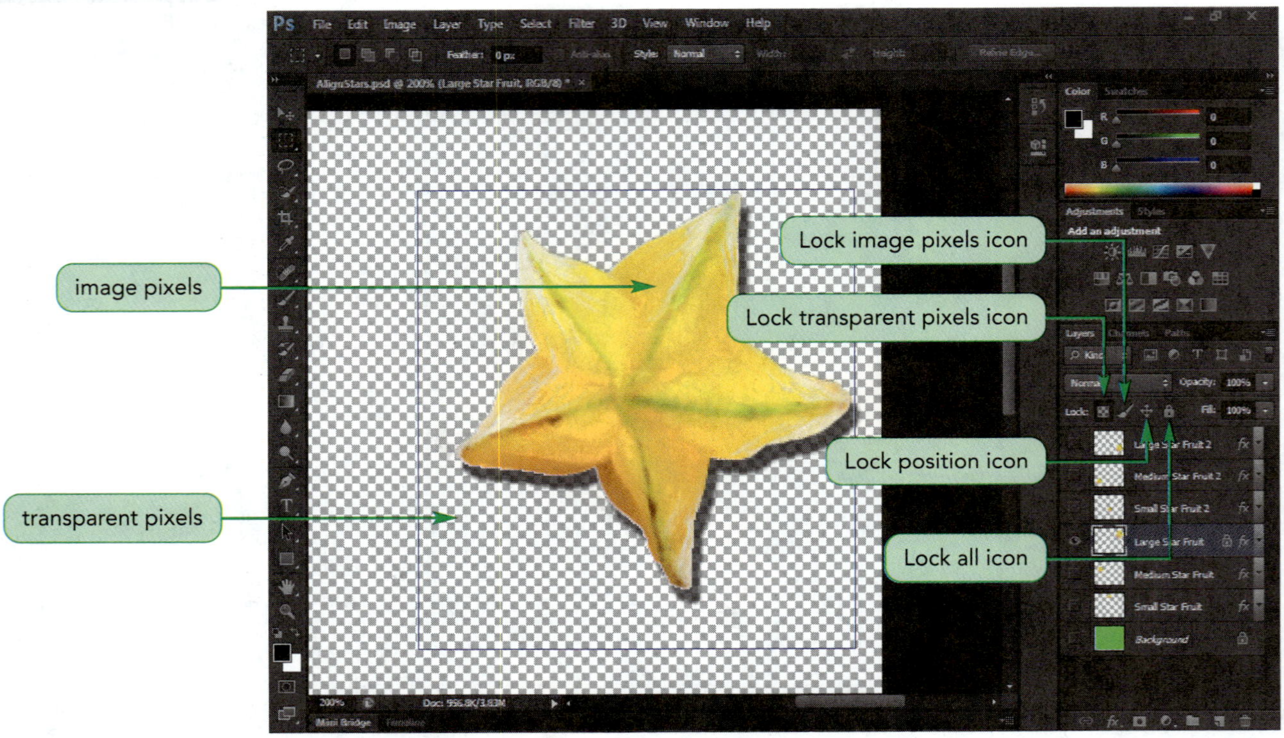

Viktar Malyshchyts/Shutterstock.com

You'll practice locking image pixels and position so you're prepared to work with and manipulate multiple layers in any future compositions you create for Kaye.

To lock pixels and position:

1. Start Photoshop while pressing the **Ctrl+Alt+Shift** keys, and click **Yes** to delete the Settings File when prompted. Reset Photoshop to the default Essentials workspace layout, and reset all tools.
2. Open **AlignStars.psd**, located in the Photoshop3\Tutorial folder, and then, in the Layers panel, click the **Large Star Fruit** layer.
3. On the menu bar, click **View**, point to **Show**, and then click **Layer Edges** to turn on the display of layer edges, and then zoom in and pan so the large star fruit is centered in the Document window.

4. Hide all of the other layers, and then in the Layers panel, click the **Lock transparent pixels** icon. The transparent pixels in the layer are now locked, but the image pixels are not.

   To see what it means to lock transparent pixels, you'll paint across the image area on the canvas using the Brush tool.

5. In the Tools panel, click the **Brush Tool** button, and then press the **D** key to reset the foreground and background colors to the default colors (black and white), if necessary.
6. On the options bar, click the **Brush Preset picker** button, click the second preset (**Hard Round**), and then type **50** in the Size box.
7. Point to the lower-left corner of the star fruit image area (within the Layer edges), press and hold the mouse button, and then drag to the upper-right corner of the image area. See Figure 3-25.

Figure 3-25 **Locking transparent pixels**

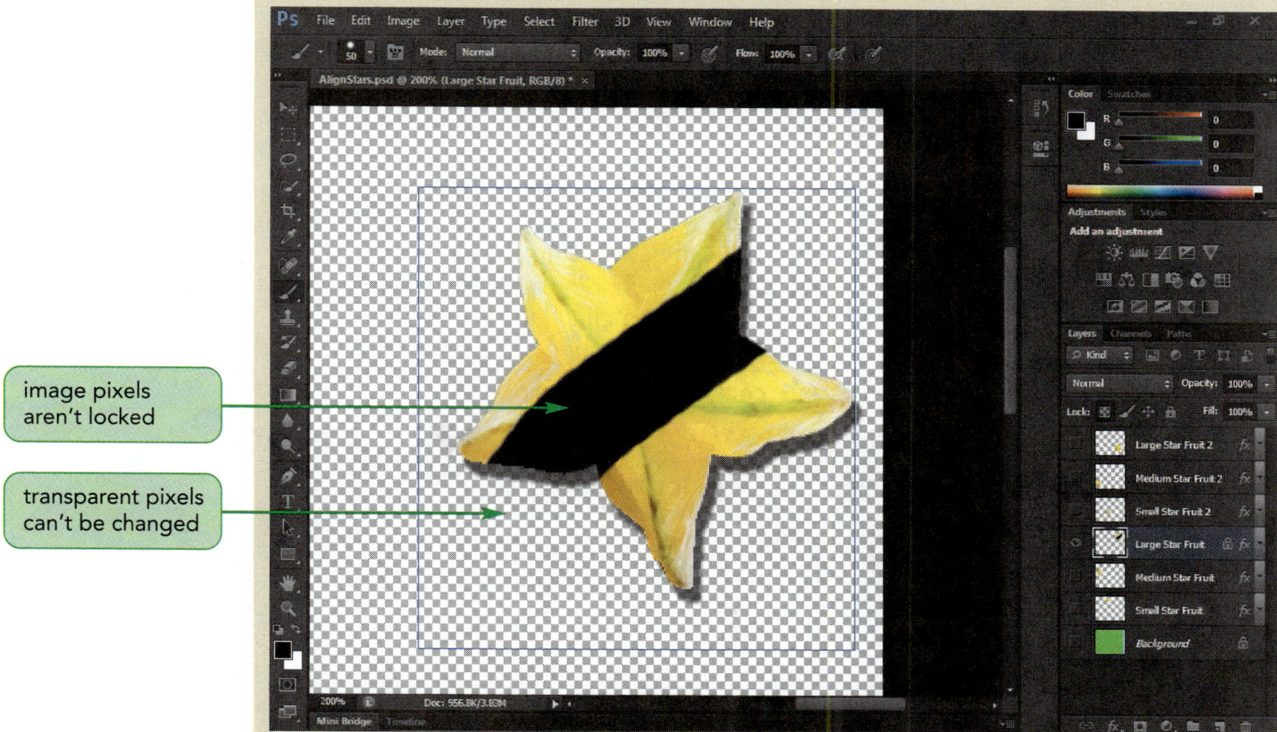

Viktar Malyshchyts/Shutterstock.com

   Although you painted a brushstroke across the entire image, including transparent pixels, the brushstroke only appears on the star fruit, not on the locked transparent pixels.

8. Click the **Small Star Fruit** layer and unhide it, and then zoom out to 100%.
9. In the Layers panel, click the **Lock image pixels** icon.
10. Use the Brush tool to try to paint across the Small Star Fruit image. A dialog box opens, informing you that you can't complete the operation. You can't paint any part of the selected layer because the image pixels are locked. Click the **OK** button to close the dialog box.
11. Select and unhide the **Medium Star Fruit** layer, and then in the Layers panel, click the **Lock position** icon.

12. Press the **V** key to activate the Move tool, and then try to drag **Medium Star Fruit** to the right on the canvas. A dialog box opens with a message that says you can't complete the operation. You can't drag the layer because its position has been locked.
13. Click the **OK** button to close the dialog box.
14. Select the Brush tool again, and paint from one point of the Medium Star Fruit to another on the canvas. Because you only locked the layer's position, not the pixels, you can still paint over the pixels.
15. Click the **Background** layer. Notice that the Background layer is locked by default.
16. Save the file as **Locked.psd** in the Photoshop3\Tutorial folder, and close the file.

Kaye suggests that you learn about layer comps so you can present a few of your ideas to her at your next meeting using a single file.

Working with Layer Comps

One of the greatest benefits of layers in Photoshop is that they give you the ability to store and experiment with many different versions of a composition in a single file using layer comps. A **comp**, short for *composition*, is a mock-up or sketch of what a final design will look like. A layer comp is the electronic version of a graphic designer's comp. A Photoshop file can have multiple layer comps. You can use layer comps to save different draft versions of your layout before deciding on a final version or as a way to present several ideas to a client. See Figure 3-26.

Figure 3-26 Working with layer comps

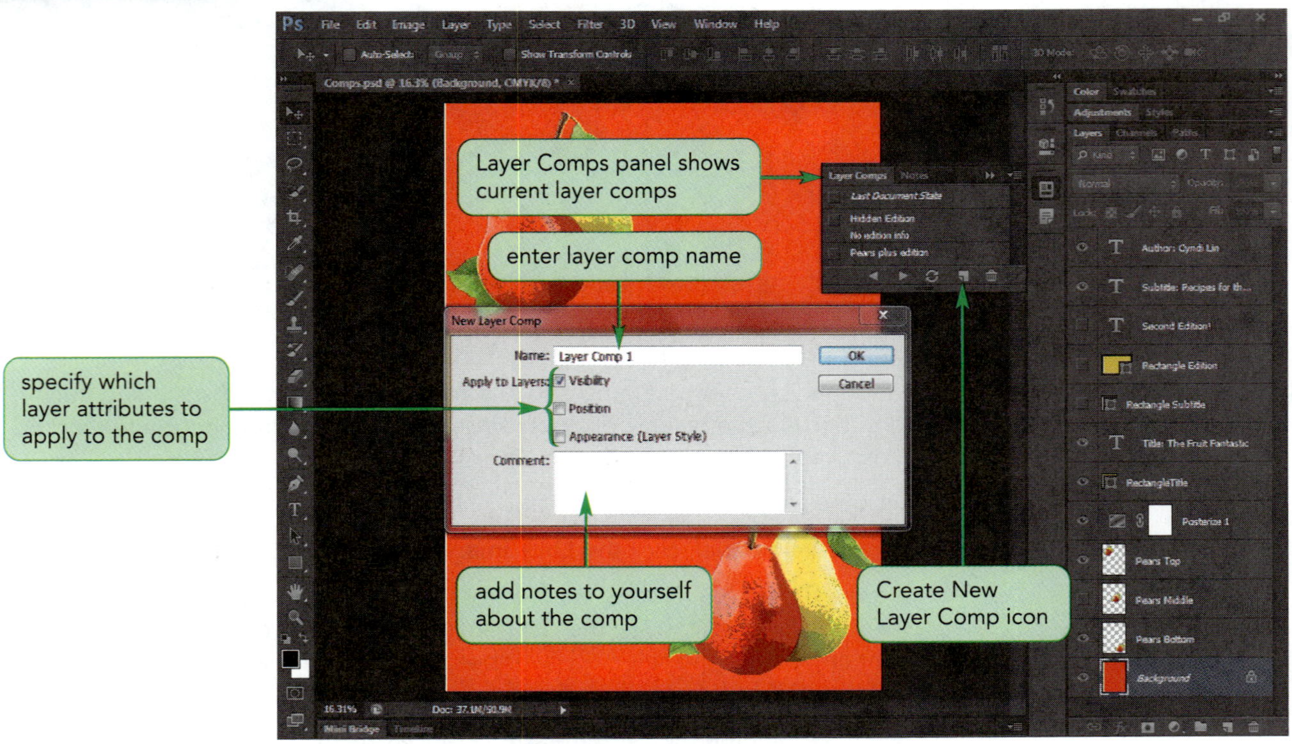

Anna Kucherova/ Shutterstock.com

In the New Layer Comp dialog box, you can give the composition a descriptive name and select the elements you want Photoshop to consider when creating the comp, including Visibility, Position, and Appearance (also called Layer Style). You can also add a comment to help you remember details about the comp—for example, notes on why you think a particular layer comp might be a good choice for the final composition, questions you might have for the client about the composition, or information about related comps.

To create a layer comp:

1. Open **FruitFantastic.psd**, located in the Photoshop3\Tutorial folder, fit the image on the screen, reset all tools, and collapse the Color and Adjustments panel groups.
2. Hide the **Second Edition!** Layer and the **Rectangle Edition** layer.
3. On the menu bar, click **Window**, and then click **Layer Comps** to open the Layer Comps panel.
4. At the bottom of the Layer Comps panel, click the **Create New Layer Comp** icon. The New Layer Comp dialog box opens.
5. In the Name box of the New Layer Comp dialog box, type **Hidden Edition**. Click the Visibility, Position, and Appearance (Layer Style) check boxes to select them, if necessary.
6. In the Comment box, type **No edition info**, and then click the **OK** button. The dialog box closes and Photoshop displays the new layer comp layout.

   Next, you'll redisplay all of the layers, and create a new layer comp called *All Visible*.
7. In the Layers panel, unhide the **Second Edition!** Layer and the **Rectangle Edition** layer.
8. At the bottom of the Layer Comps panel, click the **Create New Layer Comp** icon. Name the layer comp **All Visible**, and then click the **OK** button.

Next, you'll switch back to the Hidden Edition layer comp to see if you prefer that layout for the book cover.

To apply a layer comp to a file:

1. In the Layer Comps panel, click to the left of Hidden Edition to display that layout. See Figure 3-27.

Figure 3-27 Switching to a different layer comp

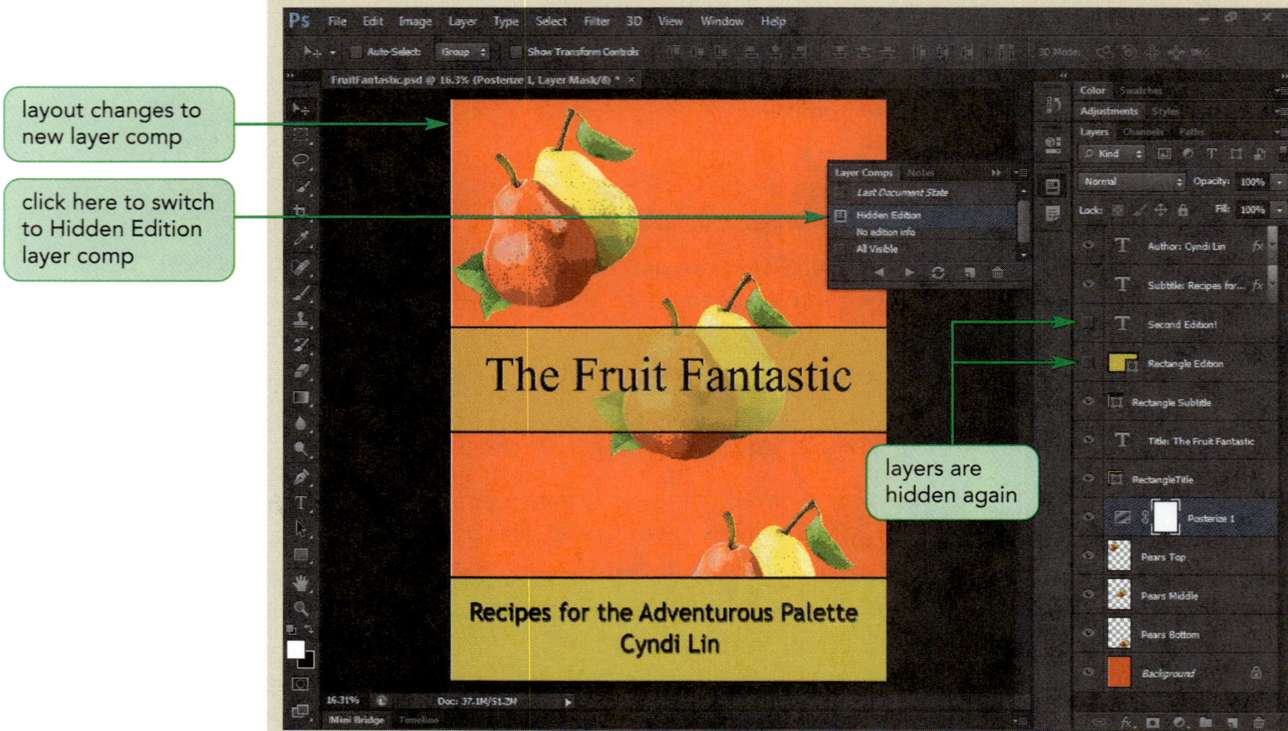

Anna Kucherova/Shutterstock.com

2. In the Layer Comps panel, click the **Apply Previous Selected Layer Comp** icon to display the **All Visible** layer comp.

After Kaye reviews your work, she decides that the layout of the Hidden Edition layer comp won't work for the cover, so you'll delete it from the file.

To delete a layer comp:

1. In the Layer Comps panel, click the **Hidden Edition** layer comp in the Layer Comps panel, and then click the **Delete Layer Comp** icon at the bottom of the Layer Comps panel.
2. Close the Layer Comps panel group.
3. Save the file as **Comps.psd** in the Photoshop3\Tutorial folder, and then close the file.

PROSKILLS

Teamwork: Using Layer Comps to Collaborate

If you work on a creative team that collaborates, layer comps can be a great tool to help you generate a final version of a composition. For example, team members can use the Comment field in a layer comp to critique a particular layout and make suggestions for improving it. They can also add text layers to a composition that include critiques or suggestions, or draw arrows and other vector objects to point out areas of the composition they would like to see changed. You can view their feedback by saving a layer comp with the comment layers visible, and then hiding the comments in a different layer comp. Alternatively, each team member can save a layer comp with his or her name in order to show the group their preferred layout, and the team can review the different options by selecting and then discussing each layer comp.

Reviewing a single file using various layer comps keeps your team's work in a single location and avoids any problems you might have with version control. Once the team has made its final decisions, you can delete any unnecessary layers and finalize the file. By using layer comps to collaborate with team members, you can create a final file that is the best it can be.

Now that you have spent some time working with layer comps, Kaye would like you to try to improve some of your compositions by experimenting with blending modes and opacity.

Working with Blending Modes and Opacity

As you have seen, the order of layers in the Layers panel affects how each layer appears in your composition. You can also change how a layer appears by blending it with the layer or layers beneath it to achieve an interesting effect. Photoshop comes with numerous blending modes.

You can also apply different opacity settings to an image to achieve additional effects. A setting of 100% means that a layer is completely opaque and nothing will show through. The lower the setting, the more transparent the layer becomes. An Opacity setting of 0% means that a layer is completely transparent.

Applying Blending Modes

When you apply a blending mode to a layer, you are specifying that you want the colors in the layer you are working with to interact in some way with all of the colors in the layers beneath it. When you work with blending modes, it helps to think of each different mode as a new experiment—such as in a chemistry class. Each mode blends the chemicals (or layer colors) of all of the layers together in a way that's unpredictable until you actually put them in the test tube and shake (apply the mode). If you make even the slightest change to one of the layers in the blend—for example, by modifying its color slightly, you have changed the chemicals in the test tube and will see a different result. See Figure 3-28.

Figure 3-28 **Different blending modes applied to same object**

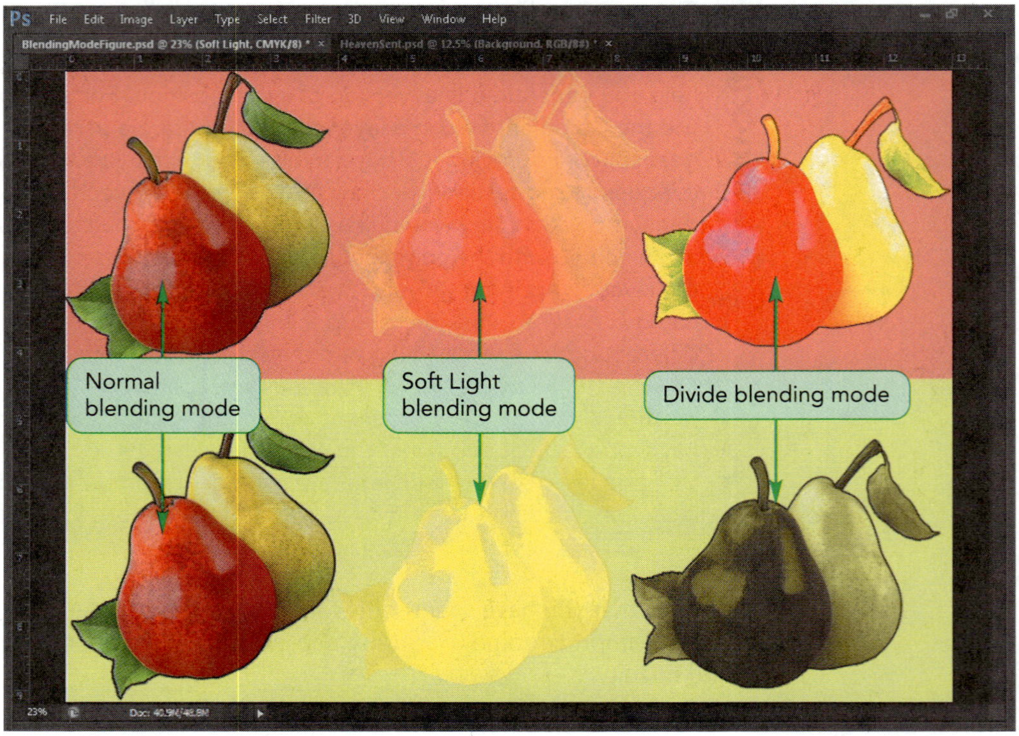

Anna Kucherova/Shutterstock.com

The upper-left and lower-left images in Figure 3-28 have the Normal blending mode applied, which is the default mode for any image you place on the canvas. With the Normal blending mode, a layer does not blend at all with the layers beneath it; the pixels in the image on the layer simply cover the pixels on any lower level layers. The middle two images have the Soft Light blending mode applied. Notice that they look completely different from each other because of the color of the layer beneath each image. The top image blends with the rose color of the rectangle layer beneath it while the bottom image blends with the yellow. The two images on the right have the Divide blending mode applied. Again, because the layers they are blending with are different colors, the result of applying the identical blending mode to identical images varies considerably. Blending modes can have dramatically different effects when applied to the same image, depending on the layers involved in the blend.

To apply a blending mode to a layer, click the layer in the Layers panel. When you do, the blending mode options become available. You can click the blending mode arrow in the Layers panel, and then choose a blending mode. After you have applied one blending mode to a layer, you can press the Ctrl key and the Down arrow key to apply the next blending mode on the list to that layer—without having to click the blending mode arrow. To go up the list, press the Ctrl key and the Up arrow key. You will often find that you need to experiment with many different blending modes to find the one you want.

You'll apply different blending modes to the artwork you're preparing for the cookbook section on star fruits to see what effects you can create.

To apply a blending mode:

1. Open **HeavenSent.psd**, located in the Photoshop3\Tutorial folder, and then show layer edges.
2. In the Layers panel, click the **Star 1** layer, and at the top of the Layers panel, click the **Set the blending mode for the layer** button and then click **Color Burn**.

   Color Burn darkens the base color and makes everything but the lightest color (the night stars) darker. However, it's probably too dark for the printed page.
3. Press and hold the **Ctrl** key, and then press the **Down arrow** key while Photoshop scrolls through the list of blending modes until **Color Dodge** is selected. Color Dodge brightens the base color and decreases the dark/light contrast.

   Trouble? If you pass Color Dodge by mistake, press and hold the Ctrl key and press the **Up arrow** key until you select Color Dodge.
4. In the Layers panel, apply the **Linear Light** blending mode to the Star 2 layer, and then apply the **Lighten** blending mode to the Star 3 layer. See Figure 3-29.

Figure 3-29 **Blending modes applied**

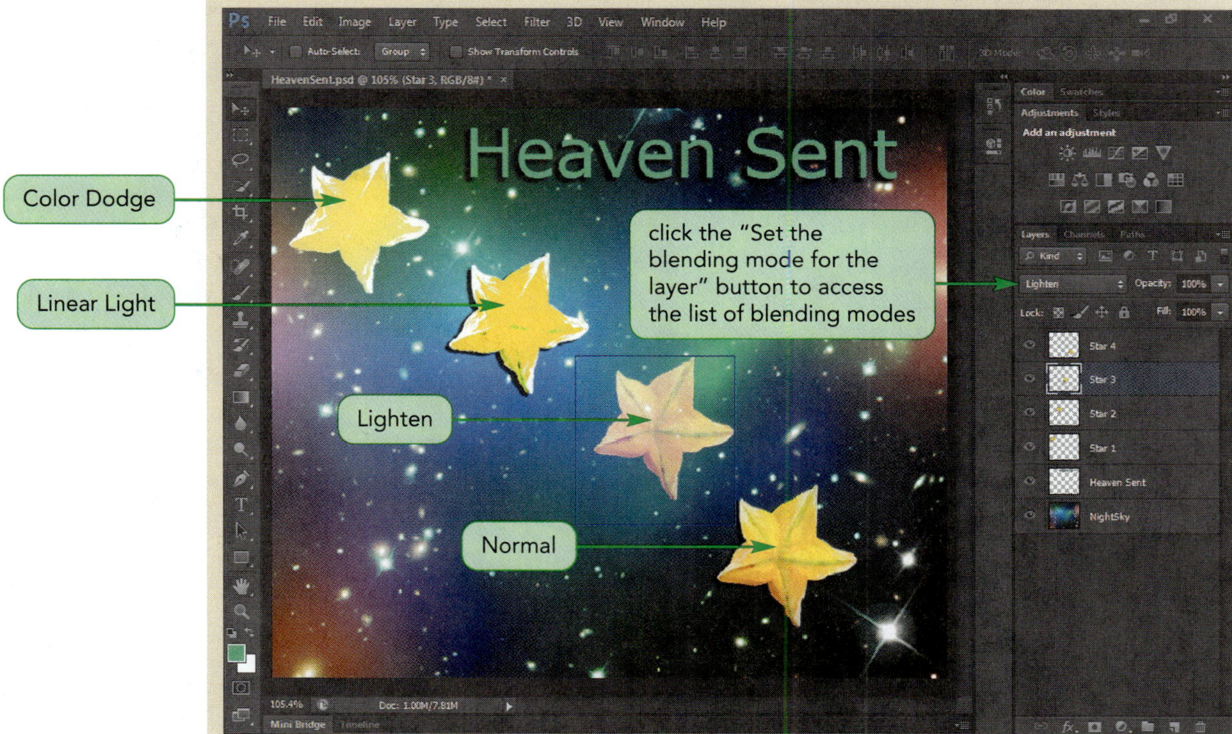

Viktar Malyshchyts/Shutterstock.com; NASA

Linear Light decreases the brightness of the star fruit's base color (the night sky). Lighten looks at the blend and base colors and selects whichever color is lighter to create the result. If a pixel is darker than the result color, Photoshop replaces it; if it's lighter, the pixel color doesn't change.

Each blending mode produces a very different effect. Next, you'll experiment with opacity settings in the Layers panel to see what other effects you can achieve when blending layers.

Changing Opacity

You can also use the Opacity setting in the Layers panel to blend layers. An Opacity setting of 100% means the layer is completely opaque or solid, with no pixels from the layer beneath it showing through. As you decrease the opacity, the layer becomes more and more transparent, showing some of the pixels on the layer beneath it. You can change the opacity by dragging the opacity slider, by typing a percentage value, or by scrubbing over the word *Opacity* in the Layers panel to change the setting. When you **scrub**, the mouse pointer changes to the scrub pointer. Scrubbing left decreases the setting, and scrubbing right increases the setting. In addition, you can press a number key to change the opacity. For example, pressing 2 changes the opacity to 20%, and pressing 5 changes the opacity to 50%.

In Figure 3-30, the first image shows the Star layer at 100% opacity. It completely hides the yellow layer beneath it. The second image shows the Star layer at 0% opacity, meaning that all of its pixels are completely transparent so the yellow layer is the only visible part of the image. In the third image, the Star layer's opacity is set to 50%, which lets some of the yellow in the Color Fill layer show through.

Figure 3-30 **Changing opacity for blending effect**

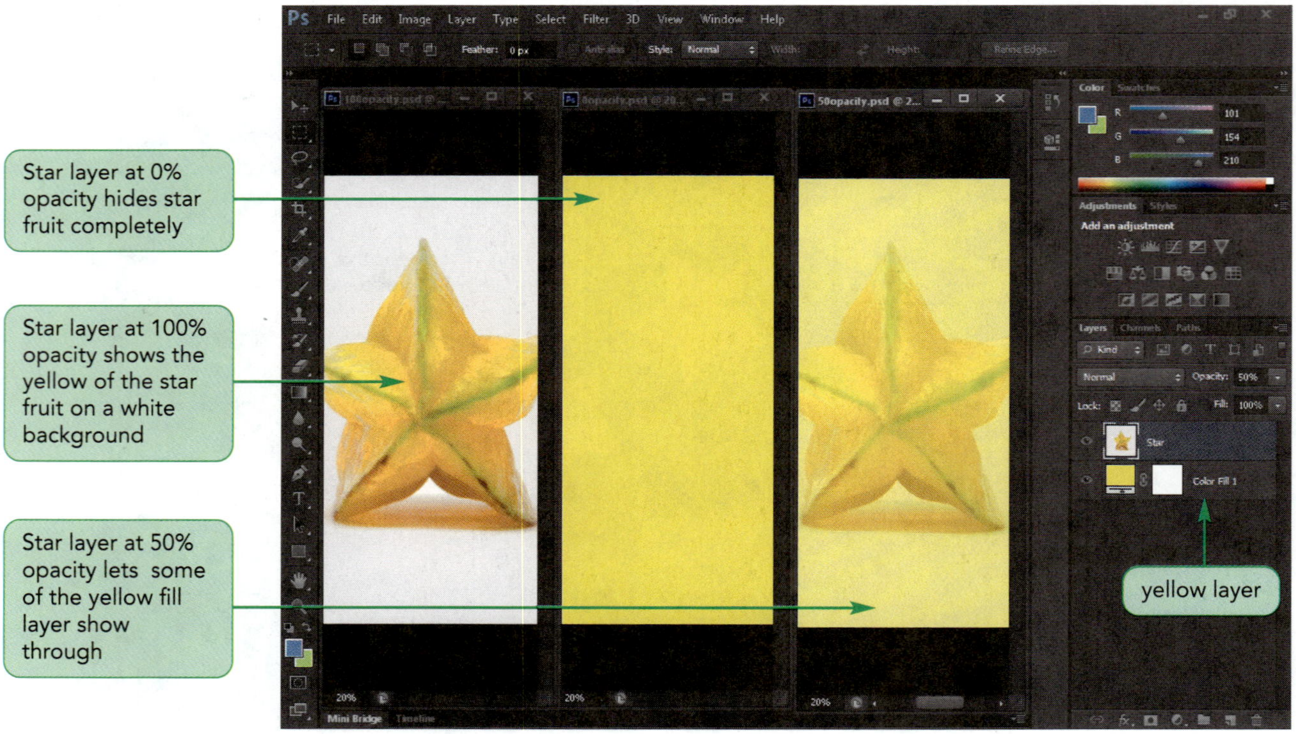

Viktar Malyshchyts/Shutterstock.com

To change the opacity to blend an image:

1. Select the **Star 4** layer, and then in the Layers panel drag the scrub pointer to the left over the word *Opacity* until the Opacity setting at the top of the Layers panel is about **70%**. At this opacity setting, some of the stars in the NightSky layer begin to show through the star fruit.
2. Press the **4** key to change the Opacity setting to 40%. More of the stars in the NightSky layer show through the Star 4 layer.

INSIGHT

Combining Settings for a Unique Effect

You'll sometimes find that a blending mode is almost what you want as an effect, but not quite. To achieve the result you want, you can combine the blending mode with opacity settings. In addition, if an object has a shadow, you can change the Fill setting rather than the Opacity setting to maintain the intensity of the shadow, but reduce the opacity of the fill. In other words, with Photoshop layers, the possibilities for achieving different effects are almost limitless, and you should take the time to explore them.

Creating Layer Groups

Earlier in the tutorial, you learned how to organize layers by changing their order in the Layers panel, by giving each layer a meaningful name, and by changing the color of layers for a visual overview of layer organization. You can also group related layers into layer groups so you can easily change the style of multiple layers at the same time or show and hide a group as necessary as you work on your composition.

REFERENCE

Grouping Layers

- In the Layers panel, click the layers you want to group, and then, on the menu bar, click Layer, and then click Group Layers.

or

- Click the layers you want to group, and then press the Ctrl+G keys.

or

- Click the Create a new group icon at the bottom of the Layers panel. Photoshop creates a new group layer.
- Drag the layers you want to add to the new group folder.

You'll organize the layers by grouping them in the HeavenSent file so Kaye can easily understand how you laid out the composition. You'll also ungroup one of the groups.

To group and ungroup layers:

1. In the Layers panel, select the **Star 1**, **Star 2**, **Star 3**, and **Star 4** layers, and then on the menu bar, click **Layer**, and then click **Group Layers**. Photoshop moves all of the selected layers into a group called Group 1 and collapses the group.

2. Click the **triangle** ▶ to the left of the Group 1 folder to expand the group and view all of the layers.
3. Select the **Heaven Sent** and **NightSky** layers, and then press the **Ctrl+G** keys. Photoshop creates a new group called Group 2 and collapses the group.
4. In the Layers panel, click the **Group 2** layer group to select it, if necessary. On the menu, click **Layer**, and then click **Ungroup Layers**. The Heaven Sent and NightSky layers are no longer in a group.

TIP

You can also press the Shift+Ctrl+G keys to ungroup a selected group or right-click the group in the Layers panel and then click Ungroup Layers on the context menu.

Next, you will finalize your work in the HeavenSent file so it is ready to present to Kaye.

Finalizing Layers

After you have created many versions of a composition and shown different layer comps to a client, you will reach the point when you are ready to finalize your work. A file with multiple layers can take up many megabytes of storage space. However, you can do a number of things to reduce file size and ensure that your work can't be accidentally changed.

Merging Layers

You can merge an adjustment layer with an underlying content layer to permanently apply the adjustment to the image. You can also merge related layers to reduce file size. When you merge image layers, the pixels on the top layer replace the pixels on the layers beneath it. Reducing the number of pixels reduces file size. To merge selected layers, you can right-click the Layers panel and click Merge Layers on the context menu, or you can select Merge Layers on the Layer menu. You can also use the Merge Visible Layers command to merge only the visible layers in the Layers panel. Note that when you merge layers that have blending modes applied, the blending modes revert to Normal in a PSD file. To merge layers and maintain blending modes, you need to either flatten the file or save the file as a JPG or other single-layer file.

To merge selected layers and visible layers:

1. In the Layers panel, click the **Heaven Sent** layer.
2. Expand the Adjustments panel, and clip a Brightness/Contrast adjustment to the Heaven Sent layer. Change the Brightness setting to **105**, and then collapse the Properties panel. The words *Heaven Sent* are now a brighter color.
3. In the Layers panel, select the **Brightness/Contrast** and **Heaven Sent** layers. On the menu bar, click **Layer**, and then click **Merge Layers**. The two layers are merged into one layer. The name of the top layer, Brightness/Contrast1, is given to the new layer.
4. Change the name of the merged layer to **Heaven Sent**.
5. In the Layers panel, hide all of the layers except for **Heaven Sent** and **NightSky**, and then click the **NightSky** layer.
6. On the menu bar, click **Layer**, and then click **Merge Visible**. The Heaven Sent and NightSky layers are merged into a single layer. See Figure 3-31.

TIP

You can also merge visible layers by right-clicking a selected visible layer and then clicking Merge Visible on the context menu.

Figure 3-31 Merging visible layers

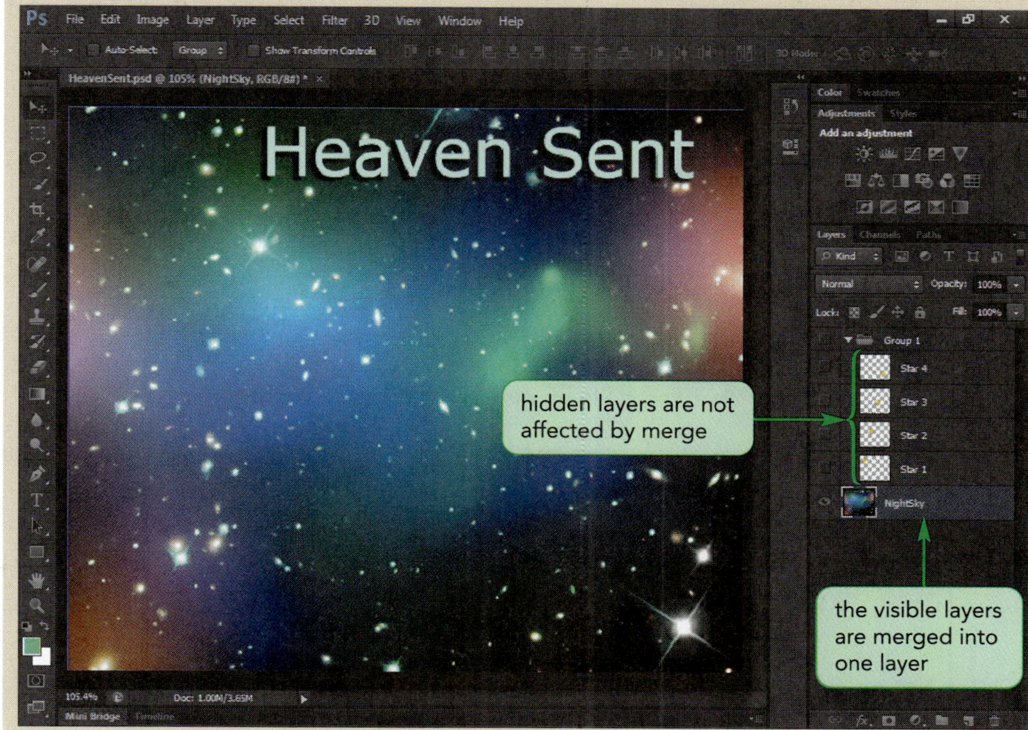

NASA

7. Unhide all of the layers.

INSIGHT

Stamping Layers vs. Merging Layers

When you stamp layers instead of merging them, Photoshop keeps the original layers intact and creates a new composite layer, called a **stamp**, with all of the selected or visible layers merged. To stamp selected layers, press the Ctrl+Alt+E keys. If you select a layer that is linked to other layers, pressing the Ctrl+Alt+E keys stamps the linked layers. You can also stamp visible layers by pressing Shift+Ctrl+Alt+E. You can use the stamp to sharpen or adjust the stamped part of the image as one layer.

Flattening an Image

TIP

When you save a PSD file in JPEG format, you flatten the image.

The final step you should take when finalizing any composition is to flatten it. If you think you might want to use the composition later and modify it, be sure to save a copy of the PSD file with all of its layers. Then flatten the image to reduce the file size and make the image portable to other file formats, such as JPEG. When you flatten an image, Photoshop merges all visible layers and throws out any hidden layers. It also replaces transparent pixels with white pixels. Once you save and close a flattened image, you cannot go back to the layered file, so it is essential that you are sure you have finished with the file before you take this last step.

As a final step before you show the HeavenSent file to Kaye, you'll flatten the composition so it has a manageable file size.

To flatten an image:

1. On the menu bar, click **Layer**, and then click **Flatten Image**. All of the layers have been flattened into a single layer called Background in the Layers panel.
2. Save the file as **FlatFile.psd** in the Photoshop3\Tutorial folder, and then close the file and exit Photoshop.

In this session, you learned how to work with layers. You selected, added, duplicated, and deleted layers and changed their properties and their visibility. You also moved, aligned, and distributed layers, and hid and unhid them. You learned how to lock layer content and how to work with layer comps and groups to improve your work flow. In addition, you learned about blending modes and opacity settings, and you finalized a file by merging layers and flattening it.

REVIEW

Session 3.2 Quick Check

1. What is a layer comp?
2. A ______________ works with the colors and opacity of one layer and combines it with the layer beneath it.
3. When you combine two or more layers into a single layer, you are ______________ the layers.
4. What is a layer group, and how would you use it?
5. You ______________ a layer by merging selected or visible layers into a new layer and leaving the original layers intact.
6. To finalize a file so it consists of only one layer, you ______________ it.

Practice the skills you learned in the tutorial using the same case scenario.

PRACTICE

Review Assignments

Data Files needed for the Review Assignments: Cover.jpg, Breads.jpg, Perfection.psd, BakeRectangle.psd, BakeRectangle2.psd

Kaye wants you to work on the graphics for another cookbook, *Baked to Perfection*. She supplies you with images to work with, and asks you to place them in a file and modify the file to develop ideas for the cover. You'll work with layers and layer comps as well as blending modes and opacity settings to create two files to present to Kaye as possible covers. Complete the following steps:

1. Start Photoshop while pressing the Ctrl+Alt+Shift keys, and click Yes to delete the Settings File when prompted. Reset Photoshop to the default Essentials workspace layout, and then reset all tools.
2. Open **Cover.jpg**, located in the Photoshop3\Review folder included with your Data Files, and save it as **BakeBook.psd** in the same folder.
3. Place **Breads.jpg**, located in the Photoshop3\Review folder, in the BakeBook.psd file. Move the image down 2.75 inches using a relative reference point.
4. Duplicate the Breads layer, using the default layer name. Move the duplicate image up to the top of the canvas so that it covers the background completely.
5. Place **Perfection.psd**, located in the Photoshop3\Review folder, in the BakeBook.psd file.
6. Place the file called **BakeRectangle.psd** in the BakeBook.psd file, and rotate it -45 degrees. Change the opacity of the BakeRectangle layer to 90%.
7. Place the file called **BakeRectangle2.psd** in the BakeBook.psd file, and change its opacity to 50%.
8. Apply the Hard Mix blending mode to the Breads copy layer, and apply the Divide blending mode to the Breads layer.
9. Save the current layer comp as **Blending Comp** and include Visibility, Position, and Appearance in the comp. Enter the comment **Blending experiment**.
10. Group the Rectangle layers, and then group the Bread layers.
11. Expand Group 2, and then ungroup the layers in that group.
12. Hide the BakeRectangle2 layer, and change the opacity of the other rectangle to 50%. Change the blending mode to Normal on both Breads layers.
13. Save the current layer comp as **No Blend** and enter the comment **Plain images**. Save BakeBook.psd.
14. Hide the Breads copy layer.
15. Draw a tan-colored rectangle on the canvas so it appears behind the *Baked to Perfection* title, and then duplicate the rectangle and move the duplicate on the canvas so it is behind the author's name at the bottom of the cover.
16. Filter the Layers panel for shape layers so only the Rectangle 1 and Rectangle 1 copy layers show. Change the name of the Rectangle 1 copy layer to **Author Background**, and then change the name of the Rectangle 1 layer to **Title Background**.
17. Display all of the layers in the Layers panel.
18. Hide the Author Background layer, merge all of the visible layers, and then delete the Breads copy layer and make the BakeRectangle2 layer visible.
19. Save the file as **BakeBook.jpg** in the Photoshop3\Review folder, using the default JPEG options. Close BakeBook.psd without saving it, and exit Photoshop.
20. Submit the results of the preceding steps to your instructor either in printed or electronic form, as requested.

Use your skills to create an interesting visual effect for an ad.

APPLY

Case Problem 1

Data Files needed for this Case Problem: NortonCo.psd, Ruins.jpg, NewHome.jpg

Norton & Company Emma Gottfried, lead architect of Norton & Company, a high-end architectural design firm, wants to launch a campaign with a "ruins to riches" theme using photo compositions of new homes rising out of ancient ruins. She gives you two photographs to work with and asks you to create a comp to present at your next meeting with her. Complete the following steps:

1. Start Photoshop while pressing the Ctrl+Alt+Shift keys, and click Yes to delete the Settings File when prompted. Reset Photoshop to the default Essentials workspace layout, and then reset all tools.
2. Open **NortonCo.psd**, located in the Photoshop3\Case1 folder, and save it as **NewRuins.psd** in the same folder. Use Figure 3-32 as a guide as you complete this exercise.

Figure 3-32 **Riches from Ruins file and Layers panel**

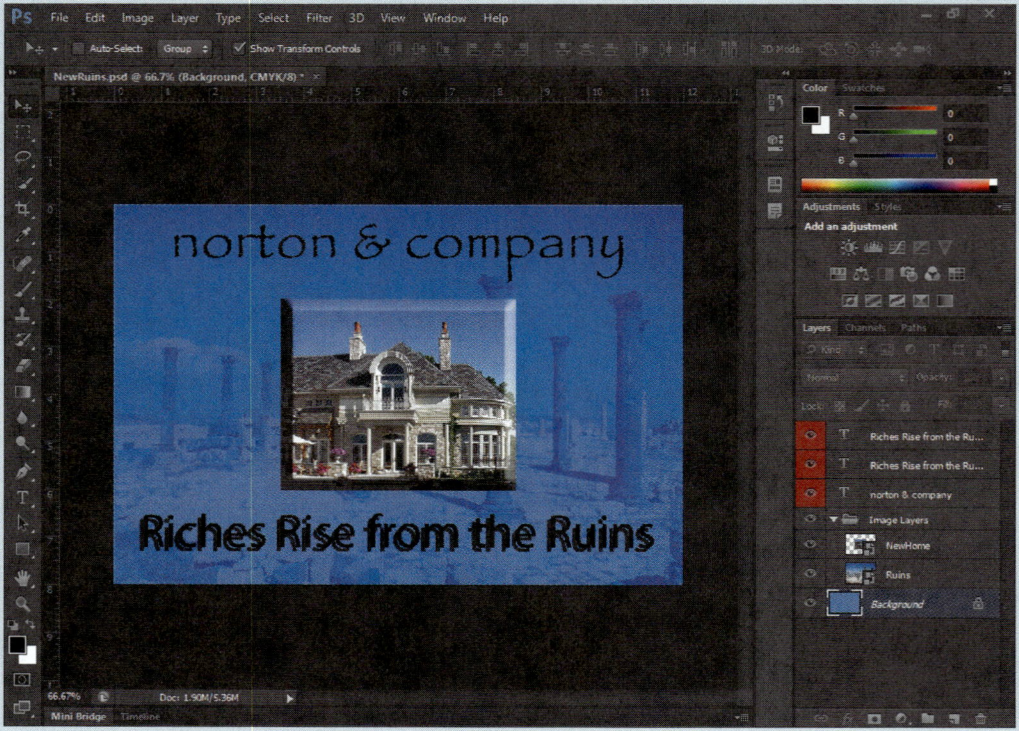

Aleksandar Tolorovic/Shutterstock.com; Ron Davey/Shutterstock.com

3. Place **Ruins.jpg**, located in the Photoshop3\Case1 folder, in the NewRuins.psd file.
4. Place **NewHome.jpg**, located in the Photoshop3\Case1 folder, on top of the Ruins image.
5. Change the Opacity of the Ruins layer to 50% and apply the Color Burn blending mode.
6. Using the Horizontal Type tool with a black Myriad Pro 72 point font, type **Riches Rise from the Ruins** at the bottom of the canvas. Use the Move tool to center the text layer below the image of the house.
7. Duplicate the text layer you just created, move it slightly down and to the left, and then change its opacity to 75%.

8. Select the Ruins layer, and using the Horizontal Type tool with any font type and size, type **norton & company** at the top of the canvas. Center the text layer above the image of the house. (*Hint*: To select a font size other than the sizes listed, you can type a value in the Set the font size box on the options bar.)
9. If necessary, rearrange the layers in the Layers panel so the text layers appear together and the image layers appear together, as shown in Figure 3-32.
10. Filter the Layers panel so that only the text layers appear, and then change the color of all of the text layers to red.
11. Turn off the filter, and put the image layers in a group called **Image Layers**.
12. Hide the Riches Rise from the Ruins copy layer, and then save the layer comp as **No Shadow**.
13. Redisplay the Riches Rise from the Ruins copy layer, and then save the layer comp as **All Layers**.
14. Save NewRuins.psd, close the file, and exit Photoshop.
15. Submit the results of the preceding steps to your instructor either in printed or electronic form, as requested.

Using Figure 3-33 as a guide, modify a composition by using what you know about layers and groups.

CREATE

Case Problem 2

Data Files needed for this Case Problem: AlwardArt.psd

Alward Art Museum You have been working on a logo for Director Guy Blanc at the Alward Art Museum. You'd like to present the file to Guy and give clear information about its organization so he can modify it as he sees fit. The file has many layers and effects, and you need to organize it so it is more manageable. Complete the following steps:

1. Start Photoshop while pressing the Ctrl+Alt+Shift keys, and click Yes to delete the Settings File when prompted. Reset Photoshop to the default Essentials workspace layout, and then reset all tools.
2. Open **AlwardArt.psd**, located in the Photoshop3\Case2 folder, and using Figure 3-33 as a guide, name and group the layers.

Figure 3-33 Alward Art file and Layers panel

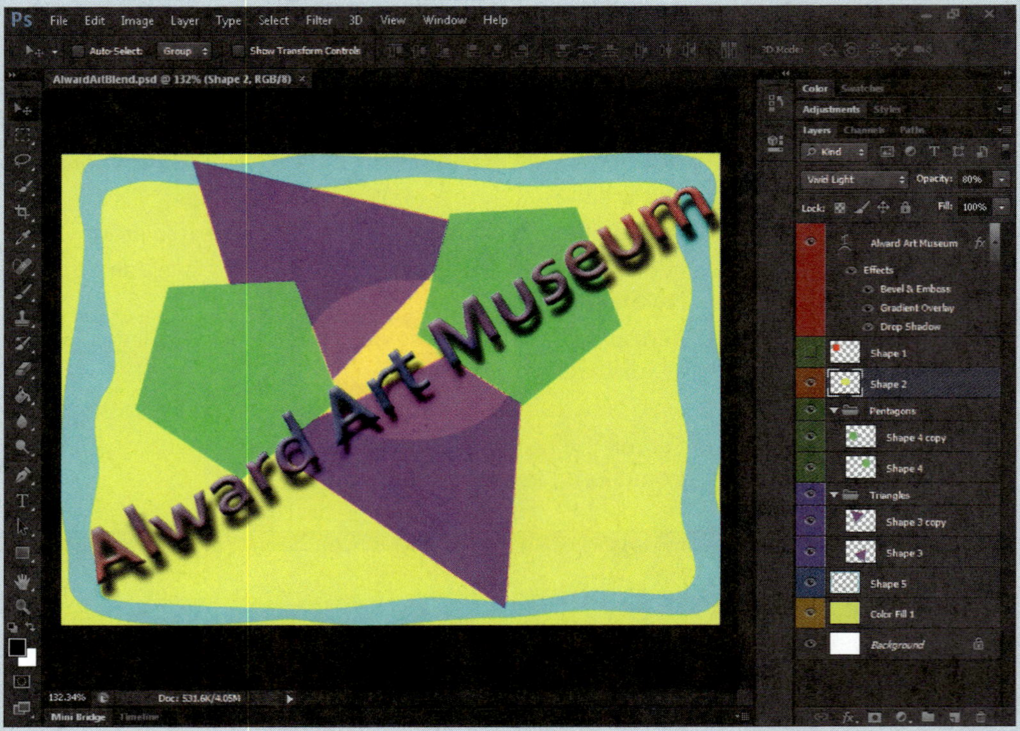

3. Move the layers so they appear in the order shown in the figure.
4. Hide layers as shown in the figure.
5. In the Layers panel, change the layer colors to match the figure.
6. Apply the blending mode and opacity shown in the Layers panel in the figure.
7. Save the file as **AlwardArtBlend.psd** in the Photoshop3\Case2 folder. Close the file, and exit Photoshop.
8. Submit the results of the preceding steps to your instructor either in printed or electronic form, as requested.

Create a unique composition by working with layers and effects.

CREATE

Case Problem 3

Data Files needed for this Case Problem: Clouds.jpg, Clouds1.jpg, Plane1.psd, Plane2.psd

Flight Plan, Inc. You are the owner of Flight Plan, Inc., a flight school in Dayton, Ohio. You will soon be meeting with an ad agency to present your ideas and launch a campaign that inspires people to learn how to fly. You'll use your Photoshop skills to combine images and work with blending modes, layers, and comps to present a couple of ideas to the agency so they will know what you want when they begin working on the campaign. Complete the following steps:

1. Start Photoshop while pressing the Ctrl+Alt+Shift keys, and click Yes to delete the Settings File when prompted. Reset Photoshop to the default Essentials workspace layout, and then reset all tools.
2. The Photoshop3\Case3 folder provided with your Data Files includes photographs of airplanes and clouds in the sky. You'll place the airplane and cloud images in a new file to create a unique composition with at least two layer comps. Use the two examples in Figure 3-34 as a reference, but use your own ideas to create the composition.

Figure 3-34 **Layer comps for Flight Plan campaign**

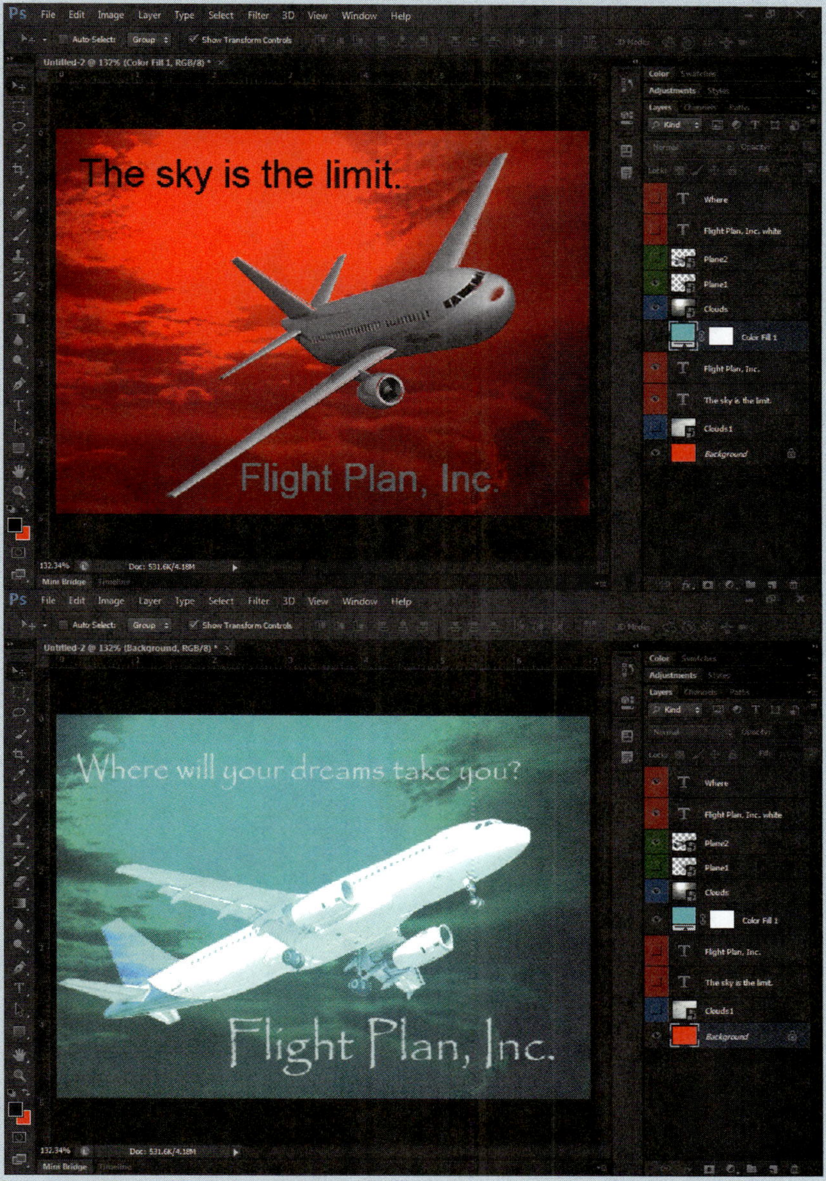

Jane Hosie-Bounar; Robert Spriggs/Shutterstock.com; ifong/Shutterstock.com

3. Create a new file using the dimensions and background color of your choosing.
4. Create a new layer and place one of the airplane images from the Photoshop3\Case3 folder on the new layer.
5. Create a new layer and place one of the cloud images from the Photoshop3\Case3 folder on the new layer.
6. Create another cloud layer and another airplane layer, using the remaining images in the Photoshop3\Case3 folder.
7. Apply blending modes and adjust the opacity of layers to achieve interesting effects. Your image does not need to match Figure 3-34.
8. Add at least two text layers and apply styles, colors, or blending modes to them. The text should include the company name and any catch phrase you think will work for the company. You can use different phrases for different layer comps.
9. Assign colors to layers to organize them, and create at least one logical group of layers in the Layers panel.
10. Lock at least two layers.

11. Hide and unhide layers to create at least two layer comps.
12. Save the file as **FlightPlan.psd** in the Photoshop3\Case3 folder.
13. Switch to your favorite comp, flatten the file, and then save it as **FlightPlan.jpg** in the Photoshop3\Case3 folder. Close the open file, and exit Photoshop.
14. Submit the results of the preceding steps to your instructor either in printed or electronic form, as requested.

Extend your skills to create a Web ad for an employment agency.

CHALLENGE

Case Problem 4

Data Files needed for this Case Problem: Keys1.jpg, Keys2.jpg

TempIT Sylvia Potter founded TempIT, an employment agency providing temporary clerical and administrative assistants to large corporations, five years ago in Denver, Colorado. You are Sylvia's administrative assistant but would like to take on more responsibility. You will use your Photoshop skills to create an interesting idea for a Web ad that you can present to Sylvia at the next staff meeting. Complete the following steps:

1. Start Photoshop while pressing the Ctrl+Alt+Shift keys, and click Yes to delete the Settings File when prompted. Reset Photoshop to the default Essentials workspace layout, and then reset all tools.
2. Create a new file of any size and background color and then extend the canvas using a second color for the extension. The extension should have room for three lines of text. Refer to Figure 3-35 for an example of a possible layer comp. Save the file as **HelpIT.psd**.

Figure 3-35 **A sample comp for TempIT**

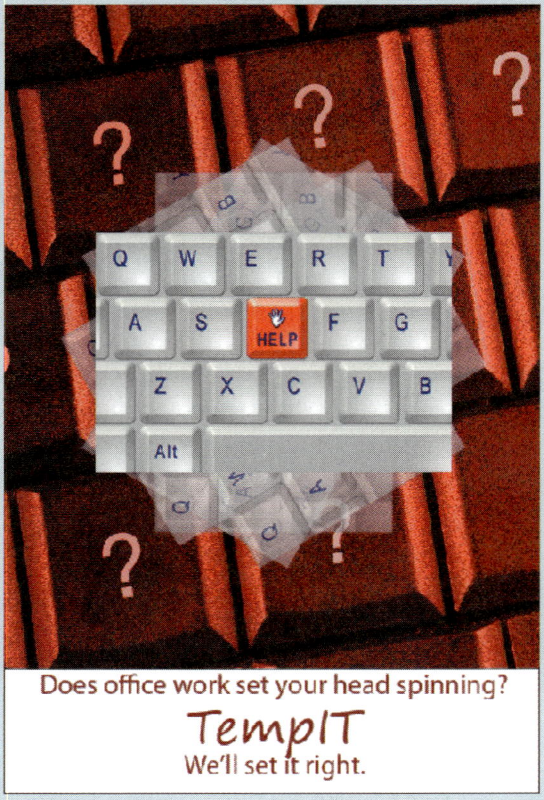

SCOTTCHAN/Shutterstock.com; keerati/Shutterstock.com

3. Use Mini Bridge to preview the images of keyboards in the Photoshop3\Case4 folder provided with your Data Files. Place one of the files in your composition, and resize it so the entire image fits in the center of the canvas.
4. Duplicate the layer containing the keyboard image, change the opacity setting, and apply a blending mode. Select the Move tool, if necessary, and using the transform controls, rotate the duplicate layer on the canvas. Create additional duplicates, and rotate each duplicate a different amount to achieve the effect of a spinning keyboard.
5. Rearrange the layers so the original keyboard layer is on top in the Layers panel and is displayed at 100% opacity.
6. Place the second keyboard file on the canvas; size and move it so it appears in the background, behind the spinning keyboards you created. Make it any size while leaving room for text at the bottom of the canvas.
7. Add text to the image on at least three layers. One layer should include the name of the company.

EXPLORE

8. Duplicate the three text layers all at once. (*Hint*: Select similar layers and then apply the Duplicate Layer command to all three layers at the same time. You will not be able to assign unique names until after the duplication.)
9. Hide the original text layers.

EXPLORE

10. Use the text style presets in the Styles panel to modify at least two of the duplicate layers. To display the presets, click the Styles panel menu button, click Text Effects 2 or Text Effects, and then replace the current styles with the Text Effects styles.
11. Apply at least two text styles to the duplicate text.

EXPLORE

12. Use the Styles panel menu to replace the Text styles with the default styles.
13. Give some of the layers more descriptive names, and group or color-code related layers.
14. Create and save at least two layer comps. Make sure to experiment with text effects, blending modes, and opacity, and use different combinations for different layer comps.
15. Save the file as **HelpIT.psd** in the Photoshop3\Case4 folder. Close the file, and exit Photoshop.
16. Submit the results of the preceding steps to your instructor either in printed or electronic form, as requested.

ENDING DATA FILES

Photoshop3 →

Tutorial

CitrusRecipes2.psd
Comps.psd
Fantastic2.psd
Fantastic3.psd
FlatFile.psd
FruitDraft2.psd
FruitFantastic3.psd
Locked.psd
StarsAligned.psd
StarsDistributed.psd

Review

BakeBook.jpg
BakeBook.psd

Case1

NewRuins.psd

Case2

AlwardArtBlend.psd

Case3

FlightPlan.jpg
FlightPlan.psd

Case4

HelpIT.psd

TUTORIAL 4

Adding Content

Adding Content and Working with Color

PHOTOSHOP

OBJECTIVES

Session 4.1

- Understand the effect of color
- Sample and set colors using color selection tools
- Change background and foreground colors
- Work with the Swatches panel
- Assign and modify layer styles using the Styles panel

Session 4.2

- Add solid color, gradient, and pattern fill layers
- Add a shape layer
- Fill pixels on a layer
- Modify shapes by adding and subtracting
- Paint with the Brush tool
- Work with Brush tool presets
- Create a work path and apply a stroke

Case | *ReCycle Bike Shop*

ReCycle Bike Shop is a used bicycle shop in Concord, Massachusetts, that also offers bicycle repair classes and mountain biking lessons. Founded in 2006 by Lee duBois, ReCycle has five employees who handle the front-of-store business, teach classes, and give mountain biking lessons. For years, Lee has been doing all of the promotion and bookkeeping; however, because the business has been growing, she has hired you to help her develop promotional materials for the shop, including posters to hang in surrounding towns, Web ads for the local Chamber of Commerce Web site, and mailers for customers who have done business with the shop in the past. She is also interested in developing a logo for the shop that can appear on a sign above the door and on all of the promotional pieces.

You'll use the color selection tools, the Paint Bucket tool, and the drawing and painting tools in Photoshop for the projects Lee has in mind. You'll also add fill layers to an image and compose an image that places your proposed sign in an illustration of the shop so Lee can see what the finished product will look like.

STARTING DATA FILES

Photoshop4 →

Tutorial

Accident.jpg
BikeSign.psd
Colorful.jpg
FillLayers.psd
FourBikes.psd
StopSign.psd
Storefront.psd
Tricycle.jpg
Upgrade.psd

Review

Gopher.jpg
Signage.psd

Case1

CD.psd
TekSell.jpg

Case2

ArchiText.psd

Case3

Easel.jpg

Case4

(none)

SESSION 4.1 VISUAL OVERVIEW

You can use the Eyedropper tool to **sample**, or copy the color of, pixels in an image so you can apply that color to another part of the image or to another image.

A **point sample** uses the color of a single pixel to set the color when you use the Eyedropper tool.

You can click the **foreground color** icon in the Color panel to open the Color Picker, where you can specify the color Photoshop uses when you work with the drawing tools.

Select the **background color** icon in the Color panel to specify the color used to extend the canvas or to create a gradient.

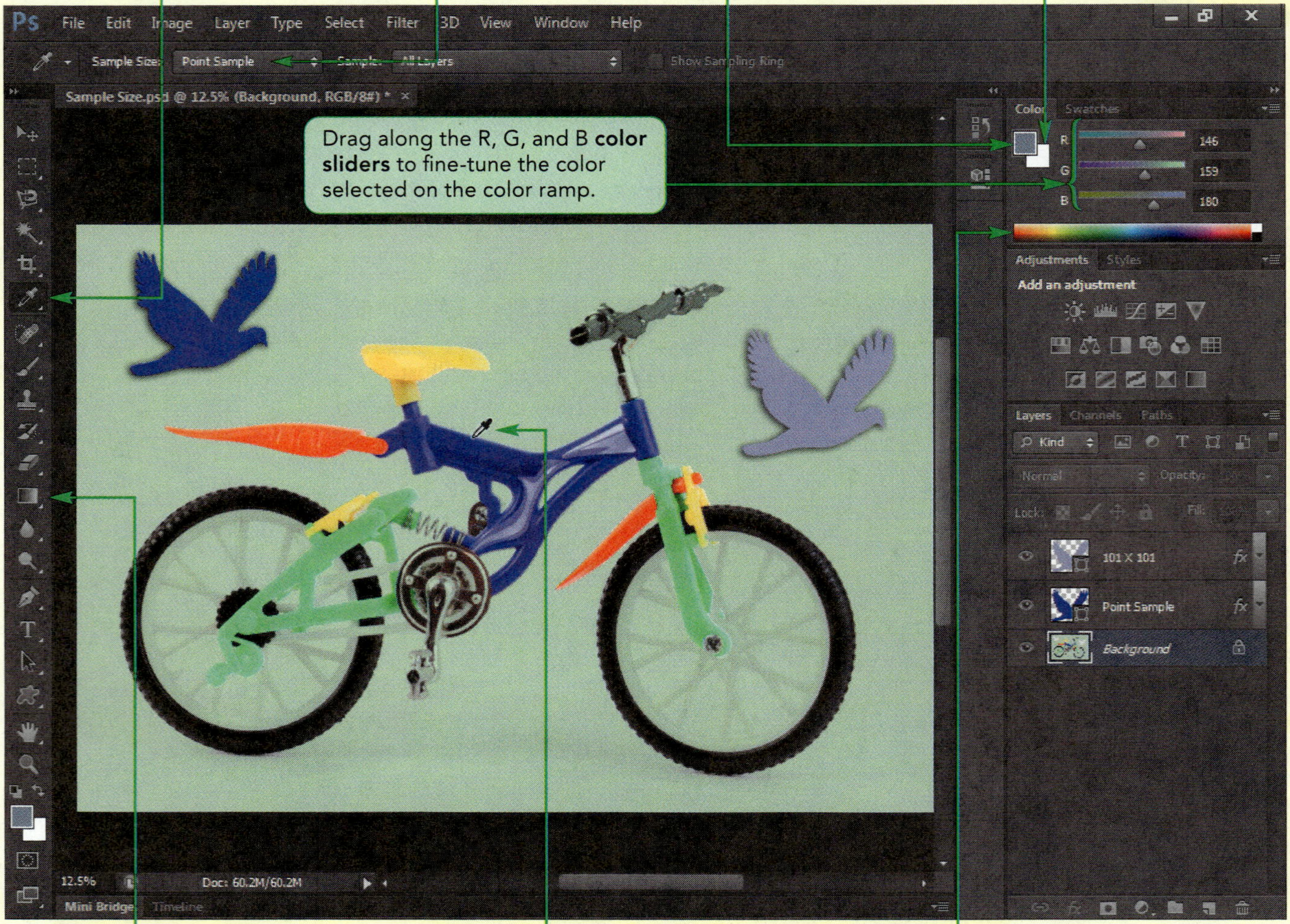

Drag along the R, G, and B **color sliders** to fine-tune the color selected on the color ramp.

The Paint Bucket tool is hidden under the Gradient tool in the Tools panel.

The pointer takes the shape of an eyedropper when you sample a color.

Click the color ramp in the Color panel to select a foreground or background color and then adjust the color using the color sliders.

Losevsky Pavel/Shutterstock.com

CONTROLLING CONTENT COLOR

The **color field** displays shades of a selected color.

The Color Picker displays the new color and compares it with the current color.

The triangle symbol indicates that the current color is **out of gamut**; it will not print properly.

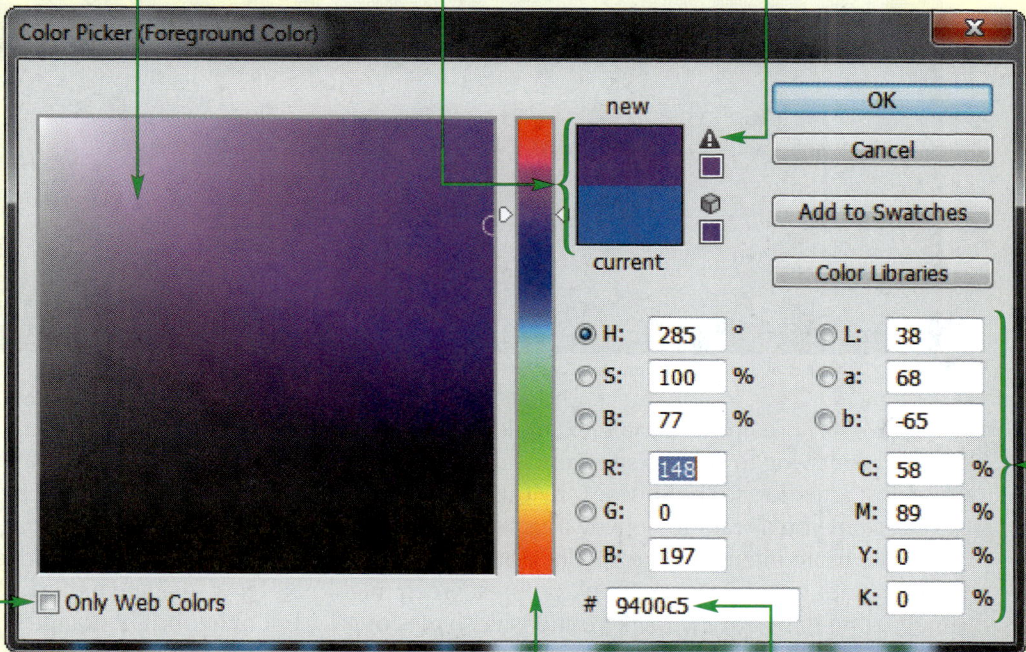

You can select Only Web Colors to display a palette of colors that will always work on a Web site, even when displayed on an older monitor.

Clicking the **color ramp** in the Color Picker dialog box displays shades of the selected color in the color field.

Hexadecimal color values are used to designate colors in HTML files for the Web; each color in the RGB color model is expressed as a unique series of numbers and letters.

Color values specify the current foreground or background color and are based on the color mode.

Understanding the Effect of Color

In the advertising world, certain brands are consistently identified with particular colors. For example, think of your favorite soft drink. Is its label red? blue? green? If your favorite soft drink has a red label, what might happen if the label were suddenly changed to yellow or pink? Would the identity of the brand change for you in some fundamental way? As you work to create the most effective compositions—that is, compositions that successfully convey your intended message or draw attention to a product you're trying to sell—you should spend some time considering the importance of color. Color can make or break a brand, can affect a viewer's mood, and can even help persuade someone to buy a product. See Figure 4-1.

Figure 4-1 **The effect of color**

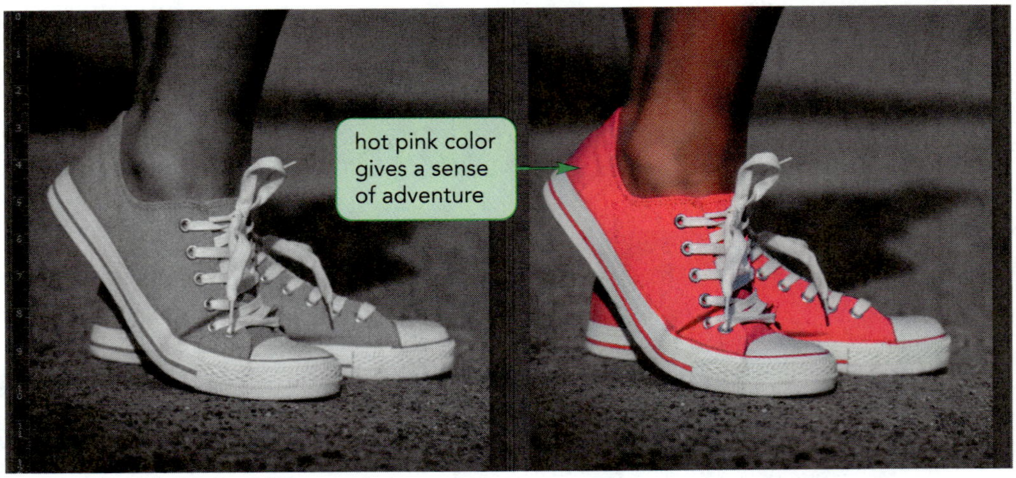

PHOTOCREO Michal Bednarek/Shutterstock.com

Figure 4-1 provides a simple example of using color to create interest. Imagine that you're trying to sell the sneakers shown in the images. Which photograph draws the most attention to the shoes? Obviously, the grayscale image does not express the excitement you'd want to convey to a potential buyer. Not only does the color image generate more interest in the product, but the hot pink shoes convey a sense of adventure that, for example, pastel pink or forest green might not. Now imagine a third image, one in which the background isn't shades of gray, but rather bright orange or some other bright color. Would that additional color draw more attention to the shoes, or less? Would it be distracting? Would it clash?

As you work with color, you might find it convenient to keep a color wheel nearby. A **color wheel** is a diagram used to the show the relationships between colors. See Figure 4-2.

Figure 4-2 Sample color wheel

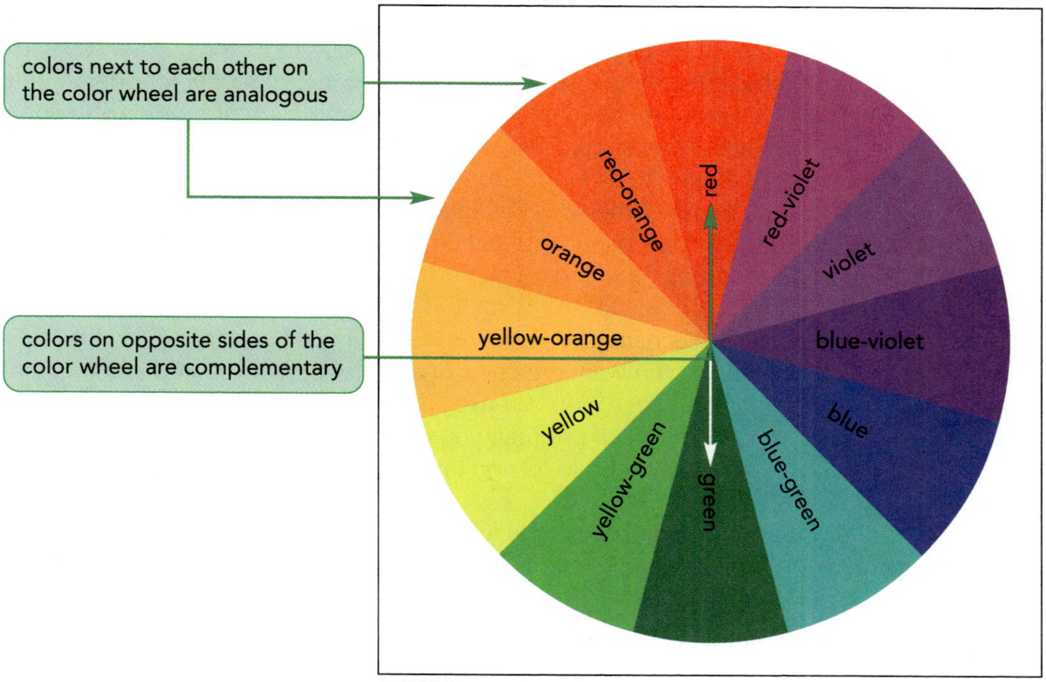

A color wheel can help you choose a **color scheme**, which is a combination of colors that work well together. Examples of color schemes include monochromatic, complementary, and analogous. A **monochromatic** color scheme uses different shades of a single color. A **complementary** color scheme includes colors that are on opposite sides of a color wheel. An **analogous** color scheme uses colors that are next to each other on a color wheel. Color schemes can also be described in terms of temperature. Certain colors, like red, orange, and yellow, convey a feeling of warmth, while others like blue and green are considered cool. **Neutral** colors are colors that aren't on a color wheel, such as browns and grays.

INSIGHT

The Psychology of Color

When working on a composition in Photoshop, you might find your choice of a color scheme dictated in part by the colors in a photograph you plan to use. However, you should also consider other factors, such as the message you want to convey, the emotions you want to elicit, or the audience you want to attract. To use color effectively, it is helpful to have some understanding of color psychology. Knowing how colors affect people—not only in your own culture, but also in other cultures—can help you convey a message or close a sale. For example, you might already know that wearing black makes you appear thinner, but did you know that it also gives you a look of authority or power? Red can elicit intense emotions, while blue and green can produce a calming effect. In certain cultures, green symbolizes paradise. Color is a powerful tool, and the more you know about it, the more effectively you'll use it. Photoshop offers a variety of tools that allow you to experiment with color to achieve the effect you want.

Using the Color Selection Tools

In Tutorial 2, you learned about different color models and the different color modes available in Photoshop. In particular, you focused on RGB, which is the standard color model for Web content, and CMYK, which is the standard model for printed output. No matter which color model you use, or which particular color mode you choose, you select colors in Photoshop using similar methods. In fact, before you use any of the drawing or painting tools in the Tools panel in Photoshop, you need to select the colors you want to use. Otherwise, by default, Photoshop will use the foreground color (shown in the Tools panel and in the Color panel) or the fill color selected on the options bar, depending on the tool you have selected. Photoshop includes many color selection tools, including the Color panel, the Color Picker dialog box, the Eyedropper tool, and the Swatches panel. Which selection tool you use depends on the task at hand. For example, if you want the color of a vector object you add to match one of the colors in a digital image, you can use the Eyedropper tool. If you want to ensure that a color is appropriate for printing, you can use the Color Picker or the Color panel, both of which display an icon to let you know if your color will be available when the image is printed.

In Photoshop, you can specify the foreground color and the background color. See Figure 4-3.

Figure 4-3 **Default foreground and background colors**

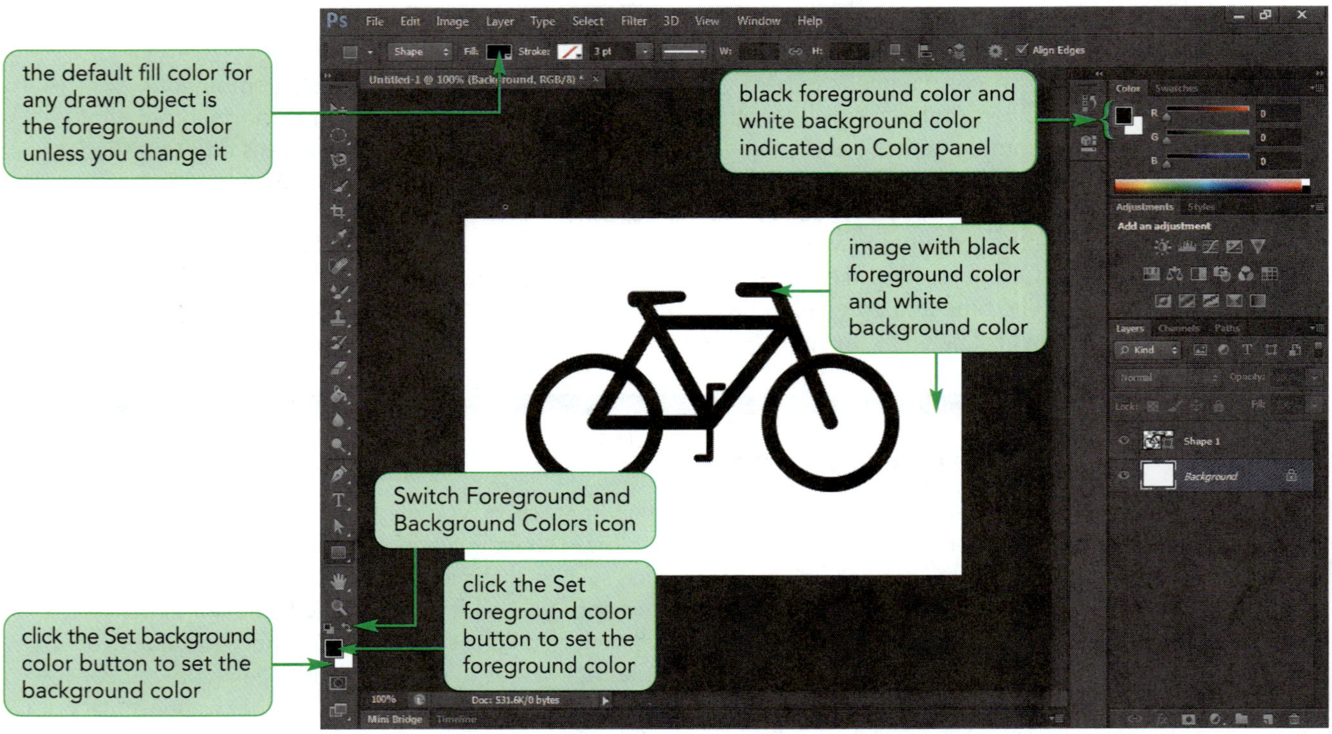

Photoshop defaults to the foreground color when you work with the drawing tools in the Tools panel. By default, the foreground color of a new file created in Photoshop is black. The background color is the color Photoshop uses to extend the canvas or, when combined with the foreground color, to create a **gradient fill**, which is a gradual blending of the foreground and background colors or of other colors determined by a gradient preset. Photoshop also uses the background color to fill empty areas of an image. By default, the background color is white. You can change the foreground and background colors at any time, and unless you restore the defaults in your next Photoshop session, your changes will remain in effect from one session to the next.

Setting the Foreground Color with the Eyedropper Tool

If you are working on a composition and want to select a color for text or a vector object based on a color or colors in a photograph, the Eyedropper tool is a good choice for setting the foreground color. See Figure 4-4.

Figure 4-4 **Sampling colors with the Eyedropper tool**

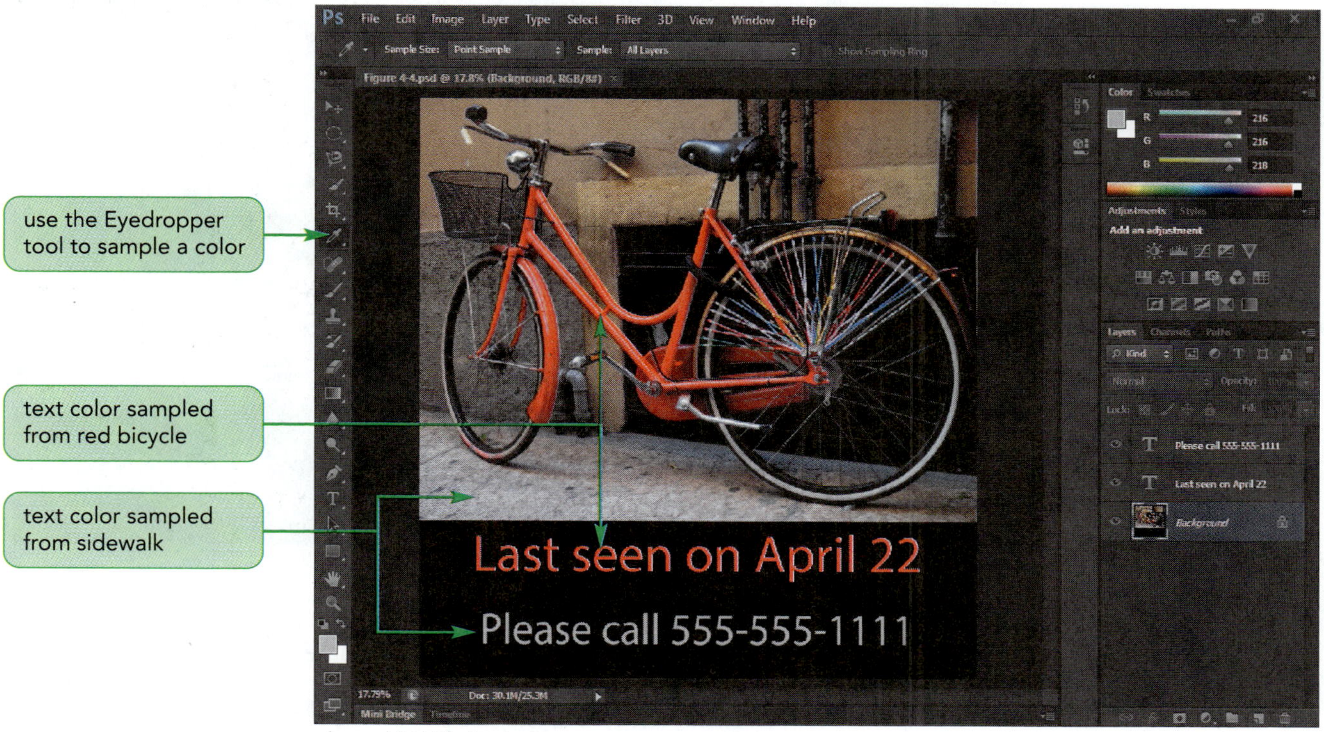

adam.golabek/Shutterstock.com

In the poster shown in Figure 4-4, the Eyedropper tool was used to sample the color of the bicycle for the top line of text. It was used again to sample the color of the sidewalk for the bottom line of text. When you sample a color, you pick up the color values for a single pixel, or for an average of pixel colors in a specified area. You can then use the sampled color to fill a vector object, to specify the color for text, or to fill a selection with the color.

You sample a color with the Eyedropper tool by selecting the layer that contains the color, activating the Eyedropper tool, and then clicking the location on the image where the color appears. To refine your selection, you can use the settings on the options bar to sample the color of a single pixel, called a point sample, or to sample the average of colors in an area of pixels, for example, a 3 × 3 pixel average or even a 101 × 101 pixel average, as shown in Figure 4-5.

TIP

You can also select a sample area by clicking the Eyedropper Tool button in the Tools panel, right-clicking the image, and then choosing a sample size from the context menu.

Figure 4-5 **Sample size causes variations in color**

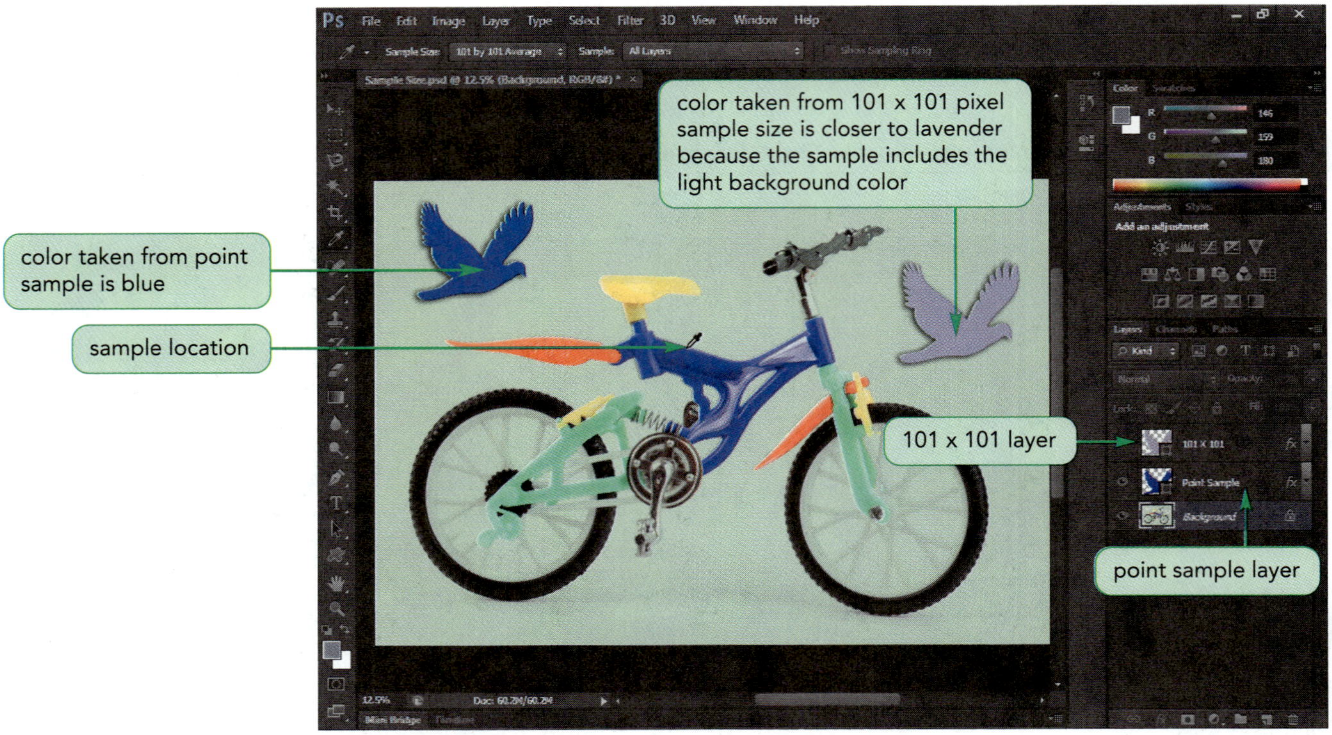

Losevsky Pavel/Shutterstock.com

Figure 4-5 shows the different results achieved by clicking the image at the same spot, but sampling areas of different dimensions. The first color sample includes only the blue of a single sampled pixel. The second sample is closer to lavender because the sample is 101 × 101 pixels, and includes the light-colored area around the bicycle. The sampled color can vary significantly at different sample sizes, so it's a good idea to experiment with a few settings if you aren't satisfied with the initial sampling.

You can also designate whether you want to sample the color on the current layer only, the current layer and the layers beneath it, or all of the layers in the document by clicking the Sample arrow on the options bar, and then clicking Current Layer, Current & Below, or All Layers. If you sample all layers, Photoshop combines the colors to come up with the sample. You can also determine whether or not Photoshop will include adjustment layers when it generates the sample color.

If you want to see the RGB and CMYK color values when you are sampling a color from an image, open the Info panel, and then, with the Eyedropper tool selected, move the mouse over different areas of the image. As you do, the numbers displayed in the Info panel change to reflect the color you are pointing to. You can open the Info panel by clicking Window on the menu bar and then clicking Info, or by pressing the F8 key.

REFERENCE

Using the Eyedropper Tool

- In the Tools panel, click the Eyedropper Tool button.
- On the options bar, click the Sample Size button to specify the size of the sample, and then click the Sample button to specify whether you want just the current layer or a combination of the image layers and adjustment layers to be used as the sample.
- Point to the area of the image from which you want to obtain a sample, and click the color you want to sample.
- Apply the sample using the Paint Bucket tool or another drawing or painting tool, or add it to the Swatches panel by clicking a blank area in the Swatches panel.

Lee is experimenting with ideas for a store logo and would like you to take one of her ideas a bit further. She has given you a simple graphic of four bicycles, currently filled with black or white, and she would like you to experiment by making them different colors. Her idea is that a multicolored image will emphasize the variety of bicycles available at the shop. You'll color the first bicycle using a color sample from the Eyedropper tool. You'll apply the sampled color to the bicycle with the Paint Bucket tool, which replaces the color of not only the pixel you click, but also all adjacent pixels with a similar color. In other words, if you click the white bicycle, the Paint Bucket tool will fill the pixel you click—plus all of the adjacent white pixels in that bicycle—with the new color, and it will leave the nonwhite pixels the same.

To sample a color using the Eyedropper tool:

1. Start Photoshop while pressing the **Ctrl+Alt+Shift** keys, and click **Yes** to delete the Settings File when prompted. Reset Photoshop to the default Essentials workspace layout, and then reset all tools.
2. Navigate to the Photoshop4\Tutorial folder provided with your Data Files, and open **Colorful.jpg** and **FourBikes.psd**.
3. Switch to the Colorful.jpg file, if necessary, and in the Tools panel, click the **Eyedropper Tool** button.
4. On the options bar, click the **Sample Size** button and select **Point Sample**, if necessary; confirm that **All Layers** is selected on the Sample button, and then click the green area near the bicycle spring, as shown in Figure 4-6.

Figure 4-6 Color sampled in one image will be applied to another

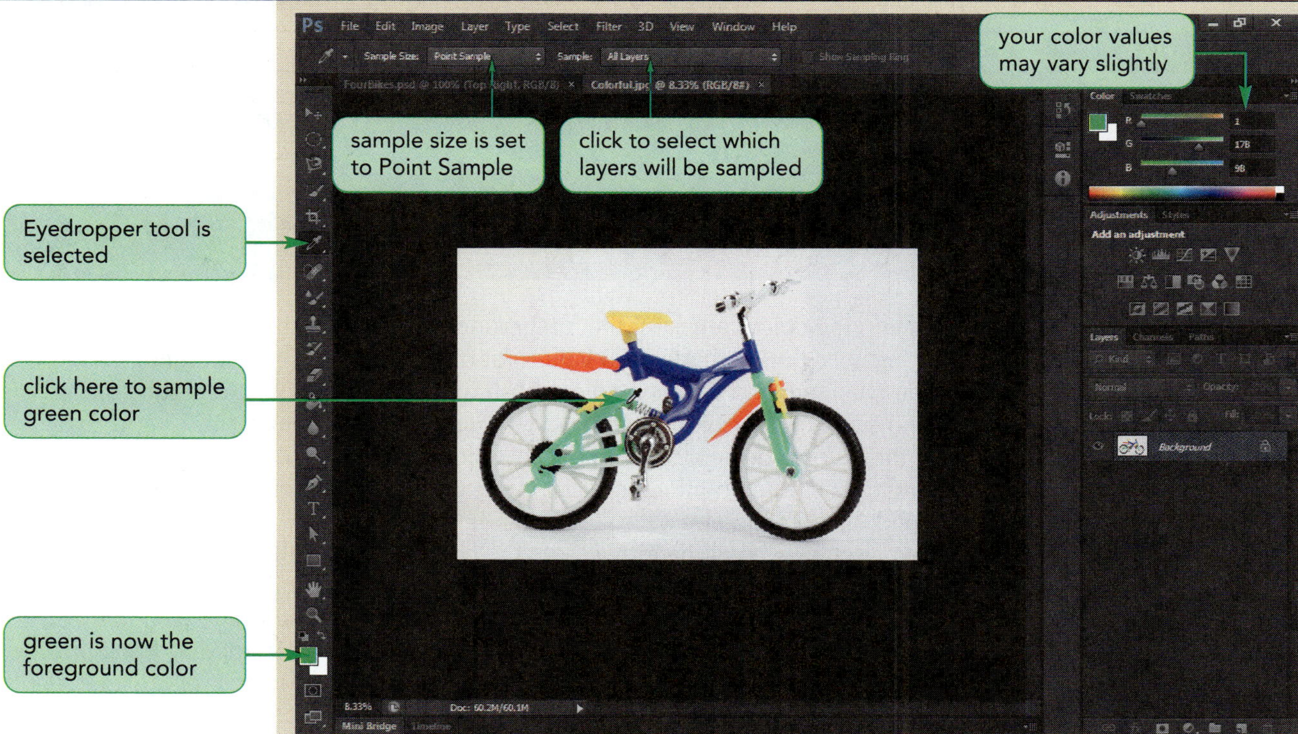

Losevsky Pavel/Shutterstock.com

The foreground color icon changes to green in the Tools panel and in the Color panel. (Don't be concerned if your color doesn't exactly match the color in the figure.)

Make sure you click the specified layer in this step and all other layer selection steps. Clicking an incorrect layer will apply the color to the wrong part of the image.

5. Switch to the **FourBikes** file, and in the Layers panel, click the **Lower Right** layer, if necessary, to make it the active layer.
6. In the Tools panel, click the **Paint Bucket Tool** button.

   Notice that the pointer shape changes to a paint bucket.

   Trouble? If you can't see the Paint Bucket Tool button, point to the Gradient Tool button in the Tools panel, click and hold the mouse button to display the hidden tool, and then click the Paint Bucket Tool button.
7. In the image, click the **lower-right bicycle**. Photoshop fills the bicycle with the sampled green color.

   Trouble? If the background or a different bicycle is filled with the green color when you click, you did not click the Lower Right layer, or you were pointing at the area around the bicycle rather than the bicycle itself. Press the Ctrl+Z keys, or click Edit on the menu bar and click Undo Paint Bucket to undo the change, and then repeat Step 7.
8. Save the FourBikes file as **FourColors.psd** in the Photoshop4\Tutorial folder, and keep it open for the next set of steps.

Setting the Foreground Color in the Color Panel

You can also use the Color panel to select a color for the foreground. In the Color panel, RGB color values are displayed if you're working in RGB mode; CMYK color values are displayed if you're working in CMYK mode. See Figure 4-7.

Figure 4-7 **Color panel showing RGB color values**

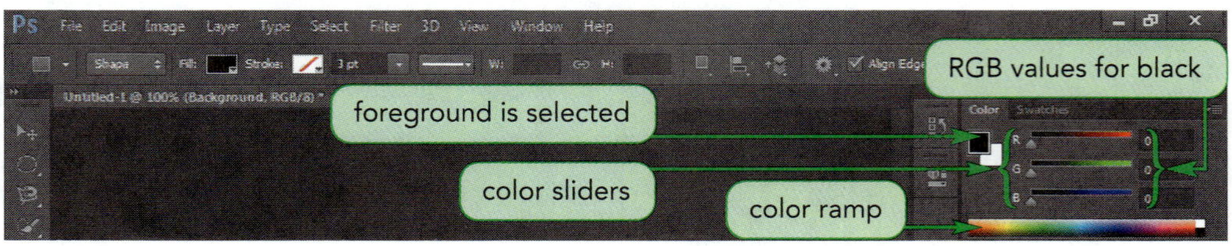

By default, the color values for the foreground color in RGB mode are R=0, G=0, and B=0 because those are the RGB values for black, the default foreground color. When you change the foreground color, those values change. You can modify the foreground color in the Color panel by entering new color values for R, G, and B; by dragging the color sliders for R, G, and B; by clicking a color in the color ramp; or by clicking the Set foreground color icon in the Color panel to open the Color Picker (Foreground Color) dialog box.

You can also use a combination of these methods to achieve the exact color you want. For example, you might click a green color in the color ramp, and then use the color sliders to adjust the levels to achieve the shade of green you want. Keep in mind, however, that some of your color manipulations might result in a color that won't print properly. You need to ensure that your color choice is within the **gamut**, or range of colors allowed by the CMYK mode. A color that won't print properly is considered out of gamut because it is a color not included in the complete set (or gamut) of print-safe colors. See Figure 4-8.

Figure 4-8 Out-of-gamut color correction

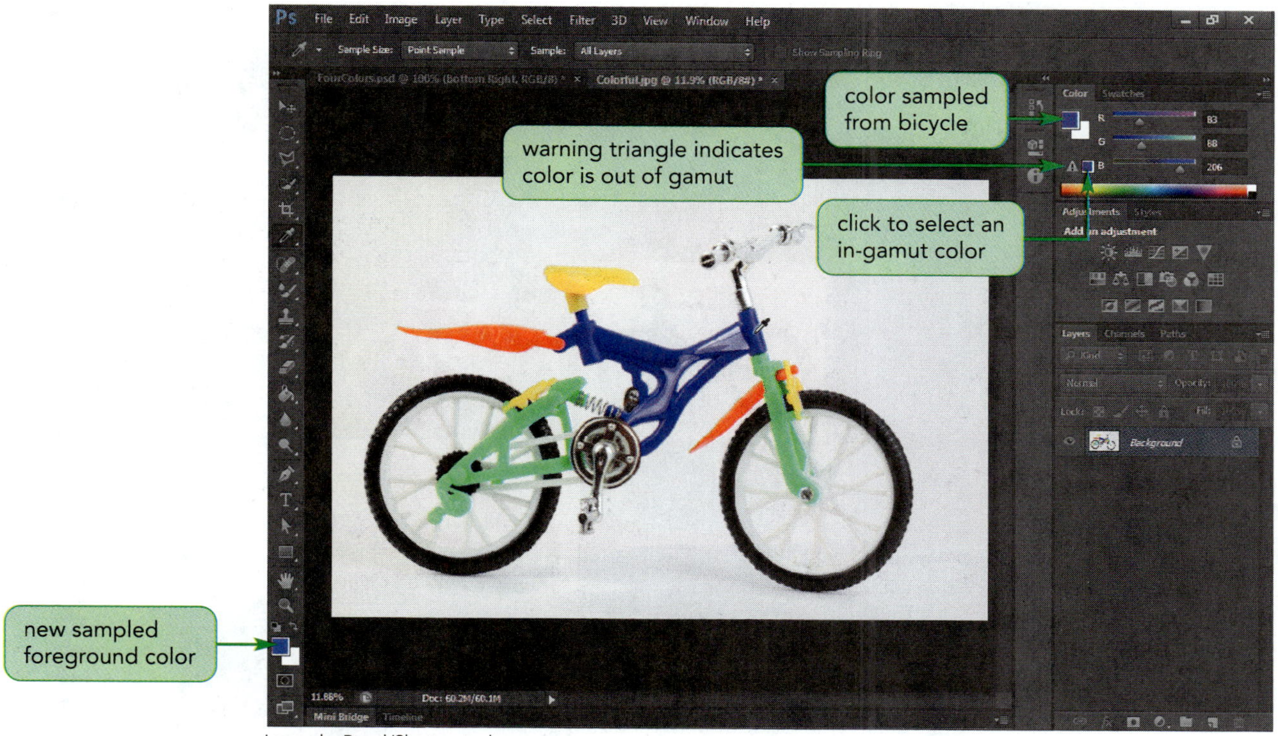

Losevsky Pavel/Shutterstock.com

In Figure 4-8, the selected foreground color is out of gamut for printing, as indicated by the triangle with the exclamation point. You can choose a new color yourself, or you can click the square to the right of the warning to have Photoshop substitute a similar color that is in gamut.

You'll use the Color panel to select a light blue color for the next bicycle.

REFERENCE

Specifying a Color in the Color Panel

- Enter color values in the boxes for R, G, and B if in RGB mode or in the boxes for C, M, Y, and K if in CMYK mode.

or

- Drag the color sliders for R, G, and B or for C, M, Y, and K.

or

- In the Color panel, click the Set foreground color icon to open the Color Picker dialog box.
- Select the color in the Color Picker dialog box, and then click the OK button.

To set a color using the Color panel:

1. In the Layers panel, click the **Lower Left** layer to select it.
2. In the Color panel, point to the **color ramp**. When the pointer is over the ramp, it changes to the Eyedropper pointer.
3. On the color ramp, click a **light blue** color. The foreground color icon changes to light blue in the Tools panel and in the Color panel.
4. Point to the **lower-left bicycle** in the image, and then click on the white area of the bicycle. Photoshop fills the bicycle with the light blue color. See Figure 4-9.

Figure 4-9 **Using the Color panel**

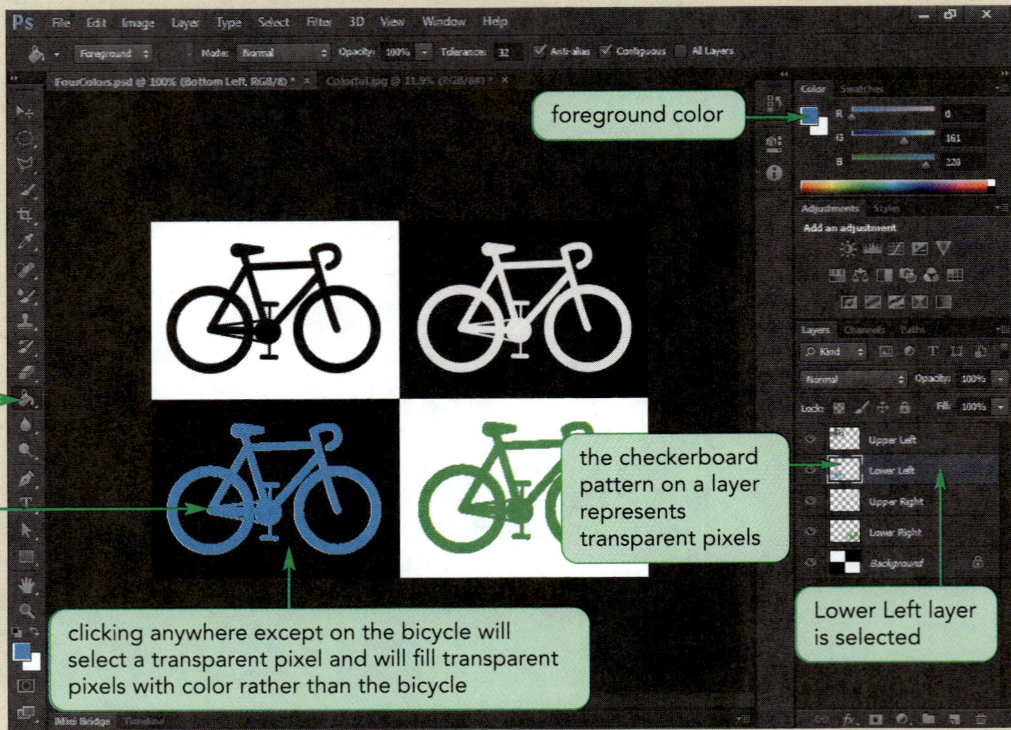

Black Images/Shutterstock.com

Trouble? If any part of the image other than the bicycle is filled with the light blue color, you have clicked a transparent part of the layer rather than the bicycle. Undo the change by pressing the Ctrl+Z keys, and then repeat Step 4.

Notice that the pointer shape is still a paint bucket because the Paint Bucket tool is still selected in the Tools panel.

INSIGHT

Understanding Web-Safe Colors

As you saw in Tutorial 2, today's color models can include millions of colors. However, in the not-so-distant past, computer monitors were limited to 256 colors. These 8-bit displays couldn't handle many of the colors available for Web design, and they used a process called dithering to mix two colors to achieve an approximation of any unavailable color. Dithering increased the time it took to upload images, and often made the Web experience less like surfing and more like a waiting game. In order to avoid dithering and slow upload times, Web designers could use **Web-safe colors**, colors that were available in any Web browser on any system. Photoshop still includes Web-safe options as color choices. For example, the Color Picker dialog box includes an Only Web Colors check box, and the Swatches panel includes palettes of Web-safe colors. Given that most computer monitors and mobile device displays can now display many more than 256 colors, you probably won't need to limit yourself to Web-safe colors, but it's good to know what they are.

You can also use the Color Picker to set a color for the foreground. To select a color in the Color Picker, click in the color ramp to display shades of that color in the color field. You can then use the color field to click a particular shade of the current color. See Figure 4-10.

Figure 4-10 Color Picker (Foreground Color) dialog box

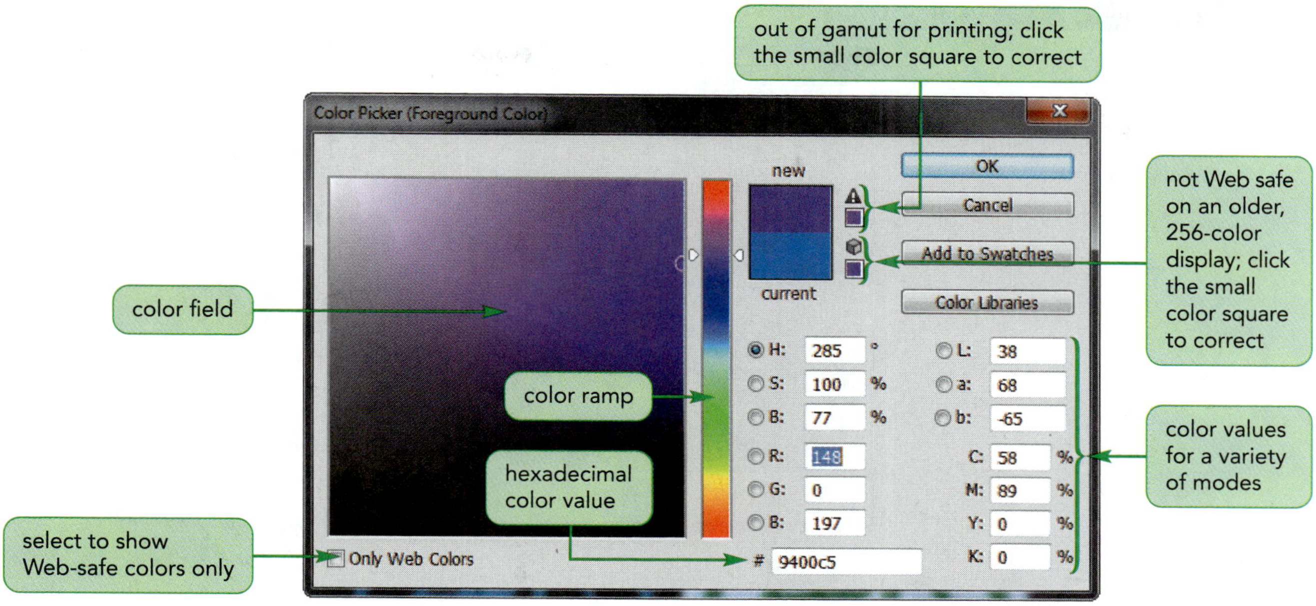

When you select the color, the Color Picker displays the color's values using different color modes, including HSB (Hue, Saturation, and Brightness), RGB, CMYK, and the color's hexadecimal color values. In a hexadecimal color value, the first pair of characters defines the red used in the color, and the next two pairs define green and blue, respectively. Hexadecimal color values are used to specify colors in **HTML (HyperText Markup Language)**, a programming language used to create Web pages. The Color Picker also displays Lab color mode values. **Lab color mode** describes colors as most people actually see them, rather than as they are interpreted by a device such as a monitor or a printer. Lab colors are considered **device independent** because a Lab color should look the same to the human eye no matter which device it's displayed on.

In addition to color values, the Color Picker displays icons that let you know if a color is either out of gamut, not Web safe, or both. To ensure that any color you choose will display correctly on an older 256-color monitor, select the Only Web Colors check box before selecting your color. If a color is out of gamut, click the "Click to select in gamut color" icon under the "Warning: out of gamut for color printing" icon to substitute a similar in-gamut color.

You'll use the Color Picker dialog box to select a yellow color for the third bicycle, and then you'll sample a color to assign to the final bicycle.

To set the foreground color using the Color Picker (Foreground Color) dialog box:

1. In the Layers panel, click the **Upper Right** layer.
2. In the Tools panel, click the **Set foreground color** icon ■. The Color Picker (Foreground Color) dialog box opens.
3. On the color ramp, click the **yellow color**, and then in the color field, click a **bright yellow**. See Figure 4-11. Note that your color values might not match the values shown in the dialog box.

Figure 4-11 Color Picker with Web-safe colors displayed

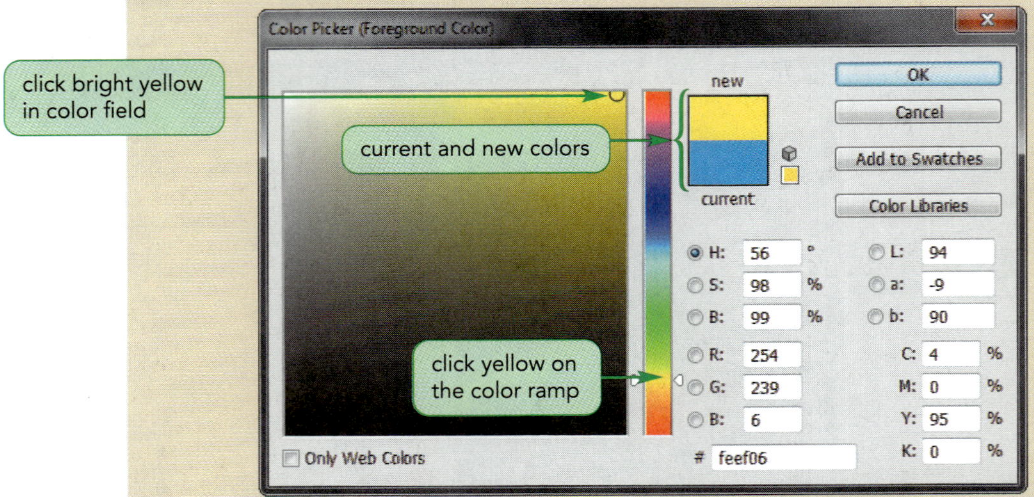

4. Click the **OK** button, and then click the **upper-right bicycle** in the image to apply the yellow color. The upper-right bicycle is now yellow.
5. Switch to **Colorful.jpg**, and sample the **red fender guard** color. In the Color panel, click the **Click to select in gamut color** icon, if necessary, and then switch back to **FourColors.psd**.
6. Click the **Upper Left** layer, click the **Paint Bucket Tool** button, and then click the **upper-left bicycle** to apply the sampled color from Colorful.jpg file.
7. Save **FourColors.psd**. See Figure 4-12.

Figure 4-12 Colors assigned to four bicycles

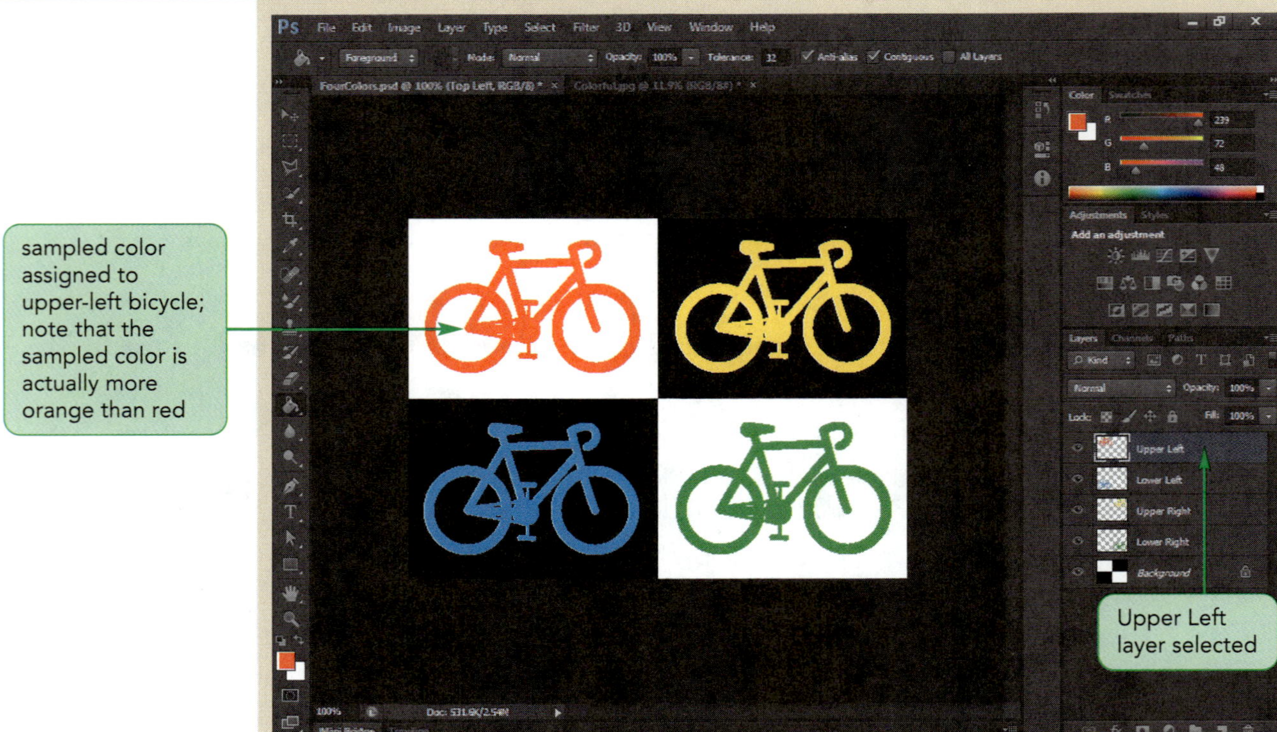

Black Images/Shutterstock.com

All of the bicycles have been assigned a color. You'll continue to work with color by assigning a new background color and then using it to extend the canvas to see if you can add interest to the logo.

Changing the Background Color

Photoshop uses the background color in combination with the foreground color to create some of the gradient presets covered later in this tutorial. You can also use the background color when you increase the canvas size of a composition, as you did in Tutorial 2. However, Photoshop only provides a background color option for increased canvas size if your composition has a Background layer. When you create a new file, Photoshop uses the current background color if you select Background Color from the Background Contents list in the New dialog box.

You can specify the background color in Photoshop using the same methods you use to specify foreground color. You can use the Color Picker (Background Color) dialog box, the Color panel, or the Eyedropper tool.

You can easily switch foreground and background colors by clicking the Switch Foreground and Background Colors button in the Tools panel or by pressing the X key. You can reset Photoshop to the default foreground and background colors by clicking the Default Foreground and Background Colors button in the Tools panel or by pressing the D key.

Lee thinks that the four-bicycle logo idea might be overkill, but wants to see if adding a border to it helps unify the colors. She suggests that you increase the size of your poster by adding a border that alternates two of the colors you used on the bicycles. To do so, you'll use the Increase Canvas Size command two times, using a different method to choose a background color each time you do.

To change the background color:

1. In the Layers panel, click the **Background** layer to make it the active layer.
2. In the Color panel, click the **Set background color** icon, which is partially hidden by the Set foreground color icon. The color values for the current background color (white) are displayed.

   Trouble? If the Color Picker (Background Color) dialog box opens, click the Cancel button.
3. In the Tools panel, click the **Eyedropper Tool** button, and then click in the upper-right yellow bicycle. Because the sample includes all of the layers in the file, Photoshop samples the yellow from the bicycle, even though the Background layer is selected, not the bicycle layer. The background color icon changes to yellow.
4. On the menu bar, click **Image**, and then click **Canvas Size**.
5. In the Canvas Size dialog box, click the **Relative** check box to select it, if necessary, type **2** in the Width box, select **Inches** as the unit of measurement, if necessary, and then type **2** in the Height box. You'll leave the Anchor setting as is so the canvas is extended equally on all four sides of the image.
6. In the Canvas extension color list, click **Background** to select it, if necessary, and then click the **OK** button to close the Canvas Size dialog box. The canvas now has a border that uses the yellow color.
7. In the Tools panel, click the **Switch Foreground and Background Colors** icon. The background color icon changes to orange.

   Next, you'll extend the canvas again using the new background color.
8. On the menu bar, click **Image**, and then click **Canvas Size**.

TIP

You can also press the X key to switch the foreground and background colors.

9. In the Canvas Size dialog box, click the **Relative** check box to select it, if necessary, type **2** in the Width box, select **Inches**, if necessary, and then type **2** in the Height box.
10. In the Canvas extension color list, click **Background** to select it, if necessary, and then click the **OK** button to close the Canvas Size dialog box. Fit the image on the screen. The canvas now has a second border that uses the orange color. See Figure 4-13.

Figure 4-13 **Extending the canvas with the background color**

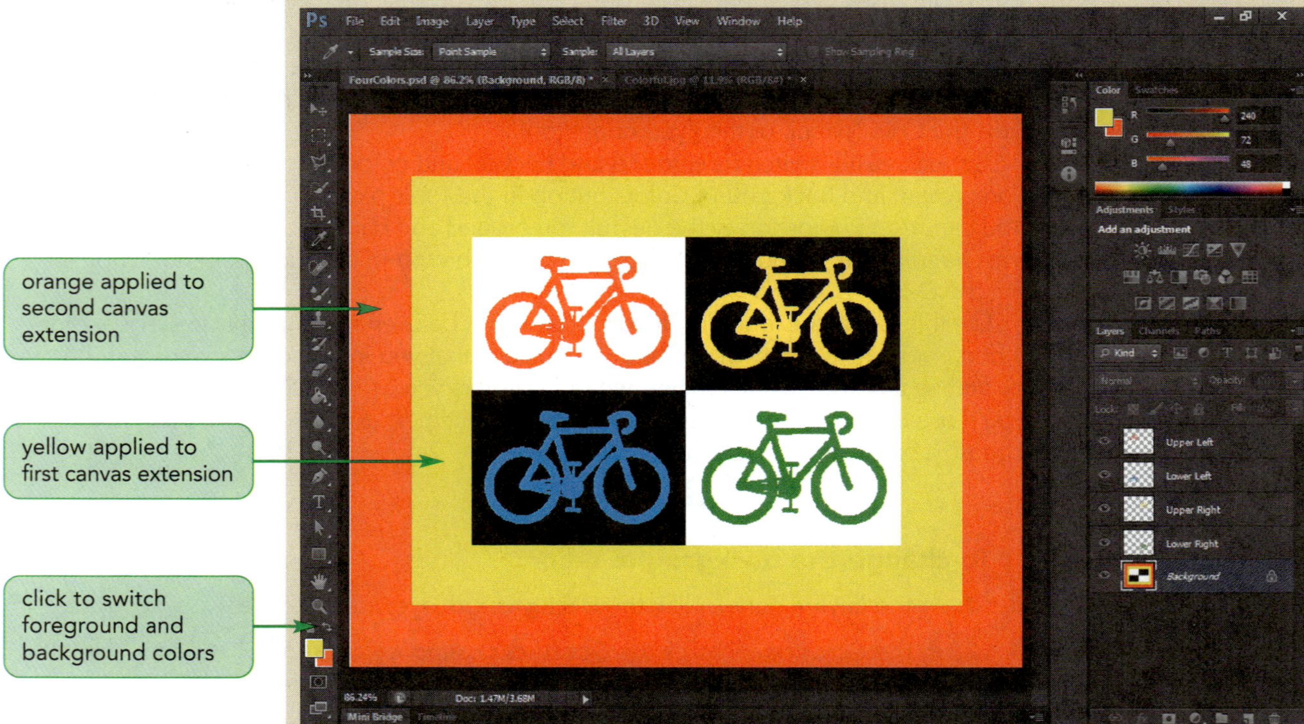

Black Images/Shutterstock.com

The canvas has been extended two times, once using yellow as the background color and then once again using orange. The image now has a border of alternating colors. You'll switch back to the default foreground and background colors before continuing your work.

11. Press the **D** key to return Photoshop to the default foreground and background colors, black and white.
12. Save the file as **FourColors.jpg**, using the default JPEG Options, in the Photoshop4\Tutorial folder. Photoshop saves the file as a JPEG and flattens the image into a single layer.
13. Close FourColors.psd without saving the file. Leave Colorful.jpg open.

PROSKILLS

Problem Solving: Making Your Work Accessible to the Color Blind

As someone using digital imaging to convey messages, you will often be faced with the challenge of trying to ensure that your work is accessible to the largest number of people possible. It's a good idea to keep in mind that some people are **color blind**, which means they don't see certain colors the same way the majority of the population sees them. There are many kinds of color blindness. Some color-blind people can't distinguish between red and green; others can't distinguish between blue and yellow; others don't see color at all (though this is extremely rare). You can create designs that accommodate the color blind in a number of ways:

- Avoid putting red and green or blue and yellow directly next to each other in a composition, if possible.
- Use textures in addition to colors to help distinguish between objects in a composition.
- Add borders to delineate separate areas in a composition or on a Web page.
- Underline text that you want to stand out, rather than relying solely on a color change.
- Vary the fonts for text that uses different colors.
- Use shapes as backgrounds for different parts of a composition.

These suggestions are helpful aids for reaching a color-blind audience, but they also present additional challenges, such as images that are too busy (because of multiple fonts and shapes), or images that aren't aesthetically pleasing to a wider audience. By following these guidelines and using the tools in Photoshop to help you solve other problems, you can create compositions that reach the widest possible audience.

Lee asks you to work on an ad that she has started for a Web campaign. She suggests you use the Swatches panel to try working with a different palette of colors.

Working with the Swatches Panel

The Swatches panel provides a library of commonly used colors that you can easily access to modify your images. The panel appears behind the Colors panel in the default Essentials workspace. You can also open the Swatches panel from any other workspace by clicking Swatches on the Window menu. See Figure 4-14.

Figure 4-14 Default Swatches panel

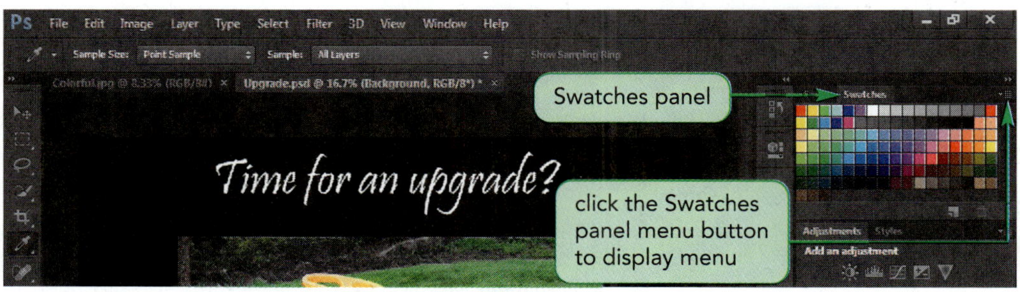

Ingvald Kaldhussater/Shutterstock.com

You can add colors to the Swatches panel so your customized palette of swatches gives you easy access to colors that you use often. To create a subset of colors with which to work, you can delete colors from the Swatches panel. You can also save the customized panel as a preset. In addition, Photoshop provides a long list of color palettes that you can choose to display in the Swatches panel based on your designing or printing needs.

TIP

To restore the default Photoshop swatches, click the panel menu button, and then click Reset Swatches.

You have the option of loading or replacing a swatches **library**, or palette of swatches, in the Swatches panel. When you load a library, it is added or **appended** to the current library of swatches at the bottom of the panel. When you replace a library, the new library takes the place of the current library in the panel, and you are prompted to save the current library if you have made any modifications to it. Whether you choose to load or replace a swatches library depends on the work you're doing. If you want to continue to work with the current swatches but need additional choices, loading a library is your best bet. If you want to restrict your choices to a single library, replace the current library. You can also customize the display of swatches in the Swatches panel to display small or large thumbnails, or to display the choices in a list.

Photoshop provides numerous libraries or color palettes that you can display in the Swatches panel. You choose a color palette based on your current project. For example, if you are creating graphics for a newspaper, you should consider displaying the ANPA color palette in the Swatches panel. ANPA stands for American Newspaper Publishers Association, and the ANPA palette displays colors commonly used in newspaper layout applications. If you are working on a printed piece, choose one of the PANTONE or other CMYK libraries. You can also display Web-safe swatches.

To select a color swatch, click a swatch to choose it as the foreground color, or press the Ctrl key and then click the swatch to choose it as the background color.

Lee wants you to revise an ad she's created for the local Chamber of Commerce Web site. She would like you to add colored rectangles behind the white text in the ad but also wants you to extend your Photoshop knowledge by working with a different palette of colors. You'll use the Swatches panel to see what a different palette looks like. You'll choose one that displays hexadecimal values for colors, which are the color values used by Web developers in their HTML code.

To customize the display of the Swatches panel:

1. Reset the Essentials workspace, click the **Swatches** panel tab, and then open **Upgrade.psd** from the Photoshop4\Tutorial folder. Photoshop displays the default Swatches panel presets using the Small Thumbnails display.
2. In the Swatches panel, click the **panel menu** button, and then click **Large List**. Photoshop displays the swatches in a list. Each swatch includes a thumbnail of the color, as well as the swatch name or color value.

Next, you'll change the Swatches panel palette to Web Spectrum to view the colors along with their hexadecimal values.

To change the color palette in the Swatches panel:

1. In the Swatches panel, click the **panel menu** button to display the list of presets, and then click **Web Spectrum**. Photoshop asks if you want to replace the current color swatches or append them to the swatches already in the panel.
2. Click the **OK** button to replace the colors in the panel with the Web Spectrum colors. The Swatches panel changes to display the new colors. Instead of names, the list displays a hexadecimal color value to the right of each swatch.

   Trouble? If you don't have the Web Spectrum palette, choose a different palette from the menu.

   Trouble? If Photoshop displays a message asking if you want to save changes to the current swatches before replacing them, click the No button.
3. Switch to the **Color** panel, click the **Set Foreground color** icon, and then switch back to the **Swatches** panel.

4. In the Swatches panel, drag the scroll box to just before the halfway point on the scroll bar, place the Eyedropper pointer over the green swatch that displays the hexadecimal values **#006600** for the green color, and then click. The foreground color changes to green.

   Trouble? If the background color changes instead of the foreground color, click the Color panel tab, and then click the Set foreground color icon in the Color panel. Switch back to the Swatches panel and repeat Step 4.

5. Click the **Background** layer to select it, if necessary. In the Tools panel, click the **Rectangle Tool** button and on the options bar, click the **Pick tool mode** button and then click **Shape**, if necessary.

6. Draw a rectangle over the "Time for an upgrade?" text. When you release the mouse button, a green rectangle appears. Because the Background layer was selected when you added the rectangle layer, the rectangle appears beneath the text on the canvas. See Figure 4-15.

Figure 4-15 Shape layer under text layer

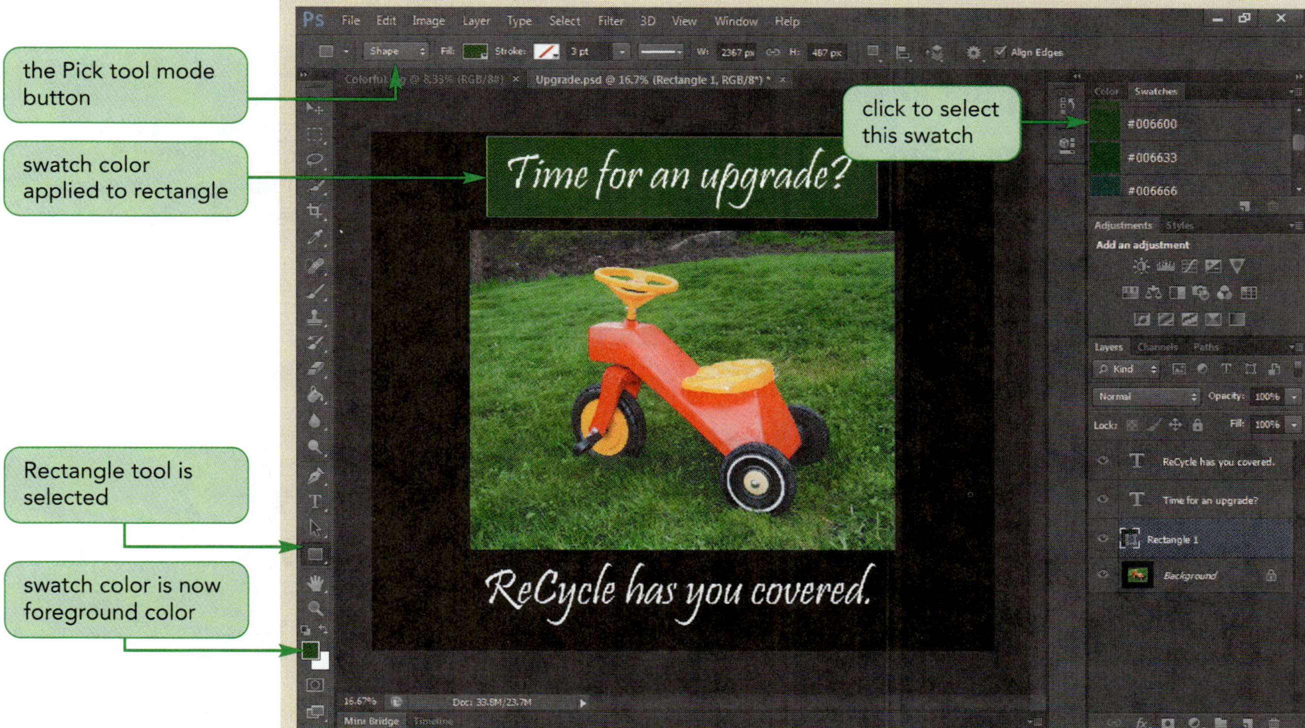

Ingvald Kaldhussater/Shutterstock.com

Notice that the Rectangle 1 layer is now the active layer in the Layers panel.

7. Draw a rectangle over the "ReCycle has you covered" text. Because the Rectangle 1 layer was selected when you added the new rectangle layer, this rectangle also appears beneath the text on the canvas.

8. To restore the original swatches, click the **panel menu** button in the Swatches panel, click **Reset Swatches**, and then click the **OK** button.

9. Click the **panel menu** button again, and then click **Small Thumbnail** to reset the display of the Swatches panel to the default.

10. Save the file as **ColorUpgrade.jpg**, using the default JPEG Options, in the Photoshop4\Tutorial folder, and then close Upgrade.psd without saving it. Leave Colorful.jpg open for the next set of steps.

Adding Colors to the Swatches Panel

You can add the current foreground color to the Swatches panel by positioning the mouse pointer over a blank area of the Swatches panel; when the Paint Bucket pointer appears, click to add the color swatch to the panel. You can also use the Create new swatch of foreground color button at the bottom of the Swatches panel, or the New Swatch command on the panel menu. Once you add a color to the Swatches panel, you can apply it as you would apply any other color.

When you add a color to the panel, it is saved with the Swatches panel as a preference. If at some point you reset your preferences, you will lose any modifications to the Swatches panel. To save a modified Swatches panel permanently, you need to save it in a library.

Lee has given you a photograph that she plans to use in a number of different campaigns, and she would like you to save some of the colors in the photograph as swatches in the Swatches panel.

To add sampled colors to the Swatches panel:

1. Reset the default Essentials workspace, and then press the **D** key to restore the default foreground and background colors.
2. In the Tools panel, click the **Eyedropper Tool** button.
3. Click the **light green chain guard** on the bicycle.
4. Click the **Swatches** panel tab, if necessary, move the mouse pointer to a blank (gray) area at the bottom of the swatches area until it becomes a Paint Bucket pointer, and then click. The Color Swatch Name dialog box opens, as shown in Figure 4-16.

Figure 4-16 Naming a color swatch

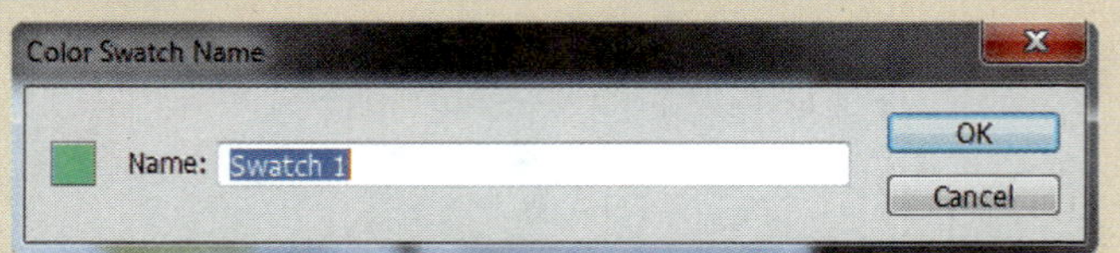

5. Type **CoolGreen** in the Name box, and then click the **OK** button. The new swatch appears as the last swatch in the Swatches panel.
6. Place the mouse pointer over the new swatch until the tooltip CoolGreen appears. The new swatch has the name you assigned.
7. Sample the **yellow seat** on the bicycle and add it to the Swatches panel as **BrightYellow**. The new swatch appears to the right of the CoolGreen swatch in the panel.
8. Sample the **red fender guard** in the image and add it to the Swatches panel as **RedFender**. The new swatch appears to the right of the BrightYellow swatch in the panel.

You'll save the modified swatches as a preset so you can use the set again in the future.

Saving Modified Swatches as a Preset

If you have swatches that you plan to reuse, for example, swatches based on a color model that you will use consistently with one campaign or for one client, it is a good idea to save them as a preset so you can reload them at any time.

To save swatches as a preset and then load them:

1. In the Swatches panel, click the **panel menu** button, and then click **Save Swatches**. The Save dialog box opens.
2. Navigate to the Photoshop4\Tutorial folder, type **ReCycleSwatches** in the File name box, and then click the **Save** button. Photoshop saves the swatches with an .aco extension in the Tutorial folder.

   You'll replace the ReCycleSwatches palette with the default palette, and then practice opening the custom palette you created.
3. In the Swatches panel, click the **panel menu** button, click **Reset Swatches**, and then click the **OK** button. Photoshop reloads the default swatches.
4. Click the **panel menu** button again, click **Load Swatches**, navigate to the Photoshop4\Tutorial folder, click the **ReCycleSwatches.aco** file to select it, and then click **Load**. The saved customized swatches are appended to the default swatches in the Swatches panel.

You can delete colors that you don't need from the Swatches panel. When you delete a swatch from a library, you need to save the library for the deletion to be permanent. If you delete a swatch by mistake, close the library without saving it and then reopen it.

You'll delete two of the colors from the Swatches panel that you know you'll never use, and you'll keep the CoolGreen swatch in the customized library.

To delete a color from the Swatches panel:

1. Point to the **BrightYellow** swatch at the bottom of the Swatches panel, press the **Alt** key so a scissors pointer appears, and then click. The swatch is deleted from the Swatches panel.

   Trouble? If you delete a different swatch accidentally, reload the ReCycleSwatches library without saving changes to the open library.
2. Repeat Step 1 to delete the RedFender swatch.
3. Reset the swatches, and save changes to the current custom swatches before closing them. Saving your changes will ensure that the ReCycleSwatches custom library includes CoolGreen so you can use it in future Photoshop sessions.

   Trouble? If you are given the choice of replacing or appending the current swatches with the default, click the OK button.

   Trouble? If you are prompted to replace the existing ReCycleSwatches.aco file, click the OK button.
4. Close Colorful.jpg without saving it.

Working with the Styles Panel

You can take the time to apply individual effects to layers in Photoshop to achieve a certain look for text or a vector object, or you can choose from a library of professionally designed styles in the Styles panel. The Styles panel, which appears behind the Adjustments panel in the Essentials workspace, includes a library of layer presets that let you change the look of a layer by applying multiple effects with a single click of the mouse. Using a style is a quick and easy way to apply multiple effects at the same time—for example, a **bevel effect**, which gives an object the appearance of a third dimension, and a gradient or a shadow. See Figure 4-17.

Figure 4-17 Style applied from Styles panel

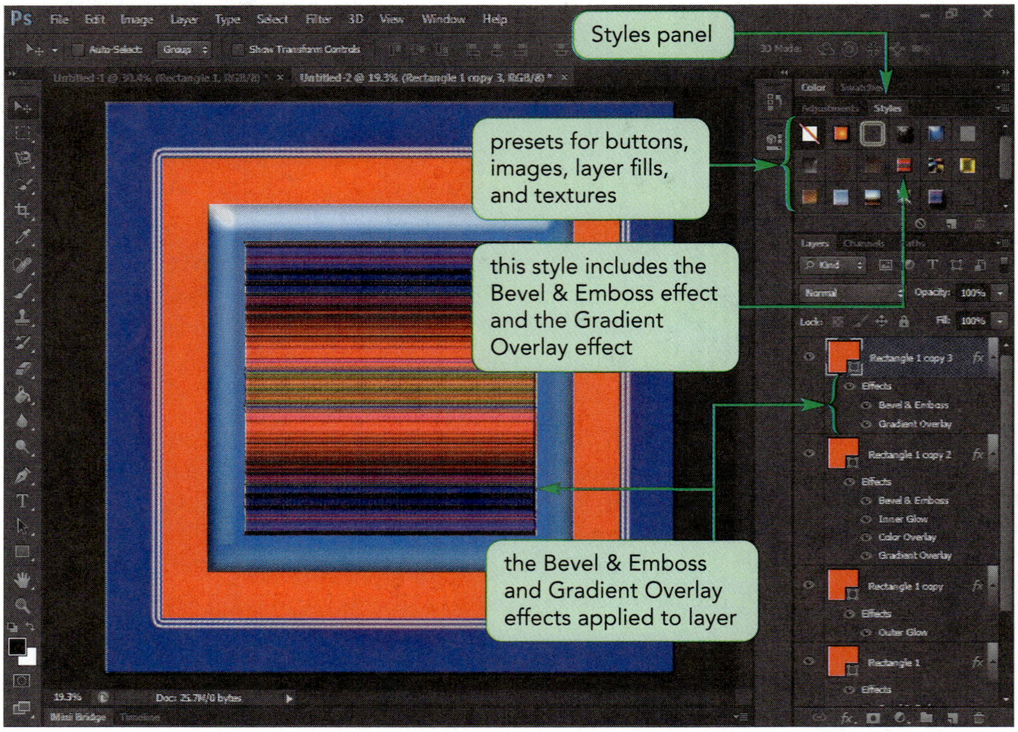

> **TIP**
> You can change the library of styles displayed in the Styles panel by selecting a new library of style presets from the Styles panel menu.

The default Styles panel library includes presets for buttons, images, layer fills, and textures. You can also choose a library with styles designed only for a particular object—for example, a library created solely for buttons or solely for text. When you assign a style to a layer, the letters *fx* appear to the right of the layer name, and the effects used in the style are listed beneath the layer in the Layers panel.

Lee would like her bicycle shop sign to be simple. She wants you to develop a sign that would consist of a bicycle silhouette that will appear on a hinged sign sticking out over the shop door—no words, just the sign. To show Lee the full effect of the sign you design, you'll place it in a vector drawing of the shop; later in the tutorial, you'll even draw the hinge that the sign will hang on.

To work with the Styles panel:

1. Reset the Essentials workspace, restore the default foreground and background colors, and then click the **Styles** tab in the Adjustments panel tab group to display the Styles panel.
2. In the Styles panel, click the **panel menu** button, click **Reset Styles**, and then click the **OK** button to replace the current styles with the default styles.

Trouble? If Photoshop displays a message asking if you want to save changes to the current styles before replacing them, click the No button.

If you hover over a style thumbnail, Photoshop displays the name of the style. However, it is difficult to tell from the names exactly what effects will be applied. To see what a style does, you need to apply it to a layer.

3. Open **BikeSign.psd**, located in the Photoshop4\Tutorial folder, display it at 100% magnification, and pan the image so the bicycle and the white background rectangle are near the center of the window.

   The file Lee provided you includes three layers: The background is a vector drawing of the storefront, the top layer is a plain bicycle silhouette on a transparent background, and the layer beneath the bicycle is a plain white rectangle.

4. In the Layers panel, click the **Bicycle** layer to select it.
5. Point to the first thumbnail in the Styles panel. Photoshop displays the style name, Default Style (None), when you point to the thumbnail. You can click this thumbnail at any point to undo any style you have applied to the layer.
6. Point to the thumbnail in the second row, fourth column, called **Blanket (Texture)**, and then click. Photoshop applies the Blanket style to the bicycle. Notice that *fx* appears to the right of the layer name in the Layers panel, and a list of effects appears indented under the layer name. Clicking a different style will replace this style with the new style.
7. Point to the thumbnail in the third row, fifth column, called **Sunset Sky (Text)**, and then click to apply this style to the bicycle. See Figure 4-18.

Figure 4-18 **Applying the Sunset Sky (Text) style**

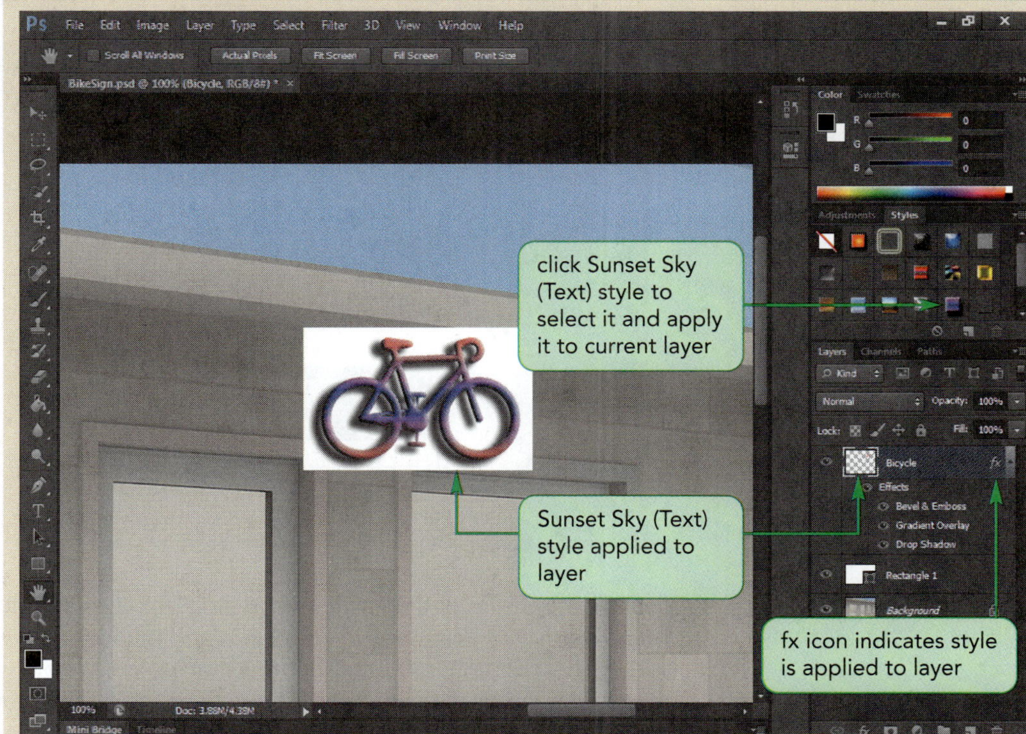

Shevchenko Nataliya/Shutterstock.com; Black Images/Shutterstock.com

Although this style was designed for text, it can be applied to any object. It includes three effects: Bevel & Emboss, Gradient Overlay, and Drop Shadow. You can hide any of these individual effects just as you can hide layers.

8. In the Layers panel, click the **Eye** icon to the left of Drop Shadow to hide that effect. The bicycle no longer has a shadow.
9. Click again in the same spot to turn the effect back on.
10. Hide the Gradient Overlay effect. The bicycle has returned to its original color, but with the Drop Shadow and Bevel & Emboss effects still applied.
11. Save the file as **SunsetBike.psd** in the Photoshop4\Tutorial folder.

You can leave a style preset as it is, or you can modify it to create a custom style preset. You'll modify the Sunset Sky (Text) style to see if you can achieve a better effect for the sign.

Using the Layer Style Dialog Box

You can modify a layer style using the Layer Style dialog box. For example, you might want to change the width of an outline (called a **stroke**) or the angle of a shadow. You can access the Layer Style dialog box by double-clicking the *fx* label to the right of the layer name, or through the Layer command on the menu bar. See Figure 4-19.

Figure 4-19 **Layer Style dialog box**

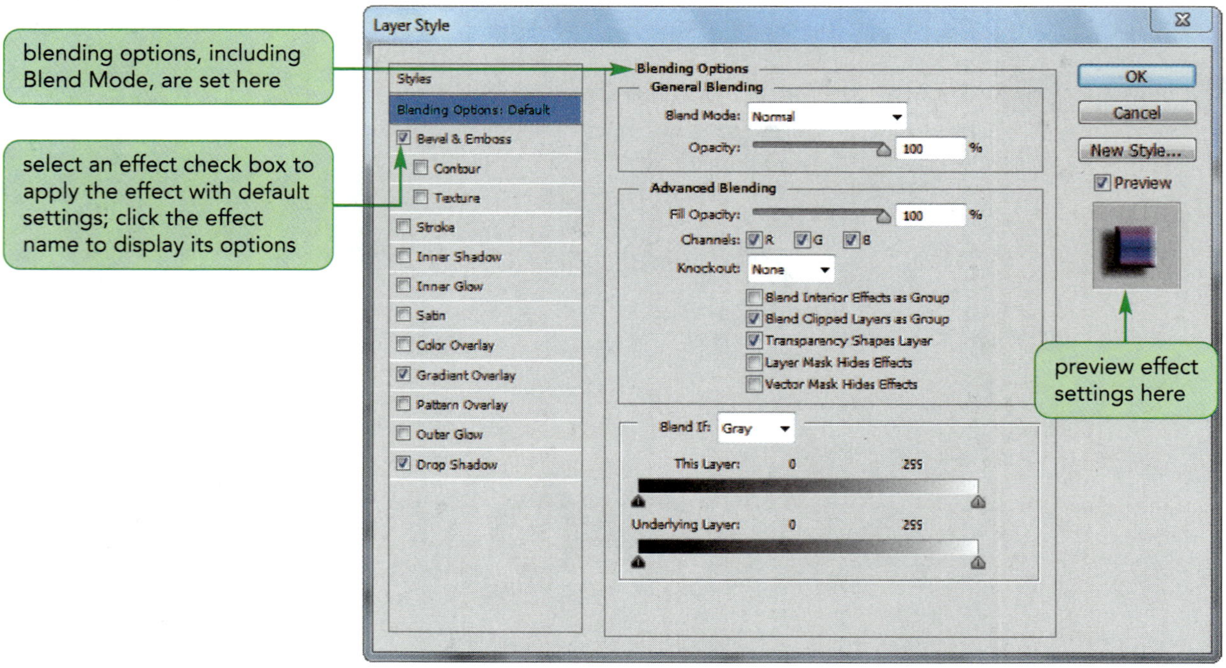

By default, the center of the Layer Style dialog box displays blending options, such as the blending modes discussed in Tutorial 3, and the fill opacity. However, the dialog box also includes a number of other options that are not visible when you first open the dialog box. In fact, the Layer Style dialog box behaves in ways you might not have seen before. On the left side of the dialog box, under the Blending Options: Default heading, you can click a check box to select an option such as Drop Shadow or Outer Glow and apply the default settings for that option. When you do, the effect is applied, but you are not given the opportunity to modify the effect. However, if you click the name of the effect rather than the check box, you select the effect and the center of the Layer Style dialog box changes to display options for the selected effect.

The effects available in the Layer Style dialog box are listed and described in the table in Figure 4-20.

Figure 4-20 **Effects in Layer Style dialog box**

Layer Style	Effect
Bevel & Emboss	Combines highlights and shadows to create a beveled effect that makes an object look three-dimensional
Stroke	Outlines the object—usually text—with a color, gradient, or pattern
Inner Shadow	Gives the layer an indented or recessed appearance by placing a shadow inside the edges of the layer content
Inner Glow	Adds a glow inside the layer content
Satin	Adds shading to the object's interior to give it the appearance of satin
Color Overlay	Fills the layer content with color
Gradient Overlay	Fills the layer content with a gradient
Pattern Overlay	Fills the layer content with a pattern
Outer Glow	Adds a glow outside the layer content
Drop Shadow	Places a shadow behind the layer; you can specify the angle and opacity of the shadow and its distance from the layer object, among the things

You've presented a draft of your sign to Lee, and she thinks it would be more effective without the gradient overlay and drop shadow. You'll experiment with different layer styles to see if you can achieve a better effect.

TIP

You can also double-click a layer thumbnail to open the Layer Style dialog box.

To use the Layer Style dialog box and save the new style:

1. In the Layers panel, double-click **fx** to the right of the Bicycle layer name. The Layer Style dialog box opens.
2. If necessary, drag the dialog box by its title bar up and to the right, and pan the document so you can see the bicycle.
3. In the Layer Style dialog box, click the **Gradient Overlay** check box to turn the effect back on. Because you clicked the check box and not the effect name, none of the Gradient Overlay effects is displayed in the right pane.

   Next, to see the options for an effect, you'll click the name of the effect rather than the check box.
4. Click **Drop Shadow**. The Drop Shadow settings are displayed in the right pane of the dialog box.

   You can change the blend mode of the shadow, its opacity, and its angle. If you would like the angle that you set to apply to all other effects so they are consistent, click the Use Global Light check box to select it. You can also change other shadow options, such as the distance from the object it is shadowing, and its size.
5. Decrease the Distance setting for the drop shadow from 10 pixels to **5** pixels. The shadow is now closer to the bicycle.
6. Click the **Drop Shadow** check box to deselect it. See Figure 4-21.

Figure 4-21 Deselecting Drop Shadow

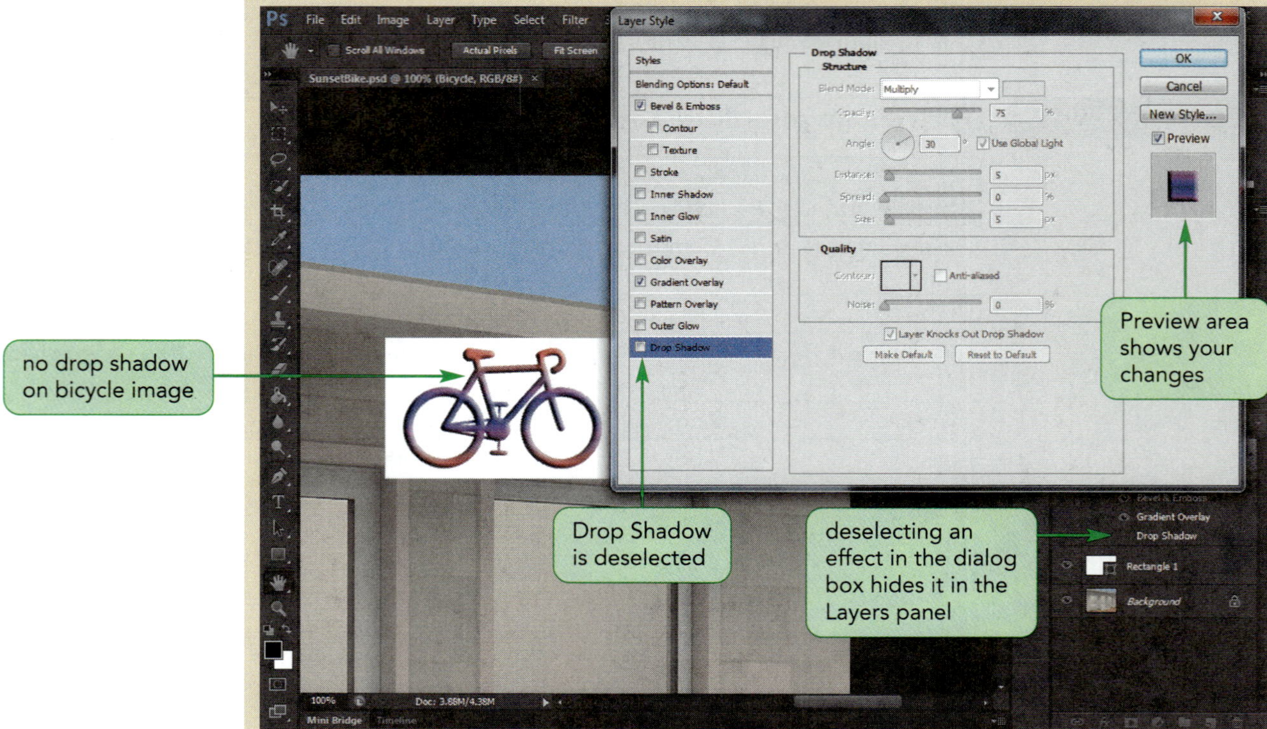

Shevchenko Nataliya/Shutterstock.com; Black Images/Shutterstock.com

In the Layer Style dialog box, the Preview area shows the effect without the drop shadow, and in the Document window, the bicycle on the sign no longer has the shadow.

7. Click the **Gradient Overlay** check box to deselect it. The bicycle appears in its original color, but it still has the Bevel & Emboss effect applied. You'll save this style so you can use it again in the future.
8. On the right side of the Layer Style dialog box, click the **New Style** button; the New Style dialog box opens.
9. Type **BikeSign** in the Name box, click the **Include Layer Effects** check box to select it, if necessary, and then click the **OK** button.
10. Click the **OK** button to close the Layer Style dialog box. The image of the bicycle on the sign now includes the new style you created.
11. Save the file as **EffectSign.jpg**, using the default JPEG Options, in the Photoshop4\Tutorial folder, close SunsetBike.psd without saving it, and then exit Photoshop.

In this session, you learned how to use the color selection tools, including the Color panel, the Color Picker, and the Eyedropper tool. You sampled colors, applied them to objects, and added them to the Swatches panel. You also worked with styles and made changes in the Layer Style dialog box to enhance parts of your image.

In the next session, you'll modify the image further so you can show Lee what your sign will look like hanging above the entrance of the store.

REVIEW

Session 4.1 Quick Check

1. By default, Photoshop uses the ____________ color when you draw or paint with one of the tools found in the Tools panel.
2. What tool in the Tools panel can you use to sample a color?
3. Define a color scheme, and give three examples of different types of color schemes.
4. ____________ is the process of mixing two colors to achieve an approximation of an unavailable color.
5. What does *gamut* mean?
6. Sometimes colors are defined by ____________ values, which are unique strings of six letters and numbers.
7. The ____________ panel displays a library of commonly used colors.

SESSION 4.2 VISUAL OVERVIEW

You can experiment with the angle of a fill to achieve different effects.

In the Gradient Fill dialog box, you can select the gradient, which can combine multiple colors.

The gradient fill style determines how the colors are laid out in the gradient. For example, they can be linear or **radial** (emanating out like a bull's eye).

Pattern fills include many different texture options.

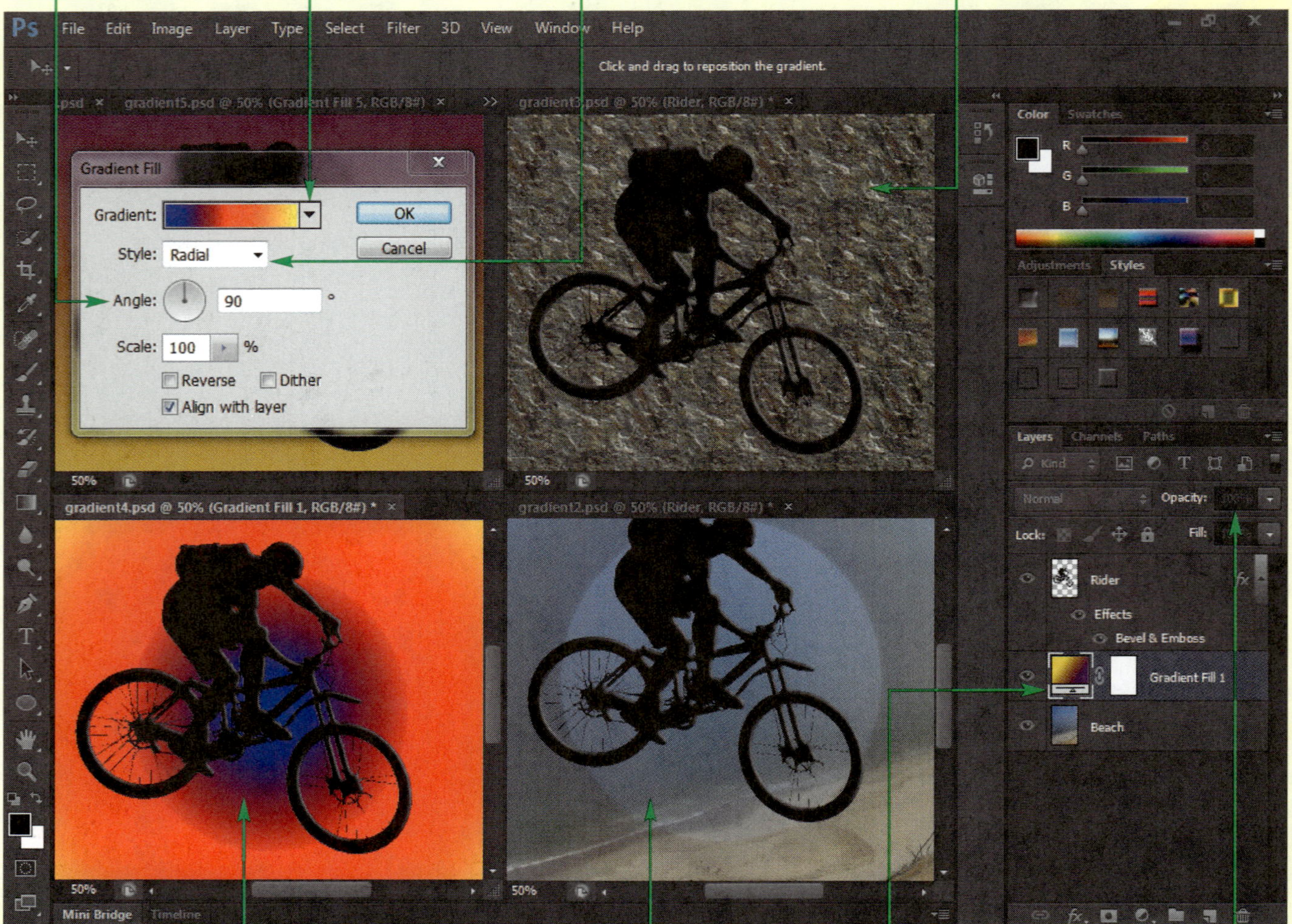

A **fill layer** is a layer filled with a solid color, a pattern, or a gradient. This gradient fill uses multiple colors.

This gradient fill layer is transparent, and affects the Beach layer beneath it, but not the Rider layer.

A gradient fill layer blends the foreground color with transparent pixels, or it blends two or more other colors.

You can let underlying layers show through by setting the opacity of a fill layer.

sn4ke/Shutterstock.com; Jane Hosie-Bounar

FILL LAYERS, SHAPES, AND PAINTING

Use the options bar to set the **diameter**, or width, of the brush tip.

The Brush Presets panel lets you preview how brush tips will look when you stroke the canvas.

You can display the panel menu to choose from many different brush preset libraries.

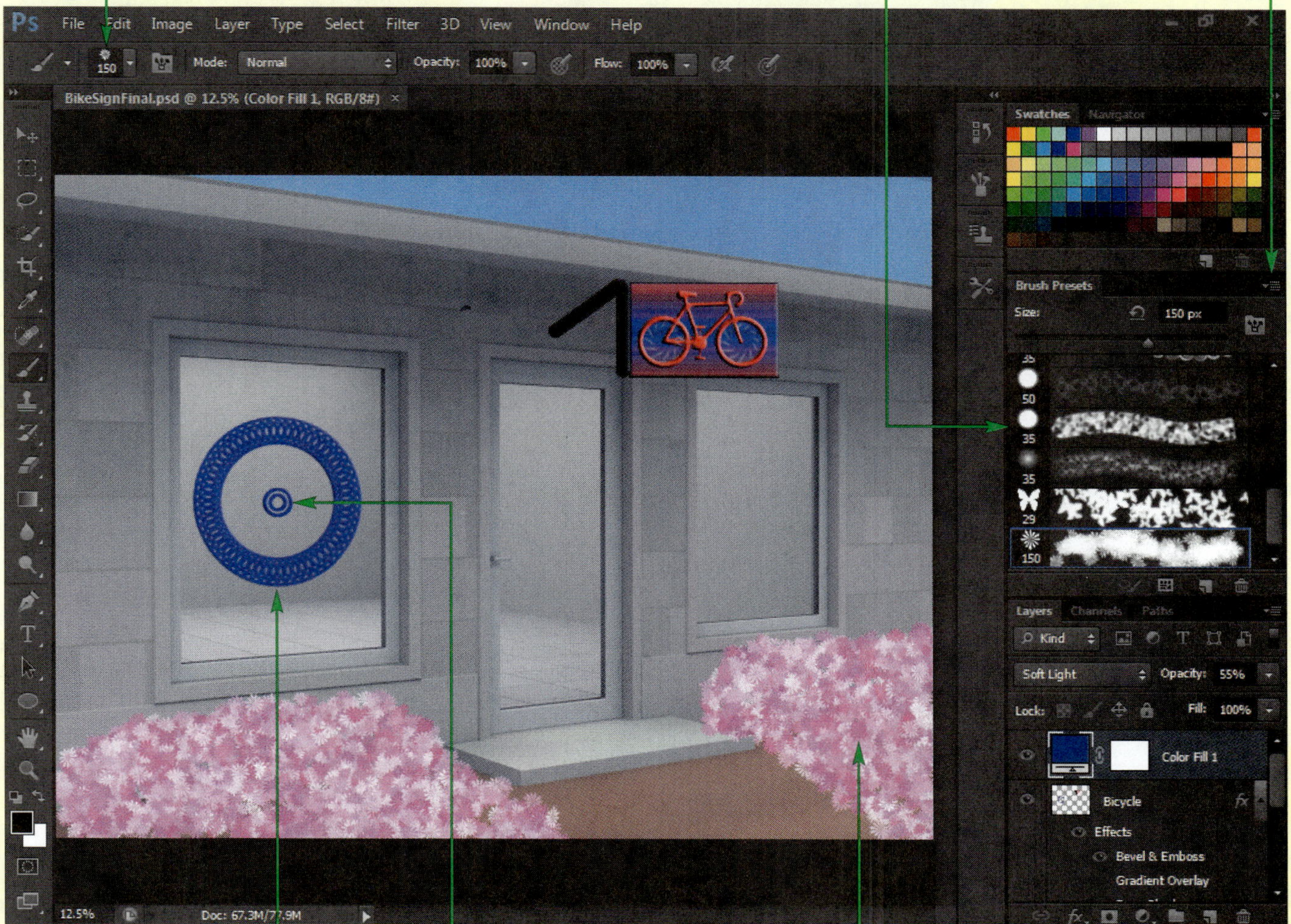

To create an exact brushstroke, create a work path and then stroke the path.

Clicking once with a brush adds a single stroke.

Brush tip choices include leaves, flowers, and other natural objects.

Shevchenko Nataliya/Shutterstock.com; Black Images/Shutterstock.com

Adding Fill Layers

You can add a fill layer to a Photoshop file using the Create new fill or adjustment layer icon at the bottom of the Layers panel. You can use fill layers to colorize black-and-white photographs or to produce interesting effects—for example, placing an image so it has a gradient or patterned background. When you add a fill layer, you set its opacity to determine how much of an effect it will have on underlying layers. You can also move a fill layer in the Layers panel so it applies to some layers and not others, as shown in Figure 4-22.

Figure 4-22 Adding a solid color fill layer

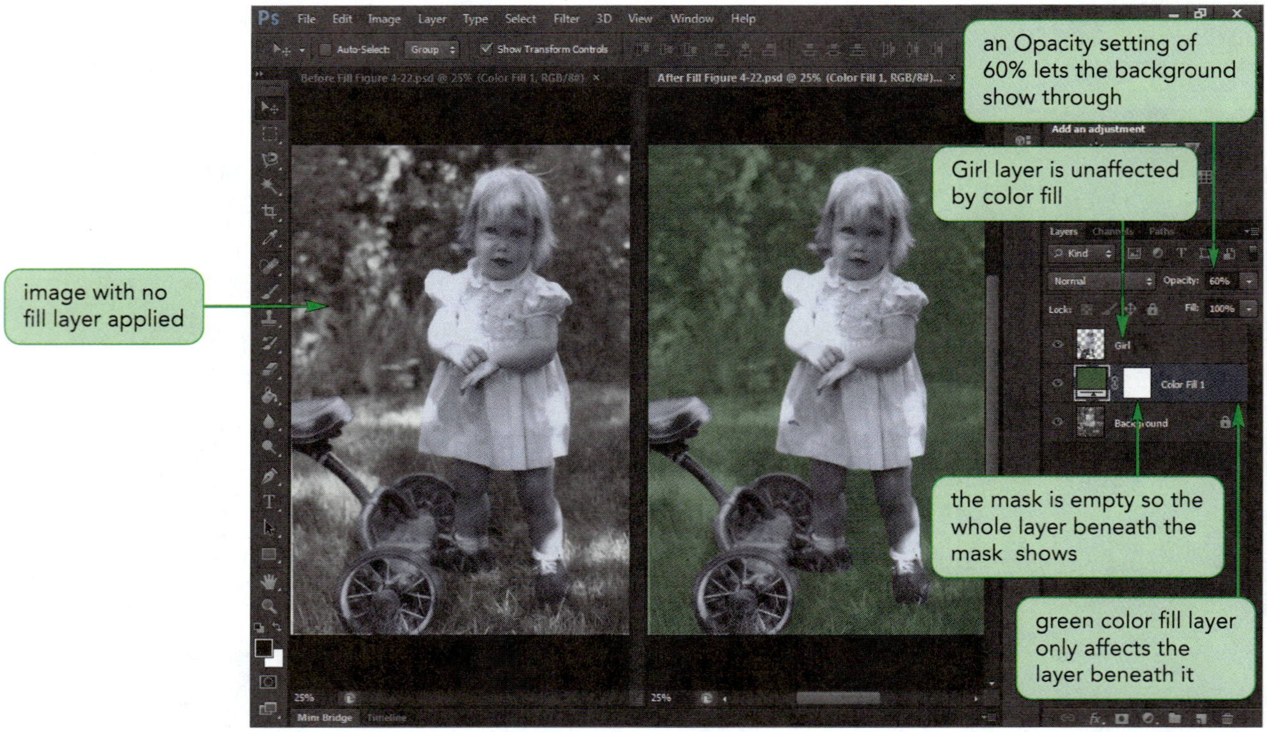

Jane Hosie-Bounar

Photoshop links every fill layer to a layer mask. A **layer mask** hides part of a layer so it doesn't show through. By default, the layer mask for a fill layer is empty so the whole layer shows through. You'll work with masks in Tutorial 5.

In Figure 4-22, the green, solid color fill layer is set at 60% opacity, and it has been placed beneath the Girl layer so it affects only the black-and-white Background layer, which is the only layer beneath it in the Layers panel. At this opacity, the fill layer makes the background photograph look as if it has been shot through a green-colored lens filter. If the fill layer were set to 100% opacity, it would completely hide the bottom layer.

You can add a gradient fill layer to produce an immediate and powerful effect in a composition without changing the pixels in any other layer. The default gradient combines the foreground color with transparent pixels; however, in the Gradient Fill dialog box, you can choose from many gradient presets, each with a different effect. You can also modify a gradient by making changes in the Gradient Fill dialog box. See Figure 4-23.

Figure 4-23 **Gradient Fill dialog box**

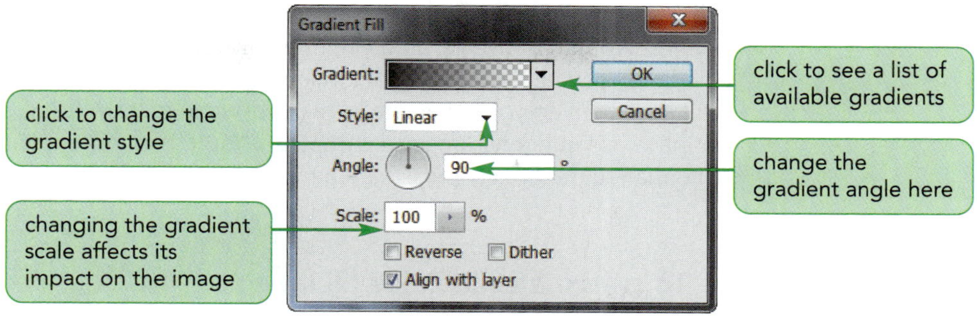

Given the number of options for changing a gradient fill, you could very easily spend hours playing with gradients to find the one that works best with your composition. Later in this session, you'll experiment with a few settings to see what works best in the image you're modifying.

A pattern fill layer works in much the same way both the solid fill and gradient fill layers work. When you add the pattern fill, it appears on its own layer in the Layers panel. Just as gradients and other layers in Photoshop include presets, so do pattern fill layers. When you first add a pattern fill layer, Photoshop applies the default pattern at 100% opacity. You can change the opacity, and you can drag the pattern fill layer in the Layers panel to change which layers it affects. To change the pattern, you use the Pattern Fill dialog box shown in Figure 4-24.

Figure 4-24 **Pattern Fill dialog box**

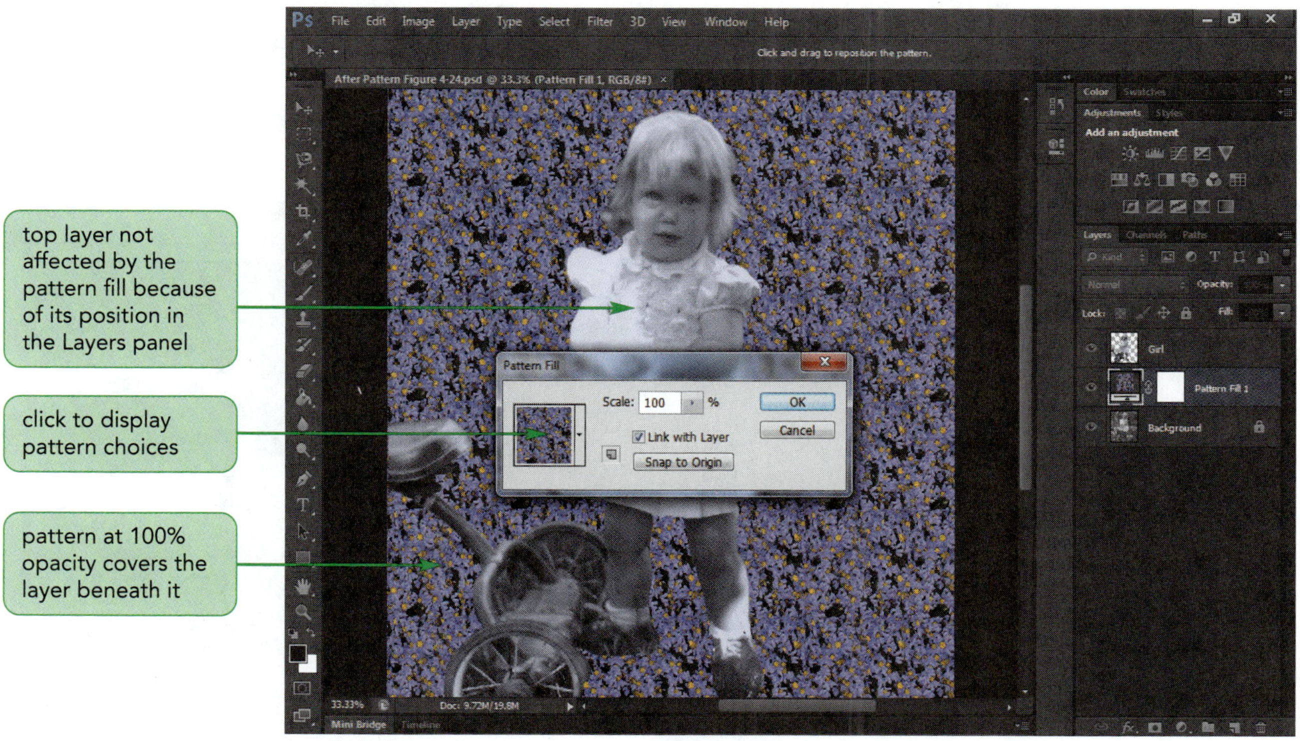

Jane Hosie-Bounar

You can choose from additional presets in the Pattern Fill dialog box by selecting a different preset group. For example, you can choose Rock Patterns, Nature Patterns, Color Paper, and different texture pattern sets. You can also modify the scale of a pattern. For example, if you modify the scale of a rock pattern, the size of the rocks in the pattern will increase by the percentage you specify in the dialog box.

Creating a Solid Color Fill Layer

Because a solid color fill layer is separate from the content it affects, it provides flexibility you wouldn't have by adjusting the color directly in the image itself. Once you add the layer, you can adjust its opacity and blending mode to achieve a variety of effects.

Lee has given you an image of the silhouette of a cyclist at a beach that she might want to use in her summer ad campaign. You'll experiment with a solid color fill layer to enhance the image and create a more dramatic effect.

To create a solid color fill layer:

1. Start Photoshop while pressing the **Ctrl+Alt+Shift** keys, and click **Yes** to delete the Settings File when prompted. Reset Photoshop to the default Essentials workspace layout, and then reset all tools.
2. Open **FillLayers.psd**, located in the Photoshop4\Tutorial folder, and then in the Layers panel, click the **Rider** layer.
3. At the bottom of the Layers panel, click the **Create new fill or adjustment layer** icon, and then click **Solid Color**. The Color Picker (Solid Color) dialog box opens. This dialog box is essentially the same as the Color Picker dialog boxes you worked with earlier.
4. In the Color Picker (Solid Color) dialog box, select any **blue** color, and then click the **OK** button. The color layer appears on top of the image so nothing shows through. You can change the opacity of the fill layer so the layers beneath it show through.
5. In the Layers panel, change the Opacity to **30%**. The rider shows through the blue layer; however, this effect would be more powerful if the layers were in a different order.
6. In the Layers panel, drag the **Color Fill 1** layer down below the Rider layer. See Figure 4-25.

Figure 4-25 Adding a fill layer

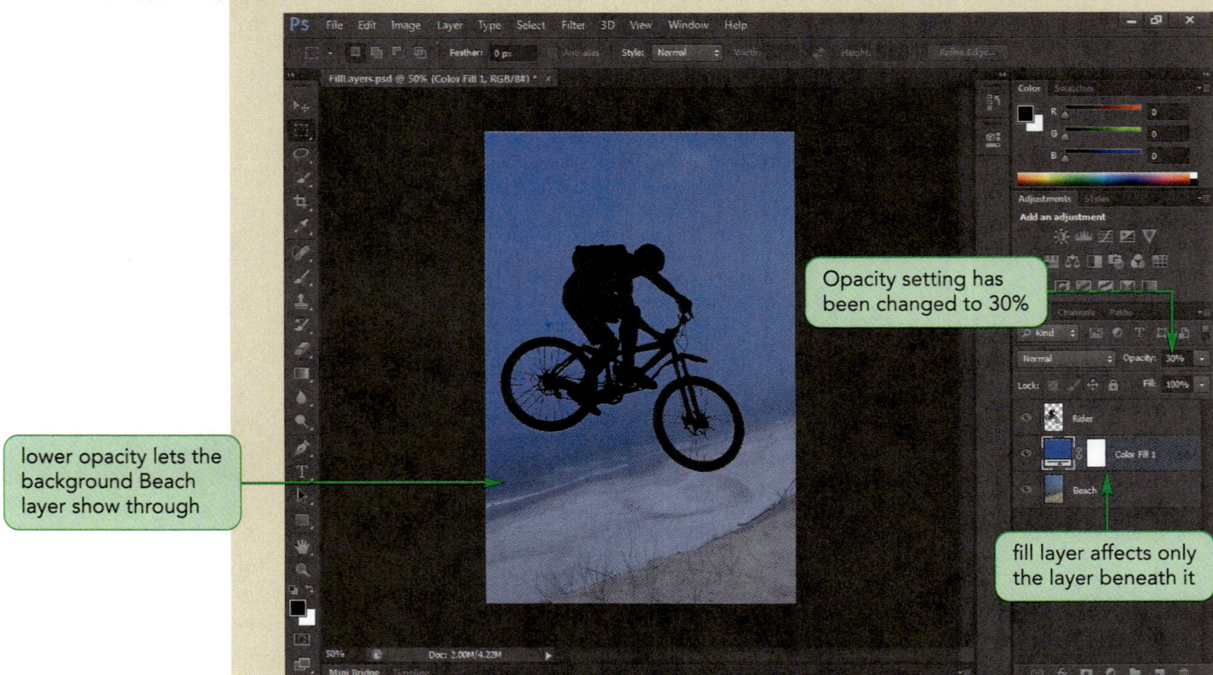

sn4ke/Shutterstock.com; Jane Hosie-Bounar

The image of the rider is now on top of the fill layer that you created, and the effect is more dramatic.

7. At the top of the Layers panel, click the **Set the blending mode for the layer** button, and then click **Divide**. The layer fill effect is brighter than it was using the Normal blending mode.

8. Save the file as **RiderEffects.psd** in the Photoshop4\Tutorial folder, and leave the file open.

Creating a Gradient Layer

You can also add a gradient layer to a composition. Gradients are an easy way to add dramatic effects to your compositions, as shown in Figure 4-26.

Figure 4-26 Gradient effects

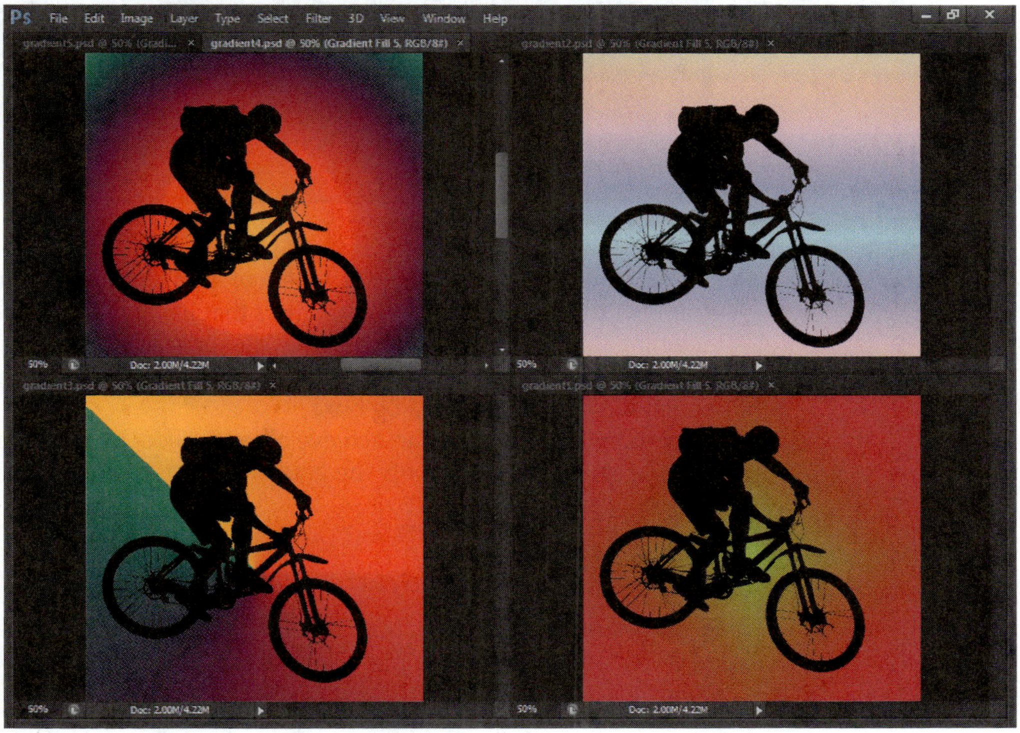

sn4ke/Shutterstock.com

When you add a gradient layer, Photoshop opens the Gradient Fill dialog box. The default gradient combines the foreground color with transparent pixels, using a Linear style, with a 90-degree angle for the gradient. Changing any of these settings changes the look of the gradient. For example, you can change the Style setting to Radial, Angle, Reflected, or Diamond. You can also choose from other gradient presets by clicking the Gradient picker button in the dialog box to display the Gradient picker. See Figure 4-27.

Figure 4-27 **Gradient picker on Gradient Fill dialog box**

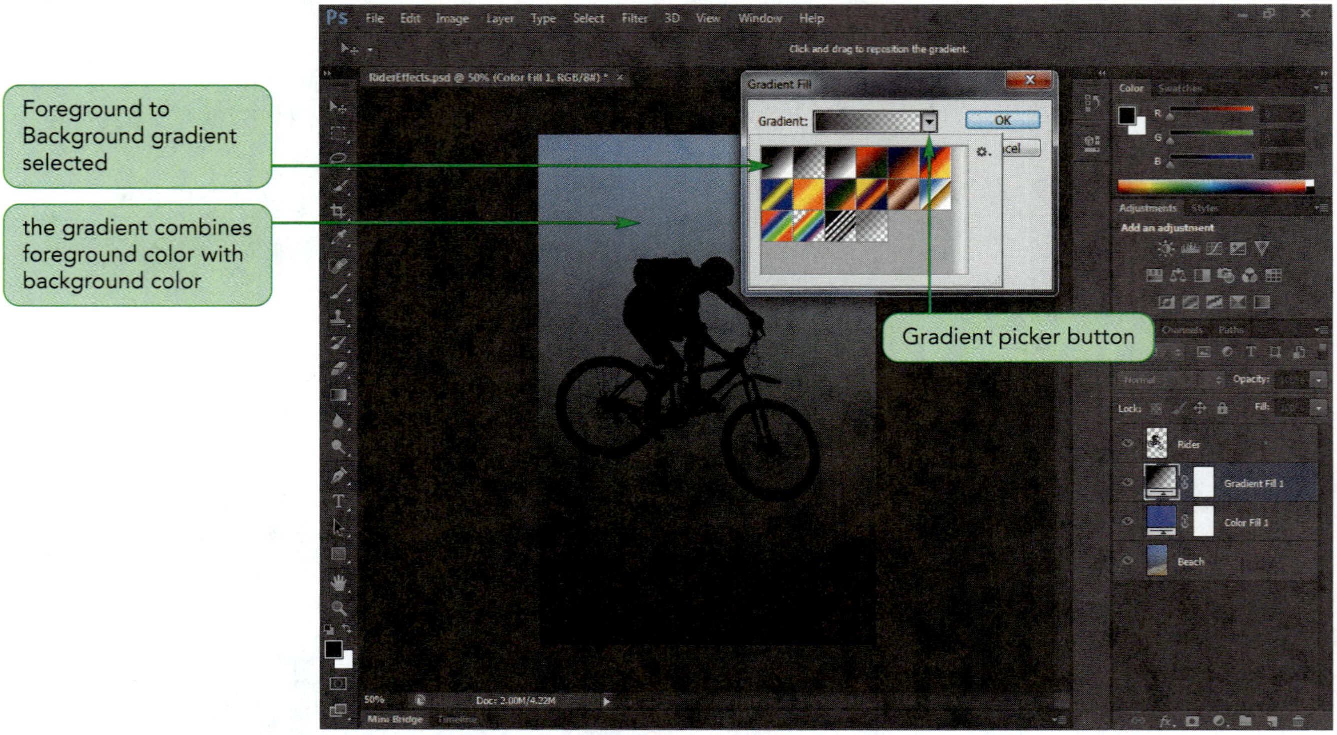

sn4ke/Shutterstock.com; Jane Hosie-Bounar

The Gradient picker displays a variety of gradient presets, some that use the background and foreground colors and others that have different color combinations, including foreground to transparent. If you apply a gradient and then decide you want to change it, you can double-click the gradient thumbnail on the gradient fill layer to reopen the Gradient Fill dialog box.

Next, you'll see if you can achieve a better effect using a gradient fill layer. You'll hide the solid fill layer so only the gradient affects the image.

To add a gradient layer:

1. In the Layers panel, hide the **Color Fill 1** layer, change the foreground color to any blue color, and make the background color black.
2. Click the **Beach** layer, click the **Create new fill or adjustment layer** icon at the bottom of the Layers panel, and then click **Gradient**. The Gradient Fill dialog box opens, and the default gradient is applied to the image.
3. In the Gradient Fill dialog box, click the **Gradient picker** button to display the Gradient picker. The first gradient choice on the list creates the gradient using the foreground color and the background color, in this case, blue and black.
4. Click the first gradient choice to see the effect. The effect is dramatic, but it completely covers the beach image and makes the cyclist hard to see. Changing the Opacity setting for the fill layer will allow more of the beach image to show through.
5. In the Gradient Fill dialog box, click the **OK** button, and then in the Layers panel, change the opacity of the layer to **30%**.

6. Double-click the **gradient thumbnail** on the Gradient Fill 1 layer. The Gradient Fill dialog box opens again. Click the **Gradient picker** button, click the **Spectrum** gradient (the first gradient in the third row), and then click the **OK** button. The Spectrum gradient is applied to the image using the gradient layer.
7. Save **RiderEffects.psd** and leave it open.

Next, you'll try a different effect by choosing from the pattern layers available in Photoshop.

Creating a Pattern Layer

Although there are only five patterns listed in the default Pattern Fill dialog box, there are many patterns to choose from if you select a different library of pattern presets. Pattern galleries include Artist Surfaces, Color Paper, Nature Patterns, and Rock Patterns, among others. When you select a pattern library, you are prompted to either replace the current patterns or append the list to the current pattern list, just as you were prompted to replace or append styles in Session 4.1.

You'll experiment with adding pattern layers to see the effects you can achieve.

To add a pattern layer:

1. In the Layers panel, hide the **Gradient Fill 1** layer, click the **Beach** layer, click the **Create new fill or adjustment layer** icon, and then click **Pattern**. The Pattern Fill dialog box opens, and Photoshop applies the default pattern fill to the image.
2. In the Pattern Fill dialog box, click the **pattern** thumbnail to open the Pattern preset picker, and then click the **More options** button to open the menu.
3. Click **Color Paper** on the menu, and then click the **OK** button to replace the current patterns with the selected patterns.

   Trouble? If you are prompted to save changes to the current patterns before replacing them, click the No button.

   The Color Paper patterns are displayed in the Pattern preset picker.
4. Scroll down the list and then click the **Red Textured** pattern to select it. See Figure 4-28.

Figure 4-28 Pattern preset picker on Pattern Fill dialog

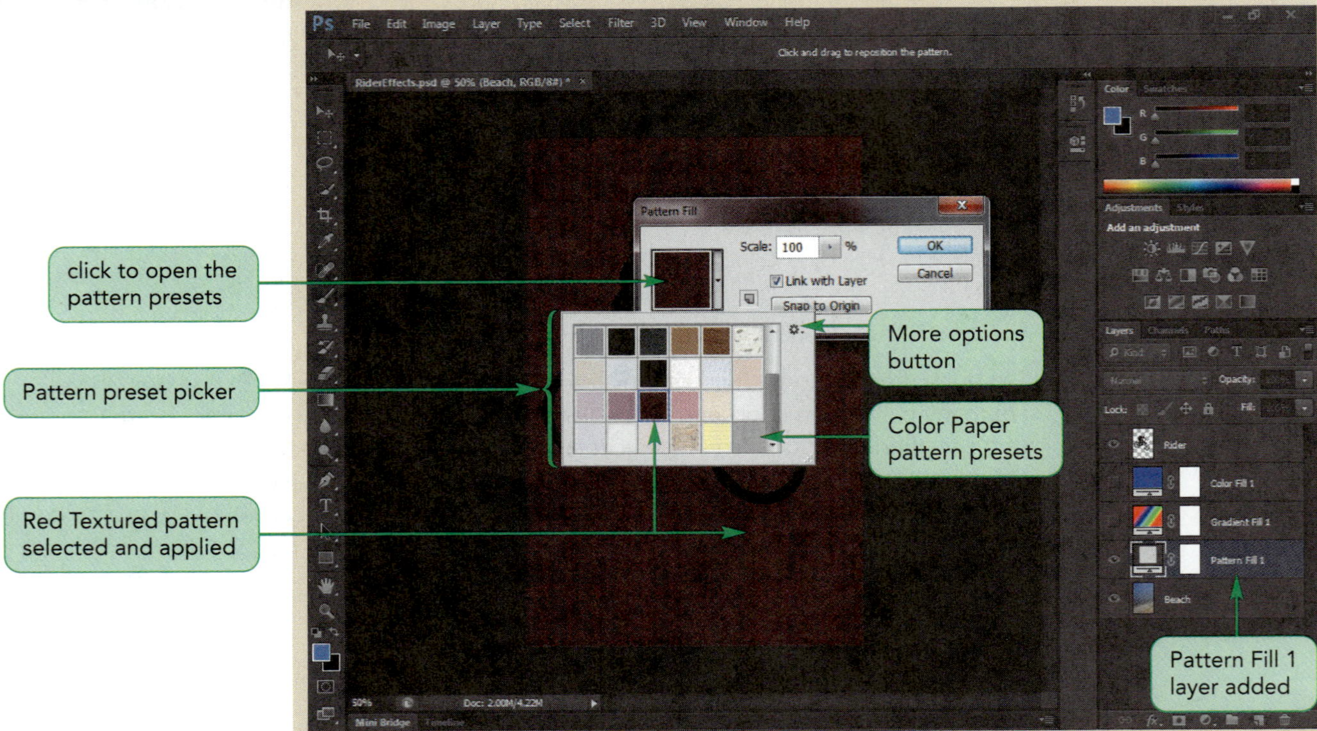

sn4ke/Shutterstock.com

The pattern appears in the dialog box and is applied to the image. The effect is interesting, but it's not the effect you had in mind. You'd like to add a sense of outdoor mountain adventure to the image.

5. Click the **More options** button to open the menu again, click **Rock Patterns**, and then click the **OK** button. The rock patterns replace the paper patterns.

6. Click **Stones** (the second pattern) to select it, change the scale to **200%**, and then click the **OK** button.

Of the three layer fills you tried, the gradient fill best conveys the excitement that Lee wants for her summer ad campaign, so you'll hide the pattern fill layer and redisplay the gradient fill.

7. In the Layers panel, hide the Pattern Fill 1 layer, redisplay the Gradient Fill 1 layer, and then save **RiderEffects.psd** and close the file.

Adding Shape Layers vs. Filling Pixels on a Layer

You've already seen that Photoshop includes a number of drawing tools that you can use to enhance a composition. Now that you know what a fill layer is, and understand what a mask does, you can delve more deeply into options available to you when using the drawing tools. For example, you can choose to add a shape to an image by making a nondestructive edit (by adding a vector shape on a separate layer) or by making a destructive edit (by adding a raster shape, which fills in the pixels on a layer). See Figure 4-29.

Figure 4-29 **Shape mode versus Pixels mode**

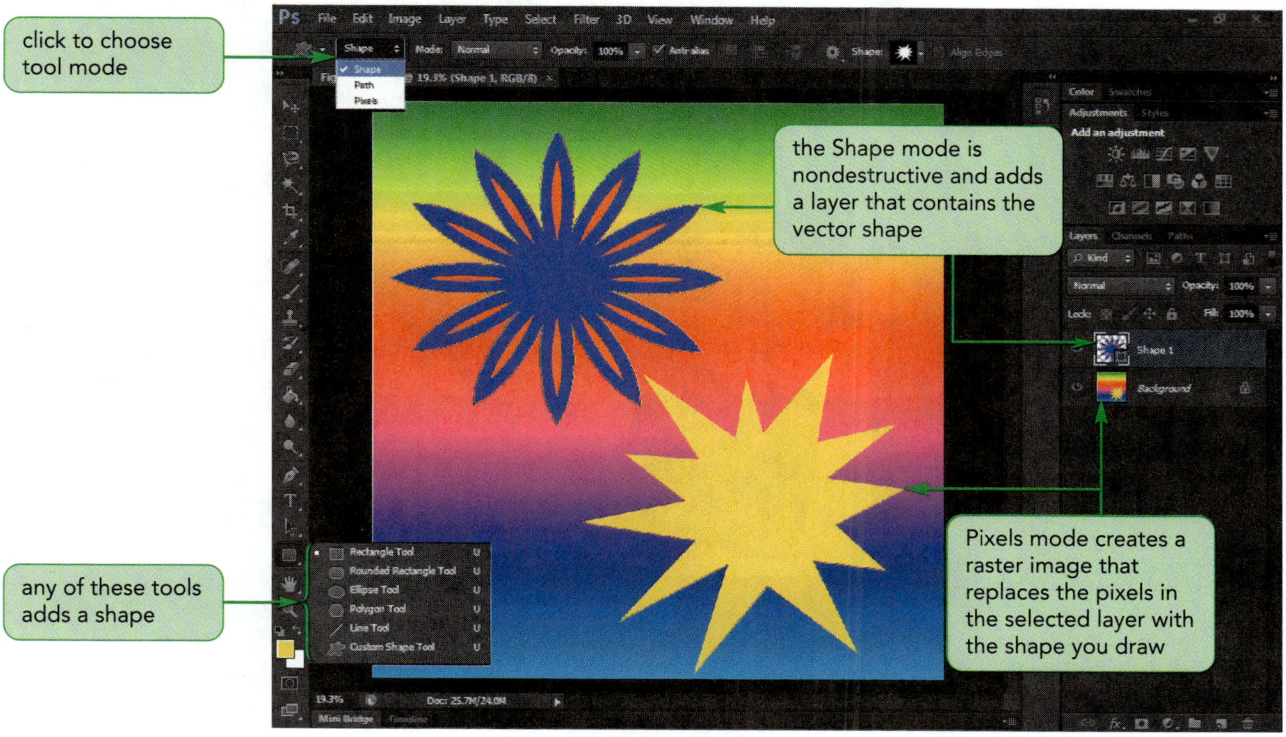

When you draw a vector shape such as the rectangle you added in Session 4.1 or the purple flower shown in Figure 4-29, you are adding a shape layer. **Shape layers**, also called vector layers, are a form of nondestructive editing because they don't alter the pixels on the layer or layers beneath them. When you select the Shape tool mode on the options bar, you are choosing to add a vector shape on a shape layer. You can also add a raster shape to a layer using the same drawing tool but a different tool mode. Pixels mode places the shape you draw directly on a layer as a raster or bitmap object, overwriting the pixels beneath it. The yellow Starburst shape in Figure 4-29 appears directly on the multicolored Background layer that contains it. It consists of pixels that are painted over the original pixels on the layer. Adding the Starburst to the Background layer is an example of destructive editing.

The third option for adding a shape is the Paths option, which is covered later in this tutorial. If you draw a shape with the Paths option selected on the options bar, you are creating a temporary work path.

Specifying Fill and Stroke Options for a Vector Shape

When you add a shape using the Shape tool mode, you can specify the fill of a shape before you draw it, or, if it is selected, after you draw it. Like the layers you added earlier in this tutorial, a shape layer can be filled with a solid color, with no color (transparent), with a gradient, or with a pattern. To select the fill color, you click the Fill button on the options bar. See Figure 4-30.

Figure 4-30 Shape fills

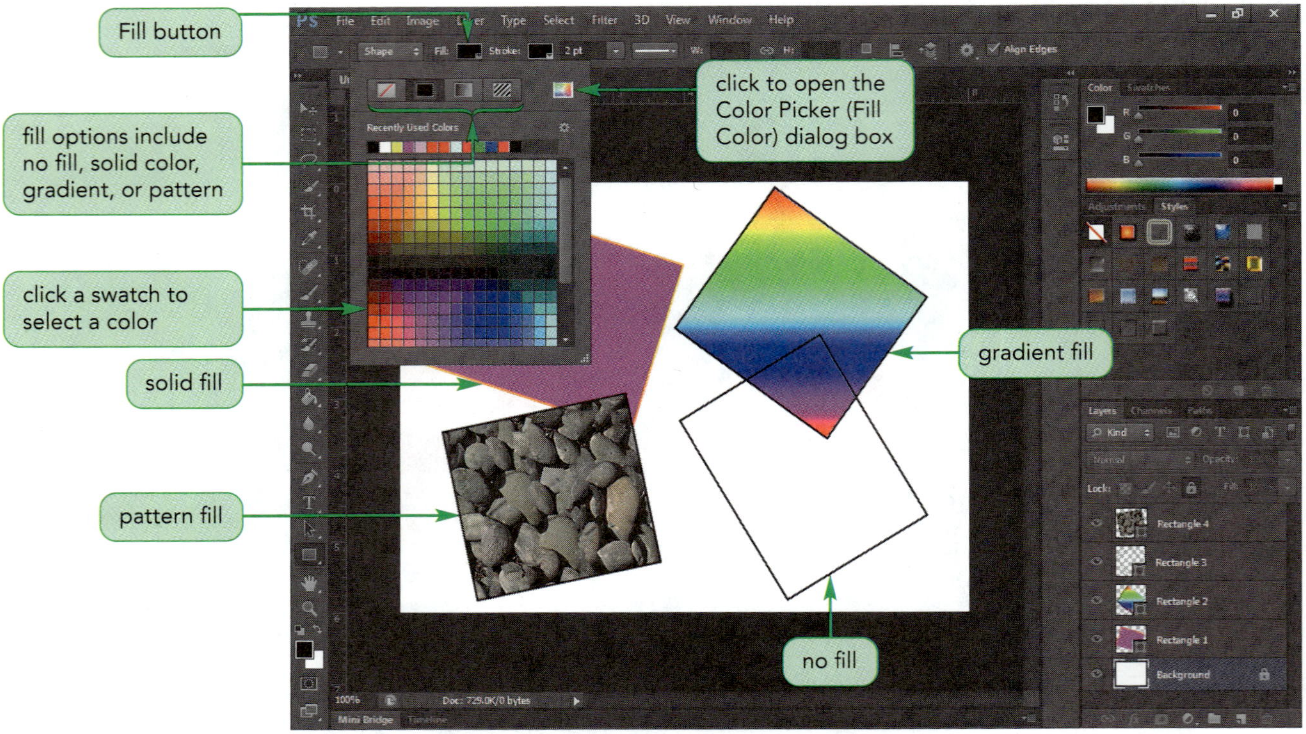

You also have a wide choice of settings for the stroke used to draw a vector shape. A stroke can be a solid color, or it can be transparent, a gradient, or a pattern. Other stroke options include width and line type (for example, solid, dashed, or dotted), as well as alignment, caps, and corner options. See Figure 4-31.

Figure 4-31 Stroke options

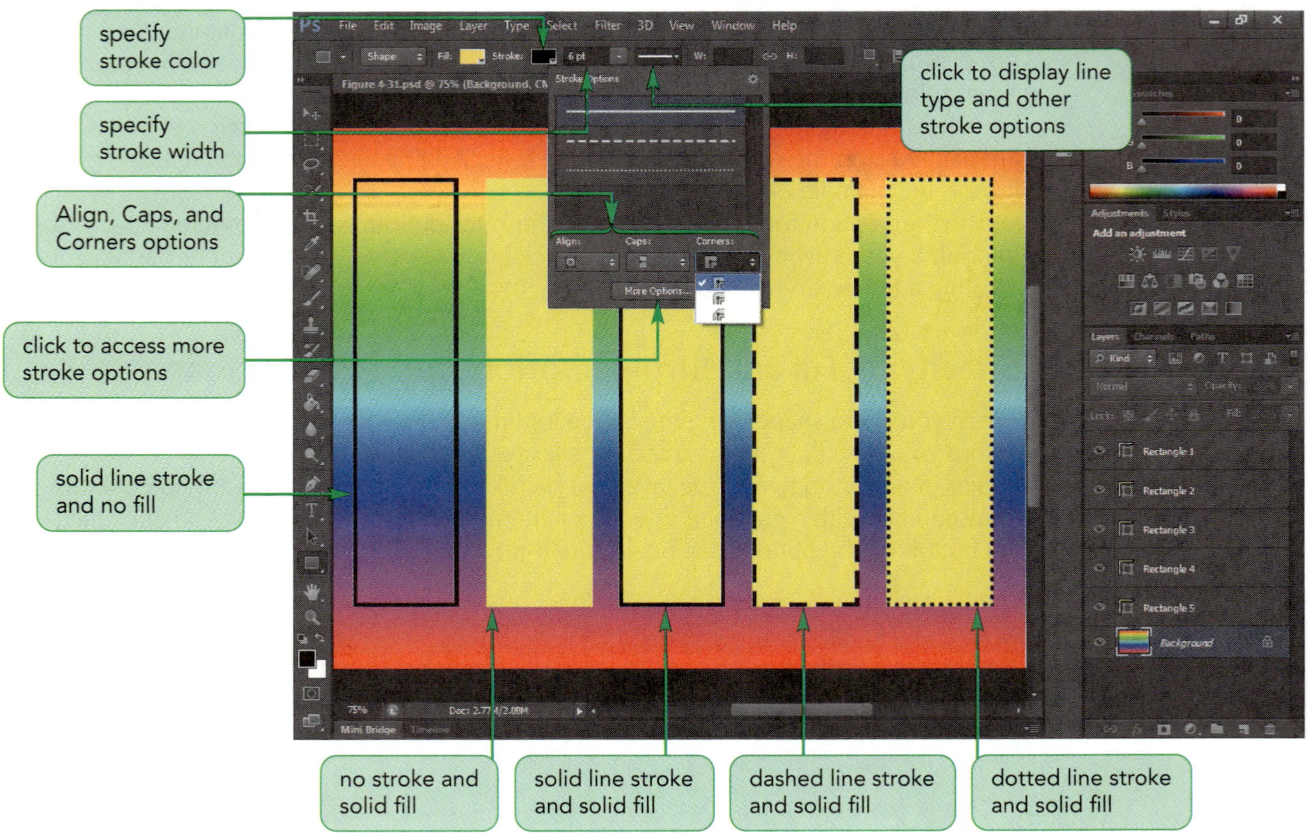

The Align options determine whether the stroke is aligned at the center of the path of the pointer as you drag, or inside or outside the path. The Caps settings let you specify how the ends of stroked paths are finished. Caps options include Butt, Round, or Square. The Corners setting determines whether a corner is mitered (square), rounded, or beveled. If you click the More options button in the Stroke Options panel, you can specify additional custom options, such as the distance between dots or dashes in a stroke, or the point size of the dots or dashes.

Adding a Shape Layer (Vector Objects)

You have already added a rectangle shape to an image. In this section, you'll learn about the different kinds of shapes you can add to a composition. To add a shape layer, click one of the shape tools in the Tools panel to select it. When the tool is selected, the options bar lets you choose to draw a shape layer (a vector object), to draw a path, or to fill the drawn object with pixels (a bitmap, or raster, object). Figure 4-32 describes the vector, path, and fill options on the options bar as well as the options for creating complex shapes by combining, intersecting, and excluding shapes as you draw.

Figure 4-32 **Shape options bar buttons**

Button	Name	Effect
	Shape	Specifies tool mode options, including Shape, Path, and Pixels
	Fill	Specifies the fill color as well as whether the fill is a solid color, pattern, or gradient
	Stroke	Specifies the stroke width
	Set shape stroke type	Specifies stroke type as a solid line, a dashed line, or a dotted line; also specifies stroke alignment, caps, and corners
W:	Set shape width	Specifies shape width and unit of measurement, either Pixels, Inches, Centimeters, Millimeters, Points, or Picas
	Link shape width and height	Constrains width and height proportions; if the width changes, the height changes proportionally, and vice versa
H:	Set shape height	Specifies shape height and unit of measurement, either Pixels, Inches, Centimeters, Millimeters, Points, or Picas
	Path operations	Specifies whether to put the shape on a new layer or to combine, subtract, intersect, exclude, or merge shapes in the same layer
	Path alignment	Specifies alignment and distribution options
	Path arrangement	Specifies arrangement of shapes on the canvas to control visibility, from front to back
	More options	Specifies whether a shape is unconstrained as it is drawn or has a fixed size or proportions and whether or not it is drawn from the center
	Align Edges check box	Aligns the edges of new shapes with existing shapes

To draw a shape, you must first activate the desired drawing tool in the Tools panel, and then select the Shape tool mode and stroke type on the options bar.

Before you begin to draw, click the Path operations button on the options bar and make sure New Layer is selected. As you drag the mouse pointer on the canvas, an outline of the object appears. When you release the mouse button, the object is filled with the fill color specified on the options bar, and the shape appears on its own layer in the Layers panel. To specify drawing options, click the More options button on the options bar to choose additional specifications. For example, if you are drawing a rectangle, you can constrain it to a square by selecting the Square option button. You can also specify a fixed or proportional size or select the From Center check box so you can start your drawing at the center and drag outward.

INSIGHT

Rasterizing a Vector Shape

Many of the digital image-editing tools in Photoshop manipulate pixels. What does this mean if you want to modify a vector shape using these tools? As you learned in Tutorial 1, a vector graphic is a collection of points, lines, curves, and shapes stored as a set of mathematical instructions. It is not pixel based. Therefore, to use the tools that manipulate pixels, you need to rasterize the image—or change it into a raster object. To rasterize a vector image, right-click the layer in the Layers panel, and then click Rasterize Layer. You can then use any of the pixel-editing tools to enhance or refine the shape on the layer.

Next, you'll add a vector shape to an image. Then, you'll copy the style that you created for the bicycle in the previous session and apply it to the sign in the image as well, so you can show Lee what your sign will look like over the doorway of the store.

To draw a vector shape:

1. Open **Storefront.psd**, located in the Photoshop4\Tutorial, display it at 50% magnification, and center the bicycle image in the Document window.
2. Restore the default background and foreground colors, press the **X** key to switch the background and foreground colors, and then click the **Background** layer in the Layers panel, if necessary.
3. In the Tools panel, click the **Rectangle Tool** button, and on the options bar, confirm that the fill color is white (the foreground color).
4. On the options bar, click the **Stroke** button, click the **Solid Color** icon, and click the **Black** color swatch (the last shape in the second row), if necessary.
5. On the options bar, highlight the current stroke width, type **2**, and then press the **Enter** key. The stroke width is now 2 points.
6. On the canvas, draw a rectangle so it contains the bicycle, as shown in Figure 4-33.

Figure 4-33 **Drawing a rectangle shape layer**

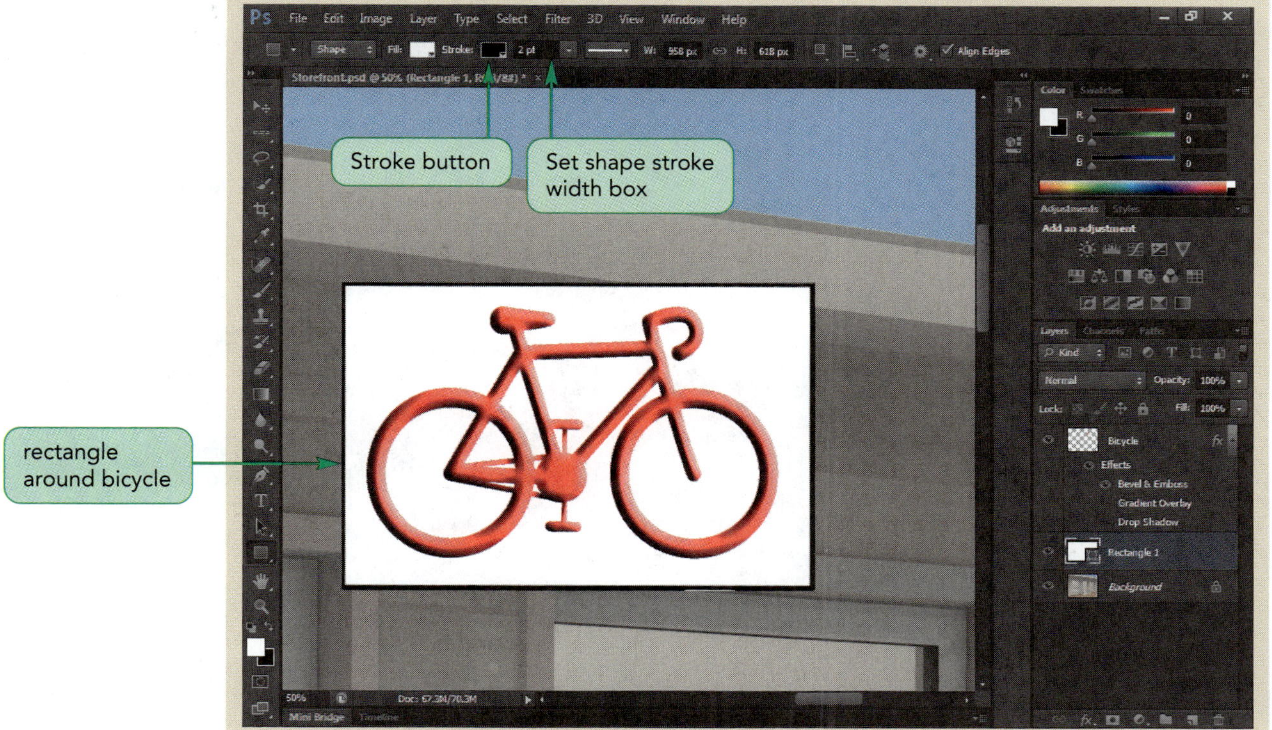

Shevchenko Nataliya/Shutterstock.com; Black Images/Shutterstock.com

7. Change the name of the new layer from Rectangle 1 to **Sign**.

   Next you'll copy the style applied to the Bicycle layer and paste it on the Sign layer.

8. In the Layers panel, right-click the **Bicycle** layer and then click **Copy Layer Style** on the context menu. Then, right-click the **Sign** layer and click **Paste Layer Style**. The sign now has the Bevel & Emboss effect that you applied to the bicycle. Note that the effects that were hidden for the Bicycle layer are still hidden for the Sign layer. Click to the left of Gradient Overlay to turn that effect on for the Sign layer. See Figure 4-34.

Figure 4-34 Copying and pasting the Bicycle layer style

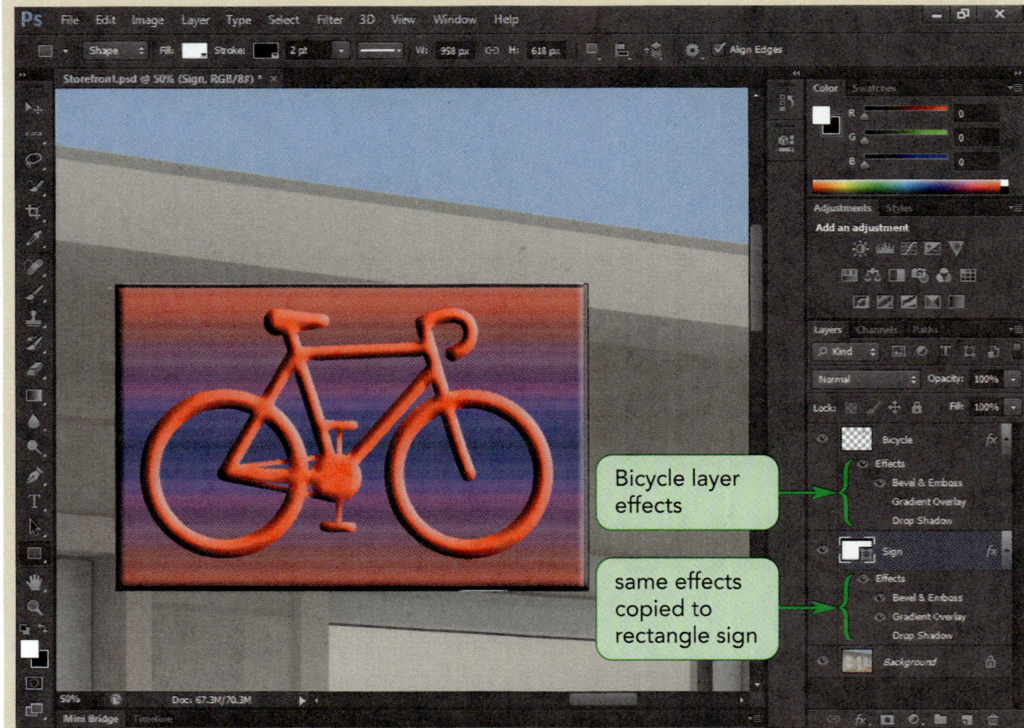

Shevchenko Nataliya/Shutterstock.com; Black Images/Shutterstock.com

9. Save the file as **BikeSignFinal.psd** in the Photoshop4\Tutorial folder, and leave the file open.

INSIGHT

Using the One-Click Method

If you select one of the shape tools in the Tools panel and click the canvas rather than drag to create the shape, the Create *Shape* dialog box opens, where *Shape* is the name of the shape you're drawing, for example, Polygon or Ellipse. In the Create *Shape* dialog box, you can specify a number of different shape attributes. For example, in the Create Polygon dialog box, you can specify the width, the height, and the number of sides of your polygon. You can also specify whether or not you want smooth corners. If the polygon you want to draw is a star, you can select the Star check box, and then specify a percentage value for the indents around the star. If you select the Custom Shape tool and then click the canvas, the Create Custom Shape dialog box includes From Center and Preserve Proportions check boxes, as well as Width and Height boxes. Once you have finished specifying shape settings in the Create *Shape* dialog box and have clicked the OK button, Photoshop draws the shape on the canvas at the location you clicked, and applies the settings you specified. The one-click method is yet another way Photoshop lets you work with vector objects, and it can be an excellent method for creating an object when you know its exact specifications.

To draw more complex shapes, you can modify existing vector layers using one of the Path operations options. See Figure 4-35.

Figure 4-35 Excluding, subtracting, combining, and intersecting

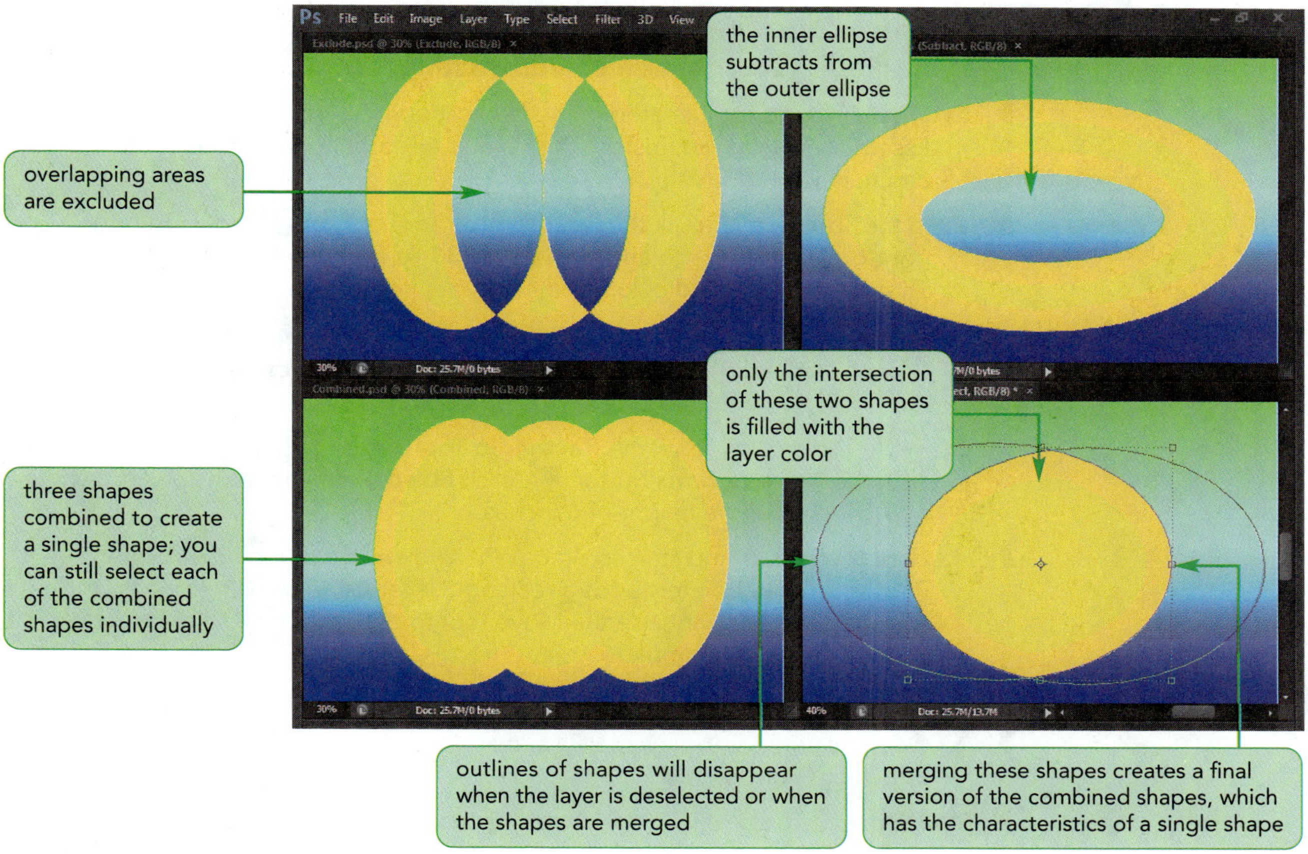

TIP

You can also leave the New Layer option selected and press the Shift key to add to the shape layer.

For example, to add to an additional vector object, select the Combine Shapes option on the Path operations menu, and then draw an additional shape. The new shape appears on the same layer as the existing shape, and the two shapes are combined to create a new shape. However, you can still select each of the combined shapes individually if you want to change the way they are arranged on the layer. To select individual shapes used in a combined shape, you use the Path Selection tool in the Tools panel, which functions much like the Move tool.

You can subtract from a shape you have drawn by clicking the Subtract Front Shape option on the Path operations menu, and then drawing a new shape on top of the original shape. When you release the mouse button, the new shape you drew is subtracted from the original shape so the color on the layer beneath it shows through. You can also achieve the same effect by leaving the New Layer option on the Path operations menu selected and pressing the Alt key to subtract from the shape layer.

You can click Intersect Shape Areas on the Path operations menu to create a shape that is the intersection of two or more shapes that you draw. If you click the Exclude Overlapping Shapes, intersecting areas are transparent, and areas outside of the intersections are opaque (or filled).

Finally, you can merge shapes after you have finished combining, subtracting, and intersecting separate shapes to create the final drawing. Once you merge shapes, they have the characteristics of a single shape and can no longer be selected individually using the Path Selection tool. To merge shapes into a final drawing, click the Merge Shape Components option on the Path operations menu.

Lee has asked you to stop work on the sign for now so you can work on an image of a tricycle that she needs immediately. She plans to use it in one of her ads, and wants you to frame the image using the drawing tools. You'll use the vector tools and options to create a frame around the tricycle.

To modify a vector shape by subtracting:

1. Open **Tricycle.jpg**, located in the Photoshop4\Tutorial folder, reset the Essentials workspace, restore the default foreground and background colors, and reset all tools.
2. In the Tools panel, click the **Eyedropper Tool** button, and then right-click in the image and click **31 by 31 Average** in the context menu. Then, sample the **red** color on the tricycle, near the pedal.

   Trouble? If the red color is assigned as the background color, press the D key to reset the colors, and then click the Set foreground color icon in the Color panel to make it active. Repeat Step 2.
3. In the Tools panel, click the **Rectangle Tool** button. On the options bar, click the **More options** button, click **Fixed Size**, and then specify a width of **8.5** inches and a height of **6** inches.
4. Click the canvas and start to drag. When you move the mouse pointer, Photoshop immediately adds a rectangle layer using the dimensions you specified. If necessary, use the Move tool to drag the rectangle so that it covers the canvas completely.
5. In the Tools panel, click the **Ellipse Tool** button.
6. On the options bar, click the **Path operations** button, and then click **Subtract Front Shape**.
7. On the options bar, click the **More options** button, click **Proportional**, enter a width to height proportion of **4** to **3**, and then click the **From Center** check box to select it.
8. In the Document window, display the rulers, and then place guides at 4.25 inches on the horizontal ruler and 3 inches on the vertical ruler.
9. Position the mouse pointer over the intersection of the guides. The mouse pointer now has a minus sign to the right of the crosshairs, indicating that the shape you draw will subtract from the previous shape.
10. Click at the intersection of the guides, and drag to draw an ellipse over the rectangle. Release the mouse button when the ellipse is about 1/4 inch from the top and bottom edges of the rectangle. The ellipse is subtracted from the rectangle when you release the mouse button, exposing the image underneath. See Figure 4-36.

Figure 4-36 **Subtracting a shape**

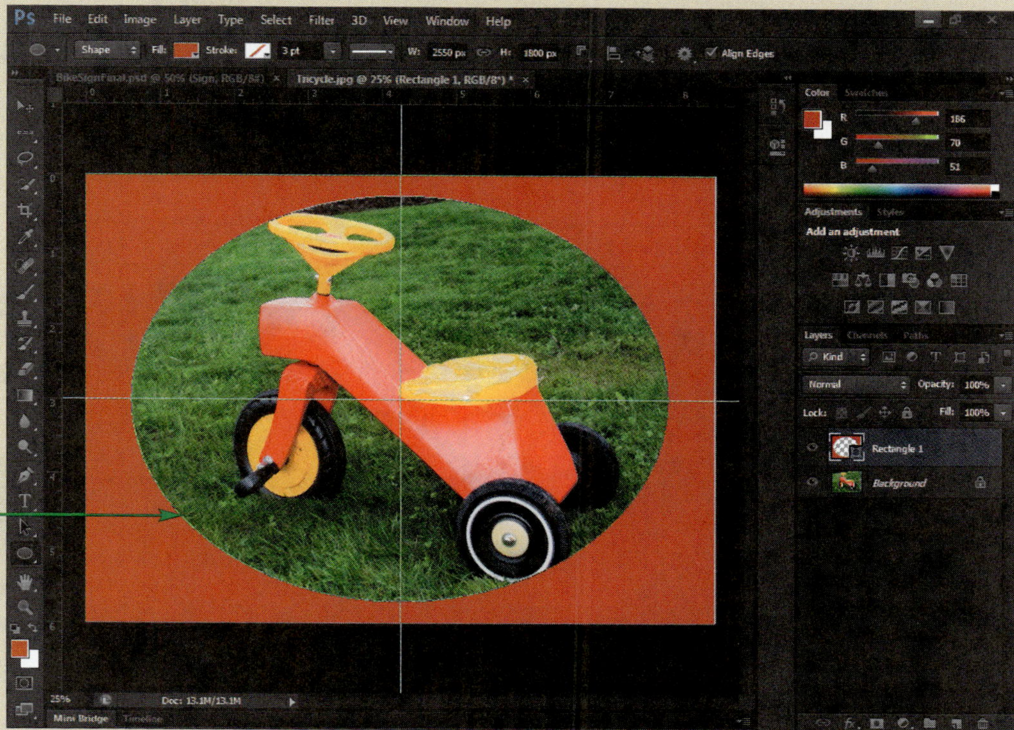

Ingvald Kaldhussater/Shutterstock.com

11. In the Styles panel, click the **BikeSign** thumbnail (the last thumbnail on the Styles panel) to apply that style to the Rectangle 1 layer.
12. Save the file as **FrameTrike.psd** in the Photoshop4\Tutorial folder and then close the file.

You can switch from one option to another on the options bar as you draw to create a complex shape that is the result of adding, subtracting, and intersecting geometric objects. Next, you'll use a combination of standard shapes and add them together to create a shape that combines a Stop sign, a bicycle, and images of pedestrians. Lee wants to use it as one of the signs inside her store.

To modify a vector shape by subtracting and merging:

1. Open **StopSign.psd**, located in the Photoshop4\Tutorial folder, size it to fit the screen, and click the **Background** layer, if necessary.
2. In the Tools panel, click the **Polygon Tool** button.

   Trouble? If you can't find the Polygon Tool button, right-click the Ellipse Tool button, and then click the Polygon Tool button on the list of hidden tools.
3. On the options bar, select a **black** fill color, if necessary, a **black** stroke color, and then, in the Sides box, type **8**.

4. Click beneath the *T O* in STOP, press and hold the mouse button, and drag to draw an octagon. With the mouse button still depressed, drag left or right to rotate the polygon until its top edge runs parallel to the top of the canvas. Release the mouse button. The STOP text is not very visible because it is the same color as the octagon. See Figure 4-37.

   Trouble? If your octagon is not positioned correctly, use the Move tool to reposition it.

Figure 4-37 **Drawing a polygon**

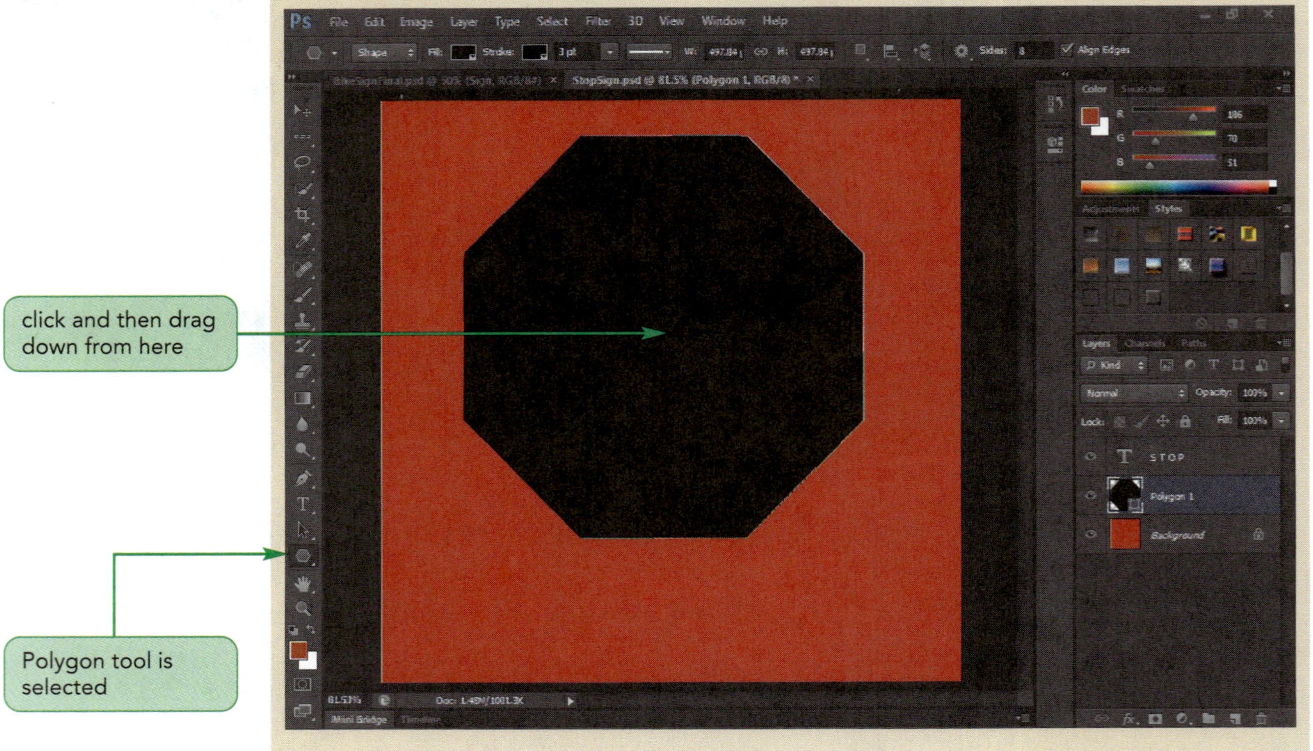

5. Click the **Polygon Tool** button in the Tools panel, if necessary, and then on the options bar, click the **Path operations** button, and click **Subtract Front Shape**. Click in the center of the octagon, and then drag to create another slightly smaller octagon on top of the original one. Drag left or right to rotate the polygon until its top edge runs parallel to the top of the canvas, but don't worry about centering it exactly. You'll adjust its position in the next step using the Path Selection tool, which lets you select a single shape on the layer, rather than the entire layer contents.
6. In the Tools panel, click the **Path Selection Tool** button, point to the second octagon, and then drag it into position. See Figure 4-38.

Figure 4-38 Placing the second octagon

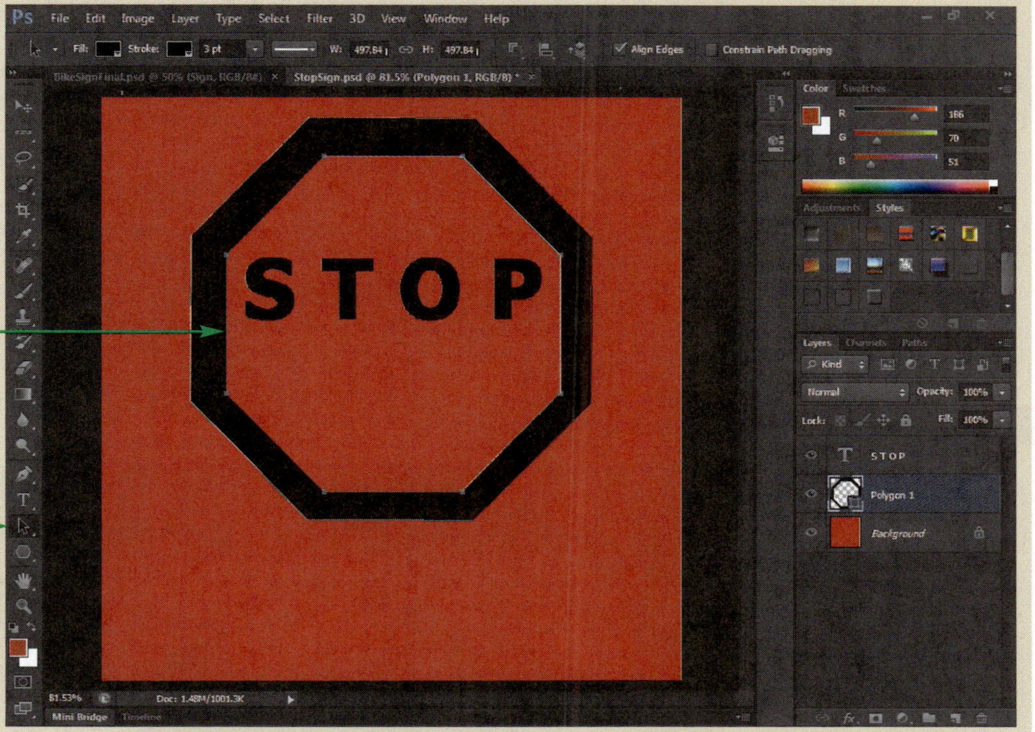

Next, you'll merge two octagons on the layer so that they have the characteristics of a single shape.

7. With the **Polygon 1** layer selected, click the **Path operations** button on the options bar, and then click **Merge Shape Components**.
8. In the Tools panel, verify that the **Path Selection Tool** button is selected, click on a black area of the merged shapes, and drag. Press the **Ctrl+Z** keys to undo the move. Both shapes move together, indicating that they have been merged; Photoshop considers them a single shape, and you can no longer use the Path Selection tool to select them individually.

Next, you'll add two custom shapes to the drawing and combine them into a single shape.

To combine two custom shapes:

1. In the Layers panel, click the **Background** layer, and then in the Tools panel, click the **Custom Shape Tool** button. On the options bar, click the **Custom Shape picker** button, and then click the **More options** button. Photoshop comes with a variety of different custom shapes.
2. Click **Symbols**, and then click the **OK** button to replace the current shapes.

   Trouble? If Photoshop displays a message asking if you want to save changes to the current shapes before replacing them, click the No button.
3. In the Custom Shape panel, double-click the **School** shape (two people walking), the last shape in the second row.
4. On the options bar, click the **More options** button, and then click **Defined Proportions** to constrain the proportions of the people, and click the **More options** button again to close the list.

5. On the options bar, set the fill and stroke colors to **white**.
6. Click in the image under the *S* and drag down and to the right to add the symbol.
7. On the options bar, click the **Path operations** button and then click **Combine Shapes**. The next shape you draw will be added to the people shape that you already drew.
8. Click in the image under the *P* and drag down and to the left to add the symbol a second time. Press the **V** key to select the Move tool, and confirm that the Show Transform Controls check box is selected. Both symbols appear on a single layer and are treated as a single shape. Because they have not been merged, you can still move them individually on the canvas using the Path Selection tool. See Figure 4-39.

Figure 4-39 **Combining shapes**

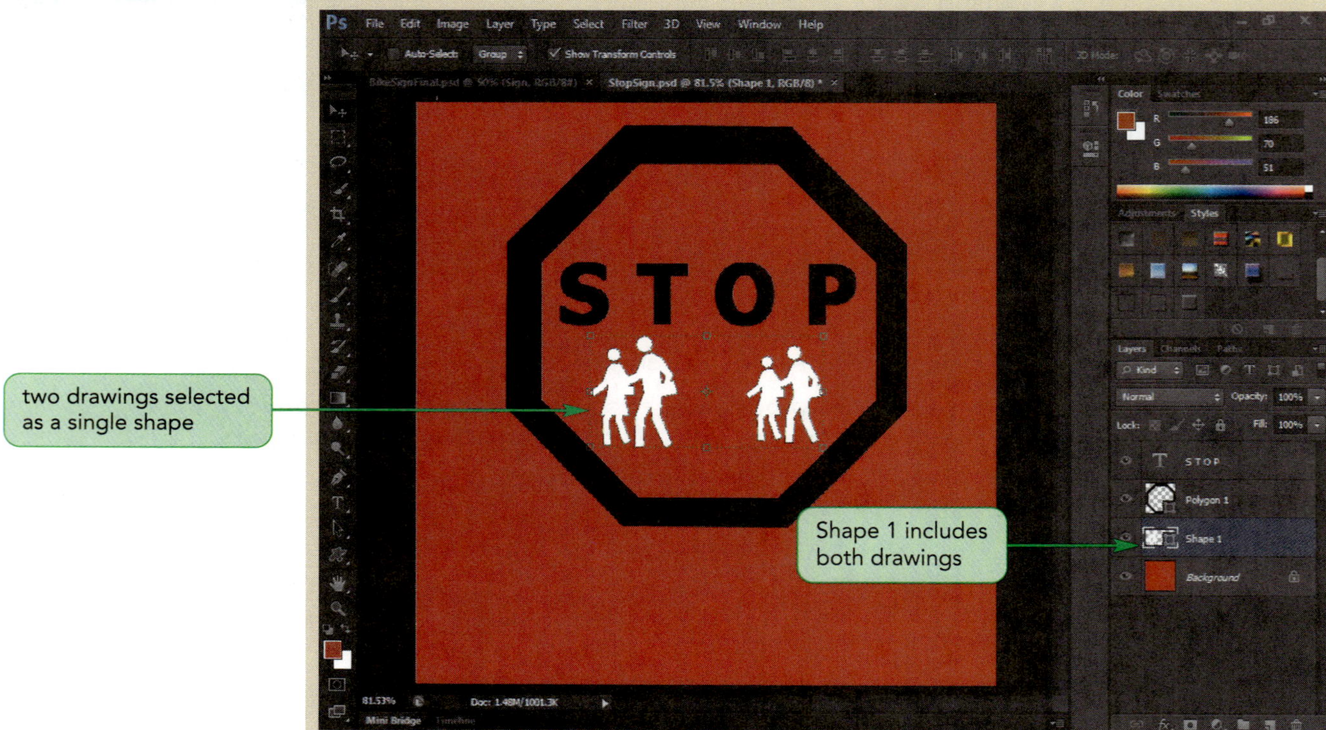

9. Save the file as **Pedestrians.psd**, and close it. You'll show the sign to Lee to see if she wants to use it in the store.

Next, Lee wants you to add a symbol to a JPEG image she has put together for her latest campaign encouraging people to replace their old bicycles. You'll draw a bitmap shape over the background pixels to add a drawing without adding a new layer.

Using Fill Pixels (Bitmap/Raster Objects)

To draw a bitmap (or raster) shape, you select the tool with which you want to draw, for example, the rectangle or ellipse, and then select the Pixels tool mode on the options bar. As implied by the name, when you draw the shape using the Pixels tool mode, you are modifying the pixels in the area of your drawing by filling them with the foreground color. As such, you are making a destructive edit. When working in Pixels tool mode, you drag the mouse pointer on the canvas to draw the object. As you draw, an outline of the object appears. When you release the mouse button, the object appears filled with the foreground color on the current layer, replacing the pixels beneath it.

To draw a bitmap shape:

1. Open **Accident.jpg**, located in the Photoshop4\Tutorial folder, and save it as **IsItTime.jpg**, using the default JPEG Options, in the same folder.
2. Using the Eyedropper tool, take a point sample of the red text to set it as the foreground color.
3. In the Tools panel, click the **Custom Shape Tool** button.
4. On the options bar, click the **Custom Shape picker** button, and then double-click the **Question Mark** symbol (the second symbol in the second row).
5. On the options bar, click the **Pick tool mode** button, and then click **Pixels**. The pixels in the Background layer will be hidden by the pixels you add to the canvas as fill.
6. Click the **More options** button, click **Unconstrained**, and click the **From Center** check box to select it. Click the **More options** button again to close the list.
7. Click at the intersection of the two guides, and drag down and to the right to create a question mark. When you release the mouse button, the new pixels replace the original pixels on the Background layer. Once you save the file and close it, you will not be able to undo this change. See Figure 4-40.

Figure 4-40 Drawing a bitmap shape

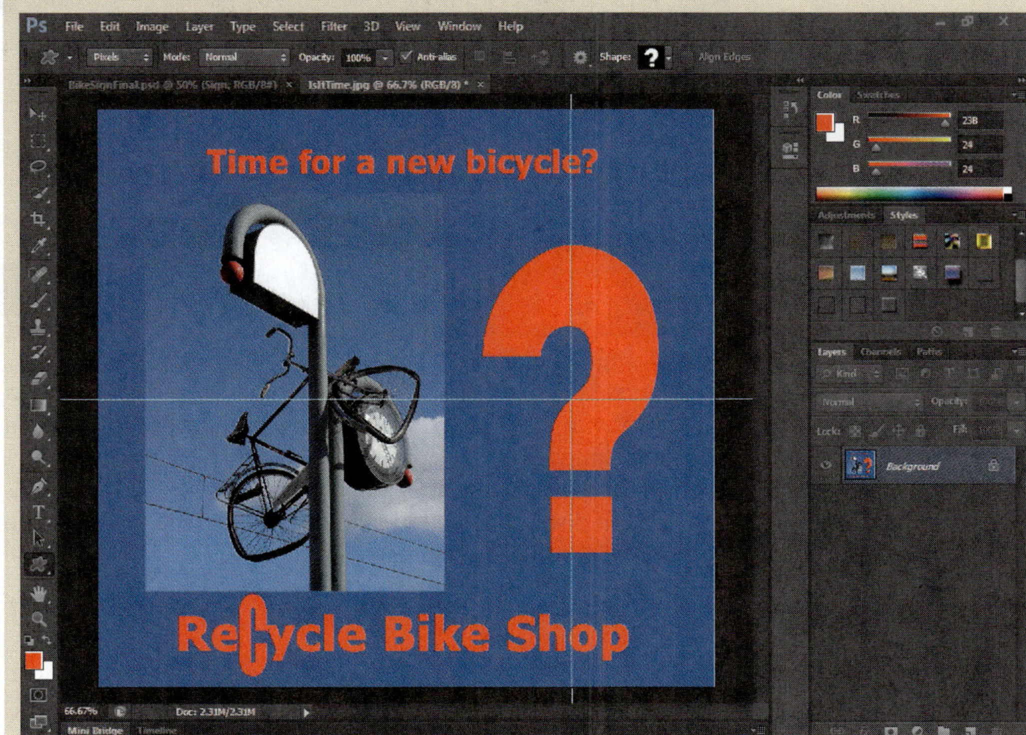

Björn Erlandsson/Shutterstock.com

8. Save **IsItTime.jpg**, and leave the file open.

Using the Brush Tool

The Brush and Pencil tools in Photoshop let you paint or draw on your images. If you are using a mouse, you have less control over your brushstrokes and pencil strokes than you would if you were using a Tablet PC with a **stylus**, which lets you write or draw directly on the screen. However, both tools are still valuable image-editing tools.

The Brush tool produces strokes that are **anti-aliased**—that is, even though you are working with pixels, your brushstrokes will have a smooth rather than a jagged appearance because Photoshop adds pixels to blend the edges into the background. Because anti-aliasing adds pixels, anti-alias settings increase file size. The **hardness** of the Brush tool is related to the amount of anti-aliasing applied to the brushstroke. A setting of 100% uses the least anti-aliasing, but still produces smooth edges. The Pencil tool is never anti-aliased; as a result, it can sometimes produce jagged or pixelated edges. See Figure 4-41.

Figure 4-41 **Brush and pencil strokes**

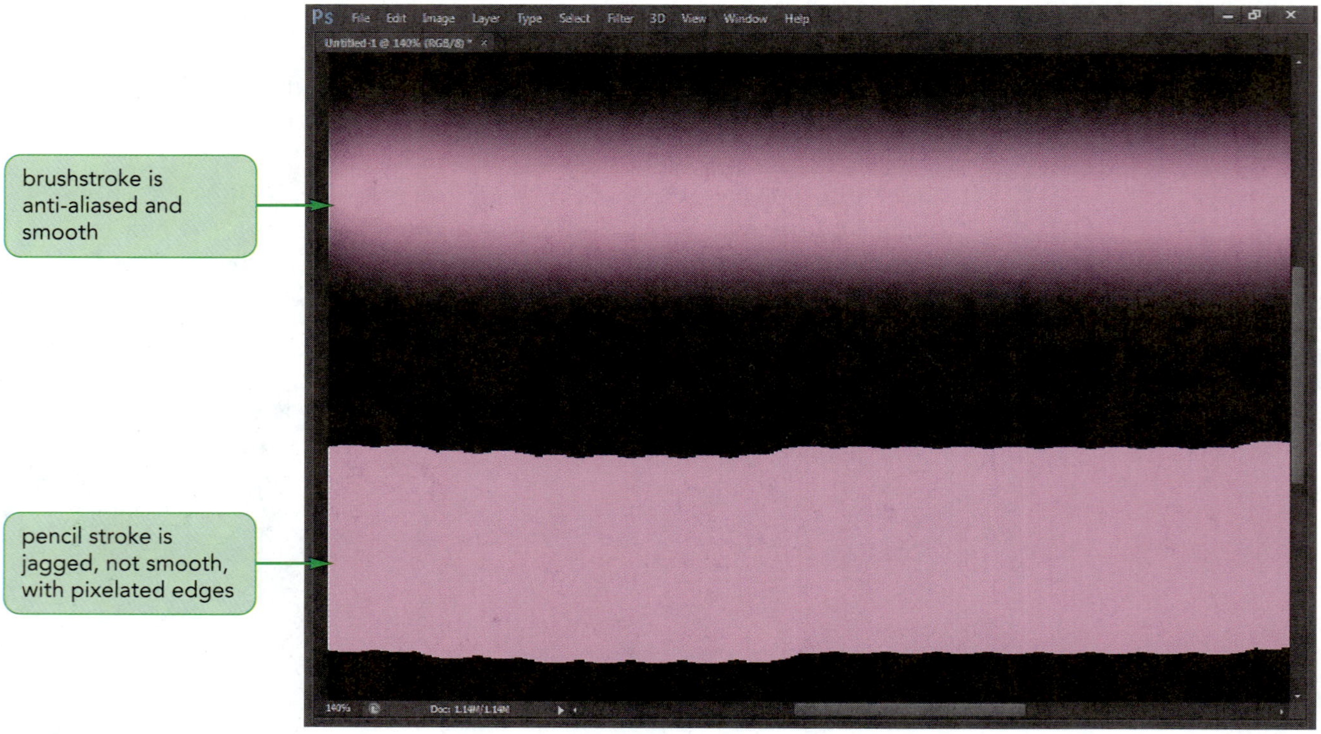

In Figure 4-41, the top stroke was drawn with the Brush tool and the bottom stroke was drawn with the Pencil tool. Both strokes have identical diameter (width) and hardness settings. However, notice how different they look. The brushstroke is smooth because it is anti-aliased. The pencil stroke has hard edges and is not anti-aliased; in fact, you can distinguish the individual pixels along the edges. In this section, you'll focus on the Brush tool, but the skills you learn can also be applied to the Pencil tool.

Choosing Brush Settings and Adding Brushstrokes

When you select the Brush tool, the options bar displays the Brush tool options shown in Figure 4-42.

Figure 4-42 Brush tool options

Button	Name	Use To
	Tool Preset picker	Display the presets for the Brush tool, such as "Airbrush soft round 50% flow." You can choose to display presets for the current tool or for all of the tools.
	Brush Preset picker	Specify the size and the hardness for the brush or choose from a variety of presets, including Chalk, Dune grass, Stars, and certain preset brush hardness and size settings.
	Toggle the Brush panel	Expand and collapse the Brush panel display.
	Mode	Choose a painting mode for the brush.
	Opacity	Set brush opacity.
	Tablet pressure	Control brushstroke opacity based on the pressure you place on the tablet rather than via Brush panel opacity settings (this only applies when you are working on a tablet computer).
	Flow	Set the flow rate, or the amount of paint on the brush; a low percentage paints as if you have just dipped the brush lightly in paint, and a high percentage saturates the brush.
	Enable airbrush-style build-up effects	Turn on airbrush mode.
	Always use Pressure for Size	Control brushstroke size based on the pressure you place on the tablet rather than Brush panel opacity settings (this only applies when you are working on a tablet computer).

The Brush Preset picker displays a library of brush settings. You can set the diameter of the brush (measured in pixels) as well as the hardness of the brush. A brush with a high hardness setting will paint on the canvas in much the same way a physical paint brush with hard bristles will paint. Strokes will appear firm and full, with little space showing between the virtual bristles. A brush with a low hardness setting will paint like a brush with softer bristles. See Figure 4-43.

Figure 4-43 **Working with brush presets**

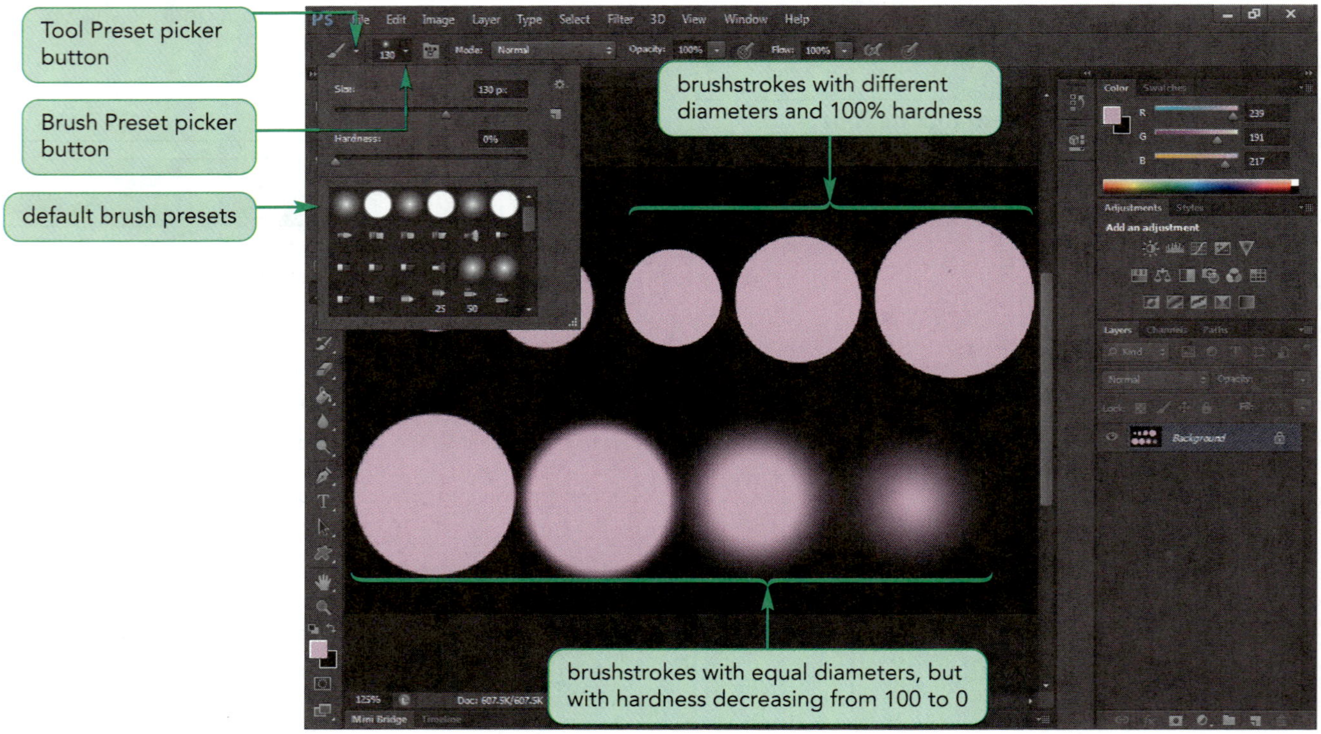

You can use the Brush Preset picker to choose from a variety of presets; however, the Brush Presets panel is a more convenient way to work with presets, and is covered later in this tutorial.

To paint with the Brush tool, set the foreground color you want to use, select the layer on which you want to paint, click the place you want to begin your brushstroke, and then drag the mouse to complete the stroke. When you have finished the first stroke, release the mouse button. You can repeat this procedure for each stroke in your composition.

You can also paint in straight lines with the Brush tool by using the click-Shift-click method. To draw a straight line, click the place on the canvas where you want to begin the stroke. Release the mouse button. Position the mouse over the point where you want to end the stroke and then Shift-click. Photoshop fills in the area between the first place you clicked and the last place you Shift-clicked with a straight brushstroke.

You'll use the Brush tool to add a chalky border to the image of the wrecked bicycle, much like the outline police might add at a crime scene. Lee wants to see if modifying that image will strengthen the material for her "Time for a Replacement?" campaign.

TIP

You can also press the B key to activate the Brush tool.

To paint using the Brush tool:

1. Ensure that IsItTime.jpg is open in the Document window.
2. In the Tools panel, click the **Brush Tool** button. The options for the Brush tool appear on the options bar.
3. Press the **X** key to switch the foreground and background colors and set the foreground color to white.
4. On the options bar, click the **Brush Preset picker** button. The Brush Preset picker displays the default size (13 pixels) and hardness (0%) for the Brush tool.

5. Change the brush size to **50** pixels, and then drag the brush pointer ○ around the bicycle as if you are outlining the victim's body at a crime scene. See Figure 4-44.

Figure 4-44 **Adding a brushstroke**

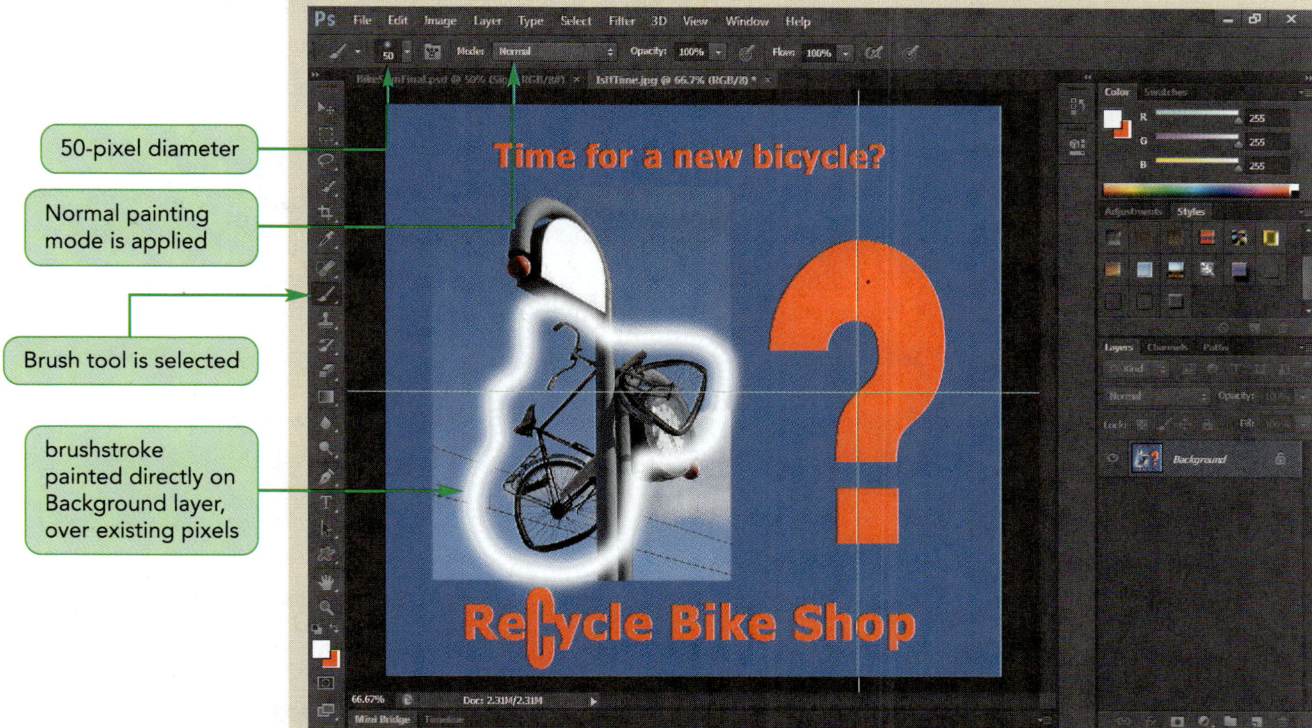

Björn Erlandsson/Shutterstock.com

The brushstroke appears directly on the Background layer. The result is that the underlying pixels have been replaced, just as they were replaced when you used the Pixels tool mode to draw a shape.

6. Change the brush size to **30** pixels, click the **Mode** arrow, and then click **Dissolve**.
7. Drag slightly outside the stroke you just painted. Changing the mode results in a completely different effect.
8. Save **IsItTime.jpg** and then close it.

Now that you have had some practice working with brushstrokes, you'll switch back to the sign file so you can finish up that project for Lee. You'll use the Brush tool to add straight lines to your sign image to create a hinge to hang the sign. Because you'll add the lines to a layer that has a Bevel & Emboss effect, the lines you draw will also have a Bevel & Emboss effect.

To draw straight lines with the Brush tool:

1. Display **BikeSignFinal.psd** at 20% magnification in the Document window, pan the image so that the bicycle sign is at the right side of the Document window, and then select the **Bicycle** layer if necessary.

2. Press the **D** key to reset the foreground and background colors to the default, and reset all of the tools.
3. Open the **Brush Preset** picker and set the size of the brush to **90** pixels and the hardness to **100%**.
4. Position the brush pointer ◯ just to the left of the upper-left corner of the sign and then click. Photoshop adds the first point in the straight line you'll draw.
5. Position the brush pointer ◯ at the left of the lower-left corner of the sign, press and hold the **Shift** key, and then click.

   Photoshop draws a straight brushstroke along the left side of the sign. To "attach" the sign to the storefront, you'll draw another straight brushstroke from the upper-left corner to the storefront.
6. Position the brush pointer ◯ just to the left of the upper-left corner of the sign slightly overlapping the top of the brushstroke you just drew, and then click.
7. Position the brush pointer ◯ at the center of the wall above the door, press and hold the **Shift** key, and then click. The sign appears to be attached to the building by a wrought iron hanger. Because you added the brushstrokes to the Bicycle layer, the Bicycle layer style is applied to the brushstrokes. See Figure 4-45.

Figure 4-45 **Painting in a straight line**

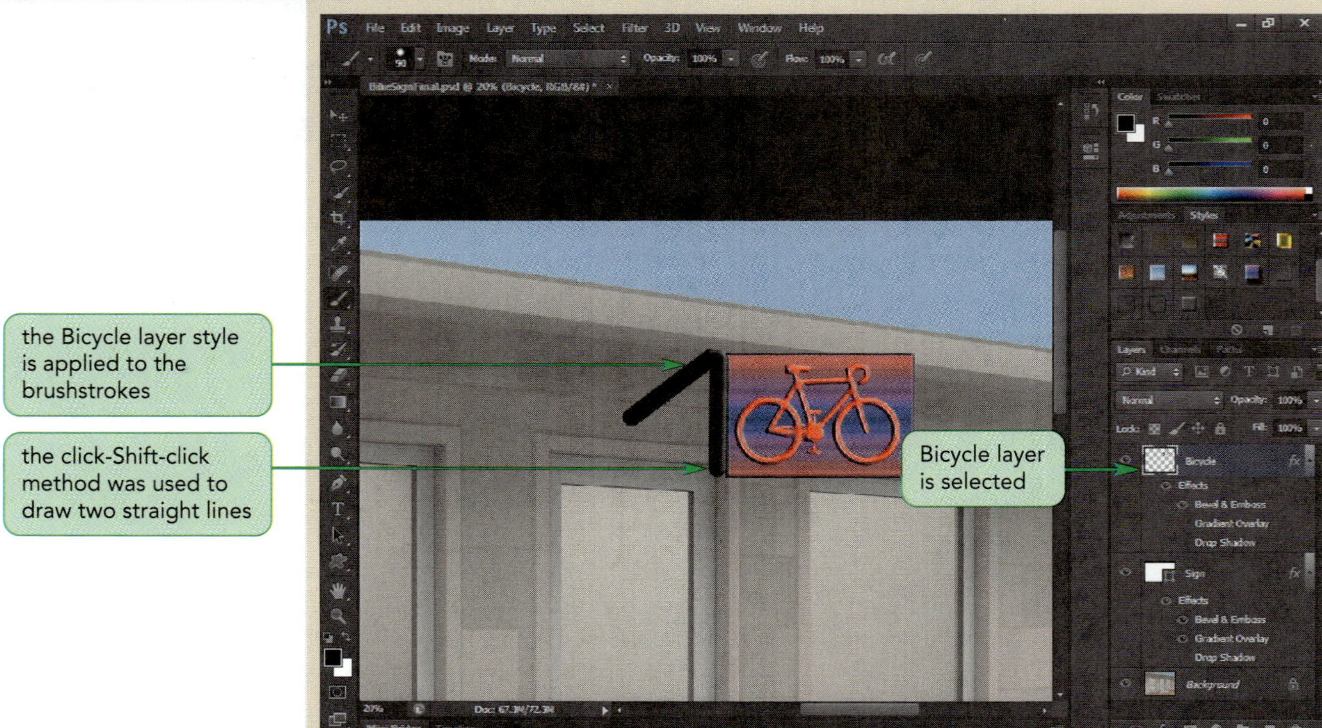

Shevchenko Nataliya/Shutterstock.com; Black Images/Shutterstock.com

8. Save **BikeSignFinal.psd**, and keep the file open.

PROSKILLS

Verbal Communication: Understanding a Client's Needs Up Front

Before you begin working on a digital composition for a client, you must ensure that you fully understand what the client is looking for. To do so, you need to set up strong and reliable lines of communication, which will involve you not only offering your advice and expertise, but also listening to what the client is *really* saying. Helping your client clearly communicate his or her needs to you is essential before you dive into any project. For example, if your client asks you to create an ad for a magazine, that information should be just a starting point. You need to ask clarifying questions, such as: Is the ad aimed at a certain demographic or group? Is the magazine a conservative business magazine, an interior decorating magazine, or is it for teens—with an emphasis on pop culture? Are you trying to convey a certain mood? Should the text be in a particular font or color? Listen carefully, and give your client time to fully explain their vision for the ad. Even after your client has provided more details, it's a good idea to make sure you really understood what you were told. It can be helpful to use phrases such as "What I understood is" or "Let me see if I heard you correctly" to be sure you really know what's required.

By asking clarifying questions and restating your understanding of the client's needs, you can iron out many potential wrinkles ahead of time. That will save you time and effort in the short term, and in the long run, it will result in a happy client who will be more likely to request your services again—and recommend you to others.

Working with Brush Presets

The Brush and Pencil presets offer a great variety of brushstrokes and pencil shapes for you to choose from. The most convenient way to work with presets is to use the Brush panel or the Brush Presets panel. The Brush panel displays the brush tip shape and lets you modify size, angle, and roundness settings. The Brush Presets panel previews the brush tip shape and shows you what a brushstroke will look like. In this section, you'll work with the Brush Presets panel. It appears by default in the Painting workspace, so you'll switch to that workspace. See Figure 4-46.

Figure 4-46 Working with brush presets in the Painting workspace

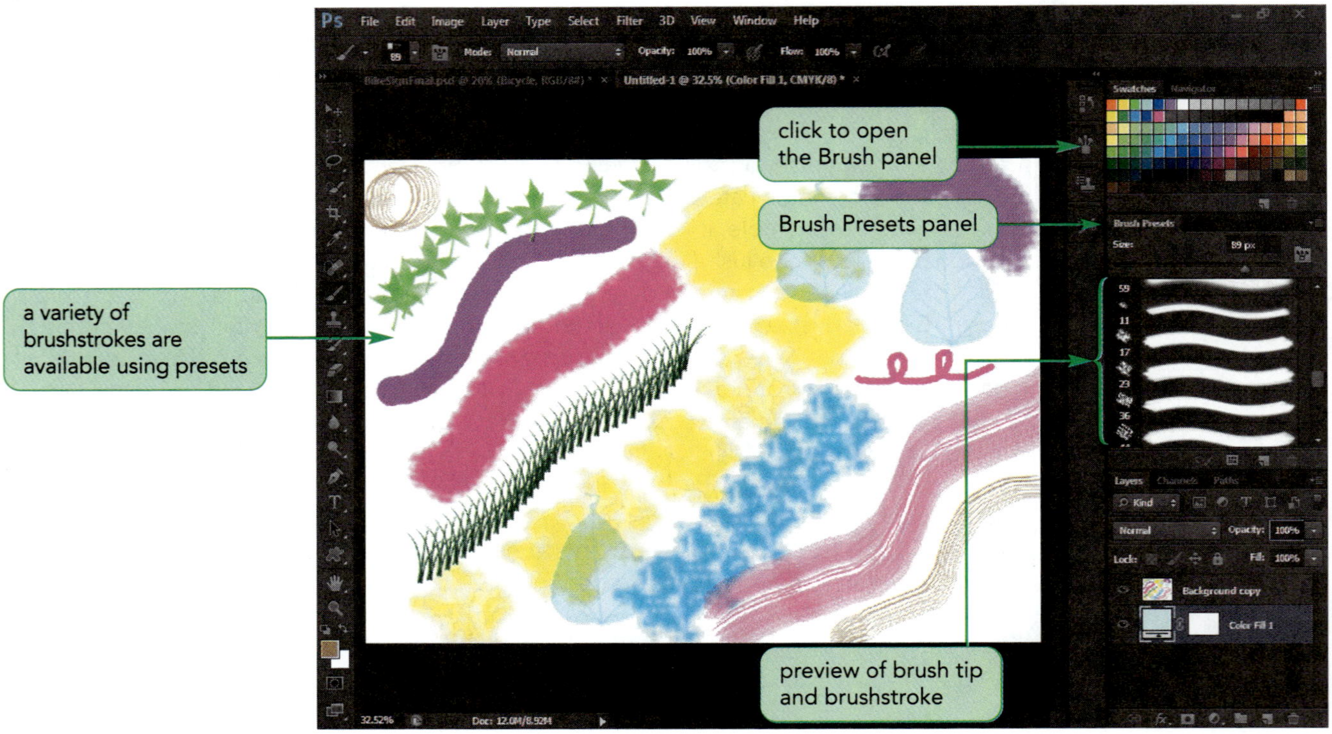

With the Brush tool, not only can you choose brush tips with different diameters and hardness settings, but you can also choose different paints as well. For example, you can choose a preset that mimics oil paint, one that mimics spray paint, or one that mimics chalk. You can also choose brush tips that paint leaves, spirals, butterflies, and other shapes.

Loading Other Presets

Photoshop provides numerous libraries of brush presets, and as a result, you have hundreds of choices for brushes. As you become more experienced in Photoshop, you'll develop a sense of which brushes you need for which effects, but as a novice, it's a good idea to experiment with as many presets and preset modifications as possible. Loading a brush preset library is basically the same as loading any other library. You do it from the panel menu, and, as with the Color, Swatches, and Styles panels you've already worked with, you need to determine whether you want to append the library to the current library, or use it to replace the current library. You can also modify any preset in any library and save it as a custom preset or, if you decide that you don't want to keep the changes you have made to a set of brush presets, you can reset the Brush panel by clicking Reset Brushes on the panel menu.

To load a preset library:

1. In the Layers panel, click the **Bicycle** layer, if necessary, click **Window** on the menu bar, point to **Workspace**, and then click **Painting** to display the most commonly used panels for painting. Click **Window** on the menu bar, point to **Workspace**, and then click **Reset Painting**, to reset the workspace.

   The Brush Presets panel is expanded above the Layers panel. The Brush panel is minimized to an icon.

2. In the Brush Presets panel, click the **panel menu** button, and then click **Assorted Brushes**.
3. Click the **OK** button to replace the current brushes with the new brushes. Click the **No** button if asked to save the current brushes.
4. In the Tools panel, click the **Brush Tool** button, and in the Brush Presets panel, scroll down until you see the Dashed Circle 2 preset shown in Figure 4-47, and then click the **Dashed Circle 2** preset to select it.

Figure 4-47 Selecting the Dashed Circle 2 brush preset

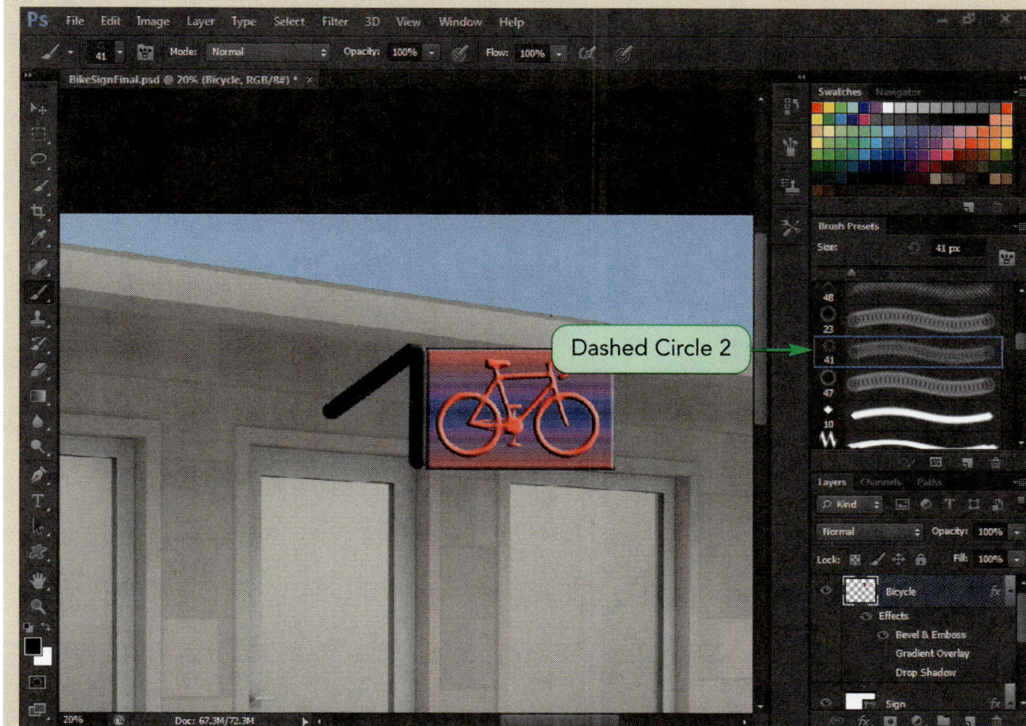

Shevchenko Nataliya/Shutterstock.com; Black Images/Shutterstock.com

The Dashed Circle 2 preset includes a brush diameter of 41 pixels; however, you can change the brush diameter to customize the preset.

5. In the Brush Presets panel, change the brush diameter to **330** pixels.
6. In the Tools panel, set the foreground color to white.
7. On the canvas, click in the front tire of the bicycle. The Dashed Circle 2 brush adds a white dashed circle to the image, which creates the appearance of tire spokes.
8. Click in the rear tire to add the dashed circle there as well.
9. Save the file.

Using a Brush Preset to Stroke a Path

When you draw a shape in Photoshop, you can use the Paths option on the options bar to specify that the shape is a temporary work path. A **work path** provides a temporary outline on a layer. You can use the outline to define a path for a variety of tasks, including erasing the area defined by the path, or stroking the path with the Brush or

Pencil tool. To create a work path and apply a stroke to it, you select the desired shape tool in the Tools panel, draw the shape, and then use the Stroke Path command on the context menu to display the Stroke Path dialog box and a list of tools you can use for the stroke. If you select the Brush option, Photoshop uses the current brush settings to draw a brushstroke around the work path. Once you have added the stroke, you can delete the work path from the Paths panel or save it for future sessions.

You'll create a circular work path and stroke it with a concentric circle brushstroke to show Lee an idea you have about painting a design on the store window.

TIP

To display a list of preset names rather than sample strokes, select the Text Only option from the Brush Presets panel menu.

To create a work path and apply a stroke:

1. In the Brush Presets panel, select the 32-pixel **Concentric Circles** preset (the fifth option in the list).
2. At the top of the Brush Presets panel, change the brush size to **200** pixels, and then in the Tools panel, set the foreground color to a **dark blue**.
3. In the Document window, zoom out to about **12.5%** and then click in the center of the store window on the left. Photoshop adds a single brushstroke to the window (a concentric circle).
4. Click two more times in exactly the same spot. Notice that the circles get darker, as if you are adding additional coats of paint.
5. In the Tools panel, select the **Ellipse Tool** button, and on the options bar, click the **Pick tool mode** button, and then click **Path**.
6. On the options bar, click the **More options** button, select the **Circle** and **From Center** options, and then click in the center of the circle you just painted and drag out to create the path.
7. Right-click the work path to open the path context menu. See Figure 4-48.

Figure 4-48 Path context menu

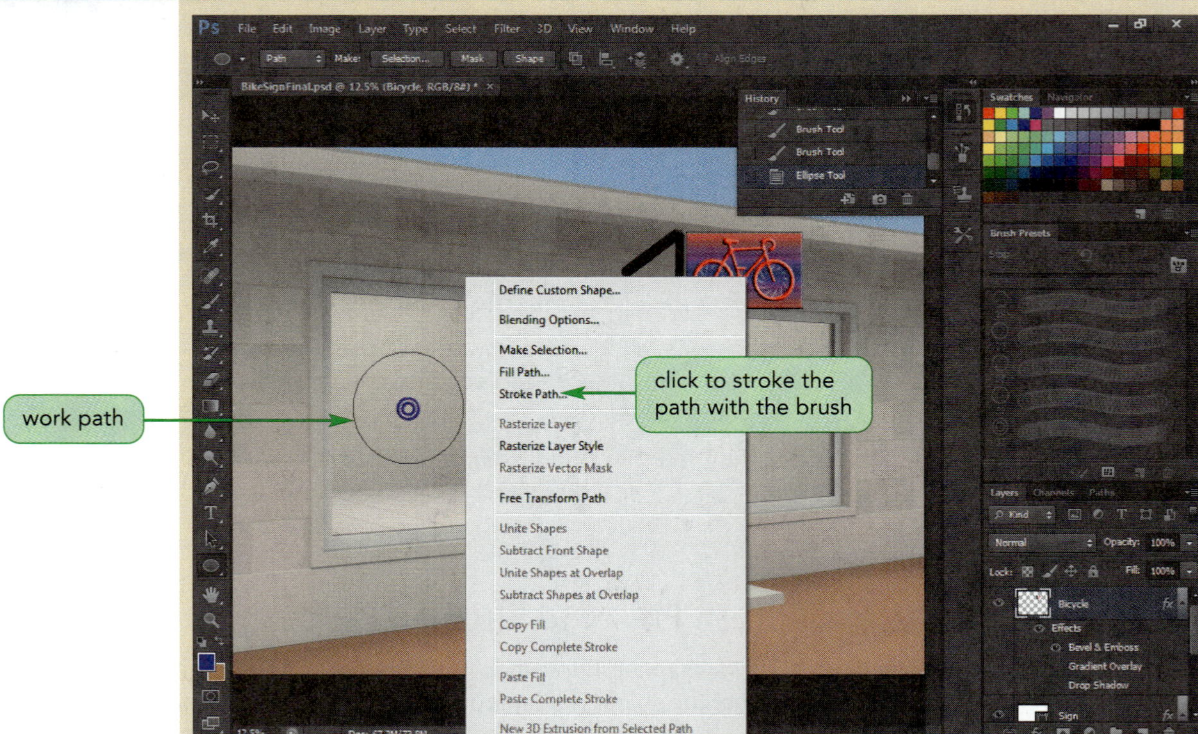

Shevchenko Nataliya/Shutterstock.com; Black Images/Shutterstock.com

Photoshop displays options for working with the work path. You can fill the path, make it a selection, or you can stroke it.

8. On the context menu, click **Stroke Path** to open the Stroke Path dialog box. Click the **Tool** arrow, click **Brush**, and then click the **OK** button to accept Brush as the tool you'll use to stroke the path.
9. Photoshop adds a brushstroke that follows the path of the circle you drew. In the Layers panel group, click the **Paths** tab. Photoshop lists a single work path in the Paths panel. Work paths are saved when a file is saved. Because you won't need this work path in the future, you'll delete it.
10. Select the **Work Path** path, if necessary, and then press the **Delete** key. The path is deleted from the panel and from the image, but the circular brushstroke remains. See Figure 4-49.

Figure 4-49 **Brushstroke on path**

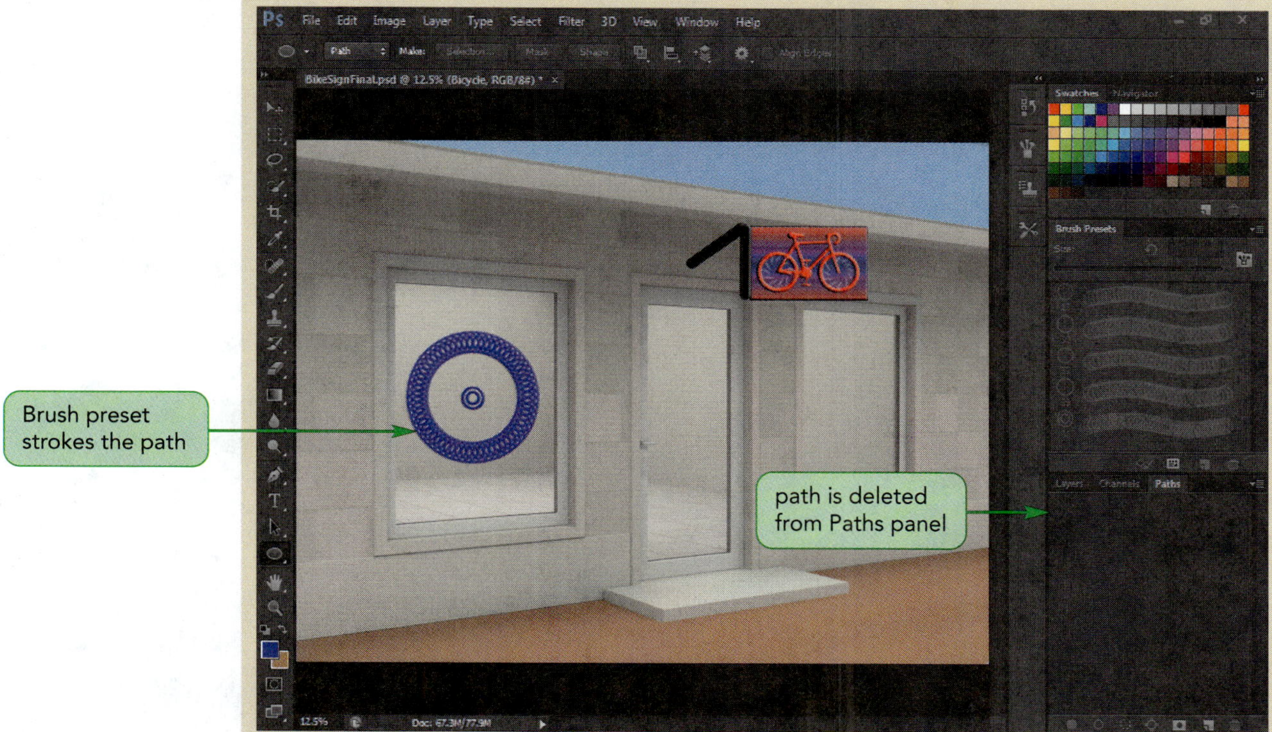

Shevchenko Nataliya/Shutterstock.com; Black Images/Shutterstock.com

Creating a Custom Preset

You can create a custom preset and save it so you can use it in future Photoshop sessions. To create a custom preset, select the brush preset you want to modify and change the settings, such as diameter and hardness, until you achieve the effect you want. When you are satisfied with your changes, you can use the New Brush Preset command on the panel menu for the Brush Presets panel to save the custom preset. You can then save a set of presets as a library using the Save Brushes options on the panel menu. Photoshop adds an .abr extension to any brush preset library you save. If you decide that you don't want to keep the changes you have made to a set of brush presets, you can reset the Brush panel without saving your changes.

Lee is happy with the work on the bike sign you have shown her so far and is planning to use your image of the storefront in an upcoming meeting with other members of the team. However, she would like you to add some color to the image to create some excitement. You'll use a customized preset to add azalea bushes to achieve a colorful effect.

To create a new brush preset:

1. Reset the Painting workspace, and reset the background and foreground colors to the default colors.
2. Fit the image to the screen, select the **Background** layer, set the foreground color to a **bright pink**, and then press the **B** key to activate the Brush tool.
3. In the Brush Presets panel, click the **panel menu** button, and click **Special Effect Brushes**, and then click the **OK** button. Click the **Azalea** preset (the first one on the list) to select it, and change the diameter to **150** pixels.
4. In the image, drag on the ground and in front of the building, avoiding the front step. See Figure 4-50.

Figure 4-50 Creating azalea bushes with brush preset

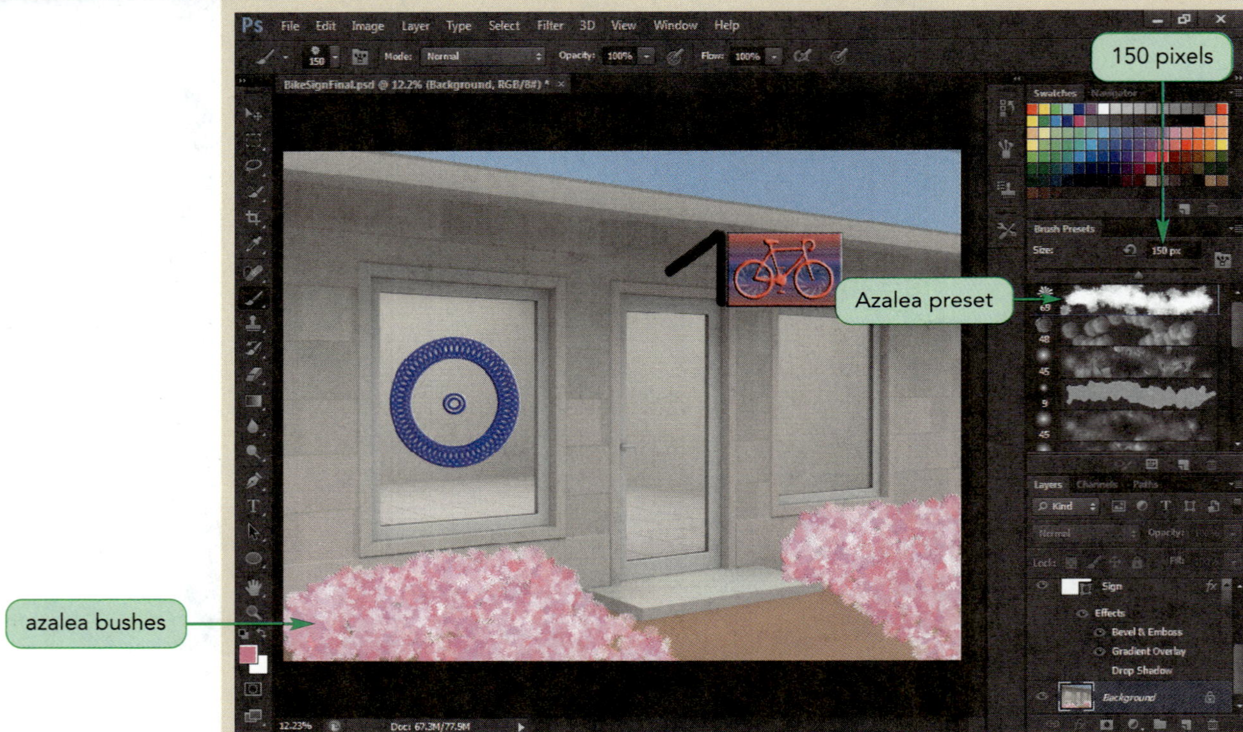

Shevchenko Nataliya/Shutterstock.com; Black Images/Shutterstock.com

5. In the Brush Presets panel, click the **panel menu** button, and then click **New Brush Preset**.
6. Type **150 px azalea** in the Name box, click the **Capture Brush Size in Preset** check box to select it, if necessary, and then click the **OK** button to save the new preset. Finally, you'll add a layer and apply a blending mode to give your illustration more depth.
7. In the Layers panel, click the **Bicycle** layer, if necessary, and add a **dark blue** fill layer. Set the opacity to **55%**, and add a **Soft Light** blending mode.
8. Save the **BikeSignFinal.psd** file, close it, and then exit Photoshop.

INSIGHT

Making a Brush Preset from an Image

You can create a custom brush preset by selecting part of an image and using the Define Brush Preset command on the Edit menu. For example, in a photograph of a pile of shells, you could select a single scallop shell and then use the Define Brush Preset command to save it as a preset. Photoshop adds the new preset to the Brush panel and shows a preview of the brushstroke at the bottom of the panel. Note that if you open an image but don't select an area, Photoshop uses the entire image as the preset, which might not be your intention. You might want to save a custom brush preset to create an effect that you plan to use in multiple files. Rather than repeating the same steps for every file, you can use the brush preset to add the desired effect.

In this session, you learned how to add color, gradient, and pattern fill layers to your compositions. You also learned how to add shapes to a layer and how to modify them by combining, excluding, and merging shapes. You worked with brushes and brush presets. In the next tutorial, you'll learn how to select, remove, and tweak content and work further with layer masks to create more sophisticated images.

REVIEW

Session 4.2 Quick Check

1. What is a gradient?
2. True or False. You cannot apply a blending mode to a Fill layer.
3. When you are drawing a shape such as a rectangle, what effect does the Proportional setting have?
4. To create a "hole" in a geometric shape that you draw, you can select the __________ __________ __________ option on the Path operations menu.
5. True or False. If you use the Shape tool mode and draw directly on an image, you are altering the pixels on the layers beneath your drawing.
6. To draw or paint a straight line, you can click at the beginning of the line, press the __________ key, and then click at the end of the line.
7. You can save the modifications you make to a brush as a brush __________.

Practice the skills you learned in the tutorial using the same case scenario.

PRACTICE

Review Assignments

Data Files needed for the Review Assignments: Signage.psd, Gopher.jpg

Lee likes the sign you proposed for the entrance to her store, and would like you to submit some ideas for signs to place in various areas inside and outside the store. For starters, she'd like a sign to place above the bicycle rack in the parking lot. Because she thinks the bike shop sign worked well with no words, she would like you to do something similar for the new signs. Complete the following steps:

1. Start Photoshop while pressing the Ctrl+Alt+Shift keys, and click Yes to delete the Settings File when prompted. Switch to the Painting workspace, and then reset the Painting workspace. Reset all tools.
2. Open **Signage.psd** and **Gopher.jpg**, located in the Photoshop4\Review folder included with your Data Files, and arrange the Document windows so the files are displayed side by side.
3. Using a point sample of the yellow color from the gopher tortoise sign, fill the Signage file background with yellow. If the color is out of gamut, adjust it so it is in gamut.
4. Close Gopher.jpg without saving it. Save Signage.psd as **NoCars.psd** in the Photoshop4\Review folder.
5. Using Figure 4-51 as a guide and with the Shape tool mode selected on the options bar, draw a 'No' Sign shape with a 10-inch diameter, a red fill, and no stroke. (*Hint*: You can find the 'No' Sign custom shape in the Symbols shapes preset library for the Custom Shape tool.) Center the sign shape on the canvas, and apply the Blue Glass (Button) style to it. Hide the color Overlay effect and the Gradient Overlay effect.

Figure 4-51 **Sample sign for ReCycle Bike Shop parking lot**

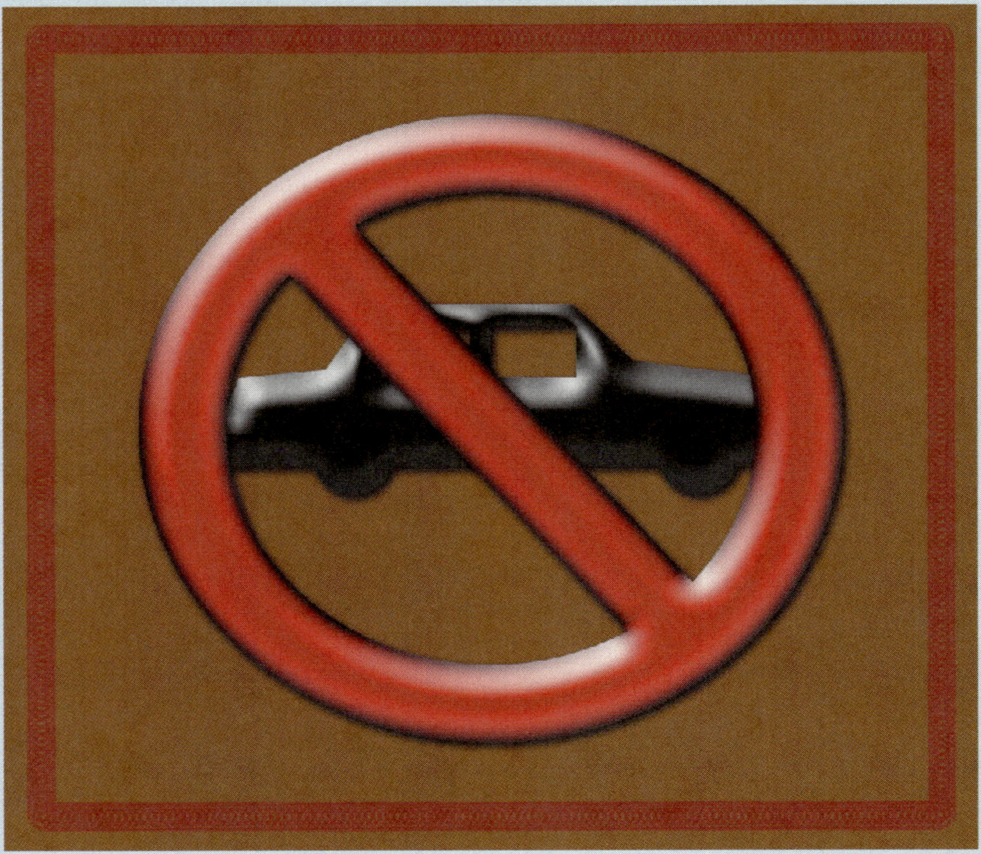

6. Right-click the new shape layer, and then select the Rasterize Layer option. Then, open the Layer Style dialog box, and add a Drop Shadow effect with a Size setting of 10 pixels. Close the Layer Style dialog box.
7. Add a Car 1 custom shape inside the sign shape using a black fill and no stroke. (*Hint*: You can find the Car 1 custom shape in the Symbols shapes preset library.) Copy the layer style from the 'No' Sign layer to the car layer. If necessary, rearrange the layers in the Layers panel so that the car shape is behind the sign shape on the canvas, and then deselect all the layers.
8. Display the rulers, and add guides at 1/2 inch and 11 1/2 inches on the vertical ruler and at 1/2 inch and 13 1/2 inches on the horizontal ruler. Add a new empty layer, and then use the Rectangle tool to draw a path over the guides.
9. In the Tools panel, select the Brush tool, and switch to the Assorted Brushes presets. Select the Concentric Circles brush preset, and then sample the red used for the 'No' Sign, and set it as the foreground color.
10. Select the Rectangle tool again, right-click the path you created with the Rectangle tool, confirm that Brush is selected in the Stroke Path dialog box, and then click the OK button.
11. Delete the path, and clear the guides.
12. Select the car layer, and create the windows in the car by selecting the Subtract Front Shape path operation. (*Hint*: Make sure you are drawing a shape and not a path.)
13. Save the **NoCars.psd** file, and close the file.

Use your skills to create a composition for a technology business.

APPLY

Case Problem 1

Data Files needed for this Case Problem: TekSell.jpg, CD.psd

TekSell Founded in 2008, TekSell is an online technology retail business that sells computer hardware and software. TekSell's owner, Jose Ruiz, has hired you to create a new look for the company's Web site. For your initial meeting with Jose, you plan to present a few ideas for the page background and possible navigation buttons. In this exercise, you'll create two sample buttons and a proposed page background. Complete the following steps:

1. Start Photoshop while pressing the Ctrl+Alt+Shift keys, and click Yes to delete the Settings File when prompted. Reset Photoshop to the default Essentials workspace layout, and then reset all tools.
2. Open **TekSell.jpg**, located in the Photoshop4\Case1 folder provided with your Data Files, and save it as **TekSellWeb.psd**.
3. You'll start by creating the "look" you will propose for the Web page background. Add a gradient fill layer to the Background layer using the Color Harmonies 1 gradient preset library. Apply the Orange, Blue gradient from that group using a gradient angle of 180 degrees. Then, set the opacity of the gradient fill layer to 60%.

EXPLORE

4. Open **CD.psd**, located in the Photoshop4\Case1 folder, and arrange the two open files side by side. In the CD.psd file, select the CD Isolated layer, and drag it over the TekSellWeb.psd document window. After the CD Isolated layer has been added to the TekSellWeb.psd file, drag the CD Isolated layer above the Gradient Fill 1 layer, if necessary. Close the CD.psd file without saving it.

EXPLORE

5. Resize the image of the CD so it is 25% of its original size. (*Hint*: To resize the CD, select the Move Tool button, show the transform controls, click one of the transform controls in the Document window, click the Maintain aspect ratio icon on the options bar, and then type **25** in the Height box.) Then, move the individual CD to the left side of the canvas, toward the top of the extension color.

6. Apply the Striped Cone (Button) style to the CD layer. Your proposal will include using the image of the CD as a navigation button on the Web site. Modify the style you just applied so it has an Outer Glow with a size of 70 pixels.
7. Below the CD image you added, draw a circle shape with a red fill, and make it about the same size as the CD. Copy and paste the CD Isolated layer style you created onto the circle. This will be the selected state of the button you're proposing for the Web site.
8. Create a new layer above the Ellipse 1 layer, and select the Brush tool. Open the Brush Presets panel, switch to the Special Effect Brushes presets library, and select the Tumble Planets brush. Set the brush size to 250 pixels, change the foreground color to yellow, and then paint planets in one brushstroke down the side of the canvas, under the buttons.
9. Save the image, flatten it, and save it again as **TekSellWeb.jpg**, using the default JPEG settings, in the Photoshop4\Case1 folder. Submit the results of the preceding steps to your instructor either in printed or electronic form, as requested.

Use your skills to create two cover options for an architecture magazine.

APPLY

Case Problem 2

Data Files needed for this Case Problem: ArchiText.psd

ArchiText Meena Patel is the publisher of *ArchiText*, a magazine for architects, where you have recently been hired as a graphic designer. The fall issue of the magazine will include photographs and articles about a series of architecturally interesting buildings from a single city, anywhere in the world. Meena has presented a challenge to you and your colleagues: Submit a mock-up of a cover that uses a photograph of a city building and presents it in a unique way; the winner's work will be published on the cover of the fall issue. To stand out from the others who will be competing, you'll create a second version of the cover that uses mostly drawn objects instead of a photograph. Complete the following steps:

1. Start Photoshop while pressing the Ctrl+Alt+Shift keys, and click Yes to delete the Settings File when prompted. Reset Photoshop to the default Essentials workspace layout, and then reset all tools.
2. Open **ArchiText.psd**, located in the Photoshop4\Case2 folder provided with your Data Files, and save it as **ArchiText2.psd** in the same folder.

EXPLORE

3. Open a Web browser of your choice and go to the MorgueFile or the Creative Commons Web site, or another site that supplies images for free for commercial purposes. If you use Creative Commons, click the Find CC-licensed works link and then, on the Search page, confirm that the "use is for commercial purposes," and the "modify, adapt, or build upon" check boxes are selected. (You can also use one of your own images.) Search the site for images of buildings from the city of your choice. For example, search for images of buildings in Chicago by using *Chicago* as your search term. Select an image in any format with which you would like to work. Before you download the image, check the licensing information to make sure that it can be remixed without attribution and used for commercial purposes. Download the image and save it as **CityShot.jpg** in the Photoshop4\Case2 folder.
4. Return to Photoshop, and place the **CityShot.jpg** image in the ArchiText2.psd file. Size the placed image so it fits properly in the composition, with the original text still showing. Apply any adjustment layers you think might be necessary.
5. Apply a style to the *ArchiText* text and modify it until it suits your composition. Save the modified style as ArchiStyle, and then apply it to *the city issue* text.
6. Add a Pattern or Gradient fill layer to the composition, change its settings as desired, and position the layer so it only affects the Background layer.

7. On a new layer, use the Brush tool to add brushstrokes or special effects to your cover using one or more brush presets. Make sure to position the layer so the strokes appear where you want them. Save ArchiText2.psd, and close it.
8. Create a new file with any background color using the same dimensions as the cover, 8 ½ × 11 inches. Use the CMYK color mode, 300-ppi resolution, and 8-bit color. Save the file as **ArchiText3.psd** in the Photoshop4\Case2 folder.
9. Use any combination of layers, brushstrokes, drawing tools, and color selection tools to create a page that you'll submit as an alternate cover idea. See Figure 4-52 as an example.

Figure 4-52 **Sample ArchiText cover**

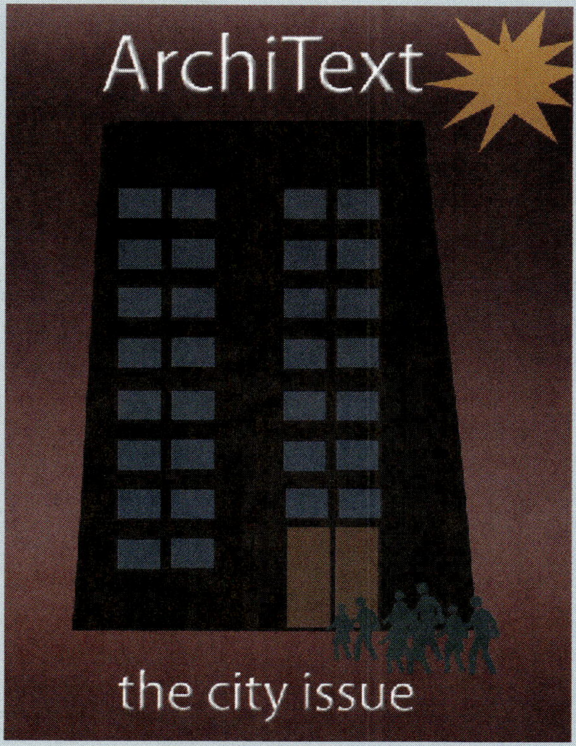

Your file should include a drawing that uses addition, subtraction, intersection, and exclusion. (*Hint*: Draw a building with windows and doors.) Be sure to include the magazine title and subtitle, as shown in Figure 4-52.

10. Flatten the image, and then save the file and close it.
11. Submit the results of the preceding steps to your instructor either in printed or electronic form, as requested.

Extend what you've learned to use the Mixer Brush to modify an image.

CHALLENGE

Case Problem 3

Data Files needed for this Case Problem: Easel.jpg

TeachOut David Jasper is the creative director for TeachOut, a company that provides distance learning solutions for schools, universities, and technical training centers. You have been hired to work with David on a series of ads that will emphasize TeachOut's goal of making learning fun. For your first project, you'll use the Mixer Brush to paint on an easel to produce an image reminiscent of a child's painting. Complete the following steps:

1. Start Photoshop while pressing the Ctrl+Alt+Shift keys, and click Yes to delete the Settings File when prompted. Reset Photoshop to the default Essentials workspace layout, and then reset all tools.
2. Open **Easel.jpg**, located in the Photoshop4\Case3 folder provided with your Data Files, and save it as **TeachOut.psd** in the same folder.
3. Add a shape layer with a white rectangle, sized to fit on the easel. Rasterize the rectangle, and then rotate it and position it so it appears to be a canvas sitting on the easel in the image. Add a shadow to the rectangle shape to give it depth and a more realistic look.
4. EXPLORE Use Photoshop Help to research the Mixer Brush. Make sure you understand the settings on the options bar, including Wet, Load, Mix, and Flow.
5. EXPLORE Create a new file with the default Photoshop settings to experiment with the Mixer Brush before you paint on the canvas in the TeachOut.psd file. Try different combinations of colors and different brushes until you understand how the options bar settings affect the mixture of colors. Save the file as **Scrap.jpg** in the Photoshop4\Case3 folder, and then close the file.
6. EXPLORE Switch back to TeachOut.psd, and using Figure 4-53 as a guide, paint an image in the style of a child's painting.

Figure 4-53 **Sample TeachOut image**

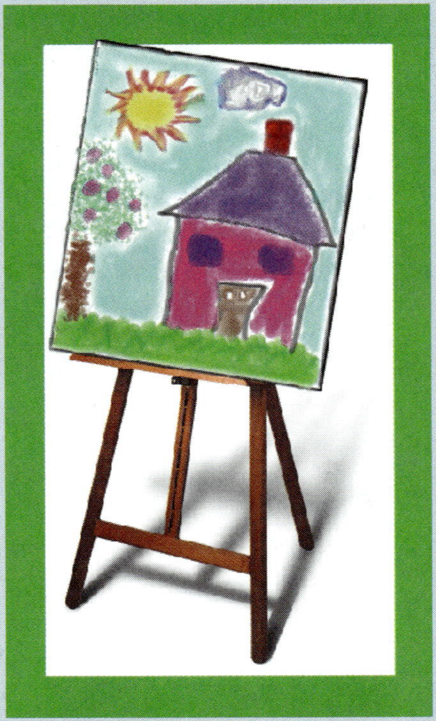

Fotocrisis/Shutterstock.com

Your painting should demonstrate that you understand how to mix colors with the Mixer Brush, and how to achieve different effects with different Wet, Load, Mix, and Flow levels. You should use at least five different colors, at least three color combinations (mixes), and three different brushes. (*Hint*: If you paint outside of the canvas by accident, use the Eraser tool to erase the paint so it is contained within the canvas edges.)

7. Change the dimensions of the document by extending the canvas one inch on all sides; sample one of the mixed colors as the canvas extension color.
8. When you are satisfied with your artwork, flatten the image and then save it.
9. Submit the results of the preceding steps to your instructor either in printed or electronic form, as requested.

Use your skills to create an original composition for a landscaping company.

APPLY

Case Problem 4

There are no Data Files needed for this Case Problem.

Prettyscapes Prettyscapes is a landscaping company with 15 employees in Boise, Idaho. Business has been growing lately, and Maya Morrisson, the owner, is interested in attracting creative talent. Maya has asked you to come up with a composition for a help wanted ad that conveys whimsy and creativity. She will provide the text. You'll use the color, drawing, and brush tools in Photoshop to show what a landscape designer might do when presented with an empty lot.

1. Start Photoshop while pressing the Ctrl+Alt+Shift keys, and click Yes to delete the Settings File when prompted. Reset Photoshop to the default Essentials workspace layout, and then reset all tools.
2. Create a new file with a white background of any dimensions.
3. Open a Web browser of your choice and go to the MorgueFile site or the Creative Commons site, or another site that supplies images for free for commercial purposes. If you use Creative Commons, click the Find CC-licensed works link and then, on the Search page, confirm that the "use is for commercial purposes," and the "modify, adapt, or build upon" check boxes are selected. (You can also use one of your own images.) In a later step, you will be adding a house to the image you download, so select an image with that in mind. Before you download the image, check the licensing information to make sure that it can be remixed without attribution and used for commercial purposes.
4. Download the image and save it as **Landscape.jpg** in the Photoshop4\Case 4 folder provided with your Data Files.
5. Return to Photoshop and place the Landscape.jpg image in your newly created file, and size it to fit.
6. On one part of the image, use the drawing tools to draw a house with windows and a door. To create the drawing, use at least two of the path operations options (creating a new layer, or combining, subtracting, intersecting, excluding, or merging shapes).
7. Use blending modes, opacity, styles, and other adjustments to modify the various shapes in your drawing. (*Hint*: For some effects, you might need to rasterize your drawn objects.)
8. EXPLORE Use any tools you choose to draw a brick walkway leading to the house.
9. EXPLORE Open one of the brush preset libraries you haven't yet used, and choose brush tips that will let you create bushes and flower beds around the house.
10. Add objects such as butterflies to your drawing using various brush presets. Make sure to vary your color choices.

11. Put any finishing touches on your composition that you'd like, flatten the image, and then save the file as **LandscapeWhimsy.psd** in the Photoshop4\Case4 folder.
12. Submit the results of the preceding steps to your instructor either in printed or electronic form, as requested.

ENDING DATA FILES

Photoshop4 →

Tutorial

BikeSignFinal.psd
ColorUpgrade.jpg
EffectSign.jpg
FourColors.jpg
FourColors.psd
FrameTrike.psd
IsItTime.jpg
Pedestrians.psd
RecycleSwatches.aco
RiderEffects.psd
SunsetBike.psd

Review

NoCars.psd

Case1

TekSellWeb.jpg
TekSellWeb.psd

Case2

ArchiText2.psd
ArchiText3.psd
CityShot.jpg

Case3

Scrap.jpg
TeachOut.psd

Case4

Landscape.jpg
LandscapeWhimsy.psd

Selecting and Modifying Content

Compositing Photos

OBJECTIVES

Session 5.1

- Modify, grow, transform, and refine a selection
- Apply an adjustment to a selection
- Copy and paste a selection
- Create complex selections
- Select a color range in an image
- Step backward and forward
- Use the History panel and the History Brush tool

Session 5.2

- Use the Lasso tool, the Magnetic Lasso tool, and the Quick Selection tool
- Save and reload a selection
- Apply Content-Aware and other fills to a selection
- Use the Content-Aware Move tool
- Add a stroke to a selection
- Work with filters and masks

Case | *Food for Change*

Food for Change, a nonprofit organization in Hartford, Connecticut, brings sustainable food systems into urban areas. Its founder, Azar Miller, created the organization in 2002, after noticing that many city-owned dirt lots were not being used. He approached city leaders with a proposal: With the help of urban and suburban youth, he would transform the lots into fruit and vegetable gardens. At the same time, he would educate youth about good nutrition, and send them into the city schools to promote urban gardening and good nutrition.

You have been hired by Azar to transform some of his photographs into compositions that he can use in brochures and fund-raising materials and on the Food for Change Web site. To make the changes Azar wants, you'll explore several Photoshop selection tools. In addition to modifying and refining selections, you'll learn how to apply an adjustment to a selection. You'll will also learn how to undo and redo actions using the Edit menu, the History panel, and the History Brush tool. You'll examine Photoshop's Content-Aware fill feature, and you'll save and reload selections. Finally, you'll experiment with filters, fills, and masks.

STARTING DATA FILES

Photoshop5 →

Tutorial
Berries.psd
Corn.jpg
GardenPath.jpg
GoodFood.jpg
GoodFood2.psd
Pumpkin.jpg
PumpkinField.jpg
Strawberry.jpg
VegetableBounty.psd
WomanInGarden.jpg

Review
4Pumpkins.jpg

Case1
Marlin.jpg
Vacation.jpg

Case2
Pitcher.psd
Vase.jpg

Case3
(none)

Case4
Smile.jpg
Spanner.jpg

SESSION 5.1 VISUAL OVERVIEW

Use the commands on the Select menu to select all of the pixels on a layer, to deselect or reselect a selection, or to invert a selection.

Click one of the Marquee tools and then drag on the canvas to create an **active selection** enclosed by an animated series of dashed lines or curves called a selection marquee.

Using the History Brush tool, you can paint over your composition and uncover part of the history state that is set as the source in the History panel.

Making adjustments to an image or combining different image files (or parts of image files) and/or vector objects in a single file is called **compositing**.

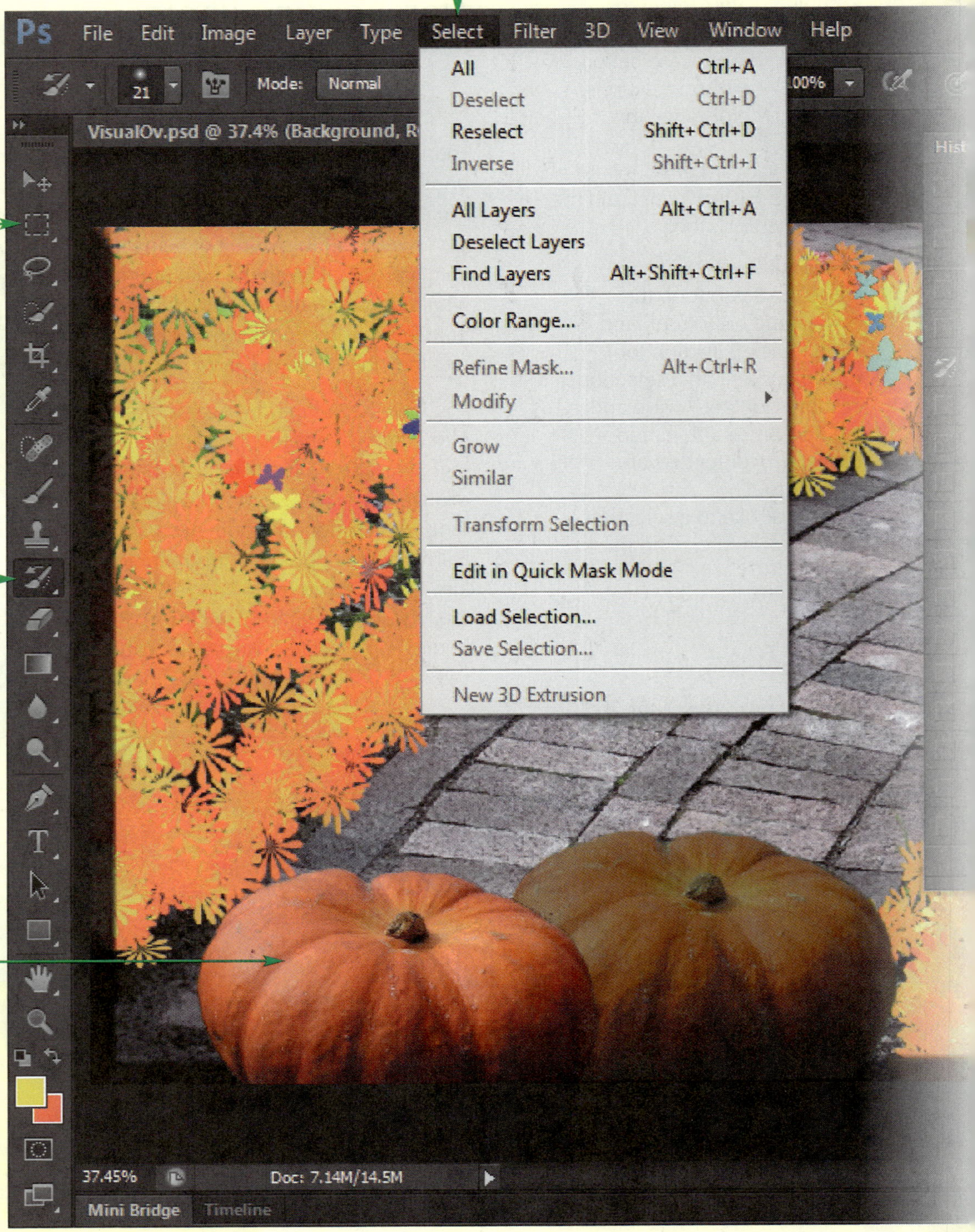

Jane Hosie-Bounar; Teodora George/Shutterstock.com

SELECTING CONTENT

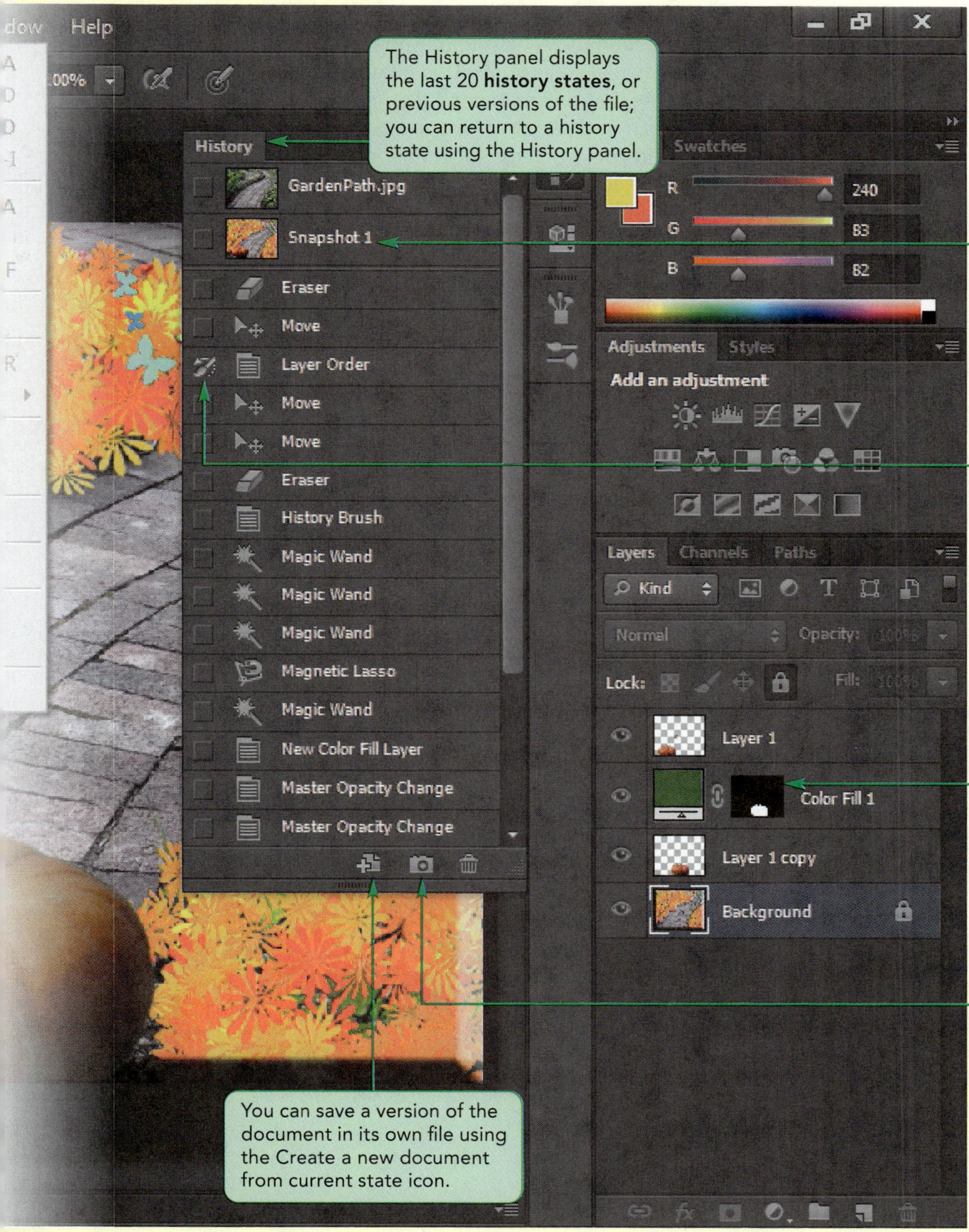

The History panel displays the last 20 **history states**, or previous versions of the file; you can return to a history state using the History panel.

You can save a **snapshot**, or a picture of what the composition looked like, at any given history state.

This history state is set as the **source** for the History Brush tool; you can use the source to revert part of an image to an earlier version.

You can make a selection, and then fill the selected pixels with color; the unselected area filled with black is the mask, which protects everything not included in the selection from changes.

Use the Create a new snapshot icon to produce a snapshot of the current history state.

You can save a version of the document in its own file using the Create a new document from current state icon.

Selecting Content for Compositing

When you work in Photoshop, much of your work will involve compositing, creating images by combining parts of different image files in a single file, or modifying an image to create a unique composition. For example, you might select a tree from one image and copy it to a photograph of an empty lot. If you do this repeatedly, you can grow a digital forest in no time. Or, you might put two people who appear in separate images into one image by selecting, copying, and pasting them into the same composition. You can also create a complex composition by starting with a single photograph to which you then apply multiple effects. Photoshop has numerous tools that let you select not only layers, but also areas of pixels in a layer. These selection tools allow you to apply different effects to different areas of an image. In Tutorial 3, you dragged a rectangular marquee around part of an image to select it, and then used the Copy and Paste commands to add your selection to another file. However, many more tools are available for making selections, as shown in Figure 5-1.

Figure 5-1 **Selection tools in Photoshop**

Icon	Tool	Use To
	Rectangular Marquee tool	Drag to select a rectangular area; select Fixed Ratio to draw a rectangle with a height/width ratio you specify, or select Fixed Size to specify the exact dimensions of the rectangle. You can also press the Shift key while drawing the selection to constrain the selection marquee to a square.
	Elliptical Marquee tool	Drag to select an elliptical area; select Fixed Ratio to draw an ellipse with a height/width ratio you specify, or select Fixed Size to specify the exact dimensions of the ellipse. You can also press the Shift key while drawing the selection to constrain the selection marquee to a circle.
	Single Row Marquee tool	Click once to select a row of pixels (one pixel high) across an image.
	Single Column Marquee tool	Click once to select a column of pixels (one pixel wide) down an image.
	Lasso tool	Drag on an image to make a freehand selection.
	Polygonal Lasso tool	Click on an image multiple times to create straight-edged selections to form the shape of a polygon.
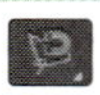	Magnetic Lasso tool	Drag a selection marquee whose border snaps to defined edges on an image—for example, a white object on a dark background.
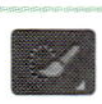	Quick Selection tool	Drag the pointer to paint your selection; as you drag, the selection grows. You can determine the sensitivity of the selection by specifying Tolerance.
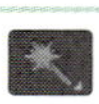	Magic Wand tool	Select an area based on a specific color; the Tolerance setting determines the color range that the tool will select.

In fact, the variety and power of the selection tools in Photoshop give you a great deal of creative license when you composite, or compose, an image. You can select an object in an image, cut it completely out of the image, and then fill in the cutout area with another object, a fill, or a gradient. You can also make a selection and apply filters and special effects only to the selection or to everything in the image *except* the selection. Figure 5-2 shows a composition created by selecting part of an image (the orange pumpkin in the middle).

Figure 5-2 **Selecting, copying, and adjusting selected pixels**

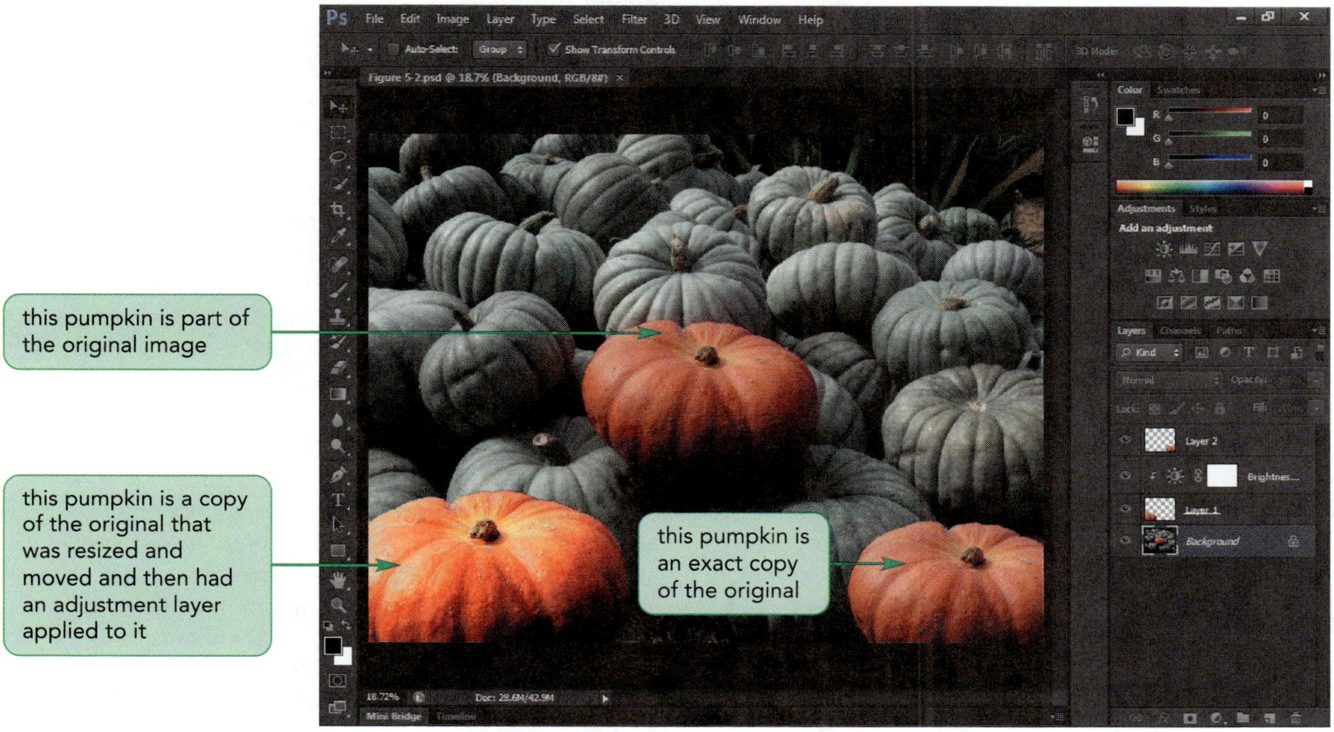

Teodora George/Shutterstock.com

The selection was copied to the Clipboard, pasted into the lower-left corner of the composition, and then resized to create the appearance of an additional pumpkin. While the new pumpkin was still selected, a Brightness/Contrast adjustment was applied only to the selection. Finally, the original pumpkin was copied and pasted again, and then dragged to the lower-right corner of the image. The end result is that an image that originally had one orange pumpkin now has three. As you can see from this simple example, the possibilities for working with selections in Photoshop are limitless.

PROSKILLS

Problem Solving: Using Photoshop to Communicate Critical Visual Data

Communicating critical visual data to clients, peers, and coworkers is an important—and sometimes challenging—task in a variety of industries, including technical fields, such as genetic research, architecture, and engineering. Using the tools in Photoshop, you can solve this problem by making adjustments to images that will focus a viewer's attention on the parts of an image that are most important. For example, imagine you are working with a researcher who will be presenting a lecture on mutations in the frog population near a hazardous waste dump. Some of the mutations are obvious, but others require a more trained eye to see. So how could you help the researcher solve the problem and make the mutations more visible to the audience? You could use the selection and adjustment tools in Photoshop to manipulate the image so that the physical features that need to be highlighted are more prominent. For example, you could darken the area around a feature, or change the contrast so that the feature stands out. Or, imagine that you're working for a structural engineer who is preparing a report that includes archived images of a building that collapsed in a minor earthquake. To highlight the weak areas of the design, you could select them and change their brightness or contrast to draw attention to them in the report. Photoshop offers a variety of tools to help solve the problem of needing to communicate critical visual data in technical and nontechnical fields. As you get more experience with Photoshop, you'll find you have more skills at your disposal to solve this type of problem in a variety of settings.

Azar would like you to work on a few compositions that show the bounty of the Food for Change program so he can present them at a government funding conference next month. He has some photographs from last summer, but he is concerned that some don't show the extent or variety of the food grown by the program, while others won't grab a viewer's attention. You'll work with the selection tools to enhance and compose images for the conference. You'll also work with the selection tools to apply effects to parts of your composition while leaving other parts unchanged.

Selecting with the Rectangular or Elliptical Marquee Tool

The Rectangular and Elliptical Marquee tools allow you to specify an exact rectangular or elliptical area by dragging on an image. These marquee tools should seem familiar to you; you use them to draw selections in much the same way you used the Rectangle and Ellipse tools to draw shapes in earlier tutorials. When you drag, Photoshop outlines the area you are selecting, and when you release the mouse button, a selection marquee indicates that the selection is active. You can press the Shift key as you drag to constrain the proportions of the selection marquee—for example, to constrain an ellipse to a circle or a rectangle to a square.

When you use either the Rectangular or Elliptical Marquee tool, you can specify settings on the options bar for the tool, as shown in Figure 5-3.

Figure 5-3 **Using Marquee tool options to create a complex selection**

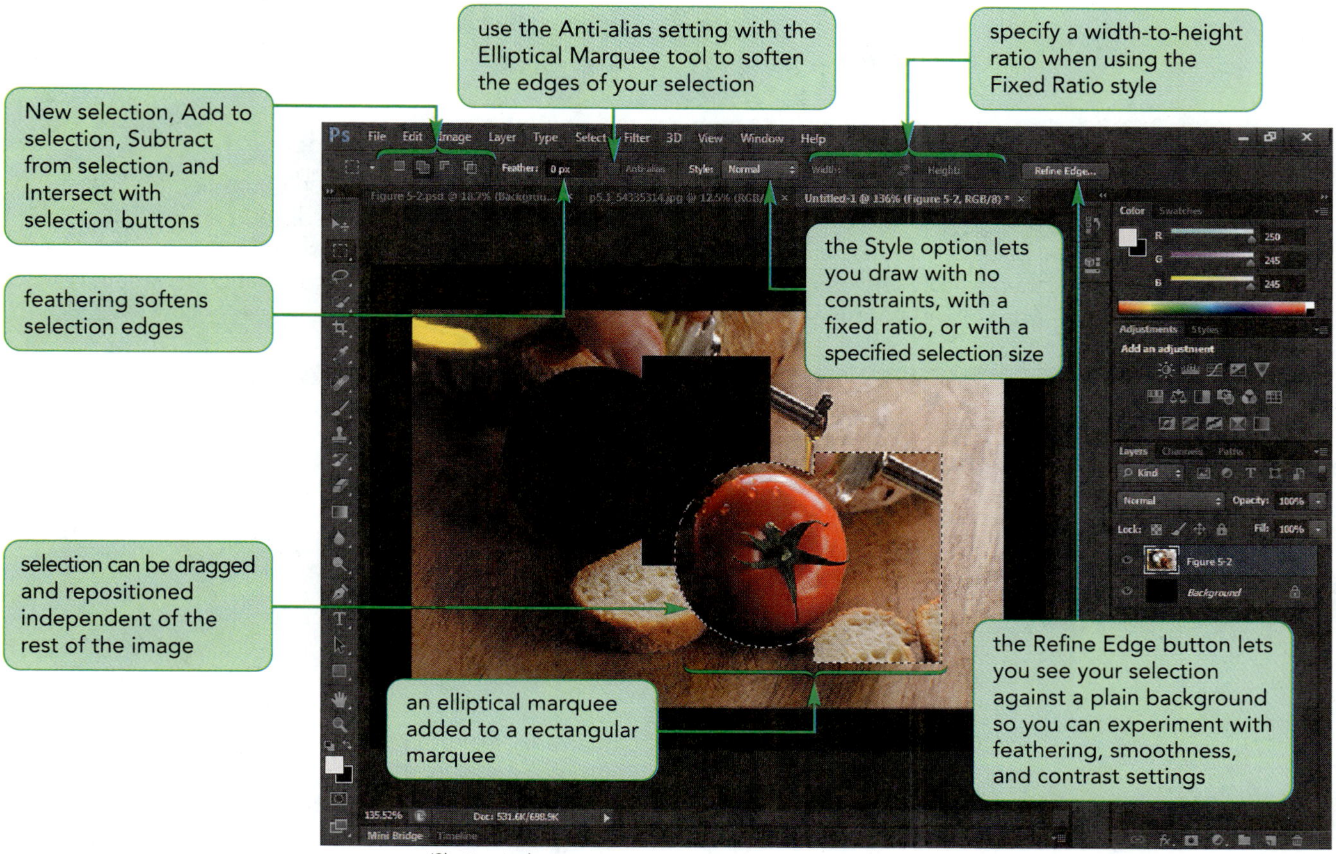

marco mayer/Shutterstock.com

The first group of settings should be familiar to you from Tutorial 4. The New selection, Add to selection, Subtract from selection, and Intersect with selection buttons behave like the New Layer, Combine Shapes, Subtract Front Shape, and Intersect Shape Areas commands you worked with when you created vector drawings. These buttons let you create complex selections by building on and subtracting from existing selections. For example, the selection in Figure 5-3 was created by drawing the first part of the selection (enclosing the tomato) with the Elliptical Marquee tool, clicking the Add to selection button on the options bar, and then using the Rectangular Marquee tool to add the rectangular area to the selection. The entire selection was then dragged down and to the right on the image, uncovering the black background beneath.

The next setting on the options bar is Feather, which you can use to soften or blur the edges of a selection. The higher the Feather setting, the softer the edges of the selection will be, which can help blend a selection into a composition. You can also modify the Feather setting in the Refine Edge dialog box to preview the setting before finalizing the selection.

The Anti-alias setting is available only with the Elliptical Marquee tool. Turning on this setting softens the pixelated edges of the curves in your selection. It is not available for the Rectangular Marquee tool because the edges of the rectangle are drawn horizontally and vertically along lines of pixels, so no jagged edges appear.

You can also specify the style of your selection. The default is the Normal style, which lets you drag a rectangle or an ellipse with no constraints. You can use Fixed Ratio to specify the width-to-height ratio of a selection. For example, a fixed ratio of Width 1 and Height 1 would draw a square or a circle. The Fixed Size option lets you specify the exact dimensions of the selection in pixels so when you click on the image, the selection marquee is created automatically. You can then drag it to its correct position. The last option on the Marquee tool options bar, Refine Edge, opens the Refine Edge dialog box, where you can fine-tune and preview your selection by modifying a number of options, including smoothness and feathering, all in one place.

Specifying a Fixed Ratio or Fixed Size Selection

As noted previously, with the Photoshop selection tools, you aren't confined to dragging on the canvas to create the selection marquee you need. You can instead specify a fixed ratio or fixed size selection when you have very specific needs, and then simply click the canvas and drag the selection marquee into position to create it. These fixed options allow you to be extremely precise.

REFERENCE

Specifying a Fixed Ratio Selection

- In the Tools panel, click the Rectangular Marquee Tool button or the Elliptical Marquee Tool button.
- On the options bar, click the Style button, and then click Fixed Ratio.
- Type ratio values in the Width and Height boxes.
- Click on the canvas, and drag to make your selection.
- Move the selection marquee to place it where you want it.

You'll work with a photograph of an arrangement of raw vegetables to create a unique, beveled image that Azar will use during his workshops around the city to emphasize that the work that Food for Change is doing is just one piece of a larger hunger and nutrition puzzle in urban areas.

To specify a fixed ratio selection:

1. Start Photoshop while pressing the **Ctrl+Alt+Shift** keys, and click **Yes** to delete the Settings File when prompted. Reset Photoshop to the default Essentials workspace layout, and reset all tools.
2. Navigate to the Photoshop5\Tutorial folder included with your Data Files, and open **VegetableBounty.psd**. Press **Ctrl+0** to fit the image to the screen.
3. Display the rulers, and then click the **Rectangular Marquee Tool** button in the Tools panel to select it, if necessary.
4. On the options bar, click the **Style** button, and then click **Fixed Ratio**. By default, Photoshop sets both the Width and Height boxes to 1, which would create a square.
5. Type **3** in the Width box, and then type **2** in the Height box. When you drag the selection, it will have a width-to-height ratio of 3 to 2.
6. In the Layers panel, select the **Vegetables** layer and then, starting at about 1" on the vertical ruler and 1" on the horizontal ruler, drag down and to the right until you're at about 5" on the vertical ruler. Photoshop creates a selection marquee with a width-to-height ratio of 3 to 2 that includes the red onion and most of the two tomatoes.
7. On the menu bar, click **Edit**, and then click **Cut**. The selection is cut from the image, and the black background shows through.
8. On the menu bar, click **Edit**, and then click **Paste**. The selection is pasted onto the center of the image on its own layer, named Layer 1.

9. In the Layers panel, double-click the **Layer 1** thumbnail to open the Layer Style dialog box, and then click **Bevel & Emboss** to select the style and display its properties.
10. In the Structure section, change the Structure Depth to **1000%**, set the Size to **100 px**, and then click the **OK** button. The cut-and-pasted selection now has a bevel and emboss effect. See Figure 5-4.

Figure 5-4 **Cutting and pasting a selection**

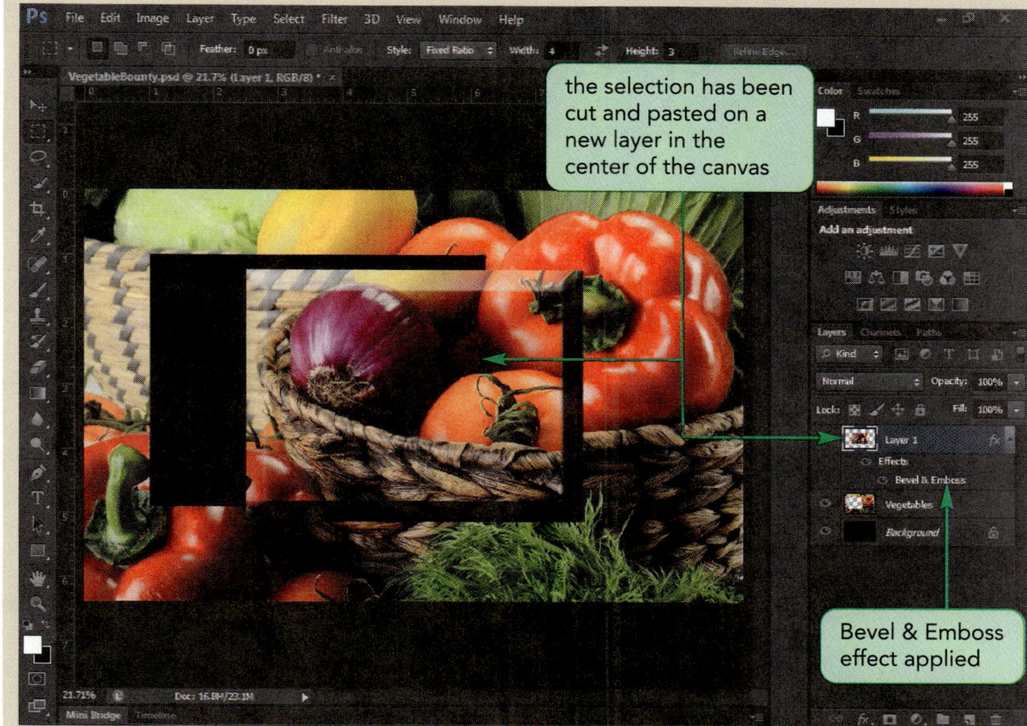

monticello/Shutterstock.com

Trouble? If you can't see the Structure Depth option, you have selected the Bevel & Emboss check box, rather than clicking the Bevel & Emboss text. Click Bevel & Emboss, and then complete Step 10.

11. Save the file as **VegetableBevel.psd** in the Photoshop5\Tutorial folder, and then close it.

You selected an area of an image using the Rectangular Marquee tool with a fixed ratio setting. Next, you'll work with a fixed size selection.

REFERENCE

Specifying a Fixed Size Selection

- In the Tools panel, click the Rectangular Marquee Tool button or the Elliptical Marquee Tool button.
- On the options bar, click the Style button, and then click Fixed Size.
- Type the width and height values you want in the Width and Height boxes, making sure to specify *px* for pixels or *in* for inches.
- Click the canvas to draw the selection marquee.
- Move the selection marquee to place it where you want it.

Next, you'll use the Elliptical Marquee tool to select an area with a fixed size. You'll make a copy of one pumpkin and then paste it into the composition so an additional pumpkin appears in the image. Azar will use the before and after versions of the image to demonstrate that it is only with contributions from the public that the bounty at Food for Change can grow and multiply.

To specify a fixed size selection:

1. Open **Pumpkin.jpg**, located in the Photoshop5\Tutorial folder, and fit the image to the screen. In the Tools panel, click the **Elliptical Marquee Tool** button.

   Trouble? If you don't see the Elliptical Marquee Tool button in the Tools panel, click and hold the Rectangular Marquee Tool button to display the hidden tools, and then click the Elliptical Marquee Tool button.

2. On the options bar, change the Feather setting to **10 px**, select the **Anti-alias** check box, if necessary, click the **Style** button, and then click **Fixed Size**. The Width and Height boxes become available.

3. Type **800 px** in the Width box, and type **600 px** in the Height box.

   The ellipse you draw will have a width of 800 pixels and a height of 600 pixels. Because you selected Anti-alias, the edges of the selection will be smooth rather than jagged or pixelated.

4. Click anywhere on the orange pumpkin. Photoshop immediately draws an elliptical selection marquee in the size you specified. Drag the **selection marquee** so it is centered over the pumpkin.

Make sure you specify pixels (*px*) and not inches (*in*). Using inches will cause Photoshop to freeze up as it attempts to draw an ellipse well beyond the bounds of the canvas.

Notice that the selection marquee is smaller than the pumpkin. You can expand a selection using commands on the Select menu, which you'll do in the next section.

Modifying a Selection

Once you have made a selection, you can modify it. The Select menu includes many commands for changing the nature and dimensions of your selection. The Grow command selects adjacent pixels of a similar color. If some of the pixels are missed by the Grow command, you can use the Magic Wand tool and the Add to selection button on the options bar to select the missing pixels. The Grow command is a good choice when the object you are selecting is quite distinct from the background it is on, but may not work as well when the background has colors within range of the object's colors. You can use the Expand command, found in the Modify option menu, to expand the selection by a specified number of pixels. The Expand command is useful if the object you are selecting has a regular shape.

You can make a selection larger or smaller, or even distort or warp a selection, using the Transform Selection command on the Select menu. Photoshop encloses your selection in a rectangle with eight handles—one handle on each corner and one handle on each side. You can resize the selection by dragging the handles. To constrain the proportions of the selection so you don't distort it, press the Shift key while you drag. When you drag, the size of the selection marquee changes. You can accept the transformation by clicking the Commit button on the options bar or by pressing the Enter key.

REFERENCE

Expanding or Growing a Selection

- Use a tool from the Tools panel to make a selection.
- On the menu bar, click Select, point to Modify, and click Expand to open the Expand Selection dialog box.
- Type a pixel value in the Expand By box, and then click the OK button.

or

- Use a tool from the Tools panel to make a selection.
- On the menu bar, click Select, and then click Grow.

Next, you'll expand and then grow the current selection to encompass the whole pumpkin.

To expand and grow the selection:

1. On the menu bar, click **Select**, and then point to **Modify**. Photoshop displays a list of commands for modifying your selection.
2. Click **Expand**. The Expand Selection dialog box opens. You can enter a pixel value to specify the size of the expansion.
3. In the Expand By box, type **100**, and then click the **OK** button. The selection marquee expands to encompass more of the pumpkin. Because the selection is still not large enough to cover all of the pumpkin, you will try the Grow option next. Before you do so, make sure your expanded selection is still centered over the pumpkin so it does not include any of the green pumpkins in the background.
4. On the menu bar, click **Select**, and then click **Grow**. The selection expands to include most of the pumpkin. See Figure 5-5.

Figure 5-5 **Expanding and growing the selection**

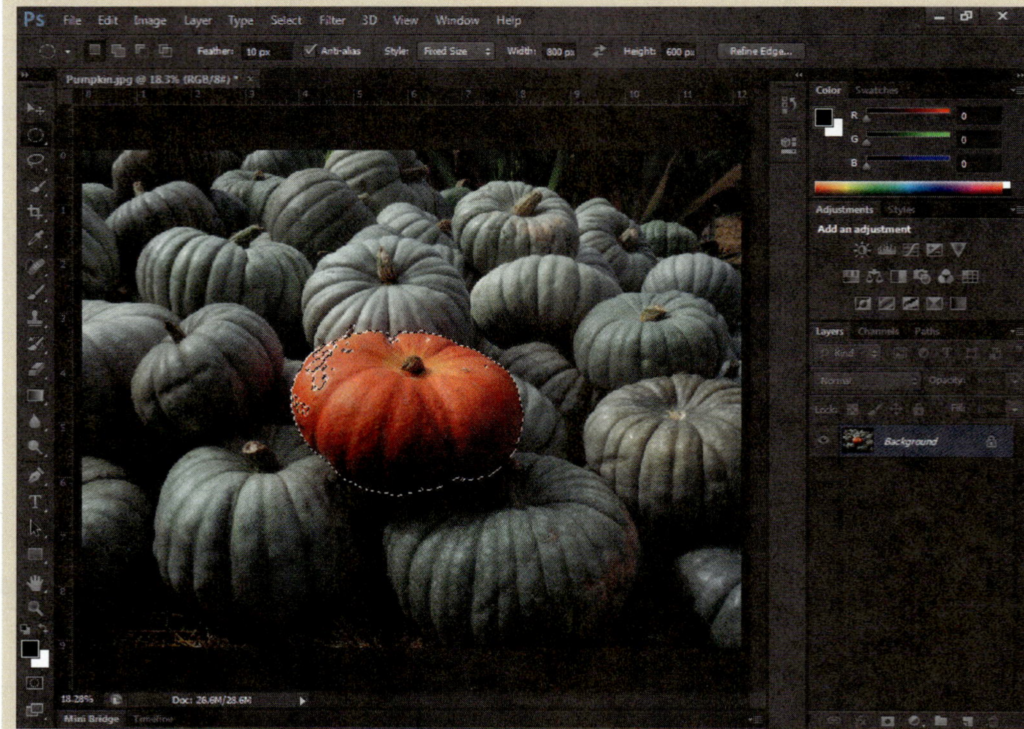

Teodora George/Shutterstock.com

Notice that the selection is no longer an ellipse because the Grow command grew the selection by finding similarly colored pixels. However, some small areas are still unselected. You'll use the Magic Wand tool to add those stray pixels to your selection.

To use the Magic Wand tool to add pixels to the selection:

1. In the Tools panel, point to the **Quick Selection Tool** button, press and hold the mouse button, and then click the **Magic Wand Tool** button.
2. On the options bar, change the Tolerance to **10**, and confirm that the **Anti-alias** and **Contiguous** check boxes are selected.

   Selecting Contiguous ensures that Photoshop selects only adjacent pixels that are the same color (orange) as the selection, rather than similarly colored pixels in the whole image.
3. On the options bar, click the **Add to selection** button. See Figure 5-6.

TIP

You can also press and hold the Shift key to temporarily select the Add to selection button. Press and hold the Alt key to temporarily select the Subtract from selection button.

Figure 5-6 **Adding pixels to the selection with the Magic Wand tool**

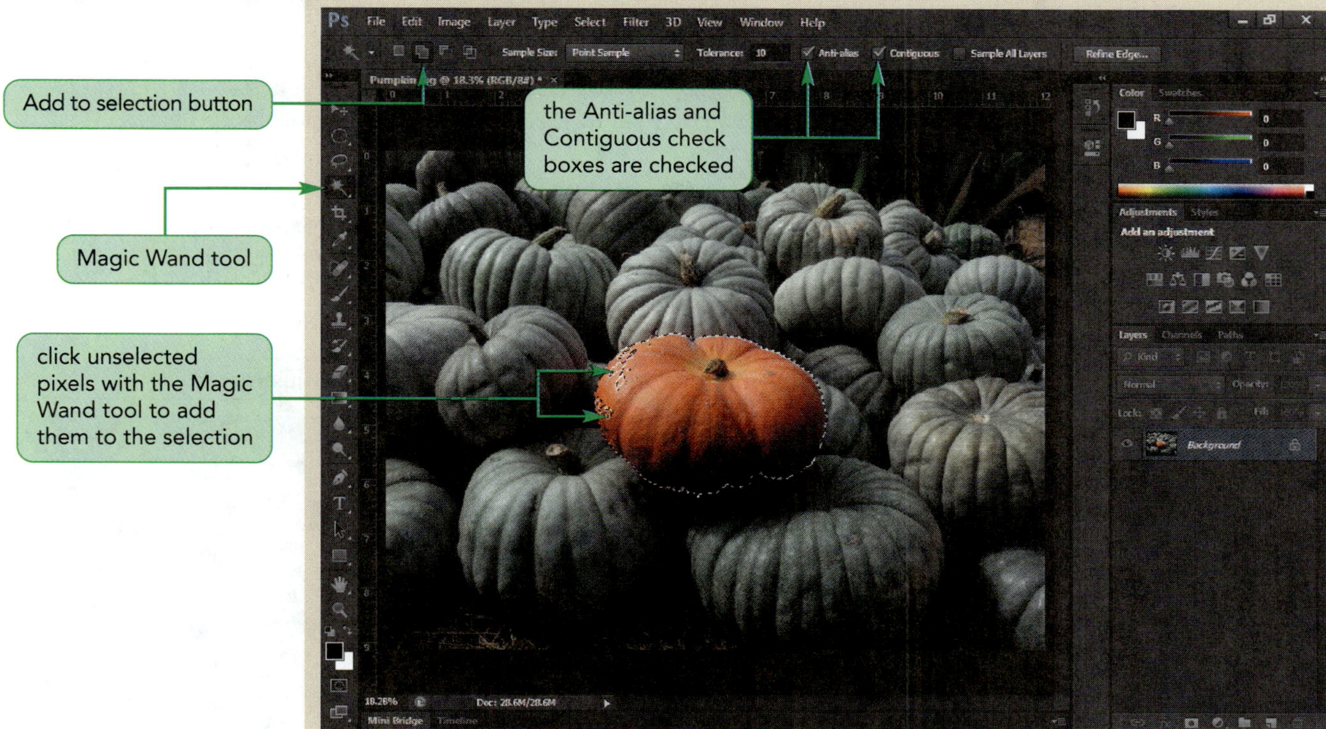

Teodora George/Shutterstock.com

4. Click on top of the pixels in the pumpkin that are not currently selected to add them to the selection. The wand pointer includes a plus sign, indicating that you are adding to the selection.

All of the pixels in the pumpkin should now be selected.

Trouble? If clicking the missing pixels doesn't add them to the selection, you have clicked one of the other options on the options bar, such as the Subtract from selection button. Click the Add to selection button, and then repeat Step 4.

Trouble? If you select pixels that shouldn't be included in the selection, press the Ctrl+Z keys or click the Subtract from selection button on the options bar, and click until only the orange pumpkin is selected.

Applying an Adjustment to a Selection

In Tutorial 3, you applied adjustments to entire layers. Photoshop also lets you adjust individual areas of an image using selections. When a selection is active, you can apply an adjustment to it, and the adjustment will affect only the selected area of the image.

Next, you'll change the color balance of the selected pumpkin so the orange is intensified. You'll then copy and paste the selection so you have two pumpkins of different shades of orange.

To apply a Color Balance adjustment to the selection:

1. In the Adjustments panel, click the **Color Balance** icon.
2. In the Properties panel, drag the **Cyan Red** slider to the right so the value in the box is +**60**. The selection marquee disappears, but it is still active. The color of the pumpkin changes to a bright orange. The unselected area of the image is unchanged.
3. Collapse the Properties panel and then in the Layers panel, click the **Color Balance 1** layer, if necessary. In the Tools panel, click the **Move Tool** button.
4. Point to the pumpkin, press and hold the mouse button, and drag the **Color Balance** adjustment up and to the left, as shown in Figure 5-7.

Figure 5-7 **Applying a color adjustment to a selection and moving the adjustment**

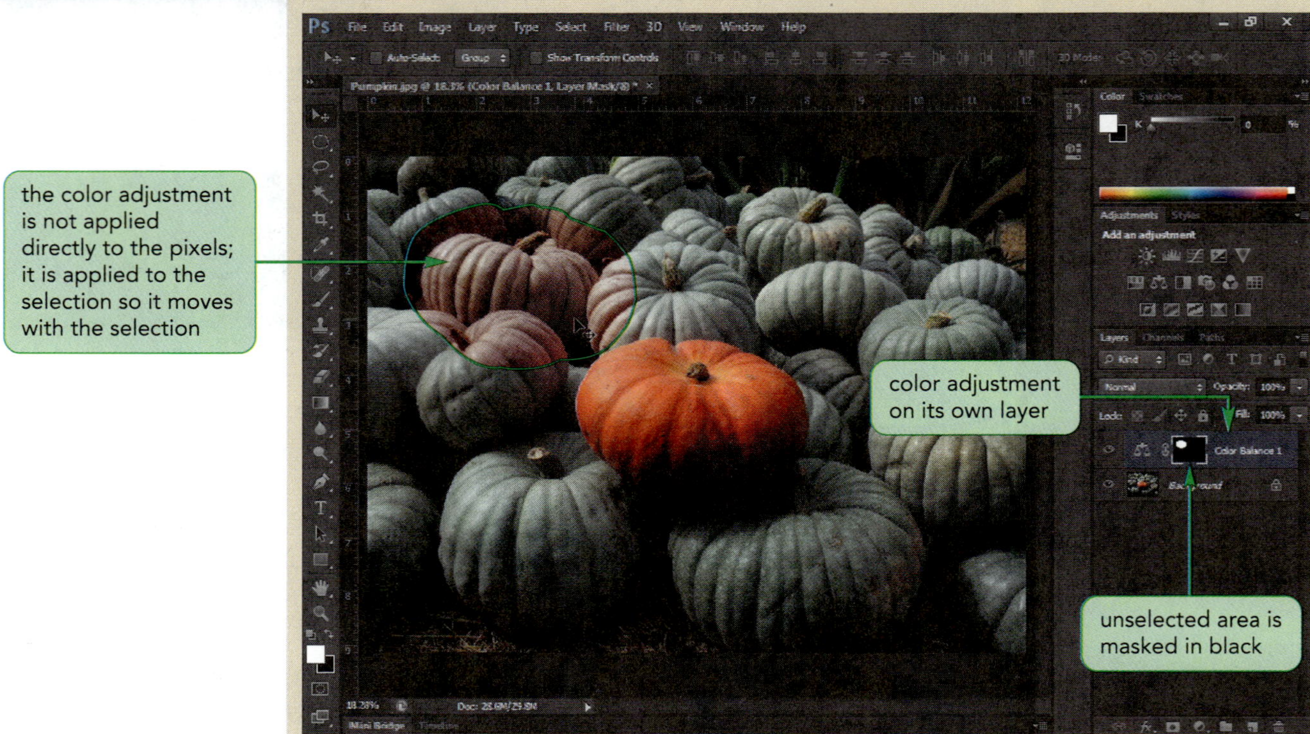

Teodora George/Shutterstock.com

The selection, along with the Color Balance adjustment, now appears above and to the left of the pumpkin. (The green outline around the Color Balance adjustment was added to Figure 5-7 to highlight the adjustment.) The colored adjustment has moved because the adjustment was applied to the selection, not to the pixels in the image.

When you made your selection and applied the adjustment, what you were actually doing was creating a mask. You can think of a mask as the inverse of a selection. A **mask** protects all of the pixels not included in the selection. As you can see on the Color Balance 1 layer, your selection (in the shape of the pumpkin) is shown in white on the thumbnail to the right in the Color Balance thumbnail. The rest of the thumbnail is black, indicating that anything you do to the selection will not affect the black areas.

You'll undo the move action you just performed, and then you'll reselect the pumpkin so you can copy and paste it in another part of the image.

To copy and paste the pumpkin selection:

1. On the menu bar, click **Edit**, and then click **Undo Move**. The Color Balance adjustment appears on top of the orange pumpkin again.
2. In the Layers panel, click the **Background** layer to select it.
3. On the menu bar, click **Select**, and then click **Reselect**. The Reselect command activates the most recent selection.
4. On the menu bar, click **Edit**, click **Copy**, click **Edit** again, and then click **Paste** to paste a second copy of the pumpkin onto the image; the copy appears on its own layer (Layer 1).
5. In the Layers panel, move the **Layer 1** layer above the Color Balance 1 adjustment layer.
6. Using the Move tool, point to the pumpkin and then drag it down and to the right. See Figure 5-8.

TIP

You can also press the Shift+Ctrl+D keys to reselect a selection. Press the Ctrl+D keys to deselect a selection.

Figure 5-8 **Two versions of the same pumpkin**

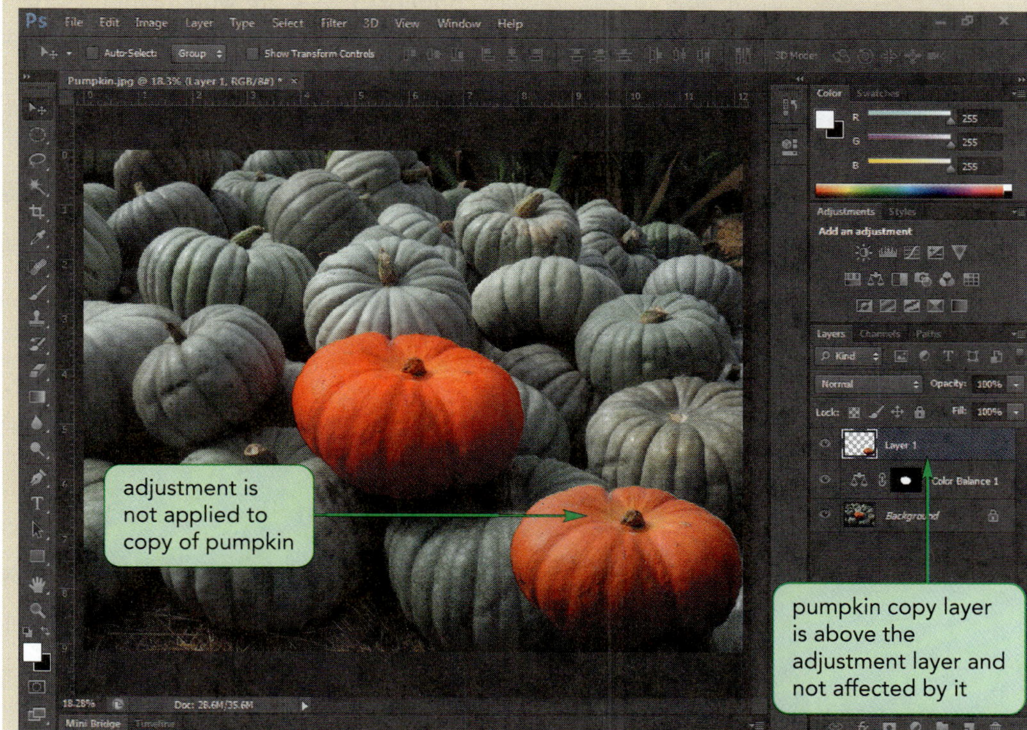

Teodora George/Shutterstock.com

Notice that the copy of the pumpkin does not include the adjustment you made because it is no longer part of the selection. It retains the less-intense orange color of the original version of the pumpkin.

7. Save the file as **TwoPumpkins.psd** in the Photoshop5\Tutorial folder, and then close the file.

Now that you have added more interest to this image, you will give this file to Azar so he can use the image in his fund-raising presentation. In the next section, you will learn how to use selection tools to make more complex selections.

INSIGHT

Refining a Selection

Once you have made a selection, you can click the Refine Edge button on the options bar to further refine the selection. Using Refine Edge, you can better see if you have picked up any unwanted pixels in your selection, and you can fine-tune the selection. Clicking Refine Edge opens the Refine Edge dialog box, which shows your selection against a white background by default. You can change the View Mode setting to a black background or another option depending on the colors of the selection. You can also adjust edge settings, such as Smooth, Feather, and Contrast, and you can shift the edge to expand the selection or contract it.

Creating Complex Selections

As you continue to work in Photoshop, you'll find that many of the individual selection tools will work just fine in certain cases. But what happens if the area or areas you need to select are very complex? If they are, you might find that a single selection tool just won't do the job. Just as you did with the Magic Wand tool earlier, you can use the buttons on the options bar to add to and subtract from selections. This Photoshop feature is useful if you want to make a complex selection that includes irregularly shaped areas containing pixels with a variety of colors.

REFERENCE

Adding to a Selection to Create a Complex Selection

- Activate one of the selection tools in the Tools panel, and set its options on the options bar.
- Drag on the canvas to make the first selection.
- On the options bar, click the Add to selection button.
- Use the same tool or select a different one, and drag on the canvas to make a selection that will be added to the first.
- Repeat until you are satisfied with the final selection.

For one of your projects for Azar, you need to select just part of an image of a strawberry plant to use in a flyer. To do so, you'll create a complex selection using both the Rectangular Marquee tool and the Elliptical Marquee tool.

To create a complex selection and paste it into a new file:

1. Open **Strawberry.jpg**, located in the Photoshop5\Tutorial folder, fit the image on screen, reset all of the tools, press the **D** key, if necessary, to reset the default colors, and display the rulers, if necessary.
2. In the Tools panel, click the **Elliptical Marquee Tool** button, and on the options bar, confirm that the **New selection** button is selected and that the Feather setting is **0 px**.
3. On the options bar, click the **Style** button, and then click **Fixed Size**.
4. Specify a Width of **1000** pixels and a Height of **1100** pixels, click the canvas to create the selection, and then drag the selection until it is positioned as shown in Figure 5-9.

Figure 5-9 **Positioning a selection**

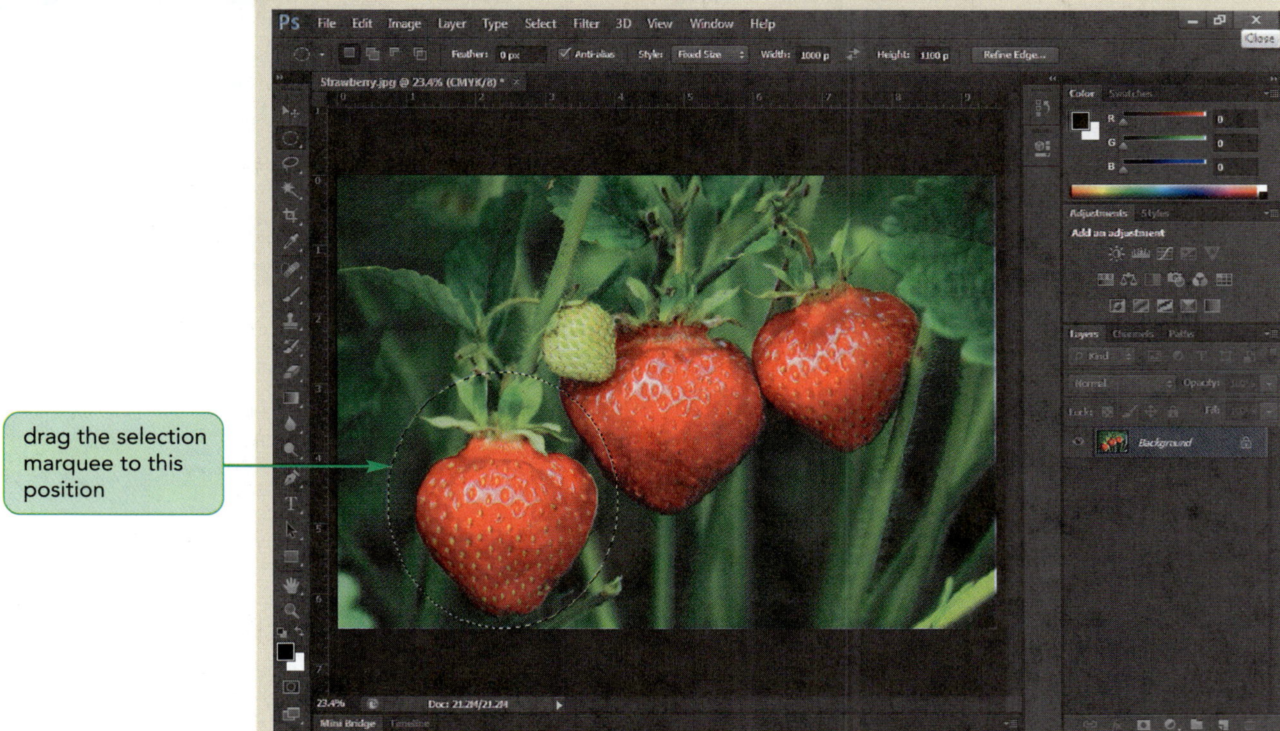

Catarina Belova/Shutterstock.com

5. In the Tools panel, click the **Rectangular Marquee Tool** button, and then on the options bar, click the **Add to selection** button. You can leave the default settings on the options bar.
6. Drag to create a rectangle, as shown in Figure 5-10.

Figure 5-10 Adding to a selection

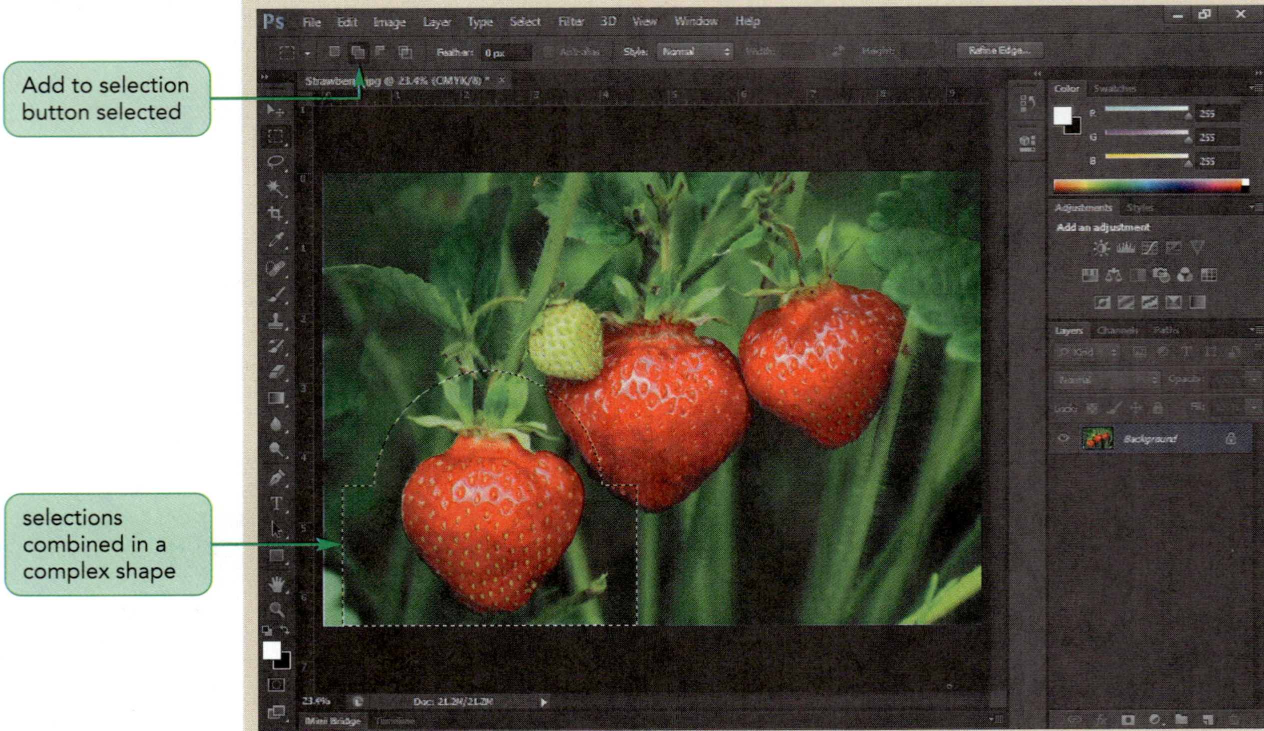

Catarina Belova/Shutterstock.com

When you release the mouse button, the two selections are combined into a single selection.

7. On the menu bar, click **Edit**, and then click **Copy**.
8. Press the **X** key to switch the foreground and background colors so the background color is black.
9. On the menu bar, click **File**, click **New**, and then create a new file using the Default Photoshop Size preset, the CMYK Color mode, and a Resolution setting of 300 ppi. Click the **Background Contents arrow** ▾, and then click **Background Color** to create a black background. Click the **OK** button.
10. Fit the image to the screen, and then on the menu bar, click **Edit** and then click **Paste** to add your selection into the new file.

    The strawberry is pasted into the file as a new layer, labeled Layer 1.
11. In the Layers panel of the new file, double-click the **Layer 1** thumbnail to open the Layer Style dialog box. Apply an Outer Glow effect to the layer with **90%** opacity; in the Elements section, set the Size to **65** pixels, and then click the **OK** button. See Figure 5-11.

Figure 5-11 Complex selection pasted in new file with Outer Glow effect applied

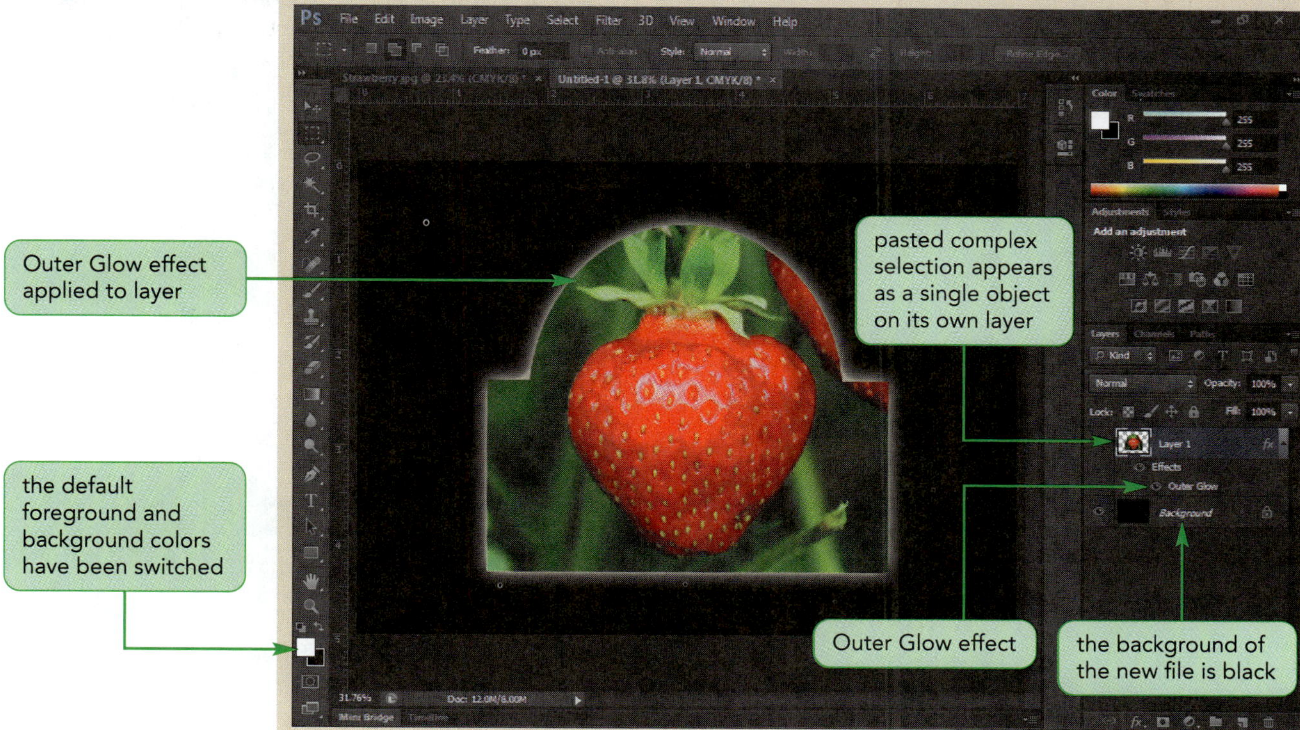

Catarina Belova/Shutterstock.com

12. Save the new file as **StrawberryGlow.psd** in the Photoshop5\Tutorial folder, and then close the file. Close Strawberry.jpg without saving it.

Selecting a Color Range

There may be times when one of the colors in an image is not quite what you want it to be. To solve this problem, you can select a color range in an image, and then adjust the color of the pixels that are in that color range—without affecting any other part of the image. In the Color Range dialog box, you can select either a sampled color or any of the RGB (red, green, blue) or CMY (cyan, magenta, yellow) colors. When you use the Color Range command to select a color in an image, Photoshop surrounds the pixels containing the color with a selection marquee. See Figure 5-12.

Figure 5-12 **Selecting a color range in the Color Range dialog box**

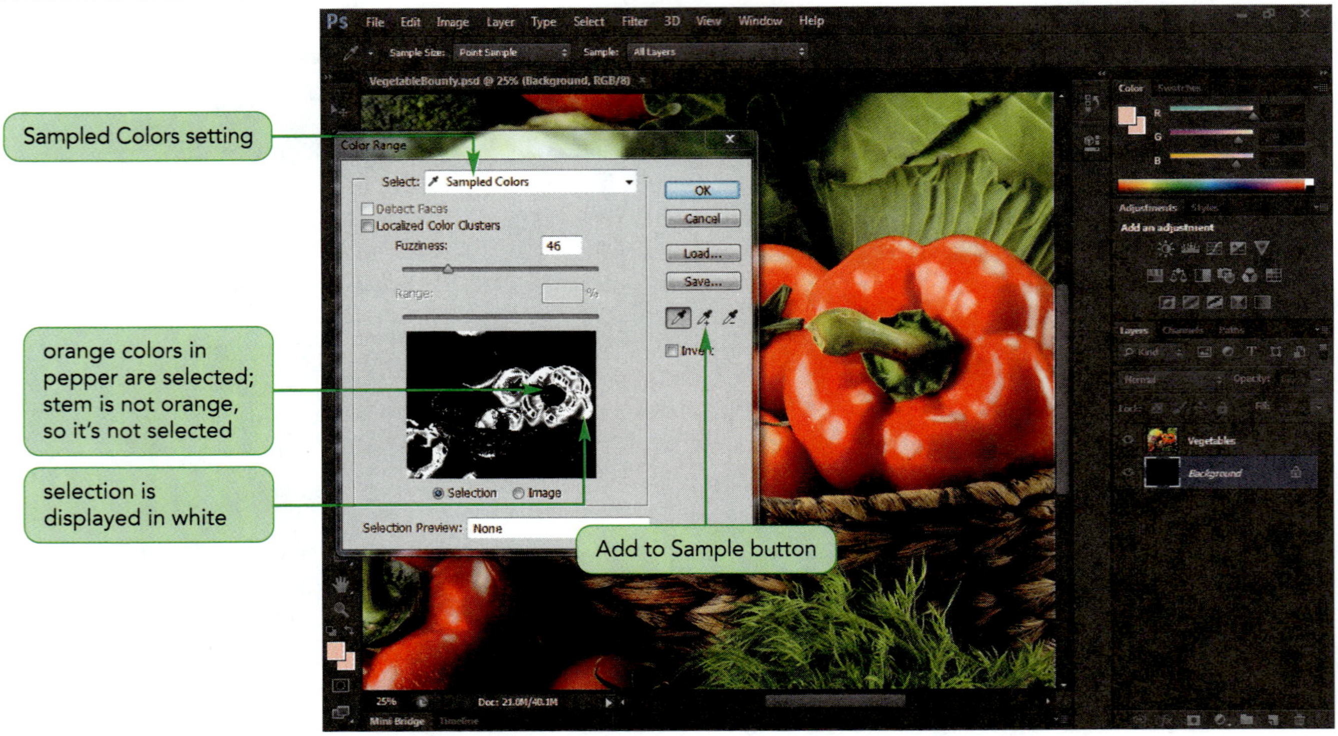

monticello/Shutterstock.com

Figure 5-12 shows a selection based on selecting a range of sampled orange colors. Notice that the selection shown in the Color Range dialog box is much more complex than a selection you could make yourself using the selection tools in the Tools panel. When you select a color range using sampled colors, you can expand your selection to include pixels that are variations in shades of the original sampled color, or even completely different colors. To do so, select the first color and then click the Add to Sample button in the Color Range dialog box. You can subtract from a sample by clicking the Subtract from Sample button and then clicking the color or shade on the canvas that you want to subtract from the selection. You can also click the Localized Color Clusters option to extend the selection only to pixels near the sampled color, and then use the Range slider to determine how near or far from the sample the selection will extend. A Range value of 100% includes the entire image. Increasing the Fuzziness setting increases the array of color values included in the selection. A low Fuzziness setting will select only colors that are very similar to the selected color. A high Fuzziness setting will select colors that are similar to the selected color—for example, oranges of different intensities. Once you select the colors you want, close the dialog box, and then modify the selection as desired—for example, by adjusting its hue, saturation, and brightness (HSB) or by applying an adjustment layer to the pixels that are part of the selection but not to the image as a whole.

Azar wants you to work with the image of the pumpkins to change it from a photograph of green pumpkins with one orange pumpkin on top to all orange pumpkins. He'd like to use the two images to show that in the Food for Change organization, every participant has an equal chance at success.

To select using a color range:

1. Open **Pumpkin.jpg**, located in the Photoshop5\Tutorial folder, display the image at a 10% zoom setting, hide the rulers, and reset all of the tools. Press the **D** key to return to the default foreground and background colors.
2. Click **Select**, and then click **Color Range**. The Color Range dialog box opens. Drag the dialog box to the right so the entire image is visible. See Figure 5-13.

Figure 5-13 Using the Color Range dialog box

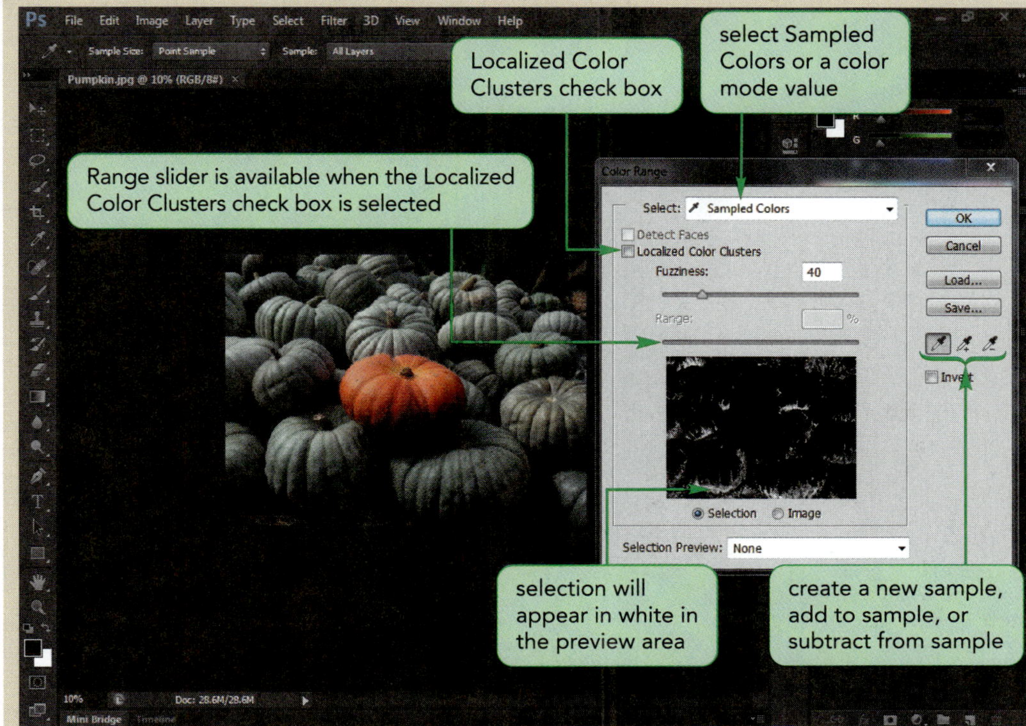

Teodora George/Shutterstock.com

3. Confirm that **Sampled Colors** is selected in the Select box at the top of the dialog box, and that the **Selection** option is selected under the preview box. The Fuzziness setting should be set at the default of **40**. Click different areas of the green pumpkins on the canvas. As you do so, the preview changes to show what areas of the image would be selected based on the sampled color. White areas show completely selected pixels, while gray areas show partially selected pixels.

   To see the effect of selecting localized color clusters, you'll select that option in the dialog box.

4. Click the **Localized Color Clusters** check box to select it, set the Range to **20%**, and then click one of the green pumpkins. Only a small area around the pumpkin you clicked shows a selection because you limited the range.
5. Drag the **Range** slider to the right until the setting is **100%**. The sampled color is once again selected in the entire image.
6. Change the Fuzziness setting to **170**. More pixels in the green pumpkins are selected.

7. Deselect the **Localized Color Clusters** check box. Notice that even more of the green pixels in the image are selected and the pixels appear white rather than gray, indicating that they are fully selected.
8. In the Color Range dialog box, click the **Select arrow** ▾, and then click **Reds**. The orange pumpkin, which includes a high red intensity value, is selected, but the green pumpkins are not.
9. Click the **Select arrow** ▾, and then click **Sampled Colors**. The green pumpkins are selected again.
10. Change the Fuzziness setting to **40**, click the **Add to Sample** button in the dialog box, and then on the canvas, click any areas of the green pumpkins that aren't selected in the dialog box. See Figure 5-14.

Figure 5-14 **Completing the selection**

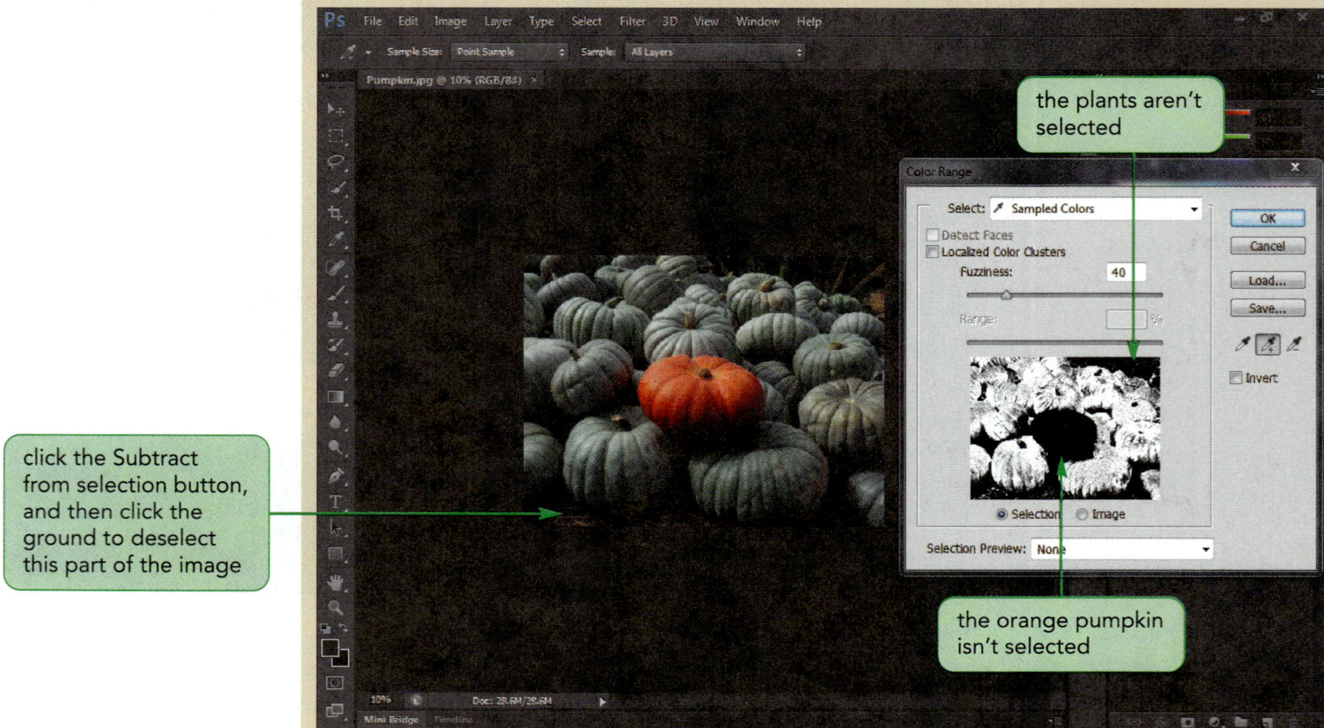

Teodora George/Shutterstock.com

Trouble? If the ground and the green stems at the top of the image are selected and appear white in the preview instead of gray, click the Subtract from Selection button, and then click the ground on the canvas so that your dialog box resembles the dialog box in Figure 5-14. Note that you might need to subtract from and add to the selection a few times to get your selection to match the selection shown in the figure.

11. Click the **OK** button. Photoshop displays a complex selection marquee. See Figure 5-15.

Figure 5-15 **Complex selection based on color**

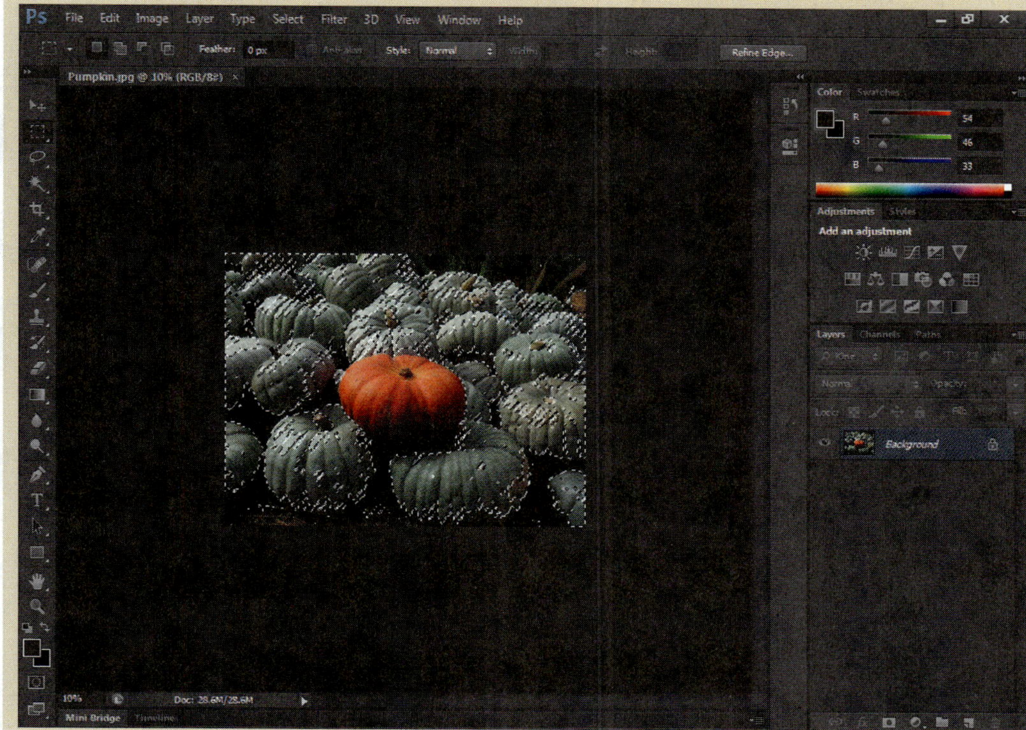

Teodora George/Shutterstock.com

You could continue to add to this selection to include additional pixels.

12. In the Adjustments panel, click the **Color Balance** icon.

13. In the Properties panel, make sure **Midtones** is selected for the Tone option, and adjust the settings to **+100** for Cyan Red, **-99** for Magenta Green, and **-100** for Yellow Blue.

14. Click the **Tone** button, select **Shadows**, and change the Cyan Red setting to **+49** and the Yellow Blue setting to **-55**. Collapse the Properties panel. See Figure 5-16.

Figure 5-16 Color Balance adjustment applied to selection

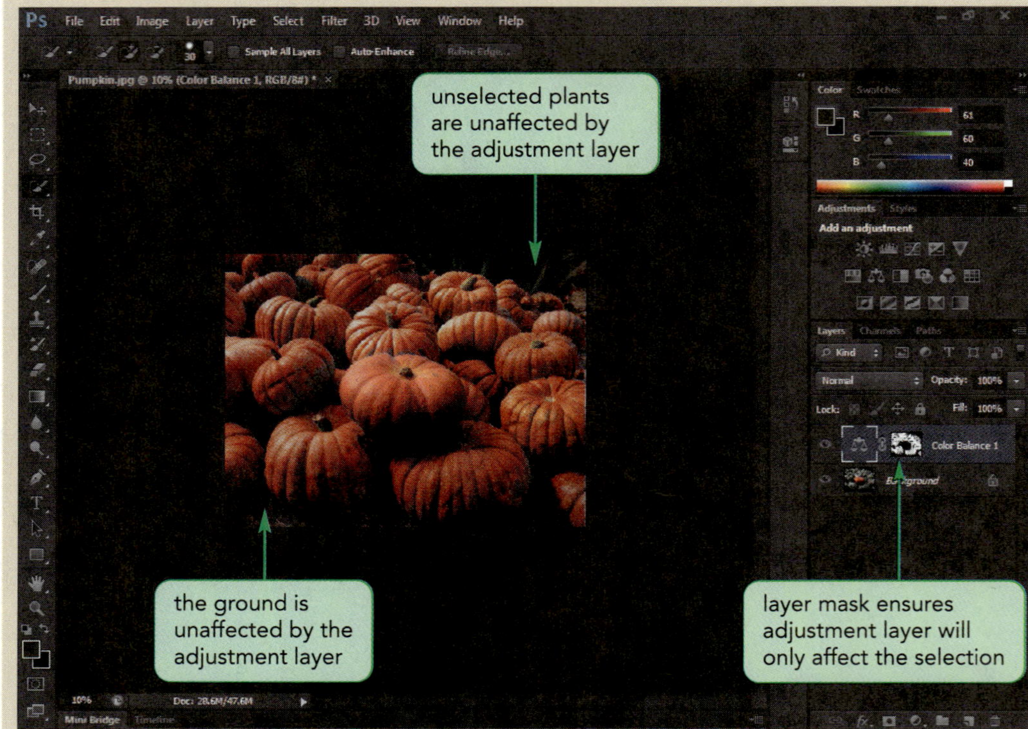

Teodora George/Shutterstock.com

The layer mask thumbnail on the adjustment layer indicates which parts of the image are affected by the adjustment. The thumbnail displays the selection in white.

15. To see more clearly how the new adjustment layer has not altered the underlying pixels in the image, hide and then redisplay the **Color Balance 1** layer. The image beneath the adjustment layer is unchanged.

16. Save the file as **AllOrange.psd** in the Photoshop5\Tutorial folder, and then close it.

The tasks Azar is giving you are getting more and more complex. You'd like to make sure you can keep track of all of your changes to a composition and not alter any files permanently until you are happy with what you've done. You'll learn about and then use undo and redo techniques to keep track of your actions so you can proceed with confidence.

Undoing and Redoing Actions

Once you master selections, you have the tools to be more creative than ever. You can apply even more complex effects and adjustments to your compositions—not just to layers, but to pixels selected in a layer. With this newfound creative license, it is helpful to know how to undo some of your changes while preserving others.

Stepping Backward and Forward

When you make a change or an adjustment that you want to reverse, you can undo it by clicking the Undo command on the Edit menu. The actual name of the Undo command varies, depending on your most recent action. For example, if your most recent action was adding a new solid color fill layer, the command name is Undo New Color Fill Layer. If you have just drawn a rectangle on the canvas, the command name is Undo Rectangle tool. Using the Undo command, you can undo only the most recent action.

Photoshop has two additional commands on the Edit menu, Step Forward and Step Backward, that let you undo a series of changes, and then redo them to whatever point you want. Using these commands can help you determine if the modifications you've made to an image have the effect you had planned.

To step forward and backward in a file:

1. Open **Pumpkin.jpg**, located in the Photoshop5\Tutorial folder, and then zoom in to view the image at 50%. Pan the image, if necessary, so that the orange pumpkin appears at the center of the canvas, and press the **D** key to reset the foreground and background colors.
2. In the Tools panel, click the **Elliptical Marquee Tool** button, and click and drag to create an elliptical marquee that partially covers the orange pumpkin. Drag the selection to center it over the pumpkin, if necessary. Don't worry if the selection marquee doesn't encompass the entire pumpkin or if your selection marquee is too large.
3. On the menu bar, click **Select**, and then click **Transform Selection**. A rectangle appears around the selection, and handles appear on the rectangle.
4. Drag the handles on the rectangle until the ellipse covers most of the pumpkin but doesn't go beyond its edges, and then click the **Commit** button on the options bar.
5. In the Tools panel, click the **Brush Tool** button, and change the brush Size setting to **150** pixels. Paint three separate strokes over the selection, starting above the selection marquee and ending below the selection marquee. See Figure 5-17.

Figure 5-17 Altering the pixels within a selection marquee

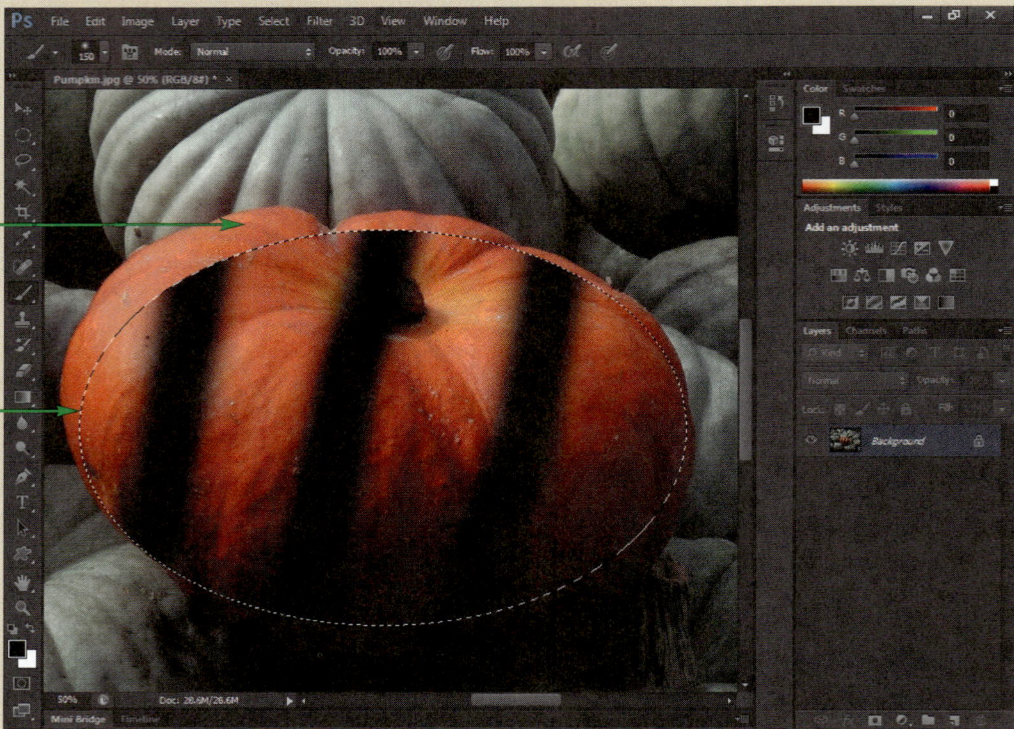

Teodora George/Shutterstock.com

As you paint, notice that none of your painting spills over the selection border. The selection contains your actions, and only lets you affect the pixels within the selection marquee.

6. On the menu bar, click **Edit**. The top menu choice is Undo Brush Tool. The third choice is Step Backward. As you have seen, you can only undo one action (in this case, the last action taken using the Brush tool). However, you can step backward up to 20 times.
7. Click **Step Backward**. The last brushstroke you added disappears from the image.
8. On the menu bar, click **Edit**, and then click **Step Backward**. The previous brushstroke disappears.
9. On the menu bar, click **Edit**, click **Step Forward**, click **Edit**, and then click **Step Forward** again. Both brushstrokes reappear. You undid and then redid two actions.
10. On the menu bar, click **Edit**, and then click **Step Backward**. The last brushstroke to reappear disappears again.

TIP

You can also press the Alt+Ctrl+Z keys to step backward. Press the Shift+Ctrl+Z keys to step forward.

Using the Step Backward and Step Forward commands works well if you're only dealing with a few actions, but what happens when you've made multiple changes to a file, and want to quickly go back to a previous state? This is where the History panel comes in.

Reverting to a Previous State Using the History Panel

The History panel provides a more flexible way to reverse changes to a composition. By default, the History panel records your 20 most recent actions and lists them in order. Each item on the list is called a history state. A snapshot of the file's original state appears at the top of the list. As you work, you can create additional snapshots to make it easy to return to a particular history state after you have made a series of changes. If you perform more than 20 actions, the earliest history states drop off the History panel and are no longer visible or reversible. See Figure 5-18.

Figure 5-18 Using the History panel

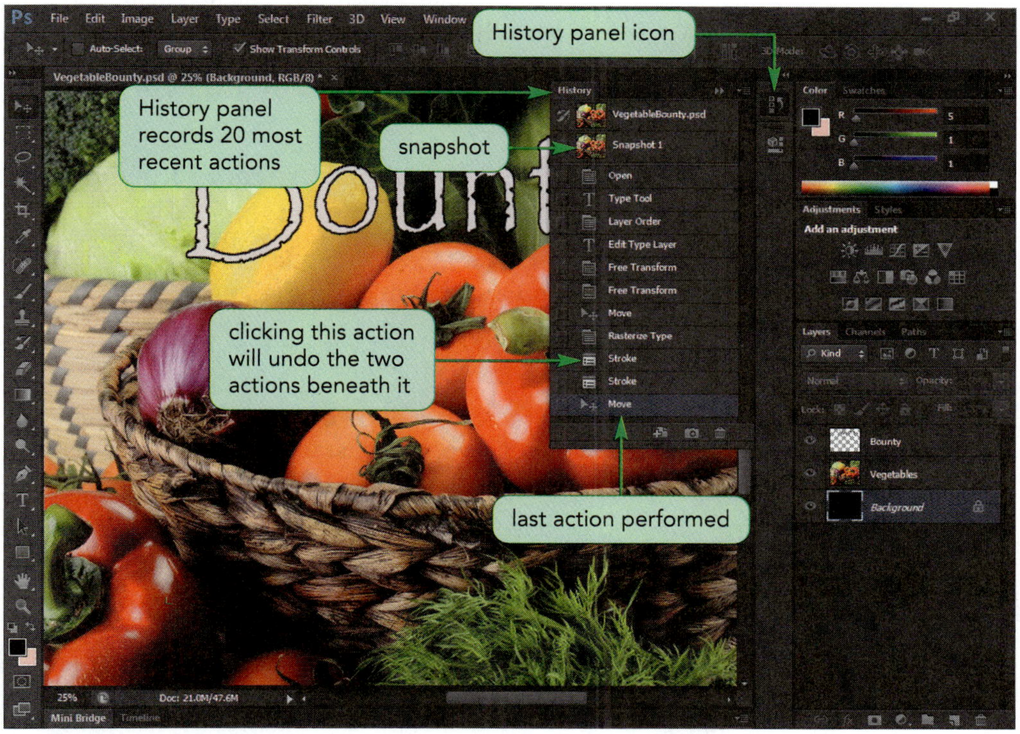

monticello/Shutterstock.com

You can click a history state in the History panel to revert your image to the state it was in when you performed that action. When you do, the states beneath that action appear dimmed in the History panel. However, they are still stored in memory, so if you want to redo all of the actions at once, you can simply click the bottom command on the panel. For example, in Figure 5-18, the last action on the list is Move. If you click the Stroke history state two rows up, Photoshop will undo the two actions beneath it in the panel. If you click the Move history state again, Photoshop will redo the final two actions in the History panel.

It's important to note, though, that if you select a history state and then perform a different action, all of the steps beneath the history state you selected are no longer in memory and are erased from the panel. Furthermore, once you close a document, all of the states and snapshots are erased and won't be available the next time you open the file.

REFERENCE

Reverting to a Previous History State Using the History Panel

- Click the History icon to the left of the Color panel, or on the menu bar, click Window, and then click History to open the History panel.
- Edit the image you are working with, and at the bottom of the History panel, click the Create new snapshot icon as needed to record specific history states.
- Click a history state or a snapshot to revert to that state.

You'll experiment with the History panel, and then modify the image of the pumpkin so Azar can use it in his nutrition presentation "Pumpkins: Not Just for Jack-o'-Lanterns," which is an outreach program that encourages schoolchildren to eat more vegetables.

To use the History panel to revert to history states, delete history states, and create snapshots:

1. Click the **History** icon to the left of the Color panel. The History panel opens, and a snapshot of the file's original state appears at the top of the list.

   Trouble? If you can't see the top of the list, drag the scroll bar up until you can.

2. Point to the bottom edge of the History panel until you see a double-headed arrow, and then, if necessary, drag down until all of the history states appear on the panel.
3. Add a horizontal brushstroke to the selection. See Figure 5-19.

Figure 5-19 States recorded in the History panel

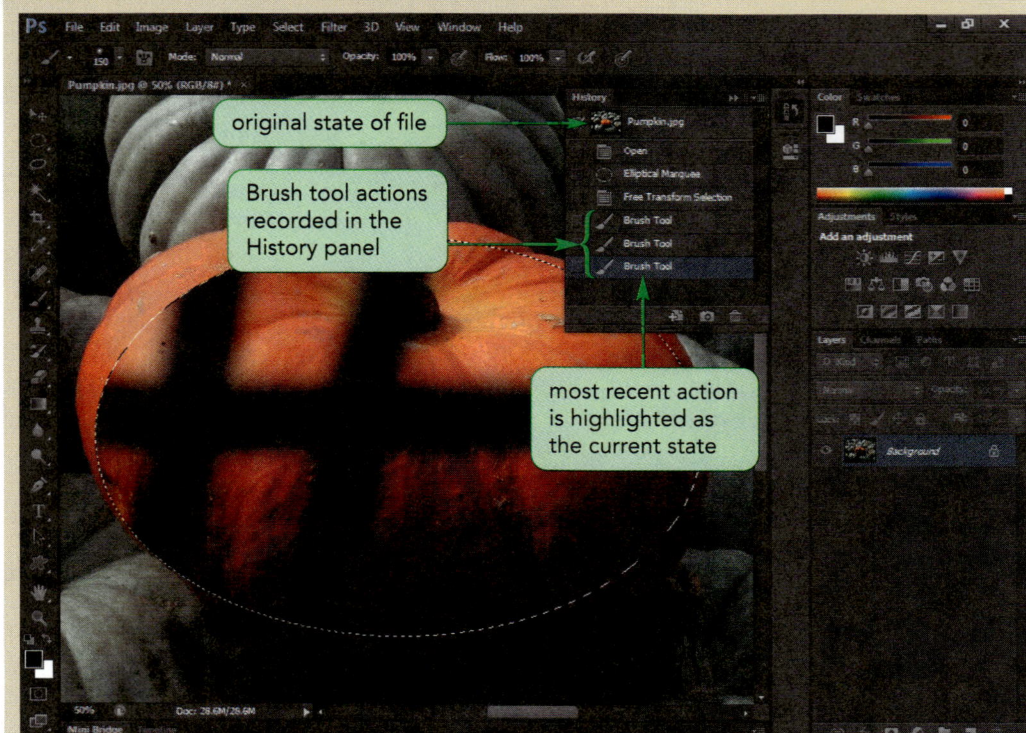

Teodora George/Shutterstock.com

Notice that an additional Brush tool history state now appears at the bottom of the panel. Because it is your most recent action, it is highlighted.

4. In the History panel, click the **Free Transform Selection** state. All of the Brush tool states appear dimmed in the History panel, and all of the brushstrokes disappear from the composition.
5. Click the **Pumpkin.jpg** snapshot at the top of the History panel. The file reverts to its original state, with no selection marquee.
6. Click the top **Brush Tool** state. One brushstroke appears on the image along with the selection marquee, but the other two brushstrokes are still not visible.
7. At the bottom of the History panel, click the **Create new snapshot** icon. A snapshot of the image in the selected state appears in the History panel beneath the image of the file in its original state. See Figure 5-20.

Figure 5-20 **Storing a state as a snapshot**

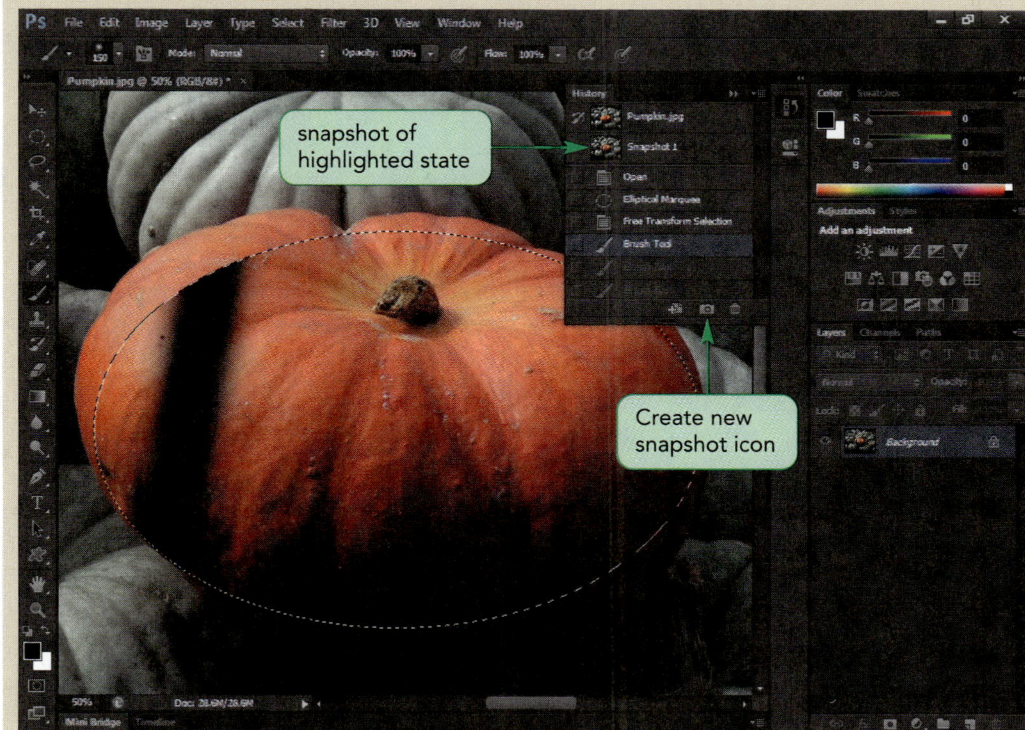

Teodora George/Shutterstock.com

You can click this snapshot at any time to revert to this state.

8. In the History panel, click the **Elliptical Marquee** state. The first brushstroke you painted disappears, and if you moved or resized the selection after you drew it, the selection marquee returns to its original location and size.

9. Click **Snapshot 1**. The document now reflects the history state of the selected snapshot.

10. Click the bottom **Brush Tool** state to select it, and then drag it to the Delete current state icon at the bottom of the panel. The Brush Tool state is deleted from the History panel, and the horizontal brushstroke is deleted from the image.

11. Click the top **Brush Tool** state in the History panel, click the **Delete current state** icon at the bottom of the panel, and then click the **Yes** button in the dialog box to confirm the deletion. Both of the remaining brushstrokes disappear from the image, and both of the Brush Tool states disappear from the History panel.

    You'll learn more about the Quick Selection tool in the next session, but for now, you'll use the Quick Selection tool to add to the selection, and then apply an effect to the inverse of the selection so the orange pumpkin stands out even more.

12. Collapse the History panel, and then in the Tools panel, click the **Quick Selection Tool** button, on the options bar, change the size of the Quick Selection pointer to **50** pixels, click the **Add to selection** button, and then click the unselected parts of the pumpkin until they are fully selected.

    Trouble? If you select more than the orange pumpkin, press the Ctrl+Z keys to undo the selection or click the Subtract from selection button on the options bar until only the orange pumpkin is selected.

13. On the menu bar, click **Select**, and then click **Inverse**. Press the **Ctrl+0** keys to fit the image on screen. Everything but the orange pumpkin is selected in the image.

14. Add a black Solid Color fill layer to the image with **75%** opacity. See Figure 5-21.

Figure 5-21 **Adding an effect to an inverse selection**

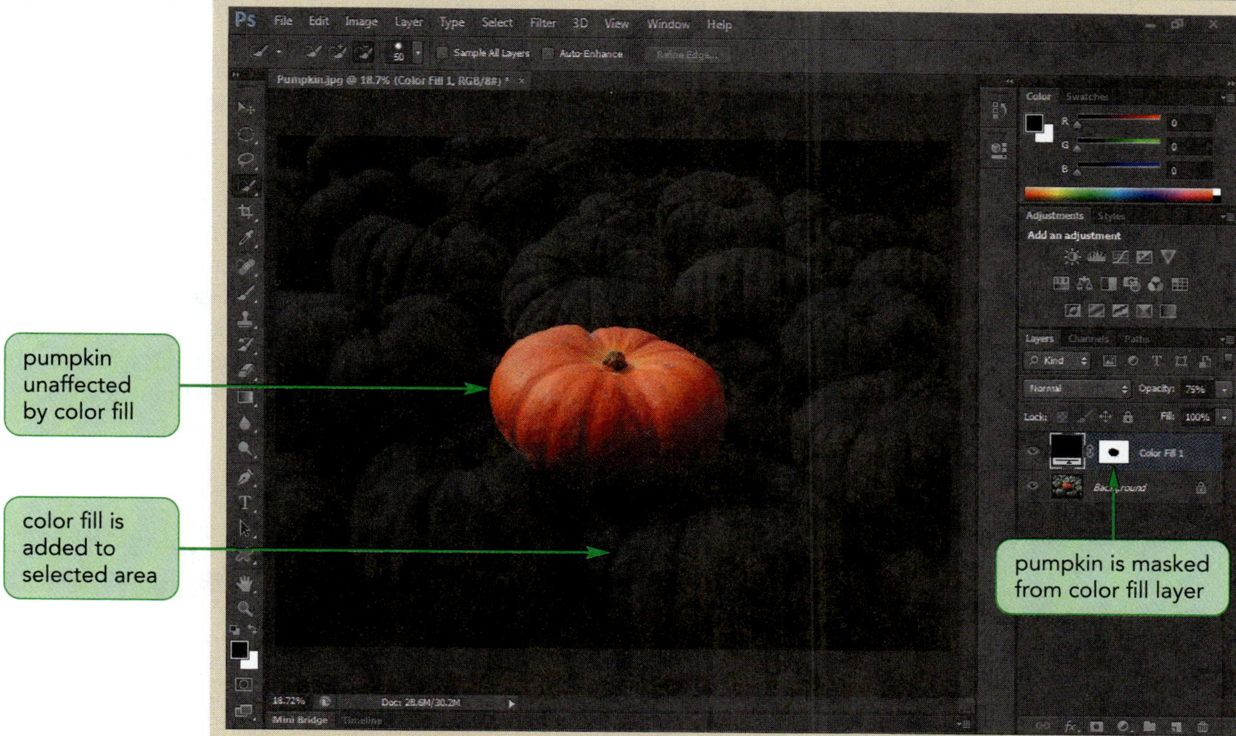

Teodora George/Shutterstock.com

The orange pumpkin stands out even more, while the rest of the image is shaded in black.

15. Save the file as **SolePumpkin.psd** in the Photoshop5\Tutorial folder, and then close the file.

INSIGHT

Changing the Number of History States Stored by Photoshop

You can increase or decrease the number of history states Photoshop stores in memory. If you decrease the number of history states, you can improve your system performance by freeing up memory. If you increase the number of history states, you have more freedom to undo multiple changes, but your system may slow down. Photoshop stores history states for every file open in memory, so if you have five files open, you can have up to 100 history states in memory by default. You can change the number of history states Photoshop stores using the Preferences command on the Edit menu. The Performance option lets you change the number of history states. The number of states you decide to store ultimately depends on your work habits and your computer system.

You can also use the History Brush tool to return an image to a previous state—or even a partial version of a previous state.

Using the History Brush Tool

The History Brush tool works in tandem with the History panel to give you very detailed control over the edits you've made to a file. You might be familiar with the phrase *to airbrush history*. In historical terms, airbrushing history means deliberately hiding the parts of a historical record that you think are unfavorable. You can think of the History Brush tool in a similar way. Imagine that you have made multiple changes to a composition, and each change is recorded as a state in the History panel. Some of your changes are perfect; you want to keep them the way they are. Others work for some areas of the image but not for others. In Normal mode, the History Brush tool lets you paint over individual areas you want to revert to a previous state while leaving other areas alone. When you paint over those areas, the brush erases the state or states on top of the image to return to the state you have chosen as the source for your brush.

To use the History Brush tool, in the History panel, click in the empty box to the left of a state that you want to "uncover" with the brush. This sets the source for the History Brush tool. You can then choose a brush tip for your brush, set the diameter, and set the Opacity and Flow percentages. If you want to paint with the selected state exactly as it appeared before the additional changes, make sure that the Opacity and Flow settings are 100% and the Mode setting is Normal so all of the details revert to the way they looked in that state.

REFERENCE

Using the History Brush Tool to Return Part of an Image to a Previous History State

- Click the History icon to the left of the Color panel, or on the menu bar, click Window, and then click History to open the History panel.
- In the History panel, click to the left of a history state to mark it with the Sets the source for the history brush icon and to make that history state the source for the brush.
- In the Tools panel, click the History Brush Tool button.
- On the options bar, specify History Brush tool options such as brush diameter, mode, opacity, and flow.
- Paint over the part of the image you want to return to the source state.

Azar wants you to work with a photograph of a pathway to one of the organization's gardens to make it look magical so that he can include it in his presentation to a group of younger children he hopes will join the program.

To use the History Brush tool to return part of an image to a previous state:

1. Open **GardenPath.jpg**, located in the Photoshop5\Tutorial folder, reset the Essentials workspace, reset the foreground and background colors to the default colors, reset all tools, open the History panel, and drag the bottom edge of the History panel down to resize it so there is room to show multiple history states. Then, drag the entire History panel to the lower-right corner of the Document window so that it is beneath the Layers panel.
2. In the Tools panel, click the **Brush Tool** button.
3. On the menu bar, click **Window**, and then click **Brush Presets** to open the Brush Presets panel.
4. In the Brush Presets panel, click the **panel menu** button, click **Special Effect Brushes**, and then click the **OK** button to replace the current brushes with the Special Effect Brushes.

   Trouble? If you are prompted to save changes to the current brushes, click the No button.
5. In the Brush Presets panel, click the **Azalea** brush tip, and change the size of the brush to **200** pixels. Change the Opacity on the options bar to **100%** if necessary.
6. Press the **X** key to switch the foreground and background colors, and then set the foreground color on the Color panel to R=**230**, G=**50**, and B=**150**. The Azalea brush uses both the foreground and background colors in its strokes.
7. Click the **Brush Presets** icon to the left of the Color panel to collapse the Brush Presets panel.
8. Paint over the garden on the left side of the brick pathway, as shown in Figure 5-22, by dragging back and forth and up and down with the mouse pointer. Keep the mouse button depressed the entire time so only one Brush Tool state is recorded in the History panel.

Figure 5-22 Recording painting actions in the History panel

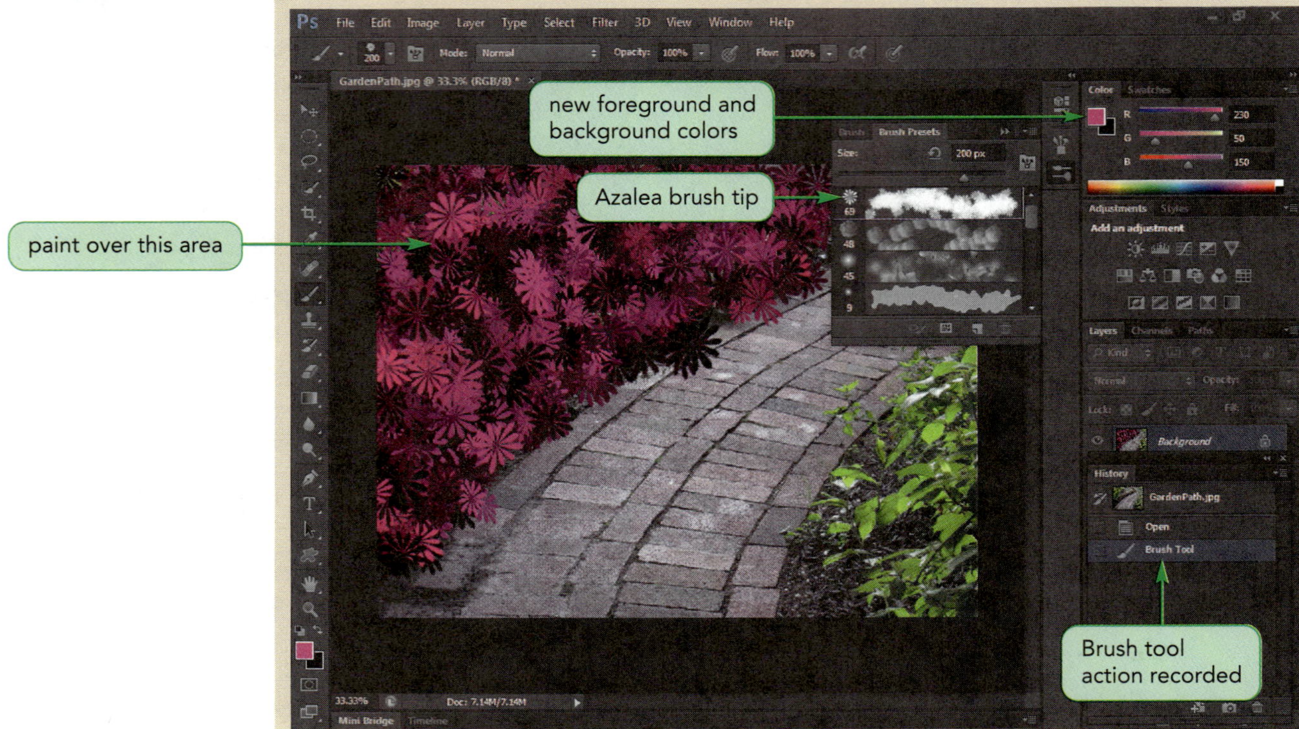

Jane Hosie-Bounar

Trouble? If you need to start over, either step backward to undo your actions, or delete the states in the History panel.

9. Click the **Brush Presets** icon to the left of the Color panel to expand the Brush Presets panel, scroll down if necessary, and then click the **Butterfly** brush tip. Set the size to **150** pixels, and change the Opacity on the options bar to **100%**, if necessary.
10. Set the foreground color to R=**140**, G=**200**, and B=**240**.
11. Keeping the mouse button depressed, drag up and down and side to side over the bed of azaleas you just painted until you've added many butterflies.

    You'll use the History Brush tool to uncover the azaleas and part of the original image.

12. In the Tools panel, click the **History Brush Tool** button, on the options bar, click the **Brush Preset picker** button, and then change the brush size to **100** pixels. Click the **Brush Preset picker** button again to close the Brush Preset picker.
13. On the options bar, confirm that the Opacity and Flow settings are 100%, and then drag down through the center of the flower bed. See Figure 5-23.

TIP

You can also press the Y key to activate the History Brush tool.

Figure 5-23 Using the History Brush tool

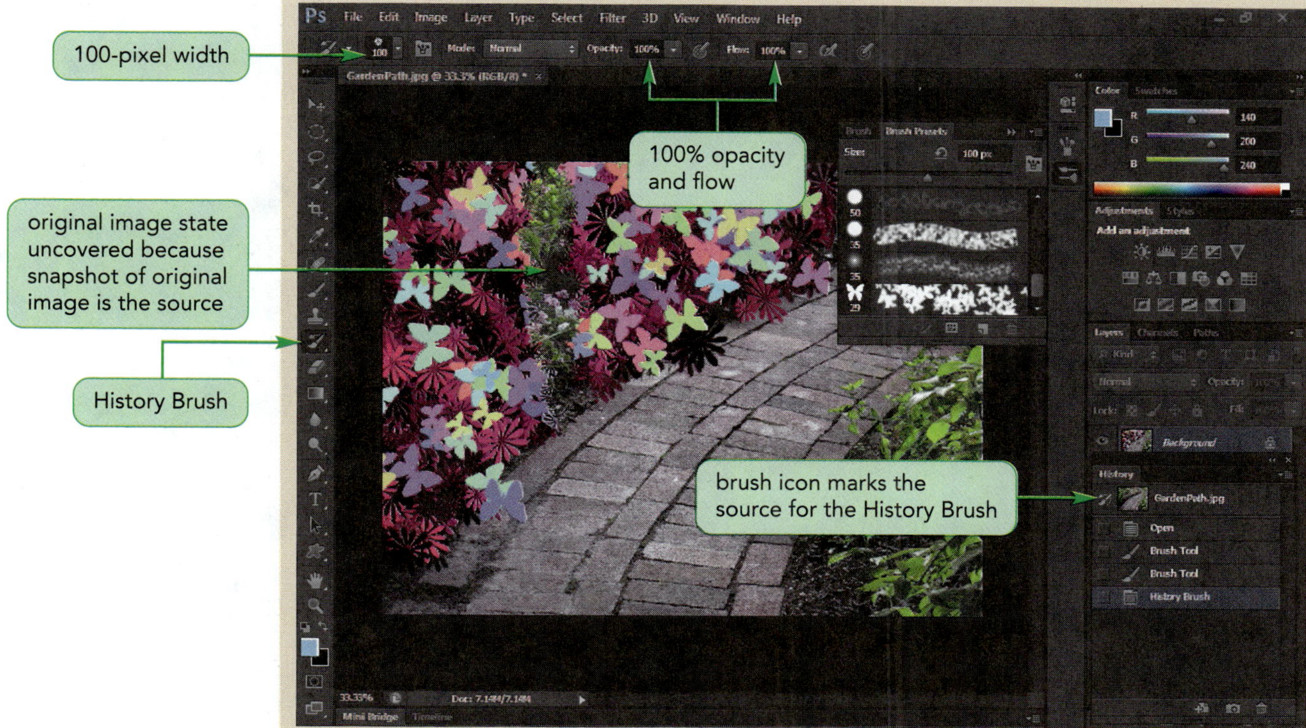

Jane Hosie-Bounar

You uncovered the original image because by default, the History Brush tool uses the original image state as its source.

14. Expand the History panel, if necessary, and then, at the bottom of the History panel, click the **Delete current state** icon, and then click the **Yes** button to confirm the deletion.

Next, you'll make the azaleas the source for the History Brush tool so it erases the butterfly brushstrokes, but not the flowers.

TIP

You can also take a snapshot of a history state, and then use that snapshot to set the source for the History Brush tool.

15. In the History panel, click to the left of the first Brush tool history state to mark it with the Sets the source for the history brush icon, and then drag over the flower bed with the brush until most of the butterflies have been painted over with the History brush. See Figure 5-24.

Figure 5-24 History erased to the state marked as the source

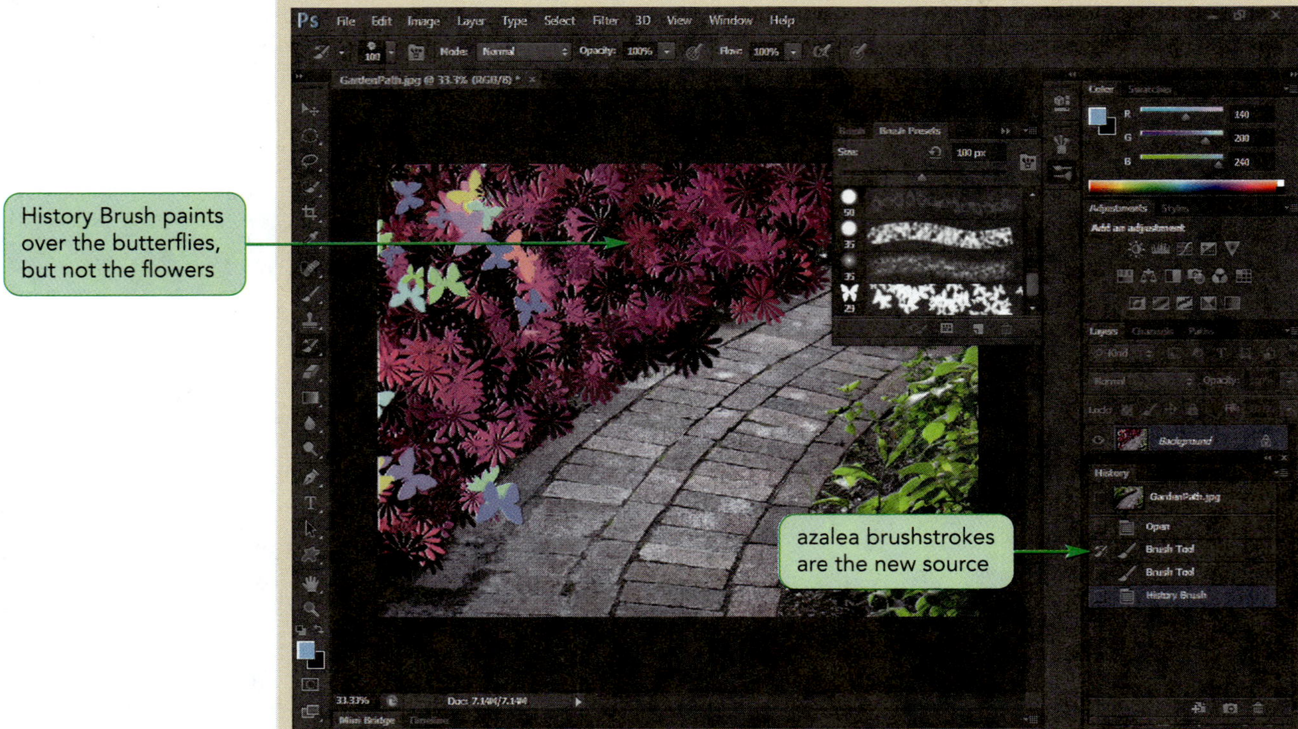

Jane Hosie-Bounar

The History Brush tool erases the butterfly brushstroke, but not the flower bed you painted. This is because you set the Azalea brushstroke state as the source for the brush.

16. Save the file as **Flowerbed.jpg**, using the default JPEG Options, in the Photoshop5\Tutorial folder, close the file, and then exit Photoshop.

INSIGHT

Using the Art History Brush Tool

The Art History Brush tool also uses history states to paint on an image, but the effect is completely different from the effect of the History Brush tool. The Art History Brush tool creates stylized artwork by essentially transforming a digital photograph into a painting using the colors of the source. Its results are often unpredictable, and if you choose to use the Art History Brush tool, you should take the time to experiment with different mode, opacity, style, and tolerance settings. Minor variations in any of these settings can create very different results.

In this session, you experimented with a variety of Photoshop selection tools. You learned how to apply an adjustment to a selection and how to copy and paste selections. You created complex selections, and explored how to select a color range in an image. You also spent time undoing and redoing actions with the Edit menu, the History panel, and the History Brush tool. In the next session, you'll explore additional selection tools, and work with filters, fills, and masks.

REVIEW

Session 5.1 Quick Check

1. A(n) ____________ encloses part of an image in a series of animated dashed lines or curves.
2. True or False. The Rectangular Marquee tool has an Anti-alias setting.
3. The ____________ setting on the options bar lets you specify a width and a height for your selection.
4. Which command increases the size of a selection by a specified number of pixels?
5. What is the purpose of a snapshot in the History panel?
6. True or False. When you save and close a file, all history states are saved with the file.
7. Which tool can you use in conjunction with the History panel to return part of an image to a previous state?

SESSION 5.2 VISUAL OVERVIEW

The Magnetic Lasso tool quickly selects the outline of a complex object on a high-contrast background and adds **fastening points** that define the selection marquee based on the frequency you specify; the **frequency** determines the distance between fastening points.

You can load a saved selection by selecting it from the Channel list.

An RGB image has a composite RGB color channel and three individual color channels (R, G, and B).

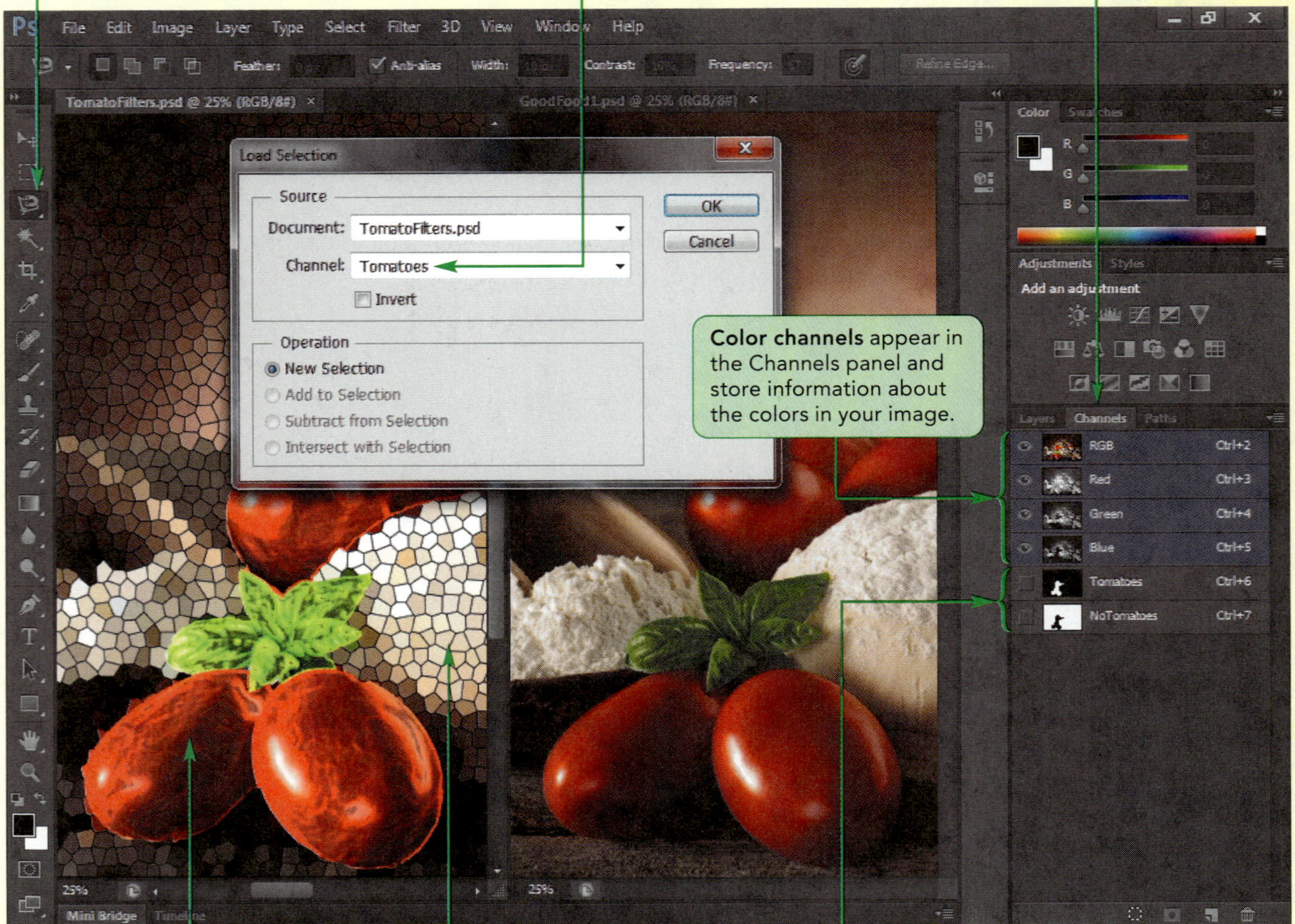

Color channels appear in the Channels panel and store information about the colors in your image.

The Diffuse Glow effect has been applied to the Tomatoes selection.

The Stained Glass effect has been applied to the NoTomatoes selection.

Selections can be saved as **alpha channels**, which store selections as masks; white indicates the selection, while black indicates the masked area.

marco mayer/Shutterstock.com

LASSO TOOLS AND FILTERS

Use selections and the Filter Gallery to apply multiple effects to the same image.

Each folder in the Filter Gallery contains multiple filter effects.

Filters come with multiple settings that you can modify before applying the filter.

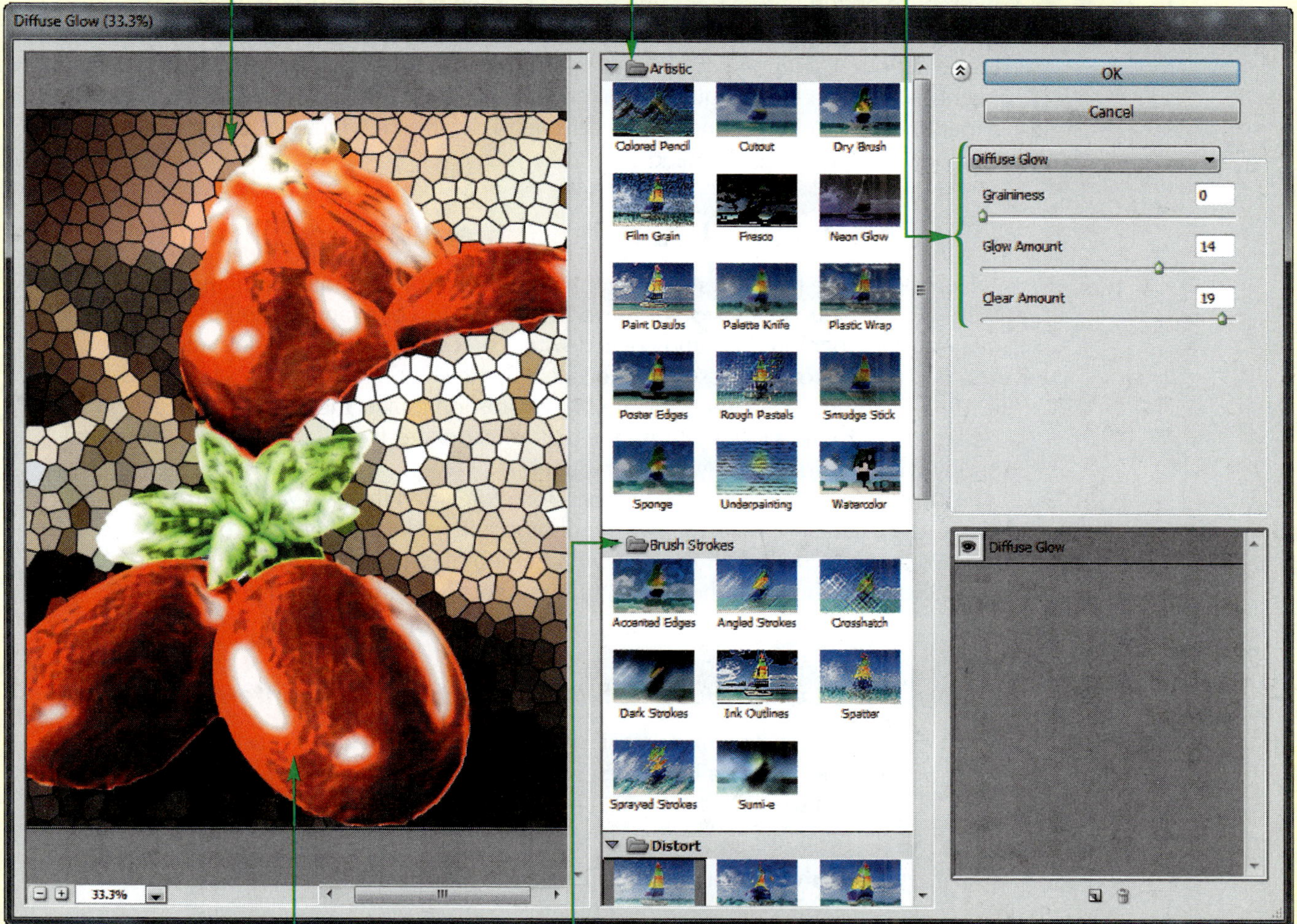

You can preview the selected filter effect before applying it.

Click a folder icon to expand or collapse the folder.

marco mayer/Shutterstock.com

Working with the Lasso Tools, Fills, and the Content-Aware Move Tool

The Lasso tools give you many options for selecting content on your canvas. Photoshop includes three Lasso tools, each with unique benefits. To use the Polygonal Lasso tool, click a starting point for your selection, and then continue to click around the selection. As you do, Photoshop connects the points you click with straight lines. You can close your selection and activate the selection marquee by double-clicking. The Magnetic Lasso tool is attracted to the defined edges of whatever object you first click on. As you move the mouse pointer, it adds points along the selection based on a frequency you specify. You can add extra points and change direction by clicking. You use the regular Lasso tool in much the same way you would draw with a brush or pencil. You simply drag on the image to create your free-form selection. When you release the mouse button, Photoshop creates the selection marquee. If you release the mouse button before returning to your starting point, Photoshop draws a straight line to the starting point from the point at which you stopped dragging to complete the selection. A selection made with the Lasso tool isn't as precise as other selection methods, but you'll find you use it often as a starting point. As you become more experienced with Photoshop, you'll be able to determine which particular tool is the best one for your selection needs.

Filling a Selection Using the Content-Aware Fill Feature

A Content-Aware fill allows you to remove objects from a photograph and replace them with similar versions of the surrounding pixels. For example, you might have a beautiful photograph of a sandy beach with a piece of trash right in the middle of it. You can use one of the Lasso tools to select the trash and some of the sand surrounding it. When you use the Content-Aware fill, Photoshop makes the trash disappear and replaces it with the sand. Because the feature generates the fill randomly, if you're not happy with the first result, you can repeat it.

Azar has given you a photograph of a tomato garden that he wants to use in his Live Green, Eat Green slide show. The photograph includes a woman, but he'd like to remove the woman and fill the area with tomato plants instead. You'll select the woman using the Lasso tool, and then you'll fill the selection using the Content-Aware fill.

To use the Lasso tool and fill the selection with content:

1. Start Photoshop while pressing the **Ctrl+Alt+Shift** keys, and click **Yes** to delete the Settings File when prompted. Reset Photoshop to the default Essentials workspace layout, and reset all tools.
2. Navigate to the Photoshop5\Tutorial folder included with your Data Files, and open **WomanInGarden.jpg**. Display the image at 25% zoom, and pan the image, if necessary, so the woman is completely in the Document window.
3. Click the **Lasso Tool** button in the Tools panel and drag a selection completely around the woman, and then release the mouse button.

   You don't need to be too exacting when you make the selection, but make sure the woman is completely selected, and that the selection includes some of the image area surrounding the woman.

A selection marquee appears around the woman. See Figure 5-25. (The green outline around the selection marquee was added to Figure 5-25 to highlight the selection marquee.)

Figure 5-25 **Selecting with the Lasso tool**

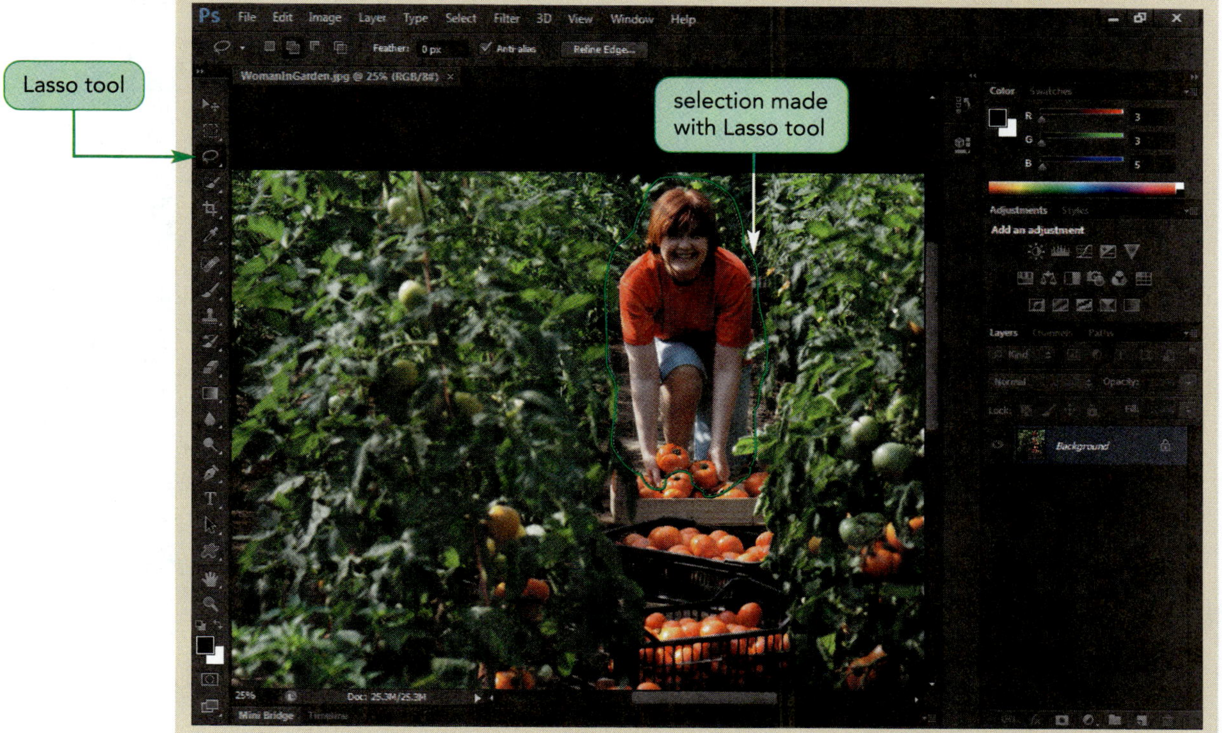

Fotokostic/Shutterstock.com

4. On the menu bar, click **Edit**, and then click **Fill**. The Fill dialog box opens.
5. In the Contents section, click the **Use** button, and click **Content-Aware**, if necessary. Set the Blending Mode to **Normal**, set the Opacity to **100%**, and then click the **OK** button. A progress bar appears while the selection is filled.
6. Press the **Ctrl+0** keys to fit the image on screen. See Figure 5-26.

Figure 5-26 **Selected area filled with surrounding content**

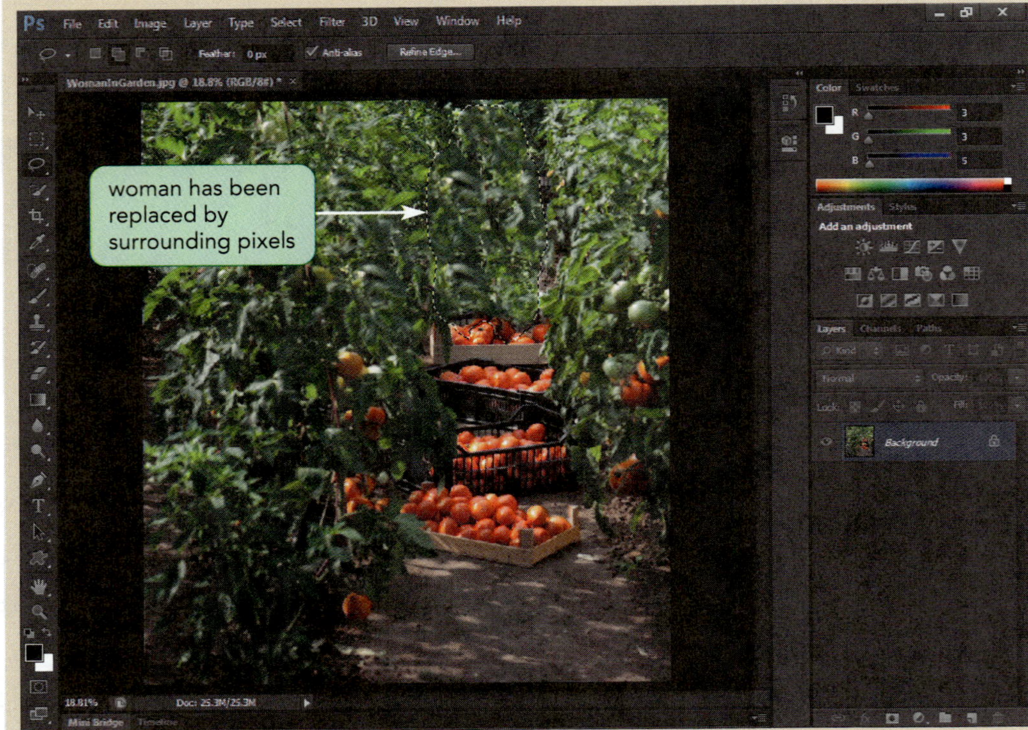

Fotokostic/Shutterstock.com

Photoshop uses the data in the area surrounding the selection to fill the selection.

7. On the menu bar, click **Select**, and then click **Deselect** to clear the selection.

   The image has been transformed from a photograph of a woman in a garden to just the garden. There is no evidence that the woman was ever there.

   Trouble? If you aren't satisfied with the way Photoshop filled in the area, repeat Steps 3 through 7. Because the results are randomly generated, the fill will look different every time.

8. Save the file as **TomatoGarden.jpg**, using the default JPEG Options, in the Photoshop5\Tutorial folder, and then close it.

Moving a Selection Using the Content-Aware Move Tool

In earlier versions of Photoshop, you could make a selection and move or cut the selected pixels, but when you did so, you were always left with an empty area on your canvas. Think back to what happened when you cut and pasted a selection in the last session: Cutting the pixels exposed the black Background layer underneath the strawberry layer because the remaining area contained only transparent pixels. Photoshop CS6 has a new tool hidden under the Spot Healing Brush tool on the Tools panel called the Content-Aware Move tool. The **Content-Aware Move tool** combines a typical move action with the magic of Content-Aware fill so that when you move a selection, the empty space left behind is automatically filled with pixels copied from the surrounding area. As a result, your image remains whole. See Figure 5-27.

Figure 5-27 **Moving a selection with the Content-Aware Move tool**

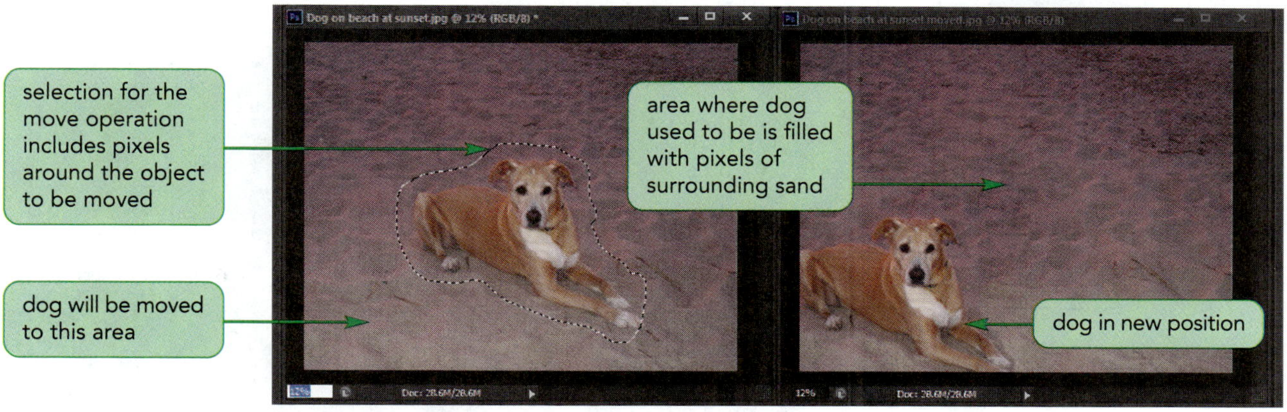

Jane Hosie-Bounar

In Figure 5-27, the dog has been moved from the center of the image to the lower-left corner of the image using the Content-Aware Move tool. In the original photo, shown on the left, the dog and some of the surrounding sand were selected with the Lasso tool. Then, using the Content-Aware Move tool, the selection was dragged down and to the left. The space where the dog was originally lying was filled with pixels from the surrounding area—the sandy beach.

Azar would like you to modify an image of a pumpkin patch so there is room for advertising copy on the left side. He suggests you move the pumpkin in the foreground to the right.

To use the Content-Aware Move tool to move a selection:

1. Open **PumpkinField.jpg**, located in the Photoshop5\Tutorial folder, fit the image on the screen, and then, in the Tools panel, click the **Lasso Tool** button, if necessary, to select it.
2. Drag a selection around the pumpkin in the foreground and its shadow, as shown in Figure 5-28. (The green outline around the selection marquee was added to Figure 5-28 to highlight the selection marquee.)

Figure 5-28 **Selecting the pumpkin to move**

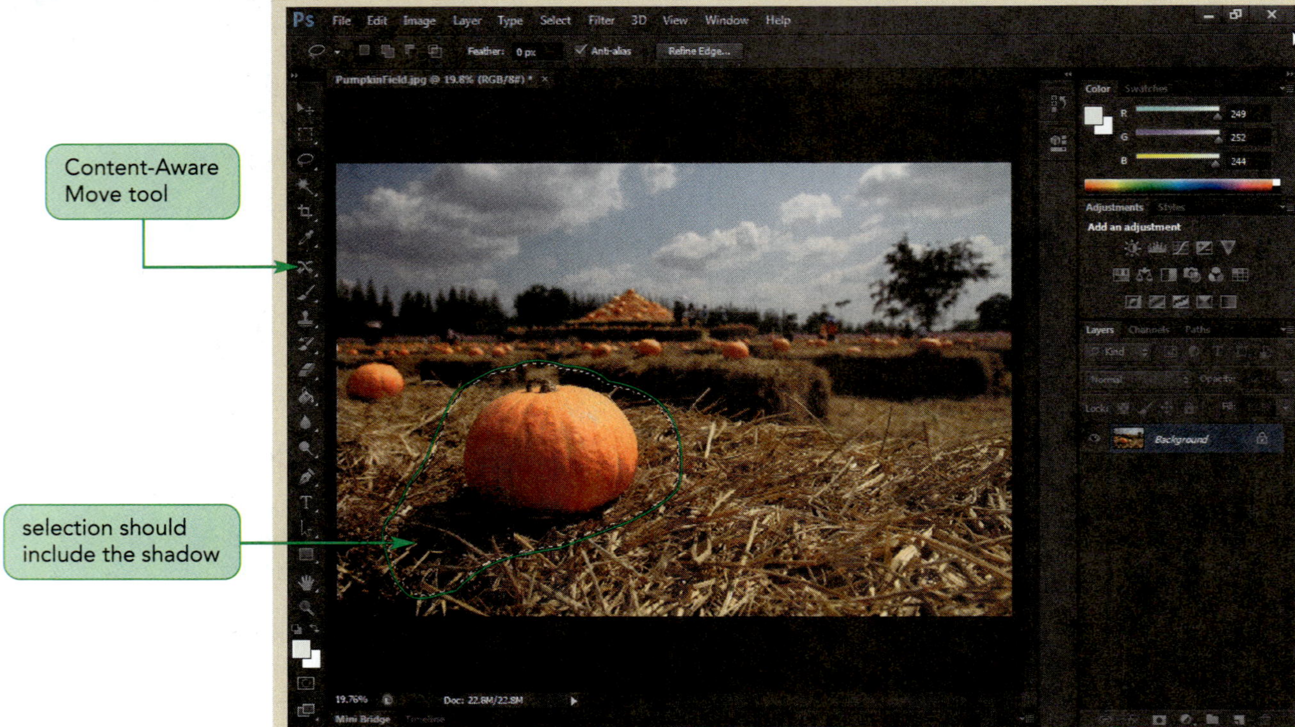

iKhai_TH/Shutterstock.com

3. In the Tools panel, click the **Content-Aware Move Tool** button. On the options bar, set the Mode to **Move**, and set the Adaptation to **Medium**, if necessary.

   Trouble? If you don't see the Content-Aware Move Tool button in the Tools panel, click and hold the Spot Healing Brush Tool button to display the hidden tools, and then click the Content-Aware Move Tool button.

4. Point to the selection. The pointer changes to. Press the mouse button, and then drag to the right until the pumpkin is in the location shown in Figure 5-29. Release the mouse button. As you drag, you can see two versions of the pumpkin.

   When you release the mouse button, you'll see a progress bar as Photoshop analyzes, moves, and replaces pixels, and then you'll see the pumpkin in its new location.

Figure 5-29 Using the Content-Aware Move tool

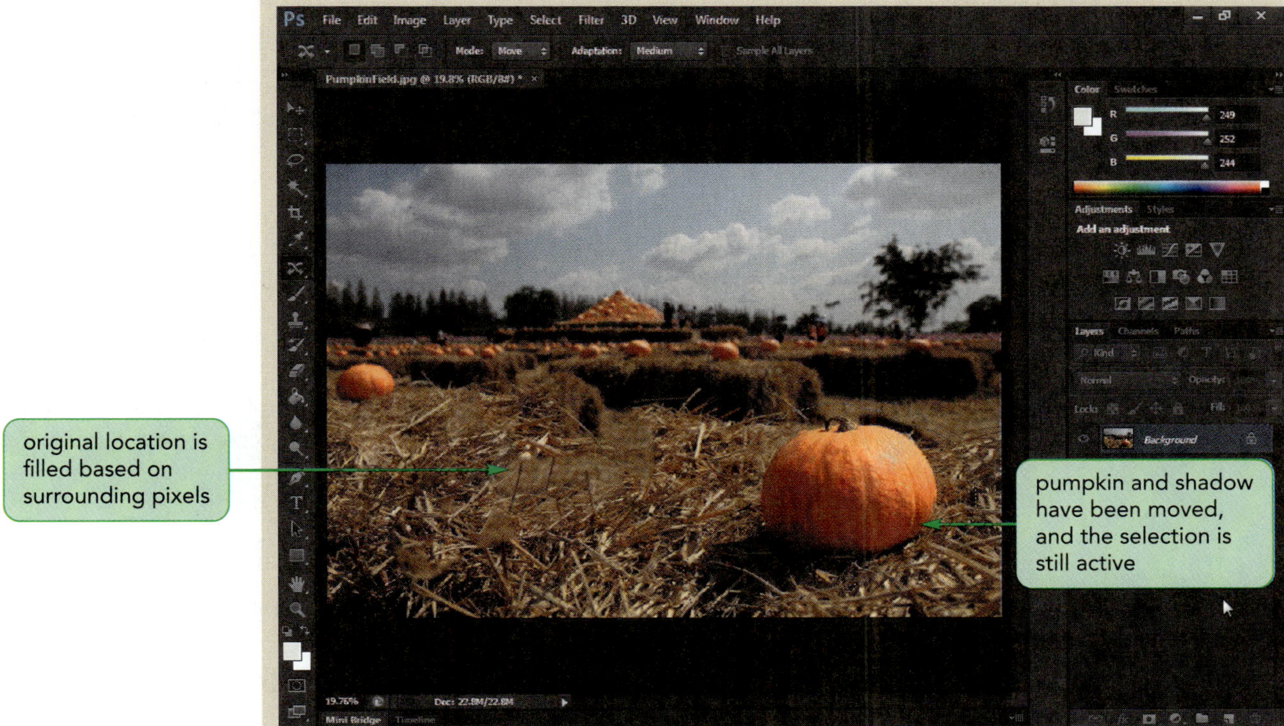

iKhai_TH/Shutterstock.com

Trouble? If you're not satisfied with the result, step backward and then experiment with different-sized selections and options bar settings. Because of the complexity of the operation, results will vary not only by image, but also by the way you draw your selection.

5. Save the file as **PumpkinMoved.jpg** using the default JPEG options, and then close it.

PROSKILLS

Problem Solving: Using an Image Without a Model Release

Problem solving is the ability to identify—and close—a gap between an existing state and a desired state. It's a critical skill to develop because no matter what your career, you're bound to encounter problems that take a creative thinker (you) to solve them. For example, imagine that you have the perfect landscape photo for a travel ad you're creating. The image includes a stunning landscape, beautiful architecture, and an old man riding his bicycle along the cobblestone road. Can you use the photograph?

The answer isn't simple. Basically, it depends. If you're using the photograph for a commercial purpose, as in this travel ad example, you would need to ask the man to sign a model release form giving you permission to use his likeness in your piece. However, if the man isn't recognizable—for example, if you've photographed his back, or if his face is cloaked in shadow, you really don't need his permission. But, assume the man in the image is fully recognizable, and that using his image is a problem you need to solve. Even without his permission, you still have a number of options. You can modify the photograph so the man is unrecognizable—for example by using Photoshop to add shadows to his face. You can also use the Content-Aware fill feature to replace the man and his bicycle with pixels from the cobblestone road. In other words, when you're experienced in digital image editing, you'll find more than one way to solve any image problem you may encounter.

Selecting Content with the Magnetic Lasso Tool

The Magnetic Lasso tool is hidden under the Lasso tool in the Tools panel. It's aptly named because it appears to use a virtual magnet to select the edges of an object in an image. When you work with the tool, it is as if the object you are selecting is metal and the selection marquee is a magnet.

As the tool draws a selection marquee, it drops fastening points along the selection marquee to hold the selection in place. The frequency determines the distance between fastening points. On the options bar, you can specify a Frequency setting between 0 and 100. For a more refined selection, increase the frequency of the fastening points. You can also specify a detection Width, which is the distance from the pointer, in number of pixels, within which you want the tool to detect edges. The Contrast setting, which ranges from 1% to 100%, determines how sensitive the tool is to edges. A low Contrast setting detects low contrast edges, whereas a high setting detects edges with a sharp contrast. Unlike with the Lasso tool, you do not need to hold down the mouse button when making a selection using the Magnetic Lasso tool. You click to set the first fastening point, and then move the mouse pointer to outline the selection. As you do, Photoshop adds fastening points at the frequency you specified. You can add fastening points manually by clicking as you make your selection. You can delete the most recent fastening point by pressing the Backspace key. When you have finished making your selection, you can modify its pixels or fill it with surrounding content or with a pattern, color, or gradient. To fill a selection, you can use the Fill command on the Edit menu, which fills a selection on the current layer, rather than adding the fill to a separate layer as you did earlier in this tutorial. If you fill a selection with a pattern, you can choose a **scripted pattern**, which applies a special effect to the pattern you select, such as displaying it as a spiral or a weave.

REFERENCE

Using the Magnetic Lasso Tool

- In the Tools panel, click the Magnetic Lasso tool.
- On the options bar, click the New selection, Add to selection, Subtract from selection, or Intersect with selection button.
- Specify a Feather setting, and select or deselect the Anti-alias check box.
- Specify a Width for edge detection, the Contrast percentage for detecting either low-contrast or high-contrast edges, and the Frequency at which fastening points will appear.
- Click on the image to set the first fastening point, and then move the mouse pointer along the edges of your selection.
- Click at the last fastening point to close the selection marquee.

Azar has an image of corn that he wants to use in his presentation, where he includes various recipes, including many for corn. The image has a blue sky, and he has asked you to give the background a rainbow effect to support his slide text: *The gold at the end of the rainbow*. You'll select the corn cob, select its inverse to select the sky, and then apply a pattern fill to the selection.

To use the Magnetic Lasso tool and fill the selection with color:

1. Open **Corn.jpg**, located in the Photoshop5\Tutorial folder, and then, in the Tools panel, click the **Magnetic Lasso Tool** button.
2. On the options bar, confirm that the Feather setting is **0 px**, select the **Anti-alias** check box, if necessary, set the Width to **1 px**, set the Contrast to **10%**, if necessary, and set the Frequency to **80**. A frequency of 80 will drop fastening points very close together along the edges of the selection.
3. Start by clicking the tip of the corn cob, move the mouse pointer down and to the right until you reach the edge of the canvas, and then move the mouse pointer down until you reach the lower-right corner of the canvas. Stay at the edge, or even slightly outside of the image, so the fastening points are along the edges of the photograph.
4. Move the pointer to the left, and then up slowly along the edge of the ear of corn until you reach the top, and then click when you reach the first fastening point to close the selection marquee. The selection marquee encloses the corn cob in a selection. See Figure 5-30.

   Trouble? If you find that the selection marquee strays from the outlines of the corn cob, use the Magic Wand tool and the Add to selection button and the Subtract from selection button, as necessary, to refine your selection.

TIP

You can restart a selection by pressing the Esc key, and then clicking to create the first fastening point again.

Figure 5-30 **Using the Magnetic Lasso tool**

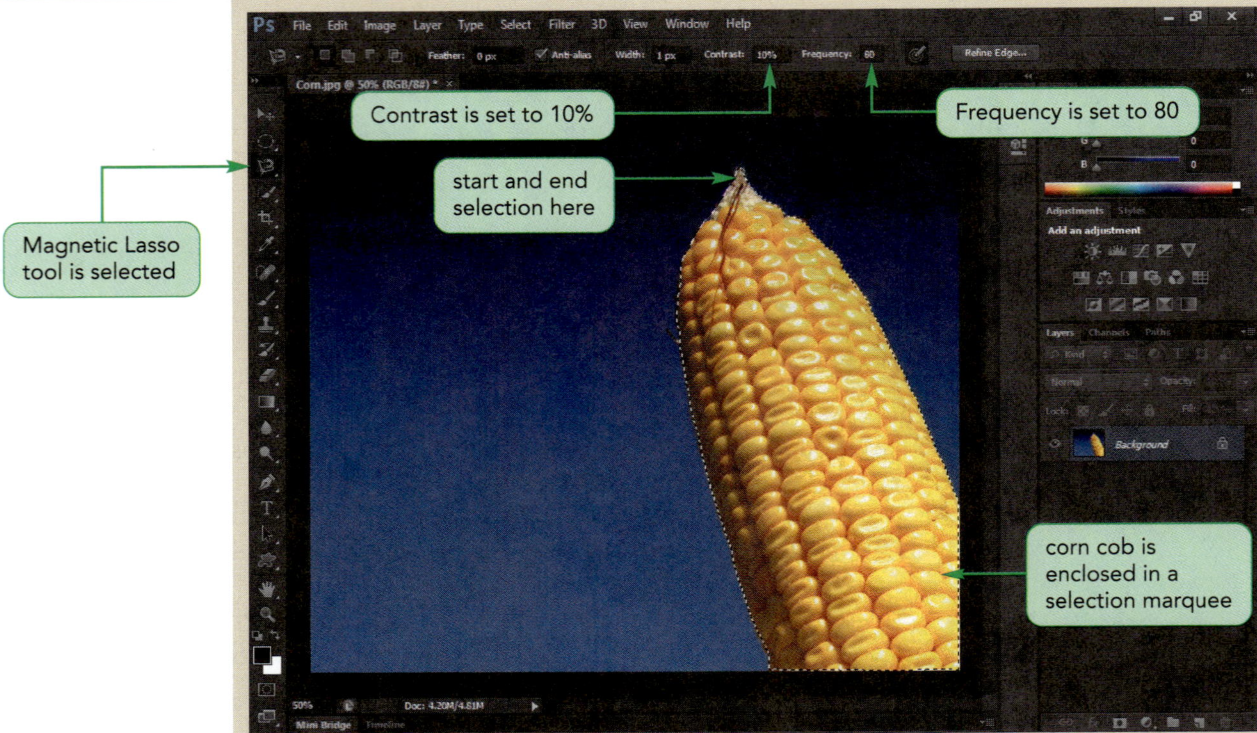

Zeljko Radojko/Shutterstock.com

Make sure you click to close the selection marquee. If you don't click, the tool will continue to drop fastening points, even outside of the canvas, and you'll be unable to choose any commands or tools.

5. On the menu bar, click **Select**, and then click **Inverse** to select every part of the image except the corn cob.
6. Click **Edit**, and then click **Fill**. In the Fill dialog box, click the **Use** button, and then click **Pattern**.
7. Click the **Custom Pattern arrow**, click the **Tie Dye thumbnail**, the second pattern in the first row, and then click the **Custom Pattern arrow** again to close the list.

   Trouble? If the Tie Dye thumbnail is not visible, click the More options button and then click Reset Patterns.

8. At the bottom of the Fill dialog box, click the **Scripted Patterns** check box to select it, click the **Script arrow**, click **Spiral**, and then click the **OK** button.
9. On the menu bar, click **Select**, and then click **Deselect** to clear the selection. See Figure 5-31.

Figure 5-31 **Filling a selection with a scripted pattern**

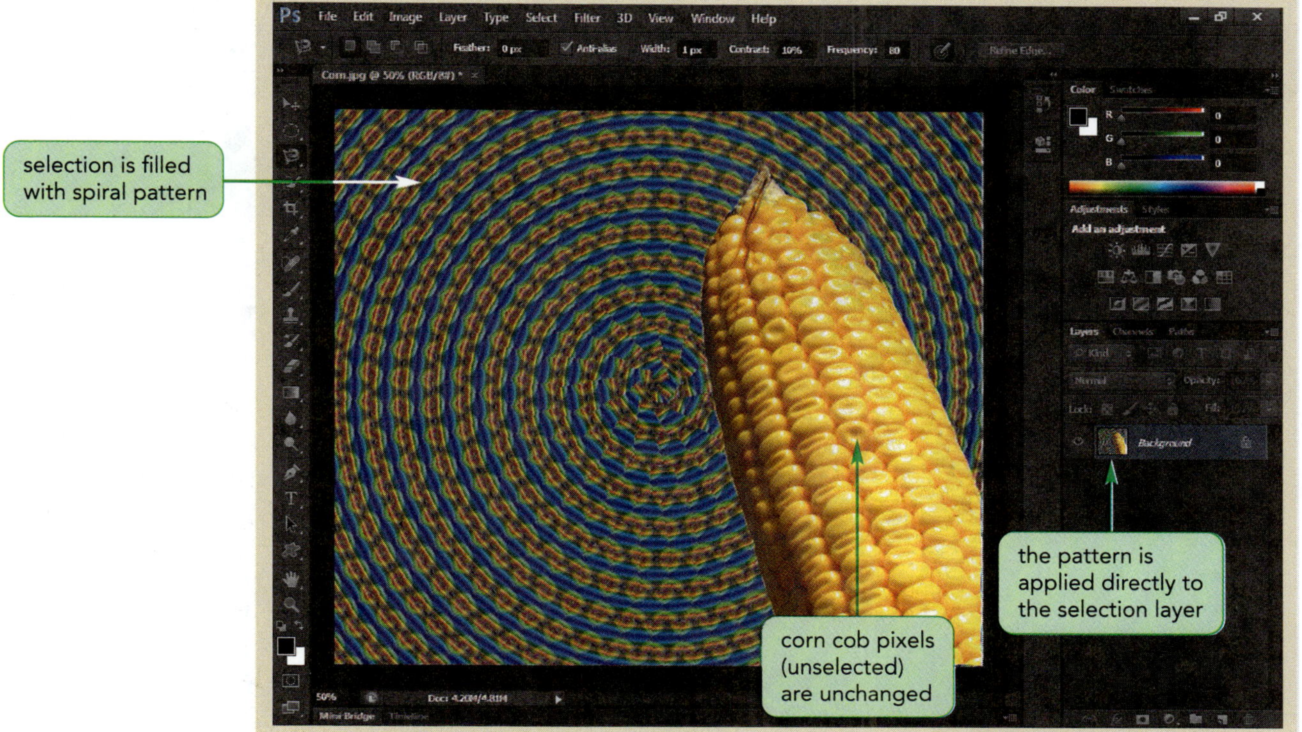

Zeljko Radojko/Shutterstock.com

The sky has changed from blue to a colorful swirling effect because of the pattern fill you added to the selection. If you had been unable to isolate the selection, the pattern fill would have affected both the corn cob and the sky.

Notice that the Fill command added the pattern pixels to the current layer, and did not add a fill layer.

10. Save the modified file as **SwirledCorn.jpg** using the default JPEG options.

Although you've created an interesting pattern, Azar wants you to try to achieve a rainbow effect behind the ear of corn.

11. Click **Edit** on the menu bar, and then click **Step Backward**, and then click **Edit** and **Step Backward** again. The pattern fill is removed from the image.

12. In the Layers panel, add a new Gradient fill layer to the Layers panel, and in the Gradient Fill dialog box, select the **Spectrum** gradient, set the Angle to **45** degrees, and then click the **OK** button. See Figure 5-32.

Figure 5-32 Creating a rainbow gradient fill

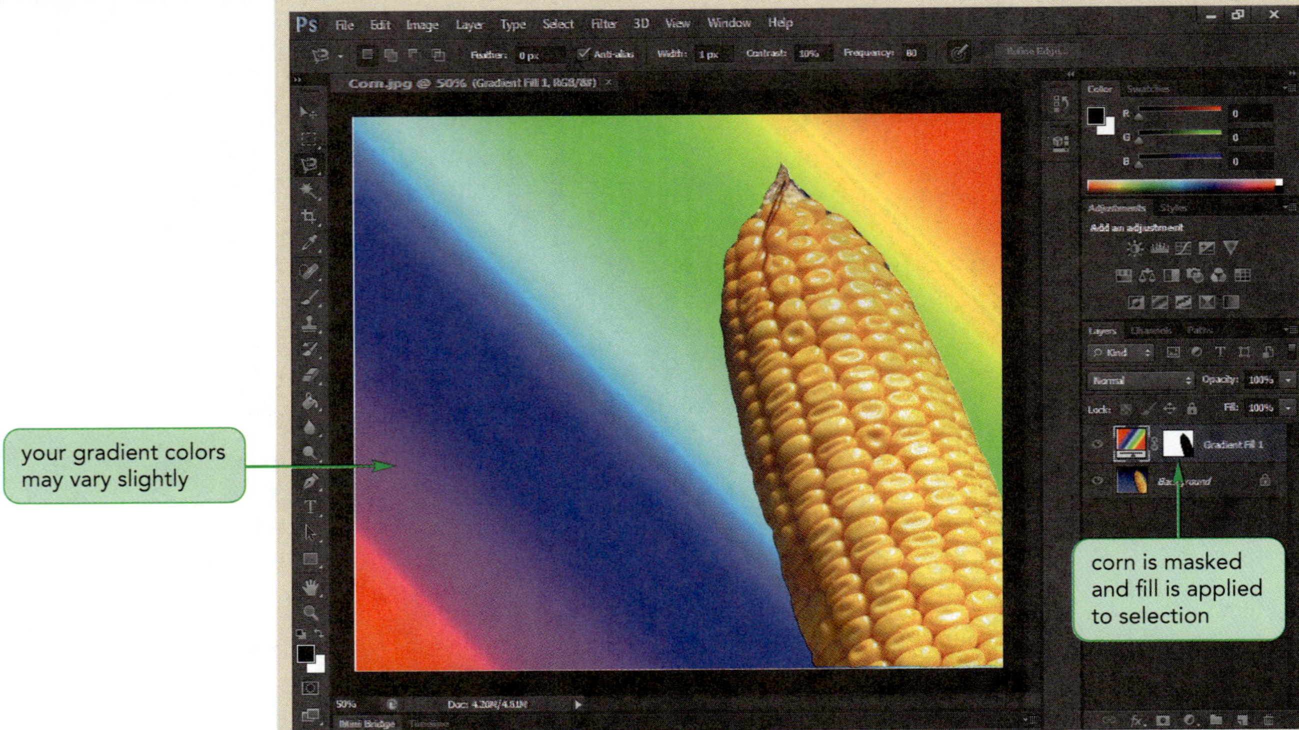

Zeljko Radojko/Shutterstock.com

The gradient fills the selected area, and provides a rainbow effect behind the ear of corn.

13. Save the file as **RainbowCorn.psd** and then close the file.

Saving and Reloading a Selection

You can save a selection with a file so you can use it the next time you open the file. For example, if you want to experiment with many different effects on a single selection, you can save the first effect in a file with a new name, reopen the original file, load the saved selection, and then try a different effect. Photoshop saves the selection as a new layer in the Channels panel, which you'll explore later in this tutorial. See Figure 5-33.

Figure 5-33 Loading a selection

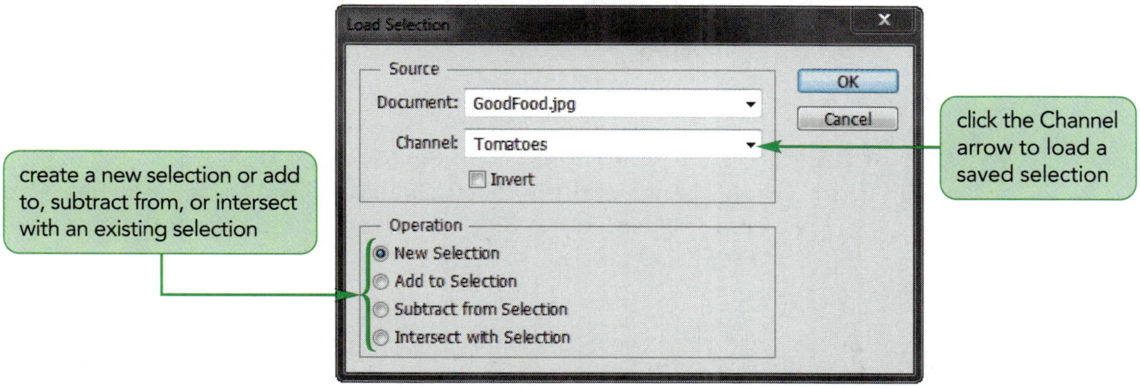

You can choose a selection from the Channel list in the Load Selection dialog box. You can use the saved selection to add to, subtract from, or intersect with an active selection. You can also simply load the selection you saved with the file.

REFERENCE

Saving and Loading a Selection

- In the Tools panel, activate any selection tool and make a selection on the image.
- On the menu bar, click Select, and then click Save Selection.
- In the Save Selection dialog box, type a name for the selection in the Name box, and then click the OK button.
- On the menu bar, click Select, and then click Load Selection.
- In the Load Selection dialog box, click the Channel arrow, and then click the name of the selection you want to load.
- In the Operation section of the Load Selection dialog box, click New Selection, Add to Selection, Subtract from Selection, or Intersect with Selection.
- Click the OK button.

Selecting with the Quick Selection Tool

You can select part of an image by painting it with the Quick Selection tool. The Quick Selection tool expands to select the edges of any object in an image that you paint over to enclose it in a selection marquee. It works well when you want to select areas with defined edges. It is also a good tool for adding pixels to a partial selection, as you did in the first session with the pumpkin. When you use the Quick Selection tool, you can specify its diameter. A larger diameter gives you less control over the tool, but if you are selecting a large area, it's more efficient. You can also select Sample All Layers to create the selection using all of the layers in the file rather than just the active layer. If you select Auto-Enhance, Photoshop automatically reduces the roughness around the border of the selection.

Azar has asked you to create two images that showcase the quality of last summer's tomato crop for Food for Change. To do so, you'll create two compositions. In one, you'll use the Quick Selection tool to make a selection and then select the inverse so you can change all of an image except the tomatoes to black and white to make them stand out. In the second composition, you'll place a stroke or outline around the tomatoes to make them stand out in the image.

TIP

You can also press the [key to reduce the brush size in 5-pixel increments.

To use the Quick Selection tool and save the selection:

1. Open **GoodFood.jpg**, located in the Photoshop5\Tutorial folder, and then zoom to about **35%** and pan it as necessary, so you can work with the tomatoes in the image.
2. Reset all of the tools, reset the Essentials workspace, and then, in the Tools panel, click the **Quick Selection Tool** button. By default, the New selection button is selected on the options bar, and the brush size is set to 30 pixels.
3. Open the Brush picker and drag the slider to the left to change the brush size to **20 px**. Close the Brush picker.
4. Point to the top of the tomato on the lower right, click and drag the mouse down to the bottom of that tomato. Photoshop selects most of the tomato, but it also selects some of the tabletop. See Figure 5-34.

Figure 5-34 Using the Quick Selection tool

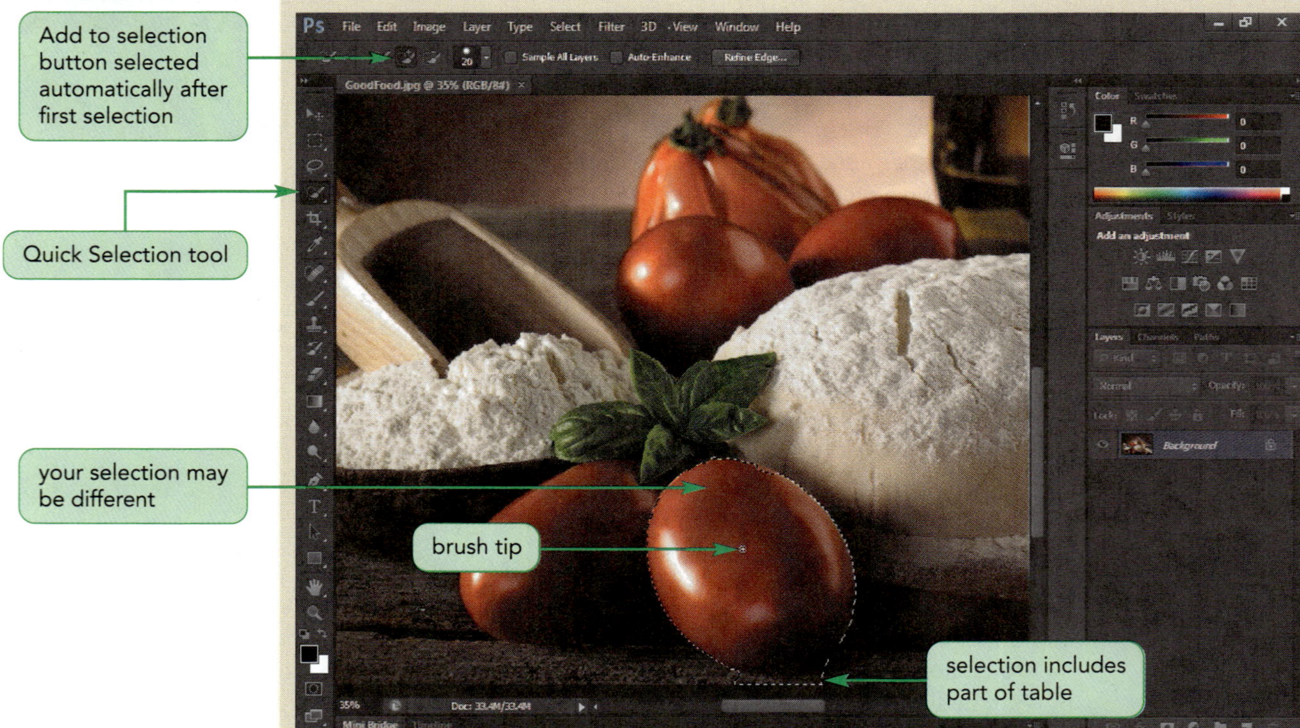

marco mayer/Shutterstock.com

You need to select the other tomatoes as well, and then refine the selection to get rid of the areas that aren't part of the tomatoes. The Add to selection option has been automatically selected on the options bar so the next selection you make will be added to the current one.

5. Drag over the tomato on the left. Photoshop joins the selections, as shown in Figure 5-35.

Figure 5-35 Selections are joined

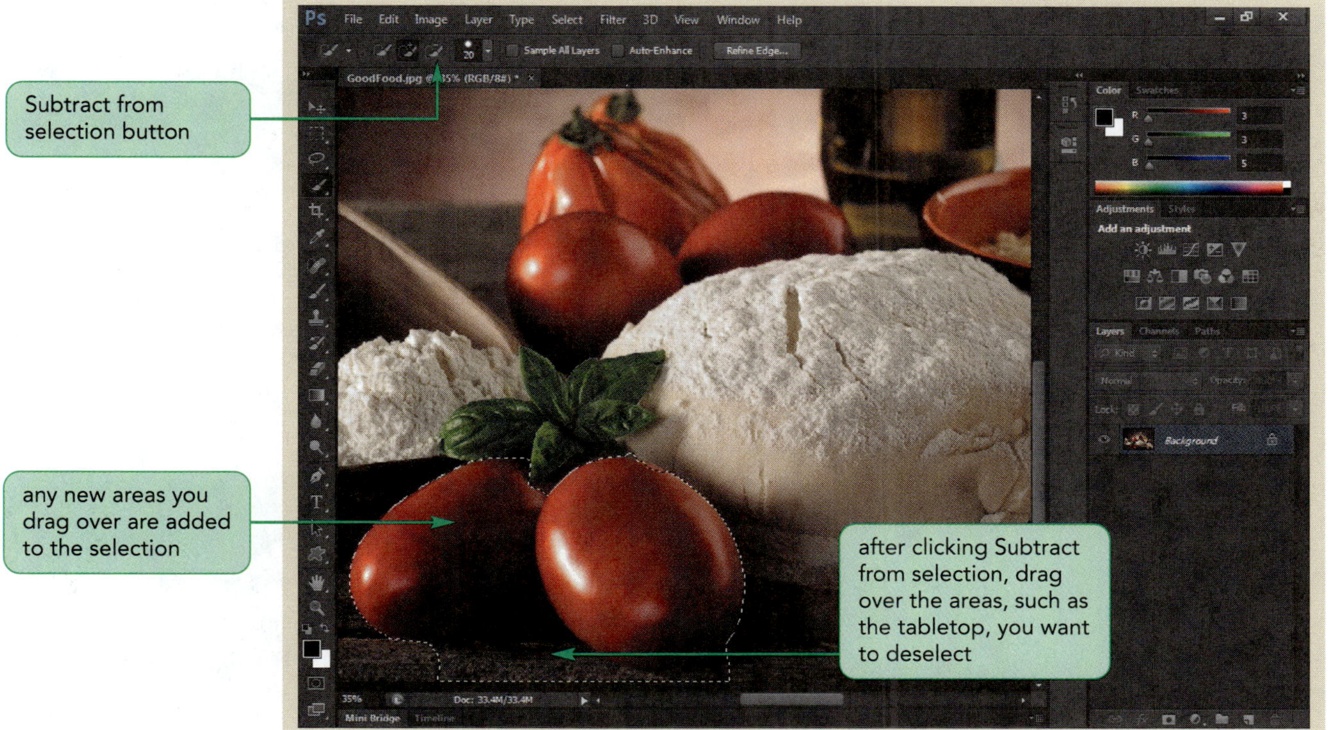

marco mayer/Shutterstock.com

You can subtract from your selection using the Subtract from selection button on the options bar.

6. On the options bar, click the **Subtract from selection** button, and then drag in the areas you want to deselect.

Trouble? If you accidentally deselect part of one of the tomatoes, or if you were unable to select the complete tomato in your first selection, you can use the Add to selection button to add it back to the selection.

Photoshop deselects the shadowed parts of the selection so now the selection marquee encompasses only the tomatoes.

7. Continue to add to the selection until you have selected all of the tomatoes and the basil leaves in the image, as shown in Figure 5-36. You'll save this selection to use later.

Figure 5-36 Selection is complete

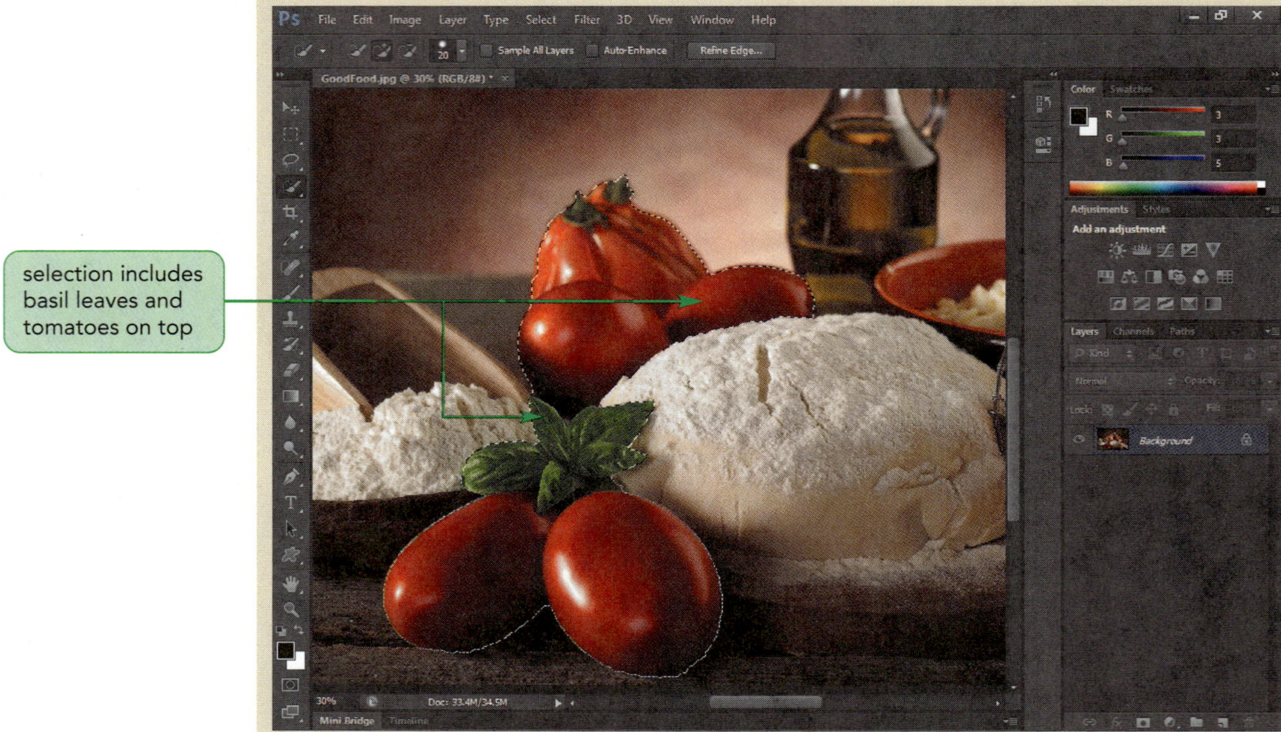

marco mayer/Shutterstock.com

8. On the menu bar, click **Select**, click **Save Selection**, and then in the Save Selection dialog box, type **Tomatoes** in the Name box. Click the **OK** button. The selection is saved with the file so you can use it later.
9. Save the file as **GoodFood1.psd** in the Photoshop5\Tutorial folder.

Next, you'll select the inverse of the tomato selection so you can apply an effect that makes the tomatoes stand out.

To select the inverse of the selection:

1. Zoom out so you can see the entire image. On the menu bar, click **Select**, and then click **Inverse**. Photoshop changes the selection so all of the image *except* the tomatoes is now selected.
2. On the menu bar, click **Image**, click **Adjustments**, and then click **Black & White**.
3. In the Black and White dialog box, click the **OK** button to accept the default settings.
4. On the menu bar, click **Select**, and then click **Deselect**. See Figure 5-37.

Figure 5-37 Applying the Black and White adjustment to a selection

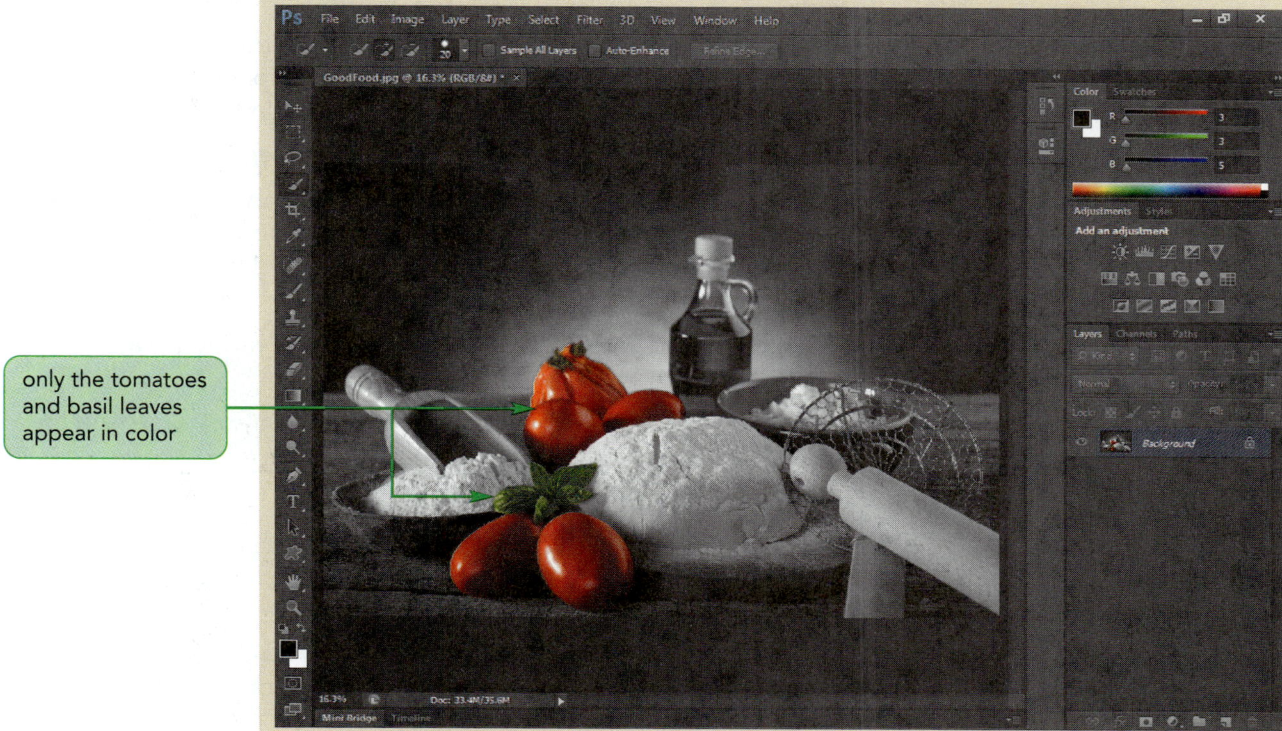

marco mayer/Shutterstock.com

All of the areas in the image except the tomatoes are now black and white. Using this kind of effect in a composition immediately draws attention to the area of the image on which you want the viewer's eyes to focus.

5. Save the file as **BlackWhiteRed.psd** in the Photoshop5\Tutorial folder, and close it.

Next, you'll work with the same image, and apply a different effect so you have two options to show to Azar at your next meeting.

Stroking a Selection

You can make a selection stand out by **stroking** it, or drawing a border around it. To do so, you select an area of the image with any of the selection tools—or load a saved selection—and use the Stroke option on the Edit menu. In the Stroke dialog box, you can specify the width, color, and location of the stroke, as well as its blending mode and opacity.

You'll add a stroke to the tomato selection you saved earlier to see if you like the effect.

To load the saved tomatoes selection and add a stroke to the selection:

1. Open **GoodFood1.psd**, located in the Photoshop5\Tutorial folder and zoom to **25%**. Photoshop displays the original image of the tomatoes. Although you can't see the selection you saved earlier, it has been saved with the file.
2. On the menu bar, click **Select**, and then click **Load Selection**.
3. Confirm that **Tomatoes** appears in the Channel box, and then click the **OK** button. Photoshop selects the tomatoes and basil in the image using the selection marquee you saved with the file. You'll expand the selection, and then you'll add a stroke to the selection to make it stand out.
4. On the menu bar, click **Select**, point to **Modify**, and then click **Expand** to open the Expand Selection dialog box.
5. In the Expand By box, type **20** and then click the **OK** button to expand the selection by 20 pixels.
6. On the menu bar, click **Edit**, and then click **Stroke**.
7. In the Stroke dialog box, specify a Width of **20 px**, and then click the Color box to open the Color Picker (Stroke Color) dialog box. Select a **yellow** color and then click the **OK** button to close the Color Picker (Stroke Color) dialog box.
8. In the Stroke dialog box, under Location, click the **Outside** option button. Under Blending, click the **Mode arrow**, and then click **Dissolve**. See Figure 5-38.

Figure 5-38 **Stroking a selection**

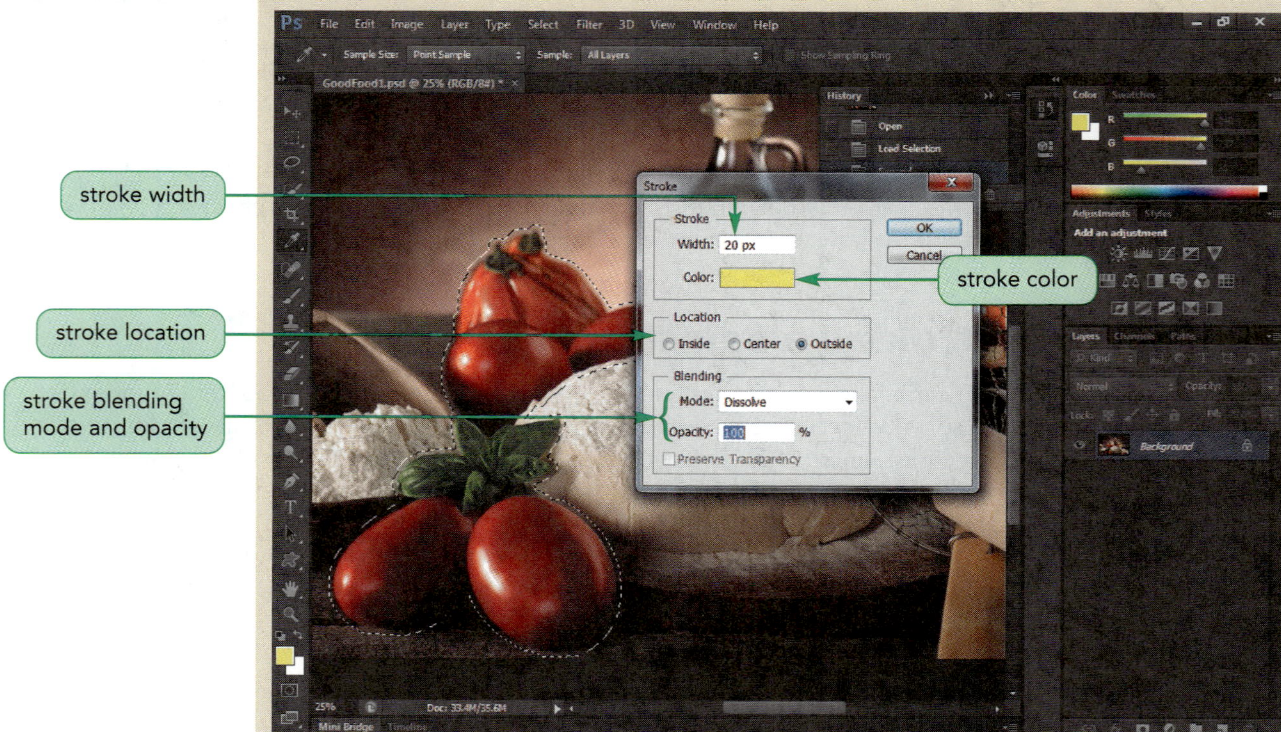

marco mayer/Shutterstock.com

9. Click the **OK** button, and then deselect the tomatoes. See Figure 5-39.

Figure 5-39 Selection with stroke added

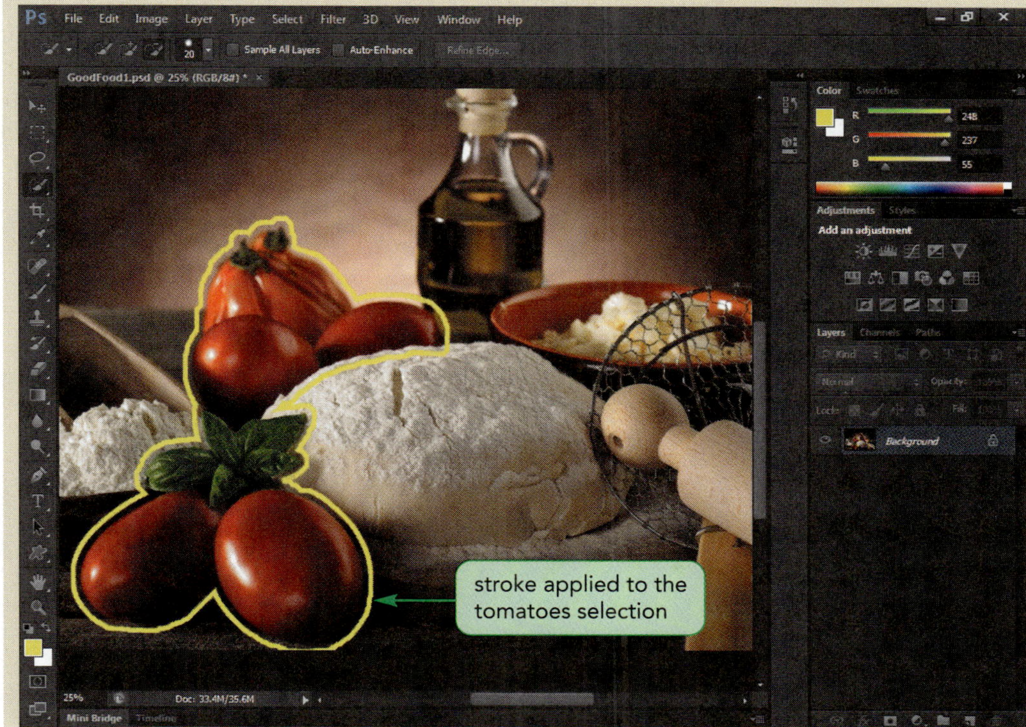

marco mayer/Shutterstock.com

10. Save the file as **Stroke.psd** in the Photoshop5\Tutorial folder, and then close the file.

When you next meet with Azar, you'll show him the two versions of the file to see which one he prefers. Next, you'll explore filters and masks.

Working with Filters and Masks

Photoshop includes more than enough filter options to fill a book. In this session, you'll focus on just a few of the available filters. However, once you understand how to apply them, you'll be able to experiment with many more. You can access all of the available filters from the Filter menu. Some commands open a dialog box specific to the filter; other commands are applied when you click them. Still other commands open the Filter Gallery, where you can modify and preview different filters.

TIP

Some filters can only be applied to RGB images. If you are working on a piece for print, work on it in RGB mode and then switch to CMYK mode after you have applied any filters.

You can apply a filter effect to an entire image, to a layer, or to a selection on a layer. In this session, you'll apply different filters to different selections. When you apply an effect to a selection, you are actually working with a mask. The mask ensures that the filter is only applied to the selected area. Sometimes filter results can be a little over the top, but if you experiment with them, you'll see the variety and creativity you can achieve using these tools.

Understanding Masks

If you have ever painted a room, you know that there's a certain amount of preparation that has to take place before you actually put your paintbrush in the paint and the brush on the wall. Certain areas of the room—for example, the doors, windows, and molding—need to be protected, and to protect these areas, you'll most likely use masking tape. Photoshop carries the metaphor of masking tape into the digital image-editing world. Masking an area keeps it safe from any digital paint you apply. You saw a masking effect in Session 5.1 when you selected an area on an image, and then added brushstrokes: The brushstrokes were contained in the selection and did not spill over onto the rest of the image.

You might be wondering what a mask actually looks like in Photoshop. Masks are stored in the Channels panel, which appears behind the Layers panel in the Essentials workspace. See Figure 5-40.

Figure 5-40 Channels panel

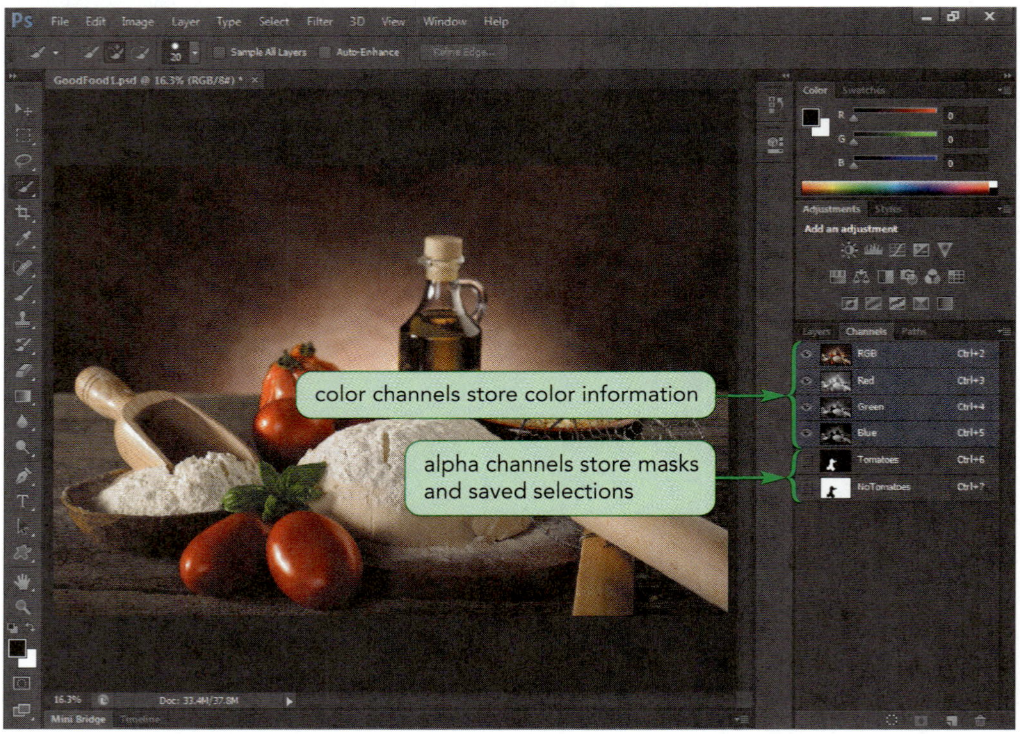

marco mayer/Shutterstock.com

The Channels panel stores a variety of information, including color information. In an RGB image, Red, Green, and Blue color channels appear, as well as the combined RGB channel. For a CMYK file, the Channels panel would display Cyan, Magenta, Yellow, and Black channels in addition to the CMYK channel. You can show and hide these color channels as you work with an image file.

When you saved a selection earlier in this tutorial, Photoshop saved it as a mask, also called an alpha channel, titled Tomatoes in the Channels panel. On any alpha channel thumbnail, the masked part of the image is black, indicating that it is protected, and the unmasked part of the image is white, indicating that it is editable. In Figure 5-40, notice that in addition to the color channels, there are two other channels. One, called Tomatoes in the figure, masks the tomatoes and basil. It was created by selecting the tomatoes and basil, and then saving the selection. The other channel in Figure 5-40 is called NoTomatoes, and it masks the rest of the Image. It was created by inverting the original selection, and then saving the new selection. You'll continue to work with masks in this tutorial as you apply filters from the Filter Gallery.

INSIGHT

Working with Color Channels

The color channels in the Channels panel give you a high level of control over color adjustments. You can use them to change the color balance in an image by modifying them individually. For example, you can modify the Red channel to achieve one effect or the Blue channel to achieve another. If you have a photograph with too much red in it, you can select the Red color channel in the Channels panel and modify its settings individually to reduce the red output. Having this kind of flexibility when you modify a photograph helps to ensure that you get exactly the effect you want.

Using the Liquify Filter

The Liquify filter is available directly from the Filter menu. You can use the Liquify filter to distort or correct an image. You can create swirls; you can stretch certain areas; you can even bloat or pucker the image. If you want to work with all of the options available in the Liquify dialog box, select the Advanced Mode check box. The advanced options let you modify the mask from within the dialog box itself, rather than returning to the image to change your selection. The tools on the left side of the dialog box give you a variety of options for using the Liquify filter, as shown in Figure 5-41.

Figure 5-41 Liquify tools

Icon	Name	Description
	Forward Warp tool	Pushes pixels ahead of the pointer as you drag
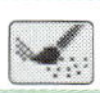	Reconstruct tool	Undoes any distortion you've applied
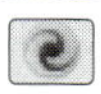	Twirl Clockwise tool	Twirls pixels clockwise; hold down the Alt key to twirl pixels counterclockwise
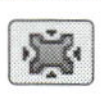	Pucker tool	Moves pixels toward the center of the mouse pointer as you click
	Bloat tool	Moves pixels away from the center of the mouse pointer as you click
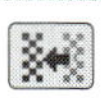	Push Left tool	Moves pixels to the left when you drag up and to the right when you drag down
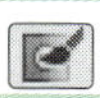	Freeze Mask tool	Protects an area from changes
	Thaw Mask tool	Thaws an area with freeze mask applied
	Hand tool	Pans an image
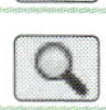	Zoom tool	Zooms in and out on an image

As you work, you can change tools to create different effects on different parts of an image. For example, you might use the Twirl Clockwise tool to create special effects in a cloudy sky or to add a whirlpool to still water.

The Freeze Mask tool in the Liquify dialog box is especially useful if you want to avoid liquifying parts of an image while working on other parts. It has a similar effect to inverting a selection to exclude it before applying an adjustment or effect. You use the Freeze Mask tool to paint a mask on the image. As with other masks in Photoshop, any area that is masked is protected. You can use the Zoom tool and the Hand tool to zoom and pan the image to paint an accurate mask. If you paint beyond the boundaries of the mask you want to create, you can "thaw" the mask by clicking the Thaw Mask tool and painting over the part of the mask you want to erase.

REFERENCE

Using the Liquify Filter

- Select the area you want to work with; if you want to liquify the whole layer, don't make any selection.
- On the menu bar, click Filter, and then click Liquify. In the Liquify dialog box, click the Advanced Mode check box to select it.
- Use the Freeze Mask tool to freeze any areas you don't want to liquify.
- Select a tool on the left side of the Liquify dialog box, and drag the mouse pointer over the image to warp, bloat, pucker, or otherwise liquify your image.
- Use the Thaw Mask tool to thaw any frozen areas, and use additional tools to add more liquify effects, if desired.
- Click the OK button to apply the effects, and close the dialog box.

Azar is planning a summer fund-raiser, and would like to send a postcard to patrons as an invitation. He supplies you with an image of strawberries, and asks you to apply an unusual eye-catching effect to the image. You'll use the Liquify filter to swirl the colors in the image around one of the strawberries.

To work with the Liquify filter:

1. Open **Berries.psd**, located in the Photoshop5\Tutorial folder, and save it as **SummerBerries.psd** in the same folder.
2. In the Layers panel, hide the Berry Fun!! layer, select the **Background** layer, and then use any of the selection tools you have learned about to select the strawberry on the left side of the image. Select only the berry, and not the leaves. Add to and subtract from the selection as necessary.

   Trouble? If you're having difficulty making exact selections, remember that you can refine your selection using the add and subtract buttons on the options bar.
3. On the menu bar, click **Select**, and then click **Inverse**. Everything but the strawberry on the left is selected in the image.
4. On the menu bar, click **Filter**, and then click **Liquify**. The Liquify dialog box opens.
5. Click the **Advanced Mode** check box to display all of the options, and then, at the bottom of the dialog box, click the **Mask Color** button, and then click **Magenta**. See Figure 5-42.

   Trouble? If the Mask Color button is unavailable, click that the Show Mask check box to select it.

Figure 5-42 Liquify dialog box

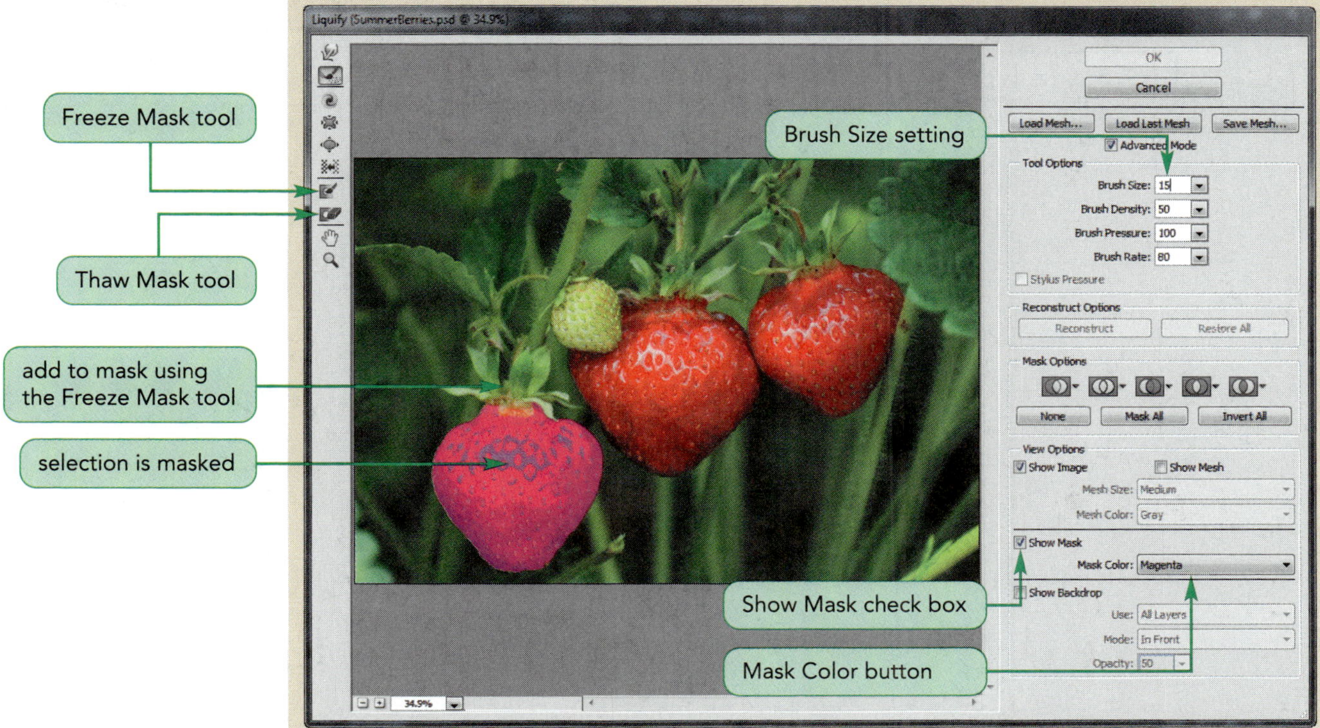

Catarina Belova/Shutterstock.com

The Liquify dialog box shows a preview of the image, with tools along the left side and settings for each tool along the right. By default, the strawberry was painted over with a red mask. The magenta color makes the mask easier to see. Your goal is to liquify the area around the strawberry to give it an impressionistic effect, while leaving one realistic berry image on the left side of the image.

In the figure, the mask of the strawberry is imperfect. You'll use the Freeze Mask tool to add the leaves to the selection, and then you'll correct any oversights on your mask.

6. In the Tools panel of the Liquify dialog box, click the **Freeze Mask Tool** button. The pointer shape for the Freeze Mask tool is a circle with a plus sign in the middle.
7. Change the Brush Size setting to **21**. You'll leave the other settings as is.
8. Drag over the leaves at the top of the strawberry to add them to the mask. As you paint, use the Hand tool and the Zoom tool to ensure that you paint every pixel of the strawberry and leaves to protect them from the filter changes. If the current brush size is inconvenient for you, use a different size.
9. If you make any errors while you paint, click the **Thaw Mask Tool** button and paint over your mistakes to erase them, and then click the **Freeze Mask Tool** button and continue painting. When you have finished applying the mask, your image should resemble Figure 5-43.

TIP

In the Liquify dialog box, you can also press the Ctrl++ keys and the Ctrl+- keys to zoom in and out, press the Ctrl+0 keys to fit the image in the dialog box, and press the Ctrl+1 keys to display the image at 100%.

Figure 5-43 **Masked area in Liquify dialog box**

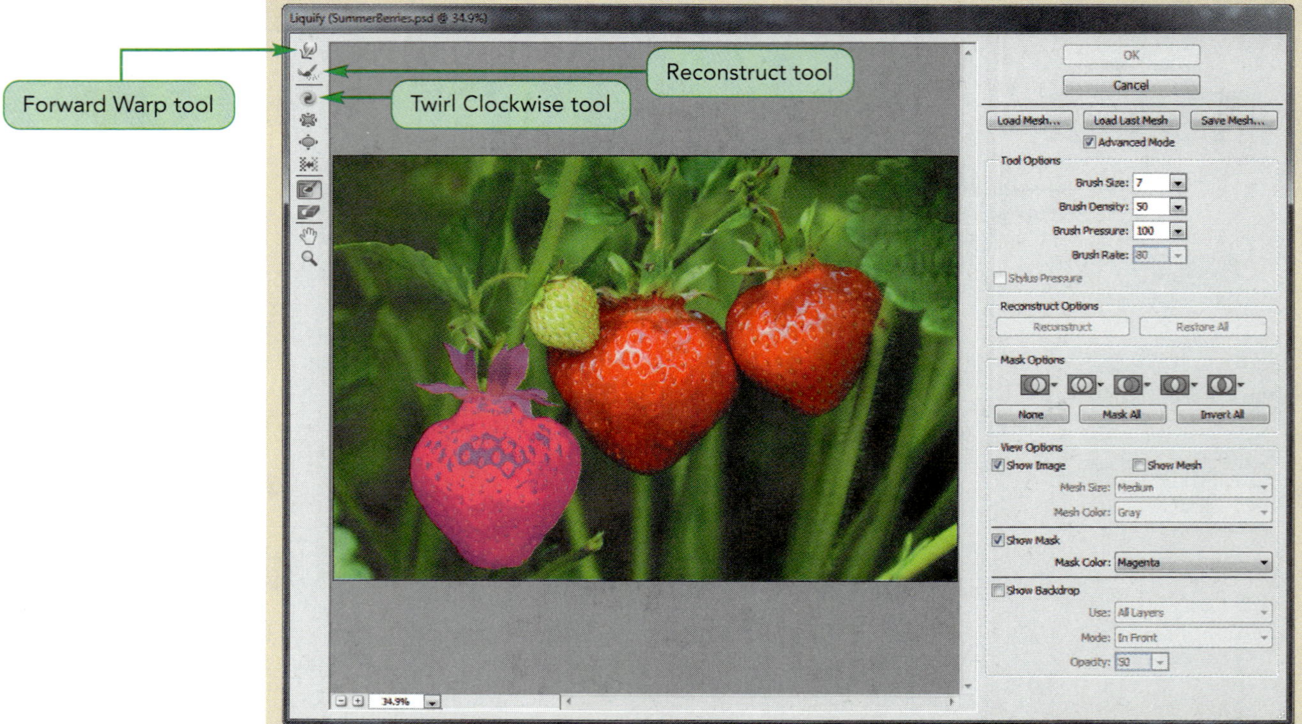

Catarina Belova/Shutterstock.com

You are now ready to liquify the unmasked parts of your image.

10. In the Tools panel of the Liquify dialog box, click the **Forward Warp Tool** button, set the brush size to **65**, point to the upper-left side of the image, and then drag the mouse pointer to the right.

The part of the image beneath the pointer is dragged to the right, as if it is made of putty.

Trouble? If the warp uncovers part of the background, which is made up of transparent pixels, undo it using the Reconstruct tool.

11. Click the **Reconstruct Tool** button, and then drag to paint over the warp you just created. Continue to drag until the image returns to its original state. (It will take several passes with the Reconstruct tool to get back to the original state.)

The Reconstruct tool works in much the same way the History Brush tool works. The history state you are reverting to is the state the image was in when you issued the Liquify command.

12. Click the **Twirl Clockwise Tool** button, and set the Brush Size to **105**.

13. Point to the middle of the strawberry on the right, and press and hold the mouse button. Look carefully inside the pointer: The image beneath the pointer has become a whirlpool and is rotating clockwise.

14. Change the Brush Rate to **100**, point to the right of the first whirlpool effect, and press and hold the mouse button. The pixels rotate more quickly than they did at a setting of 80.

15. Drag the pointer over the image, and watch the distortions take shape.

16. Continue to experiment with the different Liquify options by clicking different Liquify tools. If you are dissatisfied with a result, use the Reconstruct tool. If you would like to start over, use the Restore All button.

17. Click the **OK** button to liquify your image, and then deselect the selection. Unhide the **Berry Fun!!** layer. See Figure 5-44.

Figure 5-44 **Liquified image**

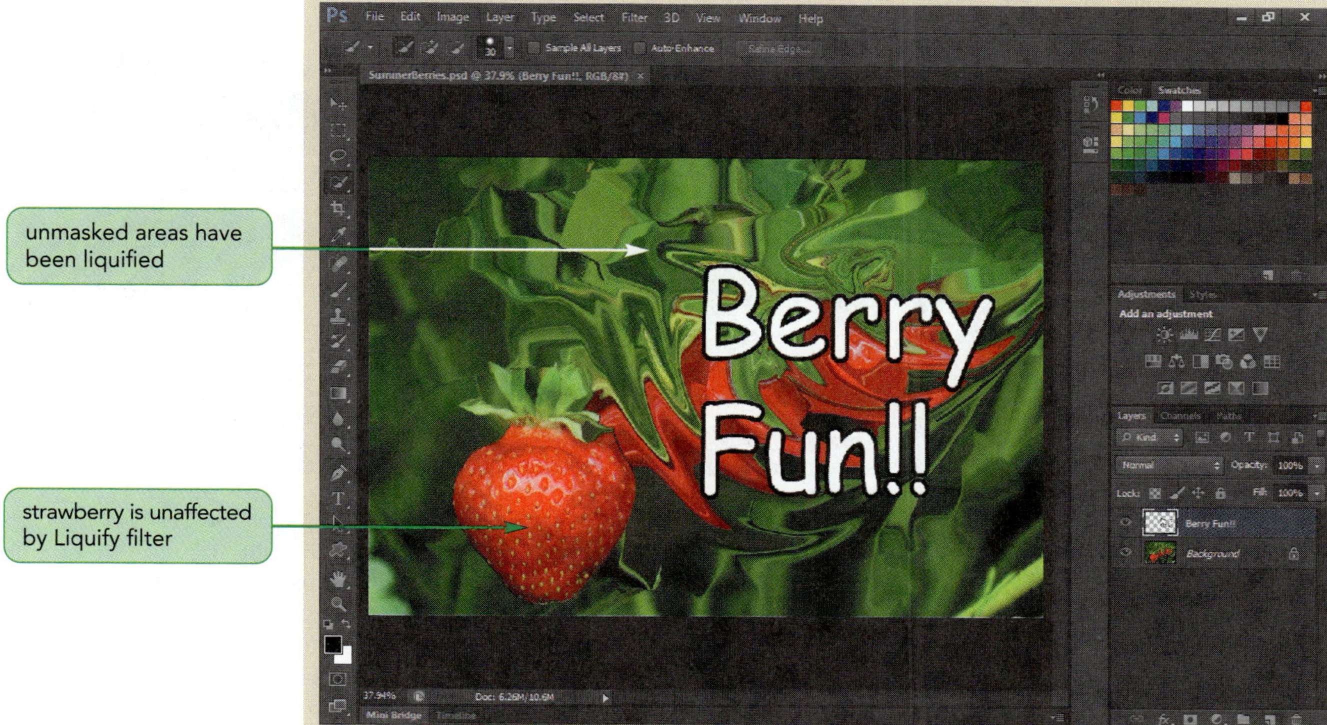

Catarina Belova/Shutterstock.com

The area surrounding the strawberry has an oil paint effect, but the strawberry itself is unchanged by the filter because you masked it.

18. Save **SummerBerries.psd**, and then close it.

Working with the Filter Gallery

The Filter Gallery includes nearly 50 filters that you can apply to an image. The filters can provide artistic effects—for example, turning your image into a colored pencil drawing or pastel painting—or distortions—making your image appear to glow or to be covered by a pane of glass. Figure 5-45 shows just a few of the effects you can achieve with filters from the gallery. All of the filters have been applied to the same image.

Figure 5-45 Four different filters applied to same image

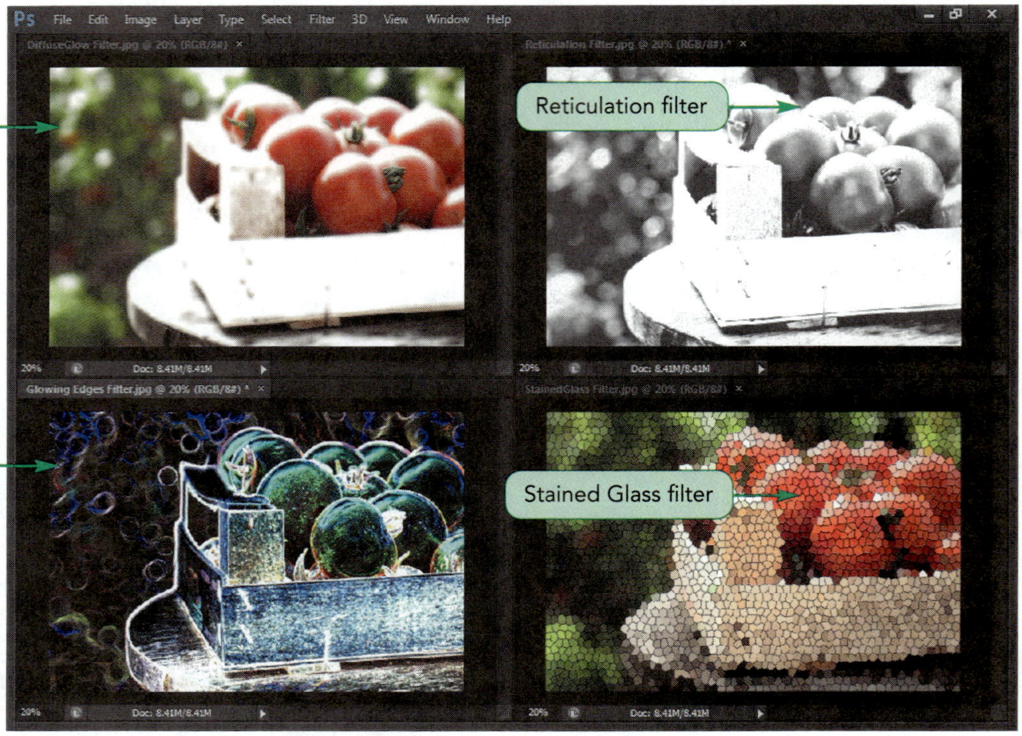

Jira Hera/Shutterstock.com

The Filter Gallery includes six categories of filter: Artistic, Brush Strokes, Distort, Sketch, Stylize, and Texture. Some filters, like the Sketch filters, use the current foreground and background colors to produce an effect. In addition, each filter has its own custom settings, which you can manipulate on the right side of the dialog box. You can also combine filters for unique effects by clicking the New effect layer icon at the bottom of the dialog box, or you can delete an effect by clicking the Delete effect layer icon. As you make changes to the filter or include additional filters, you can preview everything in the left pane of the dialog box. To see more or less of the image, you can click the Zoom Out or Zoom In icons at the bottom of the dialog box or type a zoom percentage. You can also pan the image by dragging the scroll boxes at the bottom and right side of the preview area.

To use the Filter Gallery:

1. Open **GoodFood2.psd**, located in the Photoshop5\Tutorial folder. Reset the default foreground and background colors, if necessary.
2. Click the **Channels** tab to display the Channels panel. This file includes a saved selection called Tomatoes. Notice that the tomato selection appears white on the channel thumbnail, and the rest of the image is black. This indicates that everything in the image except the tomato selection is masked.
3. On the menu bar, click **Select**, click **Load Selection**, confirm that **Tomatoes** is the selected Channel, and then click the **OK** button.
4. On the menu bar, click **Select**, click **Inverse**, click **Select** again, and then click **Save Selection**. In the Save Selection dialog box, type **NoTomatoes** in the Name box, and then click the **OK** button. Photoshop adds the new selection as an alpha channel in the Channels panel.

5. In the Channels panel, click the empty Eye icon box in the Show/Hide column to the left of the Tomatoes mask thumbnail so an Eye icon appears. Photoshop paints the masked area directly on the image using a translucent shade of red. See Figure 5-46.

Figure 5-46 Showing the mask on the image

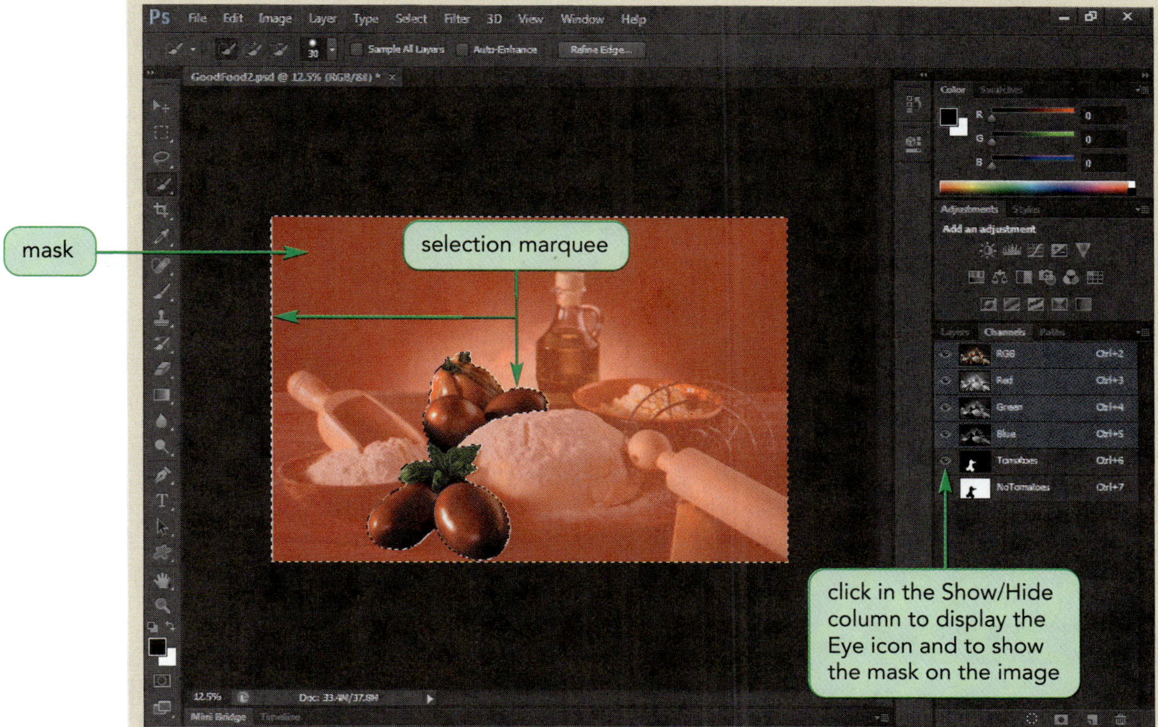

marco mayer/Shutterstock.com

You can turn on this feature whenever you want to get a clearer image of the mask so you can make modifications.

6. In the Channels panel, click the **Eye** icon to the left of the Tomatoes mask thumbnail to hide the image mask.

7. On the menu bar, click **Filter**, and then click **Filter Gallery**. The Filter Gallery opens, and the image appears in a preview window. The filter that was applied the last time the Filter Gallery was open is applied to the selection.

   Trouble? If Filter Gallery appears twice in the Filter menu, click the second instance.

8. Click the **Zoom Out** button at the bottom of the Filter Gallery, if necessary, so you can see the entire image.

9. In the middle panel of the Filter Gallery, click the **Artistic** folder to see the options available.

   Trouble? If the Artistic folder isn't visible, click the Expand icon to the left of the OK button.

10. Click the various Artistic options to preview them in the gallery. Depending on the speed of your computer, it might take some time to display the filter result. If so, Photoshop displays a progress bar at the bottom of the dialog box to the right of the zoom box.

Each of the filters has its own additional settings on the right side of the dialog box. For example, for the Colored Pencil filter, you can specify the pencil width, stroke pressure, and paper brightness.

11. Click the **Texture** folder and experiment with the different available textures. You can change the Texture settings to see their effect.

12. Click the **Stained Glass** filter. On the right side of the Filter Gallery, set the Cell Size to **25**, the Border Thickness to **5**, and the Light Intensity to **2**, and then click the **OK** button to see the filter applied to the image in the Document window. The background appears with a stained glass effect, while the tomatoes and basil still resemble a photograph.

13. Invert the selection, and then open the Filter Gallery. Photoshop applies the Stained Glass effect to the new selection because the Filter Gallery keeps the settings of the previous filter. You'll change the effect.

Trouble? If Photoshop applies a stained glass effect to the rest of the image without opening the gallery, you have selected the wrong Filter Gallery command. Photoshop lists your most recent filter command at the top of the Filter menu. Selecting it will just apply the same settings to the new selection. Undo the change, and then click the Filter Gallery command that is followed by ellipses (...).

14. Use the **Zoom Out** button to zoom the image out to **25%**. In the Filter Gallery, click the **Accented Edges** filter in the Brush Strokes folder. Set the Edge Width to **10**, set the Edge Brightness to **50**, and set the Smoothness to **11**. See Figure 5-47.

Figure 5-47 Image with two filters applied

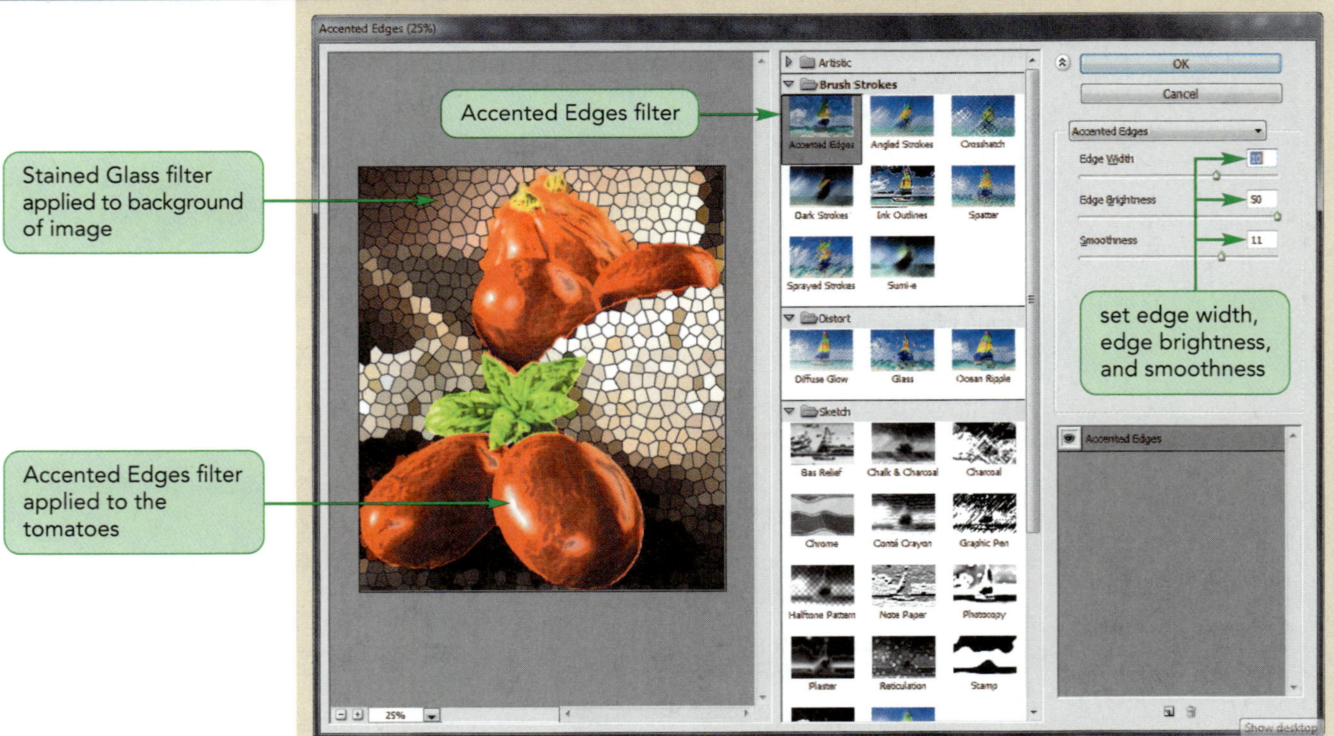

marco mayer/Shutterstock.com

15. Click the **OK** button to close the Filter Gallery.

You used selection masks, the Channels panel, and two filter effects to change a photograph into a completely different composition.

16. Deselect the tomatoes, save the file as **TomatoFilters.psd** in the Photoshop5\Tutorial folder, close the file, and exit Photoshop.

In this session, you learned how to use the Lasso tools and the Quick Selection tool to make selections. You learned how to save selections in the Channels panel and how to load selections to reuse them. You experimented with fills, including the Content-Aware fill, and you used the Content-Aware Move tool. You also learned how to work with masks and filters, including the Liquify filter and some of the filters in the Filter Gallery.

REVIEW

Session 5.2 Quick Check

1. Which tool lets you drag on the canvas to create a free-form selection marquee?
2. The ______________ fill feature lets you remove objects from an image and replace them with randomly generated versions of surrounding pixels.
3. What are fastening points?
4. True or False. Photoshop stores saved selections in the Layers panel.
5. The ______________ Selection tool works well if you want to select an area of an image with clearly defined edges.
6. To reuse a selection that you have saved, use the ______________ Selection command on the menu.
7. What does the Inverse command on the Select menu do?
8. Use the ______________ Mask tool in the Liquify dialog box to paint a mask on the part of an image you want to protect.

Practice the skills you learned in the tutorial using the same case scenario.

PRACTICE

Review Assignments

Data File needed for the Review Assignments: 4Pumpkins.jpg

Azar would like to include images in this year's annual report that emphasize his message that Food for Change not only unites urban and suburban youth, but also encourages cross-cultural understanding. He has given you an image of four pumpkins, and wants you to modify three of the pumpkins so each pumpkin has a different effect or filter, representing the variety of youth his program serves. He also wants you to create an image with two of the pumpkins that he can use for a postcard campaign at Halloween. Complete the following steps:

1. Start Photoshop while pressing the Ctrl+Alt+Shift keys, and click Yes to delete the Settings File when prompted. Reset Photoshop to the default Essentials workspace layout, and reset all tools.
2. Open **4Pumpkins.jpg**, located in the Photoshop5\Review folder provided with your Data Files.
3. Select the Background layer, if necessary, and then select the front pumpkin in the image, using the Elliptical Marquee tool with a fixed size of 1000 pixels by 1100 pixels. Then, use the Quick Selection tool to select the whole pumpkin. Don't include the stem when you make your selection.
4. Save the selection as **Pumpkin2**, and then deselect the pumpkin.
5. Select the pumpkin to the left of the first pumpkin you selected. Don't include any part of the first pumpkin you selected. Save the selection as **Pumpkin1**, and then deselect the pumpkin.
6. Select the pumpkin on the far right, but do not include any part of the first pumpkin you selected. Save the selection as **Pumpkin3**.
7. Load the Pumpkin1 selection, and on the Layers panel, add a new solid color fill layer with a green color fill at 50% opacity.
8. Open the History panel and take a snapshot of the current file.
9. Apply a Liquify filter to the second pumpkin using the Pumpkin2 selection. (*Hint*: Make sure to select the Background layer before you open the Liquify dialog box.) Try the Twirl Clockwise tool with a Brush Size of 225, a Brush Density of 100, a Brush Pressure of 100, and a Brush Rate of 100.
10. Load the Pumpkin3 selection, and apply the Chrome Filter (found in the Sketch folder) with a Detail setting of 7 and a Smoothness of 5.
11. Save the file as **Diversity.psd** in the Photoshop5\Review folder.
12. Revert the file to the snapshot you took in Step 8, then save the file as **GreenPumpkin.psd** in the same folder.
13. Load both the Pumpkin1 and Pumpkin2 selections. (*Hint*: When loading the second selection, make sure to select the Add to Selection option button in the Load Selection dialog box.) Then add to the combined selection by selecting the stems of the two pumpkins.
14. Select the Background layer, make the background color in the Tools panel black, and then copy the selection to the Clipboard.
15. Create a new file that is 10 inches wide and 8 inches high, select the Background Color as the Background Contents, and then click the OK button.
16. Paste the Clipboard contents into the new file.
17. Save the file as **2Pumpkins.psd** in the Photoshop5\Review folder, and then close both files.

Use your skills to select parts of an image to create interesting effects.

APPLY

Case Problem 1

Data Files needed for this Case Problem: Vacation.jpg, Marlin.jpg

Lake Shares Shirley Beaghan is the marketing director for Lake Shares, an online time-share company specializing in waterfront properties. She wants you to take two images and combine them to create a whimsical image for the Web site. You'll use selection tools and filter effects. Complete the following steps:

1. Start Photoshop while pressing the Ctrl+Alt+Shift keys, and click Yes to delete the Settings File when prompted. Reset Photoshop to the default Essentials workspace layout, and reset all tools.
2. Open **Vacation.jpg** and **Marlin.jpg**, located in the Photoshop5\Case1 folder provided with your Data Files.
3. In the Marlin.jpg file, select the marlin using the selection tools of your choice, copy it to the Clipboard and then, using Figure 5-48 as a guide, paste it into the Vacation image four times. Resize, rotate, and reposition three of the copies of the marlin so they appear to be jumping out of the water beyond the beach umbrella.

Figure 5-48 **Sample Lake Shares Web site image**

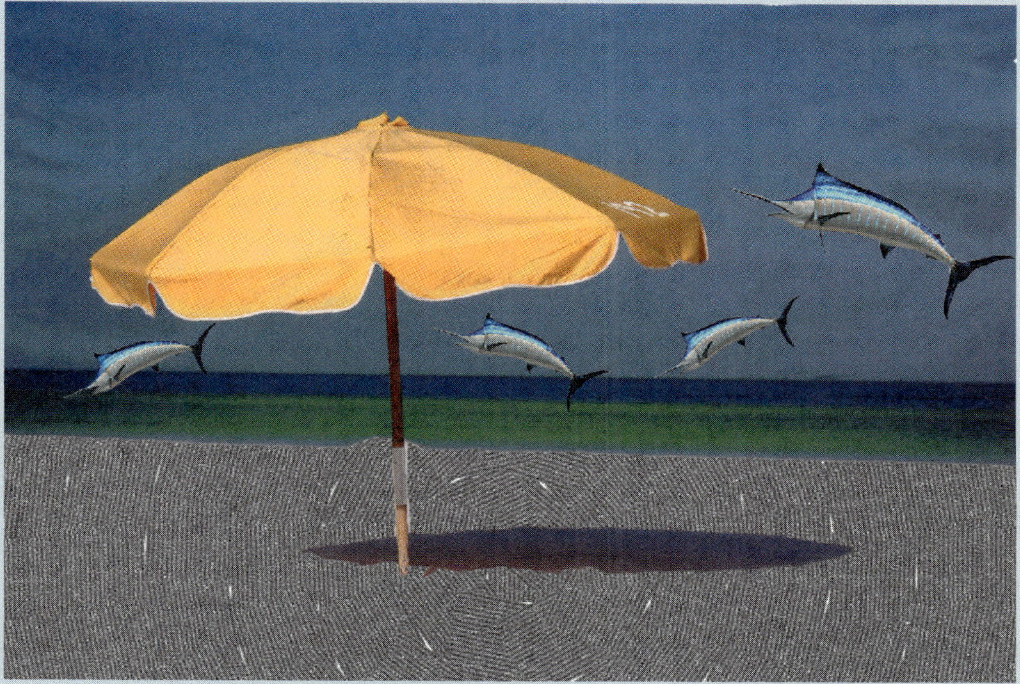

Danny Rehbein/Shutterstock.com; Paul Brennan/Shutterstock.com

4. Reposition the fourth copy of the marlin to the right of the top of the umbrella, and transform and rotate it so it is slightly larger than the fish in the water and appears to be jumping into the photograph from the right side of the image.
5. Select the Background layer, open the Liquify dialog box, and in Advanced Mode, use the Mask All button under Mask Options to mask the entire image. Thaw the part of the mask that covers the sky. (*Hint:* Remember that if you accidentally thaw outside the sky, you can use the Freeze Mask tool to repair the mask.)
6. Apply any of the Liquify filters to the sky.
7. Use the Color Range command to select some of the water tones, and add a bright green color fill layer to the selection. Make sure to lower the opacity so some of the texture of the water shows through.

8. Select the sand (but not the shadow on the sand) and fill it with a scripted pattern of your choosing.
9. Apply any other effects to other parts of the image, and then save the image as **BeachShow.psd** in the Photoshop5\Case1 folder.

Using Figure 5-49 as a guide, combine images in a single composition.

CREATE

Case Problem 2

Data Files needed for this Case Problem: Pitcher.psd, Vase.jpg

PierCeramics You are the owner of PierCeramics, a ceramics studio on Sanibel Island in Florida. You have many photographs of your work, and think you might be able to turn those photographs into digital art to sell along with your pottery. You'll experiment with selections, filters, and effects using two photographs of your pottery. Complete the following steps:

1. Start Photoshop while pressing the Ctrl+Alt+Shift keys, and click Yes to delete the Settings File when prompted. Reset Photoshop to the default Essentials workspace layout, and reset all tools.
2. Open **Pitcher.psd**, located in the Photoshop5\Case2 folder provided with your Data Files.
3. Apply a scripted pattern fill to the area around the pitcher, and apply a filter to the pitcher. Save the file as **PatternPitcher.psd** and close it.
4. Open **Vase.jpg**, located in the Photoshop5\Case2 folder.

Figure 5-49 **Sample PierCeramics image**

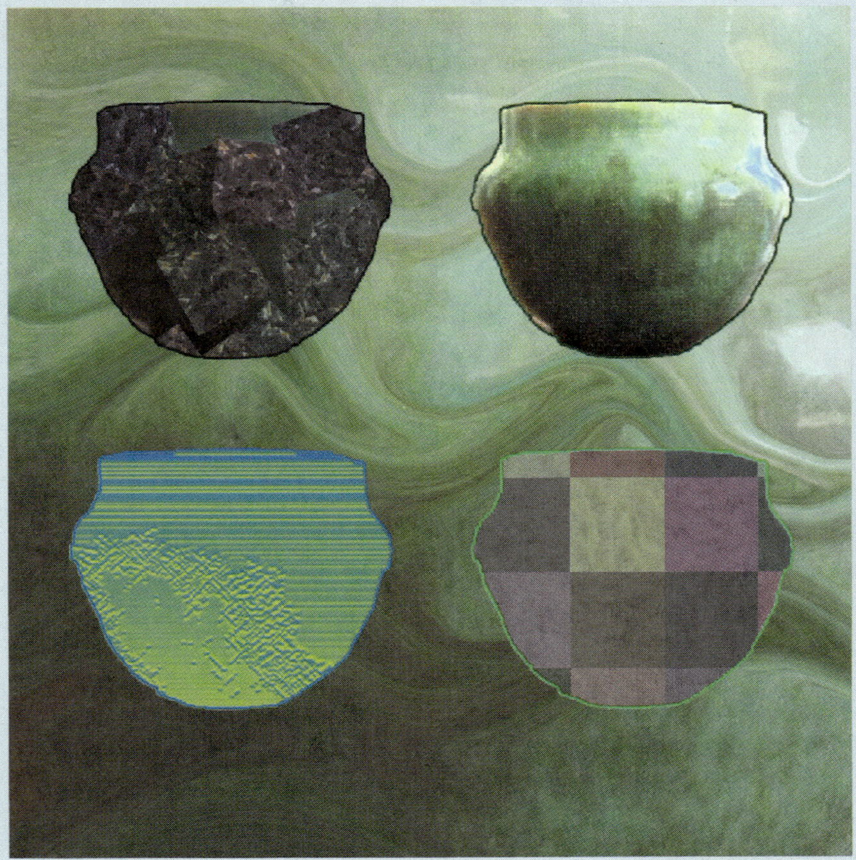

Jane Hosie-Bounar

5. Using Figure 5-49 as a guide, create a new file with a transparent background and the following settings: Width: 10 inches, Height: 10 Inches, Resolution: 180 ppi, and Color Mode: RGB.
6. Select the vase in Vase.jpg, and copy it into the new file five times. Change the size of the vase on the first layer so it extends beyond the edge of the canvas on all four sides and acts as a background for the other layers.
7. Apply a Liquify filter to the background vase.
8. Arrange and resize the other vases so that they are all visible on the canvas. (*Hint*: If you want them all to be the same size, select all four layers in the Layers panel before resizing.)
9. Apply different filters to two of the vases, and adjust the filter settings until you achieve the effects you want. (*Hint:* Some of the filters use the foreground and background color to achieve an effect, so experiment with different colors until you achieve the effect you want.)
10. Take a snapshot of the current state in the History panel.
11. Apply two different scripted fills to the other two vases. (*Hint:* Remember that you must select each vase on its layer before applying a fill or the whole layer will be filled.) In Figure 5-49, the lower-right vase uses a light marble cross weave fill. The upper-left vase uses a black marble random fill.
12. Add a 5-pixel stroke around each of the four vases. Use different colors for each of the strokes.
13. Save the file as **FilterVase.psd** in the Photoshop5\Case2 folder.
14. Return the file to the previous history state captured in the snapshot.
15. Create a new document based on the current history state. (*Hint:* Use the Create new document from current state icon at the bottom of the History panel.)
16. Flatten the new document image. Save the new file as **NoFill.psd**, and then close the file.
17. Return to the final history state by selecting the last entry in the History panel. Apply a Brightness/Contrast adjustment to lighten up the background to your liking, and then save FilterVase.psd in the Photoshop5\Case2 folder and close it.

Extend your skills to transform images for a bookstore.

CHALLENGE

Case Problem 3

There are no Data Files needed for this Case Problem.

GoBooks Gary Smith is the owner of a small bookstore in Shawano, Wisconsin. He has asked for your help in developing a poster he will display in the storefront window for the month of January that shows that books can take you anywhere—even when you're snowed in. Your focus for the first poster is children's books. You'll use one landscape image and at least two "character" images from the Web or your own collection to create the poster. Complete the following steps:

1. Start Photoshop while pressing the Ctrl+Alt+Shift keys, and click Yes to delete the Settings File when prompted. Reset Photoshop to the default Essentials workspace layout, and reset all tools.
2. Go to the MorgueFile or the Creative Commons Web site and search for a landscape or cityscape photograph with which you would like to work. Alternatively, use one of your own photographs of a landscape or cityscape. You'll be adding filters and effects to change a real landscape into a storybook landscape. Before you download any images, check the licensing information to make sure that they can be remixed without attribution and used for commercial purposes. Download the landscape image you have chosen.

3. Find images of at least two "characters" for your poster. Your characters can be animals, insects, plants, statues, tea pots—whatever you feel comfortable working with. Download the character images you have chosen.
4. Confirm that all the images you have downloaded are the same resolution before you combine them. If they aren't, change their resolution before combining the files.
5. Using WordPad, which is available from the Accessories menu of the All Programs menu in Windows 7, create a new document and keep a record of the steps you take to create the final image. You don't need to record steps that you later undo. Save the document as **Process.rtf** in the Photoshop5\Case3 folder.
6. Using the skills you learned in this tutorial, create a composition that you think would catch a customer's eye. The focus of this exercise is to mix realistic photographic images with images that have been altered to look painted or computer generated. Use selection tools, filters, fills, and the drawing tools for your composition. Use the Brush tools and the History Brush tool to refine your work.
7. In any font, add a headline to the poster that reads **Go Books Go Anywhere**.
8. EXPLORE — Warp the title text. To do so, click the Create warped text button on the options bar for one of the Text tools, and then click a Style setting such as Bulge.
9. EXPLORE — Transform or warp at least one of the characters you place in the landscape, either by resizing, rotating, or warping it. (*Hint*: To warp a selection, make an initial selection, click Select on the menu bar, and then click Transform Selection. On the options bar, click the Switch between free transform and warp modes button. When you are in warp mode, warp the selection by dragging one of the handles on the selection.)
10. EXPLORE — Use Puppet Warp to change the position of the limbs of one of your characters. (*Hint:* On the menu bar, click Edit, and then click Puppet Warp to add pins to one of the animals or objects in the poster and manipulate them. For example, click to place anchor pins in a knee joint or elbow, then click in a different spot to add a pin, and then drag that second pin to warp the limb.) In Figure 5-50, the wild turkey's legs have been manipulated with the Puppet Warp feature in all four copies of the turkey.

Figure 5-50 Sample GoBooks poster

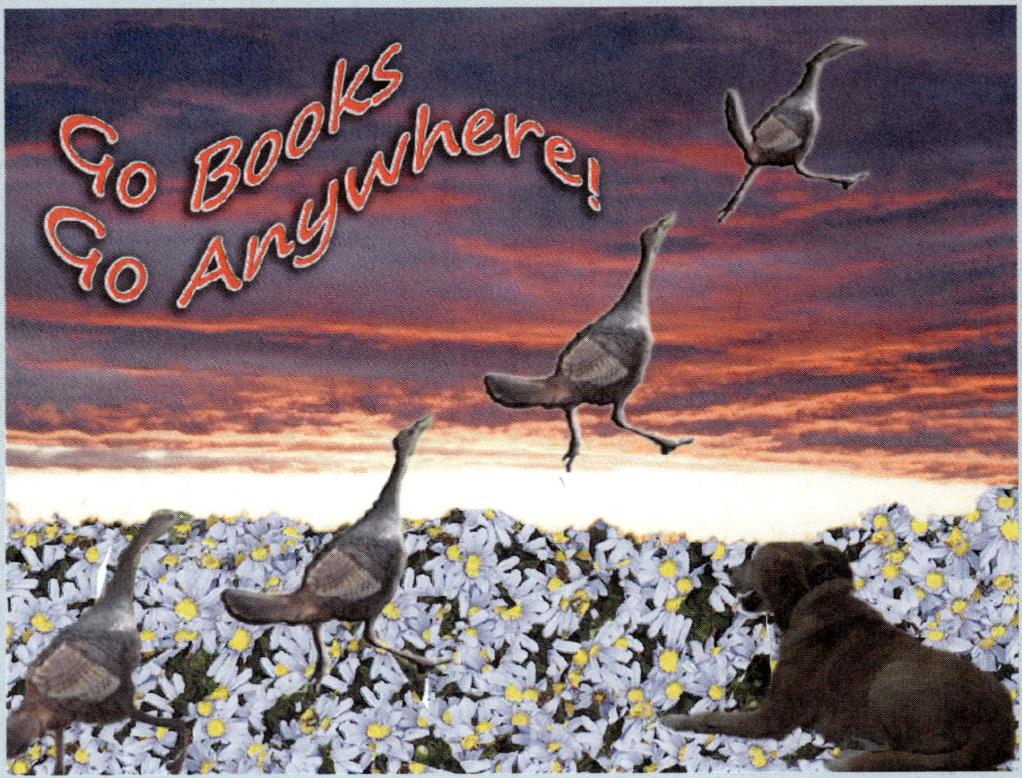

Jane Hosie-Bounar

11. Save Process.rtf in the Photoshop5\Case 3 folder.
12. Save the file as **GoBooks.psd** in the Photoshop5\Case3 folder, and exit Photoshop.

Use your compositing skills to create an eye-catching image.

CREATE

Case Problem 4

Data Files needed for this Case Problem: Smile.jpg, Spanner.jpg

DBF Dental Aisha Gomez is the marketing manager for DBF Dental, a dental supply company in Chicago, Illinois. The company's customer base includes dentists and orthodontists in Iowa, Wisconsin, Indiana, and Minnesota. Recently, another dental supply company has moved into the area. However, there have been reports of inferior products from some of DBF's former customers who switched suppliers. Aisha wants you to develop a new campaign that addresses this issue and tries to win back the customers. You'll create an image that uses humor to address the topic. Complete the following steps:

1. Start Photoshop while pressing the Ctrl+Alt+Shift keys, and click Yes to delete the Settings File when prompted. Reset Photoshop to the default Essentials workspace layout, and reset all tools.
2. Create a new 300-ppi file with dimensions and a background color of your choosing. Place **Smile.jpg**, located in the Photoshop5\Case4 folder, on the canvas of your new file so it fits, and then rasterize the Smile layer. Flatten the image and then save the file as **DBFDental.psd**.
3. Use your compositing skills to create an image that uses the unexpected or the humorous to get your point across, as shown in the example in Figure 5-51. The sample image also uses the file called Spanner.jpg, included with your Data Files. You can use this file, or find another image to get your humorous message across.

Figure 5-51 **Sample DBF Dental ad**

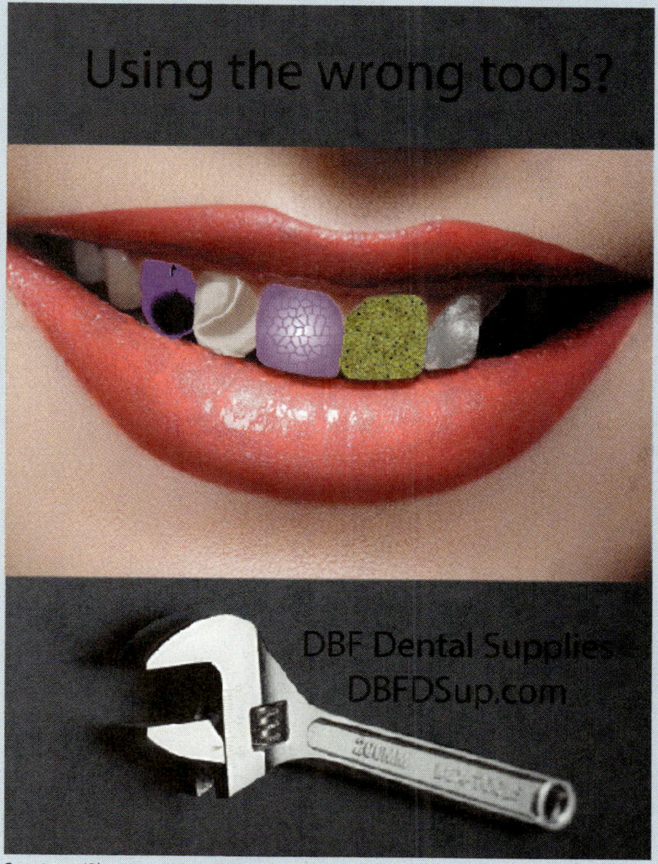

Seprimor/Shutterstock.com; Garsya/Shutterstock.com

4. Save your selections as channels and name them. For example, save each tooth as its own selection.
5. Save at least two layer comps that show different ideas or arrangements. If you want to create different fill effects for the same selection, make sure to apply the fill to its own layer so you can turn it on and off.
6. When you have finished editing the file, save it, and exit Photoshop.

ENDING DATA FILES

Photoshop5 →

Tutorial

AllOrange.psd
BlackWhiteRed.psd
Flowerbed.jpg
GoodFood1.psd
PumpkinMoved.jpg
RainbowCorn.psd
SolePumpkin.psd
StrawberryGlow.psd
Stroke.psd
SummerBerries.psd
SwirledCorn.jpg
TomatoFilters.psd
TomatoGarden.jpg
TwoPumpkins.psd
VegetableBevel.psd

Review

2Pumpkins.psd
Diversity.psd
GreenPumpkin.psd

Case1

BeachShow.psd

Case2

FilterVase.psd
NoFill.psd
PatternPitcher.psd

Case3

GoBooks.psd
Process.rtf

Case4

DBFDental.psd

TUTORIAL 6

Designing with Text

Using Text and Text Effects

OBJECTIVES

Session 6.1
- Work with text layers and the Type tools
- Use the Typography workspace to enter and modify point type and paragraph type
- Assign fonts and other text formats
- Work with vertical text
- Check spelling, and find and replace text

Session 6.2
- Apply a style to text
- Set tracking and scaling for individual characters
- Specify a baseline shift
- Bend text to a closed path
- Apply a clipping mask to fill text with an image, pattern, and gradient

Case | *RC Investments*

You have taken a summer internship with a small investment firm called RC Investments, which was founded in 1979 by Rose Clarke's father, Richard. In 2009, Rose took over the company, which helps middle-income people manage their assets by developing an investment strategy best suited to their needs. Rose was the sole employee when she took over the firm, but word of mouth has helped her grow the firm to five investment professionals. She has asked you to create a marketing campaign to help her increase the firm's client base. You'll use the Photoshop Typography workspace and many of the text tools and features to create comps that you'll present to her for the proposed campaign. You'll add text to images and modify text fonts; you'll also adjust the scaling and tracking, alignment, and rotation of text. Finally, you'll apply styles to text and fill text with images, gradients, and color.

STARTING DATA FILES

Photoshop6 →

Tutorial
Money.psd
RCPath.psd
RCVertical.psd
RightChoice.psd

Review
RCRetire.psd

Case1
Fireworks.jpg
Shuttle.jpg

Case2
Gourmet.jpg

Case3
Luxury.jpg

Case4
Soccer.jpg

SESSION 6.1 VISUAL OVERVIEW

The **font size** is the height of the text measured in points. A **point**, abbreviated as *pt*, is 1/72 of an inch.

Use settings in the Paragraph panel to **align** (or line up) text at the left, right, or center edges of a text bounding box.

The Hyphenate setting determines whether a word breaks across two lines.

Left-aligned text lines up at the left edge of the text box you draw with the Horizontal Type tool.

To add interest to the copy in a composition, you can apply effects to the text; for example, this text has a style from the Styles panel applied.

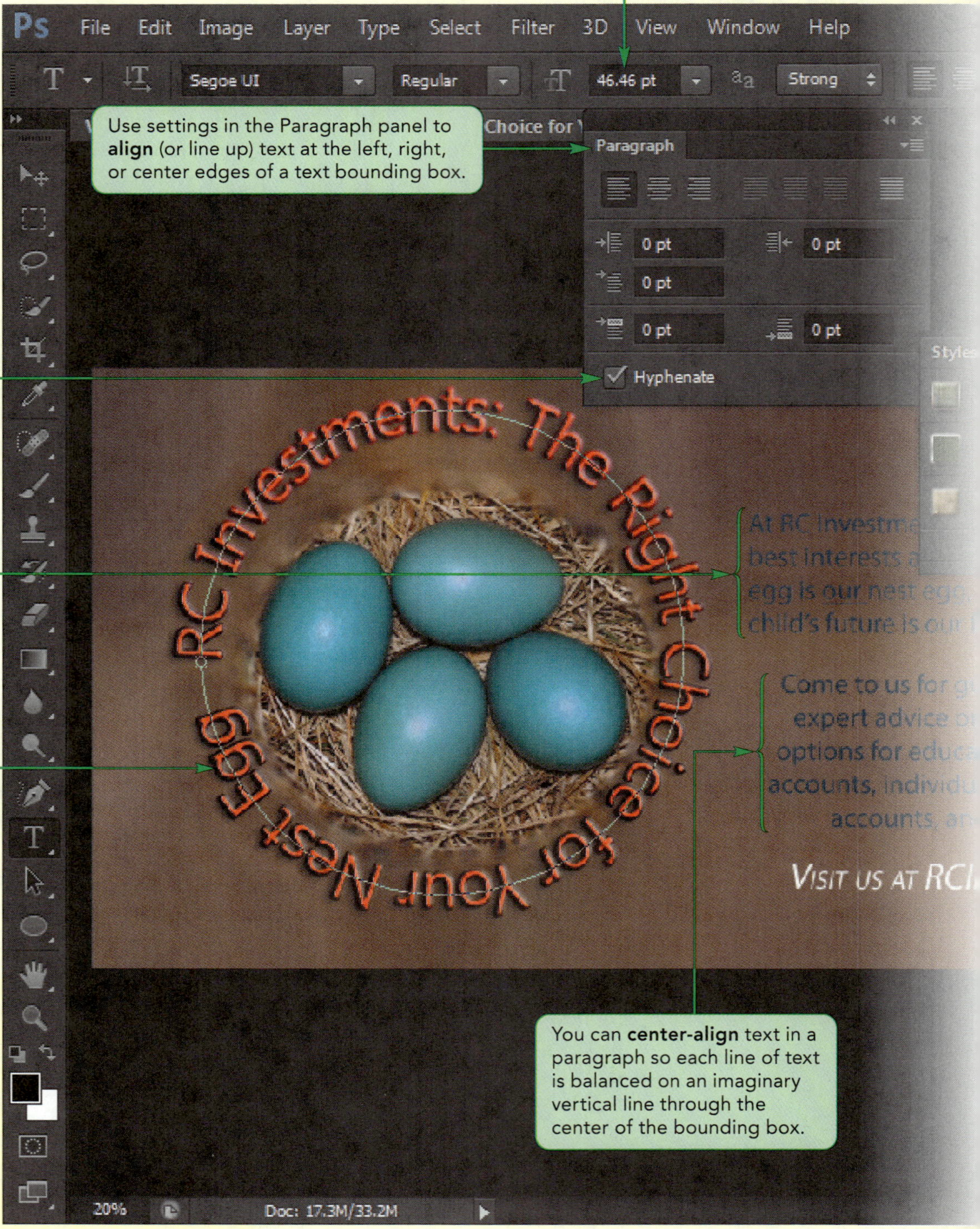

You can **center-align** text in a paragraph so each line of text is balanced on an imaginary vertical line through the center of the bounding box.

Steven Russell Smith Photos/Shutterstock.com

TEXT LAYERS AND PANELS

For more control, you can modify the **kerning**, which is the spacing between a pair of characters.

You can specify font family and font style in the Character panel.

To fine-tune the appearance of text, adjust the **tracking**, which is the spacing between all of the characters in selected text or a paragraph.

Quickly apply text effects by clicking a style button.

Scale text vertically or horizontally by changing the percentage settings.

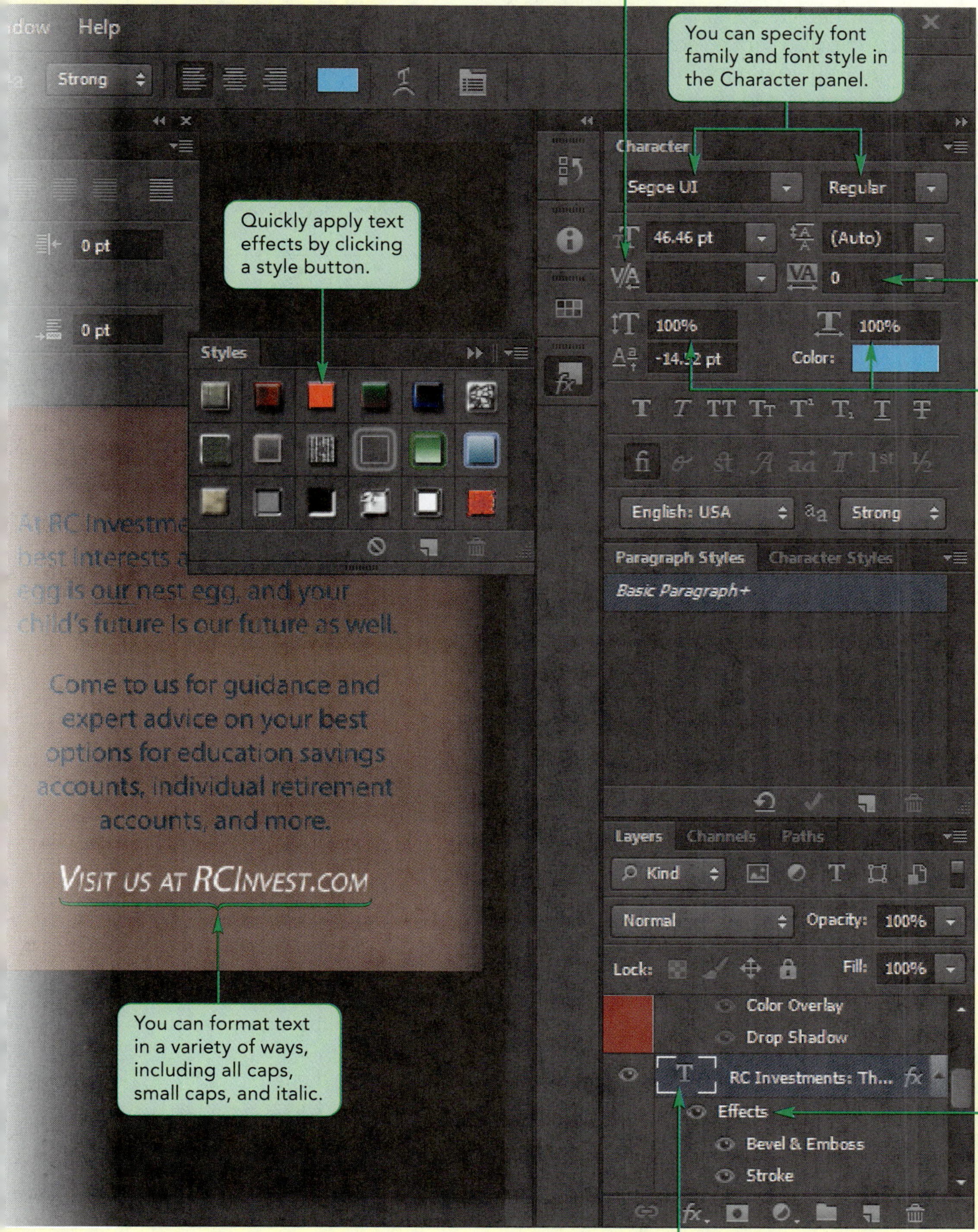

You can format text in a variety of ways, including all caps, small caps, and italic.

Text effects change the appearance of text and are listed in the Layers panel grouped with the layer to which they apply.

Text in Photoshop is stored on **text layers**.

Introducing Text Layers

Photoshop is first and foremost a digital image-editing tool, but it also provides a variety of text tools that let you format and arrange text in a document in much the same way you would format text in a page layout application. In fact, new features in Photoshop CS6, including the new Character Styles and Paragraph Styles panels, make it easier than ever to achieve the text effects you want in your compositions. When you add text to a Photoshop image, it is added as a vector object. This means that you can resize it, rotate it, stretch it, change its color, or apply a style to it without affecting its resolution. You can also stroke vector text to add an outline that makes it stand out. However, if you want to use the full set of image-editing tools available in Photoshop, you need to rasterize text to change it to a bitmap object. This gives you the flexibility to fill the text with an image, apply filters, and use other image-editing features; however, once you rasterize text, you can no longer edit it as text.

The Photoshop interface uses the terms *text* and *type* interchangeably. The tools you use to add text are called **Type tools**, but text is stored on text layers. See Figure 6-1.

Figure 6-1 Text layers in a composition

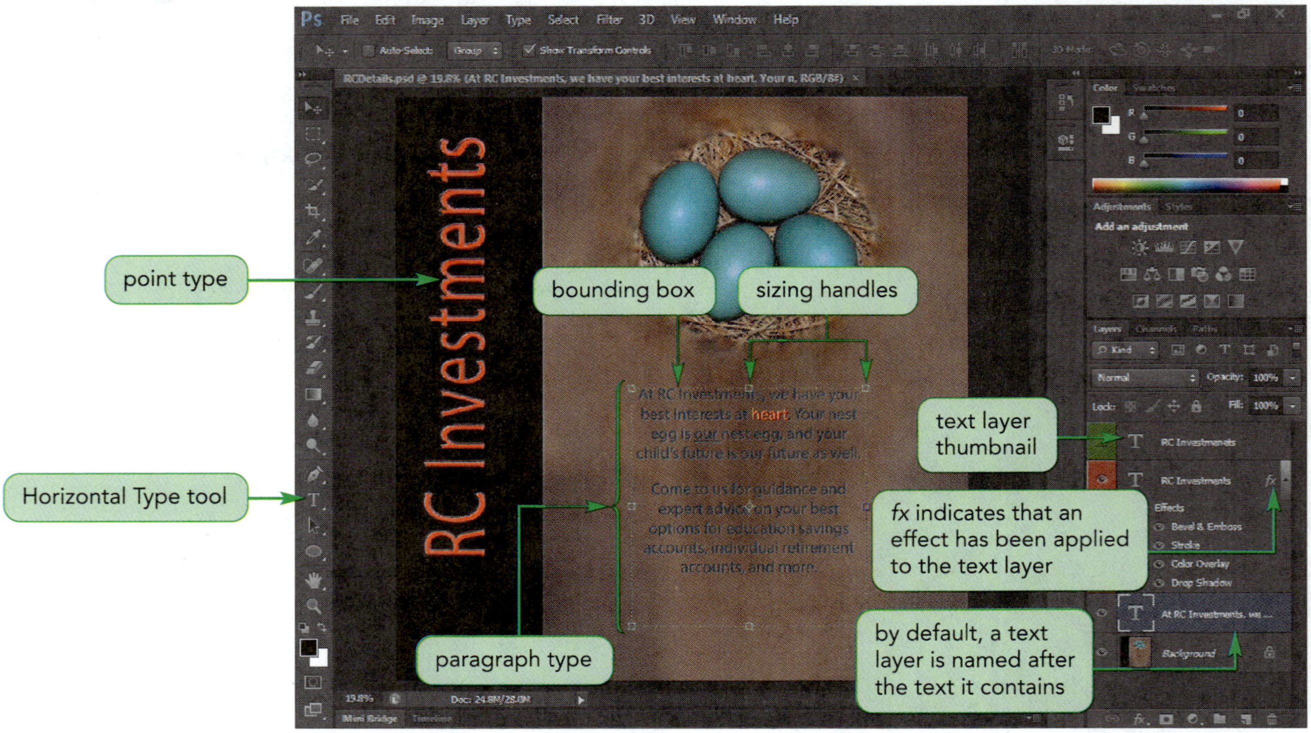

Steven Russell Smith Photos/Shutterstock.com

Text layers follow the same hierarchy rules as other layers in the Layers panel. A text layer on the canvas appears on top of any layers that it is on top of in the Layers panel. You can clip adjustments to text layers and set their opacity and blending modes. You can also select text layers, and move, group, copy, merge, and delete them.

A text layer is distinguished in the Layers panel by a Text thumbnail, which is a square with the letter *T* in it. By default, a text layer takes as its name the text that is included in the layer, but you have the option to rename the layer just as you can rename any other layer. When you apply an effect to a text layer, an *fx* appears to the right of the layer name in the Layers panel, and the details of the effect are listed beneath the layer name.

If you show transform controls when a text layer is selected, you will see that the text is contained in a bounding box. You can manipulate the bounding box in the same way you manipulate any other object. You can drag a handle to resize it, or use the rotate pointer to rotate it. When you resize a bounding box that contains text, you also resize the text.

Photoshop lets you enter two kinds of text: point type (also called character type) and paragraph type. **Point type** or **character type** is text you type after selecting one of the Type tools and clicking directly on the canvas to type. At the point you click, Photoshop adds a **baseline**, which is the line on which the text will rest as you type. The baseline extends with each new character. You can move to a new line by pressing the Enter key, and Photoshop will add a new baseline on the new line. When you have finished entering point type and move to a new task, Photoshop encloses the point type in a bounding box that you can see if you select the layer again and turn on transform controls or layer edges.

Paragraph type is text that is contained in a bounding box whose dimensions you specify by activating a Type tool and then clicking on the canvas and dragging. Once you define the dimensions of the bounding box, you can start to type, and the text will appear in the box. As you type, text wraps to a new line when it reaches the border of the bounding box. If you type more text than can fit in the bounding box, it is hidden unless you change the dimensions of the bounding box by dragging a transform control.

After you select a Type tool, you can use the options bar to define the font, font style, font size, and anti-aliasing method for the text, as well as its alignment. See Figure 6-2.

Figure 6-2 **Type tool options**

Icon	Tool	Description
	Toggle text orientation	Switches between the Horizontal and Vertical Type tools
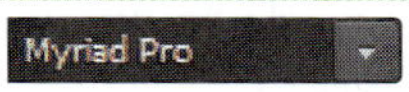	Set the font family	Lets you preview and choose from a list of fonts installed on your computer; the font name in the box varies depending on the most recent font selection
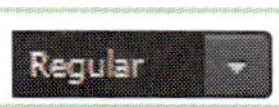	Set the font style	Applies styles such as bold, italic, and bold condensed
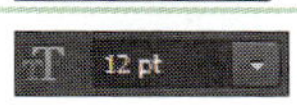	Set the font size	Allows you to select from a list of font sizes or type a custom size in the text box
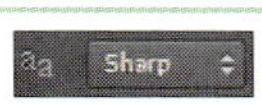	Set the anti-aliasing method	Sets the anti-alias setting, which determines the smoothness of text; settings include None, Sharp, Crisp, Strong, and Smooth
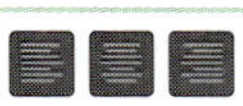	Left align text, Center text, and Right align text	Aligns text within a text bounding box on the canvas
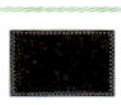	Set the text color	Opens the Color Picker (Text Color) dialog box where you can use the color ramp and color field to select a color or enter color values; the color of this icon varies depending on the most recent text color selection
	Create warped text	Opens the Warp Text dialog box, where you can apply a style and/or horizontal and vertical distortions
	Toggle the Character and Paragraph panels	Toggles between the Character and Paragraph panels

INSIGHT

Using the Typography Workspace

When you are working with a lot of text in a composition, you'll find that the Typography workspace has many of the tools you'll need. The Typography workspace provides character formatting tools in the Character panel and paragraph formatting tools in the Paragraph panel. The Character and Paragraph panels appear in the Typography workspace in their own tab group, stacked with some of the panels you are already familiar with, including the Layers, Channels, and Paths tab group. In addition, the History, Info, Swatches, and Styles panels are collapsed to icons to the left of the Character panel. You can switch between the Character and Paragraph panels depending on whether you are formatting individual characters, words, or entire paragraphs. The Typography workspace also includes a Paragraph Styles panel and a Character Styles panel, where you can store any styles that you create. Using the many tools available in the Typography workspace will streamline your workflow whenever you work with text-heavy documents or want an easy way to apply consistent formats across a composition.

You'll use both point type and paragraph type to work on the compositions you'll submit to Rose for the new RC Investments marketing campaign.

Adding and Modifying Point Type

In Photoshop, you can add two different kinds of point type: horizontal and vertical. **Horizontal type** flows from left to right along a horizontal line. You create horizontal type using the Horizontal Type tool in the Tools panel. **Vertical type** runs from top to bottom along a vertical line. You can rotate horizontal type 90 degrees so it has a vertical orientation in your composition, but when you do so, the characters themselves are also rotated 90 degrees. If you want the characters in vertical type to have a horizontal orientation, you need to enter the type using the Vertical Type tool. See Figure 6-3.

Figure 6-3 **Horizontal and vertical type**

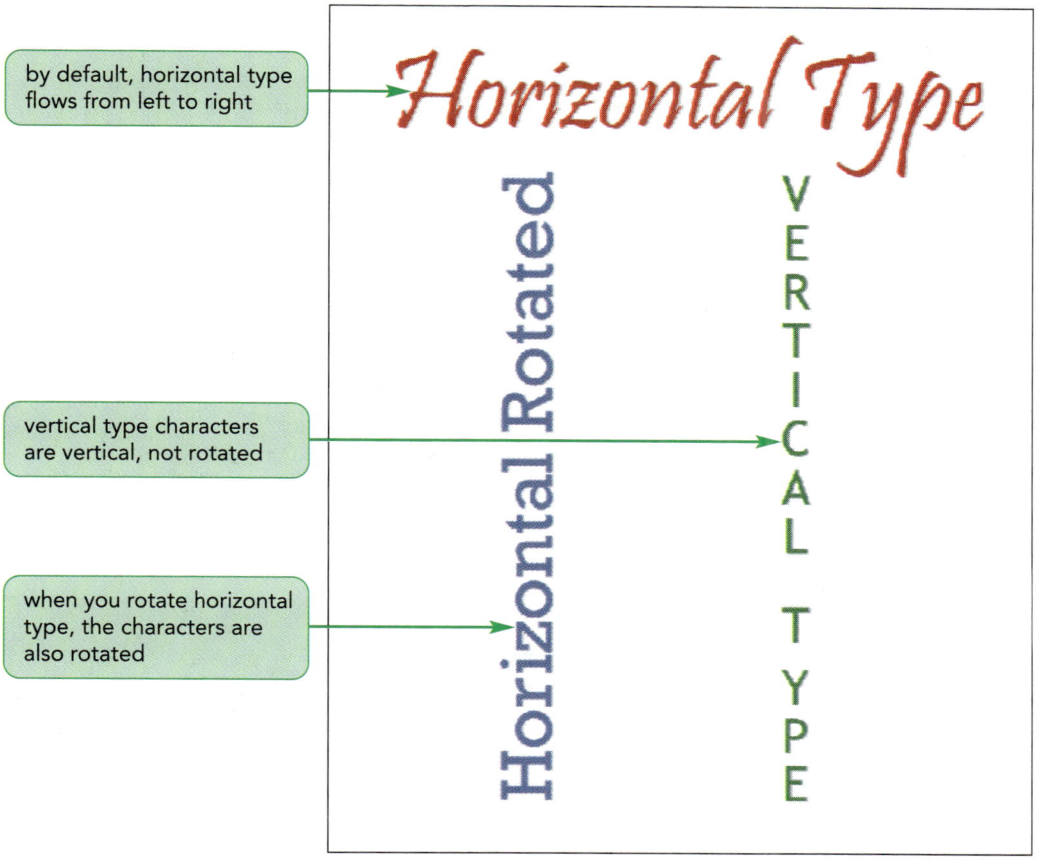

When you add point type, you are in text mode. In **text mode**, a blinking **cursor**, or vertical line, appears at the end of the text that you type, indicating that you can continue to type with the same settings. A horizontal baseline also appears under the text as you type. The type rests on that line unless you specify a baseline shift, which you will do later in this tutorial.

Once you add a point type layer, you can modify it. For example, you can change its font, font size, color, or style. Styles include Regular, Italic, Bold, and Bold Italic. If a font family doesn't include a style that you want to apply, you can apply a **faux style**, which is a style generated by Photoshop when an attribute, such as bold, is unavailable in a font family. For example, the Pristina font includes only regular characters. If you want to make a Pristina character bold, you have to use the Faux Bold button in the Character panel to have Photoshop generate a bold version of the character.

REFERENCE

Adding Point Type to an Image

- In the Tools panel, click the Horizontal Type tool or the Vertical Type tool.
- On the options bar, specify the font, font style, font size, anti-aliasing method, alignment, and color.
- Click the canvas at the location you want the text to appear, and type the text.
- On the options bar, click the Commit button.

You'll use a photograph of robin's eggs as the basis for the ad you'll present to Rose, and you'll add point type to it.

To add point type to a file:

1. Start Photoshop while pressing the **Ctrl+Alt+Shift** keys, and click **Yes** to delete the Settings File when prompted. Reset Photoshop to the default Essentials workspace layout, and then reset all tools.
2. Navigate to the Photoshop6\Tutorial folder included with your Data Files, and open **Right Choice.psd**. Press the **Ctrl+0** keys to fit the image in the window.
3. Display the rulers, and then add vertical guides at 1 1/4 inches and 2 inches on the horizontal ruler. Add two horizontal guides at 3/4 inches and 1 1/2 inches on the vertical ruler.
4. In the Tools panel, click the **Horizontal Type Tool** button T. The options bar displays settings for the Horizontal Type tool.
5. On the options bar, click the **Set the font family** button Myriad Pro. Photoshop lists the fonts available on your system. To the right of the font name, you can see a preview of the font. See Figure 6-4.

Figure 6-4 **Available fonts**

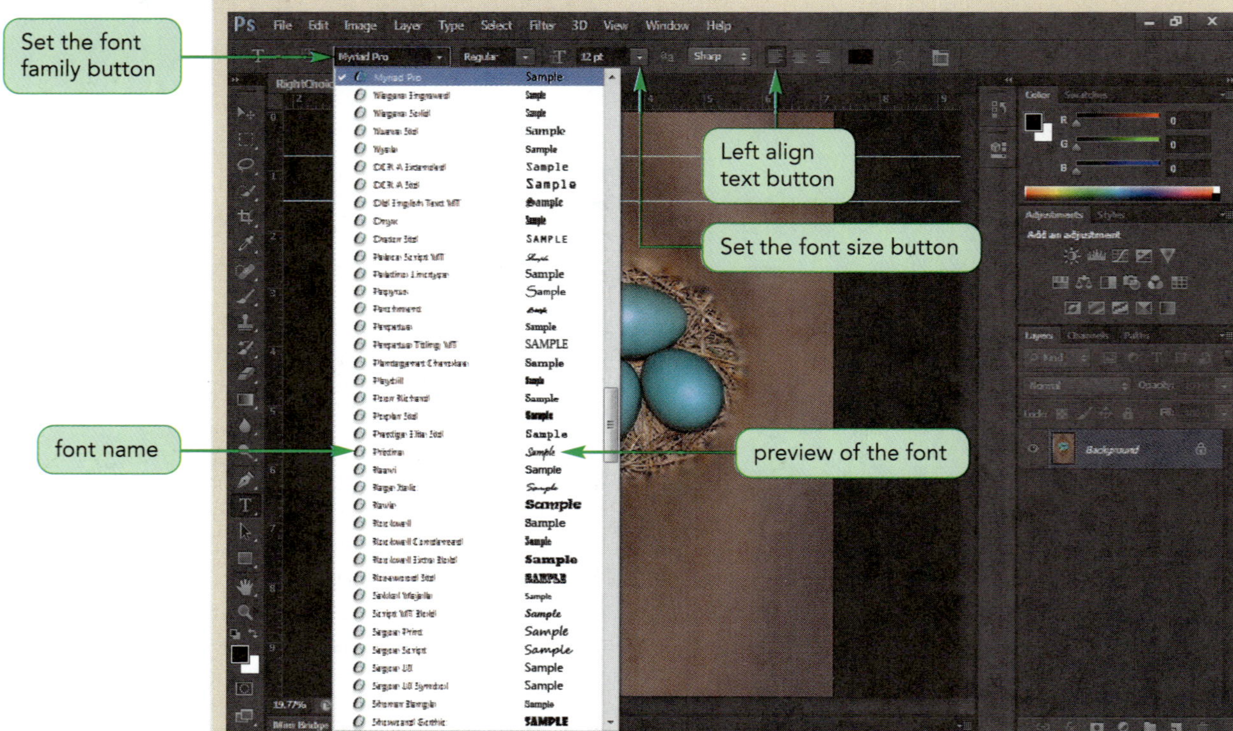

Steven Russell Smith Photos/Shutterstock.com

6. In the font family list, click **Pristina**, and on the options bar, click the **Set the font size** button 12 pt, and then click **48 pt**. Click the **Left align text** button, if necessary.

   Trouble? If you don't have Pristina, choose a different font.

7. Click the **Set the text color** button to open the Color Picker (Text Color) dialog box, and enter the following values: R=**0**, G=**102**, B=**102**. Click the **OK** button to close the dialog box.

   You are now ready to type text that will have the settings you specified.

8. Click at the intersection of the top horizontal guide and the left vertical guide, and type **Who's**. See Figure 6-5.

Figure 6-5 **Adding point type**

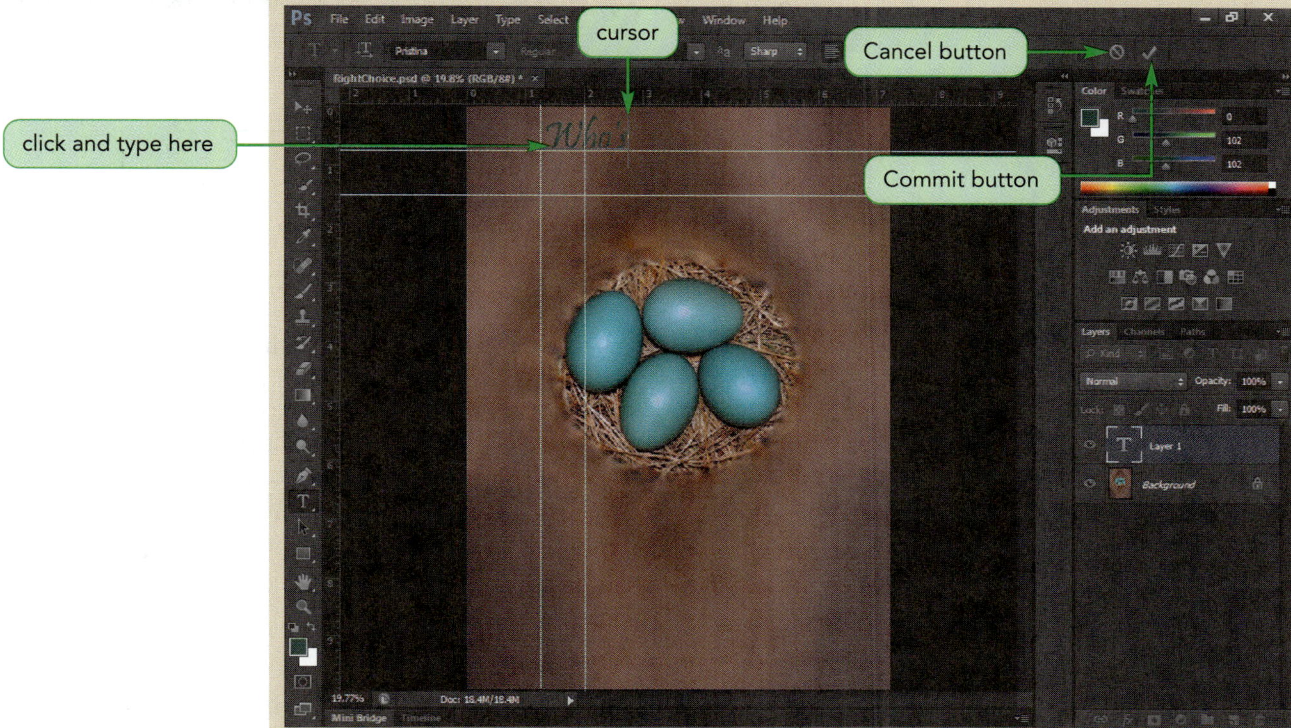

Steven Russell Smith Photos/Shutterstock.com

Because the text is left-aligned, it starts where you clicked with the mouse. If you look closely, you can see the baseline running along the bottom of the text. Photoshop adds the text on its own layer. Any new text you enter will be added to that text layer until you click the Commit button ✓, which tells Photoshop that you have finished entering text.

9. Press the **Spacebar**, and then type **watching over**, and then on the right side of the options bar, click the **Commit** button ✓.

10. Click at the intersection of the second horizontal guide and the right vertical guide, type **your nest egg?**, and then click the **Commit** button ✓.

11. Click **View** on the menu bar, and then click **Clear Guides** to get a better view of your work.

Because you didn't change any of the options on the options bar, the new text has the same formatting and size as the first text you entered.

TIP

You can click the Cancel button on the options bar to delete the text entry rather than committing it.

Working in the Typography Workspace

When you are working extensively with text in Photoshop, you might find it helpful to switch to the Typography workspace, which provides easy access to many tools for working with text. The Character panel is particularly useful, and it appears at the top of the dock in the Typography workspace. See Figure 6-6.

Figure 6-6 Character panel formatting options

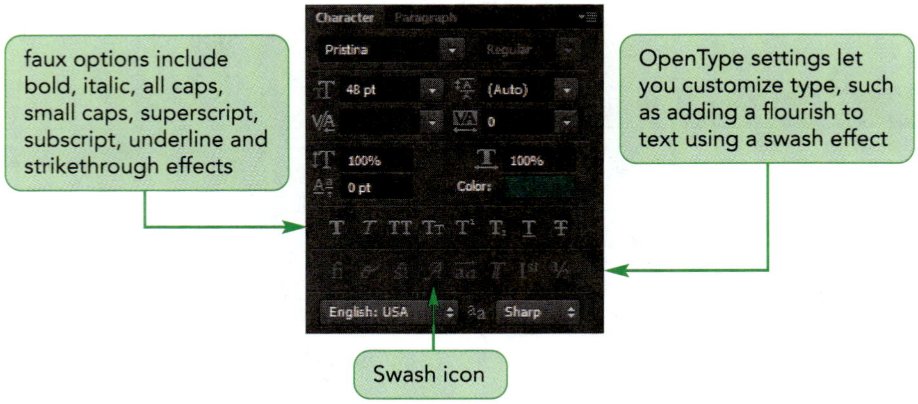

The Character panel includes options for generating faux styles, such as bold or italic. Options for working with OpenType fonts also appear in the Character panel. OpenType fonts are scalable, modifiable fonts that you can use in either a PC or a Mac environment. OpenType fonts provide a great deal of flexibility to a designer because they can be scaled to almost any size, and modified to include characters found in languages other than English. They also let you add artistic effects to type, such as a swash, which is an italic embellishment that extends a character beyond the baseline. If you've ever received a fancy wedding invitation, you've probably seen a swash or two.

You'll be making a lot of changes to the text you enter in your new composition, so you'll switch to the Typography workspace.

To switch to the Typography workspace and modify the point type:

1. On the menu bar, click **Window**, point to **Workspace**, and then click **Typography** to display the Typography workspace.
2. In the Layers panel, double-click the **your nest egg?** text thumbnail. The text is highlighted on the image. Double-clicking the thumbnail is a quick and efficient way to select the text on a layer.

   You'll change the color of the *your nest egg* text so it stands out more than it did with the color you originally assigned.
3. In the Character panel, click the **Color** button, change the color of the text to white by typing RGB values of R=**255**, G=**255**, and B=**255** in the Color Picker (Text Color) dialog box, click the **OK** button, and then click the **Commit** button on the options bar. The text is now white.
4. On the canvas, double-click within the word ***your***. Double-clicking within a word selects it. See Figure 6-7.

Figure 6-7 **Double-clicking a word to select it**

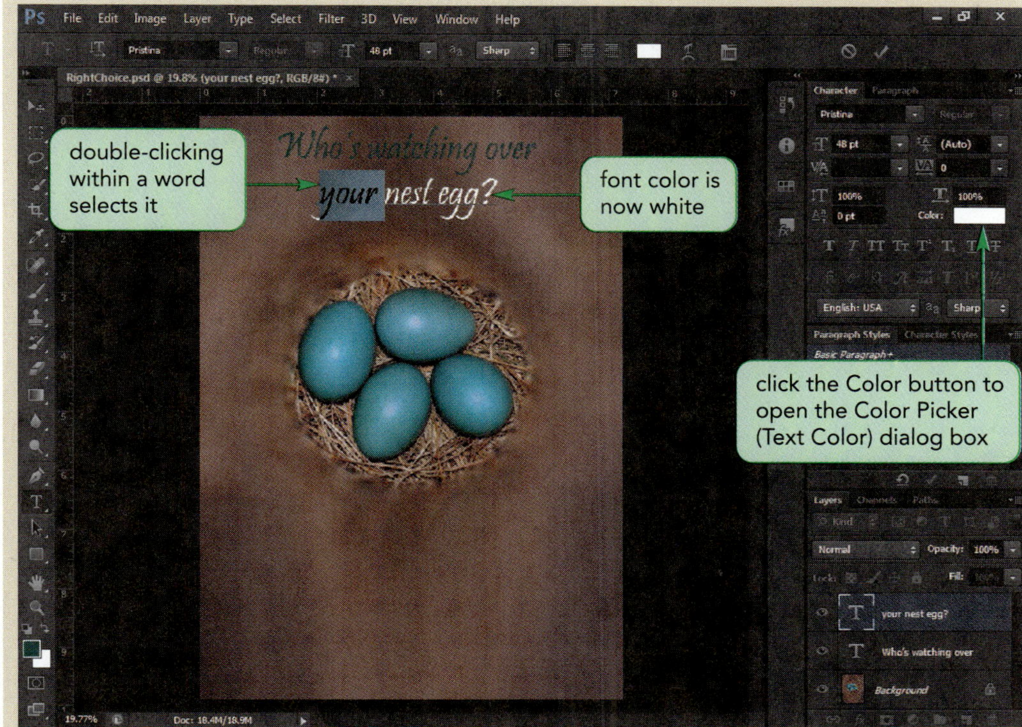

Steven Russell Smith Photos/Shutterstock.com

When a word is selected, you can edit it by typing new text, or you can change its format using the options bar or the Character panel.

5. In the Character panel, click the **Faux Bold** button, and then click the **Commit** button. The word *your* is now bold.
6. In the Layers panel, double-click the **Who's watching over** text thumbnail to select the words *Who's watching over.*
7. Click the **Swatches panel** icon to expand the panel, and then click the **White** swatch in the Swatches panel to change the text to white. Collapse the Swatches panel, and then click the **Commit** button.

   You could have also clicked the Color button in the Character panel to select the new color, but the Swatches panel provides an easier way to assign a standard text color because it avoids the dialog box.

You can also use the Character panel to format the text as all caps or small caps. The **all caps** format changes any text you type, whether you type it as uppercase or lowercase, to all capital letters in the current point size. The **small caps** option formats all letters as capital letters. The letters you type in uppercase are taller than the letters you type in lowercase, but all are capitalized. You'll add some additional text, and then change the formatting of that text to add interest to the composition.

To center text and format it as small caps:

1. Add guides at 3 1/2 inches on the horizontal ruler and at 7 inches and 9 inches on the vertical ruler. At the intersection of the top horizontal guide and the vertical guide, click to make the insertion point active, and then, on the options bar, change the font size to **60 pt** and click the **Center text** button. Type **RC Investments**.

   When the Center text option is selected on the options bar, any text that you type spreads out from the center point, which is the point where you click the mouse. See Figure 6-8.

Figure 6-8 Adding centered point type

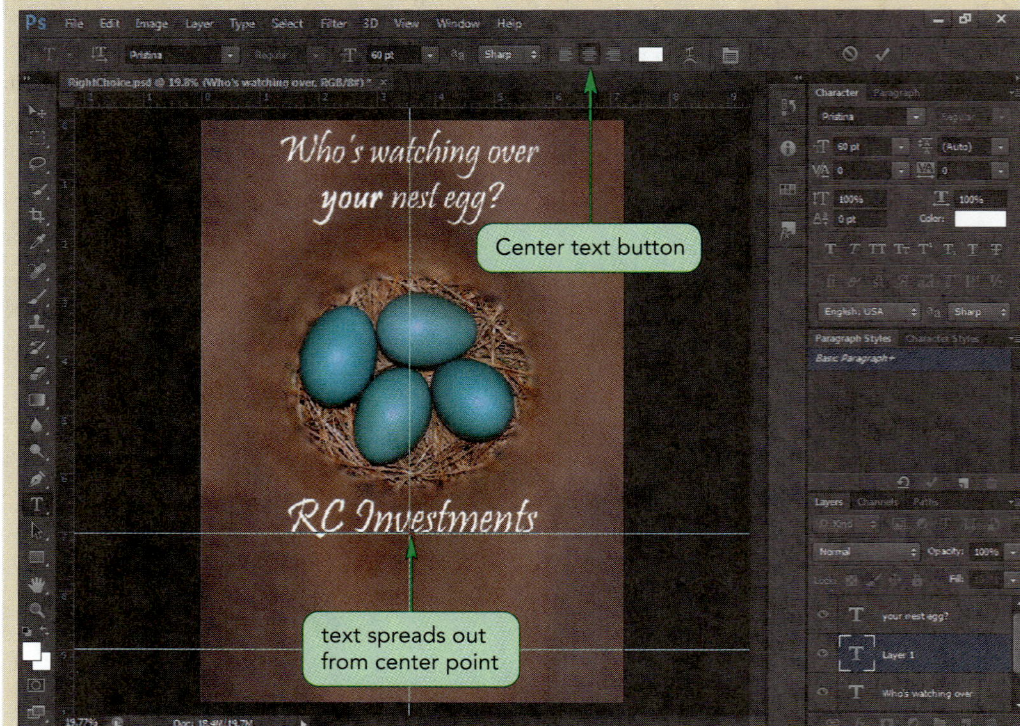

Steven Russell Smith Photos/Shutterstock.com

You can use small caps in a layout to add sophistication to your text, or to make it stand out from the other text. You'll apply it to the word *Investments* in the company name.

2. Highlight ***Investments*** by dragging the mouse over the word. In the Character panel, click the **Small Caps** button, and then click the **Commit** button. The capital *I* in the word is the same size as the capital *R* and capital *C*. However, the letters you typed as lowercase (*nvestments*) are formatted not as lowercase, but as small capital letters.
3. Using the same settings, type **The Right Choice** beneath RC INVESTMENTS at the intersection of the guides, and then click the **Commit** button.

Scaling Text Using the Character Panel

Using the Character panel, you can also scale text on a text layer. Scaling has an effect similar to changing the font size, but scaling gives you the flexibility to scale width and height separately.

REFERENCE

Scaling Text Using the Character Panel

- In the Layers panel, click the text layer you want to scale.
- If necessary, select individual words on the canvas.
- In the Character panel, in the Vertically scale box, type a scaling percentage.
- In the Character panel, in the Horizontally scale box, type a scaling percentage.
- Click outside the scale box, or press the Enter key to apply the new size.

Next, you'll scale the letters *R* and *C* in RC investments to add flair to the text on the canvas.

To scale the RC Investments text:

1. In the Layers panel, click the **RC Investments** layer, select *RC* on the canvas, and then in the Character panel, double-click in the **Vertically scale** box and type **110**. Double-click in the **Horizontally scale** box, type **120**, and then press the **Enter** key. The selected text is now 10 percent taller and 20 percent wider.
2. Click to the right of the letters *RC* and then press the **Enter** key. Photoshop adds a line break, and the *Investments* text moves to a new line below *RC*.

   Pressing the Enter key while the Text tool is active adds another line with the same point text settings as the current line. Notice that the *Investments* text is still centered at the vertical guide because the Center text button is still selected on the options bar.
3. Select the *I* in *Investments* and change the Vertically scale setting to **110%** and the Horizontally scale setting to **120%**. Select the last *s* in *Investments* and change both the Vertically scale setting and the Horizontally scale setting to **120%**, and then click the **Commit** button.

   See Figure 6-9.

Figure 6-9 Adding a line break and increasing scale

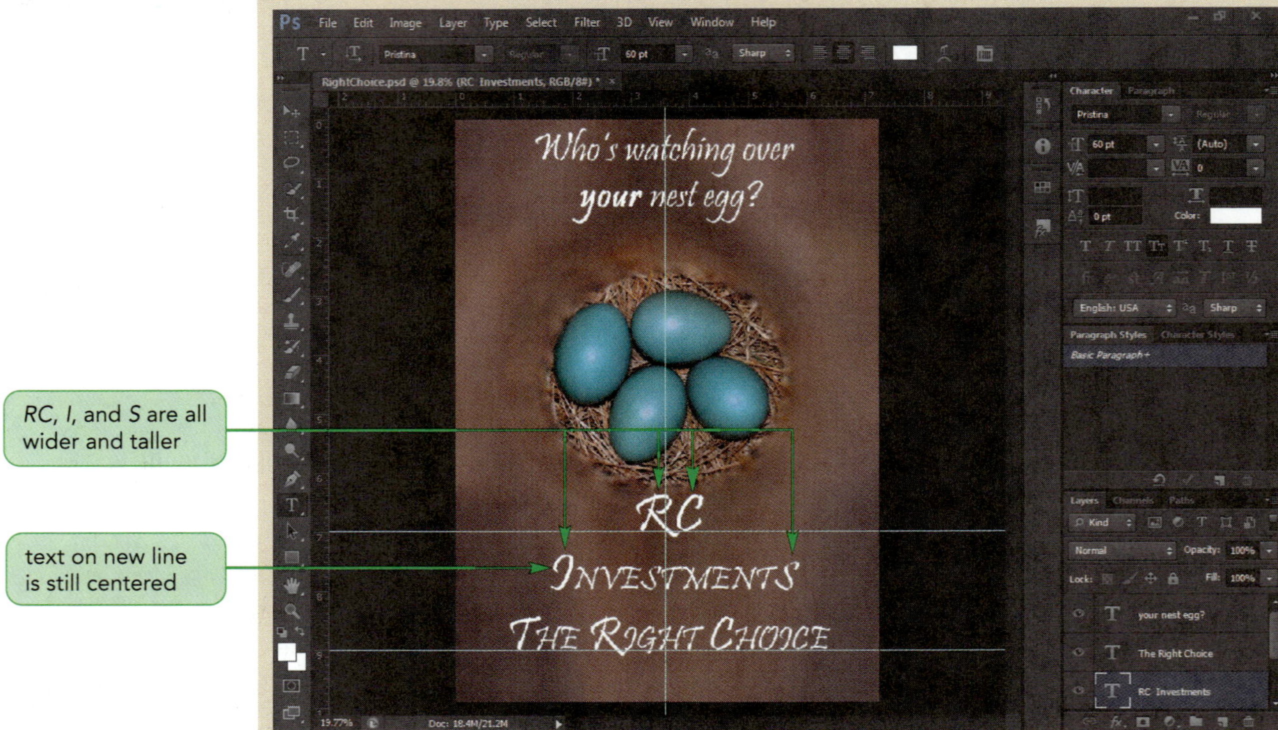

Steven Russell Smith Photos/Shutterstock.com

4. Save the file as **RCI.psd** in the Photoshop6\Tutorial folder, and leave it open for the next set of steps.

Scaling Text Using the Move Tool

You can also use the Move tool to scale text using the transform controls. The transform controls, also called selection handles, let you resize the contents of the selected layer by dragging. You drag a side control to make the text wider or narrower, and you drag a top or bottom control to make the text taller or shorter. You can maintain the width-to-height ratio by pressing the Shift key while dragging a corner handle. After you click a transform control, you can also use the W (width) and H (height) boxes on the options bar to scale text by increasing or decreasing its width and height percentages. To constrain the scaling so that it's uniform, click the Maintain aspect ratio button on the options bar before changing a percentage.

REFERENCE

Scaling Text Using the Move Tool

- In the Layers panel, click the text layer you want to scale.
- In the Tools panel, click the Move Tool button.
- On the options bar, select the Show Transform Controls check box.
- Press and hold the Shift key, and drag a corner handle to scale text uniformly.

or

- Drag any handle to change the size of the text in the direction you drag.
- Press the Enter key, or on the options bar, click the Commit button.

You'll use the Move tool and the Shift key to scale the text on the The Right Choice layer uniformly.

> **TIP**
>
> After you click a transform control, you can use the Width and Height boxes on the options bar to scale text by increasing or decreasing its width and height percentages. To constrain the scaling so that it's uniform, click the Maintain aspect ratio button on the options bar before changing a percentage.

To use the Move tool to scale text:

1. In the Layers panel, click **The Right Choice** layer.
2. In the Tools panel, click the **Move Tool** button, if necessary, and then on the options bar, click the **Show Transform Controls** check box to select it, if necessary.
3. Press and hold the **Shift** key, click the **lower-left transform control**, and then drag the lower-left transform control up and to the right until it touches the horizontal guide. Release the mouse button, and then the Shift key. See Figure 6-10.

Figure 6-10 Resizing text by dragging transform controls

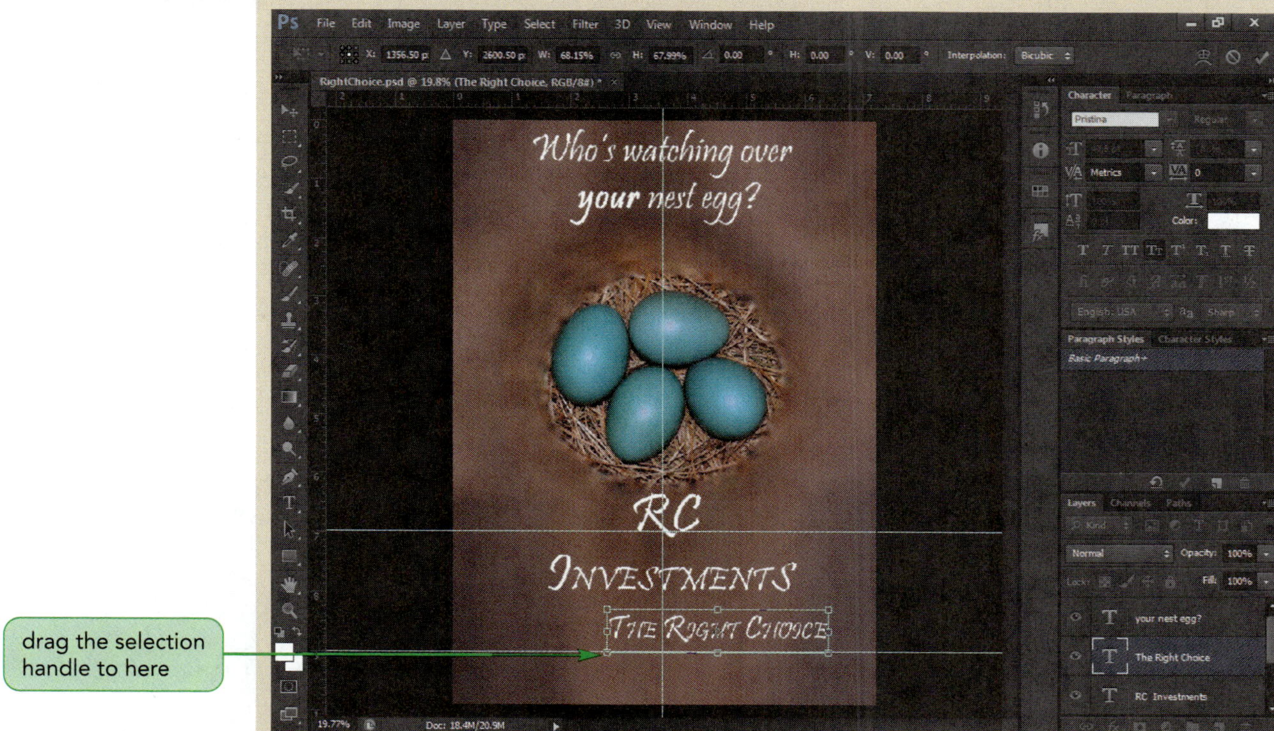

Steven Russell Smith Photos/Shutterstock.com

Trouble? If the text doesn't have similar proportions to Figure 6-10, you released the Shift key before releasing the mouse button. Cancel the transformation by clicking the Cancel button on the options bar, and then repeat Step 3.

4. Click the **Commit** button.
5. With the **The Right Choice** layer still selected, move the text to the left so it is centered beneath the word *INVESTMENTS*.
6. Save the RCI.psd file and close it.

You can emphasize text in a composition by typing it using a vertical orientation, so it is read from top to bottom. Next, you'll experiment with adding vertical text to a variation of the image you used for the previous composition.

Working with Vertical Point Type

Using vertical instead of horizontal type is another way to draw attention to a word or words in a composition. Obviously, you wouldn't apply vertical text to entire paragraphs. That would just frustrate your audience. However, a company name or catch phrase running vertically in a composition is an excellent way to make it stand out.

You will create another sample RC Investments ad for Rose using vertical type for the company name to add interest to the layout. You'll work with two kinds of vertical text. First, you'll enter horizontal type and rotate it 90 degrees to see if you like that effect. Then, you'll enter text using the Vertical Type tool, which adds the text from top to bottom.

To rotate horizontal type to a vertical position:

1. Open **RCVertical.psd**, located in the Photoshop6\Tutorial folder, size it to fit the window, and then save it as **RCDetails.psd** in the same folder.
2. Extend the canvas so you add an additional 2 1/2 inches to the left side of the canvas. Use black as the canvas extension color. (*Hint*: Click the Relative check box and anchor the existing image on the right.) The canvas now includes a 2 1/2 inch wide black bar along the left side. This is where you'll place the company name.
3. In the Tools panel, click the **Horizontal Type Tool** button, and then use the Character panel to set the font to **Myriad Pro** and the font size to **72 pt**. Click the **Small Caps** button to deselect it. Leave the other settings in the Character panel as they are.
4. On the options bar, click the **Left align text** button.
5. Click the canvas at about 8 inches on the vertical ruler and 1 inch on the horizontal ruler, and then type **RC Investments**. See Figure 6-11.

Figure 6-11 Entering font settings for horizontal type

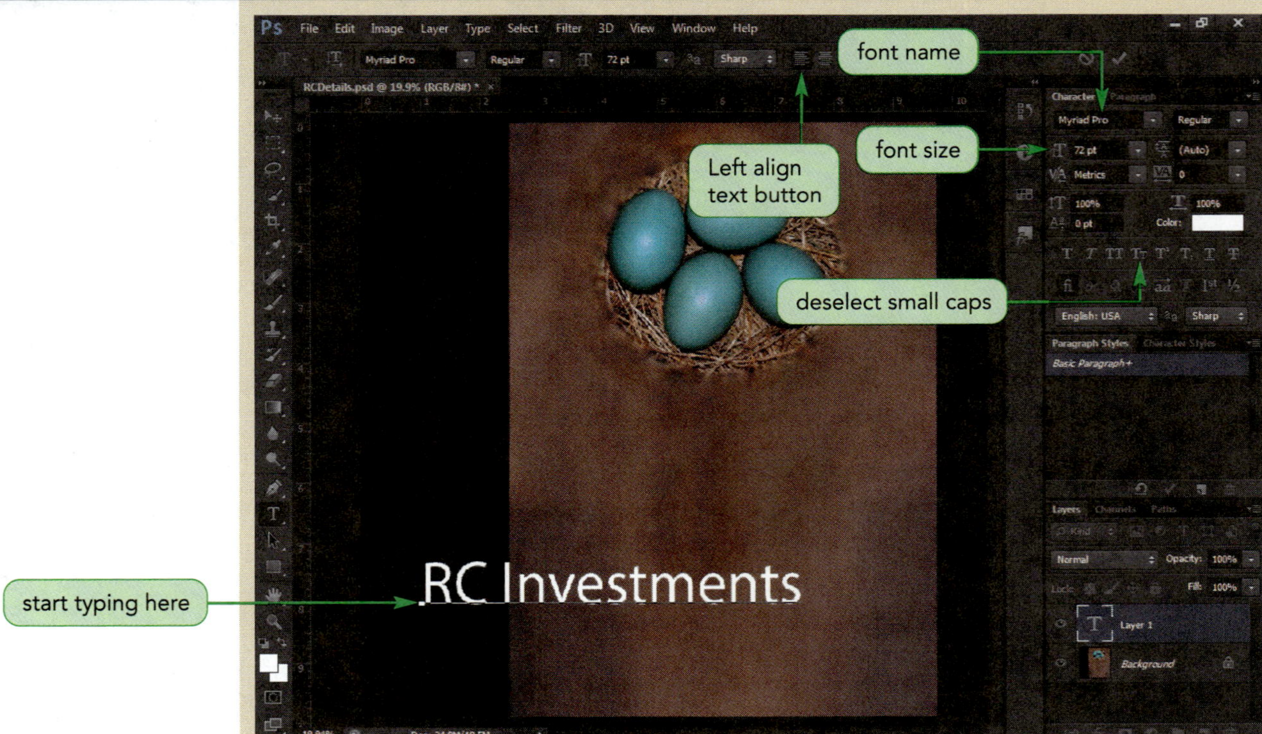

Steven Russell Smith Photos/Shutterstock.com

TIP

Pressing the Shift key while rotating the text constrains the rotation to increments of 15 degrees.

6. Click the **Commit** button. The text appears near the bottom of the image.
7. Press the **V** key to activate the Move tool, show the transform controls if necessary, and then position the mouse pointer near the upper-right transform control so it appears as a curved double-headed arrow.
8. Drag the control up and to the left until the text is at a – 45-degree angle. As you drag, the text rotates counterclockwise. See Figure 6-12.

Figure 6-12 **Rotating horizontal type**

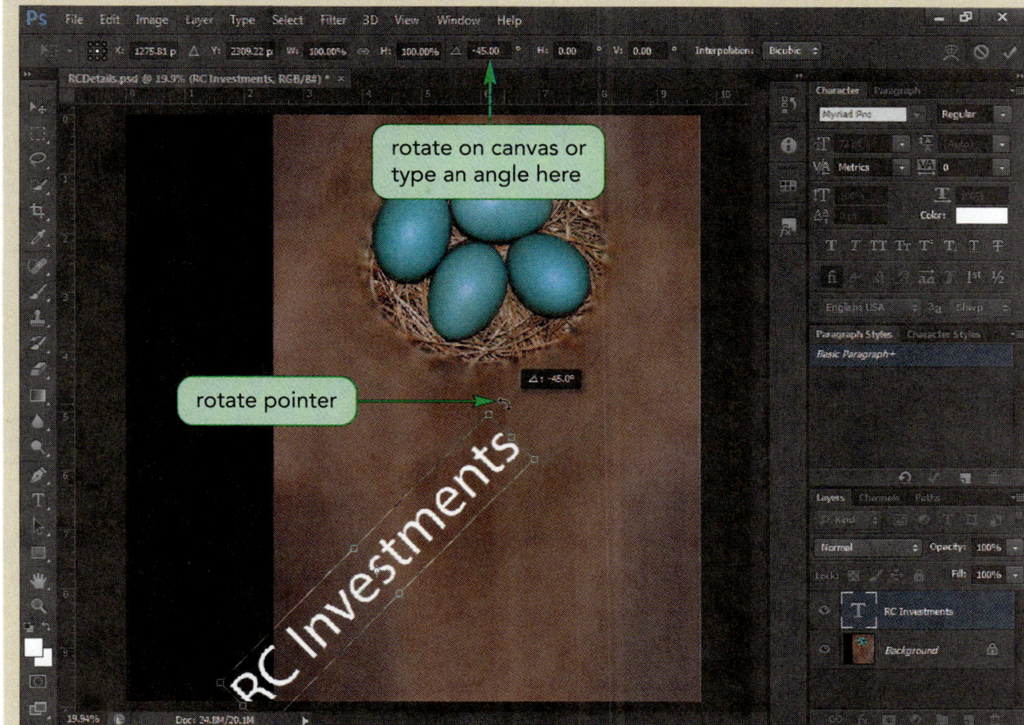

Steven Russell Smith Photos/Shutterstock.com

There will be times when you'll want to eyeball an angle of rotation until you're happy with how it looks in the image. However, if you know the angle of rotation that you want, it is easier to type it on the options bar or use the Shift key to rotate in increments.

9. On the options bar, type **-90** in the Rotate box.

   Specifying a negative number rotates the text in a counterclockwise direction. Typing a positive number rotates the text in a clockwise direction.
10. On the options bar, click the **Commit** button, and then drag the text until it appears centered in the black bar.
11. On the options bar, deselect the **Show Transform Controls** check box so you can see the full effect of the text rotation. See Figure 6-13.

Figure 6-13 **Horizontal text rotated to vertical position**

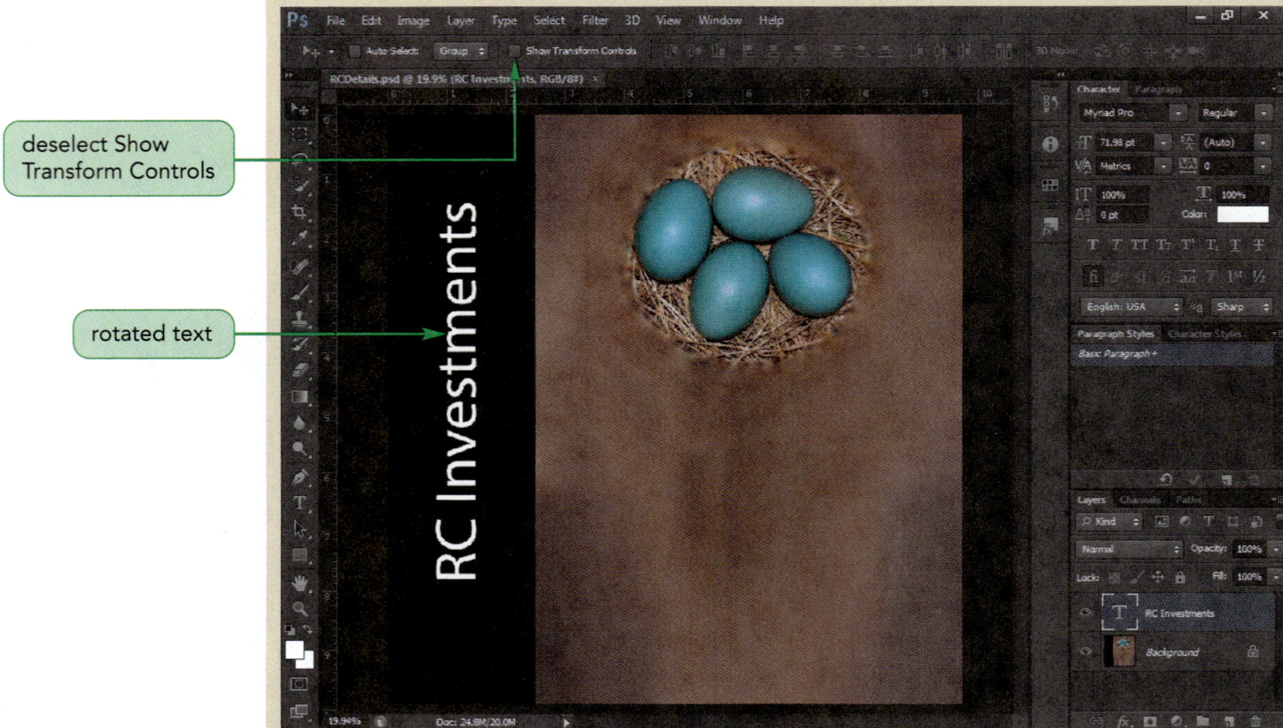

Steven Russell Smith Photos/Shutterstock.com

12. In the Layers panel, right-click the **RC Investments** layer, and then click **Red**. This layer color change will help you distinguish this layer from a similar layer you'll create next.
13. In the Layers panel, click the **Eye** icon to the left of the RC Investments layer to hide that layer.

To have some different options to present to Rose, you'll create another RC Investments layer that has vertical text in the black bar, only this time, you'll use the Vertical Type tool.

To use the Vertical Type tool to enter vertical type:

1. In the Tools panel, click the **Vertical Type Tool** button.

   Trouble? If you can't find the Vertical Type Tool button, right-click the Horizontal Type Tool button, and then click the Vertical Type Tool button.
2. On the options bar, select **Times New Roman** as the font. Click in the **Set the font size** box, highlight the current value, and then type **54**.
3. Click the canvas at about 1 inch on the horizontal ruler and ½ inch on the vertical ruler, and then type **RC Investments**. As you type, Photoshop enters subsequent letters beneath the previous letters, so the text has a vertical orientation. It also centers the letters along a vertical baseline. Click the **Top align text** button, if necessary. See Figure 6-14.

Figure 6-14 Entering vertical type

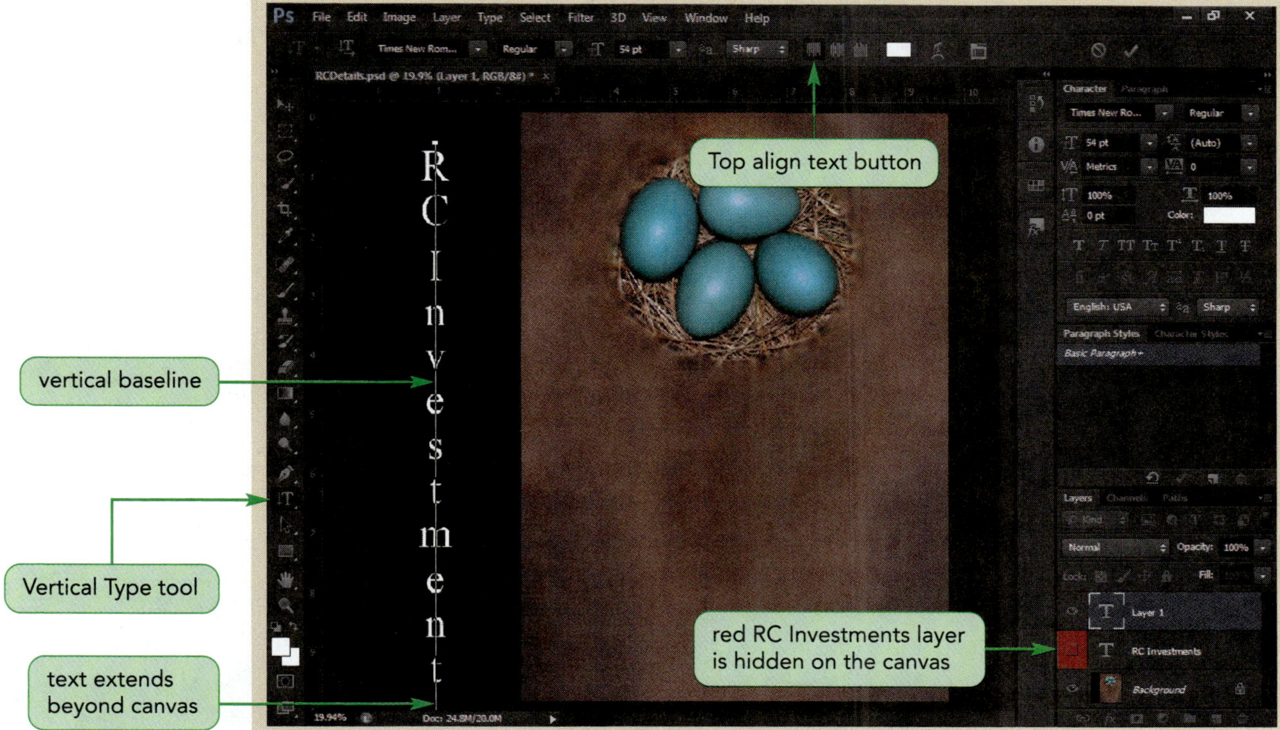

Steven Russell Smith Photos/Shutterstock.com

4. On the options bar, click the **Commit** button.

   Notice that the text has extended beyond the canvas. You'll adjust the tracking of the text to fix this problem.

Adjusting the Tracking of Vertical Text

In Photoshop, you can modify text tracking, which is the spacing between characters. The settings in the Character panel allow you to increase or decrease the spacing between the characters in selected text.

The RC Investments text is too spread out, so you will adjust the tracking so it all fits on the canvas. You'll also adjust the scaling of one of the characters so the characters line up better vertically.

To adjust the tracking and the scaling of the RC Investments text:

1. In the Layers panel, right-click the new **RC Investments** layer, and then click **Green** to change the layer color.
2. Double-click the **RC Investments** text thumbnail for the green text layer, and then in the Character panel, double-click the **Set the tracking for the selected characters** icon, and then type **-100** in the box. All of the characters now fit on the canvas, but the result still isn't satisfactory because it appears as if there is no space between *RC* and *Investments*.

3. Select the *C* and the *I*, and then in the Character panel, click the **Set the tracking for the selected characters** arrow, and then click **-50**. There is now more space between the words.

   The text now fits on the canvas, but the letter *m* seems out of place because it's much wider than the other letters in *Investments*.

4. Select the ***m***, and then in the Character panel, type **75** in the Horizontally scale box to make it narrower, and then on the options bar, click the **Commit** button.

   The text still needs work because the *I* in *Investments* is now too far from the *n*. You'll adjust the tracking between the *I* and the *n*.

5. Select the letters ***In*** within the word *Investments*, click the **Set the tracking for the selected characters box** arrow, and then click **-100**. The *I* and the *n* move closer together. Commit the change.

6. If necessary, use the Move tool to drag the text layer so it is centered in the black bar, as shown in Figure 6-15.

Figure 6-15 **Centering the vertical text**

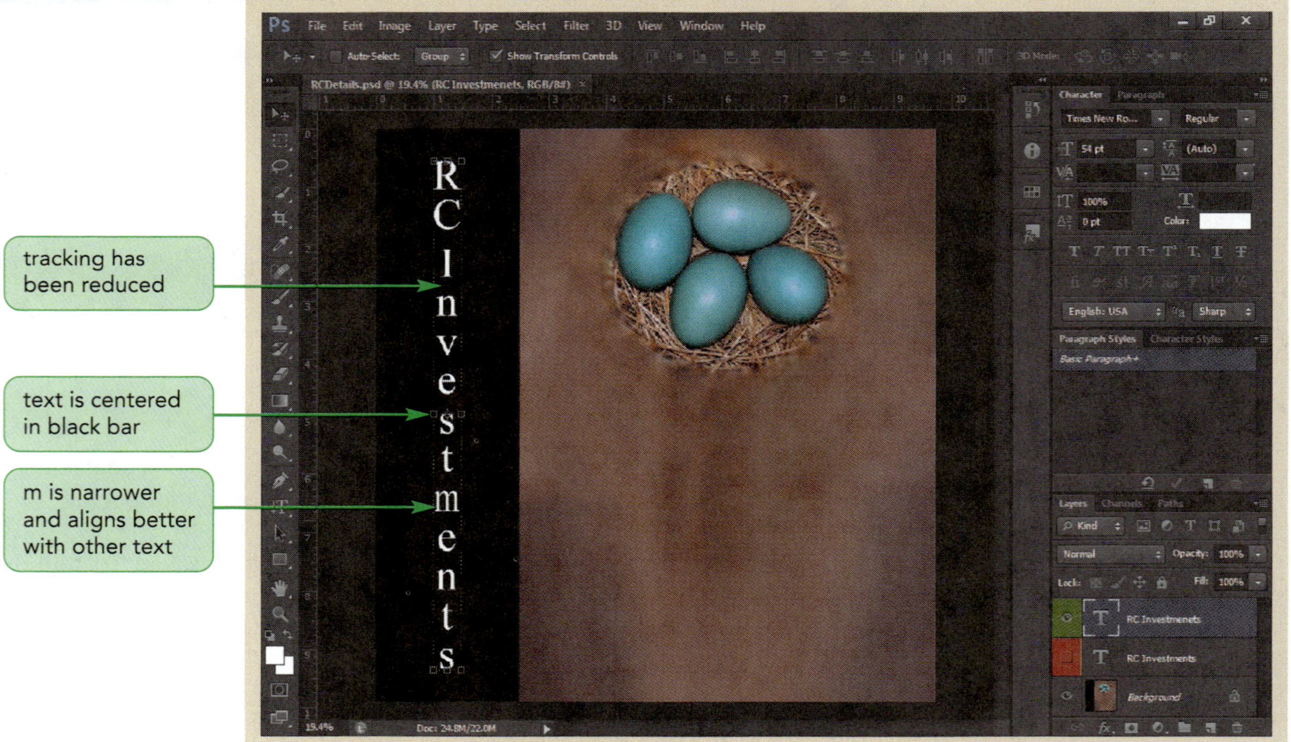

Steven Russell Smith Photos/Shutterstock.com

7. In the Layers panel, hide the green RC Investments layer, and display and select the **red RC Investments** layer. In the Tools panel, click the **Horizontal Type Tool** button, and then on the canvas, select the ***RC Investments*** text.

8. In the Character panel, increase the vertical scale of the RC Investments text to **150%**, and increase the tracking to **60**. See Figure 6-16.

Figure 6-16 Changing the vertical scale and tracking

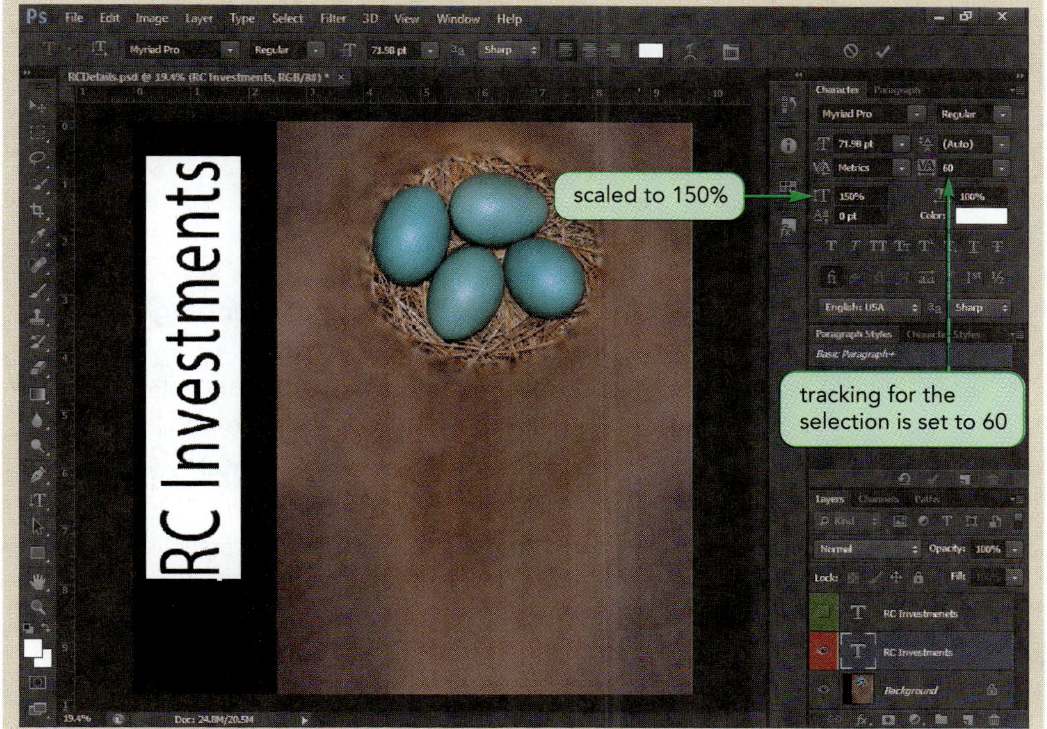

Steven Russell Smith Photos/Shutterstock.com

9. Commit the change, and then open the Layer Comps panel, and save the current view as a new layer comp called **Rotated**. Base it on Visibility and Position.
10. Hide the **red RC Investments** layer, display the **green RC Investments** layer, and save the current view as a new layer comp called **Vertical**, based on Visibility and Position. Minimize the Layer Comps panel group.
11. Save RCDetails.psd, and leave the file open.

Working with Paragraphs

TIP

You can add guides to help position a bounding box. As you drag the borders of the bounding box toward the guides, the borders snap to the guide location.

You can also work with paragraphs in a Photoshop composition. Paragraph text lets you predefine the size of the text box before you type, which is often essential when you are working with a fixed layout. To create paragraph text, select the Horizontal Type tool, and then drag on the canvas to create the bounding box that will hold the text. When you first enter it, Paragraph text behaves differently than point text. For example, if you type beyond the edges of the bounding box, the text will not appear, although as you'll see in the following steps, it's still being recorded by Photoshop.

REFERENCE

Adding Paragraph Text

- In the Tools panel, click the Horizontal Type Tool button, and on the options bar, specify the formatting options for the paragraph text.
- Click on the canvas, and drag to create a bounding box to hold the paragraph.
- Type the text in the bounding box.
- When you have finished entering text, click the Commit button on the options bar.

To enter paragraph type in a bounding box:

1. Position guides at about 5 inches and 6 1/2 inches on the vertical ruler and 4 inches and 8 inches on the horizontal ruler. Zoom the display to **25%**, and in the Layers panel, click the **Background** layer.
2. In the Tools panel, click the **Horizontal Type Tool** button T, and reset all of the tools.
3. Click the canvas at the upper-left intersection of the guides, and then drag a bounding box down to the lower-right intersection, as shown in Figure 6-17.

Figure 6-17 **Creating a bounding box**

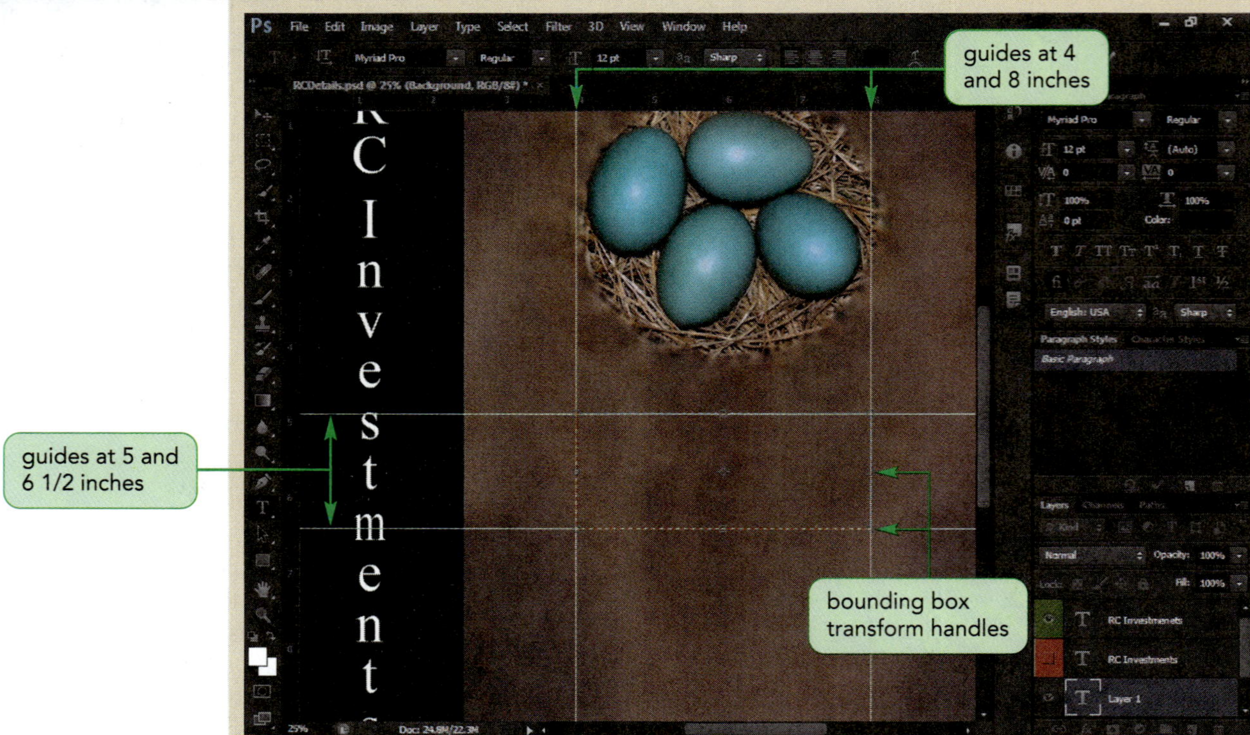

Steven Russell Smith Photos/Shutterstock.com

The bounding box has transform handles like other objects in Photoshop. An insertion point appears in the upper-left corner of the bounding box, although it might be difficult to see.

Trouble? If your bounding box doesn't fit in the guides exactly, press the Escape key and repeat Step 3. If it still doesn't fit the guides, your text might wrap differently than the text shown in the figures.

4. In the Character panel, set the font to **Myriad Pro**, if necessary, click the **Set the font size arrow**, and then click **18 pt**. If necessary, set the vertical scale to **100%**.
5. Click the **Swatches panel** icon to expand it, and then click the **Darker Cyan** swatch in the middle of the second-to-last visible row. The Color boxes in the Character panel and on the options bar display the new text color. Darker Cyan is also the new foreground color in the Tools panel.

   Trouble? If you can't find the Darker Cyan swatch, click any blue swatch in the panel.
6. Type **At RC Investments, we have your best interests at heart.** As you type, notice that the text wraps to fit in the bounding box you drew.
7. Press the **Spacebar**, and then type **Your nest egg is our nest egg, and your child's future is our future as well.**
8. Press the **Enter** key. Pressing the Enter key starts a new paragraph and moves the cursor to a new line, just as it does in a word-processing program.
9. Type **Come to us for guidance and excellent advice on your best options for** in the bounding box. The word *excellent* is hyphenated, and the rest of the text is hidden. See Figure 6-18.

Figure 6-18 Text beyond bounding box is hidden

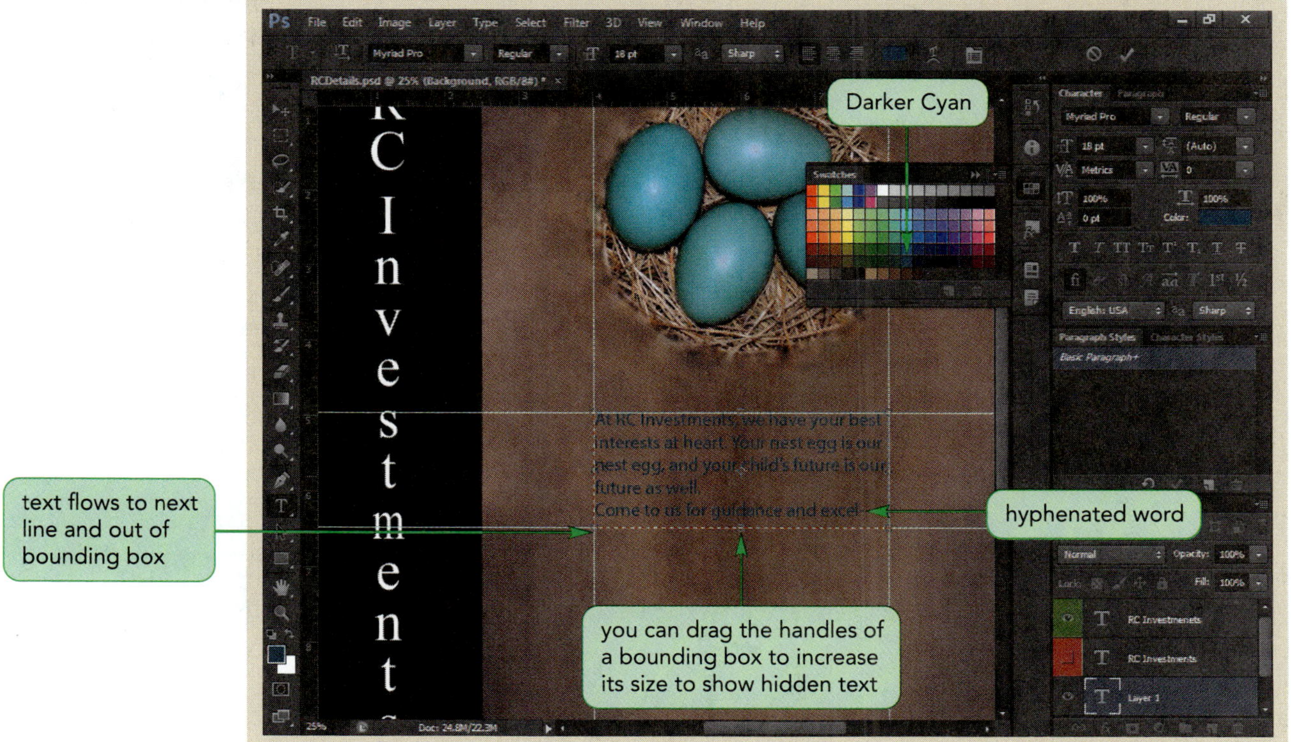

Steven Russell Smith Photos/Shutterstock.com

Trouble? If your text wraps differently, or fits the text box differently, don't worry. If there is even a slight difference in the size of the bounding box, line breaks will vary.

When you enter point type, the bounding box expands to fit the text as you add it to the canvas. However, with paragraph type, the text you type must fit in the bounding box to show up on the canvas. To display more text, you need to change the size of the bounding box.

10. Position the mouse pointer over the center-bottom handle of the bounding box, and then drag the handle down to about the 9-inch mark on the vertical ruler. The rest of the text that you typed is now visible.

You'll continue to type, and will intentionally misspell the word *education* as *edcuation* so you can correct it when you check spelling later.

11. Press the **Spacebar**, type **edcuation savings accounts, individual retirement accounts, and more.**

12. On the menu bar, click **View**, point to **Show**, and then click **Guides** to hide the guides. Collapse the Swatches panel.

13. Select all of the text and change the font size to **20 pt**, and then commit the change. See Figure 6-19.

Figure 6-19 **Paragraph text after the bounding box has been extended**

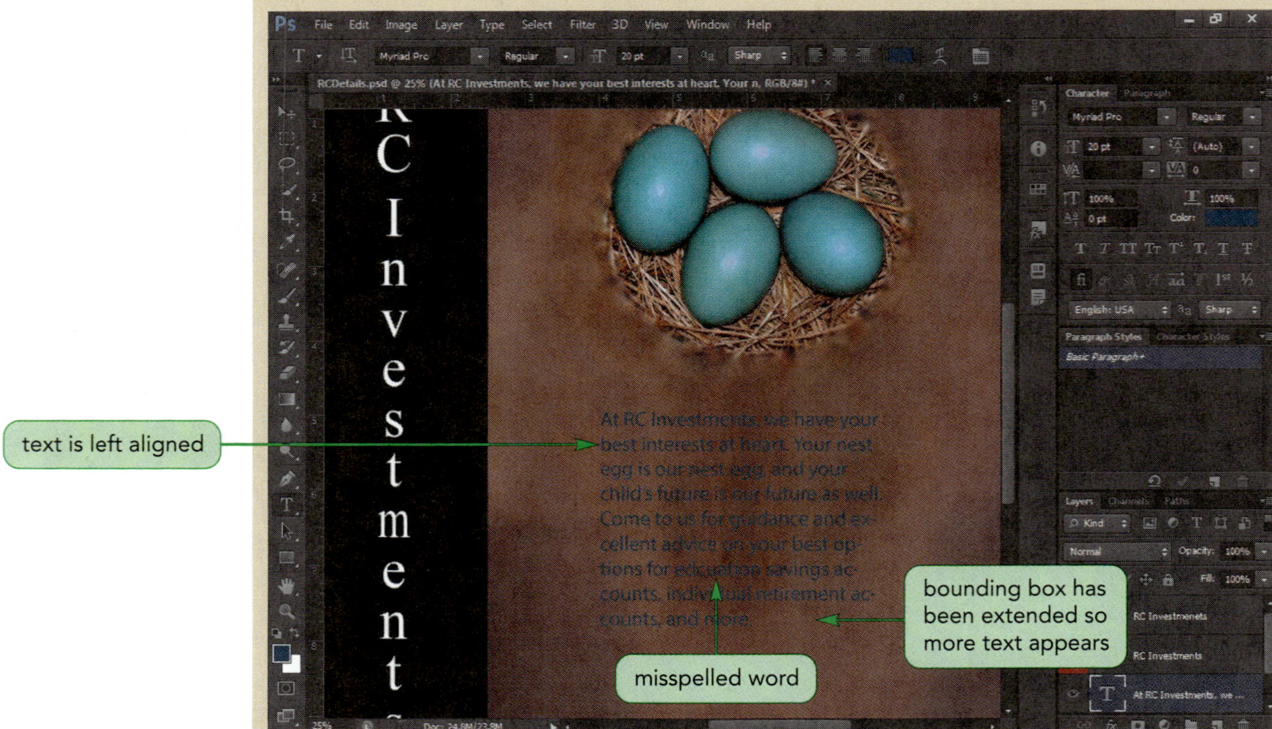

Steven Russell Smith Photos/Shutterstock.com

PROSKILLS

Decision Making: Knowing When to Justify

When formatting paragraph text, you can choose to left-align, right-align, center, or justify it. When you left-align a paragraph, text appears **flush left**, or straight along the left margin, and has a ragged right edge, like the paragraphs in this book. In Photoshop, and in word-processing programs, text is left-justified by default. When you right-align text, it appears **flush right** along the right margin, and has a ragged left edge. When you center text, both the left and right edges are ragged, and each line is centered, resulting in lines of different lengths. When you **justify** text, it is aligned flush along both the left and the right margins. This gives your paragraphs neat, symmetrical margins, but it can introduce other problems, such as loose or tight lines. In a **loose line**, text is so spread out that it is distracting to the eye because of all of the white space. White space flowing from line to line, called a **river**, can draw a reader's attention away from the content. In a **tight line**, some words are so close together that they are difficult to distinguish. In general, justifying text in a narrow column results in a great number of loose lines and is, therefore, not advised. Photoshop and most word-processing programs provide tools that let you fix the tracking and kerning of loose lines to reduce the white space between words and characters in justified text, but making adjustments line by line can be very time consuming.

So when do you use justified text, and when do you use some other alignment option? In fact, there's no simple answer. You need to determine your needs on a case-by-case basis. In general, justified text is considered formal, while unjustified text is less so. Other considerations are column width and page design. For example, how do the graphics on the page look next to justified or unjustified text? As you become more experienced working with text, you'll develop a sense of what works best in a given situation. You'll also need to weigh other factors, such as the time it takes to adjust tracking, kerning, and hyphenation in a particular design. Once you have weighed all of these factors, you'll have the information you need to make the right decision for a given project.

Next, you'll use the Paragraph panel to adjust the alignment of the paragraphs and the space between paragraphs to see if that improves the layout. You'll also turn off hyphenation to see how different line breaks affect the readability of the text.

To use the Paragraph panel to adjust alignment and hyphenation:

1. Click the **Paragraph panel** tab to display the Paragraph panel.
2. On the canvas, click in the first line of the first paragraph, and then in the Paragraph panel, click the **Center text** button. The text in the first paragraph is centered, and both the left and right margins are ragged. Notice that clicking the Center text button only affects the current paragraph.
3. Click in the second paragraph, and in the Paragraph panel, click the **Justify last left** button. See Figure 6-20.

Figure 6-20 **Adjusting text alignment**

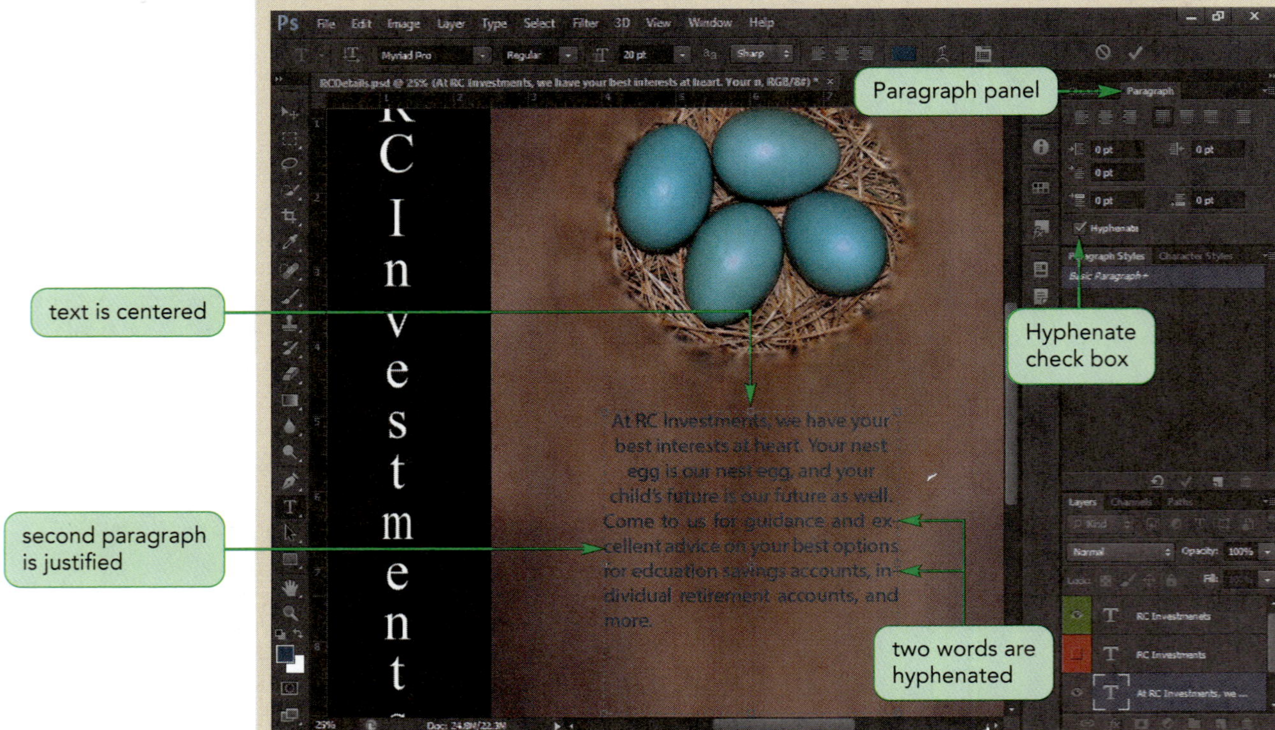

Steven Russell Smith Photos/Shutterstock.com

The text is justified, or evenly spread between the margins of the bounding box, with the last line aligned at the left margin. Two of the words in the second paragraph are hyphenated.

Trouble? If you don't see two hyphenated words, your bounding box is a different size. Continue with the remaining steps.

4. In the Paragraph panel, click the **Hyphenate** check box to deselect it. The words that were hyphenated in the second paragraph have now moved to the next line of text, without hyphenation, and the remaining text spreads out to maintain the justification. Notice that there are now more loose lines and rivers of blank space.

5. In the Paragraph panel, click in the **Add space before paragraph** box, and type **20**. Photoshop adds a 20-point vertical space before the second paragraph.

   Even with the space before the second paragraph, the text doesn't work well as it is currently formatted. Some of the words are too spread out, which makes the paragraph look sloppy. You'll use the center align option for the second paragraph so the characters and words are spaced for easier reading and so it matches the formatting of the first paragraph.

6. Click in the second paragraph, if necessary, and then in the Paragraph panel, click the **Center text** button. The text is centered, without hyphenation.

7. Commit the changes to the paragraph text. See Figure 6-21.

Figure 6-21 Paragraphs centered and separated by space

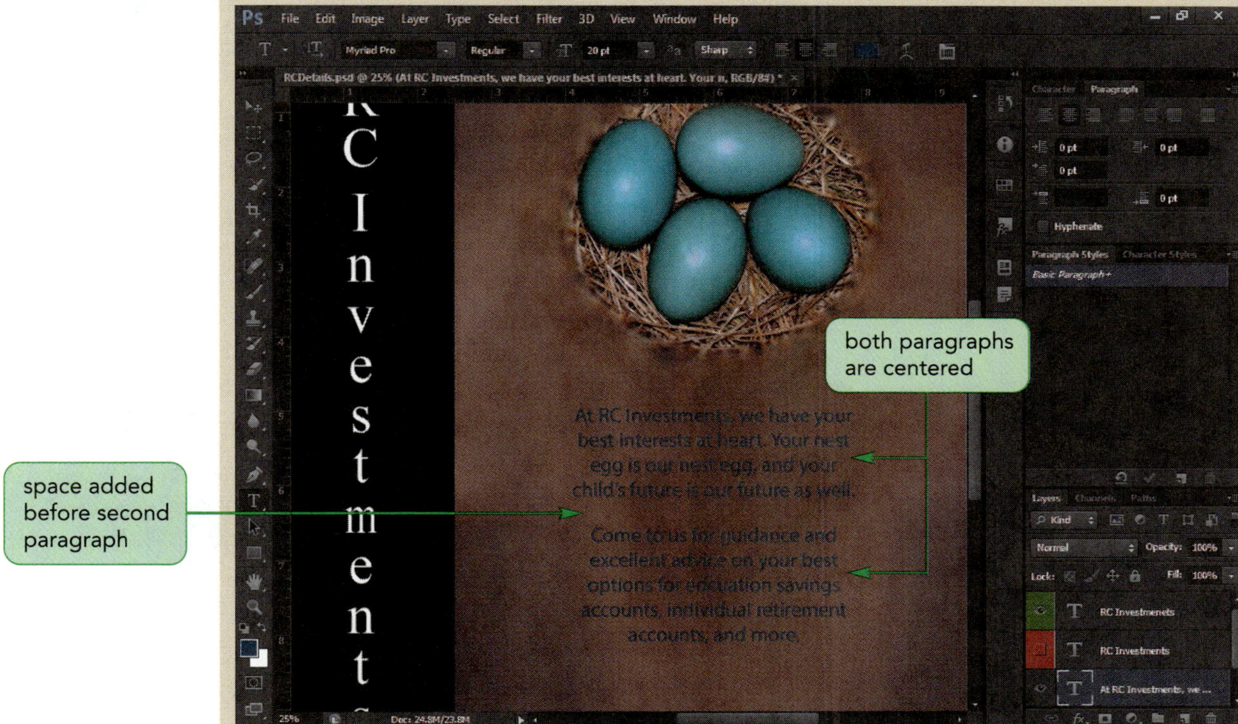

Steven Russell Smith Photos/Shutterstock.com

INSIGHT

Using Advanced Justification Settings

You can access advanced justification settings by selecting Justification from the Paragraph panel menu. Advanced justification settings let you specify Minimum, Desired, and Maximum values for word and letter spacing, as well as glyph scaling. The **Word Spacing** setting determines the space between words. You typically add space between words by pressing the Spacebar. Using advanced justification settings, you can adjust the width of that space. The **Letter Spacing** setting controls the distance between letters. A setting of 100% puts the width of a regular space between letters; 0% packs letters tightly together with no space between them. The **Glyph Scaling** setting determines the width of individual characters. Each font family has predetermined widths for characters, but you can override that setting by specifying a value between 50% and 200%. **Auto Leading** sets the leading—or the vertical space between lines of text—to 120% of the font size by default. You can change the space between lines by changing the value in the Auto Leading box.

Next, you'll format individual words in the paragraphs to make them stand out from the rest of the paragraph. You'll do this using the Character panel and the Swatches panel.

To format the paragraph text:

1. Double-click the word ***heart*** in the first paragraph.
2. Expand the Swatches panel, click any **red swatch**, and then commit the change. Collapse the Swatches panel. The word *heart* is formatted in a red font.

3. In the third line of the first paragraph, double-click the word ***our***, display the Character panel, click the **Set the font style** button Regular, and then click **Italic**.
4. Near the bottom of the Character panel, click the **Underline** button, and then click outside the word *our* to deselect it. The word *our* is italicized and underlined, while the rest of the words retain their original formatting.

Even though you entered the text you just formatted as paragraph type, you can format it the same way you format point type. In fact, after you commit either paragraph type or point type, they behave in the same manner.

Checking Spelling and Replacing Text

When you enter a lot of text in a bounding box, you'll sometimes find that you've made typing errors. You might be used to word-processing programs that mark misspelled words as you type. Photoshop doesn't have that feature, so you need to use the Check Spelling option on the Edit menu. You can also replace one word or phrase with another using the Find and Replace feature in Photoshop. This command is also on the Edit menu.

To check spelling in the paragraph text:

1. Click at the beginning of the first paragraph, to the left of the word *At*.
2. On the menu bar, click **Edit**, and then click **Check Spelling**. The Check Spelling dialog box opens, indicating that *edcuation* is not in the dictionary. Photoshop suggests that you replace the word with the correctly spelled version, *education*.

   Trouble? If the spelling suggested in the Check Spelling dialog box is not the spelling you want, or is not the word you intended, you can either type the correct spelling in the Change To box, or scroll down the list of suggestions and select one of the alternate words.

   Trouble? If a dialog box with a "Spell check complete." message appears, you either have no errors in your text, or you have not clicked at the beginning of the first paragraph. When checking spelling, Photoshop starts at the insertion point and goes to the end of the bounding box. If the insertion point is in the middle of the text, it checks only the second half of the text entry.
3. Click the **Change** button. Photoshop corrects the spelling of *education* and indicates that the spelling check is complete.

   Trouble? If Photoshop finds additional misspelled words, correct them as necessary before closing the dialog box.
4. Click the **OK** button to end the spelling check.

You can also replace text using the Find and Replace Text command on the Edit menu, which opens the Find And Replace Text dialog box. See Figure 6-22.

Figure 6-22 Find And Replace Text dialog box

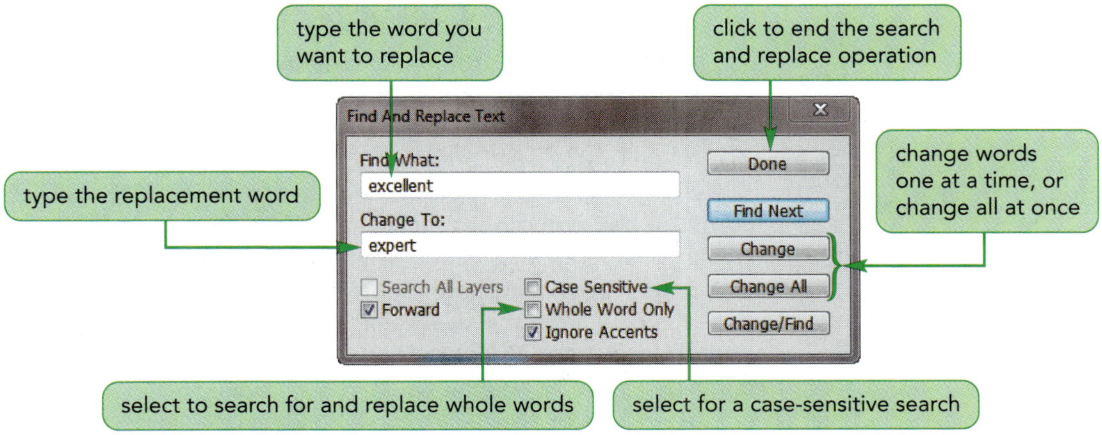

You can type the word you want to replace in the Find What box, and then type the new word in the Change To box. The Find Next button finds the next instance of the word you want to replace. The Change button replaces the word. The Change All button replaces all instances of the Find What word in one step. To change one instance of the word you want to replace and then move to the next, click the Change/Find button. You can also specify whether you want to search forward through the text, whether you want to search all layers, and whether the search should be case sensitive and should look for whole words. For example, if you specify *day* as the word to find, Photoshop will find *today*, *Monday*, and *daylight* in addition to *day*. If you specify Whole Word Only, Photoshop will only find *day*.

While the Find and Replace feature is most useful in situations in which you are working with large segments of text, you will experiment with it by replacing the word *excellent* with the word *expert* in the ad you are working on for Rose.

To find and replace text:

1. Click at the beginning of the first paragraph. On the menu bar, click **Edit**, and then click **Find and Replace Text**. The Find And Replace Text dialog box opens.
2. In the Find What box, type **excellent**, and then in the Change To box, type **expert**.
3. Click **Find Next**. Photoshop highlights the instance of *excellent* in the paragraph.
4. Click the **Change** button to change *excellent* to *expert*.
5. Click the **Done** button, and then in the Layers panel, click the **Background** layer to deselect the paragraph text.
6. Save RCDetails.psd. If you are not taking a break before the next session, leave the file open.

INSIGHT

Creating Paragraph and Character Styles

If you plan to use the same format for multiple paragraphs, it's a good idea to create and save a paragraph style so you can use it again in the future. Photoshop CS6 has a new panel, the Paragraph Styles panel, that lets you do just that. To save a paragraph style, click the Create new Paragraph Style icon at the bottom of the panel, and then double-click the new style in the list to open the Paragraph Style Options dialog box. In this dialog box, you can set character formats, indents, spacing, justification, and hyphenation, among other things. When you save the style, it is saved as a choice in the Paragraph Styles panel and can be applied to other paragraphs in your document. Because the paragraph style is saved with the document, it can also be used in future sessions. To access the style, display the Paragraph Styles panel, and select the style from the list.

You can also save character styles using the new Character Styles panel. To do so, format the text in the style you want to save, and then double-click the new style in the list to open the Character Style Options dialog box. In this dialog box, you can set character formats, including font, font style, font size, and leading, tracking, and kerning options. You can also create special styles that use all caps or small caps, among other settings.

Because you can also load styles into one document from another by selecting Load Character Styles or Load Paragraph Styles from the panel menu, using paragraph and character styles is a good way to streamline your work flow and achieve a consistent look across compositions.

In this session, you learned about text layers, and you worked with horizontal point type, vertical point type, and paragraph type. You explored the Typography workspace, and experimented with a variety of text formatting and alignment options. You also learned about character styles and paragraph styles. In the next session, you'll work with some more advanced text formatting options, including applying text styles, specifying baseline shifts, and bending text to a path. You'll also fill text with an image, a pattern, and a gradient.

REVIEW

Session 6.1 Quick Check

1. What is the difference between the way you enter paragraph type and the way you enter point type?
2. Point type is entered along a(n) ____________ that expands to accommodate new text.
3. The ____________ workspace is designed for text editing and formatting.
4. True or False. Vertical type entered with the Vertical Type tool has the same appearance as text that is entered with the Horizontal Type tool and then rotated counterclockwise 90 degrees.
5. Which setting in the Paragraph panel lets you adjust the space between words and characters?
6. What does it mean to justify the text in a paragraph?

SESSION 6.2 VISUAL OVERVIEW

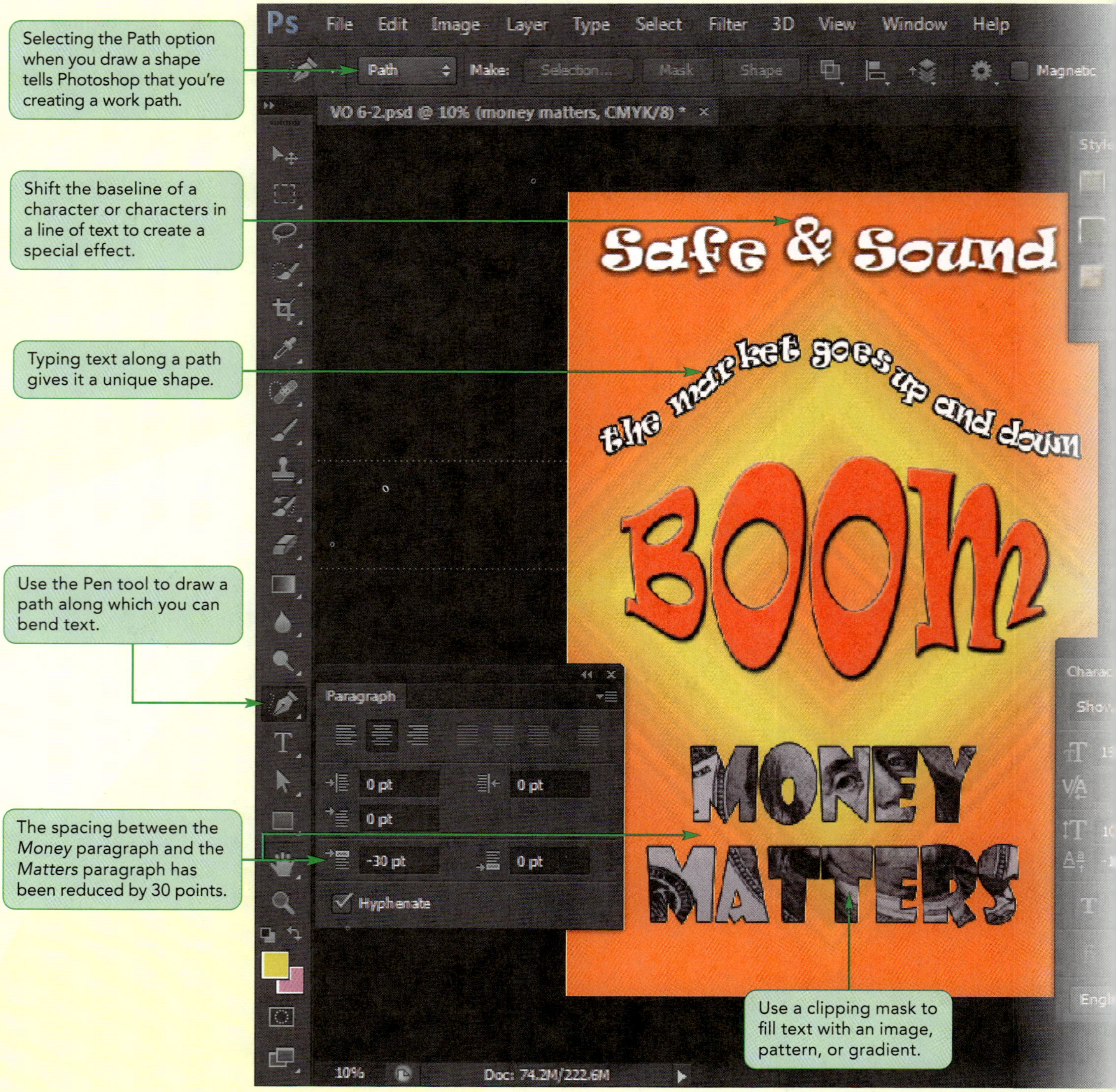

Helder Almeida/Shutterstock.com

CREATING UNIQUE TEXT

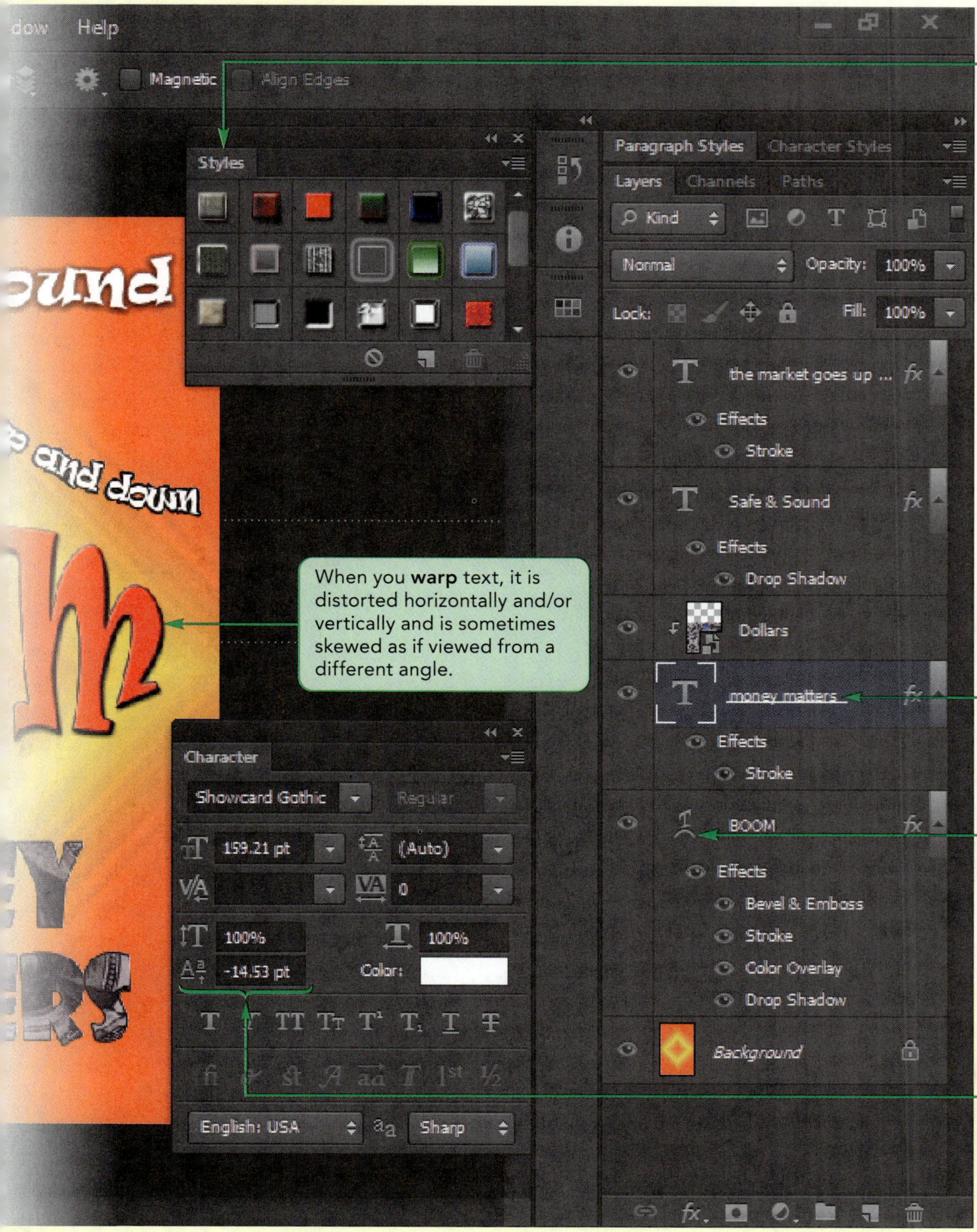

Use the Styles panel to apply preset effects to text.

When you **warp** text, it is distorted horizontally and/or vertically and is sometimes skewed as if viewed from a different angle.

The underlined text in this layer indicates that the layer is a **clipping mask**, which will mask the layer or layers above it. In this case, the image of the hundred dollar bill in the Dollars layer will be masked by the *Money Matters* text.

Warped text layers display a thumbnail indicating that the text is warped.

In the Character panel, you can set the **baseline shift**, which raises characters a specified number of points above or below the baseline.

Creating Unique Text

When you enter text in Photoshop, you can combine formatting options such as font, color, and alignment to get the look you want. However, there might be times when you want a unique look that isn't possible using the standard formatting tools. With the options available in the Styles panel, the baseline shift feature, and the text warping and bending capabilities of Photoshop, you have more powerful tools to work with to achieve interesting and unique results for your text. In addition, the ability to rasterize text and treat it as a digital or bitmap image opens up countless other possibilities as you use Photoshop's digital image-editing tools to create eye-catching text in your compositions.

Applying a Style to Text

The Styles panel has dozens of formatting presets that you can apply with the click of a button. In fact, Photoshop has style presets designed specifically for text, which are accessible via the Styles panel menu. Using the style presets allows you to experiment with different looks for the text in your composition without having to set a variety of individual effects such as shadow, bevel and emboss, and gradient fills.

The RC Investments text is too plain to draw attention to the company name in the layout you've been working on. You'll apply a text style to the company name, and then see if formatting the paragraph text with preset styles makes the layout more interesting.

To apply a style to the text:

1. If you took a break after the last session, start Photoshop while pressing the **Ctrl+Alt+Shift** keys, and click **Yes** to delete the Settings file when prompted. Switch to and reset the Typography workspace, and then reset all tools. Press the **D** key to restore the default foreground and background colors if necessary.
2. Navigate to the Photoshop6\Tutorial folder, open **RCDetails.psd**, if necessary, and fit the image on screen. Clear the guides and hide the rulers, if necessary. Double-click the Paragraph Styles tab to minimize the panel group so you can see all of the layers in the Layers panel.
3. In the Layers panel, hide the green RC Investments layer, if necessary. Display and select the **red RC Investments** layer.

   Trouble? If you are prompted to save changes to the current set of styles, click No.
4. Expand the Styles panel, click the panel menu button, and then click **Text Effects 2**. Click the **OK** button to replace the current styles. Click the **Swamp Bevel with Shadow** icon (the first effect). This effect gives the text a raised, three-dimensional look.
5. Click the **Dented Metal with Shadow** icon (third row, fourth column). This effect gives the text a shiny, metallic look.
6. Click the **Bright Red Bevel** icon (the third effect in the first row). This style adds four effects: a bevel and emboss effect, a stroke, a color overlay, and a drop shadow. Each effect in the style is listed beneath the RC Investments layer in the Layers panel. See Figure 6-23.

Figure 6-23 Applying a style

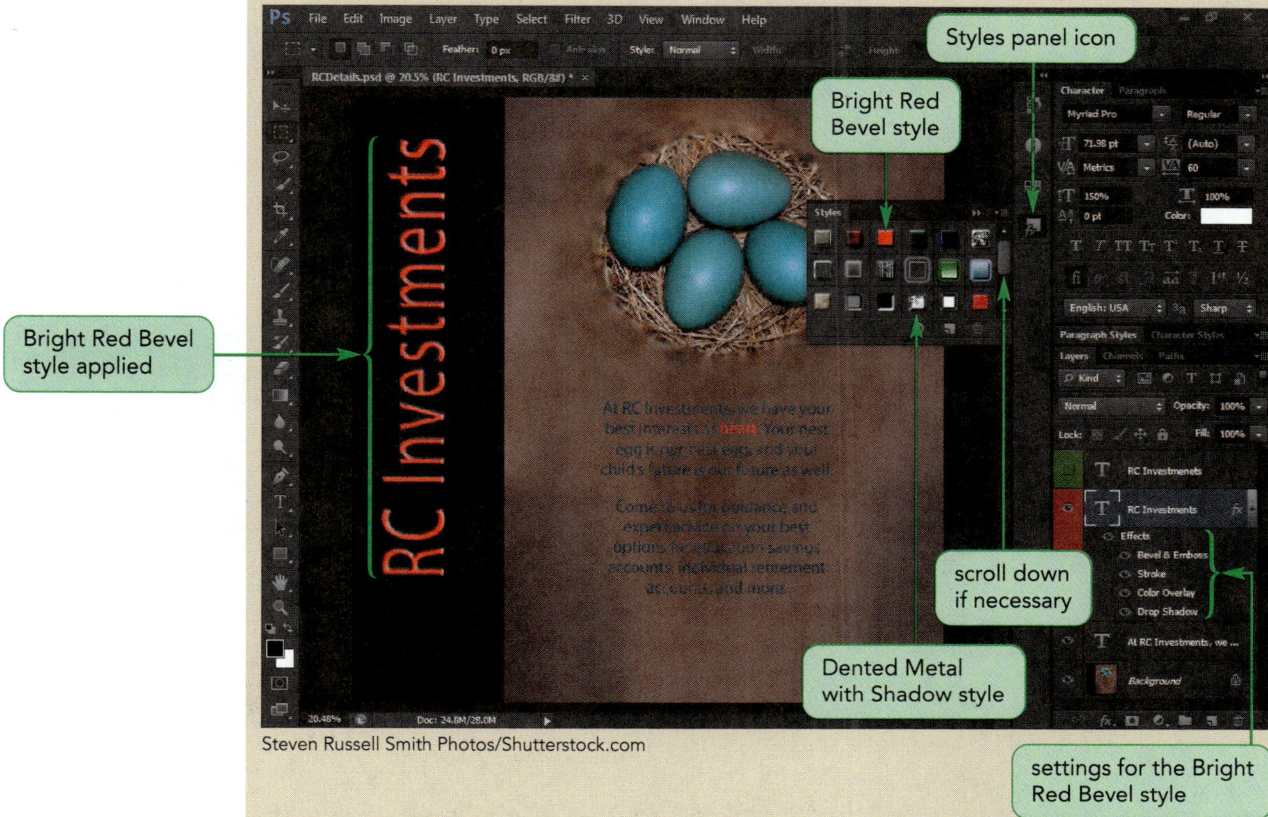

Steven Russell Smith Photos/Shutterstock.com

7. In the Layers panel, select the **At RC Investments...** layer, and then apply the **Bright Red Bevel** style to both paragraphs. Although the style made the company name stand out well on the black background, when it is applied to the paragraph, it makes the text difficult to read.

8. Apply the **Dented Metal with Shadow** style to the paragraphs. See Figure 6-24.

Figure 6-24 Style applied to paragraphs

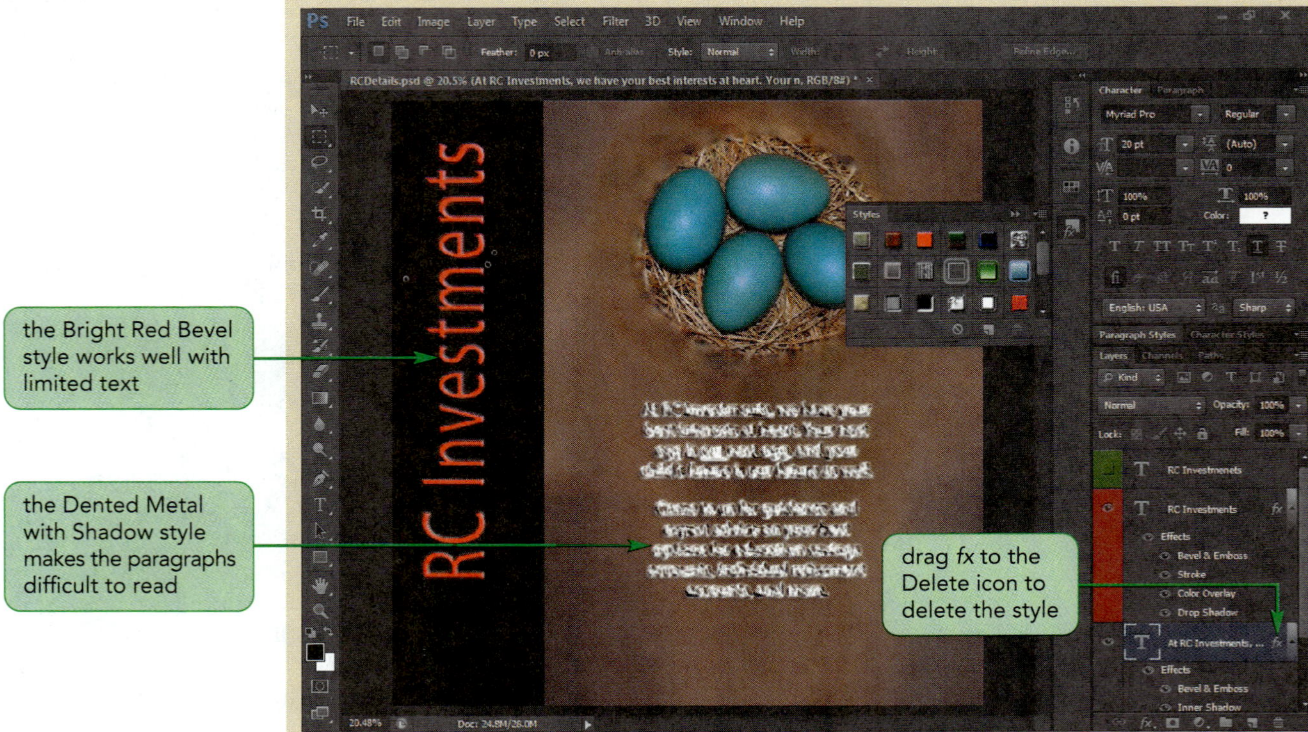

Steven Russell Smith Photos/Shutterstock.com

The Dented Metal style also makes the paragraph text difficult to read. For paragraphs with a lot of text, the simpler the better. You can get a message across much more effectively if the text itself takes center stage rather than its formatting.

9. Delete the paragraph text style you added by dragging the ***fx*** symbol at the right of the At RC Investments… text layer name to the **Delete** icon at the bottom of the Layers panel. The text returns to the formatting you applied earlier.
10. Collapse the Styles panel, save RCDetails.psd, and close it.

Scaling and Tracking Text to Achieve Balance

You can also create unique text by scaling individual characters to give words and phrases different shapes, and to achieve balance in a layout. When you adjust the tracking between characters, text shifts left or right in the text layer, changing its relation to the center point. When you change the horizontal scale of a letter or letters, you're not only changing the shape of the word, you're also shifting the text on either side as you widen or narrow the selected characters.

To adjust scaling and tracking to add shape and balance a text object:

1. Open **RCPath.psd**, located in the Photoshop6\Tutorial folder, and save it as **RightPath.psd** in the same folder; then press the **Ctrl+0** keys to fit the image on screen. Display the rulers, if necessary. This file includes an image and text.

TIP

If a text tool is active, you can also triple-click text on a selected layer directly on the canvas to select all of the text in the text object.

Trouble? If your system doesn't have the font provided in the file, accept the suggested font substitution.

2. Double-click the **Safe & Sound** text thumbnail to select all of the text, and then click on the canvas to the left of the ampersand (&) to place the insertion point.
3. Double-click the **&** to select it. See Figure 6-25.

Figure 6-25 Single character selected in text-editing mode

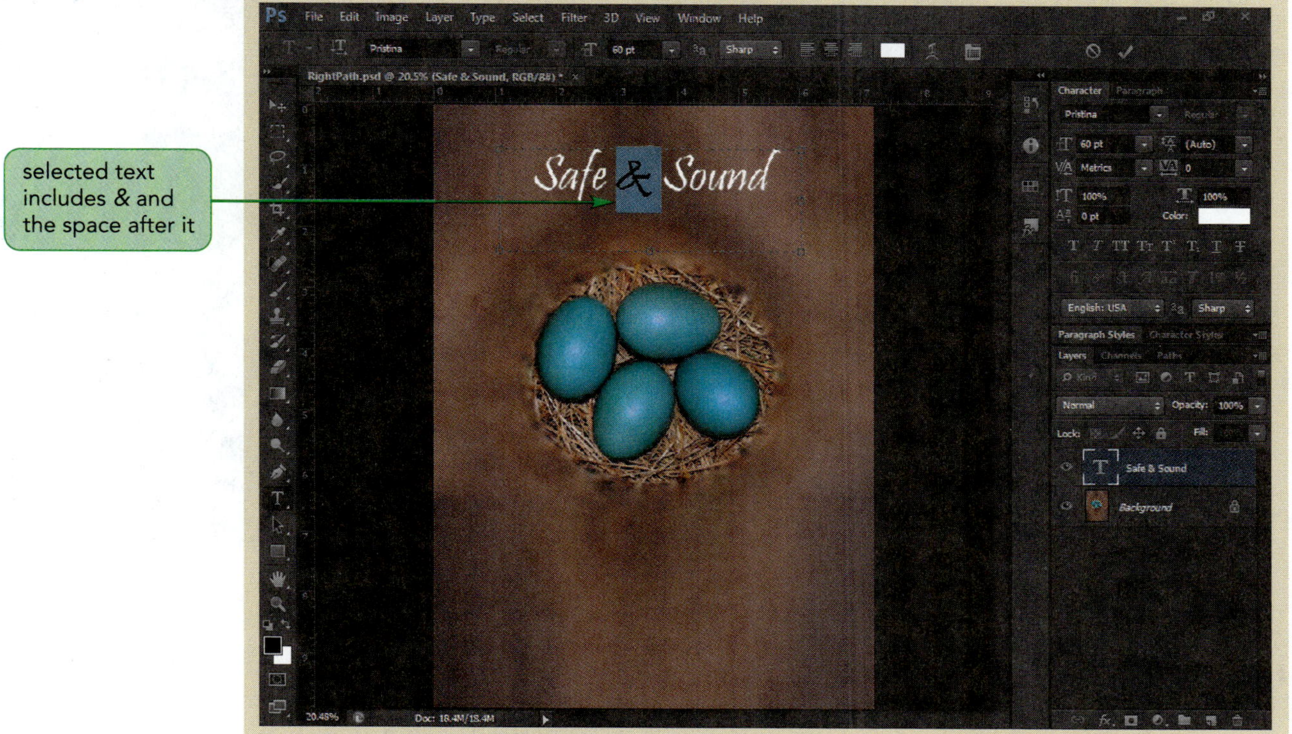

Steven Russell Smith Photos/Shutterstock.com

The & and the space after it are selected. You'll make the ampersand larger to give the text a unique shape.

4. Change the font size of the & from 60 points to **72** points, and then commit the change. See Figure 6-26.

Figure 6-26 Mixed font sizes

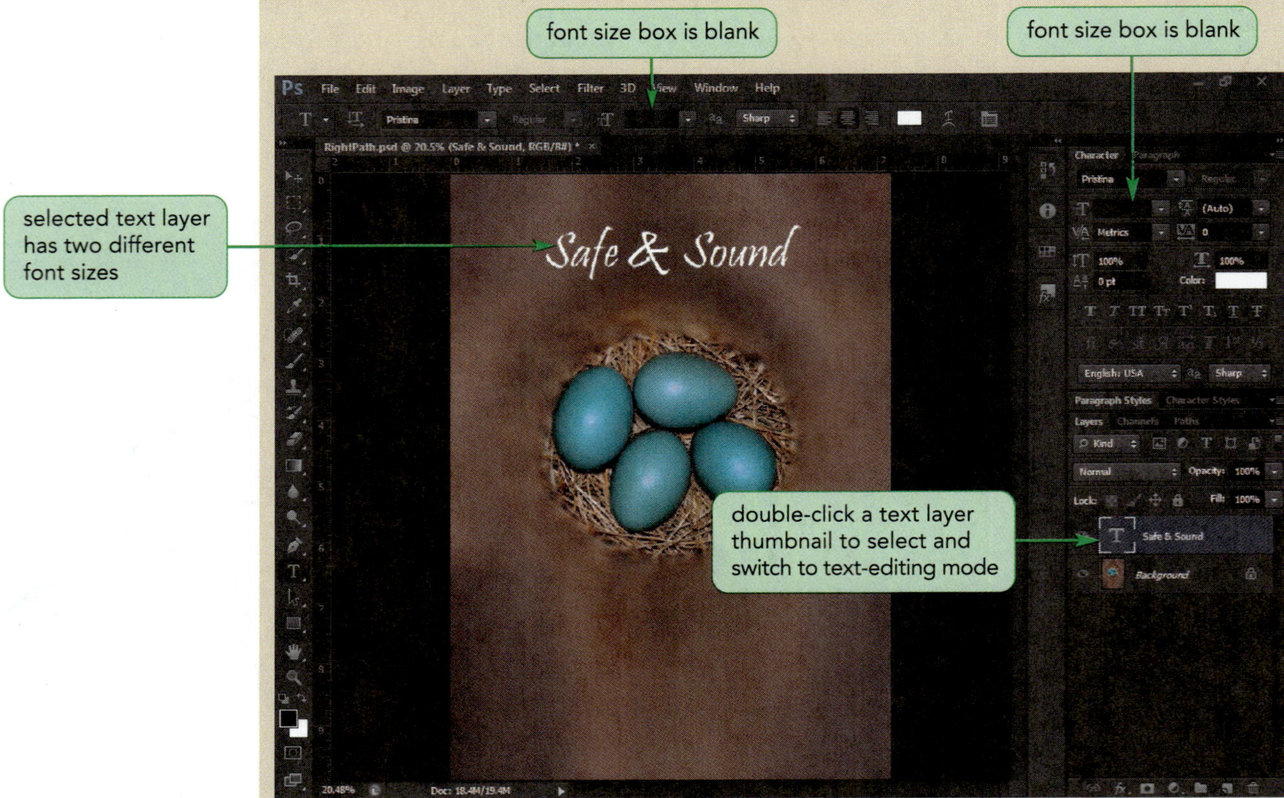

Steven Russell Smith Photos/Shutterstock.com

Because this text layer now has more than one font size applied, the Set the font size boxes are blank in the Character panel and on the options bar.

Trouble? If you can't see the Set the font size box on the options bar, make sure the Horizontal Type tool is still selected in the Tools panel.

5. Press the **V** key to activate the Move tool, and then show the transform controls, if necessary. See Figure 6-27.

Figure 6-27 **Centering text**

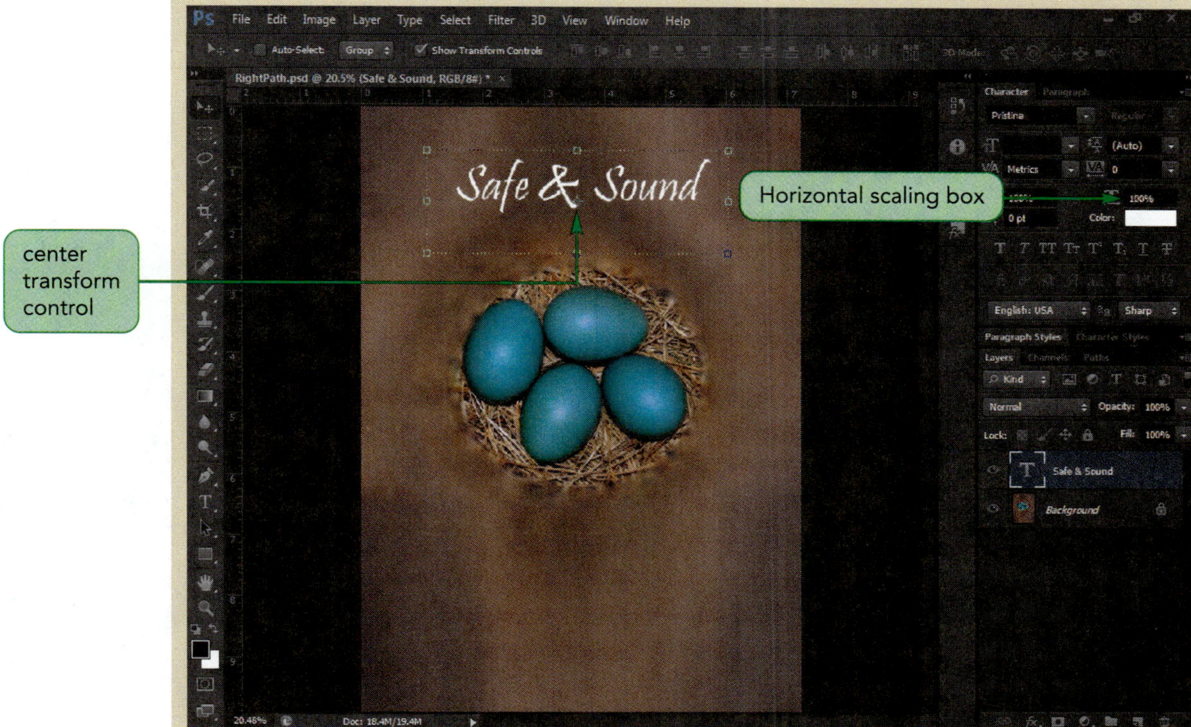

Steven Russell Smith Photos/Shutterstock.com

Notice that the center transform control, which marks the center of the text, is to the right of the ampersand. You'll change the horizontal scaling of the word *Safe* and change the tracking of individual letters and spaces to make the text more balanced around the center point.

6. In the Layers panel, double-click the **Safe & Sound** text thumbnail, and then drag on the canvas to select all of the letters in the word *Safe*.
7. In the Character panel, horizontally scale the word *Safe* to **120%**.
8. On the canvas, select the ***e*** in *Safe* and the space after the word *Safe*, and set the tracking to **60**.
9. Select the space after the *&* and select the ***S*** in *Sound*, and decrease the tracking to **-75**. Click the **Commit** button. The text is now more evenly balanced around the center point. See Figure 6-28.

TIP

You can also scrub the Set the tracking for the selected characters icon in the Character panel to adjust the tracking value by increments of 20.

Figure 6-28 **Balanced text**

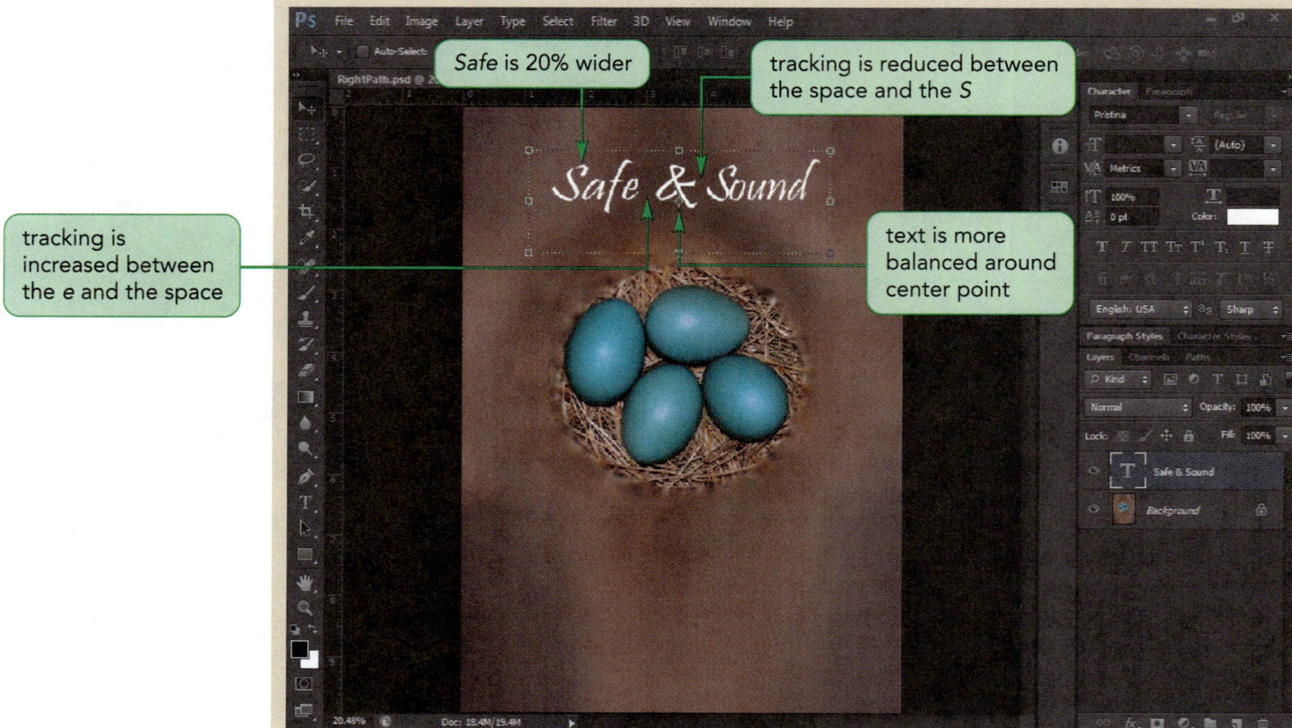

Steven Russell Smith Photos/Shutterstock.com

10. Save RightPath.psd, and keep the file open.

INSIGHT

Understanding Optical and Metrics Kerning

Kerning makes text easier to read by adding or subtracting space between pairs of characters. Just looking at the text on this page, you can probably see that some character pairs are closer together than others based on the shapes of the characters. Many of the font families you'll work with come with predefined kern pairs that handle letter pairings that might otherwise be problematic—for example, the letter *W* might be kerned differently when paired with the letter *o* than when paired with the letter *i* simply for readability. When this kerning is built in to a font family, it's called **metrics kerning**. However, some fonts don't have built-in kerning, or they have kerning for some character pairs but not others. When this is the case, you can choose the **optical kerning** option in Photoshop, and Photoshop will adjust the spacing between character pairs based on the shapes of the characters. To work with metrics and optical kerning, you can choose either Metrics or Optical, rather than a number setting, from the "Set the kerning between two characters" list in the Character panel.

Next, you'll change the baseline shift of the ampersand in the *Safe & Sound* text to give the text in the composition a more interesting shape.

Specifying a Baseline Shift

So far, all of the point text you have entered has been placed on the default baseline, indicated by *0 pt* in the Set the baseline shift box in the Character panel. However, you can assign a positive number to the baseline to shift characters above the baseline by the specified number of points. Assign a negative number to shift characters so they sit beneath the baseline.

To specify a baseline shift for the ampersand:

1. Press the **T** key to activate the Horizontal Type tool, and then select the **&** on the Safe & Sound layer.
2. In the Character panel, type **10** in the Set the baseline shift box. The ampersand moves above the rest of the text, 10 points above the baseline. You'll try a different setting to see how the ampersand looks below the baseline.
3. In the Character panel, set the baseline shift to **-15**. See Figure 6-29.

Figure 6-29 Baseline shift

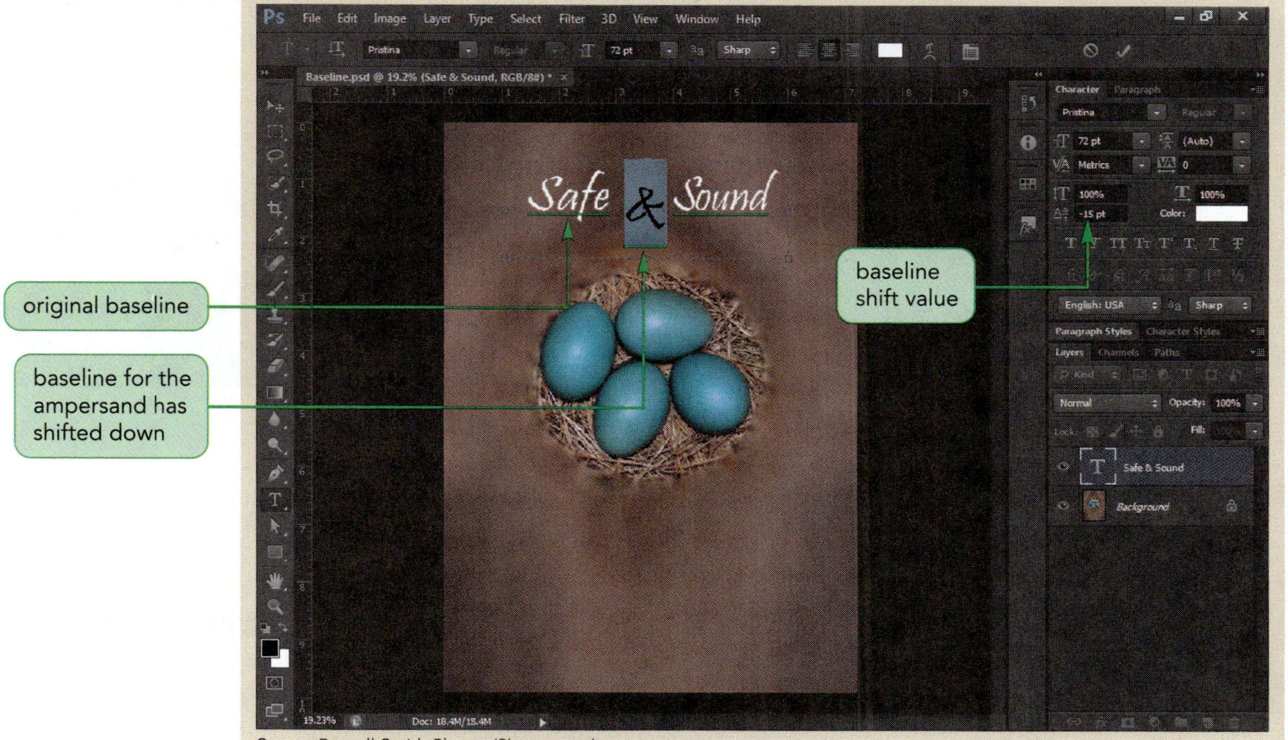

Steven Russell Smith Photos/Shutterstock.com

A negative baseline shift value moves the selection below the baseline of the other characters.

4. Commit the change, save the file as **Baseline.psd** in the Photoshop6\Tutorial folder, and keep the file open.

Warping Text

You can warp text to give it a unique shape. When you warp text, characters fill the shape of the warp style you specify. Characters no longer have a consistent font size, and depending on the warp, they might also be slightly skewed in perspective—for example, they might look as if they are being squashed or stretched vertically, horizontally, or diagonally. See Figure 6-30, which shows some of the default warp styles available in Photoshop, including Flag, Squeeze, and Bulge.

Figure 6-30 Warping text

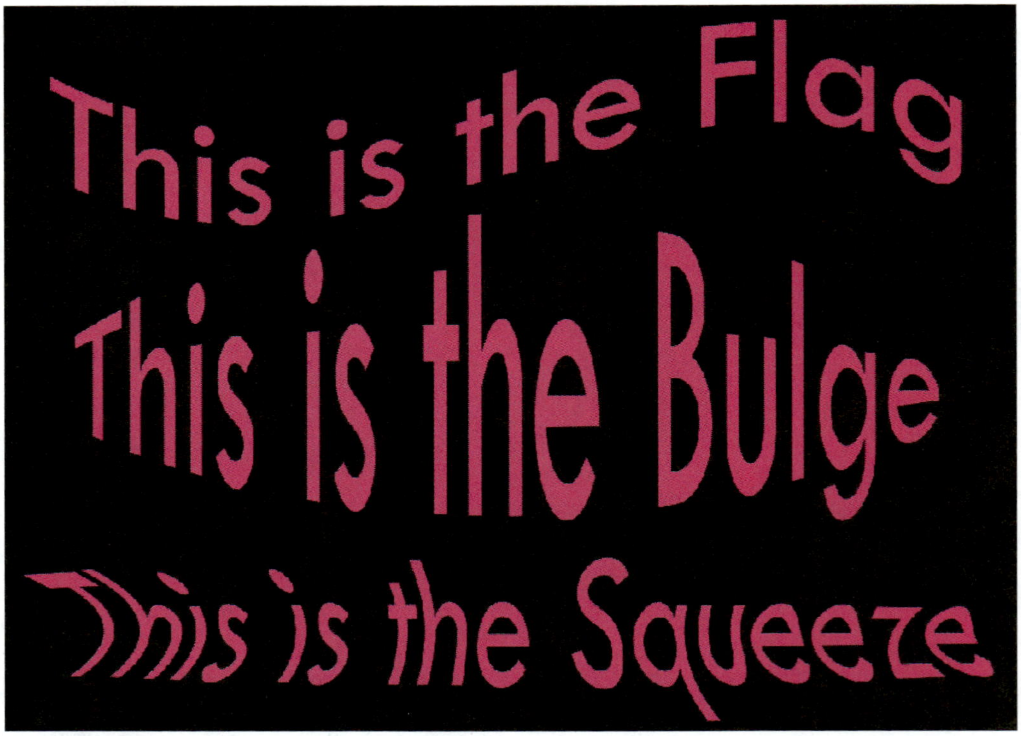

When you warp text, you can use the default settings for the specified warp, or you can modify the extent of the warp by changing the Bend percentage, or the Horizontal or Vertical Distortion. As you change the values in the Warp Text dialog box, you can see them being applied on the canvas.

REFERENCE

Warping Text

- In the Layers panel, click the text layer you want to warp, and in the Tools panel, click the Horizontal Type Tool button or the Vertical Type Tool button.
- On the options bar, click the Create warped text button.
- In the Warp Text dialog box, select the style for the warp.
- Specify a direction for the warp, and change the Bend, Horizontal Distortion, and Vertical Distortion percentages to change the warp effect, as desired.
- Click the OK button to warp the text.

You'll warp the Safe & Sound text to see if the effect works in your composition.

TIP

You can also click Layer on the menu bar, point to Type, and then click Warp Text to open the Warp Text dialog box.

To warp the Safe & Sound text:

1. In the Layers panel, click the **Safe & Sound** text layer to select it, if necessary.
2. On the options bar, click the **Create warped text** button. The Warp Text dialog box opens.
3. Drag the **Warp Text** dialog box to the right so you can see all of the canvas.
4. In the Warp Text dialog box, click the **Style** arrow, and then click **Arc Lower**. See Figure 6-31.

Figure 6-31 Arc Lower warp applied to text

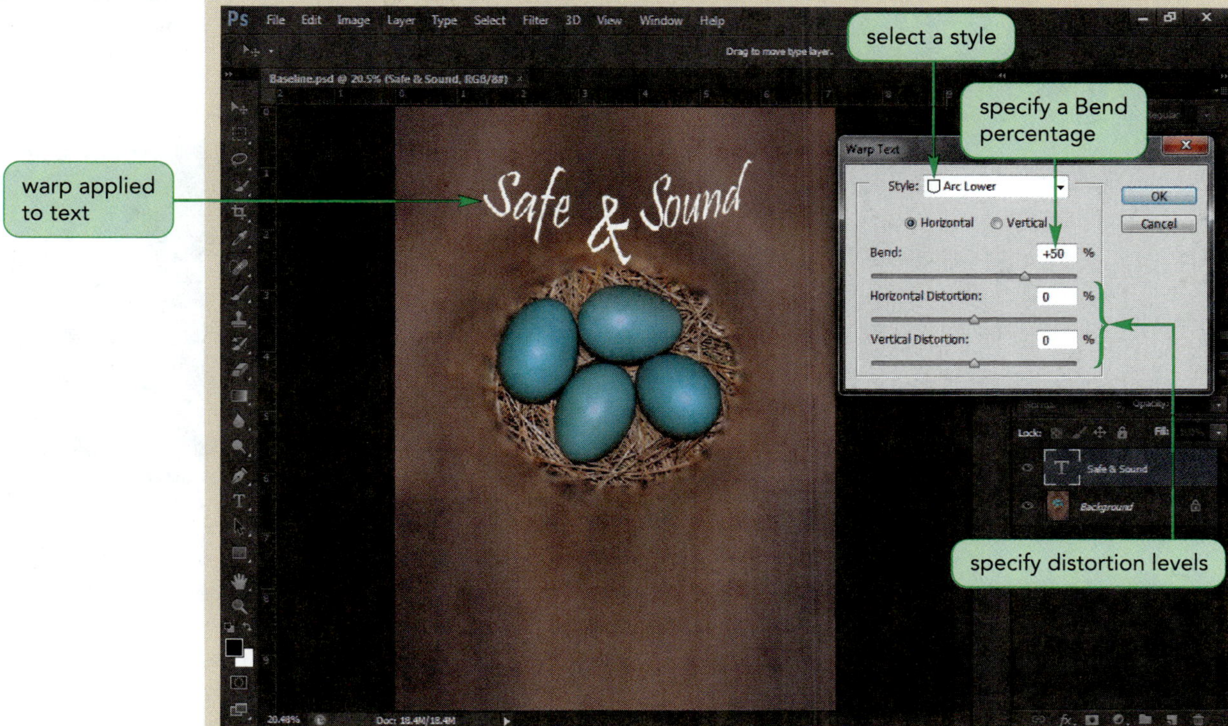

Steven Russell Smith Photos/Shutterstock.com

5. Change the Bend to -**20** and the Horizontal Distortion to -**60**. The Bend setting determines the amount of distortion applied to the text. By specifying a negative number, you reduced the distortion. The Horizontal Distortion setting changes the perspective of the warp.
6. Press and hold the **Alt** key and then click the **Reset** button in the Warp text dialog box. Photoshop removes the warp, and the settings go back to their defaults. You'll try a different warp setting to see if it works better in the composition.
7. Click the **Style** arrow, and then click **Rise**.
8. Change the Bend setting to **0**. A Bend setting of 0 applies no distortion, so the text is not affected by the warp.
9. Drag the **Bend** slider to change the Bend setting to **+55**.

   As you experiment with warp effects, you can move the text around the image without closing the dialog box. This feature lets you get the effect you want in the most efficient way.

10. On the canvas, drag the text up and to the left. See Figure 6-32.

Figure 6-32 Rise warp applied to text

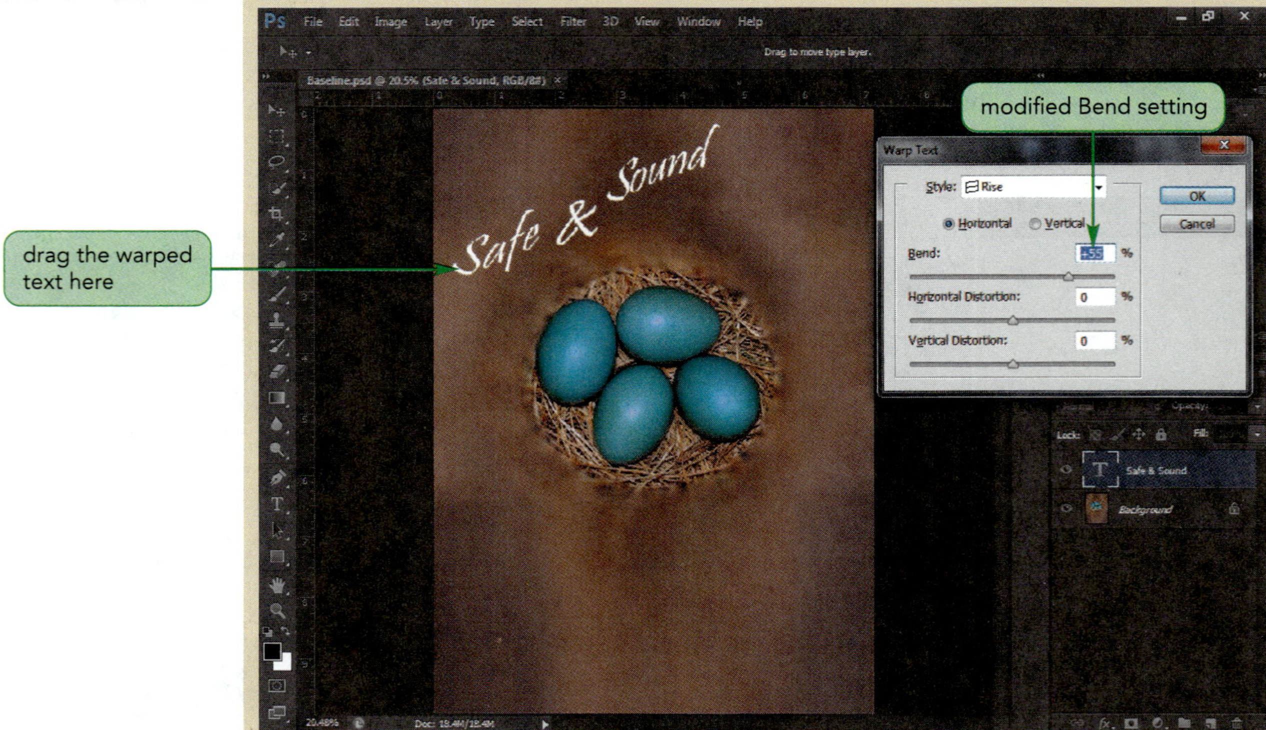

Steven Russell Smith Photos/Shutterstock.com

Trouble? If your Bend setting does not have a plus sign in front of the 55, you typed the value rather than dragging the Bend slider. Either method achieves the same result.

11. Press and hold the **Alt** key and then click the **Reset** button in the Warp Text dialog box. You'll try one more warp setting and reposition the text so it flows around the nest.

12. Click the **Style** arrow [▾], and then click **Arc Upper**. Increase the Bend setting to **+100%**, and then change the Horizontal Distortion to **0%** and the Vertical Distortion to **0%**, if necessary. Then drag the text so it is positioned as shown in Figure 6-33.

Figure 6-33 **Arc Upper warp applied to text**

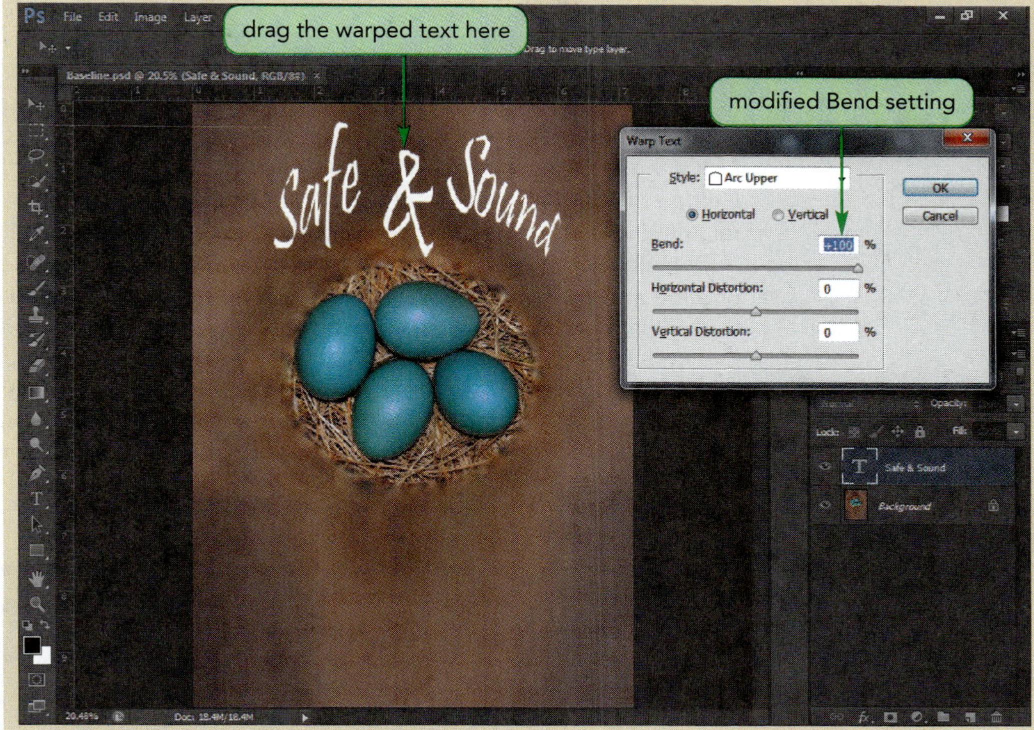

Steven Russell Smith Photos/Shutterstock.com

13. Click the **OK** button to close the Warp Text dialog box. The warp is applied to the text, and in the Layers panel, the text layer now has a different icon, indicating that the text is warped.
14. In the Layers panel, position the pointer over the **Safe & Sound** text thumbnail. Photoshop displays an "Indicates warped text layer" tip.
15. Save the file as **ArcUpper.psd** in the Photoshop6\Tutorial folder, and leave it open.

INSIGHT

Working with Placeholder Text

If your Photoshop comp includes text, you might not be the one who writes the text. Instead, you might need to get the text for your piece from some other department, such as editorial or marketing. If this is the case, and the text is not readily available, consider using **placeholder text** or **dummy text**, which lets you work with fonts and font sizes in text boxes to plan your layout. Many compositors use *lorem ipsum* text as placeholder text in templates. **Lorem ipsum** text is a standard series of Latin words. Oddly enough, if you do use lorem ipsum text, what you are doing is called **greeking**. Photoshop CS6 includes a new Paste Lorem Ipsum command on the Type menu. To fill a text box with lorem ipsum text, simply click Type on the menu bar, and then click Paste Lorem Ipsum. Photoshop fills the text box with text using the paragraph and character settings you have selected. The first sentence of the text is "This is Photoshop's version of Lorem Ipsum." The rest of the sentences are in Latin.

Adding Text Along a Path

TIP

To add and delete anchor points, you use the Add Anchor Point and Delete Anchor Point tools, which are hidden beneath the Pen tool in the Tools panel.

If the warp options in Photoshop aren't what you need for your composition, you can draw a path on the canvas and then add text to it so the text follows the path. When you create text on a path, the path becomes the baseline for any text you enter. Photoshop provides a number of tools for creating paths. You can use the Pen tool or the Freeform Pen tool to create an **open path** with a separate start point and endpoint and then manipulate individual points on the path until it takes the shape you need. Using the Pen and Freeform Pen tools often creates an initial path that is inexact. Getting the path to conform to the shape you want can be tedious, as it requires adding, deleting, and moving **anchor points**, the points that define the path.

Drawing tools like the Ellipse tool, the Rectangle tool, and the Custom Shape tool provide an easier way than the Pen tools to create interesting paths for text. When you draw a path with the Ellipse or Rectangle tool, you are creating a **closed path**, or a path in which the start point and the endpoint are one and the same. You can use the drawing tools individually, or you can combine them to create a complex path shape. In Figure 6-34, the elliptical path was created using the Ellipse tool, and the other two paths were drawn with the Pen tool.

Figure 6-34 Sharp angles and curves in a path

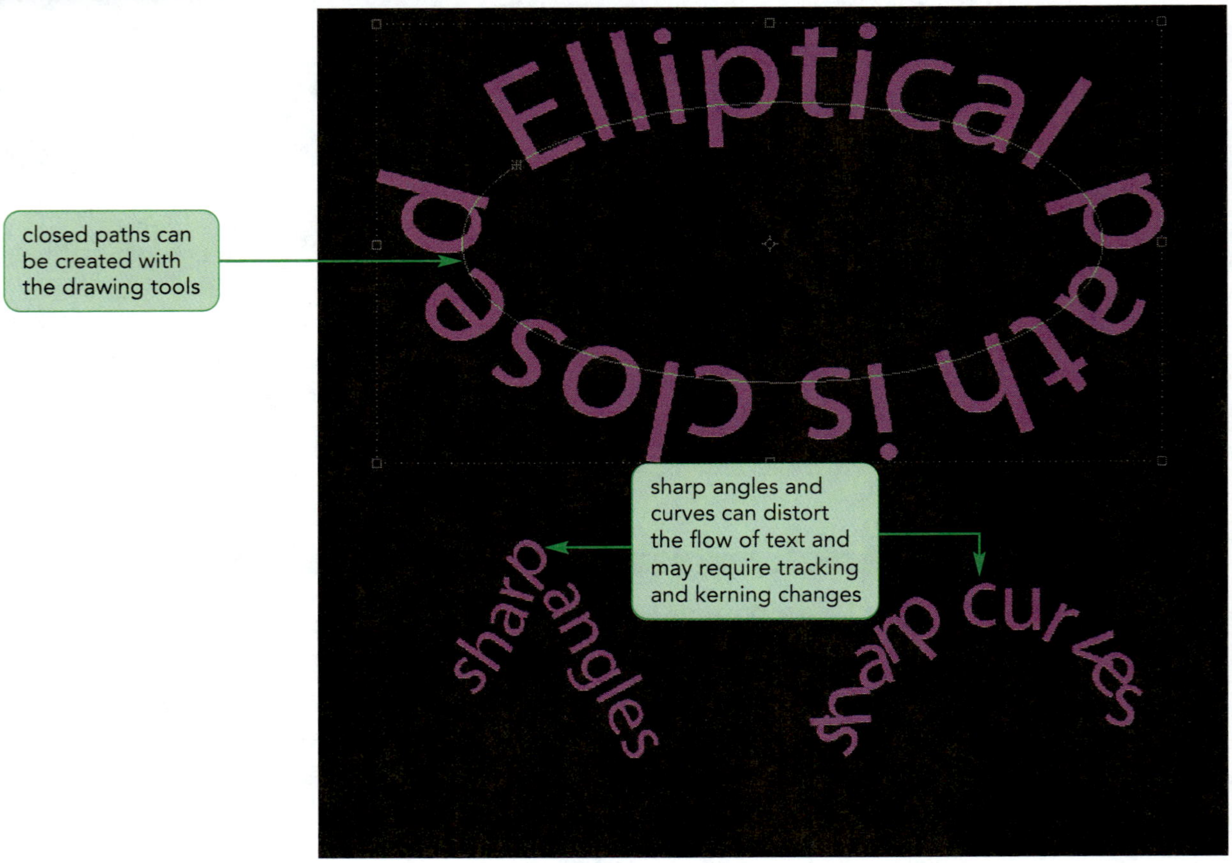

Figure 6-34 shows two of the pitfalls of aligning text to a path. Typing text along a path with a sharp angle or a sharp curve can distort the flow of text and throw characters on top of each other. Typing text along a curved or angled path often requires tracking and kerning adjustments so the text flows smoothly.

Rose would like you to try a different promotional phrase on the image of the nest. In addition, she'd also like you to wrap the text completely around the nest. You'll use the Ellipse tool to create a closed path along which you'll enter the new text.

To create the closed path and add text to it:

1. In the Layers panel, select and hide the Safe & Sound layer.
2. In the Tools panel, click the **Ellipse Tool** button.

   Trouble? If you don't see the Ellipse Tool button, right-click the Rectangle Tool button and then click the Ellipse Tool button on the context menu.
3. On the options bar, click the **Shape** button, and then click **Path**. Selecting the Path option ensures that the shape you draw will be a path rather than a shape on a new layer.
4. Click near the center of the nest. The Create Ellipse dialog box opens. Set both the width and height to **1500** pixels, verify that the **From Center** check box is selected, and then click the **OK** button.

   Photoshop adds a path in the shape of a circle around the image of the nest.
5. To ensure that the path is centered over the nest, in the Tools panel, click the **Path Selection Tool** button, point to the path, and then drag it to the location shown in Figure 6-35.

Figure 6-35 Closed path for text

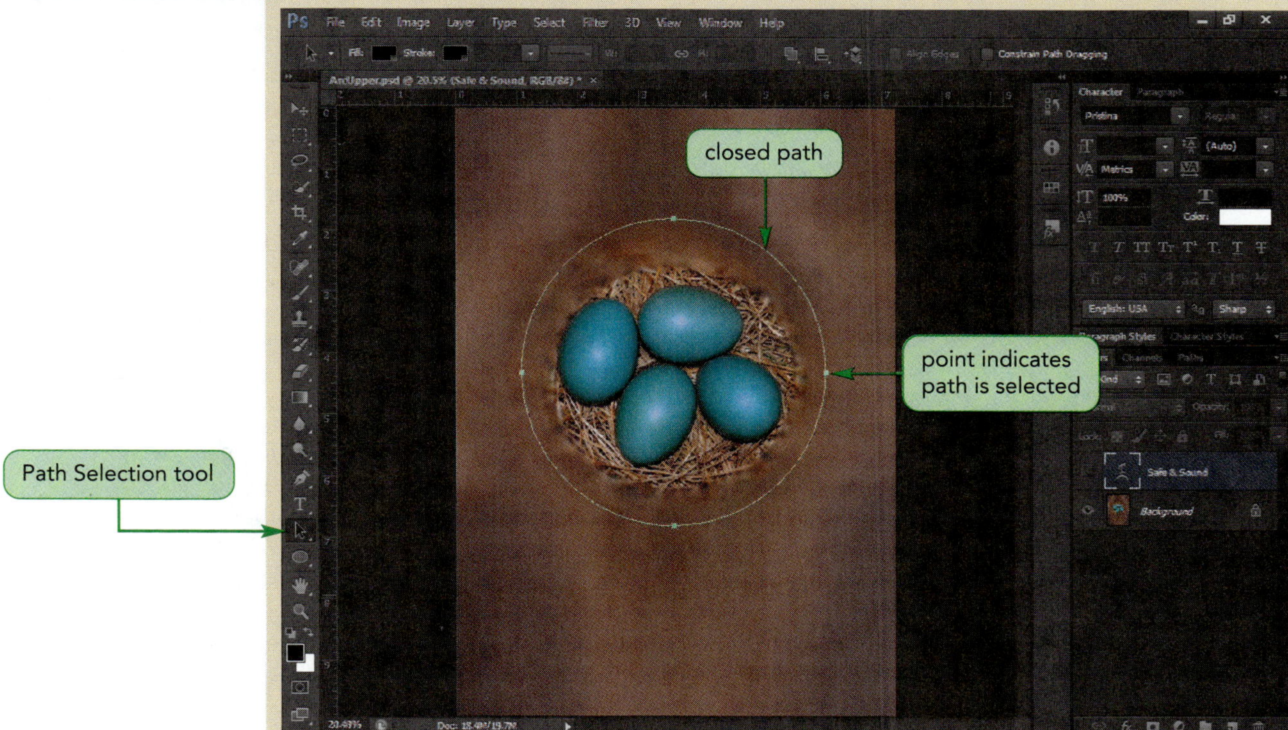

Steven Russell Smith Photos/Shutterstock.com

6. Click the **Horizontal Type Tool** button, and on the options bar, select **Segoe UI** as the font, set the font style to **Regular**, set the font size to **48** points, set the anti-aliasing to **Strong**, left-align the text, and on the options bar, set the color to any **blue**.
7. Click the left side of the path, just under the anchor point, and then type **RC Investments: The Right Choice for Your Nest Egg**. The text follows the shape of the path you drew. See Figure 6-36.

Figure 6-36 Text along a closed path

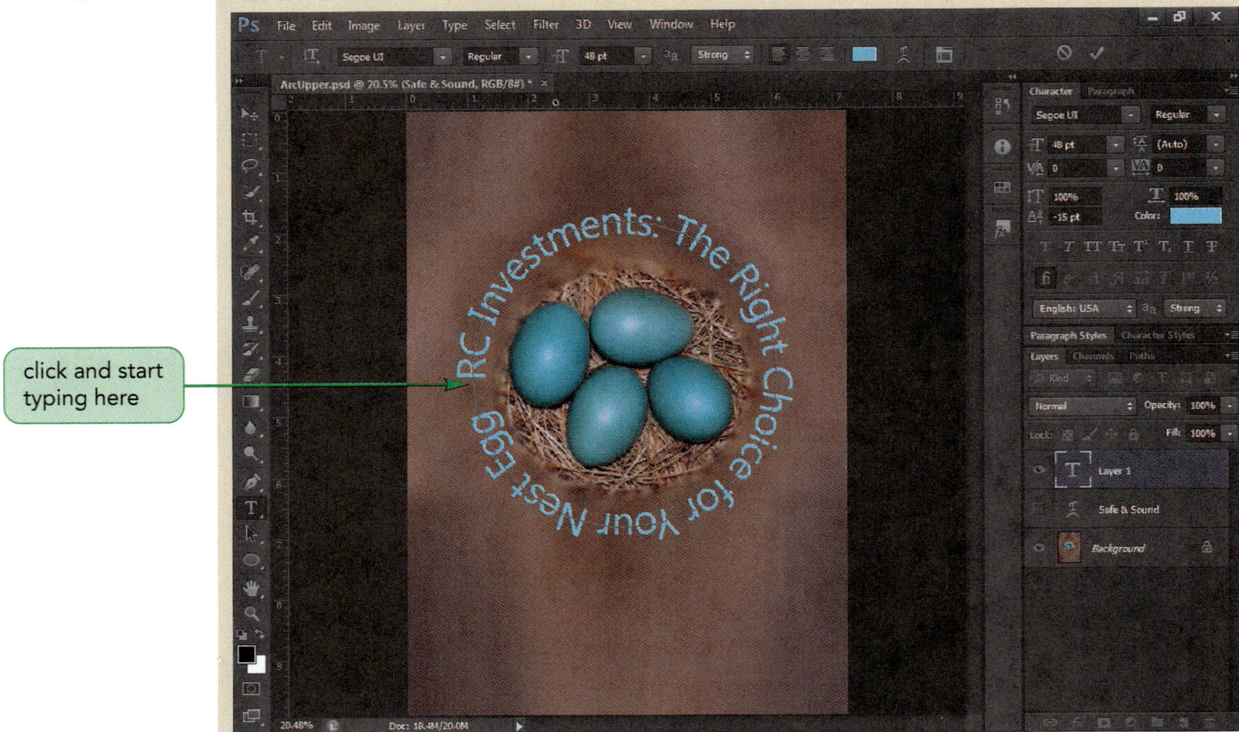

Steven Russell Smith Photos/Shutterstock.com

8. In the Layers panel, click the **Background** layer to deselect the path and commit the text. Save the file as **CirclePath.psd** in the Photoshop6\Tutorial folder, and close it.

PROSKILLS

Written Communication: Adding Copy to a Composition

If it is your responsibility to write the text in a layout yourself, you need to gather the information and details you'll need for the copy ahead of time. To do so, you can discuss the copy with managers or subject matter experts in other departments. Or, if the piece is for an external customer, contact the customer for details about their product or service. Once you have written the copy, you'll most likely need to get it approved by the department responsible for external communications, such as the Public Relations Department or the Marketing Department. You'll also need to have someone edit the text, and when the composition is complete, you should have someone proofread the copy to check it for errors.

You need to consider the context in order to make decisions about text layout and formatting. Will your composition appear in a newsletter that uses a particular font set? If so, you'll need to use a font from that set—unless, of course, your goal is to draw attention to the image in a way that is out of the ordinary. You also need to consider the nature of the brand you're writing about. If your piece is an ad, is there a specific font that the company always uses in its advertisements so the text itself is recognizable as part of the brand? Once you understand what the expectations are for written communication in your organization, you can use your image- and text-editing skills to create impressive, attention-grabbing layouts.

Rose would like to eventually work with a Web developer to create an ad that appears along the right side of some of the more popular search engines. Her idea is that three words, "Money Changes Everything," will appear one by one to grab the viewer's attention. She wants each word to have a different effect, and has asked you to create a comp that shows her some options.

Filling Text with an Image, Pattern, or Gradient

Another way you can give text a unique look is to fill it with an image, pattern, or gradient. To fill text with an image, you apply a clipping mask to the image you want the text to display. A clipping mask lets you define a mask for a layer based on the shape of another layer. When you fill text with an image, pattern, or gradient, you are actually specifying that everything *except* the text should mask the underlying image. As a result, the graphic or pattern shows through the letter shapes.

To fill text with an image:

1. Open **Money.psd**, located in the Photoshop6\Tutorial folder, and save it as **MoneyClip.psd** in the same folder. Reset the background and foreground colors to the default colors.

   Right now, only the Sunrise layer is visible. Two of the text layers are hidden, and the Money and Background layers are covered on the canvas by the Sunrise layer. You'll use the Sunrise layer to fill the first word, *Money*, with an image. First you'll add a stroke to the Money layer so that the fill is more dramatic.

2. In the Layers panel, hide the **Sunrise** layer, double-click the **Money** layer to open the Layer Style dialog box, and then add a **10-pixel**, **Outside**, **Normal**, **black** stroke to the text, as shown in Figure 6-37.

Figure 6-37 Stroke added to text

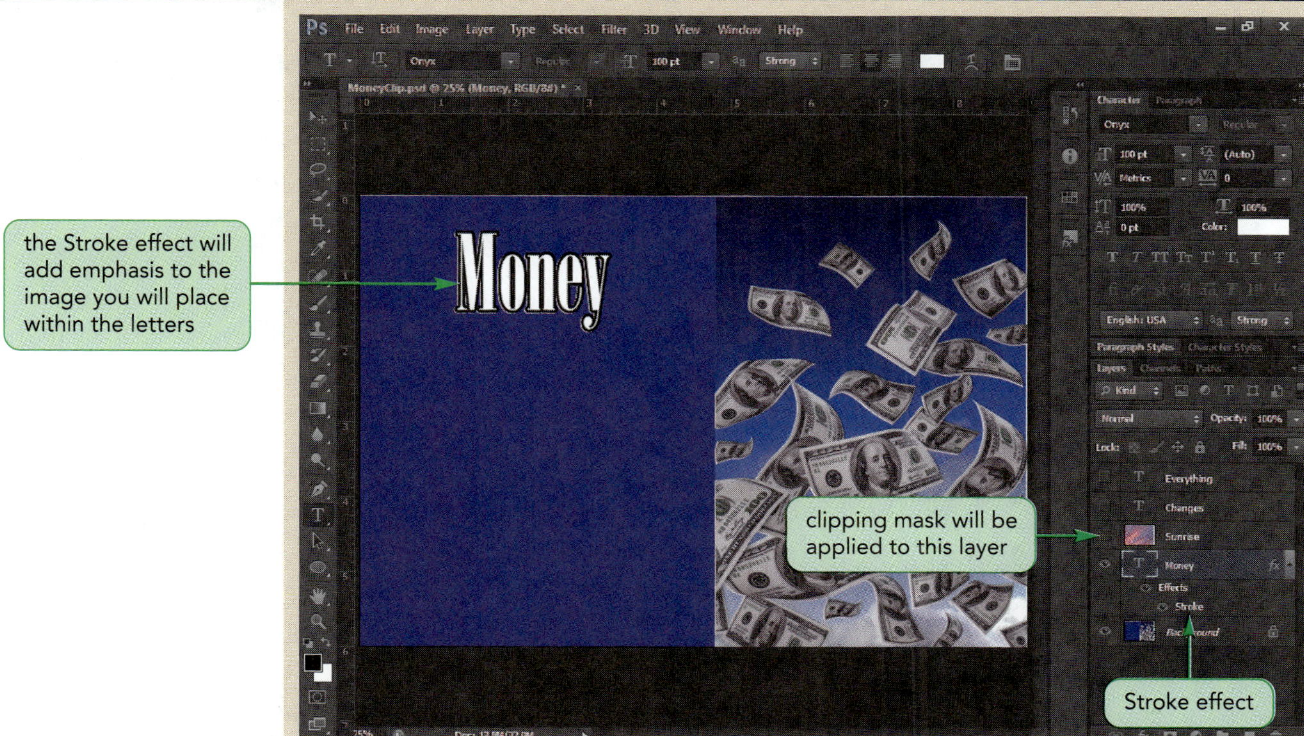

Helder Almeida/Shutterstock.com; Jane Hosie-Bounar

TIP

You can also press the Alt+Ctrl+G keys to create a clipping mask.

3. In the Layers panel, display the **Sunrise** layer and select it.
4. On the menu bar, click **Layer** and then click **Create Clipping Mask**. Photoshop uses the Sunrise image layer to fill the *Money* text. See Figure 6-38.

Figure 6-38 **Clipping mask applied to text**

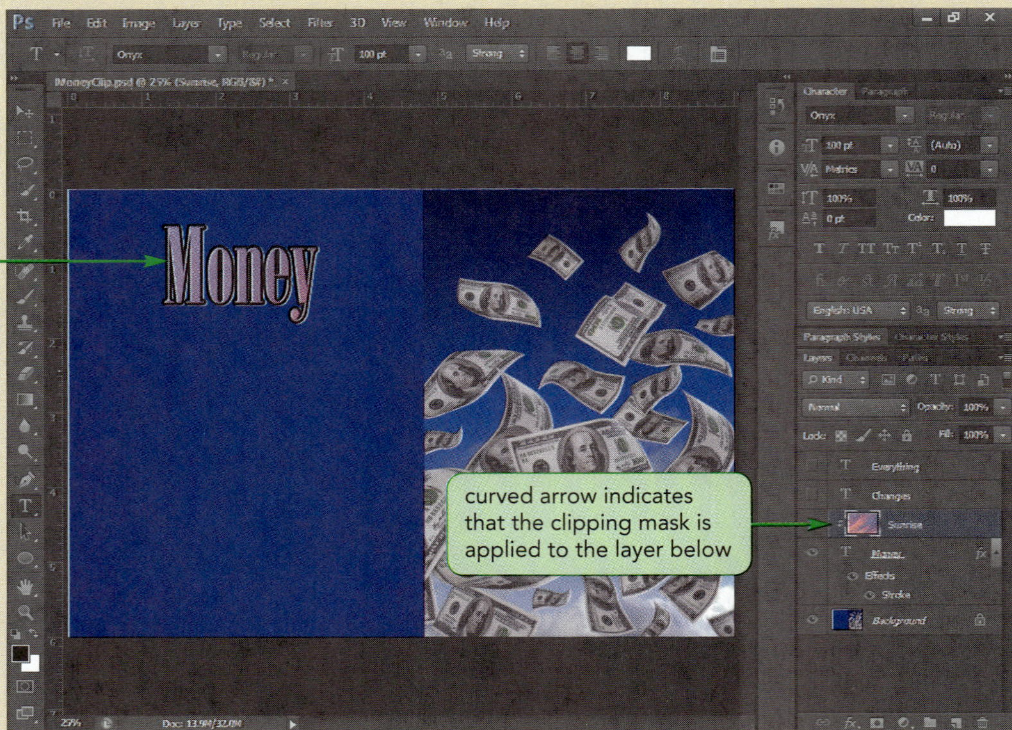

Helder Almeida/Shutterstock.com; Jane Hosie-Bounar

5. Right-click the **Sunrise** layer, and then click **Release Clipping Mask**. The image you used to mask the text now appears on top of the canvas, covering everything beneath it in the Layers panel, including the text and the background.
6. Press the **Ctrl+Z** keys to undo Step 5. The mask is reapplied.
7. Save the file, and keep it open.

You can also use a clipping mask to fill text with a gradient or a pattern. To do so, add a gradient or pattern layer above the text you want to fill, and then create the clipping mask. You'll experiment with pattern and gradient clipping mask effects to see which one will work best for RC Investments.

To fill the text with a pattern and a gradient:

1. In the Layers panel, display the **Changes** layer. You'll copy the layer style you applied to the Money layer and apply it by pasting it on the Changes layer.
2. Right-click the **Money** layer, and click **Copy Layer Style**. The layer style is copied to the Clipboard.
3. Right-click the **Changes** layer, and then click **Paste Layer Style**. The Changes layer now has a 10-pixel black stroke.

4. At the bottom of the Layers panel, click the **Create new fill or adjustment layer** icon, and then click **Pattern**.
5. In the Pattern Fill dialog box, click the **pattern** thumbnail to open the Pattern Fill preset picker, click the **More options** button to display the list of available preset libraries, click **Nature Patterns**, and then click the **Append** button to append the new presets to the current set of patterns.
6. Select the **Yellow Mums** preset (the third preset in the second row), change the Scale to **60%**, and then click the **OK** button. The layer is now filled with a pattern of yellow flowers.

   Trouble? If the Yellow Mums preset is not in the second row, position the mouse pointer over the preset thumbnails until you see *Yellow Mums*.
7. Right-click the **Pattern Fill 1** layer, and then click **Create Clipping Mask**. The *Changes* text is filled with the pattern you selected. See Figure 6-39.

Figure 6-39 **Pattern-filled text**

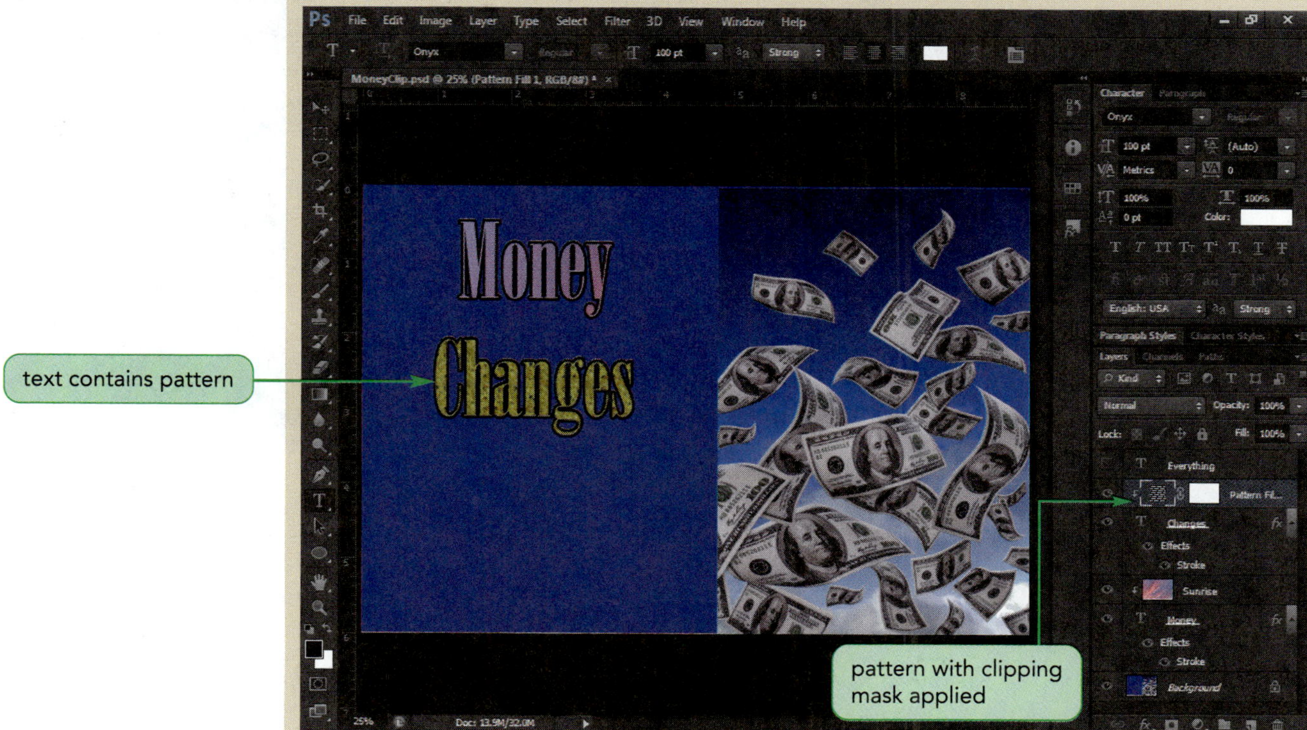

Helder Almeida/Shutterstock.com; Jane Hosie-Bounar

8. Display and then right-click the **Everything** layer, and then click **Paste Layer Style**. The Everything layer now has a 10-pixel black stroke.
9. At the bottom of the Layers panel, click the **Create new fill or adjustment layer** icon, and then click **Gradient**.
10. In the Gradient Fill dialog box, click the **Gradient** arrow, click the **Transparent Rainbow** gradient (the second gradient in the last row), change the angle to **30** degrees, and then click the **OK** button to add a gradient fill layer above the Everything layer.

Trouble? If you don't see the Transparent Rainbow gradient, click the More options button, click Reset Gradients, click the OK button, and then click the No button if you are asked if you want to save changes to the current gradients. Repeat Step 10.

11. Right-click the **Gradient Fill 1** layer, and then click **Create Clipping Mask**. The *Everything* text is filled with the gradient you selected. See Figure 6-40.

Figure 6-40 **Gradient mask applied to text**

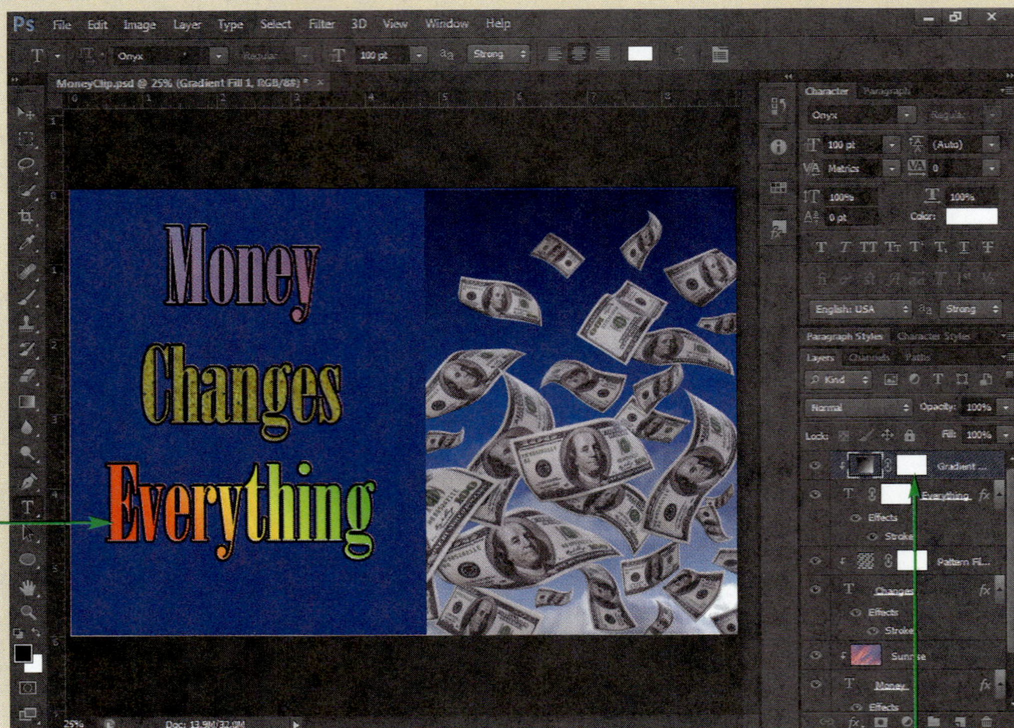

Helder Almeida/Shutterstock.com; Jane Hosie-Bounar

12. Save the MoneyClip.psd file, close it, and then exit Photoshop.

Rose is satisfied with the options you provided her for the Web ad and will send it to a Web developer for her input.

In this session, you learned how to further customize and enhance text by applying different styles using the Styles panel. You also set tracking and scaling for individual characters, specified a baseline shift, and added text to a closed path. You applied clipping masks so you could fill text with an image, a pattern, and a gradient.

REVIEW

Session 6.2 Quick Check

1. In which panel can you adjust the horizontal and vertical scale of text?
2. What is a baseline shift?
3. When you change the shape of text by applying a predefined style with bend and distortion settings, you are ______________ the text.
4. A path that has the same beginning and ending point is called a ______________ path.
5. True or False. A path can be used as the baseline for text typed on a layer.
6. The individual points along a path are called ______________ points.
7. When you fill text with a gradient, pattern, or image, you are using a(n) ______________ mask.

Practice the skills you learned in the tutorial using the same case scenario.

PRACTICE

Review Assignments

Data Files needed for the Review Assignment: RCRetire.psd

Rose wants you to create an ad directed specifically at baby boomers and their retirement accounts. She has provided you with an image and has asked you to add text that will capture the attention of potential customers and educate them about RC Investment opportunities. Complete the following steps:

1. Start Photoshop while pressing the Ctrl+Alt+Shift keys, and click Yes to delete the Settings File when prompted. Switch to and reset the Typography workspace, and then reset all tools.
2. Open **RCRetire.psd**, located in the Photoshop6\Review folder provided with your Data Files, and save it as **RCRetirement.psd** in the same folder.
3. Using the Horizontal Type tool, drag a bounding box that is about 6 1/2 inches wide and 4 inches high starting in the upper-left corner of the canvas. Use a Papyrus, Regular, 18 pt, Strong, left-aligned black font, and type the following two paragraphs (*Note*: The three spelling errors—*liesure*, *conselors*, *carreer*—are intentional):

   At RC Investments, we believe that retirement is not an end, but a beginning, a time to spread your wings and take flight, or to settle in to a life of liesure and relaxation--a life you and your investment firm have worked hard to achieve.

   Our investment conselors were there for you when you started your carreer, and we're here for you now. RC Investments. The Real Choice. The Right Choice.

4. Format both paragraphs with no hyphenation, and justify them so the last line of each paragraph is centered.
5. Add a 10-point space before the second paragraph to separate it from the first paragraph.
6. Put each of the last three phrases in its own paragraph. (*Hint*: You can press the Enter key to add a paragraph break.)
7. Adjust the tracking of the text if necessary to improve its appearance by avoiding loose and tight lines and rivers of white space. Determining when the paragraphs are acceptable will be an individual choice.
8. Use the Move tool to change the dimensions of the bounding box and reposition it on the canvas. Adjust the size of the bounding box so it is about 6 inches wide and 3 1/2 inches tall, and place it so the bounding box is centered near the top of the document.
9. Add a new text layer but change the font to 60 point and the color to white. Type **Dreams Take Flight** on the canvas as point type. Apply the Rise warp style and change the bend to 80%. Reposition the text layer so it starts just above the water on the left and rises above the sun on the lower-right side of the canvas.
10. Select the Dreams Take Flight text, and format it with an underline. Add a 2-pixel stroke effect in the Layer Style dialog box.
11. Check the spelling in the document, and correct any misspelled words.
12. Add a vertical type layer using Verdana, Italic, 24-point black font, and type **RC Investments** down the left edge of the canvas. Increase the horizontal scale of the text to 145%. Increase the vertical scale of the text to 120%. Reduce the horizontal scale of the letter *m* to 115%, and then increase the tracking between the letter *C* and the letter *I* to about 80.
13. Use a clipping mask to apply a Leaf pattern fill to the company name. (*Hint*: Use the Color Paper presets.)

14. Apply a Drop Shadow and a Bevel & Emboss effect to the RC Investments layer text using the default settings.
15. Save RCRetirement.psd, and exit Photoshop.
16. Submit the results of the preceding steps to your instructor either in printed or electronic form, as requested.

Use your skills to create special effects with text.

APPLY

Case Problem 1

Data Files needed for this Case Problem: Shuttle.jpg, Fireworks.jpg

Concord High School You've recently been hired as a teaching assistant at Concord High School in Ohio. You'll be working with the school's physics teacher, Dr. Marie Cash. She has asked you to create a series of slides meant to pique students' interest in physics. You'll add text with different special effects to an image and save a series of layer comps to see which options will work best in the slide show. Complete the following steps:

1. Start Photoshop while pressing the Ctrl+Alt+Shift keys, click Yes to delete the Settings File when prompted. Switch to and reset the Typography workspace layout, and then reset all tools.
2. Open **Shuttle.jpg**, located in the Photoshop6\Case1 folder provided with your Data Files.
3. Switch the foreground and background colors so the foreground color is white. Using the Horizontal Type tool, choose a font that you think is appropriate for a clipping mask—with a font size that is at minimum 200 points. For example, Showcard Gothic is a heavy, wide font that would work well for a clipping mask. Type **E = MC2** near the bottom of the image.
4. Apply a superscript effect to the *2* in the *E* = *MC2* text.
5. Scale the text horizontally so it fills the width of the image, but not the bar on the left side.
6. Add a new layer at the top of the Layers panel, and place **Fireworks.jpg**, located in the Photoshop6\Case1 folder, on the new layer.
7. Fill the $E = MC^2$ text with the Fireworks image you just added. You may need to drag the Fireworks layer to get the effect you want. Add a stroke of any color and size to the text.
8. Add any adjustment to the composition, if desired, and then save a layer comp called **Fireworks**, and hide any adjustment layers and the Fireworks layer.
9. Duplicate the E = MC2 layer. (*Hint*: Right-click the E = MC2 layer in the Layers panel, and select Duplicate Layer.) Reapply the original clipping mask, if necessary. Move the copy beneath the original in the Layers panel. Change the layer color of the original E = MC2 layer to red and change the color of the copy layer to green. Then, hide the red E = MC2 layer and the Fireworks layer.
10. Warp the green E = MC2 layer using the style of your choice. Fill the warped text with a pattern from the Rock Patterns preset group. Create a layer comp, and save it as **PhysicsRocks**.
11. Hide all layers except the Background layer, and then type **Physics** so it runs vertically on the left side of the canvas. (*Hint*: Use the Vertical Type tool and choose any font and any font size.) Fill the word with a gradient.

12. Type the following paragraphs at the bottom of the canvas in 24 point, Times New Roman in any color you choose:

    You might not believe it yet, but physics is fun! Or should we say phun? What other disciplines have put a man on the moon and the shuttle into orbit? And who would argue that gravity doesn't keep us grounded?

    So put on your space suits, your x-ray specs, and your thinking caps and get ready for the ride of a lifetime!
13. Check the spelling of the text you typed, but leave the spelling of *phun*.
14. Format *physics is fun!* in small caps.
15. Adjust the alignment and the paragraph spacing until you're satisfied with the results.
16. Save the file as **Physics.psd** in the Photoshop6\Case1 folder, and exit Photoshop.
17. Submit the results of the preceding steps to your instructor either in printed or electronic form, as requested.

Use your skills to create a logo and an online ad for a catering business.

CREATE

Case Problem 2

Data File needed for this Case Problem: Gourmet.jpg

No Fuss Gourmet You've recently started your own catering business. You specialize in intimate parties, and you treat food as an art form. You are going to start advertising online, and you need to create a logo and an online ad for your business. You'll experiment with the text features of Photoshop to come up with the best look for your logo, and then you'll place the logo with an image to see the full effect. Complete the following steps:

1. Start Photoshop while pressing the Ctrl+Alt+Shift keys, click Yes to delete the Settings File when prompted. Switch to and reset the Typography workspace layout, and then reset all tools.
2. Create a new file of any size, with any background color. Make sure you have enough space to experiment with at least two different logo ideas. Because you are creating the logo for the Web, you can work with a file that is 72 ppi.
3. Create two possible logos with the name of the company—No Fuss Gourmet—using different fonts, styles, fills, and effects. Adjust character spacing, font, and styles as necessary to come up with the best effect. Combine text with shapes to achieve the effect you want. Change layer order as necessary to build the logo, and then merge the layers in each logo so that the file consists of only the Background layer and the two logo layers.
4. Save the file as **Logos.psd** in the Photoshop6\Case2 folder provided with your Data Files.
5. Open **Gourmet.jpg**, located in the Photoshop6\Case2 folder, and save it as **NoFuss.psd** in the same folder.
6. To create a mock-up for an online ad, choose your favorite logo from Logos.psd, and copy it to the NoFuss image. Resize it as necessary to achieve the best effect. You can use Figure 6-41 as an example, but your composition should be unique.

Figure 6-41 Sample No Fuss Gourmet ad

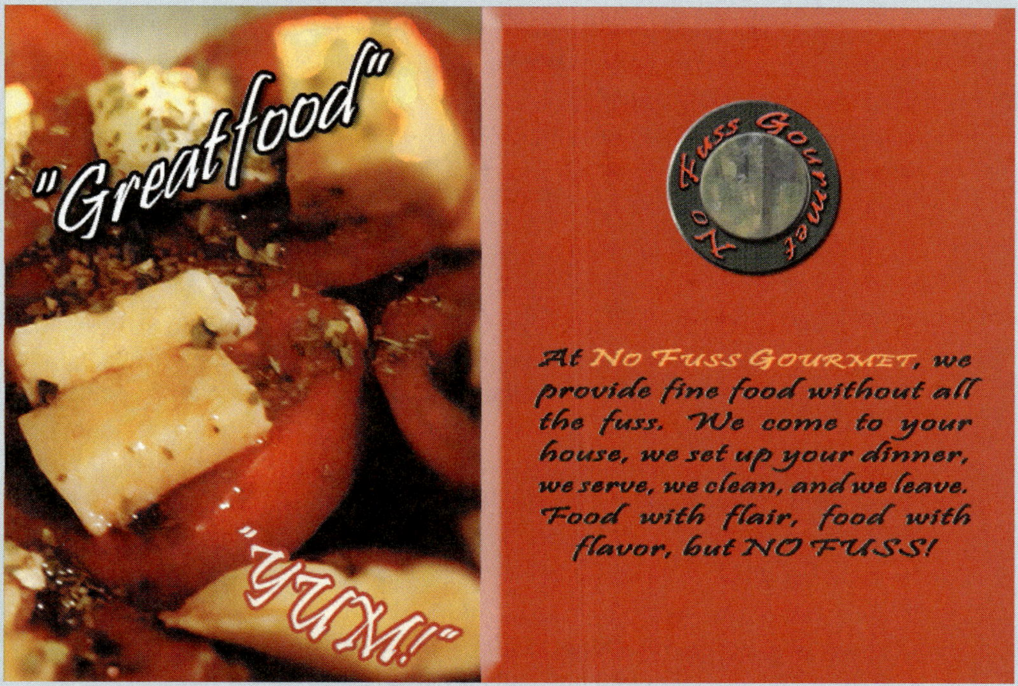

Jane Hosie-Bounar

7. Create a rectangle of any color on the right side of the image and format it with any effects you want. Move the logo so it appears on top of the rectangle, and then type the following paragraph text over the rectangle:

   At No Fuss Gourmet, we provide fabulous food without all the fuss. We come to your house, we set up your dinner, we serve, we clean, and we leave. Food with flair, food with flavor, but no fuss!

8. Format *No Fuss Gourmet* as small caps, and change the font color. In the last sentence, format *no fuss* as all caps.
9. Check the spelling in the paragraph, and replace *fabulous* with *fine*.
10. Turn off hyphenation, and justify the paragraph settings as desired.
11. On the left side of the composition, add short sample quotes from customers using warped text. Format the text with any style or stroke.
12. Save NoFuss.psd and Logos.psd, and exit Photoshop.
13. Submit the results of the preceding steps to your instructor either in printed or electronic form, as requested.

Use your skills to add text to an image for an ad campaign.

APPLY

Case Problem 3

Data File needed for this Case Problem: Luxury.jpg

Goldilocks Inn Goldilocks Inn is a small bed-and-breakfast in Ripton, Vermont. The proprietor Betsy Hemmings, hoping to attract both tourists and the parents of local college students, has asked you to create an ad for a page in the college calendar. Complete the following steps:

1. Start Photoshop while pressing the Ctrl+Alt+Shift keys, click Yes to delete the Settings File when prompted. Switch to and reset the Typography workspace layout, and reset all tools.

2. Open **Luxury.jpg**, located in the Photoshop6\Case3 folder provided with your Data Files, and save it as **Goldilocks.psd** in the same folder.
3. Extend the canvas so it measures 11 inches wide and 12 inches high. The canvas extension should be a color that you think works well with the image supplied. Anchor the image in a corner when you extend the canvas.
4. Using a font or fonts of your choosing, type the name of the inn on two different layers. For one layer, use the Vertical Type tool and for the other, use the Horizontal Type tool, but rotate the text 90 degrees. You'll save layer comps so you have a couple of choices to show to Betsy. Save the composition that shows the rotated text as a layer comp named **Horizontal** and the vertical composition as a layer comp named **Vertical**.

EXPLORE

5. Using the Vertical layer comp, apply a style to the text. Modify the style by changing at least one of its attributes. (*Hint*: Double-click an individual effect in the Layers panel to open the Layer Style dialog box with the settings for that effect displayed.)
6. Use the Type tools to type the word **Comfort** three times, one time on each front pillow, and once on the carpet. Each instance should use a different text effect. For example, warp the text, type it along a path, apply a style to it, or change its scale in some way. Rotate individual instances until you have the effect you want for each pillow and for the carpet.
7. At the bottom of the image, type the following paragraph text:

   At Goldilocks Inn, we offer all the comforts of home, with none of the hassles. Dine in our four-star dining room and enjoy the company of other guests. Or request a table in a romantic corner. Sip cognac by the common fireplace in the evening or relax in our outdoor hot tub year-round. Take a cooling dip in our pool, or heat up in the sauna.

   Goldilocks Inn is all about comfort. Comfort, comfort, and affordability. And oh, did we mention comfort?
8. Check the spelling of the paragraph text.
9. Format the inn name in small caps in the paragraph text.
10. Format the second paragraph in a way that distinguishes it from the first paragraph, and adjust the alignment and justification for each paragraph as desired.
11. Type the word **AHH!** somewhere on the composition, and fill it with a pattern.
12. Display and hide layers until you are happy with the comp, and then save the new layer comp as **Favorite**.
13. Save the file, and then convert the image to CMYK mode, rasterize it, and flatten it.
14. Save the flattened file as **Goldilocks.tif** in the Photoshop6\Case3 folder, using the default TIFF settings.
15. Submit the results of the preceding steps to your instructor either in printed or electronic form, as requested.

Extend your skills to create a logo and a poster for a soccer academy.

CHALLENGE

Case Problem 4

Data File needed for this Case Problem: Soccer.jpg

Soccer Academy You are a recent college graduate who played soccer in college. You had trouble finding a job, so you have decided to start your own business using the assets and skills you have: a degree in marketing, experience in soccer, and a flair for Photoshop. Your "soccer academy" offers classes for women who are interested in playing in recreational leagues. You'll go to their homes or to a soccer field of their choice and teach them shooting, dribbling, and strategy skills. You need to create a logo for your new business, as well as a poster that you'll hang at local community and child-care centers. Complete the following steps:

1. Start Photoshop while pressing the Ctrl+Alt+Shift keys, click Yes to delete the Settings File when prompted. Switch to and reset the Typography workspace layout, and then reset all tools.
2. Open **Soccer.jpg**, located in the Photoshop6\Case4 folder provided with your Data Files, and save it as **Academy.psd** in the same folder.
3. Extend the canvas size to add 1 ½ inches on the left side. Use black for the canvas extension color.
4. Add white vertical text along the left side of the image using the Raavi, Regular, 30-point font. Type **Soccer Academy**, and position the text so it is centered in the black bar.
5. Increase the tracking between the *r* in *Soccer* and the *A* in *Academy*.
6. Decrease the horizontal scale of the *m* in *Academy*, and increase the vertical scale of the *S* in *Soccer* and the *A* in *Academy*. Adjust the tracking between individual characters as you see fit.
7. Create a duplicate layer of the Soccer Academy layer and name it **Soccer Academy copy**. Hide the original layer.

EXPLORE

8. Change the vertical alignment so the text runs sideways from top to bottom. (*Hint*: Click the Character panel menu button, and deselect Standard Vertical Roman Alignment.) Reposition and resize the text to your liking and change settings in the Character panel as required, and then rename the layer **Sideways**.
9. Hide the Sideways layer, select and display the Soccer Academy layer, click the Character panel menu button, and select Change Text Orientation. Reposition and resize the text so it fits over the turf along the bottom of the image. Adjust the tracking so the letters aren't crowded.
10. Shift the baseline of *cc* down and shift the baseline of *de* up. Add a 10-pixel black stroke to the text.
11. Extend the canvas height by 3 inches using black, and anchor the image on the top. Using any character or paragraph settings, type the following text in a paragraph:

    New to soccer? Call us for a fun workout while learning the fundamentals of the most popular sport in the world.

    You name the place and the time and we'll be there. If you don't have access to a field in your neighborhood, no problem! We'll arrange a meeting place.

EXPLORE

12. Explore the other Paragraph panel settings, as well as the options on the panel menu, while aligning and/or justifying the text to your liking. If you don't like an effect, use the History panel to undo your change.
13. Add **555-555-5555** as a phone number somewhere on the poster. Type it along a path that you specify.
14. Type **Have a ball!** on the image so it follows the curve of the soccer ball.

EXPLORE

15. To create a logo, select the soccer ball in the Background layer and copy it to a new layer. Rearrange the layers so the Have a ball layer is on top of the new layer, and then merge the two layers. (*Hint*: Select both layers, right-click, and then click Merge Layers.) Create a new file with any color background and drag the new logo layer you just merged into the file. See Figure 6-42 for an example.

Figure 6-42 **Sample Soccer Academy logo file**

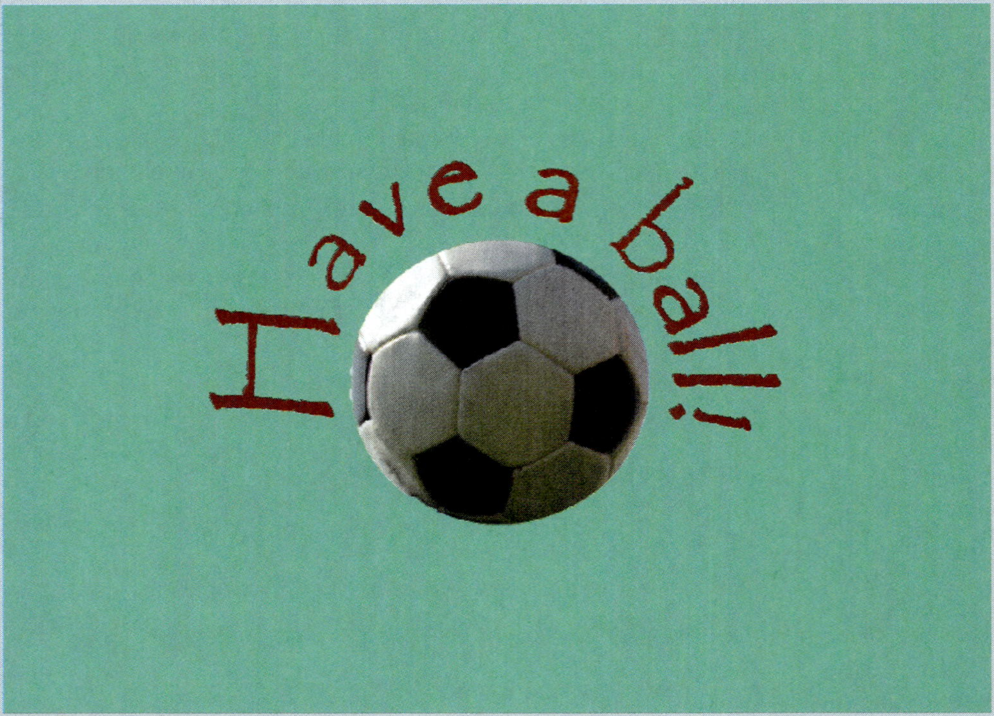

Dmitriy Shironosov /Shutterstock.com

16. Save the new file as **FinalLogo.psd** in the Photoshop6\Case4 folder.
17. Save Academy.psd, and exit Photoshop.
18. Submit the results of the preceding steps to your instructor either in printed or electronic form, as requested.

ENDING DATA FILES

Photoshop6 →

Tutorial
ArcUpper.psd
Baseline.psd
CirclePath.psd
MoneyClip.psd
RCDetails.psd
RCI.psd
RightPath.psd

Review
RCRetirement.psd

Case1
Physics.psd

Case2
Logos.psd
NoFuss.psd

Case3
Goldilocks.psd
Goldilocks.tif

Case4
Academy.psd
FinalLogo.psd

ProSkills

Teamwork

Working with a Team to Create a Campaign

Teamwork is the collaborative process by which team members work together to achieve a common goal. Often, you may find that you need to reach out to managers, to fellow employees, and to people in other departments within your organization to achieve a goal. You might also need to collaborate with a customer or with organizations outside of your company.

Knowing how to be a team player is a critical skill because many organizations rely heavily on teams to complete work tasks. Learning the different roles team members play, how they complement each other for efficient task completion, and how to lead and motivate a team toward achieving a goal can mean the difference between success and failure. Whether your team is ad hoc and short-lived, or ongoing and strategic, the ability to work effectively on a team is a professional skill you need to develop.

What Is a Team?

The Web sites of this country's most desirable employers tell potential employees they'll be working on teams from the start. At Google, the Advertising Sales team members "collaboratively shape solutions that drive their [clients'] strategic initiatives." Apple's corporate retail team is "the backbone behind Apple's retail revolution." For KPMG, one of the world's leading professional services organizations, you may be part of a multidisciplinary team or on a team that is "at the heart of our organization." But what exactly is a team?

More than just people thrown together, a team consists of individuals who have skills, talents, and abilities that complement each other and, when joined, produce synergy—results greater than those a single individual could achieve. It is this sense of shared mission and responsibility for results that makes a team successful in its efforts to reach organizational goals.

Types of Teams

In organizations, there are a variety of team types. Some are formal, while others are more informal. Some meet in person; others have members who have never met face-to-face. Depending on the work, the type of teams you work on will vary.

Formal teams are organized within the company as part of its official structure. These teams can be either horizontal or vertical. A horizontal team has members from roughly the same level in the organization. When people on a team come from different functional areas of the company—finance, information systems, sales—they are often called a cross-functional team, project team, special-purpose team, or task force because they usually have a specific problem to solve within a limited time frame. After the problem is solved, the team disbands. A vertical team, sometimes called a functional team, has a manager and subordinate workers from the same department in the company's hierarchy. The manager is in charge and directs the workers as they complete their tasks. This type of team has a much longer life because the work is not single-goal oriented. Functional teams work together to accomplish their everyday tasks.

Informal groups sometimes form in the workplace when the members choose to join forces to solve a problem, work on a task, or simply meet to talk over lunch. Because they are not appointed by management and their duties are not specifically outlined in job descriptions, there is little or no direct accountability or reporting of results to the

ProSkills

organization. For example, a group that organizes to clean up a stretch of highway outside a company's office building won't have management directing its efforts.

A virtual team is one whose members rarely, if ever, meet in person to work on team tasks. Instead, technology makes it possible for members to be geographically distant yet work as if everyone was in the same room. Some common examples of technologies used in virtual teamwork include the following:

- Corporate networks, such as intranets, as well as File Transfer Protocol (FTP) sites
- Teleconferencing—both audio and video
- Groupware and collaboration software tools, such as those found in Adobe Creative Suite and Microsoft Office 2010
- Social networks, blogs, and wikis
- Email, voice mail, and fax

Virtual teams often must work rapidly to accomplish tasks, so knowing how best to use these technologies is critical. Some virtual teams also have high turnover because members will join when their expertise is needed and then leave upon completion of their contribution. The leader may change as well, depending on the stage of work the team is completing.

The Importance of Technology in Teamwork

Each time you work in a group, decide at the outset how the team will use different technologies to communicate and document work activities. Determine how the team will organize and combine deliverable documents or presentation materials. Use whatever technology tools make the most sense for your team, your task, and your skills.

The Roles of Team Members

If a team is to be successful, individual members must see the value in their respective contributions and what the team as a whole gets out of each member's contribution. This means two important requirements must be met: task performance and social satisfaction. Task performance usually is handled by one or more members who are task specialists. Task specialists spend a lot of time and effort ensuring that the team achieves its goals. They initiate ideas, give opinions, gather information, sort details, and provide motivation to keep the team on track. Social satisfaction is handled by individuals who strengthen the team's social bonds through encouragement, empathy, conflict resolution, compromise, and tension reduction. Have you ever been on a team where the tension was high, and someone stepped in to tell a joke or tried to soften the blow of criticism? That person held the role of managing social satisfaction. Both the task specialist and social satisfaction specialist are important roles on teams. These are not the only roles, however. Other roles include team leaders, work coordinators, idea people, and critics. The roles of individual team members are not always mutually exclusive. For example, the task specialist might also be the team leader, and the idea person might also fill the social satisfaction role. As you begin working with your team in this exercise, watch how these roles are filled and how they change as your team completes its work. Perhaps you'll want to discuss up front which role each member is comfortable filling to see how complementary your collective skill sets turn out to be. What if a role is not being filled on your team? Then you'll need to figure out, as a team,

ProSkills

how to move forward so you can complete your work successfully. The following are tips that everyone should respect as work on a team begins:

- Remember that everyone brings something of value to the team.
- Respect and support each other as you work toward the common goal. When criticism or questions arise, try to see things from the other person's perspective.
- If someone needs assistance, find ways to encourage or support that person so the team is not affected.
- Deal with negative or unproductive attitudes immediately so they don't damage team energy and attitude.
- Get outside help if the team becomes stuck and can't move forward.
- Provide periodic positive encouragement or rewards for contributions.

PROSKILLS

Create a Campaign for a Business

Many organizations use Photoshop for both internal and external publications, including Web and print pieces. In this exercise, you'll work with other team members to design a logo as well as print and Web marketing pieces for a fictional business. As you decide on your business, keep the following in mind: Your main tool for this exercise will be Photoshop; therefore, the business should lend itself to striking visuals so that you have photographs and other images to manipulate for the exercise. In other words, a travel agency would probably be a better candidate than a company that provides typing services.

As a group, you'll create the following three pieces: a company logo consisting of both text and a drawing or photograph; a Web banner with text and graphics for the company's home page; and a magazine ad that includes point text and paragraph text, as well as a digital image that has been modified using special effects, adjustment layers, and the Brush tool. The ad will consist of multiple layer comps, with the goal of each team member presenting his or her comps to the group so you can come to a consensus on the best design. To create and design these pieces, your group will use the Photoshop skills and features presented in Tutorials 1 through 6.

1. Meet with your team to brainstorm and come to a consensus on what your business will be. Coming to a consensus is a necessary part of any work a team undertakes, so make sure everyone is happy with the choice. Once you have chosen a business, discuss what products and/or services it provides.
2. As a group or individually, use the Web to research businesses similar to the one your group chose. Print the home pages of the similar businesses you find, and, if you can find banner ads in other Web pages, print those. What kinds of logos do the businesses use? What kind of language do they use in their ads? Do they use a particular font and color scheme? Do you think their branding is effective?
3. As a group, discuss what color scheme might work best to promote your business and create a recognizable brand. Do you want complementary, monochromatic, analogous, or neutral colors? Any member who proposes a color scheme should begin a group discussion on the reasons for that color scheme, and what kind of audience might respond to the scheme.

4. Have each team member create a logo for the business, and set a deadline for its completion. The logo should include both text and graphics, and to create it, team members should use the Drawing tools, the Type tools, special effects, warped text or text along a path, and multiple layers. The logo should be created in the RGB color mode at 300 ppi. It will be saved at lower resolutions and in different color modes later in the exercise. The logo can include a digital image, but it must be either your own image, in the public domain, or available for commercial, royalty-free use.
5. In a team meeting, have each member present his or her logo. Spend time discussing the effectiveness of each one. At the end of the discussion, choose the two logos (we'll call them Logo1 and Logo2) that best represent the products, services, and perceived brand of the company.
6. Split the team into two groups. Team members in Group 1 will work with Logo1, and those in Group 2 will work with Logo2. Every team member should leave the meeting with a digital copy of the logo their group will be using.
7. Each team member should create a new file based on one of the Photoshop Web presets. The new file should include the placed logo and any supporting text for a Web banner for the company's home page. It can be a horizontal or vertical banner, and can include horizontal or vertical type. The final version of the file should be saved using the RGB color mode in JPEG format and should have a resolution of 72 ppi.
8. Each group should meet separately so the individual team members can present their banners to each other. Each group should then create one file and place each member's banner JPEG on a separate layer in the file. Each layer will comprise its own layer comp, which means that all other layers must be hidden when the layer comp is created. The name of the layer comp should be the name of the team member who created that particular banner. The layer comp Comment field should list what the group considered the strengths of each banner design.
9. Each group should choose its favorite banner and save the combined banner file with the favorite banner layer on top and visible, and all of the other layers hidden. To preserve the individual layers, the file should be saved in PSD format.
10. As a final step, the two groups should rejoin and all the team members should combine their efforts to lay out a magazine ad using one of the logos, point text, and paragraph text. The ad should include text along a path and/or warped text. The paragraph text can be placeholder text or can be written specifically for the ad. Either the point text or the paragraph text should include at least one character that uses a baseline shift. The ad should demonstrate knowledge of how to adjust colors; how to use fill layers, blending modes, opacity, masks, and filters; and how to use the Brush tool and the History Brush tool. Team members can work together to come up with the best design. When there is a consensus, save the ad in PSD format at 300 ppi for a CMYK print piece, and then save it in Grayscale at the appropriate resolution and as the appropriate file type for a newspaper ad.
11. Submit your team's completed files to your instructor as requested. Files should include the two logo files in digital format, the Web banner file in digital format with the multiple Web banner layers, and the magazine ad in CMYK PSD format and Grayscale JPEG format. The team should also provide written documentation that describes the role of each team member and his or her contributions to the team. This documentation should include descriptions of any challenges the team faced while completing this exercise and how the team members worked together to overcome those challenges.

GLOSSARY/INDEX

Note: Boldface entries include definitions.

D

E

F

S

T

U

V

W

Z

TASK REFERENCE

TASK	PAGE #	RECOMMENDED METHOD
Adjustment layer, add	PS 93	In the Layers panel, select a layer to adjust, click the desired adjustment in the Adjustments panel, change the settings in the Properties panel as desired
Adjustment layer, delete	PS 95	In the Layers panel, drag the adjustment layer to the lower-right corner of the Layers panel to
Background color, change	PS 185	In the Color panel or in the Tools panel, click , click again to open the Color Picker (Background Color) dialog box to select a color or click to sample a new background color
Baseline shift, specify	PS 353	Select the text, type a baseline shift value in the box in the Character panel, click
Blending mode, apply	PS 157	In the Layers panel, select the layer, click the Set the blending mode for the layer button, click the desired blending mode
Brush preset library, load	PS 226	In the Brush Presets panel, click , click a preset library
Brush preset picker, open	PS 46	In the Tools panel, click , click on the options bar
Brush preset, create	PS 230	In the Brush panel, select a brush and specify the settings, click in the Brush Presets panel, click New Brush Preset; in the Brush Name dialog box, type a name for the preset in the Name box, click the Capture Brush Size in Preset check box to select it, click OK
Brush tool, activate	PS 222	Press the B key
Brush tool, use	PS 222	In the Tools panel, click , set the options on the options bar or click to set the brush size and hardness, drag on the canvas to create a brushstroke
Brush tool, use to draw straight line	PS 223	In the Tools panel, click , set the options on the options bar or click to set the brush size and hardness; click on the canvas at the starting point for the line, press and hold the Shift key, click at the end point for the line
Canvas, extend	PS 98	*See* Reference box: Extending the Canvas
Canvas, trim	PS 100	*See* Reference box: Trimming the Canvas
Clipping Mask, create	PS 362	In the Layers panel, select a layer to serve as the clipping mask, click Layer on the Menu bar, click Create Clipping Mask
Color Balance adjustment, apply to a selection	PS 252	Make a selection in an image, click in the Adjustments panel, drag the color sliders to achieve the desired color balance
Color mode, change	PS 81	On the Menu bar, click Image, point to Mode, click a mode
Color picker, open	PS 183	In the Color panel or the Tools panel, click or , click a color on the color ramp, click a shade of that color in the color field, click OK
Color range, select localized	PS 259	On the Menu bar, click Select, click Color Range; in the Color Range dialog box, select Sampled Colors, if necessary, click the Localized Color Clusters check box, click part of the image that includes the desired color range, click OK
Color, sample using the Eyedropper tool	PS 178	*See* Reference box: Using the Eyedropper Tool

TASK	PAGE #	RECOMMENDED METHOD
Color, specify using the Color Panel	PS 181	*See* Reference box: Specifying a Color on the Color Panel
Color, specify using the Color Picker dialog box	PS 183	In the Color panel or the Tools panel, click or , click a color on the color ramp, click a shade of that color in the color field, click OK
Color, specify Web-safe colors using the Color Picker dialog box	PS 182	In the Color Picker dialog box, click the Only Web Colors check box to select it
Complex selection, create	PS 254	*See* Reference box: Adding to a Selection to Create a Complex Selection
Content-Aware Fill, use	PS 278	Make a selection in an image, click Edit on the Menu bar, click Fill; in the Fill dialog box, select Content-Aware from the Use drop-down menu, set the Blending Mode and the Opacity, click OK
Content-Aware Move tool, use	PS 281	Make a selection in an image, click in the Tools panel, drag the selection to its new location
Custom document preset, delete	PS 88	*See* Reference box: Deleting a Custom Document Preset
Custom document preset, save	PS 87	*See* Reference box: Saving a Custom Document Preset
Custom Shape picker, open	PS 48	In the Tools panel, click , click Shape: on the options bar
Document, navigate to an open	PS 15	Click the Document window tab of the desired document
Document preset, delete a custom	PS 88	*See* Reference box: Deleting a Custom Document Preset
Document preset, save a custom	PS 87	*See* Reference box: Saving a Custom Document Preset
Document window, float	PS 17	Point to a Document window tab, press and hold the mouse button, drag the tab to the middle of the workspace, release the button
Documents, arrange in Document window	PS 19	On the Menu bar, click Window, point to Arrange, click the desired arrangement option
Eyedropper tool, use	PS 178	*See* Reference box: Using the Eyedropper Tool
File, close	PS 20	On the Menu bar, click File, click Close
File, create using a preset	PS 84	*See* Reference box: Creating a New File Using a Preset
File, navigate to an open	PS 15	Click the Document window tab of the desired file
File, open	PS 8	On the Menu bar, click File, click Open, navigate to the folder containing the file, click the file, click Open
File, open recent	PS 15	On the Menu bar, click File, click Open Recent, click the filename
File, save as	PS 14	On the Menu bar, click File, click Save As, select a file type in the Save As dialog box, type the new filename in the File name box, click Save
Files, close all	PS 21	On the Menu bar, click File, click Close All
Files, display a list of open	PS 15	In the Document window, click >>
Filter Gallery, use	PS 302	On the Menu bar, click Filter, click Filter Gallery, click a folder, click a filter, adjust the settings as desired, click OK
Filter layers	PS 124	Click the desired filter icon at the top of the Layers panel
Font size, set	PS 320	Select the text, type a new font size in the 12 pt box in the Character panel
Foreground and background colors, switch	PS 185	Press the X key
Foreground color, change	PS 183	In the Color panel or in the Tools panel, click to open the Color Picker dialog box to select a color or click to sample a new foreground color

TASK	PAGE #	RECOMMENDED METHOD
Freeze Mask tool, use	PS 298	*See* Reference box: Using the Liquify Filter
Gradient fill layer, create	PS 204	At the bottom of the Layers panel, click [button], click Gradient, click [button] in the Gradient Fill dialog box, click a gradient, click OK; in the Layers panel, adjust the Opacity setting as needed
Grid, show or hide	PS 42	On the Menu bar, click View, point to Show, click Grid
Guides, add	PS 39	On the Menu bar, click View, click New Guide, click the Vertical or Horizontal option button, type a value in the Position box, click OK
Guides, add by dragging	PS 39	Drag down from the horizontal ruler to place a horizontal guide; drag over from the vertical ruler to place a vertical guide
Hand tool, use	PS 104	In the Tools panel, click [button], click in the image, drag in the desired direction
Help, access	PS 11	On the Menu bar, click Help, click Photoshop Online Help, click the link for a topic, click the subtopic hyperlink
Help, access	PS 11	Press the F1 key
Help, search	PS 13	In Adobe Community Help Search box in the Photoshop Online Help window, type a search term, press Enter, click the topic link
History Brush tool, activate	PS 272	Press the Y key
History Brush tool, use to return part of an image to a previous state	PS 270	*See* Reference box: Using the History Brush Tool to Return Part of an Image to a Previous History State
History panel, use to revert to a previous state	PS 266	*See* Reference box: Reverting to a Previous History State Using the History Panel
History state, delete	PS 266	In the History panel, click the history state, click [button]
Horizontal point type, add	PS 319	*See* Reference box: Adding Point Type to an Image
Horizontal type, rotate	PS 329	Select text with the Move tool, click the Show Transform Controls check box on the options bar, place the mouse pointer at the corner of the bounding box, drag clockwise or counterclockwise to achieve the desired rotation, click [button] on the options bar
Image resolution, change using resampling	PS 70	*See* Reference box: Changing Image Resolution Using Resampling
Image, display and pan in the Navigator	PS 105	On the Menu bar, click Window, click Navigator, drag the view box in the Navigator to pan the image
Image, flatten	PS 162	On the Menu bar, click Layer, click Flatten Image
Image, pan	PS 104	In the Tools panel, click [button], click in the image, drag in the desired direction
Image, place	PS 84	On the Menu bar, click File, click Place; in the Place dialog box navigate to and select the image you want to place, click Place, press Enter
Image, resample	PS 70	*See* Reference box: Changing Image Resolution Using Resampling
Image, rotate by a preset amount	PS 107	On the Menu bar, click Image, point to Image Rotation, select a rotation option
Image, rotate by an arbitrary amount	PS 108	On the Menu bar, click Image, point to Image Rotation, click Arbitrary, type an angle in the Angle box, select a direction option button, click OK
Image, zoom	PS 44	In the Tools panel, click [button] or press the Z key, click the image

TASK	PAGE #	RECOMMENDED METHOD
Image, zoom to 100%	PS 45	Press the Ctrl+1 keys
Image, zoom to a specified percentage	PS 45	On the status bar, double-click the current zoom percentage, type a new percentage value, press Enter
Image, zoom to fit on screen	PS 45	Press the Ctrl+0 keys
Image, zoom using a preset	PS 103	In the Tools panel, click , click a zoom preset on the options bar
JPEG, save a file as	PS 65	On the Menu bar, click File, click Save As, click the Format arrow, click JPEG (*.JPG, *.JPEG, *.JPE), click Save; in the JPEG Options dialog box, click the desired Quality setting, click the desired Format Option, click OK
Lasso tool, use	PS 278	In the Tools panel, click , drag to make a selection
Layer comp, apply	PS 153	In the Layer Comps panel, click to the left of the layer comp
Layer comp, create	PS 153	On the Menu bar, click Window, click Layer Comps, click at the bottom of the Layer Comps panel; in the New Layer Comp dialog box, type a layer comp name in the Name box, type a comment in the Comment box, click OK
Layer comp, delete	PS 154	In the Layer Comps panel, click the layer comp, click
Layer edges, display	PS 134	On the Menu bar, click View, point to Show, click Layer Edges
Layer edges, hide	PS 134	On the Menu bar, click View, point to Show, click Layer Edges to deselect it
Layer Style dialog box, open	PS 195	In the Layers panel, double-click fx or double-click the layer thumbnail, select the desired settings in the dialog box, click OK
Layer style, apply	PS 127	In the Layers panel, select a layer, click a style in the Styles panel
Layer style, copy and paste	PS 211	In the Layers panel, right-click a layer, click Copy Layer Style, right-click the layer you want to copy the style to, click Paste Layer Style
Layer(s), deselect	PS 123	On the Menu bar, click Select, click Deselect Layers
Layer, add empty	PS 126	At the bottom of the Layers panel, click
Layer, add new by copying and pasting	PS 128	In the Layers panel, select a layer, click a selection tool; in the Tools panel, drag to make a selection on the canvas; on the Menu bar, click Edit, click Copy, click Edit again, click Paste
Layer, change color in the Layers panel	PS 132	In the Layers panel, right-click the layer, click a color
Layer, change opacity of	PS 159	In the Layers panel, drag the mouse pointer over the word Opacity to the right to increase the opacity and to the left to decrease it
Layer, create a gradient fill	PS 204	At the bottom of the Layers panel, click , click Gradient, click the Gradient arrow in the Gradient Fill dialog box, click a gradient, click OK; in the Layers panel, adjust the Opacity setting as needed
Layer, create a pattern fill	PS 205	At the bottom of the Layers panel, click , click Pattern, click the pattern thumbnail in the Pattern Fill dialog box, click a pattern, click OK; in the Layers panel, adjust the Opacity setting as needed
Layer, create a solid color fill	PS 202	At the bottom of the Layers panel, click , click Solid Color, select a color in the Color Picker (Solid Color) dialog box, click OK; in the Layers panel, adjust the Opacity setting as needed
Layer, delete	PS 143	In the Layers panel, select the layer, press the Delete key
Layer, hide and redisplay	PS 141	In the Layers panel, click to the left of the layer

TASK	PAGE #	RECOMMENDED METHOD
Layer, lock entire	PS 150	In the Layers panel, select the layer, click
Layer, lock image pixels	PS 150	In the Layers panel, select the layer, click
Layer, lock position	PS 150	In the Layers panel, select the layer, click
Layer, lock transparent pixels	PS 150	In the Layers panel, select the layer, click
Layer, move to change position on canvas	PS 137	In the Layers panel, select a layer, point to the layer on the canvas, click and drag the layer to a new position
Layer, move to change visibility	PS 135	*See* Reference box: Moving a Layer in the Layers Panel to Change Its Visibility
Layer, redisplay	PS 141	In the Layers panel, click to the left of the layer
Layer, rename	PS 132	In the Layers panel, click the layer, double-click the current layer name, type a new name, press Enter
Layer, select	PS 122	Click the layer in the Layers panel
Layers, align	PS 139	*See* Reference box: Aligning Layers in a Composition
Layers, distribute	PS 140	*See* Reference box: Distributing Layers in a Composition
Layers, filter	PS 124	Click the desired filter icon at the top of the Layers panel
Layers, group in the Layers panel	PS 159	*See* Reference box: Grouping Layers
Layers, hide all but selected layer	PS 142	In the Layers panel, select a layer, press and hold the Alt key, click on the selected layer
Layers, merge selected	PS 160	Select the layers, click Layer on the Menu bar, click Merge Layers
Layers, merge visible	PS 160	On the Menu bar, click Layer, click Merge Visible
Layers, select multiple	PS 123	*See* Reference box: Selecting Multiple Layers
Layers, stamp selected	PS 161	Select the layers, press the Ctrl+Alt+E keys
Layers, ungroup in the Layers panel	PS 160	In the Layers panel, select the group, click Layer on the Menu bar, click Ungroup Layers
Liquify Filter, use	PS 298	*See* Reference box: Using the Liquify Filter
Magic Wand tool, use to add pixels to a selection	PS 250	In the Tools panel, click ; on the options bar, specify a Tolerance setting, and select or deselect Anti-alias and Contiguous as desired, click , click the pixels to be added to the selection
Magnetic Lasso tool, use	PS 285	*See* Reference box: Using the Magnetic Lasso Tool
Mini Bridge, launch	PS 73	At the bottom of the Photoshop window, click the Mini Bridge tab, click Launch Bridge
Move tool, activate	PS 43	Press the V key
Multiple files, open at once	PS 13	*See* Reference box: Opening Multiple Files at Once
Navigator, display and use to pan an image	PS 105	On the Menu bar, click Window, click Navigator, drag the view box in the Navigator to pan the image
New file, create using a preset	PS 84	*See* Reference box: Creating a New File Using a Preset
Opacity, change for a layer	PS 159	In the Layers panel, drag the mouse pointer over the word Opacity to the right to increase the opacity and to the left to decrease it
Panel dock, expand	PS 32	Click
Panel dock, minimize	PS 32	On the right side of the title bar for the docked panels, click
Panel tab, select	PS 28	Click the desired panel tab in a panel group
Panel, close	PS 31	On the title bar for the panel, click , click Close

TASK	PAGE #	RECOMMENDED METHOD
Panel, close from Window menu	PS 32	On the Menu bar, click Window, click the panel name to remove the check mark
Panel, display	PS 29	On the Menu bar, click Window, click the desired panel
Panel, move	PS 33	Point to the panel bar to the right of the panel tab, press and hold the mouse button, drag the panel group to the desired location, release the mouse button
Panels, hide all	PS 33	Press the Tab key
Panels, redisplay all	PS 33	Press the Tab key
Panels, stack	PS 34	Point to a panel bar to the right of the last panel tab, press and hold the mouse button, drag the panel group under another panel group until a blue bar appears, release the mouse button
Paragraph text, add	PS 334	*See* Reference box: Adding Paragraph Text
Pattern fill layer, create	PS 205	At the bottom of the Layers panel, click , click Pattern, click the pattern thumbnail in the Pattern Fill dialog box, click a pattern, click OK; in the Layers panel, adjust the Opacity setting as needed
Photoshop preferences, set	PS 24	*See* Reference box: Setting Photoshop Preferences
Photoshop settings file, reset	PS 7	Click , click All Programs, click Adobe Photoshop CS6 while pressing and holding the Ctrl+Alt+Shift keys; when prompted to delete the Adobe Photoshop settings, click Yes
Photoshop, exit	PS 21	On the Menu bar, click File, click Exit
Photoshop, start	PS 7	Click , click All Programs, click Adobe Photoshop CS6
Placed image, reposition using relative positioning	PS 146	On the options bar, click , right-click the X or Y box, click the desired units on the context menu, highlight the current value in the X box, type a new value, press Enter, repeat for the Y box
Placed image, resize and maintain aspect ratio	PS 145	On the options bar, click , highlight the current value in the W box, type a new value, press Enter
Placed image, rotate	PS 146	Place the mouse pointer at the corner of the placed image on the canvas, drag clockwise or counterclockwise
Placed image, rotate in 15-degree increments	PS 146	Place the mouse pointer at the corner of the placed image on the canvas, press and hold the Shift key, drag clockwise or counterclockwise to achieve the desired rotation
Point type, add to an image	PS 319	*See* Reference box: Adding Point Type to an Image
Preferences, set	PS 24	*See* Reference box: Setting Photoshop Preferences
Resolution, change using resampling	PS 70	*See* Reference box: Changing Image Resolution Using Resampling
Rulers, show or hide	PS 38	On the Menu bar, click View, click Rulers
Selection, complex	PS 254	*See* Reference box: Adding to a Selection to Create a Complex Selection
Selection, copy and paste	PS 253	Make a selection in an image, click Edit on the Menu bar, click Copy, click Edit again, click Paste
Selection, create using a color range	PS 259	On the Menu bar, click Select, click Color Range; in the Color Range dialog box, select Sampled Colors, if necessary, click the Localized Color Clusters check box, click the part of the image that includes the desired color range, click OK
Selection, expand or grow	PS 249	*See* Reference box: Expanding or Growing a Selection

TASK	PAGE #	RECOMMENDED METHOD
Selection, fixed ratio	PS 246	*See* Reference box: Specifying a Fixed Ratio Selection
Selection, fixed size	PS 248	*See* Reference box: Specifying a Fixed Size Selection
Selection, save and load	PS 289	*See* Reference box: Saving and Loading a Selection
Selection, select inverse of	PS 268	Make a selection, click Select on the Menu bar, click Inverse
Selection, stroke	PS 294	Make a selection in an image, click Edit on the Menu bar, click Stroke; in the Stroke dialog box, specify a width, color, location, blending mode, and opacity, click OK
Selection, use Magic Wand tool to add pixels to	PS 250	In the Tools panel, click [icon]; on the options bar, specify a Tolerance setting, and select or deselect Anti-alias and Contiguous as desired, click [icon], click the pixels to be added to the selection
Shape layer, create	PS 210	In the Tools panel, click a shape tool, ensure that Shape is selected on the options bar, draw the shape on the canvas
Shape, add to	PS 218	In the Tools panel, click a shape tool, click [icon], click [icon] on the options bar, draw a shape on the canvas over an existing shape
Shape, draw	PS 210	In the Tools panel, click a shape tool, ensure that Shape is selected on the options bar, draw the shape on the canvas
Shape, draw a bitmap	PS 219	In the Tools panel, click a shape tool, ensure that Pixels is selected on the options bar, draw the shape
Shape, exclude overlapping	PS 213	In the Tools panel, click a shape tool, click [icon], click [icon] on the options bar, draw the shape on the canvas
Shape, subtract from	PS 214	In the Tools panel, click a shape tool, click [icon], click [icon] on the options bar, draw the shape on the canvas over the existing shape you want to subtract from
Solid color fill layer, create	PS 202	At the bottom of the Layers panel, click [icon], click Solid Color, select a color in the Color Picker (Solid Color) dialog box, click OK; in the Layers panel, adjust the Opacity setting as needed
Spelling, check	PS 340	Click at the beginning of the text, click Edit on the Menu bar, click Check Spelling; in the Check Spelling dialog box, select the correct spelling for the first highlighted word, click the Change button, click OK when the spelling check is complete
Step backward	PS 264	On the Menu bar, click Edit, click Step Backward
Step forward	PS 264	On the Menu bar, click Edit, click Step Forward
Style, apply	PS 192	In the Layers panel, select a layer, click a style on the Styles panel
Swatches panel, add sampled color to	PS 190	Sample a color, move the mouse pointer to a blank (gray) area at the bottom of the Swatches panel, when the mouse pointer changes to [icon], click, type a swatch name in the Name box, click OK
Swatches panel, change palette preset	PS 188	On the Swatches panel, click [icon], click a preset
Swatches panel, customize display	PS 188	On the Swatches panel, click [icon], click a display option
Swatches, delete a color from	PS 191	Press the Alt key to change to the [icon] pointer, point to the color swatch and click
Swatches, load	PS 191	On the Swatches panel, click [icon],click Load Swatches, click the desired swatches preset, click Load

TASK	PAGE #	RECOMMENDED METHOD
Swatches, reset to default	PS 189	On the Swatches panel, click , click Reset Swatches
Swatches, save as a preset	PS 191	On the Swatches panel, click , click Save Swatches, type a name for the swatches, click Save
Tab group, close	PS 31	On the title bar for the panel, click , click Close Tab Group
Tab order, change	PS 16	Point to a Document window tab, press and hold the mouse button, drag the tab to the new location, release the mouse button
Text, add along a closed path	PS 359	Select a drawing tool, click on the options bar, draw a closed path on the canvas; in the Tools panel, click , specify type settings, click the path, type to add text along the path
Text, apply style to	PS 346	Select the text, click a style on the Styles panel
Text, center	PS 324	With a text tool active, click on the options bar, click
Text, find and replace	PS 341	Click at the beginning of the text, click Edit on the Menu bar, click Find and Replace Text; in the Find And Replace Text dialog box, type a word in the Find What box, type a word in the Change To box, click Find Next, click Change, click Done when finished
Text, format as small caps	PS 324	Select the text, click on the Character panel, click
Text, scale using Character panel	PS 325	*See* Reference box: Scaling Text Using the Character Panel
Text, scale using Move tool	PS 326	*See* Reference box: Scaling Text Using the Move Tool
Text, warp	PS 354	*See* Reference box: Warping Text
Tool options, set	PS 45	In the Tools panel, select a tool, select the settings on the options bar
Tool preset, delete	PS 51	On the options bar, click , click the preset, click , click Delete Tool Preset
Tool preset, save	PS 50	On the options bar, click , click , type a preset name in the Name box, select any other desired options, click OK
Tool, reset	PS 46	On the left side of the options bar, right-click the tool, click Reset Tool
Tracking, adjust	PS 331	Select the text, click in the box in the Character panel, select any existing value, type a new value
Vertical point type, add to an image	PS 319	*See* Reference box: Adding Point Type to an Image
Web-safe colors, specify in the Color Picker dialog box	PS 183	In the Color Picker dialog box, click the Only Web Colors check box to select it
Work path, create and stroke with brush	PS 228	In the Tools panel, select a drawing tool, click Path on the options bar, draw the path, right-click the path, click Stroke Path; in the Stroke Path dialog box, click the Tool arrow, click Brush, click OK
Workspace, choose a preset	PS 36	On the Menu bar, click Window, point to Workspace, click the desired workspace name; or click the Workspace switcher and then click the desired workspace name
Workspace, reset	PS 8	On the Menu bar, click Window, point to Workspace, click Reset [*workspace name*]
Workspace, switch	PS 36	On the Menu bar, click Window, point to Workspace, click the desired workspace
Zoom tool, access	PS 44	Press the Z key or click in the Tools panel